# Strategic Management

*Competitiveness and Globalization*

## CONCEPTS

# Strategic Management

## Competitiveness and Globalization

## CONCEPTS

**Michael A. Hitt**
Texas A & M University

**R. Duane Ireland**
Baylor University

**Robert E. Hoskisson**
Texas A & M University

**WEST PUBLISHING COMPANY**
Minneapolis/St. Paul   New York   Los Angeles   San Francisco

## PRODUCTION CREDITS

**Copyediting**   Sherry Goldbecker

**Text Design**   Paula Goldstein

**Illustrations**   Randy Miyake, Miyake Illustration

**Dummy Artist**   Gary Hespenheide, Hespenheide Design

**Composition**   Carlisle Communications

**Cover Image and Design**   Rosalyn M. Stendahl, Dapper Design

## WEST'S COMMITMENT TO THE ENVIRONMENT

In 1906, West Publishing Company began recycling materials left over from the production of books. This began a tradition of efficient and responsible use of resources. Today, up to 95 percent of our legal books and 70 percent of our college and school texts are printed on recycled, acid-free stock. West also recycles nearly 22 million pounds of scrap paper annually—the equivalent of 181,717 trees. Since the 1960s, West has devised ways to capture and recycle waste inks, solvents, oils, and vapors created in the printing process. We also recycle plastics of all kinds, wood, glass, corrugated cardboard, and batteries, and have eliminated the use of Styrofoam book packaging. We at West are proud of the longevity and the scope of our commitment to the environment.

Production, Prepress, Printing and Binding by West Publishing Company.

British Library Cataloguing-in-Publication Data. A catalogue record for this book is available from the British Library.

COPYRIGHT ©1995        By WEST PUBLISHING COMPANY
                       610 Opperman Drive
                       P.O. Box 64526
                       St. Paul, MN 55164-0526

02 01 00 99 98 97 96        8 7 6 5 4 3 2

Library of Congress Cataloging-in-Publication Data

Hitt, Michael A.
      Strategic management : competitiveness and globalization / Michael
   A. Hitt, R. Duane Ireland, Robert E. Hoskisson.
         p.    cm.
      Includes index.
      ISBN 0-314-04339-X (soft)
      1. Strategic planning.     2. Industrial management.
I. Ireland, R. Duane.      II. Hoskisson, Robert E.    III. Title.
HD30.28.H587   1995                                                    94-34794
658.4'012—dc20                                                         CIP

## Dedication

To Frankie for all of your encouragement, support and love.

To Mary Ann, Rebecca, and Scott, who are my constant sources of love, support and encouragement.

To Kathy for your continuous love, support and encouragement.

# ▼ Contents

 **CHAPTER   3**   The Internal Environment: Resources,
                                   Capabilities, and Core Competencies   **64**

**PART 2**
Strategic Actions:
Strategy Formulation
**97**

▼ CHAPTER **6**   Corporate-Level Strategy **160**

▼ CHAPTER **7**   Acquisition and Restructuring
                Strategies **192**

## PART 3

Strategic Actions:
Strategy
Implementation  **257**

▼ **CHAPTER 11** Strategic Leadership **316**

▼ **CHAPTER 12** Corporate Entrepreneurship and Innovation **344**

The strategic management process helps organizations identify *what* they intend to achieve and *how* they will accomplish valued outcomes. The magnitude of this challenge is greater today than historically. The global economy—an economy in which products (goods and services) flow freely among nations—continuously pressures firms to become more competitive. However, companies which increase competitiveness offer products to customers with greater value and this often enables the firm to earn above-average profits.

The strategic management process is the focus of this book. Described in Chapter 1, organizations (both for-profit companies and not-for-profit agencies) use the strategic management process to understand competitive forces and to systematically and consistently develop sustainable competitive advantages.

This book is intended for use primarily in strategic management and business policy courses. The materials presented in the 12 chapters have been thoroughly researched. Both the academic, scholarly literature and the business practitioner literature were utilized and integrated to design and write this book. The academic literature provided the foundation to develop an accurate, yet meaningful description of the strategic management process. The business practitioner literature yielded a rich base of current domestic and global examples that were used to show how the concepts, tools, and techniques of the strategic management process are applied.

Top-level managers are responsible for developing and effectively using a strategic management process in their organizations. Because they bear this responsibility, the work of top-level managers is considered in greater detail in this book than that of middle- and first-level managers.

Our treatment of the strategic management process is both traditional and contemporary. In maintaining tradition, we examine important materials that have historically been a part of understanding strategic management. For example, we thoroughly examine how to analyze a firm's external environment and internal environment as a part of the strategic management process. However, in explaining these important activities, in Chapters 2 and 3, respectively, our treatments are contemporary. In Chapter 3, for example, we emphasize the importance of identifying and determining the value-creating potential of a firm's resources, capabilities, and core competencies. The strategic actions taken as a result of understanding a firm's resources, capabilities, and core competencies have a direct link with the company's ability to establish a sustainable competitive advantage, achieve strategic competitiveness and earn above-average profits.

Our contemporary treatment is also exemplified in the chapters on the dynamics of strategic change in the complex global economy. In Chapter 5, for example, we discuss how the dynamics of competition between firms affect the outcomes achieved by individual companies. This chapter's discussion is grounded in the reality that in most industries, the strategic actions taken by a firm are influenced by a series of competitive actions and responses initiated by competitors. Thus, competition in the global economy is fluid, dynamic, and significantly influences a firm's performance. Similarly in Chapter 7, we address the dynamics of strategic change at the corporate level, specifically addressing the motivation and consequences of mergers, acquisitions and restructuring divestitures in the global economy.

We also emphasize that the total set of strategic actions known as strategy formulation and strategy implementation (see Figure 1–1 in Chapter 1) must be integrated carefully for a firm to achieve strategic competitiveness and earn above-average profits.

In addition, we examine traditional topics of strategy implementation but emphasize contemporary topics and concepts. For instance, Chapter 9 discusses how different corporate governance mechanisms (e.g., boards of directors, institutional owners, executive compensation, etc.) affect strategy implementation. The vital contributions of strategic leaders are discussed in Chapter 11. Chapter 12 addresses the important topic of corporate entrepreneurship and innovation through internal corporate venturing, strategic alliances and external acquisition or venture capital investment. Through an integration of the traditional and contemporary topics, readers of this book should be able to fully understand the strategic management process and to use it successfully in an organizational setting.

A number of contemporary topics and issues are examined in the book as well. These include total quality management (TQM), stakeholder analyses, core competencies, strategic alliances (domestic and international), speed of decision making, transnational strategy and refocusing (downsizing, downscoping, LBOs), and the importance of ethics, among others.

## Key Features of This Text

To increase the pedagogic value of this book for the reader, several features have been used. Each of these features is described below.

**Learning Objectives**   Each chapter begins with clearly stated learning objectives. These objectives inform readers of key points they should master from each chapter. To both facilitate and verify their learning, students have an opportunity to revisit each chapter's learning objectives by preparing answers to the review questions appearing at the end of each chapter.

**Opening Cases**   Following the learning objectives, each chapter begins with an opening case. These cases describe current actions taken by well-known companies including AT&T, J.C. Penney, Unifi, British Telecommunications, AMR (American Airlines), Time Warner, Shougang Corp. (A Chinese steel maker), General Motors, Sears, Oracle Corp. and Sony. The purpose of these cases is to demonstrate how a specific firm applies concepts examined in the chapter. Thus, the opening cases provide a link between the theory and application of the strategic management process in current organizations.

**Key Terms**   Key terms—those that are critical to understanding the strategic management process—are boldfaced throughout the book. In addition, definitions of these key terms appear in chapter margins.

**Strategic Focus Segments**   A minimum of three, and usually four, Strategic Focus segments are presented in each chapter. As with the opening case, the Strategic Focus segments showcase organizations that are usually familiar to readers. These segments provide additional applications of the concepts highlighted in each chapter. Each Strategic Focus describes how a company has applied a particular part of the strategic management process in order to achieve strategic competitiveness. For instance, Whirlpool's strategy in Asia is used in a Strategic Focus in Chapter 1 to demonstrate the importance of competitiveness in a global economy. Mercedes–Benz' brand name is discussed as a source of competitive advantage in Chapter 3. The recent acquisition of Rover by BMW is presented in Chapter 7 to discuss how an acquisition can be advantageous in competition. Specifically, BMW hopes to confront the Mercedes-Benz entry into the sport utility vehicle market through the Rover acquisition. Wal–Mart's entry into Mexico is explained in Chapter 8 on international strategy. Executive compensation and board involvement in strategy in Japan and the United States are compared in Chapter 9. The strategy and control system of Asea Brown Boberi (ABB), a transnational firm in electrical and power generation equipment, is explored in Chapter 10. These examples and others make the concepts in each chapter come alive for the reader and facilitate reality–based learning.

**End of Chapter Summaries**   Each chapter ends with a summary that is related to the learning objectives. These summaries are presented in a bulleted format to highlight concepts, tools, and techniques examined in each chapter.

**Review Questions**   As mentioned above, review questions are tied to each learning objective. As such, students are prompted to focus on the specific learning objectives of each chapter.

**Application Discussion Questions**   Following the review questions at the end of each chapter is a set of application discussion questions. These questions challenge readers to apply the strategic management process highlighted in the chapter. These questions are intended to stimulate thoughtful classroom discussions and to help students develop critical thinking skills. Lively debates should emerge as students discuss potential applications.

**Ethics Questions**   While competing in a global economy, firms continuously face ethical challenges and dilemmas. At the end of each chapter, readers are presented with a set of questions about ethical issues that require careful thought and analysis. Preparing answers to these questions should help students confront many of the ethical issues facing those responsible for designing and effectively using a firm's strategic management process. Discussing these difficult issues in class heightens one's awareness of the ethical challenges that are encountered in modern organizations.

**Examples**   Besides the opening cases and Strategic Focus segments, the chapters contain many other real-world examples. For instance, MCI is discussed as an example of cost leadership in relationship to its entry into the long distance telecommunication market in Chapter 4. Also, Chapter 8 has a number of examples of international competition such as Miller Beer's and Anheuser-Busch's entry into foreign markets (Mexico and Japan). Grounded in descriptions of actual organizations' actions, these examples are used to illustrate key strategic management concepts and make examining the strategic management process more real and interesting.

Besides the traditional end of book subject and name indices, a company index is provided. This index includes the names of all organizations discussed in the text for easier accessibility.

**Strategic Competitiveness and Globalization**   The title of this book highlights the importance of strategic competitiveness and globalization to our examination of the strategic management process. The strategic management process is critical to an organization's success. As described in Chapter 1, strategic competitiveness is achieved when a firm develops and exploits a sustained competitive advantage. Attaining such an advantage results in the earning of above-average profits; that is, profits that exceed the returns an investor could expect from other investments with similar amounts of risk. For example, Gillette's new product development and especially its flexible and low cost manufacturing capability have sustained its superior profitability and market leadership (see Chapter 4).

Also critical to the approach used in this text is the fact that all firms face increasing global competition. Firms no longer operate in relatively safe domestic markets as U.S. auto firms have discovered. In the past, many firms, including most in the United States, produced large quantities of standardized products. Today, companies typically compete in a global economy that is complex, highly uncertain, and unpredictable. To a greater degree than was the case in a primarily domestic economy, the global economy rewards effective performers while poor performing companies are forced to restructure significantly to enhance their strategic competitiveness. Because of conditions in the global economy, some believe the 1990s may be remembered as a time of "competitive hell" for many Western companies—a time during which many firms will struggle to continuously improve to meet customers' demands for high quality products at low prices.[1]

Success in the uncertain and difficult global economy requires specific capabilities, including the abilities to: (1) use scarce resources wisely to maintain the lowest possible costs, (2) constantly anticipate frequent changes in customers' preferences, (3) adapt to rapid technological changes, (4) identify, emphasize, and effectively manage what a firm does better than its competitors, (5) continuously structure a firm's operations so objectives can be achieved more efficiently, and (6) successfully manage and gain commitments from a culturally diverse work force.

The importance of developing and using these capabilities in the global economy of the 1990s and beyond should not be underestimated. In the opinion of General Electric's chairman, Jack Welch, firms that cannot sell a top-quality product at the world's lowest price will soon be out of business.[2]

Welch's opinion challenges firms to understand the nature of global competition and its direct and indirect effects on their operations. In some instances, firms compete directly with global competitors. For companies competing only with domestic competitors (evidence suggests that the number of these firms continues to decline), the effect of globalization is witnessed in terms of competitive standards. Indirectly, then, the global economy forces all companies—even those focused on a domestic market—to compete in terms of the world's highest standards.

Thus, we believe the strategic management process should positively affect a firm's performance. However, in the 1990s and into the 21st century, globalization will affect the nature of the strategic management process and its yield of strategic outcomes.

---

[1]Henkoff, R. 1990. How to plan for 1995. *Fortune.* December 31: 70–79.
[2]Jack Welch's lessons for success. 1993. *Fortune.* January 25: 86–93.

**Full Four-Color Format**   Our presentation and discussion of the strategic management process is facilitated by use of a full four-color format. This format provides the foundation for an interesting and visually appealing treatment of all parts of the strategic management process. Also included is a series of photographs accompanied by captions integrated with the text material to help students more graphically understand the concepts.

**Cases**   The text includes 40 case studies that represent a variety of business and organizational situations and corporate– and business–level strategic issues. For example, there are cases representing manufacturing, service, consumer goods, and industrial goods industries. Furthermore, many of the cases include an international perspective. Also, cases with high technology, entertainment, and utility firms are represented. Some cases focus specifically on social or ethical issues, while others emphasize strategic issues of entrepreneurial or small and medium-sized firms. Finally, a significant number of the cases also provide an effective perspective on the industry examined.

The cases have been carefully reviewed and personally selected by the authors. Our goal was to select cases that were well written and focused on clear and important strategic management issues. In addition, the cases represent a variety of industries and strategic issues, as well as provide a rich learning experience for those performing case analyses. The cases are multidimensional and, for the readers' convenience, a matrix listing all 40 cases and the dimensions/characteristics of each one is provided following the Table of Contents. While most of these cases are concerned with well-known national and multinational companies, several depict the strategic challenges involved in smaller and entrepreneurial firms. Given the global economy emphasized in this book, over 50 percent of the cases include an international perspective. Additionally, given that by the year 2000 approximately 50 percent of all businesses will be owned and operated by women, there are several cases that examine firms with women CEOs/owners such as Ryka, Inc. and Susan's Special Lawns. There are also cases of special interest or topics (e.g., Arizona Public Service Company, IMAX in the Soviet Union, Kentucky Fried Chicken in China). Additionally, while most cases focus on profit oriented companies, we also have cases on nonprofit organizations (e.g., The Unfinished Symphony). In summary, we have cases that represent a wide variety of important and challenging strategic issues and that provide an exciting setting for case analyses and presentations.

**Custom Cases**   A special feature of this book is the option for custom publishing. This option allows instructors to create their own set of cases for use in their courses by choosing among the 40 cases contained in this book and 23 excellent additional cases available for adoption. The 23 additional cases were chosen using the same criteria as for the 40 cases contained within this book. The 23 additional cases from which adopters may choose include:

Bieffebi SPA, Allen Bauerschmidt
Case Study: ZYX, Inc., George Whaley
Euro Disney: The Theme Park, Scott Reynolds
Father Flanagan's Boys Town, John J. Vitton

Fluent Machines A, Raymond M. Kinnunen, John Seeger, and James F. Molloy, Jr.

Fluent Machines B, Raymond M. Kinnunen, John Seeger, and James F. Malloy, Jr.

Grupo Intelecsis, Walter E. Greene

The Horn and Hardart Company, L. Richard Oliker

John Labatt Limited, George Atahnassakos

The Micro Projects Corporation Case, Arun Shanker, David C. Snook-Luther, and Don Parks

Miller and Rhoads Department Stores, Michael W. Little and Eugene H. Hunt

Northrup Corporation: A Case Study in Subcontract Management, Thomas J. Dudley and Ralph J. Melargno

Northstar Publishing Co. Inc., James C. Crew

Ontario Flower Growers, Kenneth Harling

Procter & Gamble in Eastern Europe, Lucas Birdeau and Douglas Manfield

Sidethrusters, Inc., Raymond M. Kinnunen

Sierra Research and Technology, Inc., Raymond M. Kinnunen and John A. Seeger

Sony Corp.: Transition into Multi-Media (Hardware and Software), D. A. Millet and J. Hallist

Sun Country Foods, Inc., Royston Greenwood and Lloyd Steier

Total Quality Management at Production Supply Company, Brett Schwartz, Caroline M. Fisher, and Claire Anderson

A University Considers its Mission, Philip Baron and Donald Grunewald

Vietnam: Asian Tiger or Tiger Trap?, Dave Jenkins

Will Whirlpool's Strategy Wash in Europe?, Matthew A. Ballard and Randall E. Carr

All of the cases available for customization include full case note support. Instructors can contact their West representative for information on the custom publishing option.

## Instructor Support Materials

The instructor support package is an innovative response to the growing demand for creative and effective teaching methodologies. The supplements are designed to provide a comprehensive resource package for all faculty adopting this text; the materials used will depend on the faculty member's interest areas, class size, equipment availability, and teaching experience. All supplements not prepared by the authors have been reviewed by the authors for consistency and accuracy with the textual materials.

**Annotated Instructor's Edition**　An *annotated edition of the book* has been prepared by Robert D. Nixon of Tulane University. The annotations, based on events experienced by organizations that are familiar to students, provide a number of suggestions to encourage and facilitate class discussion of important concepts from the book. In addition, there are additional company examples that may be used to further enlighten the students on a particular topic.

**Instructor's Manual**   A comprehensive *Instructor's Manual* has been prepared by Richard Menger of St. Mary's University. The instructor's manual provides a complete lecture outline for each chapter, teaching tips, detailed summaries of each opening vignette and strategic focus, summary discussion of each text figure, supplemental lectures and notes, and answers to all review and discussion questions. Ethics mini-cases and discussions of each are provided.

**Instructor Case Notes**   Professor Victoria Buenger of Vanderbilt University prepared the *Instructor's Case Notes* that accompany the text. Each case note highlights the details of the case within the framework for case analysis developed in the text. The authors chose cases that represent a myriad of strategy topics and company types. The structure of the case notes allows instructors to organize case discussions along common themes and concepts. For example, each case note details the firm's capabilities and resources, its industry and competitive environment (if applicable), and key factors for success in the industry.

   The case notes also feature aspects of the cases that make them unique. Each case is analyzed within its particular time frame. An updating epilogue is included for most of the cases. Professor Buenger also provides a summary table of all the figures and exhibits in each case. Instructors will know, at a glance, what information the students have when preparing a case.

**Test Bank**   A *comprehensive set of test questions* (true-false, multiple choice, and essay) has been prepared by Garry Bruton of the University of Tulsa.

**Transparencies**   A set of *overhead transparencies* based on the book content, featuring figures from the book text, and innovative adaptations to enhance classroom presentation has been prepared by James Fiet of Clemson University.

**WesTest™**   This supplement is a computerized version of the hard-copy test bank. WesTest includes edit and word processing features that allow test customization through the addition, deletion, or scrambling of test selections. WesTest is available in DOS, Windows, and Macintosh formats.

**Videos**   An *extensive video package* created with the assistance of Joe Michlitsch (Southern Illinois University) includes 3–5 video segments per chapter. The videos feature real companies and real cases, not company promotions.

**Video Guide**   A video guide has been developed by Joe Michlitsch to accompany the video package and provide information on length, alternative points of usuage within the text, highlights to address, and some discussion questions to stimulate classroom discussion.

**FisCAL**   For those adopters who want computer software support for case analysis, we are pleased to offer the FisCAL Business Analysis System developed by The Halcyon Group, Inc. The menu driven FisCAL software is a powerful tool that allows students to perform any or all of the following analyses:

1. Comparison of Financial Statements to Industry Norms
2. Cost-Profit-Volume Analysis including Breakeven Analysis and Operating Leverage
3. Ratio Analysis and Bankruptcy Prediction
4. Cash Market Valuation
5. Multi-period Analysis of Trends, Operating Ratios, and Cash Flow
6. Strategic Analysis for testing the feasibility of alternative strategies
7. Proforma Projections

The financial data from the following text cases have been loaded on a data disk for use with the FisCAL software:

Blockbuster Entertainment Corporation

Chrysler Corporation

Gillette and the Men's Wet-Shaving Market

The Great Atlantic and Pacific Tea Co., Inc. and the Retail Grocery Industry

Hartmarx Corporation

The Metamorphosis of Whirlpool Corporation

Ryka, Inc.: The Athletic Shoe with a "Soul"

SRC—The Next Chapter

Susan's Special Lawns

United States Gypsum Corporation

Wang Laboratories, Inc.

Adopters who request the FisCal software receive a copy of the paperback book *Profiting from Financial Statements* by the Halcyon Group, and an outstanding 45 minute videotape that describes the software capabilities and operating procedures. If you are interested in using the FisCAL software, please contact your local WEST representative or call West Publishing at 1-800-328-9424.

## West's Strategic Management Series

This is a unique series of six paperback core paperback texts authored by respected experts in their fields and edited by Michael A. Hitt, R. Duane Ireland, and Robert E. Hoskisson. These texts are appropriate as supplements to the graduate strategic management course or as additional readings for various upper division managerial courses.

*Resource-Based View of the Firm*
by Jay B. Barney, Ohio State University

*Strategic Leadership*
by Sydney Finkelstein, Dartmouth College
and Donald C. Hambrick,
Columbia University

*Corporate Strategy*
by Charles W. Hill, the University of Washington

*International Strategic Management*
by Bruce M. Kogut, the University of Pennsylvania

*Corporate Governance*
by Rita D. Kosnik, Trinity University,
and Thomas A. Turk, Chapman University

*Industry Rivalry and Coordination*
by Ken G. Smith and Curtis Grimm, both of the University of Maryland

## Acknowledgments

We gratefully acknowledge the help of many people in the development of this book. The professionalism, guidance and support provided by Rick Leyh, Editor, and his staff, in particular Alex von Rosenberg and Kara ZumBahlen, are gratefully acknowledged. We appreciate the excellent work of Garry Bruton, Vickie Buenger, Jim Fiet, Richard Menger, Joe Michlitsch and Robert Nixon in preparing the supplemental materials accompanying this book. Also, we appreciate the excellent secretarial assistance provided by Wanda Bird. In addition, we owe a debt of gratitude to our colleagues at Texas A&M and Baylor. Finally, we gratefully acknowledge the help of many who read and provided feedback on drafts of our chapters. Their insights enhanced our work. Those who contributed through reviews and evaluations are listed below:

Garry D. Bruton
University of Tulsa

Victoria L. Buenger
Vanderbilt University

Lowell Busenitz
University of Houston

Gary R. Carini
Baylor University

Roy A. Cook
Fort Lewis College

Derrick E. Dsouza
University of North Texas

W. Jack Duncan
University of Alabama-Birmingham

Karin Fladmoe-Lindquist
University of Utah

Karen A. Froehlich
North Dakota State University

Ching–Der Horng
National Sun Yat-Sen University

Sharon G. Johnson
Cedarville College

Anne T. Lawrence
San Jose State University

Franz T. Lohrke
Louisiana State University

Richard A. Menger
St. Mary's University

Joseph F. Michlitsch
Southern Illinois University
  at Edwardsville

Paul Miesing
SUNY-Albany

Douglas D. Moesel
Lehigh University

Benjamin M. Oviatt
Georgia State University

George M. Puia
University of Tampa

Michael V. Russo
University of Oregon

Ronald J. Salazar
Idaho State University

Clayton G. Smith
Oklahoma City University

David C. Snook-Luther
University of Wyoming

Kathleen M. Sutcliffe
University of Michigan

Margaret A. White
Oklahoma State University

Robert Wiseman
Arizona State University

Thomas A. Turk
Chapman University

**Final Comments** Organizations face exciting and dynamic competitive challenges as the 1990s come to a close and the 21st century appears on the horizon. These challenges, and effective responses to them, are explored in this book. The strategic management process offers valuable insights for those committed to successfully leading and managing organizations in the 1990s and beyond. We hope you will enjoy the exposure to the strategic management process provided by this book. In addition, we wish you success in your careers and future endeavors.

# PART 1

# Strategic Management Inputs

# CHAPTER 1
## Strategic Management and Strategic Competitiveness

▼

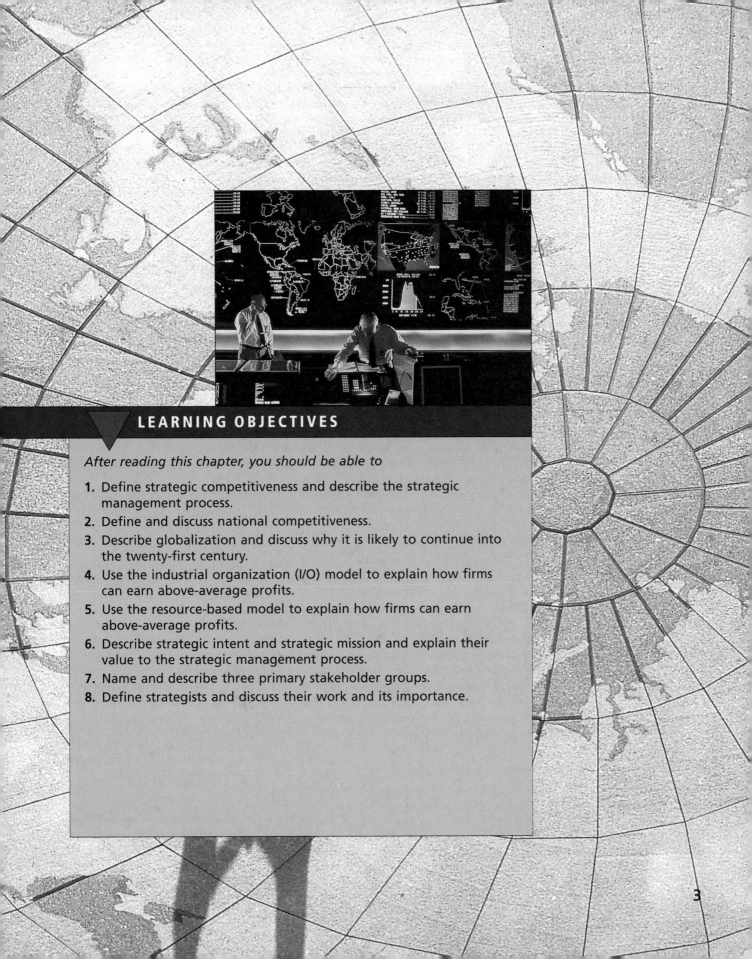

*After reading this chapter, you should be able to*

1. **Define strategic competitiveness and describe the strategic management process.**
2. **Define and discuss national competitiveness.**
3. **Describe globalization and discuss why it is likely to continue into the twenty-first century.**
4. **Use the industrial organization (I/O) model to explain how firms can earn above-average profits.**
5. **Use the resource-based model to explain how firms can earn above-average profits.**
6. **Describe strategic intent and strategic mission and explain their value to the strategic management process.**
7. **Name and describe three primary stakeholder groups.**
8. **Define strategists and discuss their work and its importance.**

## AT&T: Competing as a Global Company

On January 1, 1984, the U.S. government broke AT&T ("Ma Bell") into seven regional operating companies (which quickly become known as the Baby Bells). AT&T was left with its long-distance business, Western Electric (a manufacturer of telephone equipment), and access to Bell Labs (a world-famous research laboratory). Between 1984 and the middle of 1993, AT&T eliminated approximately 140,000 jobs, struggled to be successful in the computer business, and saw its percentage of the long-distance market fall from 90.1 percent in 1984 to 62.2 percent in 1992.

But, clearly, not all of AT&T's experiences since 1984 have been negative. On the positive side, it has made significant progress toward the objective of becoming a global company. By early 1993, over 24 percent of AT&T's sales revenues were being earned in markets outside the United States; the company wanted this figure to reach 50 percent by the year 2000.

In commenting about his firm's international sales target, Bob Allen, AT&T's CEO, noted that the 50 percent figure was not magical. What was mandatory, however, was that AT&T become a global company. In Allen's view, superior growth opportunities outside the United States, the reality that AT&T's competitors are global firms, and the need to spread the company's R&D-intensive costs across greater volume all pointed to the importance of becoming a successful global company. This intent is captured by the following AT&T goal: to bring people together and give them easy access to each other and to the information they want and need—*anytime, anywhere.*

Under Allen's leadership, AT&T took several actions to reach its goal of becoming a global company. As examples, the company (1) installed a new corporate structure to encourage cooperation among otherwise independent operating businesses, (2) devoted considerable time to supporting a set of company values (e.g., respect for individuals and dedication to helping customers), (3) ended a tradition of insularity by hiring outside executives, (4) developed new links with its unions, and (5) invested in other firms (e.g., McCaw Cellular Communications) with critical technologies or attractive market positions.

Although learning how to compete effectively against global competitors will challenge AT&T, initial feedback about the company's performance and strategic competitiveness capabilities is encouraging. In the early 1990s, many were optimistic about the firm's chances of developing a successful global strategy. For example, a Goldman Sachs analyst believed AT&T had the ability, primarily because of its experience in selling branded products, to achieve major market-share gains worldwide. According to this analyst, the "AT&T brand could be to the worldwide communications business what Coke is to the beverage business." ▲

The actions and strategies AT&T implemented to become a global company were designed to achieve strategic competitiveness and earn above-average profits.

**Strategic competitiveness** is achieved when a firm successfully formulates and implements a value-creating strategy. When a firm implements a value-creating strategy that current and potential competitors are not simultaneously implementing and when other companies are unable to duplicate the benefits of its strategy, this firm has a **sustained** or **sustainable competitive advantage.** A firm is assured of a sustained competitive advantage only after others' efforts to duplicate its strategy have ceased because they have failed.[1] Even if a firm achieves a competitive advantage, it normally can sustain this advantage only for a period of time.

A sustained competitive advantage results in investors earning above-average profits on their investments. **Above-average profits** are returns in excess of what an investor expects to earn from other investments with a similar amount of risk. Firms that are without a sustained competitive advantage or that are not competing in an attractive industry earn, at best, only average profits. **Average profits** are returns equal to those an investor expects to earn from other investments with a similar amount of risk. In the long run, an inability to earn at least average profits results in failure. Failure occurs because investors will choose to invest their funds in firms that earn at least average profits and will withdraw their investments from firms that earn less. As shown in Figure 1-1, the **strategic management process** is the full set of commitments, decisions, and actions required for a firm to achieve strategic competitiveness and earn above-average profits.[2]

The strategic management process is dynamic in nature. Relevant and accurate *inputs,* from analyses of the internal and the external environments, are required for effective and efficient strategy formulation and implementation *actions.* In turn, effective and efficient *strategic actions* are a prerequisite to achieving the desired *strategic outcomes* of strategic competitiveness and above-average profits.

Feedback about a firm's strategic actions comes from various sources. The degree to which a company has become strategically competitive and the level of profits it has earned yield valuable feedback. Feedback is also provided by a firm's stakeholders. Effective feedback helps firms continuously adjust and refine their strategic inputs and strategic actions.

In the remaining chapters of this book, we use the strategic management process to explain what firms should do to achieve strategic competitiveness and earn above-average profits. Through these explanations, it becomes clear why some firms achieve competitive success, while others do not.

▲ **Strategic competitiveness** is achieved when a firm successfully formulates and implements a value-creating strategy.

▲ **Sustained** or **sustainable competitive advantage** occurs when a firm implements a value-creating strategy that current and potential competitors are not simultaneously implementing and when other companies are unable to duplicate the benefits of its strategy.

▲ **Above-average profits** are returns in excess of what an investor expects to earn from other investments with a similar amount of risk.

▲ **Average profits** are returns equal to those an investor expects to earn from other investments with a similar amount of risk.

▲ The **strategic management process** is the full set of commitments, decisions, and actions required for a firm to achieve strategic competitiveness and earn above-average profits.

## The Challenge of Strategic Management

Achieving strategic competitiveness and earning above-average profits are challenging—for firms as large as AT&T and as small as your local dry cleaners. The fact that only 2 of the 25 largest U.S. industrial corporations in 1900 are still competitive attests to the rigors of business competition (the remaining 23 companies have failed, have been merged with other firms, or are no longer of significant size relative to their competitors).[3]

Additional evidence of strategic management's challenge is suggested by the data in Table 1-1. Notice that across all industries, over 62 percent of U.S. businesses fail within their first six years. Thomas J. Watson, Jr., formerly the chairman of IBM, once cautioned people to remember that "corporations are expendable and that success—at best—is an impermanent achievement which can always slip out of hand."[4]

**FIGURE 1–1** **The Strategic Management Process**

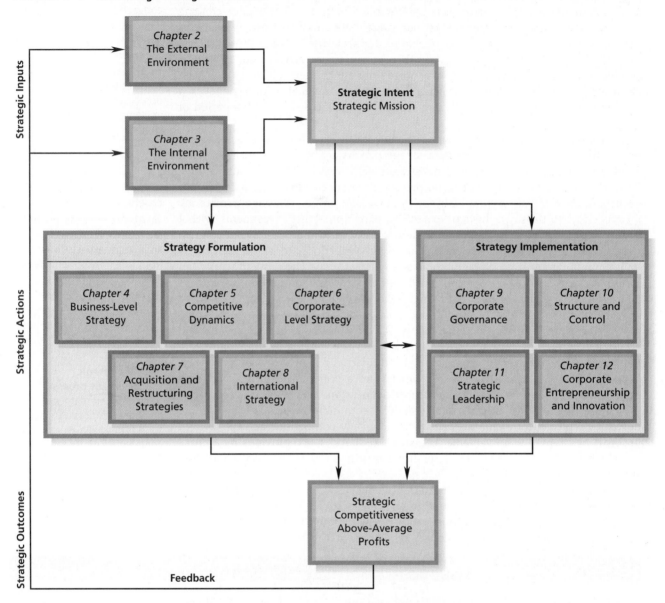

More recently, Andrew Grove, head of Intel, observed that only paranoid companies survive and succeed. Such firms know that current successes do not guarantee future strategic competitiveness and above-average profitability. Accordingly, these companies strive continuously to improve so they can remain competitive.[5] To be strategically competitive and earn above-average profits in the future as a global company, AT&T must compete differently than it did as a semi-public U.S. monopoly. As a global service business, AT&T must develop and implement a value-creating strategy that global competitors cannot duplicate easily.

Several topics are discussed in this chapter. First, to establish the context within which the strategic management process is used, the interrelated issues of

| TABLE 1–1 | | | |
|---|---|---|---|
| **U.S. Business Survival Rates (Percent)** | | | |
| | *Years of Survival* | | |
| | Up to 2 | *Between 2 and 4* | *Between 4 and 6* |
| Construction | 77.1 | 45.6 | 35.2 |
| Finance, insurance, real estate | 74.2 | 46.2 | 36.0 |
| Manufacturing | 78.7 | 56.2 | 46.2 |
| Retail trade | 75.6 | 48.1 | 37.0 |
| Services | 75.4 | 46.5 | 37.3 |
| Transportation, communications, public utilities | 75.7 | 46.2 | 37.0 |
| Total: All industries | 76.1 | 47.9 | 37.8 |

*Source:* U.S. Small Business Administration Office of Advocacy, 1992, *The State of Small Business: A Report of the President* 1992, Washington D.C.: 195

national competitiveness, the global economy, and globalization are addressed. In recent years, firms' competitiveness in the global economy has been emphasized in the United States and is an important topic in countries throughout the world.[6] In a **global economy,** goods, services, people, skills, and ideas move freely across geographic borders.[7] A global economy is relatively unfettered by artificial constraints, such as tariffs, and significantly expands a firm's competitive landscape.

▲ In a **global economy**, goods, services, people, skills, and ideas move freely across geographic borders.

With information about national competitiveness, the global economy, and globalization as a foundation, we next examine two models. Each of these models suggests conditions organizations should study to gain the *strategic inputs* needed to select *strategic actions* in the pursuit of superior profitability.

The emphases of these two models differ. The first model suggests that the *external environment* should be the primary determinant of a firm's strategic actions. The key to this model is locating and competing successfully in an attractive (that is, profitable) industry. The second model suggests that a firm's unique internal resources and capabilities are the critical link to strategic competitiveness. Specifically, this model suggests that resources and capabilities that are valuable, rare, imperfectly imitable, and non-substitutable indicate the strategies a firm should formulate and implement in the pursuit of superior profitability. Thus, in this second model, a firm's *internal environment* is the primary determinant of its strategies. These two approaches suggest that successful competition requires a keen understanding of a firm's external *and* internal environments.

Resulting from analyses of its external and internal environments is the information required for a firm to maintain strategic fit and to develop its strategic intent and strategic mission (fit, intent, and mission are defined later in this chapter). As shown in Figure 1-1, strategic intent and strategic mission influence strategy formulation and implementation actions.

Finally, this chapter's discussion turns to a consideration of the stakeholders that organizations serve. The degree to which stakeholders' needs are met increases directly with enhancements in a firm's strategic competitiveness and increases in the amount it earns beyond average profits. Closing the chapter are brief introductions to organizational strategists and the elements of the strategic management process.

## National Competitiveness

**National competitiveness** is the degree to which a country produces goods and services that meet the test of international markets, while simultaneously maintaining or expanding the real income of its citizens.[8] National competitiveness is important in the global economy. For example, in national economies based on private enterprise principles, the collective competitive successes or failures of individual business firms influence the degree to which citizens can be protected, educated, and served.

For many decades, the United States was the world's most competitive nation. The stock of physical and human capital the United States accumulated during the second century of its existence (roughly from the Civil War to the close of World War II) was the foundation for the country's competitiveness over a period of several decades. Before 1940, U.S. savings and investment rates were among the highest in the world and 10 times higher than those in Japan. In addition, the country's education system was widely thought to be better than those of all other nations. The superior skills of U.S. managers were instrumental in the country's ability to dominate key industries, such as steel and automobiles.[9]

By 1950, the United States' per capita gross national product (GNP) was 4 times greater than Germany's and 15 times that of Japan.[10] This was a time period during which U.S. companies benefited from having the world's highest-skilled workers, the largest amount of investment capital, the best technology, the best managers, and the largest domestic market.[11] The few goods and services imported from Japan and Germany did not threaten Americans' jobs, nor did U.S. exports endanger Japanese and German workers' jobs.[12]

As the world entered the 1960s, its economy was experiencing the beginning of profound changes. The amount of international trade among nations was increasing. No longer as dominant as it once was, the United States began trading with and competing against Japan and a host of European nations whose productivity rates were growing rapidly. The savings rates in many of these countries were increasing dramatically, even doubling in some cases. At the same time, the U.S. savings rate first stabilized and then began a long, steady decline. While U.S. educational standards started to slip, those in Japan and many European nations were being strengthened.[13] As the 1960s came to a close, Japan and European countries had substantially reduced their competitiveness gap with the United States. Instead of being markets for U.S. firms' exports, companies from Japan and Europe became strong competitors in the world markets.[14] In response, some companies, notably those in the United States, sought protection from foreign competition through governmental actions (e.g., tariffs and other protectionist policies).

The beginning of the 1970s saw still other significant changes in the world's economy. International trade among nations continued to increase, exposing U.S. and other domestic markets to extensive and rigorous competition. The competitiveness of the United States continued to decline as its previously sheltered domestic markets were exposed to the strategic actions of effective foreign competitors. Evidence of the decline of U.S. competitiveness is the fact that it entered the 1980s as the world's largest creditor nation, but finished the decade as the largest debtor nation.

As the 1980s came to a close, business firms across the world, but especially those in private enterprise economies, could no longer expect to be protected from the rigors of international competition by tariffs or a domestic government's political and economic power. Some U.S. industries (e.g., airlines and telecommunications) had been deregulated, encouraging entry from new domestic and foreign competitors. In order to sell their goods and services, successful companies were expanding into international markets. Other indicators of the development of a global economy include the emergence of the European Community (EC) as a trading entity, the evolution and passage of the North American Free Trade Agreement (NAFTA) and the General Agreement on Tariffs and Trade (GATT), and the coalescing of Asian countries as potent competitors.

## National Competitiveness Rankings in the Early 1990s

By the end of 1992, several indicators of U.S. national competitiveness caused concern. Consider the following conditions in the United States at the end of 1992: (1) Its savings rate was the lowest of most major industrial countries and was less than half of Japan's, (2) its investment rates were less than half of Japan's and below those of all major competing nations, and (3) its students ranked among the lowest on standardized international tests (compared to Canada, China, France, Great Britain, Italy, Korea, and Taiwan). Only 5 percent of U.S. high school seniors were prepared for college-level mathematics.[15]

In terms of national competitiveness, some evidence suggested that Japan was the world's most competitive nation at the close of 1992 (see Table 1-2). Calculated by the Institute for Management Development in Lausanne, Switzerland, the World Competitiveness Scoreboard ranks countries in terms of their ability to compete in international markets.

**Japan's Competitiveness**   The complexity of national competitiveness is reflected by the fact that even though Japan ranked first in the 1992 World Competitiveness Survey, its corporations were encountering competitive challenges. The veneer of competitive invincibility of some automobile manufacturers, such as Nissan and Toyota, was beginning to disappear. To cope with a slowdown in the global automobile market and remain strategically competitive, both companies aggressively cut costs during 1993. Plants were closed, and workers were laid off. A Nissan employee suggested that his company was having the same problems that affected U.S. car manufacturers some 10 years earlier.[16]

Honda Motor Company's experiences, however, suggest caution in cutting costs to remain competitive and profitable. Historically, Honda was proud of being

| ▼ **TABLE 1–2** |
| --- |
| **The 1992 World Competitiveness Scoreboard** |
| 1. Japan |
| 2. United States |
| 3. Denmark |
| 4. Switzerland |
| 5. Germany |
| 6. Netherlands |
| 7. Austria |
| 8. New Zealand |
| 9. Sweden |
| 10. Belgium |
| *Source:* Based on information from: T. Martin, and D. Greenwood, 1993. The World Economy in Charts. *FORTUNE,* the WEFA Group, July 26: 96, © 1993 Time Inc. All rights reserved. |

*Automobile manufacturers compete on a global basis. The Ford Escort, Saturn's products, and the Toyota Corolla compete to satisfy customers. In recent years, Ford Motor Company and General Motors have reduced the perceived gap in performance dimensions between cars produced by U.S. and Japanese companies. Because of their size, the automobile manufacturers often affect the overall global competitiveness of the United States and Japan.*

the leanest automobile company. But, in early 1993, some officials thought the firm might have become too lean. To control operating costs, the sales, service, and parts support for dealers was reduced, but it cut too deeply. As a result, Honda failed to meet its dealers' needs. To correct the problem, the company expanded sales training and introduced dealer incentives.[17]

Japan is facing other competitiveness concerns. For example, the nation's creative ability has been questioned. Japanese companies have excelled at improving existing production methods and products. However, Japanese firms have not consistently pioneered the development of new products. In the words of a Japanese executive, "there's not much left uncopied, and we are all facing the much tougher question of what to do next."[18]

Thus, Japan's future growth and competitiveness, some believe, "depend[s] on how effectively [it] can master the more daunting tasks of inventing new products, markets, and even whole businesses."[19] Because the 1990s have found many Japanese companies with unprofitable businesses, excessive manufacturing capacity, and payrolls swollen by lifetime employment policies, changing their focus from production efficiency to product innovations may be difficult.[20] Watson's suggestion that success is impermanent is equally apropos for Japanese and for U.S. corporations.

**Current Markets and Future U.S. Competitiveness**  The changes in the world economy are of keen interest to firms seeking strategic competitiveness. For example, Europe, instead of the United States, is now the world's largest single market. If countries from the former Soviet Union and other Eastern bloc nations are included, the European market has a gross domestic product (GDP) of $5 trillion with 700 million potential customers.[21] In addition, by 2015, China's total GDP will be greater than Japan's, although its per capita output will be much lower.[22] Some believe that the United States, Japan, and Europe are relatively equal contenders seeking to be the most competitive nation, or group of nations, in the twenty-first century. Achieving this status will allow the "winner's citizens to have the highest standard of living."[23]

Following his analysis of the U.S. manufacturing sector, the director of economic research at the Hudson Institute concluded that "the U.S. looks very competitive indeed in labor costs, return on capital, manufacturing growth and productivity, and exports."[24] In support of this position, the analyst noted that from 1981 to 1989, manufacturing output rose by 5.2 percent per year, up from 2.8 percent per year between 1971 and 1980. These output gains compared favorably to other nations' achievements. The 1981–1989 annual gains were 2.6 percent in Germany and 6.7 percent in Japan. Moreover, from 1980 to 1989, the cumulative increase in U.S. labor productivity in manufacturing was 42.9 percent (as compared to a 26 percent gain from 1970 to 1979). The labor productivity gains (from 1980 to 1989) in Germany were 22.3 percent and in Japan, 59.3 percent. Thus, as a whole, U.S. manufacturing firms are becoming more strategically competitive. Moreover, the trade deficits the nation experienced during the 1980s and early 1990s were concentrated in only a few industry sectors—namely, apparel, other consumer goods (e.g. food, household goods), and automobiles.[25]

Furthermore, in 1990, a full-time U.S. worker produced $49,600 worth of goods and services per year. In terms of equivalent purchasing power, a German worker produced $44,200; a Japanese worker, $38,200; and a British worker, $37,100. Worker productivity is the ultimate yardstick of international competitiveness.[26] Additionally, between 1987 and 1992, "the United States, France, the

Netherlands, Austria, Norway and New Zealand registered the largest gains in international competitiveness, measured by relative unit labour costs, while Canada, Australia, Italy, Sweden, Spain and the United Kingdom have registered the biggest losses."[27]

There is little doubt that many U.S. firms were less globally competitive during the 1970s and 1980s and that concern about U.S. competitiveness remains.[28] In addition, only one-fifth of U.S. companies in a position to export actually do so.[29] On the other hand, U.S. firms have the necessary capability to regain leadership positions in the global economy. Moreover, some firms are now effectively using this capability to achieve strategic competitiveness. Examples of strategic actions some U.S. companies are using to be strategically competitive in the global economy are presented in the Strategic Focus. Notice that each firm is trying to develop a sustainable competitive advantage.

To achieve global competitiveness, a firm must view the world as its marketplace—that is, the arena in which it intends to exploit its competitive advantages. A commitment to globalization creates a sense of direction that can serve the firm well. The Federal-Mogul Corporation, for example, defines itself as follows: "Federal-Mogul Corporation is a global distributor and manufacturer of a broad range of precision parts, primarily components for automobiles, light and heavy duty trucks, farm and construction vehicles, and industrial products."[30] Similarly, Johnson & Johnson (J&J) defines itself as "the world's leading health care products corporation, with an unsurpassed global presence." In 1992, J&J earned approximately one-half of its $13.75 billion in sales and $1.63 billion in net earnings from its international operations (the firm sells products in 158 countries).[31] These pronouncements indicate that Federal-Mogul and Johnson & Johnson intend to be active participants in global markets. If their strategies are based on sustained

## STRATEGIC FOCUS

### Achieving Strategic Competitiveness in the Global Economy

In recognition of marketplace opportunities and competitive realities, U.S. brewers continue to become more global in their pursuit of superior profitability. Adolph Coors Company established a joint venture with New Zealand's Lion Nathan and built a brewery with Jinro in Korea that opened in 1994. Anheuser-Busch purchased 18 percent of Grupo Modelo, the Mexican producer of Corona beer. The company also has alliances with China's Tsingtao Brewery Company and Kirin Brewery, a Japanese firm. One reason for these actions is that the rest of the world's market is three and one-half times larger than the U.S. market and is growing rapidly.

The recent success of American computer and semiconductor manufacturers in the Japanese market is another indicator of how globally competitive U.S. firms can be. Between 1990 and 1993, U.S. semiconductor manufacturers virtually doubled their share of the Japanese market to almost 20 percent. These gains were achieved through competitive advantages based on the basics—quality, uniqueness, performance, and price. In today's world of more graphic and powerful hardware and software, IBM, Dell, Apple, and Compaq are all making significant inroads into the Japanese PC market. The companies' progress has been earned through the development of sophisticated machines, the introduction of a new Japanese-language version of Microsoft's Windows software, and the ability to offer sharply lower prices.

competitive advantages, these companies will achieve strategic competitiveness and earn above-average profits. As suggested by our discussion of national competitiveness, the world's economy continues to become more *globalized*.

## The March of Globalization

▲ **Globalization** is the spread of economic innovations around the world and the political and cultural adjustments that accompany this diffusion.

**Globalization** is the spread of economic innovations around the world and the political and cultural adjustments that accompany this diffusion. Globalization encourages international integration. For example, financial capital might be obtained in one national market and used to buy raw materials in another one. Manufacturing equipment bought from a third national market can be used to produce products that are sold in yet a fourth market.[32] Thus, globalization increases the range of opportunities for firms.

The increasing economic interdependence among industrialized countries, the growing needs of developing countries, and the disintegration of barriers to the flow of money, information, and technology across country borders facilitate international market integration and globalization. These conditions force global companies to think seriously about the strategies they need to implement to develop sustained competitive advantages. Often, the strategies that result in a sustained competitive advantage are ones through which a firm becomes leaner, more flexible, and more focused on providing cost-effective goods and services to sophisticated customers in an interconnected world.[33]

The internationalization of markets makes it increasingly difficult to distinguish between a domestic and a global company. For example, in a recent year, Honda Motor Company (1) employed 14,000 people in the United States; (2) sold 660,000 units in the United States, 480,000 (73 percent) of which it produced there; (3) manufactured its automobiles with 75 percent local U.S. content (parts/assemblies manufactured in the United States); (4) purchased $2.9 billion worth of parts from U.S. suppliers; (5) paid $2.5 billion in federal income tax; (6) invested $3 billion in a research and development center in the United States; and (7) exported 40,000 cars from its U.S. facilities to other nations' markets. At the same time that Honda was manufacturing cars in Marysville and East Liberty, Ohio, Chrysler Corporation was producing minivans in Canada, LeBarons in Mexico, and Dodge Stealths in Japan.[34]

Banco Economico S.A. is the oldest private-sector banking institution in Latin America. Established in Salvador, Brazil, in 1834, the firm had 793 service facilities in its home country at the end of 1992. At the same time, however, it had offices in New York, London, and the Cayman Islands. These offices, coupled with Banco Economico's worldwide network of correspondent banking relationships, were established to help the firm meet its objective of satisfying customers' financial needs in a rapidly changing global economy.[35]

Given their operations, these three companies should not be thought of as Japanese, American, and Brazilian, respectively. All three are more accurately classified as global companies.

### The Continuation of Globalization

Some believe that because of its enormous economic benefits, globalization will not be stopped. It has been predicted, for example, that genuine free trade in manufactured goods among the United States, Europe, and Japan would add 5 to 10 percent to the Triad's annual economic output; free trade in the Triad's service sector would boost aggregate output by another 15 to 20 percent.[36] Realizing these potential gains in economic output requires a commitment from the industrialized nations to cooperatively stimulate the higher levels of trade necessary for global growth. Eliminating national laws that impede free trade is an important stimulus to increased trading among nations.[37]

Global competition has increased standards of performance in terms of many dimensions, including those of quality, cost, productivity, product introduction time, and smooth, flowing operations.[38] Moreover, it is critical to understand that these standards are not static and are exacting, requiring continuous improvement from a firm and its employees. As they accept the challenges posed by these increasing standards, effective firms commit to doing what is necessary to be strategically competitive. It is through acceptance of these challenges that companies increase their capabilities and individual workers sharpen their skills.[39]

Global markets are attractive strategic options for some companies, but they are not a single source of strategic competitiveness. In fact, for most companies, even for those capable of competing successfully in global markets, it is critical that they remain committed to their domestic market. In the words of the director of economic studies at the Brookings Institution, "imported goods are components of a larger share of goods produced and sold in the United States, and international trade is likely to grow in significance. Still, the great bulk of the goods and services Americans consume and invest in is entirely domestic."[40]

Thus, companies throughout the world are challenged to become more strategically competitive in their domestic markets. However, because the benchmark for strategic competitiveness relates to global standards, firms that increase their ability to compete domestically simultaneously improve their global competitiveness.

Strategically competitive companies have learned how to apply competitive insights gained locally (or domestically) on a global scale. These companies do not impose homogeneous solutions in a pluralistic world. Instead, they nourish local insights so they can, as appropriate, modify and apply them in different regions around the world.[41]

An example of a global strategy to achieve strategic competitiveness and earn above-average profits is described in the Strategic Focus. Whirlpool is committed to satisfying the needs of different local markets while competing as a global company.

There are two important models intended to describe the key strategic inputs to a firm's strategic actions. The industrial organization, or I/O model, suggests that the conditions and characteristics of the external environment are the *primary* inputs to and determinants of strategies firms should formulate and implement to earn above-average profits. Alternatively, the resource-based model argues that a firm's internal resources and capabilities represent the *foundation* for development of a value-creating strategy. Resources and capabilities that serve as a source of competitive advantage over a firm's rivals are called **core competencies.**[42] According to the resource-based model, core competencies are actually the *primary* determinants of a firm's value-creating strategy. Especially in large companies, core competencies are often related to functional skills.[43] For example, the research and development function is a core competence for Merck (pharmaceuticals); at Philip Morris (tobacco and food), the marketing function is a core competence.[44]

The resource-based model assumes that firms within an industry control different resources and that these resources are not necessarily perfectly mobile

▲ **Core competencies** are resources and capabilities that serve as a source of competitive advantage over a firm's rivals.

### Whirlpool's Global Strategy

Whirlpool is the world's largest home appliance manufacturer. To expand its sales and to have an anchor location for its global strategy in the Asian region, the company recently established its Asian headquarters in Singapore. Prior to this time, Whirlpool sold products—refrigerators, air conditioners, dishwashers, and washing machines—in Asia that had not been designed with the local market in mind. To become more competitive, the firm decided a change was necessary. In the words of Robert Frey, president of Whirlpool Asia, "You can only do so much with an imported product. We decided we needed a design, manufacturing and corporate presence in Asia to underscore our commitment to the Asian market and to drive our global strategy in the region. You can't do that long distance. . . . [Moreover,] we felt that if we wanted to maintain our global leadership and significantly expand our market share, we had to make the decision to develop and design products to local tastes and to make them locally."

To date, Whirlpool has taken several actions to achieve its goals. A centralized operation in Singapore, with approximately 200 sales, marketing, finance, manufacturing, and technical employees, has been established. Among other responsibilities, this group is asked to design and manufacture appliances specifically for the Asian market. To pursue the possibility of forming alliances with local partners in the greater China region, offices have been set up in Hong Kong, Japan, and India. In the near future, the company plans to establish four or five manufacturing plants in Asia, either individually or with a local partner.

across firms. Through willful choices and actions, resources and capabilities can be consciously and systematically developed into core competencies.[45] In the resource-based model, core competencies are the foundation for selecting a strategy, achieving strategic competitiveness, and earning above-average profits. The development, nurturing, and application of core competencies throughout a firm may be highly related to strategic competitiveness for global companies.[46]

## The I/O Model of Superior Profitability

From the 1960s through the 1980s, the external environment was a *primary* determinant of strategies firms selected to be successful.[47] The I/O model explains the dominant influence of the external environment on firms' strategic actions.

Grounded in the economics discipline, the I/O model has three underlying assumptions. First, the external environment (especially the industry and competitive environments) is assumed to impose pressures and constraints that determine the strategies that would result in superior profitability. Second, most firms competing within a particular industry, or within a certain segment of an industry, are assumed to control similar strategically relevant resources and pursue similar strategies in light of those resources. The I/O model's third assumption is that resources used to implement strategies are highly mobile across firms. Because of resource mobility, any resource differences that might develop between firms will be short-lived.

Thus, in terms of the I/O model, firms are challenged to find the most attractive industry in which to compete. Because most firms are assumed to have similar strategically relevant resources, that are mobile across companies, competitiveness generally can be increased only when they find the industry with the highest profit potential and learn how to use their resources to implement the strategy required by the structural characteristics in that industry. The *five forces model of competition* is an analytical tool used to help firms with this task. Mentioned only briefly here, this tool is examined in detail in Chapter 2.

The five forces model suggests that an industry's profitability potential is a function of the interactions among five forces (suppliers, buyers, competitive rivalry among firms currently in the industry, product substitutes, and potential entrants to the industry).[48] Using this tool, a firm is challenged to understand an industry's profit potential and the strategy it should implement to establish a defensible competitive position, given the industry's structural characteristics. Typically, this model suggests that firms can earn above-average profits by offering either no-frills products at low prices (a cost leadership strategy) or differentiated products for which customers are willing to pay price premiums (a differentiation strategy).[49] Cost leadership and differentiation strategies are addressed fully in Chapter 4.

As shown in Figure 1-2, the I/O model suggests that superior profitability is earned when firms implement the strategy dictated by the characteristics of the general, industry, and competitive environments. Companies that develop or acquire the internal skills needed to implement strategies required by the external environment are likely to succeed, while those that do not are likely to fail. As such, superior profitability is determined by the external characteristics, rather than the firm's unique internal resources and capabilities.[50]

Formulating and implementing strategies that will not allow the firm to exploit marketplace opportunities, or reduce the impact of threats, is ill-advised. A company cannot expect to achieve strategic competitiveness or earn above-average profits without an understanding and alignment of its strategic actions with the general, industry, and competitive environments.

When a firm successfully matches its resources with external environmental opportunities, or uses them to reduce or eliminate the impact of threats, it is said to achieve **strategic fit.** Actions once taken by Dillard's Department Stores demonstrate attempts to maintain strategic fit. In the early 1990s, Dillard's changed its merchandising strategy. Basically, a decision was made to offer more private-label merchandise, much of which was to be purchased from overseas manufacturers, and to depend less on brand names. As explained by William Dillard, founder and CEO, these actions were taken to reduce costs and remain competitive, given the economic realities of the day. In the early 1990s, customers wanted to purchase high-quality clothing products, but at lower prices. Private-label merchandise represented an option to satisfy this demand. Thus, conditions in the external environment shaped Dillard's merchandising strategy. Responding as it did allowed Dillard's to maintain a strategic fit with its external environment.[51]

▲ **Strategic fit** is achieved when a firm successfully matches its resources with external environmental opportunities or uses them to reduce or eliminate the impact of threats.

## The Resource-Based Model of Superior Profitability

The resource-based model assumes that each organization is a collection of unique resources and capabilities that provides the basis for its strategy and is the primary source of its profitability. Additionally, it is assumed that over time, firms acquire

**FIGURE 1–2**   The I/O Model of Superior Profitability

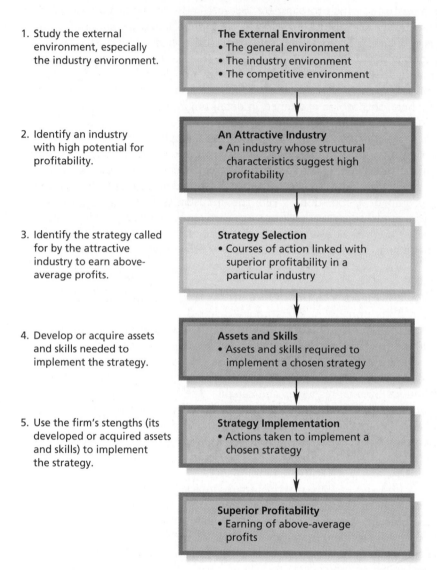

1. Study the external environment, especially the industry environment.

**The External Environment**
- The general environment
- The industry environment
- The competitive environment

2. Identify an industry with high potential for profitability.

**An Attractive Industry**
- An industry whose structural characteristics suggest high profitability

3. Identify the strategy called for by the attractive industry to earn above-average profits.

**Strategy Selection**
- Courses of action linked with superior profitability in a particular industry

4. Develop or acquire assets and skills needed to implement the strategy.

**Assets and Skills**
- Assets and skills required to implement a chosen strategy

5. Use the firm's stengths (its developed or acquired assets and skills) to implement the strategy.

**Strategy Implementation**
- Actions taken to implement a chosen strategy

**Superior Profitability**
- Earning of above-average profits

different resources and develop unique capabilities. As such, all firms competing within a particular industry may not possess the same strategically relevant resources and capabilities. The resource-based model also assumes that resources may not be highly mobile across firms. The differences in resources, which other firms may not be able to attain or easily duplicate, and the particular way they are used within a firm form the basis of competitive advantage.[52]

**Resources** are inputs into a firm's production process, such as capital equipment, the skills of individual employees, patents, finance, and talented managers. In general, a firm's resources can be classified into three categories—physical, human, and organizational capital.[53]

Individual resources alone may not yield a sustainable competitive advantage. For example, a sophisticated piece of manufacturing equipment may become a strategically relevant resource only when its use is integrated effectively with other

▲ **Resources** are inputs into a firm's production process, such as capital equipment, the skills of individual employees, patents, finance, and talented managers.

aspects of a firm's operations (such as marketing and the work of employees). But, in general, it is through the combination and integration of sets of resources that sustainable competitive advantages are formed. **Capability** is the capacity for a set of resources to integratively perform a task or an activity. Capabilities are the result of an integrated set of resources.[54]

▲ **Capability** is the capacity for a set of resources to integratively perform a task or an activity.

The resource-based model of competitive advantage is shown in Figure 1-3. In contrast to the I/O model, the resource-based view is grounded in the perspective that a firm's internal environment, in terms of its resources and capabilities, is more critical to the determination of strategic actions than is the external environment. Instead of focusing on the accumulation of resources that are necessary to implement the strategy dictated by conditions and constraints in the external environment (I/O model), the resource-based view suggests that a firm's unique resources and capabilities provide the basis for a strategy. The strategy chosen should allow the firm to best exploit its core competencies relative to opportunities in the external environment.

**FIGURE 1–3   The Resource-Based Model of Superior Profitability**

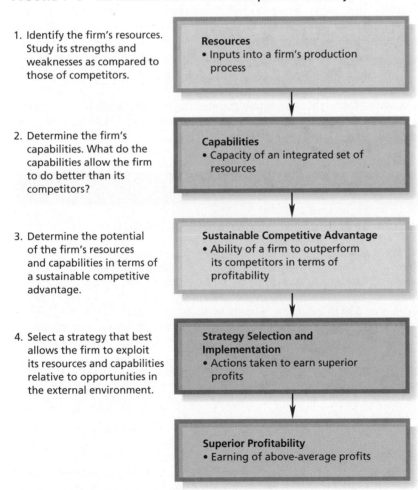

1. Identify the firm's resources. Study its strengths and weaknesses as compared to those of competitors.

> **Resources**
> • Inputs into a firm's production process

2. Determine the firm's capabilities. What do the capabilities allow the firm to do better than its competitors?

> **Capabilities**
> • Capacity of an integrated set of resources

3. Determine the potential of the firm's resources and capabilities in terms of a sustainable competitive advantage.

> **Sustainable Competitive Advantage**
> • Ability of a firm to outperform its competitors in terms of profitability

4. Select a strategy that best allows the firm to exploit its resources and capabilities relative to opportunities in the external environment.

> **Strategy Selection and Implementation**
> • Actions taken to earn superior profits

> **Superior Profitability**
> • Earning of above-average profits

*SOURCE: Adapted from Robert M. Grant, 1991, The resource-based theory of competitive advantage: Implications for strategy formulation, California Management Review 33 (Spring): 114–135 © 1991 by the Regents of the University of California. Reprinted from the California Management Review, Vol. 33, No. 3. By permission of the Regents.*

*These employees are participating in a training and development program offered at Motorola University. In the complex and challenging global economy, a company's human resources can be an important source of competitive advantage. Through its training and development efforts, Motorola may be able to develop a work force that is a core competence for the firm.*

Not all of a firm's resources and capabilities have the potential to be the basis of sustained competitive advantage. This potential is realized when resources and capabilities are valuable, rare, imperfectly imitable, and non-substitutable. Resources (as used here, this term includes capabilities) are valuable when they allow a firm to exploit opportunities and/or neutralize threats in its external environment; they are rare when possessed by few, if any, current and potential competitors; they are imperfectly imitable when other firms cannot obtain them; and they are non-substitutable when they have no strategic equivalents.[55] When these criteria are met, resources and capabilities become core competencies and serve as the basis of a firm's sustained competitive advantage, its strategic competitiveness, and its ability to earn above-average profits. These criteria are discussed in greater detail in Chapter 3.

A wide range of resources and capabilities can be the foundation for core competencies. But, in the global economy, the skills of a firm's labor force are increasingly critical to developing a sustained competitive advantage.[56] However, employing skilled workers does not necessarily result in competitive advantage. Only through establishing firm-specific patterns of training and combining the human resources with other resources and capabilities can firms expect their workers to become a core competence. One company's efforts to train and develop its workers are described in the Strategic Focus.

Motorola is known to provide some of the most effective training in the United States. Some achievements (e.g., the doubling of sales per employee) suggest that the firm's training-based efforts are successful. If these efforts are resulting in a work force that is valuable, rare, imperfectly imitable, and non-substitutable, Motorola has developed a core competence that may be providing the foundation for its value-creating strategy.

## STRATEGIC FOCUS

### Training and Development at Motorola University

In 1992, Motorola spent 3.6 percent of its payroll (this amounted to $120 million) on education and training. On the average, each Motorola employee devotes 36 hours per year to formal education and training activities. A key reason the firm is willing to engage in such training is the belief that every $1 spent on education returns $30 in productivity gains within three years. Supporting this belief are two significant accomplishments: the doubling of sales per employee between 1987 and 1992 and the 47 percent increase in profits over the same time period.

Motorola's training programs, in which employees throughout the firm's global work force participate, are held at what is known as Motorola University. Located in Schaumburg, Illinois, with regional campuses in Austin, Texas, and Phoenix, Arizona, Motorola offered 102,000 days of training in 1992 to employees and to its suppliers and customers. The university is a collection of computer-equipped classrooms and laboratories. Most courses offered at the university are highly technical (for example, one course is called Fractional Factorial Experiments). Through courses of this type, factory workers study the fundamentals of computer-aided design, robotics, and customized manufacturing. However, to make them even more capable, employees also complete "soft" courses, such as those dealing with communicating effectively and working cooperatively.

## Strategic Intent and Strategic Mission

Resulting from analyses of a firm's internal and external environments is the information required to form a strategic intent and develop a strategic mission (see Figure 1-1). Both intent and mission are linked with strategic competitiveness.

## Strategic Intent

**Strategic intent** is the leveraging of a firm's internal resources, capabilities, and core competencies to accomplish what may at first appear to be unattainable goals in the competitive environment.[57] Strategic intent is about winning competitive battles and striving to obtain global leadership. It exists when all employees and levels of a firm are committed to the pursuit of a specific (and significant) performance criterion. Some argue that strategic intent provides employees with the only goal worthy of personal effort and commitment—to unseat the best or remain the best, worldwide.[58] Strategic intent exists when people believe fervently in their product and industry and when they are focused totally on doing what they do better than competitors.[59]

The following examples offer expressions of strategic intent. Intel seeks to become the premier building-block supplier to the new computer industry. Microsoft believes that its "holy grail" is to provide the Yellow Pages for an electronic marketplace of on-line information systems. Komatsu intends to encircle Caterpillar (a key competitor), Canon desires to "beat Xerox," and Honda strives to become a second Ford (a company it identified as a pioneer in the automobile industry). The CEO of Pep Boys does not believe in friendly competition; instead, he wants to dominate the competition and, by doing so, put them out of business. At Procter & Gamble (P&G), employees participate in a program the CEO calls "combat training." The intent of the program is to focus on ways P&G can beat the competition.[60]

Strategic intent may even be described metaphorically. In a recent *Annual Report,* Reebok International showed a series of pictures depicting an athlete crossing a high-jump bar. In her own handwriting, the athlete described her commitment to being the best and to winning:

> "It's about raising the bar. I can jump higher. I know it. I can see it. I'm stronger, faster, I've learned more. The key is to focus, to concentrate on each basic element that goes into a jump. Jumping is my gift and it's a privilege to improve the gift. When everything works right, when you're focused and relaxed, it's kind of like flying. One thing that keeps you involved in jumping is that you are always trying to clear the next height. Even if you miss, you come away from every jump knowing you can go higher."[61]

The words of this athlete appear to reflect Reebok's intent to focus and concentrate on every part of its business in order to constantly improve its performance and, by doing so, earn above-average profits.

But it is not enough to know only our own strategic intent. Organizational effectiveness demands that we also identify our competitors' strategic intent. Only when others' intentions are understood can a firm become aware of competitors' resolve, stamina, and inventiveness (traits linked with effective strategic intents).[62] The success of some Japanese companies may be grounded in a keen and deep understanding of customers, suppliers, partners, and competitors' strategic intentions.[63] It is possible, for example, that other automobile manufacturers' market

▲ **Strategic intent** is the leveraging of a firm's internal resources, capabilities, and core competencies to accomplish what may at first appear to be unattainable goals in the competitive environment.

shares would have been less negatively affected had they fully understood their Japanese competitors' intentions, commitments to innovativeness and product quality, and stamina.

## Strategic Mission

As our discussion shows, strategic intent is *internally focused*. It is concerned with identifying the resources, capabilities, and core competencies on which a firm can base its strategic actions. Strategic intent reflects what a firm is capable of doing as a result of its core competencies and the unique ways they can be used to develop a sustained competitive advantage and earn above-average profits.

▲ **Strategic mission** is a statement of a firm's unique purpose and the scope of its operations in product and market terms.

Strategic mission flows from strategic intent. It is an application of strategic intent. Externally focused, **strategic mission** is a statement of a firm's unique purpose and the scope of its operations in product and market terms.[64] A strategic mission provides general descriptions of the products a firm intends to produce and the markets it will serve using its internally based core competencies. The interdependent relationship between strategic intent and strategic mission is shown in Figure 1-4.

An effective strategic mission establishes a firm's individuality and is exciting, inspiring, and relevant to all stakeholders.[65] The strategic mission, based on the firm's strategic intent, informs employees of the general directions the firm is taking. Together, strategic intent and strategic mission provide insights required to formulate and implement the firm's strategies. Examples of strategic missions are shown in Table 1-3.

Thus, a firm's intent and mission provide the guidance necessary to achieve the desired strategic outcomes shown in Figure 1-1. When strategically competitive and earning above-average profits, a firm has the capacity to more than satisfy its stakeholders' interests. The groups of stakeholders that a firm serves are examined in the next section.

## Stakeholders

▲ **Stakeholders** are the individuals and groups who can affect and are affected by the strategic outcomes achieved and who have enforceable claims on a firm's performance.

**Stakeholders** are the individuals and groups who can affect and are affected by the strategic outcomes achieved and who have enforceable claims on a firm's performance.[66] Claims against an organization's performance are enforced through a stakeholder's ability to withhold participation essential to a firm's survival, competitiveness, and profitability.[67]

Thus, organizations have dependency relationships with their stakeholders. However, firms are not equally dependent on all stakeholders; as a consequence, every stakeholder does not have the same level of influence. The more critical and valued a stakeholder's participation is, the greater a firm's dependency on it. Greater dependence, in turn, results in more potential influence for the stakeholder over a firm's decisions and actions.

▲ **Shareholders** are those who have invested capital in a firm in the expectation of earning at least a satisfactory, or average, return on their investments.

Grounded in laws governing private property and private enterprise, the most obvious stakeholders are **shareholders**—those who have invested capital in a firm in the expectation of earning at least a satisfactory, or average, return on their investments. However, modern organizations serve many in addition to those with financial interests. Firms are challenged to identify their stakeholders and the objectives each values and to determine what should be done (i.e., what strategies

**FIGURE 1–4**  **The Interdependent Relationship Between Strategic Intent and Strategic Mission**

**Strategic Intent**
• Winning competitive battles through deciding how to leverage resources, capabilities, and core competencies.

**Strategic Mission**
• An application of strategic intent in terms of products to be offered and markets to be served.

▼ **TABLE 1–3**

## Strategic Mission Statements

| | |
|---|---|
| *AT&T* | We are dedicated to being the world's best at bringing people together—giving them easy access to each other and to the information and services they want and need anytime, anywhere. |
| *Baldor Motors and Drives* | Our mission is: To be the best (as determined by our customers) marketers, designers and manufacturers of electric motors and drives. To achieve this, we must:<br>• Provide better value to our customers than any of our competitors.<br>• Attract and retain competent employees dedicated to reaching our common goals and objectives.<br>• Produce good, long-term results for our shareholders. |
| *Frito-Lay Inc.* | To best satisfy America's snacking needs by providing fun foods within arm's reach. |
| *Harsco Corporation* | The mission of Harsco Corporation is to be a world class competitor in the domestic and international manufacturing and marketing of diverse goods and industrial services, principally for defense, industrial, commercial and construction applications. The Corporation is committed to providing innovative engineering solutions to specialized problems, emphasizing technology and close attention to customer service. In accomplishing its mission, the Corporation will build upon the base of experience acquired during its long association with manufacturing and industrial services. Growth will be achieved through acquisition and internal development within a framework that balances risk of diversification against continued prudent management of current businesses. |
| *Southwest Airlines Co.* | The mission of Southwest Airlines is dedication to the highest quality of Customer Service delivered with a sense of warmth, friendliness, individual pride and Company Spirit. |

*Sources:* Company Annual Reports.

should be formulated and implemented) to accomplish those objectives. Satisfied stakeholders continue to support firms that meet or exceed their expectations.

## Classification of Stakeholders

▲ **Capital market stakeholders** are shareholders and the major suppliers of a firm's capital.

▲ **Product market stakeholders** are the firm's primary customers, suppliers, host governments, and unions representing the work force.

▲ **Organizational stakeholders** are all of a firm's employees, including both non-managerial and managerial personnel.

The parties (individuals and groups) involved with a firm's operations can be separated into three groups of stakeholders.[68] As shown in Figure 1-5, these groups are the **capital market stakeholders** (shareholders and the major suppliers of a firm's capital), the **product market stakeholders** (the firm's primary customers, suppliers, host governments, and unions representing the work force), and the **organizational stakeholders** (all of a firm's employees, including both non-managerial and managerial personnel).

Each of these stakeholder groups expects those making strategic decisions in a firm to provide the leadership through which their valued objectives will be accomplished. But these groups' objectives often differ from one another, sometimes placing managers in situations where trade-offs have to be made. As a single performance criterion, return on investment (ROI) demonstrates the most extreme case of differences in interests primarily between parts of two stakeholder groups—capital market and product market stakeholders—and the decision challenges these differences create.

Shareholders want the return on their investment (hence, their wealth) to be maximized. This could be accomplished at the expense of investing in a firm's future. Gains achieved by reducing investment in research and development, for example, could be returned to shareholders (thereby increasing the short-term

**FIGURE 1–5  Groups of Organizational Stakeholders**

return on their investments). However, a short-term enhancement of shareholders' wealth can negatively affect the firm's future competitive ability. Sophisticated shareholders, with diversified portfolios, may sell their interests if a firm fails to invest in its future. Those making strategic decisions are responsible for a firm's survival in both the short and the long terms. Accordingly, it is in neither their interests (as organizational stakeholders) nor those of product market stakeholders for investments in the company to be unduly minimized.

In contrast to shareholders, customers prefer that investors receive a minimum return on their investments. As such, customers could have their interests maximized when the quality and reliability of a firm's products are improved, but without a price increase. High returns to customers might come at the expense of lower returns negotiated with capital market stakeholders.

Because of potential conflicts, each firm is challenged to manage its stakeholders. When earning above-average profits, this challenge is lessened substantially. With the capability and flexibility provided by above-average profits, a firm can more easily satisfy all stakeholders simultaneously.

When earning average profits, a firm may find the management of stakeholders to be more difficult. In these situations, trade-offs must be made. With average profits, a firm is unlikely to maximize the interests of all stakeholders. The objective becomes one of at least minimally satisfying each stakeholder. Trade-off decisions are made in light of how dependent the firm is on the support of the stakeholder groups. An example of how stakeholders can demand satisfaction of their claims on a firm's performance is provided in the next subsection. A firm earning below-average profits does not have the capacity to minimally satisfy all stakeholders. The managerial challenge in this case is to make trade-offs that minimize the amount of support lost from stakeholders.

In the next three subsections, additional information is presented about the stakeholder groups that firms manage.

**Capital Market Stakeholders**   Both shareholders and lenders expect a firm to preserve and enhance the wealth they have entrusted to it. The returns expected are commensurate with the degree of risk accepted with those investments (i.e., lower returns are expected with low-risk investments; higher returns are expected with high-risk investments).

If lenders become dissatisfied, they can impose stricter covenants on subsequent capital borrowing. Shareholders can reflect their dissatisfaction through several means, including the sale of their stock. When aware of potential or actual dissatisfactions among capital market stakeholders, a firm may respond to their concerns. The firm's response to dissatisfied stakeholders is affected by the nature of its dependency relationship with them. The greater and more significant the dependency relationship, the more direct and significant a firm's response will be. Citicorp's actions demonstrate this point.

Citicorp was long known as a bank not clearly focused on profitability. In the words of one analyst, "Traditionally, [Citicorp] has been run for growth and for revenue generation and for the fiefdoms of its managers, at all levels. It has not been run for profitability."

In the middle of 1993, Citicorp's capital market stakeholders reacted to this means of operating the bank. Probably because of the importance of the bank's dependency relationship with these stakeholders, its strategists responded aggressively. During a spring banking conference with Solomon Brothers, Citicorp's chairman announced that one of the bank's key goals had become "to deliver shareholder value, on a sustained basis." In part, Citicorp made this commitment to retain its capital market stakeholders' support.[69] At least in the short run, this additional support for the capital market stakeholders may come at the expense of returns to the other stakeholders.

**Product Market Stakeholders**    Initial observation of customers, suppliers, host governments, and unions representing workers might suggest little commonality among their interests. However, close inspection suggests that all four parties can benefit as firms engage in competitive battles. For example, depending on product and industry characteristics, marketplace competition may result in lower product prices charged to a firm's customers and higher prices paid to its suppliers (the firm might be willing to pay higher supplier prices to assure delivery of the types of goods and services linked with competitive success).

Generally speaking, customers, as stakeholders, demand reliable products at the lowest possible price. Suppliers seek assured customers willing to pay the highest sustainable prices for the goods and services they receive. Host governments want companies willing to be long-term employers and providers of tax revenues, without placing excessive demands on public support services. Union officials are interested in secure jobs, under ideal working conditions, for employees they represent. Recall, as mentioned in the opening case, that one of AT&T's actions to implement a global strategy was the development of effective links—working relationships—with its unions. Thus, product market stakeholders are generally satisfied when a firm's profit margin yields the lowest acceptable return to capital market stakeholders (i.e., the lowest return lenders and shareholders will accept and still retain their interests in the firm).

All product market stakeholders are important in a competitive business environment. However, in many firms, customers are being emphasized. At AT&T, for example, one of the company's upper-level executives cautions those with whom he works to ask why customers (or competitors, for that matter) are not being discussed after the first 15 minutes of any meeting. If they are not being discussed after a second 15-minute period, the executive believes people should leave the meeting.[70] This proposed action appears to be consistent with AT&T's "dedication to helping customers" (mentioned in the opening case). Moreover, the recommended action reflects a belief that focusing on customers is linked with earning above-average profits.

**Organizational Stakeholders**    Employees, non-managerial and managerial, expect a firm to provide a secure, dynamic, stimulating, and rewarding career environment. These stakeholders are usually satisfied working for a company that is growing and developing their skills. Workers who learn how to productively use rapidly developing knowledge are thought to be critical to organizational success. In a collective sense, the education and skills of a nation's work force may be its dominant competitive weapon in a global economy.[71]

In a global economy, the strategic management process is important to both nations and their individual firms. In the next section, we describe the people responsible for the design and execution of strategic management processes. Various names are given to these people—top-level managers, executives, strategists, the top management team, and general managers are examples. Throughout this book, these names are used interchangeably. But, in all cases, they describe the work of a person responsible for and involved with implementing a firm's strategic management process and helping the firm earn superior profits.

As is discussed in some detail in Chapter 3, the work of these people is critical. In fact, top-level managers can be a source of sustained competitive advantage. Moreover, the decisions and actions these people make to combine resources to create capabilities can often be a source of competitive advantage.[72]

## Organizational Strategists

Small organizations may have a single strategist. In many cases, this person owns the firm and is deeply involved with its daily operations. At the other extreme, large, diversified firms have many top-level managers. In addition to the CEO and other top-level officials (e.g., chief operating officer and chief financial officer), they have strategists in charge of individual business units.

Typically, stakeholders have high expectations of strategists, particularly the CEO. For example, in the middle of 1993, Leonard Roberts was chosen as Radio Shack's new CEO. Based on his previous successes as chairman and CEO first of Arby's and then of Shoney's, Roberts was expected to help Radio Shack complete the sale of its manufacturing businesses, improve its sagging profit margins, and increase its sales. Although confident of Roberts's abilities, analysts believed accomplishing these objectives would be difficult in a slow-growth, yet increasingly competitive, global business environment.[73] Roberts' impact on Radio Shack is yet to be fully determined.

As leaders, top-level managers use various means to influence and motivate others to be a part of the activities for which they bear the final responsibility. Among them are the firm's governance structure and its structure and control mechanisms (these topics, along with strategic leadership and corporate entrepreneurship and innovation, are examined in detail in Part III of this text).

Top-level managers play critical roles in firms' efforts to achieve desired strategic outcomes (see Figure 1-1). In fact, some believe that every organizational failure is actually a failure of those who hold the final responsibility for the quality and effectiveness of a firm's decisions and actions.[74] Thus, it can be argued that organizations fail when executives do not create a sustained competitive advantage.

Decisions for which strategists are responsible include how resources will be developed or acquired, at what price they will be obtained, and how they will be used. Strategists' decisions also influence how information flows in a company, the strategies a firm chooses to implement, and the scope of its operations. Additionally, how strategists complete their work and their patterns of interactions with others significantly influence the way a firm does business and affect its ability to develop a sustained competitive advantage. How a firm does business is captured by the concept of organizational culture. Critical to strategic leadership practices and the implementation of strategies, **organizational culture** refers to the core values shared by all or most of the managers and employees. It is the "social energy that drives—or fails to drive—the organization."[75] As we discuss in Chapters 2, 11, and 12, organizational culture is a potential source of sustained competitive advantage for a firm.[76]

After evaluating available information and alternatives, top-level managers must frequently choose from among similarly attractive alternatives. The most effective strategists have the self-confidence required to select the best alternatives, allocate the required level of resources to them, and effectively explain to interested parties why certain alternatives were selected.[77]

▲ **Organizational culture** refers to the core values shared by all or most of the managers and employees. It is the "social energy that drives—or fails to drive—the organization."

When choosing among alternatives, strategists are accountable for treating employees, suppliers, customers, and others with fairness and respect. Nonetheless, firms cannot succeed without people who, following careful and sometimes difficult analyses, are willing to make tough decisions—the types of decisions that result in strategic competitiveness.[78]

## The Work of Effective Strategists

Perhaps not surprisingly, hard work, thorough analyses, and common sense are prerequisites to an individual's success as a strategist.[79] The former CEO of Apple Computer, John Sculley, tries to sleep an hour "here and there." In describing the reality of work in the 1990s, Sculley suggested that sleeping through the night is an outmoded remnant of the agrarian and industrial ages. "People don't live that way anymore," Sculley stated. "It's a 24-hour day, not an 8-to-5 day."[80]

In addition to hard work, thorough analyses, and common sense, effective strategists must be able to think clearly and ask many questions. Their strategic effectiveness increases as they find ways for others to also think and inquire about what a firm is doing and why. But, in particular, top-level managers are challenged to "think seriously and deeply . . . about the purposes of the organizations they head or functions they perform, about the strategies, tactics, technologies, systems, and people necessary to attain these purposes, and about the important questions that always need to be asked."[81] Through this type of thinking, strategists, in concert with others, increase the probability of identifying bold, innovative ideas. When these ideas lead to the development of core competencies that are valuable, rare, imperfectly imitable, and non-substitutable, they become the foundation for exploiting environmental opportunities in the pursuit of strategic competitiveness in the global economy.

Our discussion highlights the nature of a strategist's work. Instead of simplicity, the work is filled with ambiguous decision situations—situations for which the most effective solutions are not always easily determined.[82] However, the opportunity suggested by this type of work is appealing. These jobs offer exciting opportunities to dream and to act. The following words, given as advice by his father to Steven J. Ross, the former chairman and co-CEO of Time-Warner, describe the excitement of a strategist's work: "There are three categories of people—the person who goes into the office, puts his feet up on his desk, and dreams for 12 hours; the person who arrives at 5 A.M. and works for 16 hours, never once stopping to dream; and the person who puts his feet up, dreams for one hour, then does something about those dreams."[83] Strategists have opportunities to dream and to act, and the most effective ones provide a vision (dream) to effectively elicit the help of others in creating a firm's sustainable competitive advantage.

## The Strategic Management Process

As shown in Figure 1-1, the parts of the strategic management process are highly interdependent. Through study of its external (Chapter 2) and internal (Chapter 3) environments, a firm identifies marketplace opportunities and threats and determines how to use its core competencies to achieve strategic competitiveness and earn superior profits. With this knowledge, the firm forms its strategic intent in order to leverage its resources, capabilities, and core competencies and win battles in the global economy. Flowing from strategic intent, the strategic mission specifies, in writing, the products a firm intends to produce and the markets it will serve when leveraging its resources, capabilities, and core competencies.

A firm's strategic inputs provide the foundation for its strategic actions—the actions required to formulate and implement strategies. As strategic actions, both formulation and implementation are critical to achieving strategic competitiveness and earning above-average profits. Formulation and implementation issues must be considered simultaneously.

Today, cross-functional teams often are formed to simultaneously consider all issues related to the development, production, and marketing of new products. This integrated approach allows a firm to focus consistently on both formulation and implementation issues as it completes actions intended to result in desired strategic outcomes. Through integrated strategic actions that are based on valid and reliable strategic inputs, the firm achieves strategic competitiveness and earns above-average profits.

Figure 1-1 shows the topics we examine to study the interdependent parts of the strategic management process. In Part II of this book, actions related to the formulation of strategies are explained. The first topic studied is the formulation of strategies at the business-unit level (Chapter 4). A diversified firm, one competing in multiple product markets and businesses, has a business-level strategy for each distinct product market area. A company competing in a single product market has but one business-level strategy. In all instances, a business-level strategy describes a firm's actions designed to exploit (in the marketplace) its competitive advantages over rivals. But, as is explained in Chapter 5, business-level strategies are not formulated and implemented in isolation. Competitors respond to and try to anticipate each other's actions. Thus, the dynamics of competition are an important input to and component of the formulation and implementation of all strategies, but especially to business-level strategies.

For the diversified firm, corporate-level strategy (Chapter 6) is concerned with determining the businesses in which the company intends to compete, how resources are to be allocated among those businesses, and how the different units are to be managed. Other topics vital to strategy formulation, particularly in the diversified firm, include the acquisition of other companies and, as appropriate, the restructuring of the firm's portfolio of businesses (Chapter 7), and the selection of an international strategy that is consistent with the firm's resources, capabilities, and core competencies and with its external opportunities (Chapter 8).

To examine more direct actions taken to implement strategies effectively, we consider several topics in Part III of this book. First, different mechanisms used to govern firms are considered (Chapter 9). With demands for improved corporate governance voiced by various stakeholders (e.g., shareholders), organizations are challenged to manage in ways that will result in the satisfaction of stakeholders' interests and the attainment of desired strategic outcomes. Finally, the matters of structures and actions needed to control a firm's operations (Chapter 10), the patterns of strategic leadership appropriate for today's firms and competitive environments (Chapter 11), and the link among corporate entrepreneurship, innovation, and strategic competitiveness (Chapter 12) are addressed.

The strategic management process calls for disciplined approaches to the development of sustainable competitive advantages, which will be the cornerstone of competitive success in the 1990s and into the twenty-first century. Mastery of the strategic management process will effectively serve readers and the organizations for whom they choose to work.

## Summary

- Through their actions, firms seek strategic competitiveness and above-average profits. Strategic competitiveness is achieved when a firm has developed and learned how to successfully implement a value-creating strategy. Above-average profits—returns in excess of what investors expect to earn from other investments with similar levels of risk—allow a firm to simultaneously satisfy all of its stakeholders.

- Dynamic in nature, the strategic management process is used by firms to become strategically competitive and earn superior profits. Thus, the parts of the strategic management process are interdependent. Each part must be completed successfully in order for the desired strategic outcomes (competitiveness and superior profitability) to be achieved.

- The competitiveness of the world's nations has changed during the twentieth century. The United States no longer dominates the world's marketplace. Today, the United States, Europe, and Japan are relatively equal contenders striving to be the most competitive nation, or group of nations, during the twenty-first century. For a nation to be the world's most competitive, its firms must learn how to establish and successfully exploit sustainable competitive advantages in an increasingly global economy.

- Globalization—the spread of economic innovations around the world and the political and cultural adjustments that accompany this diffusion—increases the range of possibilities for firms to establish sustainable competitive advantages. Because of globalization, firms can examine opportunities throughout the world to establish a sustainable competitive advantage.

- Due to the world's vast economic potential (such as that among the United States, Europe, and Japan), globalization is likely to continue. Globalization also increases the standards of performance (in terms of quality, price, product introduction times, and so forth) companies must meet or exceed to be strategically competitive. Developing the ability to satisfy these global performance standards also helps firms compete effectively in their important domestic markets.

- There are two major models of what a firm needs to do to earn superior profits. The industrial organization (I/O) model argues that the external environment is the primary determinant of the firm's strategy. Superior profitability is earned when the firm locates in an attractive industry and successfully implements the strategy (typically either cost leadership or differentiation) dictated by the characteristics of that industry. The resource-based model assumes that each firm is a collection of unique resources and capabilities. These resources and capabilities are the source of the firm's strategy and its profitability. Superior profitability is earned when the firm uses its valuable, rare, imperfectly imitable, and non-substitutable resources and capabilities (called core competencies) to establish a sustainable competitive advantage over its rivals.

- Strategic intent and strategic mission are formed in light of the information and insights gained from studying a firm's internal and external environments. The strategic intent describes how resources, capabilities, and core competencies will be leveraged to achieve desired goals in the competitive environment. The strategic mission is an application of strategic intent. The mission is used to specify the product markets and customers a firm intends to serve through the leveraging of its resources, capabilities, and core competencies. Thus, the strategic mission is based on the firm's strategic intent.

- Stakeholders are the individuals and groups who can affect and are affected by a firm's strategic outcomes. Because a firm is dependent on the continuing support of stakeholders (shareholders, customers, suppliers, employees, host governments, etc.), they have enforceable claims on the company's performance. When a firm is earning above-average profits, it can adequately satisfy all stakeholders' interests. However, when a firm is earning only average profits, its strategists must carefully manage all stakeholder groups in order to retain their support. A firm that is earning below-average profits must minimize the amount of support it loses from dissatisfied stakeholders.

- Organizational strategists are responsible for the design and execution of an effective strategic management process. Strategists alone can be a source of sustainable competitive advantage. The work of strategists demands decision trade-offs, often among attractive alternatives. Successful top-level managers work hard, conduct thorough analyses of situations, and constantly ask the right questions, of the right people, at the right time.

## Review Questions

1. Why should a citizen of a particular nation be interested in the strategic competitiveness of individual business firms in that nation?
2. What is national competitiveness? What conditions appear to account for the decline in the United States' competitiveness during the 1970s and 1980s?
3. What is globalization? What are the realities that continue the march toward globalization?
4. According to the I/O model, what should a firm do to earn superior profits?
5. What does the resource-based model suggest a firm should do to be strategically competitive and earn above-average profits?
6. What are the differences between strategic intent and strategic mission? Are these differences important? Why or why not?
7. What are stakeholders? Why can they influence organizations? Do stakeholders always have the same amount of influence over an organization? Why or why not?
8. Who are organizational strategists? Describe the work you would anticipate from a strategist if you were to observe one for a day.

## Application Discussion Questions

1. As reported in the opening case, the early feedback concerning AT&T's global strategy was encouraging. Go to your library to study AT&T's current performance. What percentage of its sales revenues is now being earned globally? Compared to its competitors (e.g., MCI), how profitable is it today?
2. Through library research, locate a ranking of nations' competitiveness. Is Japan still ranked number one? Describe factors and actions you believe account for any changes between the rankings you found and those shown in Table 1-2.
3. Whirlpool Corporation's global strategy in Japan and other parts of Asia was described in one of the Strategic Focus segments. Use materials in your library, and other sources available to you, to describe the results being achieved currently through this global strategy. Has Whirlpool established other plants in Southeast Asia? If so, does it have partners in these ventures?
4. Select an organization (e.g., school, club, church) that is important to you. Describe the organization's stakeholders and the degree of influence you believe each has over the organization.
5. Are you a stakeholder at your university or college? If so, of what stakeholder group, or groups, are you a part?
6. Think of an industry in which you wish to work. In your opinion, which of the three primary stakeholder groups is the most powerful in that industry today? Why?
7. Assume you have been appointed the new CEO for General Motors. As the firm's new chief strategist, describe the first actions you will take. Be prepared to defend your actions.
8. Reject or agree with the following statement: "I think managers have little responsibility for the failure of business firms." Justify your view.
9. Do strategic intent and strategic mission have any meaning in your personal life? If so, describe it. Are your current actions being guided by an intent and a mission? If not, why not?

## Ethics Questions

1. Can a firm achieve sustained competitive advantage and thereby strategic competitiveness without acting ethically? Explain.
2. What are a firm's ethical responsibilities if it earns above-average profits?
3. What are some of the critical ethical challenges to firms competing in the global marketplace?
4. How should ethical considerations be included in analyses of a firm's internal and external environments?
5. Can ethical issues be integrated into a firm's strategic intent and mission? Explain.
6. What is the relationship between ethics and stakeholders?
7. What is the importance of ethics for organizational strategists?

## Notes

1. J. B. Barney, 1991, Firm resources and sustained competitive advantage, *Journal of Management* 17, no. 1: 99–120.
2. A. D. Meyer, 1991, What is strategy's distinctive competence? *Journal of Management* 17, no. 4: 821–833.
3. C. J. Loomis, 1993, Dinosaurs, *Fortune,* May 3, 36–42.
4. Ibid., 36.
5. S. Sherman, 1993, The secret to Intel's success, *Fortune,* February 8, 14.
6. M. E. Porter, 1992, America's investment famine, *Economist,* June 27, 89–90.
7. P. Gyllenhammar, 1993, The global economy: Who will lead next? *Journal of Accountancy* 175:61–67.
8. M. Kotabe and E. P. Cox III, 1993. Assessment of global competitiveness: Patent applications and grants in four major trading countries. *Business Horizons* 36, no. 1: 57–64.
9. *First Annual Report of the Competitiveness Policy Council,* 1992 (Washington, D.C.: U.S. Government Printing Office), 18–57.
10. L. C. Thurow, 1992, Who owns the twenty-first century? *Sloan Management Review* 33, no. 3: 5–17.
11. Ibid., 10.
12. Ibid., 5.
13. *First Annual Report of the Competitiveness Policy Council:* 26–29.
14. G. Capoglu, 1990, The internationalization of financial markets and competitiveness in the world economy, *Journal of World Trade* 24, no. 2: 111–118.
15. *First Annual Report of the Competitiveness Policy Council,* 26–29.
16. J. Kahn, 1993, Downshifting in Japan, *Dallas Morning News,* August 8, H1.
17. A. Taylor III, 1993, The dangers of running too lean, *Fortune,* June 14, 113–118.
18. B. R. Schlender, 1993, Japan: Hard times for high tech, *Fortune,* March 22, 93.
19. E. Thornton, 1993, Japan's struggle to be creative, *Fortune,* April 19, 129.
20. E. Thornton, 1993, Japan's struggle to restructure, *Fortune,* June 28, 84–88; A. Taylor III, 1993, U.S. automakers keep on truckin', *Fortune,* July 26, 12.
21. J. C. Madonna, 1992, If it's markets you need, look abroad, *New York Times Forum,* January 5, F13.
22. T. A. Stewart, 1993, The new face of American power, *Fortune,* July 26, 70–86.
23. Thurow, Who owns the twenty-first century? 5.
24. A. Reynolds, 1991, Competitiveness and the global capital shortage, *Business Horizons* 34, no. 6: 23.
25. M. N. Baily, 1993, Made in the U.S.A., *Brookings Review* 11, no 1: 36–39.
26. U.S. tops in productivity, 1992, *Dallas Morning News,* October 13, D1.
27. Measurement and implications of changes in OECD countries' international competitiveness, 1992, *OECD Economic Outlook* 52 (December): 50.
28. Baily, Made in the U.S.A., 37.
29. Madonna, If it's markets you need, F13.
30. Federal-Mogul Corporation, 1992, *Annual Report,* 2.
31. Johnson & Johnson, 1992, *Annual Report,* 31–32.
32. W. W. Lewis and M. Harris, 1992, Why globalization must prevail, *McKinsey Quarterly* 2: 114–131; B. G. Resnick, 1989, The globalization of world financial markets, *Business Horizons* 32, no. 6: 34–41.
33. H. S. Dent, Jr., 1993, Global strategic alliances, *Fortune,* August 8 (Special Advertising Section), S2–S19.
34. M. G. Harvey, 1993, "Buy American": Economic concept or economic slogan? *Business Horizons* 36, no. 3: 40–46.
35. Banco Economico, 1992, *Annual Report,* 2–3.
36. Lewis and Harris, Why globalization must prevail, 115.
37. J. Nesmith and E. Jaspin, 1993, Japan's patents pending no more, *Waco Tribune-Herald,* January 24, A1, A10; L. S. Richman, 1994, What's next after GATT's victory? *Fortune,* January 10, 66–70.
38. B. J. White, 1988, The internationalization of business: One company's response, *Academy of Management Executive* 2, no. 1: 29–32.
39. L. T. Perry, 1991. Taking an offensive stance, *Exchange* Summer: 3–7.
40. H. J. Aaron, 1992, Comments included in a debate called "How real is America's decline?" *Harvard Business Review* 70, no. 5: 172.
41. G. Das, 1993, Local memoirs of a global manager, *Harvard Business Review,* 71, no. 2: 38–47.
42. A. A. Lado, N. G. Boyd, and P. Wright, 1992, A competency based model of sustainable competitive advantage: Toward a conceptual integration, *Journal of Management* 18, 77–91; R. M. Grant, 1991, The resource-based theory of competitive advantage: Implications for strategy formulation, *California Management Review* 33 (Spring): 114–135; M. A. Hitt and R. D. Ireland, 1986, Relationships among corporate level distinctive competencies, diversification strategy, corporate structure, and performance, *Journal of Management Studies* 23: 401–416.
43. M. A. Hitt and R. D. Ireland, 1985, Corporate distinctive competence, strategy, industry and performance, *Strategic Management Journal* 6, no. 3: 273–293; C. C. Snow and L. G. Hrebiniak, 1980, Strategy, distinctive competence, and organizational performance, *Administrative Science Quarterly* 25: 317–336.

44. M. A. Hitt and B. W. Keats, 1992, Strategic leadership and restructuring: A reciprocal interdependence, in R. L. Phillips and J. G. Hunt (eds.), *Strategic leadership: A Multiorganizational-Level Perspective* (Westport, Conn.: Quorum Books), 45–61.

45. Barney, Firm resources, 101; Lado, Boyd, and Wright, A competency based model, 78.

46. Hitt and Keats, Strategic leadership, 54.

47. This discussion is drawn primarily from Barney, Firm resources; Grant, Resource-based theory; Lado, Boyd, and Wright, A competency based model.

48. M. E. Porter, 1980, *Competitive Strategy* (New York: Free Press); M. E. Porter, 1985, *Competitive Advantage* (New York: Free Press).

49. Lado, Boyd, and Wright, A competency based model, 94.

50. Porter, *Competitive Strategy.*

51. M. Halkins, 1993, Dillard's shifting merchandising strategy, *Dallas Morning News,* May 17, D1, D7.

52. Barney, Firm resources; Grant, Resource-based theory; Meyer, What is strategy's distinctive competence? 823.

53. Grant, Resource-based theory; Meyer, What is strategy's distinctive competence?; Barney, Firm resources.

54. Grant, Resource-based theory, 119–120.

55. Barney, Firm resources.

56. Thurow, Who owns the twenty-first century?; J. A. Klein, G. Edge, and T. Kass, 1991, Skill-based competition, *Journal of General Management* 16, no. 4: 1–15.

57. G. Hamel and C. K. Prahalad, 1989, Strategic intent, *Harvard Business Review* 67, no. 3: 63–76.

58. Ibid., 66.

59. Sherman, The secret to Intel's success, 14.

60. M. Loeb, 1993, It's time to invest and build, *Fortune,* February 22, 4; S. Sherman, 1993, The new computer revolution, *Fortune,* June 14, 56–84; Hamel and Prahalad, Strategic intent, 64; A. Taylor III, 1993, How to murder the competition, *Fortune,* February 22, 87–90; Z. Schiller, 1992, No more Mr. nice guy at P&G—not by a long shot, *Business Week,* February 3, 54–56.

61. Reebok, 1992, *Annual Report,* 2–12.

62. Hamel and Prahalad, Strategic intent, 64.

63. M. A. Hitt, D. Park, C. Hardee, and B. B. Tyler, 1994, Understanding strategic intent in the global marketplace, *Academy of Management Executive,* in press.

64. R. D. Ireland and M. A. Hitt, 1992, Mission statements: Importance, challenge, and recommendations for development, *Business Horizons* 35, no. 3: 34–42.

65. A. D. DuBrin, and R. D. Ireland, 1993, *Management and Organization,* 2d ed. (Cincinnati: Southwestern), 140.

66. R. E. Freeman, 1984, *Strategic Management* (Boston: Pitman), 53–54.

67. G. Donaldson and J. W. Lorsch, 1983, *Decision Making at the Top: The Shaping of Strategic Direction* (New York: Basic Books), 37–40.

68. Ibid., 37.

69. C. J. Loomis, 1993, The Reed that Citicorp leans on, *Fortune,* July 12, 90–93.

70. D. Kirkpatrick, 1993, Could AT&T rule the world? *Fortune,* May 17, 55–66.

71. S. Lee, 1993, Peter Drucker's fuzzy future, *Fortune,* May 17, 136; Thurow, Who owns the twenty-first century? 6.

72. D. C. Hambrick, 1989, Guest editor's introduction: Putting top managers back in the strategy picture, *Strategy Management Journal* 10: 5–15; Lado, Boyd, and Wright, A competency based model, 83.

73. T. S. Threlkeld and M. Wrolstad, 1993, Restaurant exec to head Radio Shack, *Dallas Morning News,* July 8, D1, D2.

74. J. O. Moller, 1991, The competitiveness of U.S. industry: A view from the outside, *Business Horizons* 34, no. 6: 27–34.

75. M. A. Hitt and R. E. Hoskisson, 1991, Strategic competitiveness, in L.W. Foster (ed.), *Advances in Applied Business Strategy,* (Greenwich, Conn.: JAI Press), 1–36.

76. J. B. Barney, 1986, Organizational culture: Can it be a source of sustained competitive advantage? *Academy of Management Review* 11, no. 3: 656–665.

77. R. D. Ireland, M. A. Hitt, J. C. Williams, 1992, Self-confidence and decisiveness: Prerequisites for effective management in the 1990s, *Business Horizons* 35, no. 1: 36–43.

78. Gary Belis, 1993, Beware the touchy–feely business book, *Fortune,* June 28, 147; A. E. Pearson, 1988, Tough-minded ways to get innovative, *Harvard Business Review* 66, no. 3: 99–106.

79. K. W. Chilton, M. E. Warren, and M. L. Weidenbaum (eds.), 1990, *American Manufacturing in a Global Market* (Boston: Kluwer Academic Publishers), 72.

80. A. Deutschman, 1993, Odd man out, *Fortune,* July 26, 42.

81. T. Levitt, 1991, *Thinking About Management* (New York: Free Press), 9.

82. B. Dumaine, 1993, The new non-manager managers, *Fortune,* February 22, 80–84.

83. M. Loeb, 1993, Steven J. Ross, 1927–1992, *Fortune,* January 25, 4.

CHAPTER 2

# The External Environment: Opportunities, Threats, Industry Competition, and Competitor Analysis

▼

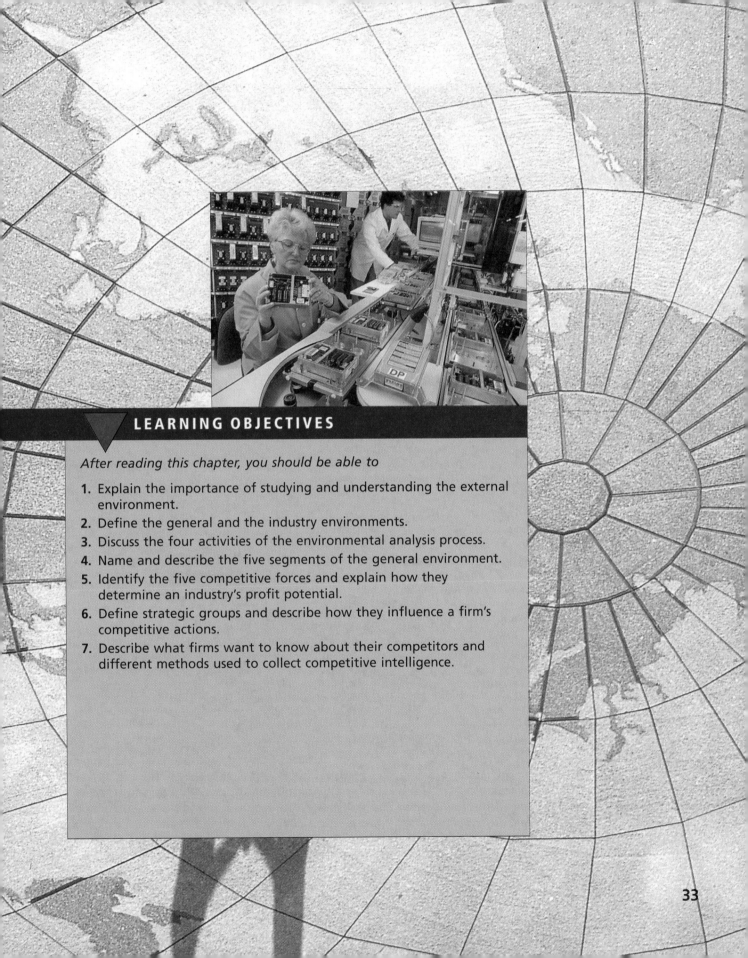

*After reading this chapter, you should be able to*

1. Explain the importance of studying and understanding the external environment.
2. Define the general and the industry environments.
3. Discuss the four activities of the environmental analysis process.
4. Name and describe the five segments of the general environment.
5. Identify the five competitive forces and explain how they determine an industry's profit potential.
6. Define strategic groups and describe how they influence a firm's competitive actions.
7. Describe what firms want to know about their competitors and different methods used to collect competitive intelligence.

## Learning to Compete Successfully in Japan

**TRW**

A large, diversified firm, TRW competes in three major markets—automotive, aerospace and information. In 1985, Joe Gorman, TRW's new chief executive officer (CEO), decided that selling to Japanese manufacturers was critical to the future success of his firm's automobile parts business. This decision was reached after careful study of what was occurring, and what was expected to occur, in the American and world automobile markets. As a summary of what his firm's analysis showed, Gorman observed the following: "All [a person] had to do was look at parking lots around America. We all knew what was happening. Given the trend lines, [I concluded that] we might as well go out of the automotive business if we [couldn't provide] the Japanese [automobile manufacturers] with some major portion of our products."

Based on his belief that Japanese automobile manufacturers would continue to sell their products successfully in the United States and globally, Gorman initiated a string of decisive actions. First, the firm's direct sales force in Japan was expanded. While helpful, this action alone was insufficient. Of greater benefit to TRW was the decision to invest heavily in joint ventures with companies supplying parts to Nissan's and Toyota's U.S.-based manufacturing plants. Because of the high quality of products sold to these plants, TRW was able to sell its outputs to Nissan and Toyota (and eventually to other manufacturers as well) in Japan.

Over the years, TRW became even more committed to the goal of selling automobile parts to Japanese manufacturers in addition to its regular domestic and European customers. The company now supplies a full range of products, including valves, steering systems, air bags, electronic components, and seat belts, to its Japanese customers. An inspection of electronic components is shown on page 33. With the exceptions of some air-bag-system components and a few electronics, TRW manufactures all of these products in Japan. Serving as the foundation for the company's success is its air-bag technology. This technology has been extremely successful, resulting in TRW's ability to supply air-bag triggering sensors for 50 percent of the cars Japanese firms sell to other nations and for 35 percent of the cars they sell in Japan. Because of these accomplishments, TRW expects its sales to Japanese companies to reach $1.5 billion by 1997 (the comparable sales figure in 1992 was $500 million). ▲

**A**s noted in the first chapter, the environmental conditions facing firms today are different from those of past decades. Many companies now compete in global, rather than domestic, markets. Technological changes and the explosion in information-gathering and -processing capabilities demand more timely and effective competitive actions and responses.[1] The rapid sociological changes occurring in many countries affect labor practices and the nature of products demanded by increasingly diverse consumers. Governmental policies and laws impact where and how firms choose to compete. Firms must be aware of and understand the implications of these environmental realities to be effective competitors in the global economy.

In high-performing, strategically competitive organizations, people seek patterns to help them understand their external environment, and it may be different from what they expect.[2] It is vital for decision makers to have a precise and accurate understanding of their company's competitive position. For example, one of the first decisions Louis Gerstner, Jr., made when chosen as IBM's CEO from outside the firm was to visit with each member of IBM's senior management team. A key reason for these visits was to learn about each business area's competitive standing in the industry (or industries) in which it competed.[3]

Strategic decision makers know that understanding their firm's external environment helps to improve a company's competitive position, increase operational efficiency, and win battles in the global economy.[4] It is likely that the 1,162 percent increase in the price of Coca-Cola's stock during Roberto Goizueta's first 12 years as the company's CEO would not have occurred had Goizueta and his top executives not maintained an effective understanding of the firm's external environment. For example, with a long history of a major global presence, Coca-Cola continues to pursue opportunities in many international markets. Goizueta observed that his company's extension into world markets is just beginning. In 1993, for example, the firm's top 16 markets accounted for 80 percent of its volume, but those markets covered only 20 percent of the world's population.[5]

As suggested in this chapter's opening case, TRW's CEO understood his firm's current external environment and future conditions. The company might have preferred to continue selling most of its automobile parts to domestic customers. However, an analysis of the external environment highlighted the global nature of the automobile parts business. Because of these environmental trends, Gorman concluded that TRW could no longer be successful in the automobile parts business by selling products only to its domestic customers. In his view, environmental changes and trends mandated that TRW learn how to sell its products to Japanese firms. Gorman also knew that to build and operate its Japanese plants, TRW would have to adapt methods of operation to Japan's culture, laws, and traditions.

TRW's commitments and actions also are clear indicators of its strategic intent (recall our discussion of strategic intent in Chapter 1). The company wanted to gain a competitive advantage in an evolving global marketplace for automobile parts. The strategic direction pursued to achieve global leadership suggests high levels of resolve, stamina, and inventiveness as TRW established and successfully operated manufacturing facilities in Japan (resolve, stamina, and inventiveness are critical parts of strategic intent).

In this chapter, we discuss the external environment. Through an integrated understanding of the external and the internal environments, firms gain information needed to understand the present and predict the future.[6] As shown in Figure 2–1, a firm's external environment has two major components—the general and the industry environments.

## The General Environment and the Industry Environment

The **general environment** is composed of elements in the broader society that can influence an industry and the firms within it.[7] We group these elements into environmental *segments* called the demographic, economic, political/legal, sociocultural, and technological segments. Examples of *elements* analyzed in these five segments are shown in Table 2–1. Firms cannot directly control these elements.

▲ The **general environment** is composed of elements in the broader society that can influence an industry and the firms within it.

**FIGURE 2-1   The External Enviornment**

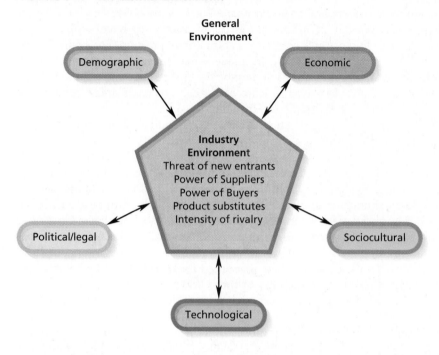

Because of this, the strategic challenge is to understand each segment and its implications so appropriate strategies can be formulated and implemented.

The **industry environment** is the set of factors—the threat of new entrants, suppliers, buyers, product substitutes, and the intensity of rivalry among competitors—that influence a firm and its competitive actions and responses. In total, the interactions among these five factors determine an industry's profit potential. The challenge is to locate a position within an industry where a firm can favorably influence these factors or where it can successfully defend against these factors' influence. The greater a firm's capacity to favorably influence its industry environment, the greater the likelihood that it will earn above-average profits.

We also discuss in this chapter how companies gather and interpret information about their competitors. Called competitor analysis, a firm's understanding of its current competitors complements the insights provided by study of the general and the industry environments. In combination, the results of these three analyses influence the development of a firm's strategic intent, strategic mission, and strategic actions.

The focus in analysis of the general environment is the future; in analysis of the industry environment, it is understanding the factors and conditions influencing a firm's profitability; and in analysis of competitors, it is predicting the dynamics of competitors' actions, responses and intentions. Although each analysis is discussed separately, a firm's financial performance improves when the insights from analyses of the general environment, the industry environment, and competitors are integrated.

In the next section, we discuss the importance of adopting a global perspective when analyzing an external environment.

▲ The **industry environment** is the set of factors—the threat of new entrants, suppliers, buyers, product substitutes, and the intensity of rivalry among competitors—that influence a firm and its competitive actions and responses.

---

### ▽ TABLE 2–1

## The General Environment: Segments and Elements

| | |
|---|---|
| *Demographic Segment* | • Population size<br>• Age structure<br>• Geographic distribution<br>• Ethnic mix<br>• Income distribution |
| *Economic Segment* | • Inflation rates<br>• Interest rates<br>• Trade deficits or surpluses<br>• Budget deficits or surpluses<br>• Personal savings rates<br>• Business savings rates<br>• Gross domestic product |
| *Political/Legal Segment* | • Anti-trust laws<br>• Taxation laws<br>• Deregulation philosophies<br>• Labor training laws<br>• Educational philosophies and policies |
| *Sociocultural Segment* | • Women in the work force<br>• Work force diversity<br>• Attitudes about quality of work life<br>• Concerns about the environment<br>• Shifts in work and career preferences<br>• Shifts in preferences regarding product and service characteristics |
| *Technological Segment* | • Product innovations<br>• Process innovations<br>• Applications of knowledge<br>• Focus of private and government-supported R&D expenditures<br>• New communication technologies |

---

## Globalization

The trend toward globalization affects a firm's study of the external environment. This trend views the world as becoming nationless and borderless.[8] One outcome of globalization is the emergence of many customers who demand products (goods or services) with the highest quality, latest technology, and speediest delivery—all at the lowest cost. Often consumers also expect products to reflect status, provide comfort, and save their time.[9]

Because of its pervasive impact, we do not treat the global environment as a separate segment of the general environment. Rather, we integrate globalization into discussions of the demographic, economic, political/legal, sociocultural, and technological segments. For example, to understand the sociocultural segment, sociocultural trends across several countries must be identified and studied and their implications assessed. Only through an integrated analysis can firms understand the full range of issues associated with operating in a nationless and borderless business environment. In many multinational firms, environments are studied in the context of the global business environment, rather than in terms of a domestic environment only.[10] The process of external environmental analysis is discussed next.

## External Environmental Analysis

Most firms face external environments that are growing more turbulent, complex, and global, making them increasingly difficult to interpret.[11] To cope with what are often ambiguous and incomplete environmental data and to increase their understanding of the general environment, firms engage in a process called external environmental analysis. This process includes four activities—scanning, monitoring, forecasting, and assessing (see Table 2–2)—and should be conducted on a continuous basis.[12]

▲ **Opportunities** are conditions in the general environment that may help a company achieve strategic competitiveness.

▲ **Threats** are conditions in the general environment that may hinder a company's efforts to achieve strategic competitiveness.

An important objective of studying the general environment is identification of opportunities and threats. **Opportunities** are conditions in the general environment that may help a company achieve strategic competitiveness. **Threats** are conditions in the general environment that may hinder a company's efforts to achieve strategic competitiveness. In essence, external environmental opportunities represent *possibilities,* while threats are potential *constraints.*

To analyze the general environment, several sources are used. Included among these are a wide variety of printed materials (e.g., trade publications, newspapers, business publications, the results of academic research and of public polls); attendance and participation in trade shows; the content of conversations with suppliers, customers, and employees of public-sector organizations; and even business-related "rumors" provided by many different people.[13] Additional sources of information and data include individuals in "boundary spanning" positions who interact with external constituents such as salespersons, purchasing managers, public relations directors, and human resource managers. Decision makers should verify the validity and reliability of the sources on which their environmental analyses are based.[14]

In some companies, especially large ones, groups are given the task of studying the external environment. These groups bear the final responsibility for conducting environmental analyses and identifying opportunities and threats. However, the quality of their work is enhanced when everyone working in the firm is encouraged to provide inputs. Given the complexity and ambiguity of the business environment, information from all sources can be important.

### Scanning

▲ **Scanning** entails the study of all segments in the general environment. Through scanning, firms identify early signals of potential changes in the general environment and detect changes that are already under way.

**Scanning** entails the study of all segments in the general environment. Through scanning, firms identify early signals of potential changes in the general environment and detect changes that are already under way.[15] When scanning, analysts typically deal with information and data that are ambiguous, incomplete, and unconnected.

In the 1990s, for example, analysts in financial institutions are observing several changes in the general environment. First, some government officials and security analysts believe a combination of personal savings, private pensions, and Social Security income may be insufficient to support U.S. baby boomers' (those born between 1947 and 1964) retirement. The first of the baby boomer generation will retire in 2011. These retirements will push the total number of retirees from 25

| TABLE 2–2 | |
|---|---|
| **Components of the External Analysis** | |
| *Scanning* | • Identifying early signals of environmental changes and trends |
| *Monitoring* | • Detecting meaning through on-going observations of environmental changes and trends |
| *Forecasting* | • Developing projections of anticipated outcomes based on monitored changes and trends |
| *Assessing* | • Determining the timing and importance of environmental changes and trends for a firm's strategies and their management |

million in 1991 to over 33 million in 2011.[16] Changes in life styles and health care systems may result in longer average life spans for the baby boomers. Combining this information with data gleaned from scanning other environmental segments (e.g., the demographic, sociocultural, and political/legal segments) could help analysts in financial institutions determine trends to monitor, forecast, and assess. Resulting from these efforts might be identification of an opportunity for a financial institution to effectively serve the baby boomers' retirement needs.

## Monitoring

When **monitoring,** analysts observe environmental changes to see if, in fact, an important trend is emerging.[17] Critical to successful monitoring is an ability to detect meaning in different environmental events. For example, an emerging trend regarding education might be suggested by changes in federal and state funding for educational institutions, changes in high school graduation requirements, and changes in the content of high school courses. In this instance, analysts would determine whether these different events suggest an educational trend and, if so, whether other information and data should be studied to monitor this trend.

▲ **Monitoring** occurs when analysts observe environmental changes to see if, in fact, an important trend is emerging.

## Forecasting

Scanning and monitoring are concerned with what is taking place in the general environment at a point in time. When **forecasting,** analysts develop feasible projections of what might happen, and how quickly, as a result of the changes and trends detected through scanning and monitoring.[18] For example, analysts might forecast the time that will be required for a new technology to reach the marketplace. Or they might forecast the length of time before different corporate training procedures are required to deal with anticipated changes in the composition of the work force or how much time will elapse before changes in governmental taxation policies affect consumers' purchasing patterns.

▲ **Forecasting** takes place when analysts develop feasible projections of what might happen, and how quickly, as a result of the changes and trends detected through scanning and monitoring.

## Assessing

The objective of **assessing** is to determine the timing and significance of the effects of environmental changes and trends on the strategic management of a

▲ **Assessing** determines the timing and significance of the effects of environmental changes and trends on the strategic management of a firm.

firm.[19] Through scanning, monitoring, and forecasting, analysts are able to under-stand the general environment. Going a step further, the intent of assessment is to specify the implications of that understanding for the organization. Without assessment, analysts are left with data that are interesting, but of unknown relevance.

As explained in the chapter's opening case, TRW's CEO concluded that the trend of U.S. consumers buying Japanese automobiles had important implications for his company. In light of this assessment, appropriate actions were taken, ultimately resulting in TRW's success in manufacturing and distributing automobile parts in Japan.

## Environmental Analysis and Rationality

The environmental analysis process includes elements of subjectivity. People are not totally rational—as analysts and decision makers. Personal biases and assump-tions influence the study of the general environment. For example, we may choose to study only a limited range of environmental conditions and may screen out unpleasant alternatives in scanning and monitoring.[20]

An organization's nature can also affect the process of environmental analysis. A firm's past experiences, organizational structure, rules and procedures, and available resources affect its perceptions of market opportunities and threats.[21]

Those responsible for analyzing the general environment should be aware of errors because of subjectivity. Because a firm's strategic inputs, actions, and outcomes are affected by how analysts and strategists perceive the general environment, this awareness is critical.[22] To reduce the potential for errors from subjectivity, analysts should regularly seek inputs from multiple sources (people and written documents) and ask for frequent feedback regarding the results of their analysis of the general environment.

Next, we discuss important *segments* of the general environment.

## Segments of the General Environment

The general environment is composed of segments (and their individual elements) external to the firm (see Table 2–1). While the degree of impact varies, these elements affect each industry and its firms. For analysts, the challenge is to scan, monitor, forecast, and assess those elements in each segment that are of the greatest importance to their firm. Results should include recognition of environmental changes, trends, opportunities, and threats. Opportunities are then matched with a firm's core competencies. When these matches are successful, the firm achieves strategic competitiveness and earns above-average profits. This matter is discussed further in Chapter 4.

### The Demographic Segment

▲ The **demographic segment** is concerned with a population's size, age structure, geographic distribution, ethnic mix, and income distribution.

The **demographic segment** is concerned with a population's size, age structure, geographic distribution, ethnic mix, and income distribution.[23] As noted previously, firms must analyze the demographics of the global society, rather than only those of the domestic population. In the following materials, each demographic element is discussed briefly.

**Size**  Observing the demographic changes in populations highlights the importance of this environmental segment. For example, in some advanced nations, there is negative population growth (except for the effects of immigration). In some countries, including the United States and several European nations, couples are averaging fewer than two children. Such a birth rate will produce a loss of population over time (even with the population living longer on average).[24] Population loss may require that a country increase immigration to have an adequate labor pool.

In contrast to advanced nations, the rapid growth rate in the populations of some Third World countries is depleting those nations' natural resources and reducing citizens' living standards. This rapid growth rate in the populations of some Third World countries may be a major challenge in the 1990s and into the twenty-first century.

**Age Structure**  In some countries, and certainly in the United States, the population's average age is increasing. Contributing to this change are declining birth rates and increasing life expectancies. Among other outcomes, these changes create additional pressures on health care systems. Beyond this, they may suggest numerous opportunities for firms to develop goods and services to meet the needs of an increasingly older population.

It has been projected that some people alive today might live to the age of 200 or more. If such a life span becomes a reality, a host of interesting issues will emerge. For example, there will be significant effects on individuals' pension plans and potential opportunities and threats for financial institutions.[25]

**Geographic Distribution**  For several decades, the United States has experienced a population shift from the North and East to the West and South. Similarly, the trend of moving from metropolitan to nonmetropolitan areas continues. Among their other effects, these changes impact local and state governments' tax bases. In turn, the locations of business firms are influenced by the degree of support different taxing agencies offer.

Affecting the geographic distribution of populations throughout the world are the capabilities from advances in communications technology. For example, through computer technologies, people can remain in their homes and communicate with others in remote locations to complete their work. In these instances, people can live where they prefer while being employed by a firm located in an unattractive location. As much as 25 percent of U.S. employees will work out of their homes by the year 2000.[26]

**Ethnic Mix**  The ethnic mix of countries' populations continues to change. Within the United States, the ethnicity of states, and of cities within the states, varies significantly. For business firms, the challenge is to be aware of and sensitive to these changes. Through careful study, firms can develop and market goods and services intended to satisfy the unique needs and interests of different ethnic groups.

Ethnic mix changes also affect a work force's composition. In the United States, for example, it is projected that by the mid-1990s, only 15 percent of the new workers entering the work force will be Caucasian males. The remainder of those entering the work force during the 1990s will be Caucasian, U.S.-born women (42 percent) and immigrants and U.S.-born minorities (43 percent).[27] The Hispanic population is predicted to be the fastest-growing segment of the U.S.

work force in the 1990s. By the year 2000, Hispanics will account for 9.2 percent of the work force, up from 7.8 percent in 1991. Because a labor force can be critical to competitive success, firms are challenged to work effectively with an increasingly diverse labor force.[28] Diversity in the work force is also a sociocultural issue.

In fact, effective management of a culturally diverse work force can produce a competitive advantage. For example, heterogeneous work teams have been shown to produce more effective strategic analyses, more creativity and innovation, and higher-quality decisions than homogeneous work teams.[29] Because of these potential outcomes, a number of companies promote cultural diversity in their work force and facilitate effective management of such diversity through specialized management training. Among these companies are American Express, Northern States Power Company, General Foods, US West, and British Petroleum. For example, US West has all of its employees (over 60,000) attend a diversity training program.[30]

**Income Distribution**    Understanding how income is distributed within and across populations informs firms of different groups' purchasing power and discretionary income. Study of income distributions suggests that while living standards have improved over time, there are variances within and between nations.[31]

Of interest to firms are the average incomes of households and individuals. Being aware of these figures yields strategically relevant information. The following Strategic Focus shows how income distribution patterns in a local community played an important role in founding and operating a successful small business.

## The Economic Segment

Clearly, the health of a nation's economy affects the performance of individual firms and industries. As a result, strategists study the economic environment to identify changes, trends, and their strategic implications.

▲ The **economic environment** refers to the nature and direction of the economy in which a firm competes or may compete.

The **economic environment** refers to the nature and direction of the economy in which a firm competes or may compete.[32] As shown in Table 2–1, indicators of an economy's health include inflation rates, interest rates, trade deficits or surpluses, budget deficits or surpluses, personal and business savings rates, and gross domestic product. However, because of the interconnectedness of the global financial community, analysts often must also scan, monitor, forecast, and assess the health of other countries' economies. For example, the economic status of nations with which the United States exchanges many products, such as Japan and Germany, can affect the overall health of the U.S. economy. In this regard, some worry that billions of dollars, yen, and deutsche marks move across national borders without much control by central banks. The delicately balanced global financial system permitting these easy transfers might contribute to an international economic crisis if the balance in the system was lost.[33]

The interrelatedness of different national economies was illustrated by the 1994 economic summit among the G-7 nations when President Clinton called on Germany and Japan to stimulate their economies to promote job growth in other countries. Furthermore, agreements to lower or eliminate trade barriers between nations, such as the North American Free Trade Agreement (NAFTA), have potentially significant economic consequences for the nations involved.

## STRATEGIC FOCUS

### Building Homes for Middle-Income People

After studying the residential real estate market in Santa Fe, New Mexico, Walton Chapman decided that the community had a shortage of mid-priced homes relative to the number of people with middle incomes. Chapman believed that city ordinances were the unintentional cause of this condition.

In the late 1960s, Santa Fe's ordinances required only gravel streets and septic tanks on one-acre sites. However, for one-half-acre sites, builders had to provide street paving, curbs, gutters, and sewers, making these homes nearly as expensive as those built on the larger, one-acre lots. At the other extreme, builders were constructing $20,000 homes, with five units per acre.

Chapman believed that these ordinances prevented the building of homes for those with middle level incomes. To develop and market his vision of a successful product—custom-designed single units for middle-income people—Chapman searched Santa Fe for one-half-acre lots. Critical to the success of his efforts was the necessity of controlling costs. Through serious negotiations with city officials, Chapman gained exemptions from some of the more expensive ordinances that applied to one-half-acre lots. Chapman also worked hard to gain favorable financing from local institutions. These accomplishments allowed Chapman to build and sell attractive, mid-priced homes to a large group of ready buyers. When established in 1966, Chapman's firm had four employees. Recently, the company was a $7 million per year home builder with 60 employees.

Economic issues also can have significant influences on political and legal issues. For example, some argue that the United States cannot afford to cancel favored-nation status for China, even though it has threatened to do so because of perceived human rights concerns. To take such action might have significant negative economic consequences for the United States and its firms.

## The Political/Legal Segment

The **political/legal segment** is the arena in which organizations and interest groups compete for attention and resources and the body of laws and regulations guiding these interactions.[34] Essentially, this segment represents how firms and other organizations try to influence government and how government entities influence them. Constantly changing, this segment (see Table 2-1) influences the nature of competition. Because of this, firms must carefully analyze a new administration's business-related policies and philosophies. Anti-trust laws, taxation laws, industries chosen for deregulation, labor training laws, and the degree of commitment to educational institutions are areas where an administration's policies can affect the operations and profitability of industries and individual firms.

Viewpoints regarding government philosophies and policies (federal, state, and local), the most effective means of competition, and the ideal relationship between government and business can vary substantially. In addition to political perspectives, these viewpoints are affected by the nature of the industry in which

▲ The **political/legal segment** is the arena in which organizations and interest groups compete for attention and resources and the body of laws and regulations guiding these interactions.

a firm competes. For example, health care organizations were quite interested in the Clinton administration's program ideas regarding the nature and delivery of health care services in the United States.

As the 1990s come to a close, business firms across the globe are confronted by an interesting array of political/legal questions and issues. For example, the debate about an industrial policy (e.g., better management of the economy versus deregulation) for the United States has yet to reach a final conclusion. Similarly, debate continues over trade policies. Some believe a nation should erect trade barriers to protect its domestic products. Others argue that free trade across nations serves the best interests of individual countries and their citizens. With the completion of the NAFTA and the GATT agreements, there seems to be a trend toward free trade.

There have been numerous debates regarding the use of tariffs to restrict the sale of foreign automobile products in the U.S. market. In mid-1993, Nissan Motor Corp. challenged the Treasury Department's 1989 decision to classify the firm's Pathfinder as a two-door sport utility vehicle. When classified this way, the product was assessed a 25 percent tariff. Instead, Nissan argued, the Pathfinder is more like a station wagon than a two-door sport utility vehicle. If so classified, the tariff would be only 2.5 percent. The outcome was of keen interest to U.S. automobile manufacturers (i.e., the Pathfinder competes with the Ford Explorer) and was expected to affect the resolution of a debate on whether the United States should increase tariffs on foreign minivans and sport utility vehicles.[35]

The end of the Cold War and the emergence of more democratic societies present challenges and opportunities—for business firms and government agencies. Strategists in both sectors must continue to search for policies, laws, and regulations through which the well-being of the nation and its industries, business firms, and individual citizens can be best served.

The Strategic Focus concerned with the McCurdy Fish Co. shows how vulnerable one small U.S. business firm was to changes in its regulatory environment. Given that no complaints were received in a 20-year period about the products processed by McCurdy's company, coupled with the opinion of the Canadian fish official, questions regarding the FDA actions should be expected. According to one analyst from the Washington, D.C.–based National Fisheries Institute, Americans' phobia about contaminated food may have forced the agency to deal aggressively with a situation that had a small probability of health risk. In fact, when asked if he would eat fish from the McCurdy Fish Co., this analyst said, "Sure. I'm sure it was perfectly safe."[36]

Officials at the FDA must scan, monitor, forecast, and assess their external environment. For example, the results of an environmental analysis identified a potential threat at McCurdy Fish Co. (that is, a health risk) to the public the agency is charged to serve. The challenge for these decision makers is to verify that their agency's policies and procedures balance the interests of the public and those of the firms it regulates.

## The Sociocultural Segment

▲ The **sociocultural segment** is concerned with different societies' social attitudes and cultural values.

The **sociocultural segment** is concerned with different societies' social attitudes and cultural values. Because attitudes and values are a society's cornerstone, they often drive demographic, economic, political/legal, and technological changes. Firms are challenged to understand the meaning of attitudinal and cultural changes across many global societies.

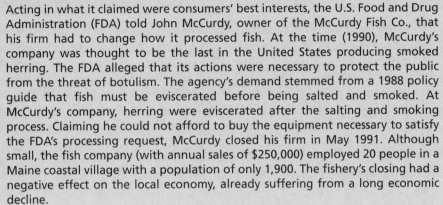

## STRATEGIC FOCUS

### The Regulatory Environment and the McCurdy Fish Co.

Acting in what it claimed were consumers' best interests, the U.S. Food and Drug Administration (FDA) told John McCurdy, owner of the McCurdy Fish Co., that his firm had to change how it processed fish. At the time (1990), McCurdy's company was thought to be the last in the United States producing smoked herring. The FDA alleged that its actions were necessary to protect the public from the threat of botulism. The agency's demand stemmed from a 1988 policy guide that fish must be eviscerated before being salted and smoked. At McCurdy's company, herring were eviscerated after the salting and smoking process. Claiming he could not afford to buy the equipment necessary to satisfy the FDA's processing request, McCurdy closed his firm in May 1991. Although small, the fish company (with annual sales of $250,000) employed 20 people in a Maine coastal village with a population of only 1,900. The fishery's closing had a negative effect on the local economy, already suffering from a long economic decline.

In McCurdy's view, the FDA overreacted to situations concerning other fish. He argued that the FDA was inappropriately applying standards set for freshwater whitefish, which had been blamed for three cases of botulism in the 1980s (all three cases resulted in deaths), to the processing of smoked herring. To support his position, McCurdy noted that his firm had produced almost 3 million pounds of herring—roughly 54 million fillets—in his 20 years as the company's owner without a single report of food poisoning. He also observed that "tons" of smoked herring enter the U.S. market from Canada each year. Some of these herring are processed in the same manner as at McCurdy's company.

The vice president of the Fisheries Council of Canada agreed with McCurdy. According to this official, the process used by the McCurdy Fish Co. had been traditional and was still in use throughout the world. Furthermore, there is no statistical evidence supporting the position that smoked herring processed in this manner pose a botulism threat.

A significant work force trend in many countries concerns diversity. In the United States, for example, 76.3 million women are expected to participate in the labor force by 2011.[37] In addition, a large percentage of new entrants into the work force will be ethnic minorities, as explained earlier. As a result, the work force will become increasingly diverse.

The influx of women and the increased ethnic and cultural diversity in the work force yield exciting challenges and significant opportunities. Included among these are the needs to combine the best of both men's and women's leadership styles for a firm's benefit and to identify ways to facilitate all employees' contributions to their firms.[38] To change what has been called a "corrosive atmosphere" in some companies, CEOs and other senior-level managers have started to provide training to nurture women's and ethnic minorities' leadership potential. Changes in organizational structure and management practices also may be required to eliminate subtle barriers that may exist. Managing diversity effectively may require accommodating special needs. Learning to manage diversity in the domestic work force can increase a firm's effectiveness in managing a globally diverse work force, as it acquires more international operations. The results achieved from these commitments to promote and manage diversity enhance a company's performance.[39]

Another important trend is that many women now choose to start their own businesses, oftentimes because of frustration in dealing with the "glass ceiling" (a subtle barrier to the advancement of women and ethnic minorities in corporations). In 1969, there were 1.2 million female entrepreneurs in the United States. By 1982, this number reached 2.4 million, and in 1991, it exceeded 3 million. During this period (1969–1991), the number of female entrepreneurs increased five times faster than the number of male entrepreneurs. In addition, this rate of increase was three times greater than that of women entering the work force. If this rate of start-ups continues, one-half of U.S. businesses will be owned by women by the year 2000.[40]

This same phenomenon is evidenced in Japan. Recently, five of every six new Japanese businesses were established and owned by women. Because women hold almost 99 percent of the clerical positions in Japan, the ownership trend has important implications for Japanese companies.[41]

## The Technological Segment

▲ The **technological segment** includes the institutions and activities involved with creating new knowledge and translating that knowledge into new outputs—products, processes, and materials.

Pervasive and diversified in scope, technological changes impact many parts of societies. These effects occur primarily through new products, processes, and materials. The **technological segment** includes the institutions and activities involved with creating new knowledge and translating that knowledge into new outputs—products, processes, and materials.

Given the rapid pace of technological change, it is vital that firms carefully study different elements in the technological segment. Many automobile manufacturers, for example, may be interested in Mazda Corp.'s efforts to design and produce environmentally friendly products. This effort is exemplified by the company's attempt to perfect a hydrogen-fueled engine.[42]

Similarly, different types of firms are interested in the technologies automobile manufacturers are developing to produce an electric car. This development is stimulated in large part by California's mandate that by 1998 two percent of the cars a company sells in the state must be zero-emission vehicles (ZEVs). Thus, automobile companies are aggressively developing technologies through which ZEVs can be produced and sold profitably. By 2003, 10 percent of cars sold in California must be ZEVs. Because California is the largest car market in the world (accounting for about 15 percent of U.S. sales), this mandate has become a force in the development of new technologies. The primary technological challenge is the building of a light, but powerful, battery that requires relatively infrequent recharges. To cope with the challenge of a commercially feasible electric car, Chrysler, Ford, and General Motors formed a consortium, leading to speculation that the companies might jointly build a national "supercar."[43]

Another technology with important implications for business is the internet, sometimes referred to as the Information Superhighway. The internet is a global web of some 25,000 computer networks. Companies such as GE, IBM, J.P. Morgan, Merrill Lynch, Motorola, Schlumberger, and Xerox use the internet. It provides a quick, inexpensive means of global communication (i.e., with strategic alliance partners) and access to information. For example, IBM engineers often use the internet to communicate with their counterparts when doing development work for other companies. The internet provides access to experts on such topics as chemical engineering and semiconductor manufacturing, to the Library of Con-

## STRATEGIC FOCUS

### Sophisticated Technology and Police Work

Two firms long known for their technologies, Texas Instruments and Hughes Aircraft, have combined their skills to produce a commercial product. The skills used to design and commercialize this product for a nondefense customer were originally developed in the companies' defense units.

Called the vision enhancement system (VES), the commercial product produced by these two companies is used in police patrol cars. The system features a roof-mounted infrared camera (which was used successfully in the Persian Gulf War) and a holographic projection capability. The system detects anything giving off heat. In addition to spotting people who are hiding, VES allows police to see glowing tire tracks left behind by a speeding vehicle. Because it is so heat sensitive, the system even detects hidden weapons, such as a gun or a knife, glowing from the heat of a subject's hand. Images spotted by the infrared camera are projected onto a small television screen for the front-seat passenger of a patrol car and onto a dollar-bill-size piece of glass mounted in front of the driver's eyes. Although expensive, VES may prove to be a valuable tool for field police officers.

gress, and even to satellite photographs. Other information available on the internet includes SEC filings, Commerce Department data, Census Bureau information, new patent filings, and stock market updates.[44] Therefore, the internet may be an excellent source of data on a firm's external environment.

Analysts should monitor the environment for the development of important technologies. Firms should also be open to opportunities to use their current technologies in new ways. Firms sometimes identify an opportunity to use their technological skills to produce products for new customers. An example of this is shown in the Strategic Focus describing the development of the vision enhancement system.

A key objective of analyzing the general environment is identification of anticipated significant changes and trends among external elements. With a focus on the future, the analysis of the general environment allows firms to identify opportunities and threats. However, to participate successfully in that future, a firm must operate effectively in both the short and the medium time periods. Critical to these operations is an understanding of a firm's industry environment and its competitors.

## Industry Environment Analysis

An **industry** is a group of firms producing products that are close substitutes. In the course of competition, these firms influence one another. Typically, industries include a rich mix of competitive strategies that companies use in pursuing strategic competitiveness and superior profitability.[45]

Compared to the general environment, the industry environment has a more direct effect on strategic competitiveness and profitability. The intensity of industry competition and an industry's profit potential (as measured by the long-run return

▲ An **industry** is a group of firms producing products that are close substitutes.

on invested capital) are a function of five competitive forces—the threat of new entrants, suppliers, buyers, product substitutes, and the intensity of rivalry among competitors (see Figure 2–2).

American Airlines continuously examines its general and industry environments, making decisions in light of anticipated changes and trends. In the early to middle 1990s, for example, the firm's CEO concluded that conditions and trends in the *industry environment* would make it impossible for high-cost airlines to survive over the next 15 to 20 years. Based on this projection, the CEO proposed several courses of action affecting the composition of American's fleet and the structure of its labor force. These actions were intended to help the firm reduce its operating costs and become more competitive.[46]

Developed by Michael Porter, the five force model expands the arena for competitive analysis. Historically, when studying the competitive environment, firms concentrated on companies with which they competed directly. But today competition is viewed as a grouping of alternative ways for customers to obtain desired results, rather than being limited to direct competitors.

The five force model recognizes that suppliers could become a firm's competitor (by integrating forward), as could buyers (by integrating backward). Similarly, firms choosing to enter a new market and those producing products that are adequate substitutes could become competitors for an existing company. Because the characteristics of an industry's environment shape a firm's strategy, environmental analysts seek to determine the relative strength of each of the five competitive forces.

## Threat of New Entrants

New entrants to an industry can threaten existing competitors. New entrants bring additional production capacity. Unless product demand is increasing, additional

**FIGURE 2–2** **The Five Force Model of Competition**

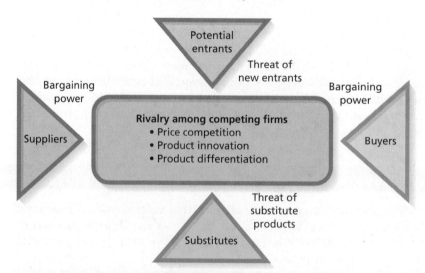

SOURCE: *Adapted and reprinted with permission of The Free Press, an imprint of Simon & Schuster from COMPETITIVE STRATEGY: Techniques for Analyzing Industries and Competitors by Michael E. Porter, Fig. 1–1, p. 4. Copyright 1980 by The Free Press.*

capacity holds consumers' costs down, resulting in less sales revenues and lower profitability for all firms in the industry. Often, new entrants have substantial resources and a keen interest in gaining a large market share. As such, new competitors may force existing firms to be more effective and efficient and to learn how to compete on new dimensions (e.g., computer-driven distribution channels). The likelihood firms will enter an industry is a function of two factors—barriers to entry and the reactions expected from current industry participants. When firms find entry into a new industry difficult or when firms are at a competitive disadvantage entering a new industry, entry barriers exist.

**Barriers to Entry** Existing competitors try to develop barriers to market entry. Alternatively, potential entrants seek markets where the entry barriers are relatively insignificant. Current industry participants protect their profitability with entry barriers; the absence of entry barriers increases the probability a new entrant can operate profitably in an industry. There are several potentially significant entry barriers.

*Economies of Scale* As the quantity of a product produced during a given time period increases, the cost of manufacturing each unit declines. These benefits are referred to as *economies of scale*.

Scale economies can be gained through most business functions (e.g., marketing, manufacturing, research and development, and purchasing). New entrants face a dilemma when existing competitors have scale economies. Small-scale entry places them at a cost disadvantage. However, large-scale entry, where the new entrant manufactures large volumes of a product to gain scale economies, risks strong reactions from established competitors.

Although still important in some industries (automobile manufacturing, for example), the competitive realities of the 1990s and the approaching twenty-first century may reduce the significance of scale economies as an entry barrier. Many companies now can customize their products for large numbers of small customer groups. Customized products are not manufactured in the volumes necessary to achieve economies of scale. Customization is made possible by new flexible manufacturing systems. Companies manufacturing multiple customized products learn how to respond quickly to customers' interests, rather than developing scale economies.

*Product Differentiation* Over time, customers may come to believe that an existing firm's product is unique. This belief can result from service to the customer, effective advertising campaigns, or the firm being first to market a particular product. In fact, many firms such as Coca-Cola and PepsiCo spend significant amounts of money on advertising to convince potential customers of the distinctiveness of their products. The belief that a firm's product is unique results in loyal customers who have strong brand identification. Typically, new entrants must allocate significant resources over a long period of time to overcome existing customer loyalties. To combat the perception of uniqueness, new entrants frequently offer their products at lower prices. However, this can result in lower profitability for the new entrant or, in the short run, even a loss.

*Capital Requirements* Competing in a new industry requires investment of a firm's resources. In addition to physical facilities, capital is needed for inventories, marketing activities, and other critical business functions. Although competing in a new industry may appear attractive, the capital required for successful market entry may not be available.

*Switching Costs*   Switching costs are the one-time costs customers incur when buying from a different supplier. The costs of buying new ancillary equipment and of retraining employees, and even the psychic costs of ending a relationship, may be incurred in switching to a new supplier. If switching costs are high, a new entrant must offer either a substantially lower price or a much better product to induce buyers. Usually, the more established the relationship, the greater the switching costs. For example, the costs of switching to a new college or university are not great after completing the first year. However, switching costs become quite significant if only a senior year remains.

*Access to Distribution Channels*   Over time, industry participants typically develop effective means of distributing products. Once developed, firms nurture their relationship with distributors. Such nurturing creates switching costs for distributors.

   Access to distribution channels can be a strong entry barrier for potential new entrants, particularly in consumer nondurable goods industries (e.g., in grocery stores, shelf space is limited). Thus, new entrants must persuade distributors to carry their products—either in addition to or in place of existing firms' products. Price breaks and cooperative advertising allowances may be used for this purpose. However, their use reduces the new entrant's potential to earn superior profits.

*Cost Disadvantages Independent of Scale*   In some instances, established competitors have cost advantages that new entrants cannot duplicate. For example, proprietary product technology, favorable access to raw materials, favorable locations, and government subsidies may provide such cost advantages.

   Successful competition requires new entrants to find ways to reduce these factors' strategic relevance. For example, the impact of a favorable location can be reduced by offering direct delivery to the buyer (a number of food establishments, with unattractive locations, deliver goods directly to the consumer). In another case, an automobile dealership developed a new advertising scheme to overcome the problem of its unfavorable location. Recognizing the reality of its situation, the dealership's advertisements encourage customers to shop at the dealership with the "world's worst location." Customers are also told that the dealer's low prices and superior service compensate for the inconvenience of an inferior location.

*Government Policy*   Through licensing and permit requirements, governments can control entry into an industry. Liquor retailing, banking, and trucking are examples of industries where governments' decisions and actions affect industry entry. Also, governments restrict entrance into some utility industries because of the need to provide quality service to all and the capital requirements necessary to do so.

**Expected Retaliation**   Concluding that a company is able to overcome the competitive disadvantages posed by entry barriers does not suggest that a final decision has been reached. Decision makers will also anticipate existing competitors' reactions to a new entrant. If retaliation is expected to be swift and vigorous, a decision could be reached against entry. Strong retaliation can be anticipated from firms with a major stake in an industry (this stake could be a function of a company having fixed assets with few, if any, alternative uses), from firms with substantial resources, and when growth in the industry is slow or constrained. Sometimes a company will publicly announce its intentions. For example, it is well known that General Electric (GE) intends to hold either the largest or, at worst, the second largest share of each market in which it competes. Thus, new entrants probably can expect strong retaliation from GE.

## Bargaining Power of Suppliers

Raising prices and reducing the quality of goods sold are potential means through which suppliers can exert power over firms competing within an industry. If unable to recover cost increases through its pricing structure, a firm's profitability is reduced by the suppliers' actions. A supplier group is powerful when

- it is dominated by a few large companies and is more concentrated than the industry to which it sells;
- satisfactory substitute products are not available to buyers;
- buyers are not a significant customer for the supplier group;
- suppliers' goods are critical to buyers' marketplace success;
- the effectiveness of suppliers' products has created high switching costs for buyers; and
- suppliers are a credible threat to integrate forward into the buyers' industry (e.g., a clothing manufacturer might choose to operate its own retail outlets). Credibility is enhanced when suppliers have substantial resources and provide buyers with a highly differentiated product. The decision by Ralph Lauren to operate retail outlets in selective markets is a credible threat to certain segments of the retail clothing industry.

## Bargaining Power of Buyers

Firms seek to maximize the return on their invested capital. Buyers prefer to purchase products at the lowest possible price—at which the industry earns the lowest acceptable rate of return on its invested capital. To reduce their costs, buyers bargain for higher quality, greater levels of service, and lower prices. These outcomes can be achieved by encouraging competitive battles among firms in an industry. A buyer group is powerful when

- it purchases a large portion of an industry's total output;
- the product being purchased from an industry accounts for a significant portion of the buyers' costs;
- it could switch to another supplier's product at little, if any, cost; and
- the suppliers' products are undifferentiated or standardized, and it poses a credible threat to integrate backward into the suppliers' industry. Large grocery chains threatening to sell products under their private labels present a credible threat to integrate backward.

## Threat of Substitute Products

In a sense, firms compete against any firms producing substitute products. Capable of satisfying similar customer needs, but with different characteristics, substitute products place an upper limit on the prices firms can charge. Thus, substitute products perform the same or a similar function or service. In general, the threat of substitute products is strong when customers face few, if any, switching costs and when the substitute product's price is lower and/or its quality and performance capabilities are equal to or greater than the industry's products. To reduce the attractiveness of substitute products, firms are challenged to differentiate their offerings along dimensions that are highly relevant to customers (e.g., price, product quality, service after the sale, and location).

As an alternative or substitute, Nutrasweet places an upper limit on the prices sugar manufacturers can charge. Nutrasweet and sugar perform the same service, but with different characteristics. Other product substitutes include fax machines instead of overnight delivery of correspondence and plastic containers instead of glass jars.

## Intensity of Rivalry Among Competitors

In many industries, firms compete actively with one another to achieve strategic competitiveness and superior profitability. Achieving these outcomes demands success relative to a firm's rivals. Thus, competition among rivals is stimulated when one or more firms feel competitive pressure or when they identify an opportunity to improve their market position. Competition among rivals is often based on price, product innovation, and other actions to achieve product differentiation (such as extensive customer service, unique advertising campaigns, and extended product warranties).

Because firms in an industry are mutually dependent, one firm's actions often invite retaliation from competitors. An industry in which this pattern of action and reaction (competitive actions and responses) occurs repeatedly is the deregulated airline industry. Quick reactions to one firm's price cuts are normal in this industry. Similarly, reactions to the introduction of innovative products, such as frequent flyer programs, usually are swift. Originated by American Airlines, virtually all major airlines rapidly developed a similar offering. Thus, in the airline industry, as in many industries, firms often *simultaneously* use two or all three of the principal means of competition (price cuts, product/service innovations, and different means of differentiation) used by rivals when trying to gain a favorable marketplace position. The *intensity* of competitive rivalry among firms is a function of several factors, as described in the following subsections.

*In many industries, firms compete actively with one another to gain an advantage over competitors. When one company gains an advantage, such as was the case with American Airlines' introduction of its frequent flyer program, competitors often try to eliminate that advantage by duplicating its competitor's actions. Along with many others, United Airlines responded to American Airlines' innovation by offering its own frequent flyer program.*

**Numerous or Equally Balanced Competitors**   Industries populated by many participants tend to be characterized by intense rivalry. With many participants, often a few firms believe they can take actions without eliciting a response. However, other firms generally notice these actions and choose to respond. Frequent patterns of actions and responses result in intense rivalry.

At the other extreme, industries with only a few firms of equivalent size and power also tend to have high degrees of competitive rivalry. The resource bases of these firms permit vigorous actions and responses. The marketplace battles between Coca-Cola and PepsiCo exemplify an intense rivalry between relatively equivalent competitors.

**Slow Industry Growth**   When a market is growing, firms are challenged to use resources effectively to serve an expanding customer base. In this instance, fewer actions may be taken to attract competitors' customers. The situation changes, however, when market growth either slows or stops. Under these conditions, rivalry becomes much more intense, as an increase in one firm's market share may come at the expense of competitors' shares.

*When facing markets that are either not expanding or are growing very slowly, firms often compete on the basis of price. In response to declining growth rates in their markets, Burger King, McDonald's, and Wendy's are pricing their products aggressively. By suggesting to customers that their products offer value at a low price, each of these firms hopes to gain market share from their competitors (each of the items on Wendy's value menu is priced under $1.00).*

To protect their market shares, firms engage in intense competitive battles. Such battles introduce instability into the market, often reducing profitability in the industry. Parts of the fast food industry are characterized by this situation. In contrast to years past, the market for these products is growing more slowly. To expand market share, many of these companies (e.g., McDonald's, Burger King, and Wendy's) are competing aggressively in terms of pricing strategies, product introductions, and product and service differentiation.

**High Fixed or Storage Costs**   When fixed costs account for a large part of total costs, companies are challenged to utilize most, if not all, of their productive capacity. Operating in this manner allows the costs to be spread across a larger volume of output. Such actions by many firms in an industry can result in excess supply. To reduce inventories, companies typically reduce product prices and offer product rebates as well as other special discounts. These practices often intensify rivalry among competitors. This same phenomenon is observed in industries with high storage costs. Perishable products, for example, rapidly lose their value with the passage of time. When inventories grow, perishable goods producers often use pricing strategies to sell their products quickly.

**Lack of Differentiation or Switching Costs**   Differentiated products engender buyer identification, preferences, and loyalty. Industries with large numbers of companies that have successfully differentiated their products are less rivalrous. However, when buyers view products as commodities (i.e., as products with few differentiated features or capabilities), rivalry intensifies. In these instances, buyers' purchase decisions are based primarily on price and service.

The effect of switching costs is identical to that described for differentiated products. The lower the buyers' switching costs, the easier it is for competitors to attract them (through pricing and service offerings). High switching costs, however, at least partially insulate firms from rivals' efforts to attract their customers.

**Capacity Augmented in Large Increments**   In some industries, the realities of scale economies dictate that production capacity should be added only on a large scale (e.g., in the manufacture of vinyl chloride and chlorine). Additions of substantial capacity can be disruptive to a balance between supply and demand in the industry. Price cutting is often used to bring demand and supply back into balance. However, achieving balance in this manner has a negative effect on the firms' profitability.

**Diverse Competitors**   Not all companies seek to accomplish the same goals, nor do they operate with identical cultures. These differences make it difficult to identify an industry's competitive rules. Moreover, with greater firm diversity, it becomes increasingly difficult to pinpoint competing firms' strategic intent. Often firms engage in various competitive actions, in part to see how their competitors will respond. This type of competitive interaction can reduce industry profitability.

**High Strategic Stakes**   Competitive rivalry becomes more intense when attaining success in a particular industry is critical to a large number of firms. For example, diversified firms' successes in one industry may be important to their effectiveness in other industries in which they compete. This is the case when firms follow a corporate strategy of related diversification (where the separate businesses are interdependent—this strategy is explained in detail in Chapter 6).

High strategic stakes can also exist in terms of geographic locations. For example, Japanese automobile manufacturers are committed to a significant presence in the U.S. marketplace. Because of the stakes involved, for Japanese and U.S. manufacturers, rivalry in the automobile industry is quite intense. On a local level, increased rivalry may be observed (e.g., in the form of price competition) following entry into the marketplace by a new bookstore with a location adjacent to a college or university.

▲ **Exit barriers** are economic, strategic, and emotional factors causing companies to remain in an industry even though the profitability of doing so may be in question.

**High Exit Barriers**   Sometimes companies continue to compete in an industry even though the returns on their invested capital are low or even negative. Firms making this choice face high exit barriers. **Exit barriers** are economic, strategic, and emotional factors causing companies to remain in an industry even though the profitability of doing so may be in question. Common sources of exit barriers are

- specialized assets (assets with values linked to a particular business or location),
- fixed costs of exit (e.g., labor agreements),
- strategic interrelationships (mutual dependence relationships between one business and other parts of a company's operations, such as shared facilities and access to financial markets),
- emotional barriers (aversion to economically justified business decisions because of fear for one's own career, loyalty to employees, and so forth), and
- government and social restrictions (common outside the United States, restrictions based on government concerns for job losses and regional economic effects).

The higher the exit barriers, the greater the probability that a firm will engage in destabilizing competitive actions (e.g., price cuts, extensive promotions, etc.).

## Interpreting Industry Analyses

Industry analyses can be challenging and are a product of careful study and interpretation of information and data from multiple sources. A wealth of industry-specific data is available to those analyzing an industry. Successful analysts learn to focus quickly on the most significant items, discarding information lacking strategic relevance in the process.

In general, the stronger the competitive forces, the lower the profit potential for firms in an industry. An *unattractive industry* has low entry barriers, suppliers and buyers with strong bargaining positions, strong competitive threats from product substitutes, and intense rivalry among competing firms. These industry attributes make it very difficult for firms to achieve strategic competitiveness and earn superior profits. Alternatively, an *attractive industry* has high entry barriers, suppliers and buyers with little bargaining power, few competitive threats from product substitutes, and relatively moderate rivalry.[47]

To serve their firm effectively, top executives must understand the structure of the industry in which their company competes. This understanding helps them select competitive strategies that allow their firm to positively influence the competitive forces or to prevent these forces from reducing its profitability.

Next we describe strategic groups. The possibility of strategic groups must be explored to fully understand the industry in which the company competes.

## Strategic Groups

Over 20 years ago, Michael Hunt studied the home appliance industry. He introduced the term *strategic groups* to describe competitive patterns observed in that industry. While he found differences in firms' characteristics and strategies, Hunt also discovered that many firms were following similar strategies. He chose to label those groups following similar strategies strategic groups.[48] Formally, a **strategic group** is "a group of firms in an industry following the same or a similar strategy along the [same] strategic dimensions."[49] These strategic dimensions include the extent of technological leadership, the degree of product quality, pricing policies, the choice of distribution channels, and the degree and type of customer service. Thus, membership in a particular strategic group defines the essential characteristics of a firm's strategy.[50] While the strategies of firms within a group are similar, they are different from the strategies being implemented by firms in other strategic groups.

The notion of strategic groups is popular for analyzing an industry's competitive structure.[51] Contributing to its popularity is Porter's assertion that strategic group analysis is a basic framework that should be used in diagnosing competition, positioning, and the profitability of firms within an industry.[52]

Use of strategic groups for analyzing industry structure requires that dimensions relevant to firms' performance within an industry (e.g., price and image, as shown in Figure 2–3) be selected. Plotting firms in terms of these dimensions helps to identify groups of firms competing in similar ways. In the example shown in Figure 2–3, Dodge, Chevrolet, and Toyota form a strategic group, as do Mercedes, Porsche, and Lincoln. The products in each of these groups are similar in price and image (within the group).

▲ A **strategic group** is "a group of firms in an industry following the same or a similar strategy along the [same] strategic dimensions."

**FIGURE 2–3**  **Strategic Groups**

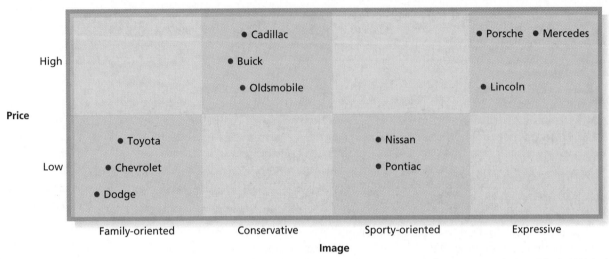

SOURCE: Adapted by permission from John C. Mowen, "Beyond Consumer Decision Making," Journal of Consumer Marketing, *Winter 1988 (vol. 5, no. 2), pp. 22–23.*

There are several implications of the strategic group concept. First, a firm's major competitors are those within its strategic group. Because firms within a group are selling similar products to the same customers, the competitive rivalry among them can be intense. The more intense the rivalry, the greater the threat to each firm's profitability. Second, the strengths of the five competitive forces differ across strategic groups. Large, established restaurants, for example, have greater strength as buyers than do small, localized food establishments. As a result, firms within the various strategic groups have different pricing policies. Third, the closer the strategic groups in terms of strategies followed and dimensions emphasized, the greater the likelihood of competitive rivalry between the groups. For example, Nissan and Pontiac are more likely competitors for Dodge than for Mercedes and Porsche. In contrast, strategic groups that differ significantly in terms of strategic dimensions and strategies do not compete directly. Mercedes and Dodge are not direct competitors, nor are Pay-Less and Cole-Haan shoes.

## The Value of Strategic Group Analysis

Opinions vary about the value of strategic group analysis for understanding industry dynamics and structure. As noted earlier, Porter believes that this analytical tool provides critical information for understanding how to compete successfully within an industry. Others, however, oppose this viewpoint. For example, some argue that there is no convincing evidence that strategic groups exist or that a firm's performance depends upon membership in a particular group.[53]

Another criticism of strategic groups is suggested by Figure 2–3. The automobile companies included in the figure manufacture many products with varying attributes. Dodge, for example, manufactures some relatively inexpensive cars with a family orientation. However, the firm also sells the Dodge Stealth, a sports car that is expensive and not a family-oriented product. Thus, the variances in many firms' product lines make it difficult to capture the nature of a company's outputs through study of a few strategic dimensions.

These criticisms notwithstanding, strategic group analysis yields benefits. It helps in the selection and partial understanding of an industry's structural characteristics, competitive dynamics, evolution, and strategies that historically have allowed companies to be successful within an industry.[54] As is always the case, a tool's strengths and limitations should be known before it is used.

Having an understanding of the general environment, the industry environment, and strategic groups, the final activity in the study of the external environment is competitor analysis. The results of this effort provide important insights about a firm's competitors.

## Competitor Analysis

As we discussed, an analysis of the industry environment reflects the potential, or the lack thereof, for profit. Understanding an industry environment alerts firms to potential sources of competition and to other companies' possible competitive actions and responses and their effects on profitability.

As a complement to an analysis of the industry, competitor analysis focuses on each company with which a firm competes directly. Although important in all industry settings, competitor analysis is especially critical for firms facing one or a few powerful competitors.[55] For example, Coca-Cola and PepsiCo are keenly interested in understanding each other's objectives, strategies, assumptions, and capabilities, as are Eastman Kodak and Fuji. In successful companies, the process of competitor analysis is used to determine

- what drives the competitor (as shown by its *future objectives*),
- what the competitor is doing and can do (as revealed by its *current strategy*),
- what the competitor believes about itself and the industry (as shown by its *assumptions*), and
- what the competitor's capabilities are (as shown by its *capabilities*).[56]

Information on these four issues helps strategists prepare an anticipated response profile for each competitor (see Figure 2–4). Thus, the results of an effective competitor analysis help a firm understand, interpret, and predict its competitors' actions and initiatives.[57] Moreover, the results should provide answers to the questions, grouped by key categories, shown in Table 2–3.

Critical to effective competitor analysis is the gathering of needed information and data, referred to as competitor intelligence. Analysts are challenged to ethically obtain information and data that inform them about competitors' objectives, strategies, assumptions, and capabilities. Intelligence-gathering techniques commonly considered to be both legal and ethical include (1) obtaining publicly available information (e.g., court records, competitors' help-wanted advertisements, annual reports, financial reports of publicly held corporations, and Uniform Commercial Code filings) and (2) attending trade fairs and shows (to obtain competitors' brochures, view their exhibits, and listen to discussions about their products).

At the other extreme, certain techniques—eavesdropping, trespassing, blackmail, and the theft of drawings, samples, or documents—are unethical and

**FIGURE 2–4  Competitor-Analysis Components**

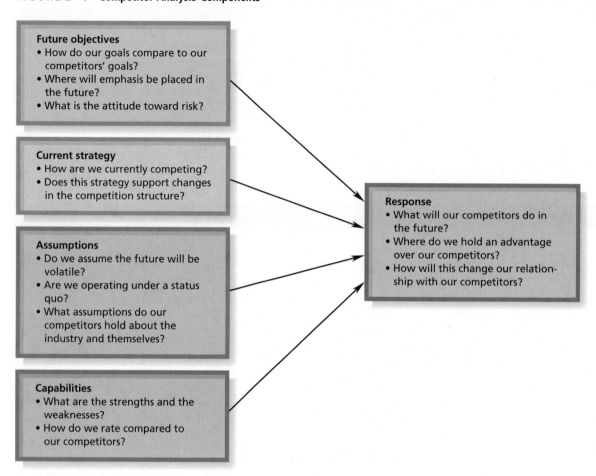

**Future objectives**
- How do our goals compare to our competitors' goals?
- Where will emphasis be placed in the future?
- What is the attitude toward risk?

**Current strategy**
- How are we currently competing?
- Does this strategy support changes in the competition structure?

**Assumptions**
- Do we assume the future will be volatile?
- Are we operating under a status quo?
- What assumptions do our competitors hold about the industry and themselves?

**Capabilities**
- What are the strengths and the weaknesses?
- How do we rate compared to our competitors?

**Response**
- What will our competitors do in the future?
- Where do we hold an advantage over our competitors?
- How will this change our relationship with our competitors?

SOURCE: Adapted and reprinted with permission of The Free Press, an imprint of Simon & Schuster from COMPETITIVE STRATEGY: Techniques for Analyzing Industires and Competitors by Michael E. Porter, Fig. 3–1, p. 49. Copyright 1980 by The Free Press.

considered to be illegal.[58] Shown in Table 2–4 are questionable intelligence-gathering techniques. While they are legal, decision makers must determine if their use is ethical. In highly competitive environments, employees may feel greater pressure to rely on these techniques. Interestingly, evidence suggests that most business people believe their competitors use questionable intelligence-gathering techniques far more frequently than they do.[59] Perhaps an appropriate guideline is to use intelligence-gathering techniques that respect the principles of common morality and the right of competitors not to reveal certain information about their products, operations, and strategic intentions.[60]

As with analysis of the general environment, analyses of the industry and competitors should result in the identification of opportunities and threats for the focal firm. A procedure for identification of opportunities and threats is explained in the Introduction to Preparing an Effective Case Analysis.

▼ **TABLE 2–3**

### Questions About Competitors

| | |
|---|---|
| *Customers* | • Who are our competitors' major customers?<br>• Where are their customers located?<br>• How much does each customer buy from our competitors? |
| *Distribution* | • How do your competitors get their products to the market? |
| *Marketing* | • What pricing, product, or regional marketing strategies are our competitors using? |
| *Sales* | • How large are our competitors' sales forces?<br>• What are their sales terms and conditions? |
| *Advertising* | • Where do our competitors advertise?<br>• How much do they spend on advertising? |
| *Finances* | • Are our competitors profitable?<br>• If so, by how much?<br>• What are their overhead costs? |
| *Operations* | • What are the size, location, and capacity of their facilities?<br>• How efficiently do they produce their products? |
| *Organization* | • What is their organizational structure?<br>• Are they decentralized?<br>• Who makes the key decisions? |
| *Research and Development* | • What patents and trademarks do they own?<br>• What new products are they working on?<br>• How much do they spend on research and development? |
| *Strategic Plans* | • What are their long- and short-term plans?<br>• Will they retain their core business or expand into other markets?<br>• Do they intend to acquire other businesses? |

*Source:* T. Eisenhart, 1989, Where to go when you need to know, *Business Marketing* 74, no. 11: 40. Reprinted with permission from the 1989 issue of *Business Marketing*. Copyright, Crain Communications Inc.

▼ **TABLE 2–4**

### Questionable Intelligence-Gathering Techniques

| | |
|---|---|
| *Use Buyers Under False Pretext* | • Ask buyers for information about competitors on the pretext of better serving the buyer. |
| *Implement Aggressive Confrontation Tactics* | • Seek competitor information at conferences or professional meetings by means beyond careful listening or "wining and dining" competitors' employees (e.g., aggressive probing and questioning of competitors' employees to obtain particular information). |

*(continued on next page)*

▽ **TABLE 2-4**

### Questionable Intelligence-Gathering Techniques (*continued*)

| | |
|---|---|
| *Hire a Competitor's Key Employees* | • Hire a knowledgeable person away from a competitor in order to get information about the competitor's inventions or technological innovations. |
| *Conduct Phony Job Interviews* | • Conduct a job interview for a nonexistent position in the hope that a competitor's disgruntled, but knowledgeable, employees will apply for the job and volunteer inside information. |
| *Use an Impostor* | • Pay someone to pose as someone else (such as a student, management consultant, government inspector, or reporter) to obtain information about competitors. |
| *Acquire a Competitor's Trash* | • Purchase a competitor's trash in order to obtain the competitor's documents, analyze its rejects, etc. |

*Source:* K.A. Rehbein, S.A. Morris, R.L. Armacost, and J.C. Hosseini, 1992, The CEOs' view of questionable competitor intelligence gathering practices, *Journal of Managerial Issues* 4, no. 4: 593. Reprinted from the *Journal of Management Issues,* published by Pittsburgh State University, Pittsburgh, KS 66762.

## Summary

- Firms' external environments are often challenging and complex. Because of their effect on performance, firms must develop the skills required to identify the opportunities and the threats existing in their external environments.
- The external environment has two major parts—the general environment (elements in the broader society that affect industries and their firms) and the industry environment (factors—the threat of entry, suppliers, buyers, product substitutes, and the intensity of rivalry among competitors—that influence a firm and its competitive actions and responses). Further informing a firm's understanding of the external environment is the study of competitors.
- Environmental analyses often must assume a nationless and borderless business environment.
- The external environmental analysis process includes four steps—scanning, monitoring, forecasting, and assessing. Analysis of this environment leads to the identification of opportunities and threats.
- Analysts do not always study the environment in a totally objective manner. Effective analyses are conducted by those who recognize their personal biases and assumptions and try to overcome those limitations.

- The general environment includes five segments (demographic, economic, political/legal, sociocultural, and technological). For each, the objective is to identify and study the strategic relevance of different changes and trends. The trend toward globalization complicates this task and expands its boundaries.
- As compared to the general environment, the industry environment has a more direct effect on a firm's efforts to achieve strategic competitiveness.
- The five forces model of an industry includes characteristics that determine the industry's profit potential. Through study of the five forces, firms select a position in the industry in which they can match their core competencies with an opportunity to achieve strategic competitiveness and earn superior profits.
- Different strategic groups exist within industries (a strategic group is a group of firms that follow the same strategy or similar strategies along the same strategic dimensions). The competition within each strategic group is more intense than is the competition between strategic groups.
- Managers should understand their firm's position, relative to competitors, in terms of the important strategic dimensions.

- Competitor analysis informs a firm about the objectives, strategies, assumptions, and capabilities of the firms with which it competes.
- Different techniques are available for gathering the intelligence (information and data) needed to understand competitors' actions and intentions. Analysts must determine the appropriate and ethical techniques for use in their firm.

## Review Questions

1. Why is it important for firms to study and understand the external environment?
2. What are the differences between the general environment and the industry environment?
3. What is the environmental-analysis process? What do analysts try to learn as they scan, monitor, forecast, and assess?
4. What are the five segments of the general environment? Explain the differences among them.
5. Use information in the chapter as your justification for accepting or rejecting the following statement: "There are five competitive forces that determine an industry's profit potential."
6. What is a strategic group? Of what value is the strategic-group concept in choosing a firm's strategy?
7. Why do firms seek information about competitors, and how is that information best collected?

## Application Discussion Questions

1. Given the importance of understanding an external environment, why do some managers, and their firms, fail to do so? Provide an example of a firm that poorly understood its external environment, and discuss the outcomes.
2. Select a firm and describe how you characterize the nature of external environments facing it. As someone who will soon enter the business world, how do you react to these environmental conditions? Why?
3. Describe how it would be possible for one firm to think of a condition in the general environment as an opportunity, while a second firm sees that condition as a threat. Provide an example of an environmental characteristic that could be perceived in this way.
4. Choose a firm in your local community. What courses of action would you follow, and what materials would you read, to understand its industry environment? Why?
5. Select an industry and describe what firms could do to create barriers to entry in this industry.
6. What conditions would cause a firm to retaliate aggressively against a new entrant in the airline industry?
7. Is it possible for an industry to exist with only a single strategic group? If so, how would this be possible? Please provide an example of such an industry.

## Ethics Questions

1. How can a firm apply its "code of ethics" in the study of its external environment?
2. What ethical issues, if any, may be relevant in a firm's monitoring of its external environment?
3. For each segment of the general environment, identify an ethical issue to which companies should be sensitive.
4. What is the importance of ethical practices between a firm and its suppliers and distributors? Explain.
5. In an intense rivalry, how can a firm undertake ethical practices and yet maintain its competitiveness? Discuss.
6. While differences in strategies may exist between strategic groups, should commonly accepted ethical values/practices be the same across strategic groups within an industry?
7. What are the primary ethical issues associated with competitor intelligence practices?

## Notes

1. G. Hamel and C.K. Prahalad, 1989, Strategic intent, *Harvard Business Review* 67, no. 3: 63–76; C.J. Fombrun, 1992, *Turning Points: Creating Strategic Change in Organizations* (New York: McGraw-Hill), 13.

2. N.M. Tichy and S. Sherman, 1993, *Control Your Own Destiny, or Someone Else Will* (New York: McGraw-Hill); The post-capitalist executive: An interview with Peter F. Drucker, 1993, *Harvard Business Review* 71, no. 3: 114–122.

3. Lou Gerstner's first 30 days, 1993, *Fortune,* May 31, 57–62.

4. Fombrun, *Turning Points,* 16, 18.

5. M. Loeb, 1993, Here's a real wealth builder, *Fortune,* May 31, 6.

6. M. Robert, 1993, *Strategy Pure and Simple* (New York: McGraw-Hill), 3.

7. L. Fahey and V.K. Narayanan, 1986, *Macroenvironmental Analysis for Strategic Management* (St. Paul: West), 49–50.

8. K. Sera, 1992, Corporate globalization: A new trend, *Academy of Management Executive* 6, no. 1: 89–96.

9. R. Henkoff, 1990, How to plan for 1995, *Fortune,* December 31, 70–77; Sera, Corporate globalization, 89.

10. J.F. Preble, P.A. Rau, and A. Reichel, 1988, The environmental scanning practices of U.S. multinationals in the late 1980s, *Management International Review* 28, no. 4: 4–14.

11. W.P. Anthony, R.H. Bennett, N. Maddox, and W.J. Wheatley, 1993, Picturing the future: Using mental imagery to enrich strategic environmental assessment, *Academy of Management Executive* 7, no. 2: 43–56; Fombrun, *Turning Points,* 14.

12. J.F. Preble, 1992, Environmental scanning for strategic control, *Journal of Managerial Issues* 4: 254–268; K. Gronhaug, and J.S. Falkenberg, 1989, Exploring strategy perceptions in changing environments, *Journal of Management Studies* 26: 349–359.

13. Fombrun, *Turning Points,* 77; Gronhaug and Falkenberg, Exploring strategy perceptions, 350.

14. L.S. Richman, 1993. Why the economic data mislead us, *Fortune,* March 8, 108–114.

15. Fahey and Narayanan, *Macroenvironmental Analysis,* 37.

16. S. Shepard, 1993, Baby boom could bust retirement system, *Waco Tribune Herald,* May 23, 1A; How America will change over the next 30 years, 1993. *Fortune,* May 2, 12.

17. Fahey and Narayanan, *Macroenvironmental Analysis,* 39.

18. Ibid., 41.

19. Ibid., 42.

20. Fombrun, *Turning Points,* 5, 88; Anthony, Bennett, Maddox, and Wheatley, Picturing the future, 45.

21. Gronhaug and Falkenberg, Exploring strategy perceptions, 350.

22. Fombrun, *Turning Points,* 12.

23. Fahey and Narayanan, *Macroenvironmental Analysis,* 58.

24. E. Cornish, 1990, Issues of the '90s, *Futurist* 24, no. 1: 29–36.

25. Ibid., 35.

26. R.I. Kirkland, 1991, Get ready for a new world of work, *Fortune,* February 11, 136–141.

27. M. McLaughlin, 1989, A change of mind, *New England Business,* April, 42–53.

28. How America will change over the next 30 years, 12; The labor secretary speaks out on training and the two-tier work force, 1993, *Fortune,* March 8, 11.

29. T. Cox and S. Blake, 1991, Managing cultural diversity: Implications for international competitiveness, *Academy of Management Executive* 5, no. 3: 45–56.

30. J.P. Fernandez, 1993, *The diversity advantage* (New York: Lexington Books).

31. Cornish, Issues of the '90s, 32.

32. Fahey and Narayanan, *Macroenvironmental Analysis,* 105.

33. D. Leebaert, 1990, Top economic trends of the 1990s, *Management Review* 79, no. 1: 21–23; Cornish, Issues of the '90s, 32.

34. Fahey and Narayanan, *Macroenvironmental Analysis,* 139, 157.

35. J.M. Moses, 1993, Nissan's challenge to 25% tariff may have effect on trade debate, *Wall Street Journal,* May 5, B14.

36. B. Bowers, 1993, FDA regulatory tide swallows up McCurdy Fish Co., *Wall Street Journal,* May 18, 2B.

37. How America will change over the next 30 years, 12.

38. J.B. Roesner, 1991, Ways women lead, *Harvard Business Review* 69, no. 3: 119–125.

39. F.N. Schwartz, 1992, Women as a business imperative, *Harvard Business Review* 70, no. 2: 105–113; B. Geber, 1990, Managing diversity, *Training,* July, 23–30; C. Torres and M. Bruxelles, 1992, Capitalizing on global diversity, *HR Magazine,* December, 30–33.

40. A.L. Dolinsky, 1992, Long term entrepreneurs' patterns: A national study of black and white female entrepreneurs, *Rothman Ink* 13: 3; E.H. Buttner, 1993, Female entrepreneurs: How far have they come? *Business Horizons* 36, no. 3: 59–65.

41. A.B. Fisher, 1993, Japanese working women strike back, *Fortune,* May 31, 22.

42. Mazda looks ahead optimistically after suffering setback with Amati, 1993, *Dallas Morning News,* November 29, 2H.

43. The greening of Detroit, 1991, *Business Week,* April 8, 54–60; W. McWhirter, 1993, Off and humming, *Time,* April 26, 53.

44. R. Tetzeli, 1994, The internet and your business, *Fortune,* March 7, 86–96.

45. M.E. Porter, 1990, *Competitive Strategy* (New York: Free Press); R.E. Miles and C.C. Snow, 1986, Network organizations: New concepts for new forms, *California Management Review* 28, no. 2: 62–73.

46. D. Blake, 1993, It's touch and go for airline, *Waco Tribune Herald,* June 6, 1B, 6B.

47. Much of the preceding discussion of competitive forces is based on Porter, *Competitive Strategy.*

48. M.S. Hunt, 1972, Competition in the major home appliance industry, 1960–1970 (doctoral diss., Harvard University).

49. Porter, *Competitive Strategy,* 129.

50. J. McGee and H. Thomas, 1986, Strategic groups: A useful linkage between industry structure and strategic management, *Strategic Management Journal* 7, no. 2: 141–160; R.K. Reger and A.S. Huff, 1993, Strategic groups: A cognitive perspective, *Strategic Management Journal* 14, no. 2: 103–123.

51. J.B. Barney and R.E. Hoskisson, 1990, Strategic groups: Untested assertions and research proposals, *Managerial and Decision Economics* 11: 198–208.

52. R.M. Grant, 1991 *Contemporary Strategy Analysis* (Cambridge, England: Blackwell Publishers), 79.

53. Barney and Hoskisson, Strategic groups, 202.

54. Grant, *Contemporary Strategy Analysis,* 80.

55. S. Ghoshal and D.E. Westney, 1991, Organizing competitor analysis systems, *Strategic Management Journal* 12, no. 1: 17–31.

56. Porter, *Competitive Strategy,* 49.

57. S.A. Zahra and S.S. Shaples, 1993, Blind spots in competitive analysis, *Academy of Managerial Executive* 7, no. 2: 7–28.

58. K.A. Rehbeing, S.A. Morris, R.L. Armacost, and J.C. Hosseini, 1992, The CEO's view of questionable competitor intelligence gathering practices, *Journal of Managerial Issues* 4: 590–603.

59. W. Cohen and H. Czepiec, 1988, The role of ethics in gathering corporate intelligence, *Journal of Business Ethics* 7, no. 2: 199–203.

60. L.S. Paine, 1991, Corporate policy and the ethics of competitor intelligence gathering, *Journal of Business Ethics* 10, no. 4: 423–436.

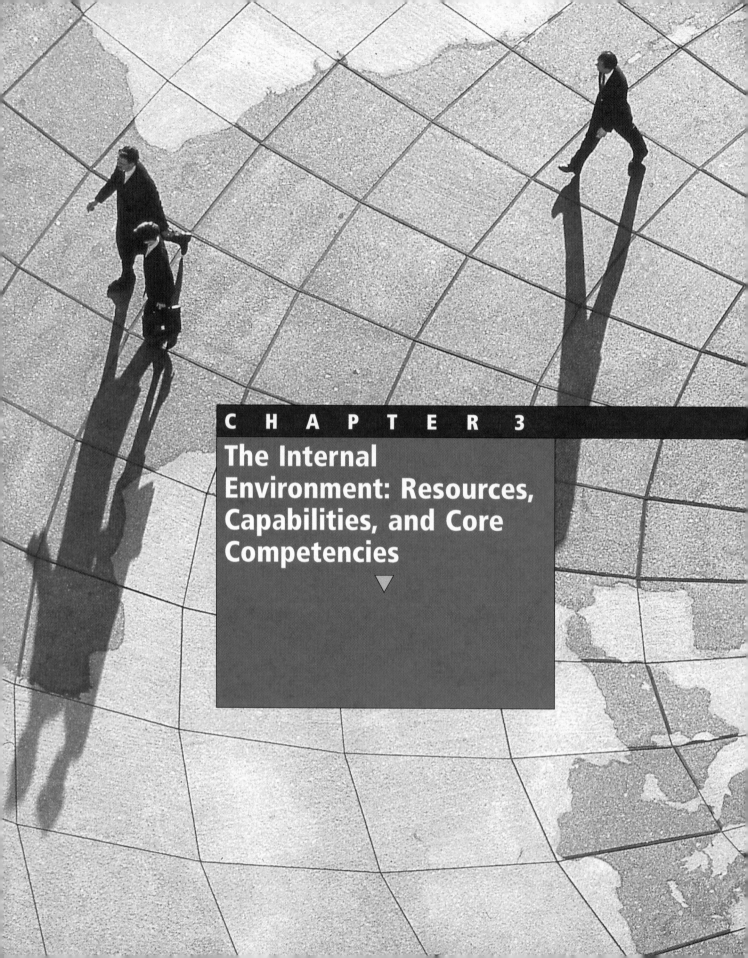

# CHAPTER 3

# The Internal Environment: Resources, Capabilities, and Core Competencies

▽

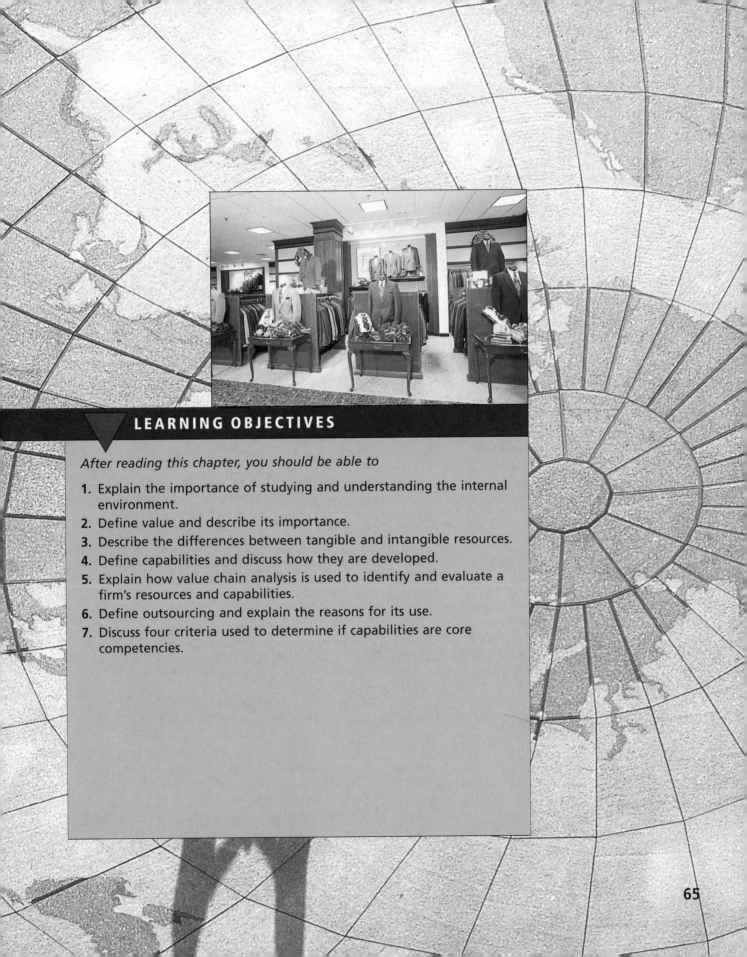

## LEARNING OBJECTIVES

*After reading this chapter, you should be able to*

1. Explain the importance of studying and understanding the internal environment.
2. Define value and describe its importance.
3. Describe the differences between tangible and intangible resources.
4. Define capabilities and discuss how they are developed.
5. Explain how value chain analysis is used to identify and evaluate a firm's resources and capabilities.
6. Define outsourcing and explain the reasons for its use.
7. Discuss four criteria used to determine if capabilities are core competencies.

## The Development of Competitive Advantage at JC Penney

Like Sears, Roebuck and Co., JCPenney has long been well known in U.S. retailing. For decades, these two firms profitably served the needs of mainly middle-income and small-town Americans for both soft goods (e.g., clothing) and hard goods (e.g., washers and dryers). However, the emergence of competitors that were capable of offering high-quality merchandise at attractive prices (such as Wal-Mart), coupled with broader societal changes in the general environment, created serious competitive problems for both JCPenney and Sears. Compared to Sears, JCPenney has moved rapidly to cope strategically with key changes taking place in the general and the industry environments.

By the early 1980s, William R. Howell, JCPenney CEO, had decided that his firm could no longer compete as it had historically. A failure to change, Howell believed, would result in continued decline in the firm's strategic competitiveness and profitability. In particular, Howell, and others in the firm, concluded that the modern-day JCPenney customer wanted stylish and trendy products—not just practical ones. Accordingly, Howell visited with manufacturers of trendy merchandise to see if they would use JCPenney as a distributor of their premium-priced, highly advertised goods. During these visits, people were told that JCPenney was going to change; stores were to be remodeled, many hard goods (dishwashers and auto parts, for example) would no longer be stocked, and the "cheap polyester stuff was going out the window."

For the most part, responses to Howell's requests were negative. The reason given by representatives of Liz Claiborne, Botany 500, and the maker of Arrow shirts was typical of the feedback Howell received: Upscale customers, such as Macy's and Bloomingdale's, would not want the same merchandise sold to JCPenney that was sold to them. This response forced JCPenney to examine its internal environment for sources of competitive advantage. Although some companies (including Levi Strauss, Vanity Fair, and Phillips-Van Heusen) did agree to sell to JCPenney, Howell concluded that creating a fashion image for the firm's private-label brands was the key to improving JCPenney's competitiveness.

Stafford and Worthington are examples of the house brands JCPenney chose to position competitively against national brands (Liz Claiborne, the Gap, and Hart Schaffner & Marx, for example). Critical to competing successfully against these brands was the decision to develop clothing lines for well-defined customer groups, such as professional women. To create unique and genuine identities for individual items that would appeal to targeted customer groups, JCPenney hired designers and assigned managers to each brand. By holding manufacturers to exacting design and production specifications, JCPenney is able to obtain high-quality goods to sell under its private label. It does not retain companies that fail to satisfy its exacting standards.

Once manufactured, each new item is test-marketed meticulously. Technology is one means used to do this. For example, a completed design for a new product, such as a sweater, is often beamed by satellite to 16 stores in different regions. JCPenney employees show the design to selected customers and carefully note their reactions. Based on this feedback, changes that are important to customers are made before stores stock an item. ▲

As is true for all firms, JCPenney is interested in developing a *sustainable competitive advantage*. A sustainable competitive advantage is achieved when firms implement a value-creating strategy that is grounded in their own resources, capabilities, and core competencies (terms defined in Chapter 1). The strategic actions described in the opening case are those JCPenney has taken to develop a stronger competitive advantage.

In the words of CEO William R. Howell, "our private brands are our competitive advantage."[1] Stating this differently, JCPenney has used its resources to form capabilities, some of which have been identified as the firm's core competencies. In turn, these competencies—the design, manufacture, and sale of private-label fashion merchandise—have been designated as a source of competitive advantage for the firm. Thus, it appears that JCPenney is implementing a strategy that exploits *its* firm-specific core competencies, relative to environmental opportunities. The relationship JCPenney seems to have established between its core competencies and its external environmental opportunities may result in strategic competitiveness and superior profitability.

Is JCPenney's strategy working? Is private-label fashion merchandise, as designed, manufactured, and distributed through the use of JCPenney's core competencies, proving to be a source of competitive advantage? And if the firm has developed a competitive advantage, is it sustainable?

Early evidence is encouraging. In 1992, JCPenney earned $777 million on revenues of $18 billion. In the same year, the Sears Merchandise Group lost $1.3 billion. From 1991 to 1992, JCPenney's profits increased 47 percent on a retail sales gain of only 11 percent. Sales were predicted to increase by 5 percent during its fiscal 1994 year, partially due to the continuing success of its private-label offerings.[2] But, JCPenney's top-level managers can conclude that the firm has developed a *sustained* competitive advantage only when current and potential competitors lack the ability or the desire to duplicate the benefits of its strategy.[3]

JCPenney's improving performance may have allowed the firm to pursue a business opportunity that became available suddenly when Sears announced the closing of its catalog operations. JCPenney's decision to focus on selected parts of Sears' catalog products was received favorably by analysts, who in 1993 estimated that the firm would add at least $300 million to its total 1994 sales figure through its catalog operations.[4] Catalog sales may be another environmental opportunity that JCPenney can pursue profitability because it has the core competencies to exploit this opportunity.

In a further extension of its apparent competencies in catalog sales, JCPenney also decided, in late 1993, to distribute catalogs to potential customers of two stores that are to open in Monterey and Leon, Mexico, in 1995. JCPenney was the first department store to offer catalogs to Mexican customers.[5] Apparently, JCPenney's strategists believe that its core competencies can be used to exploit an emerging environmental opportunity in the global economy.

Woolworth Corp., another U.S. retailer, also is striving to use its resources, capabilities, and core competencies to achieve strategic competitiveness. The relationships among these building blocks of strategic advantage for Woolworth Corp. are described in the following Strategic Focus.

As our discussions show, JCPenney's strategy differs from Woolworth's. JCPenney is striving to establish private-label brands and exploit its catalog sales capability globally, while Woolworth Corp. is seeking to establish specialty stores to serve particular customer niches. Both firms are trying to obtain sustainable competitive advantage through the implementation of strategies based on *their*

## The Development of Competitive Advantage at Woolworth Corp.

In the latter part of 1993, Woolworth Corp. made announcements signaling changes in its strategy. Woolworth executives thought that these changes were necessary in light of the firm's core competencies and the opportunities and threats in its external environment.

Among Woolworth's announcements were those indicating that almost 1,000 stores would be closed and 13,000 jobs eliminated. One result of these closures was the termination of Woolworth's century-old tradition of operating "dime stores" in towns throughout North America. According to Woolworth's CEO, generally unfavorable economic conditions and continuing shifts in consumers' shopping preferences left the firm no choice other than to close the stores.

With fewer stores, Woolworth Corp. believed it was in a better position to exploit its core competencies more successfully. A key strategic decision made by the firm's top-level managers was that Woolworth Corp would use its competencies to expand aggressively into additional specialty stores. Already successful with some specialty businesses, including Northern Reflections women's apparel stores, Foot Locker, and the RX Place (a chain of deep-discount drugstores), company leaders decided that the specialty format was an environmental opportunity that could be successfully exploited through Woolworth's core competencies.

Does Woolworth Corp. possess the core competencies required to successfully implement its emerging strategy? Even if it does, will this strategy result in a sustainable competitive advantage? Answers to these questions will be provided with the passage of time and through study of Woolworth's ability to defend itself against competitors' attempts to imitate its strategy.

At least in the short run, some analysts responded positively to the intended changes in Woolworth's strategy. One analyst, for example, noted that Woolworth Corp. introduced over 40 different specialty stores between 1973 and 1993 and that its profitability improved each time it opened a new type of specialty store.

*particular* resources, capabilities, and core competencies. Thus, top-level managers in these firms are doing what is expected of them: They are guiding their companies toward strategies that appear to be grounded in their unique core competencies. Superior profitability results when firm-specific core competencies are leveraged properly to take advantage of environmental opportunities.

As we have noted, the sustainability of the competitive advantages gained through the implementation of their firm's strategies is an important issue for both JCPenney's and Woolworth's top-level managers. But even if these firms' advantages are sustainable at a point in time, they will not last forever.[6] Eventually, other companies will be able to duplicate the benefits of JCPenney's and Woolworth's strategies, erasing these firms' competitive advantages in the process. It is not a question of *if* such duplication will occur, but rather of *when*. Thus, the challenge for JCPenney and Woolworth Corp., as it is for every firm, is to create "tomorrow's competitive advantages faster than competitors mimic the ones you possess today."[7] Only when firms are able to develop a continuous stream of competitive advantages can they achieve strategic competitiveness, earn above-average profits, and remain ahead of their competitors.[8]

In Chapter 2, the general environment, the industry environment, and rivalry among competing firms were examined. Armed with knowledge about their firm's environments, strategists have a better understanding of *what a company might do*—that is, the marketplace opportunities it might choose to pursue and the goods or services necessary to pursue them.

In this chapter, the focus is on the firm itself. Through an analysis of the internal environment, a firm determines *what it can do*—that is, the actions permitted by its resources, capabilities, and core competencies. The proper matching of what a firm *can do* with what it *might do* allows the development of strategic intent and strategic mission and the selection of a value-creating strategy. When implemented effectively, such a strategy is the pathway to strategic competitiveness and superior profitability. Outcomes resulting from internal and external environmental analyses are shown in Figure 3–1.

Several topics are examined in this chapter. First, the importance and the challenge of studying a firm's internal environment are addressed. Following these introductory materials are discussions of the roles that resources, capabilities, and core competencies play in developing sustainable competitive advantage and in formulating and implementing strategies. Included in these discussions are descriptions of the techniques used to identify and evaluate resources and capabilities and the criteria used to select a firm's core competencies from among its capabilities.

As shown in Figure 1–1, strategic intent and strategic mission, coupled with insights and understandings gained through analyses of the internal and the external environments, determine the strategies a firm will select and the actions it will take to implement them successfully. In the final part of this chapter, we briefly describe the relationship between intent and mission and a firm's strategy formulation and implementation actions.

## The Importance of Internal Analysis

In the world of global competition, traditional sources of competitive advantage, such as labor costs, capital costs, and raw materials, are ineffective. The key reason for this is that the advantages created by these sources can be overcome easily through a global strategy.[9] Thus, the demands and the nature of global competition make it necessary for top-level managers to rethink the concept of the corporation.[10] Earning strategic competitiveness in the 1990s and into the twenty-first century requires a different managerial mindset.[11] Critical to this type of mindset is

**FIGURE 3–1** Outcomes from External and Internal Environmental Analyses

By studying the external environment, firms identify
• what they *might* choose to *do*

By studying the internal environment, firms determine
• what they *can do*

the view that a firm is a *bundle* of heterogeneous resources, capabilities, and core competencies[12] that can be used to create an exclusive market position.[13] This view suggests that individual firms possess at least some resources, and particular capabilities, that other companies do not have, at least not in the same combinations. Resources are the source of capabilities, some of which are a firm's core competencies. By using their core competencies, firms are able to perform value-creating activities *better* than competitors or perform value-creating activities that competitors cannot duplicate.

In the 1990s and beyond, managers will be evaluated in terms of their ability to identify, nurture, and exploit firm-specific core competencies, as JCPenney and Woolworth Corp. have sought to do.[14] One way to do this is through the establishment and use of appropriate internal structures and processes.[15] In the final analysis, a corporatewide obsession with the development and use of core competencies may characterize companies able to compete successfully on a global basis during the 1990s and the twenty-first century.[16]

By exploiting their core competencies and meeting the demanding standards of global competition, firms create value for their customers. Jack Welch, General Electric's chief executive officer (CEO), believes that the 1990s are the *value decade*—a time during which global competition prevents firms from succeeding when they are unable to produce and sell a high-quality product at the world's lowest price.[17] **Value** entails the attributes provided by companies in the form of goods and services for which customers are willing to pay. In Chapter 4, we note that value is provided by a good's low cost, by its highly differentiated features, or by a combination of low cost and high differentiation, as compared to competitors' offerings. Core competencies, then, are actually a value-creating system[18] through which a company tries to achieve strategic competitiveness and earn above-average profits. These relationships are shown in Figure 3–2.

During the last several decades, strategic management was concerned *largely* with understanding the characteristics of the industry in which a firm was competing and, in light of those characteristics, how it should position itself relative to competitors. It is possible that the focus on industry and competitive strategy variables understated the role of organizational resources and capabilities in developing sustainable competitive advantage.[19] Furthermore, some now believe that a firm's core competencies, rather than the results of an analysis of its general, industry, and competitive environments, should be the foundation for the choice of its strategies.[20] Moreover, the nature of a company's core competencies is a significant determinant of firm profitability.[21] One reason for this different focus is a renewed understanding that the attractiveness of an industry ultimately depends on the nature of a firm's resources, capabilities, and core competencies.[22]

▲ **Value** entails the attributes provided by companies in the form of goods and services for which customers are willing to pay.

## The Challenge of Internal Analysis

The identification, development, protection, and deployment of resources, capabilities, and core competencies might appear to be relatively easy. However, such is not the case.[23] In fact, this work is as challenging and difficult as any other with which managers are involved. The decisions managers make when analyzing a firm's internal environment are significant in that they affect a firm's ability to develop sustainable competitive advantages.[24]

To manage the development and use of core competencies, managers carefully evaluate resources and capabilities to identify those that are a firm's core

**FIGURE 3–2  Components of Internal Analysis**

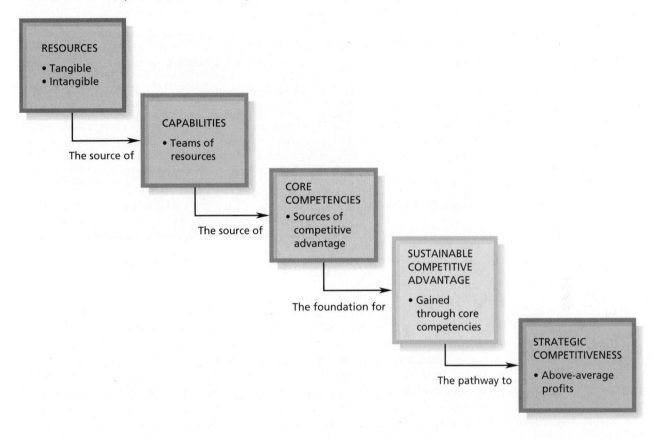

competencies. Doing this requires courage, self-confidence, integrity, and a willingness to hold people accountable for their work.[25]

Strong position statements sometimes result from a manager's analysis of a firm's performance and its internal environment. For example, in 1992, Honda Motor's sales fell 4.3 percent in the United States and 9.3 percent in Japan. In light of this, Honda's president, Nobuhiko Kawamoto, stated the following: "I definitely do not think that Honda is an excellent company. In fact, the present Honda is ill. Success has led to 'large company disease.' For those employees who are inflexible and refuse to do what they have to do, the only option is to fire them."[26] Thus, Honda's president suggested that a portion of one of the firm's resources—its people—was a source of incompetence.

Difficult managerial decisions concerning resources, capabilities, and core competencies are characterized by three conditions—uncertainty, complexity, and intraorganizational conflicts (see Figure 3–3).

Managers face *uncertainty* in terms of the emergence of new proprietary technologies, rapidly changing economic and political trends, changes in societal values, and shifts in consumer demands. Such environmental uncertainty increases the *complexity* and the range of issues managers examine when studying the internal environment. Managerial biases about how to cope with uncertainty affect decisions about the resources and the capabilities that will become the foundation of the firm's competitive advantage. Finally, *intraorganizational conflict* surfaces when

**FIGURE 3–3   Conditions Affecting Managerial Decisions About Resources, Capabilities, and Core Competencies**

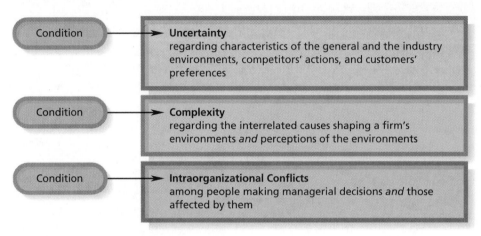

*Source: Adapted from R. Amit and P.J.H. Schoemaker, 1993, Strategic Assets and Organizational Rent,* Strategic Management Journal, *14: 33.*

decisions are made about core competencies that are to be nurtured and about how the nurturing is to take place.

When making decisions affected by these three conditions, managers should use their judgment. **Judgment** is a capacity for making a successful decision when no obviously correct model or rule is available or when relevant data are unreliable or incomplete.[27] Moreover, through judgment, managers have the capacity to make and execute decisions about resources, capabilities, and core competencies in a *timely* manner. A criticism of Robert Stempel, former CEO of General Motors (GM), was that he was slow to make changes in GM's resource base. Even after the decision was made to reduce the company's work force, for example, Stempel failed to eliminate jobs as quickly as called for by the analysis of GM's competencies and threats in its external environment.[28]

Significant changes in resources and capabilities, such as those experienced by GM, affect a company's power and social structure. In the face of such changes, there is often inertia or resistance to change. Firms should not deny the necessity of such changes to assure strategic competitiveness, but many managers experience denial. **Denial** is an unconscious coping mechanism used to block out and not initiate major changes that may have some pain associated with them.[29] Involving many people in decisions about changes can reduce denial and intraorganizational conflict.

▲ **Judgment** is a capacity for making a successful decision when no obviously correct model or rule is available or when relevant data are unreliable or incomplete.

▲ **Denial** is an unconscious coping mechanism used to block out and not initiate major changes that may have some pain associated with them.

## Resources, Capabilities, and Core Competencies

Our attention now turns to descriptions of resources, capabilities, and core competencies. The discussion that follows suggests that resources, capabilities, and core competencies form the foundation of a sustainable competitive advantage.

## Resources

Resources have been defined differently. One writer, for example, defines them as "anything which could be thought of as a strength or weakness of a given firm."[30] Others think of resources as the stocks of available factors that are controlled or owned by a firm.[31] As noted in Chapter 1, **resources** are inputs into a firm's production process, such as capital equipment, the skills of individual employees, patents, finance, and talented managers.[32] Comprehensive in scope, resources encompass a broad spectrum of individual, social, and organizational phenomena.[33]

Individually, resources typically do not result in a *sustainable* competitive advantage. A professional football team may benefit from employing the league's most talented running back. However, it is only when the running back fully integrates his running style with the blocking schemes of the offensive linemen and the team's offensive strategy that a sustainable competitive advantage may develop. Similarly, a firm's production technology, if not protected by patents or other constraints, can be purchased or imitated by competitors. But when that production technology is integrated with other resources to form a capability, a core competence may develop that can result in sustained competitive advantage. Thus, it is through the *integration* of several resources that a sustainable competitive advantage is created. More is said about this matter in the discussions of capabilities and core competencies.

Some of a firm's resources are tangible, while others are intangible. **Tangible resources** are assets that can be seen, touched, and/or quantified. **Intangible resources** range from the intellectual property rights of patents, trademarks, and copyrights to the people-dependent or subjective resources of know-how, networks, organizational culture, and a firm's reputation for its goods or services and the ways it interacts with people (e.g., employees, suppliers, and customers).[34] There are four types of tangible resources (see Table 3–1) and three types of intangible resources (see Table 3–2).

▲ **Resources** are inputs into a firm's production process, such as capital equipment, the skills of individual employees, patents, finance, and talented managers.

▲ **Tangible resources** are assets that can be seen, touched, and/or quantified.

▲ **Intangible resources** range from the intellectual property rights of patents, trademarks, and copyrights to the people-dependent or subjective resources of know-how, networks, organizational culture, and a firm's reputation for its goods or services and the ways it interacts with people (e.g., employees, suppliers, and customers).

### TABLE 3–1

#### Tangible Resources

| | |
|---|---|
| *Financial Resources* | • The firm's borrowing capacity <br> • Its ability to generate internal funds |
| *Physical Resources* | • Sophistication and location of a firm's plant and equipment <br> • Access to raw materials |
| *Human Resources* | • The training, experience, judgment, intelligence, insights, adaptability, commitment, and loyalty of a firm's individual managers and workers |
| *Organizational Resources* | • The firm's formal reporting structure and its formal planning, controlling, and coordinating systems |

*Sources:* Adapted from J.B. Barney, 1991, Firm resources and sustained competitive advantage, *Journal of Management* 17, 101; and R.M. Grant, 1991, *Contemporary Strategy Analysis* (Cambridge, England: Blackwell Business), 100–102.

▼ **TABLE 3-2**

**Intangible Resources**

| | |
|---|---|
| *Technological Resources* | • Stock of technology such as patents, trademarks, copyrights, and trade secrets as well as<br>• Knowledge required to successfully apply it |
| *Resources for Innovation* | • Technical employees<br>• Research facilities |
| *Reputation* | • Reputation with customers<br>  • Brand name<br>  • Perceptions of product quality, durability, and reliability<br>• Reputation with suppliers<br>  • For efficient, effective, supportive, and mutually beneficial interactions and relationships |

*Sources:* Adapted from R.M. Grant, 1991, *Contemporary Strategy Analysis* (Cambridge, England: Blackwell Business), 101–104; and R. Hall, 1992, The strategic analysis of intangible resources, *Strategic Management Journal* 13: 136–139.

**Tangible Resources**   Compared to intangible resources, tangible resources can be identified more readily and their value estimated. As tangible resources, a firm's borrowing capacity, the status of its plant and equipment, and many of its employees' attributes (including the amount and type of training and experiences they have had) are visible to all. The value of many tangible resources can be established through financial statements. However, financial statements do not account for the value of all of a firm's assets in that they disregard some intangible resources. As such, sources of a firm's *sustainable* competitive advantage often are not reflected on its financial statements.

⬥ The **strategic value of resources** is indicated by the degree to which they can contribute to the development of capabilities, core competencies, and, ultimately, a sustainable competitive advantage.

Managers are challenged to fully understand the strategic value of their firm's tangible and intangible resources. The **strategic value of resources** is indicated by the degree to which they can contribute to the development of capabilities, core competencies, and, ultimately, a sustainable competitive advantage. For example, as a tangible resource, a distribution facility will be assigned a monetary value on the firm's balance sheet. However, the real value of the facility as a resource is grounded in other factors, such as its proximity to raw materials and customers and, in the final analysis, its ability to be a part of a team of resources that becomes a capability.

As shown in Figure 3–2, resources are the source of a firm's capabilities. Capabilities are the source of a firm's core competencies, which are the foundation for the development of sustainable competitive advantage. On a relative basis, intangible resources, as compared to tangible resources, are a superior source of core competencies. In fact, because they tend to be invisible, intangible resources may be the only source of core competencies that can result consistently in sustainable competitive advantage.[35]

**Intangible Resources**   Because they are less visible, more difficult for competitors to understand and imitate, and a likely source of sustainable competitive advantage, managers prefer to use intangible resources as the foundation for a firm's capabilities and core competencies. This view has been derived, in part, through the results of research completed with practicing managers.[36]

In one study, upper-level executives were asked to identify the capabilities they believed were the source of their firm's sustainable competitive advantage. The managers identified well over 30 sources of competitive advantage. By a significant margin, the most important of these was an intangible resource—the company's *reputation for quality*.[37] This finding was confirmed in a survey of 847 CEOs of companies in the United Kingdom. Designed to understand CEOs' perceptions of the relative importance of various intangible resources to a firm's overall success, the results of this study confirmed the importance of company reputation. Company reputation was ranked first by the CEOs, in terms of importance, among 13 intangible resources.[38]

**Brand Names** As listed in Table 3–2, brand names, as an intangible resource, may be the most important link to sustainable competitive advantage for many companies, but especially those producing and selling either consumer durable goods (e.g., automobiles) or consumer nondurable goods (e.g., foods and household items).[39] When effective, brand names inform consumers of the performance characteristics and/or attributes associated with a particular good or service. When products with strong brand names provide superior value to customers across time, consumers tend to consistently purchase the brand-name product, rather than competing firms' offerings.

When the name of their brand yields a competitive advantage, a company will nurture the core competencies on which that advantage is based. Such nurturing is visible to the public through consistent advertising messages. These messages are often presented, in part, through slogans. Marlboro cigarettes, for example, have long been a brand-name product for Philip Morris. The image and attributes of this product have historically provided perceived value to a certain group of customers. McDonald's is another brand name representing product characteristics and attributes for which customers are willing to pay (recall the advertising slogan "What you want is what you get at McDonald's").

Recall from the opening case that JCPenney's CEO believes that its private-label merchandise is the source of the firm's competitive advantage. To support the private-label brand names as a competitive advantage, JCPenney launched a $60 million "Doing It Right" campaign. Through additional television advertising, the firm focused on its Stafford, Worthington, Hunt Club, and Arizona brand names. This major campaign also showed customers JCPenney's testing facilities and informed them that "Before you try it on, we try it out."[40] The intent of this campaign was to tell customers that Penney's private-label brands were products of high quality that had been designed to yield superior value.

Mercedes-Benz has been one of the world's most valuable brand names.[41] To support its brand name, Daimler-Benz, the manufacturer of Mercedes automobiles, has consistently informed the public, through advertising, that its cars "are engineered like no other in the world." As evidence of the reliability of its automobiles and as testimony to the quality of its engineering, the company provides customers with special recognition when their Mercedes has been driven a certain number of miles (1 million miles, for example). However, as the next Strategic Focus indicates, Mercedes has experienced difficulty in maintaining the viability of its brand name in the face of stiff competition.

## Mercedes-Benz and Its Brand Name as a Source of Competitive Advantage

Mercedes-Benz, a key part of the German conglomerate Daimler-Benz, is one of the world's most valuable brand names. But, in late 1993, Mercedes was redesigning how it would conduct its business and sought to alter slightly the image associated with its brand name, while retaining the benefits the name had provided for most of the firm's 100 plus-year history. Mercedes' declining sales performance created the need for these changes.

Mercedes' sales, which accounted for 60 percent of Daimler-Benz's 1992 sales revenues, peaked in 1991. By the middle to the late part of 1993, evidence of Mercedes' sales declines appeared in many of its markets. In Western Europe, for example, sales fell 23.2 percent in the first eight months of 1993. In contrast, the declines for BMW (18.5 percent) and Britain's Jaguar (5.1 percent) in Western Europe during the same eight-month period were less severe. In the United States, sales during the first three quarters of 1993 were down 8.8 percent from 1992 figures. This performance compared poorly to increases in U.S. sales achieved during the same time period by BMW (17.1 percent) and Jaguar (36.4 percent). Declines in units sold in the United States are critical to Mercedes because the U.S. market accounts for 12 percent of its total sales revenues. These sales declines contributed significantly to the $579 million loss Daimler-Benz reported at the end of the first half of 1993.

According to some analysts, Mercedes failed to understand the significance of rapidly changing conditions in the luxury segment of the automobile business. As perhaps the world's preeminent automaker, Mercedes long ignored signs that its costly and outdated ways of competing no longer yielded a sustainable competitive advantage. One consultant observed that Mercedes misjudged both the competitive danger of the Japanese manufacturers moving into the upscale segment in the marketplace and the "speed at which customers would respond." Because the Japanese producers of luxury cars had significant cost and productivity advantages over Mercedes, they were able to provide high-quality cars at competitive prices. Mercedes' new CEO, Helmut Werner, who joined the company in May, 1993, commented that Mercedes "was guilty of over-engineering cars and maybe of overpricing them as well." An example of this type of product could be the 12-cylinder 600SEC (which, in 1993, carried a $133,300 price tag in the United States).

In response to its competitive difficulties, Mercedes announced changes in late 1993. By the end of 1994, the company intended to eliminate 25,700 jobs from its work force of 169,080. Included in this reduction was the loss of as many as 4,000 jobs at the company's Stuttgart headquarters (this was the first headquarters reduction in the firm's history).

Of perhaps greater significance to Mercedes' future is Werner's decision regarding the value-creating strategies he wants the company to implement. Instead of implementing a strategy that calls for the company to produce only costly luxury cars, Werner expressed a desire for Mercedes to "become an exclusive, full-manufacturer offering high quality vehicles of all shapes and sizes." Sample products Werner believes Mercedes should design and produce include what are known as minivans and four-wheel-drive sport-utility vehicles in the United States. He also wants the company to have an entry (by 1995) in super-small city cars. Super-small city cars are a market segment that is rare outside of Japan.

What happened to Mercedes? Is its powerful brand name no longer a source of competence and, ultimately, of sustainable competitive advantage? Mercedes' experiences appear to be similar to those of other producers of brand-name products that have encountered competitive difficulties. As an intangible resource, brand names should be viewed as one pathway through which products of superior value can be offered to customers. Overengineered and overpriced automobiles, regardless of the manufacturer's brand name, do not offer superior value to customers. Can Mercedes be successful through the intended value-creating strategy described in the Strategic Focus? Possibly so, although the difficulty of implementing the strategy outlined by the firm's CEO is obvious. The challenge for Mercedes is to reduce its costs and broaden its marketplace appeal, while retaining and emphasizing those qualities—technology, safety, and performance—for which its brand name is famous. If Mercedes can do this—that is, if it can relearn how to control its costs and deliver its well-known automobiles to customers at a competitive price—there appears to be a high probability that the company can regain a sustainable competitive advantage.

The competitive value yielded by brand names is created by a combination of resources and capabilities that are somewhat invisible to competitors. However, this value is created only through careful and private nurturing of firm-specific resources, capabilities, and core competencies.

In the early 1990s, the products being produced by private-label makers were creating significant competitive pressures for those with famous brand names. In fact, during this time, "private label makers, whose offerings look and taste more like the 'Real Thing' every day but cost 15% to 40% less, [were] making life miserable for companies such as PepsiCo, Procter & Gamble, and H.J. Heinz."[42] By the latter part of 1993, store brands had grown to 18 percent of supermarket sales, causing some analysts to conclude that it was no longer possible for "juicy" price premiums to be earned by famous-label goods. As such, many customers may have decided that some brand-name products no longer provided *superior* value. Many private-label goods were offering customers a combination of features, including price and quality, that yielded greater value than the features associated with brand-name products. Thus, private-label manufacturers may have discovered ways to create a competitive advantage relative to brand-name products.

The responses from brand-name-product makers were swift and, in some cases, dramatic. Philip Morris, for example, reduced the price of Marlboros by 40 cents per package. Because this competitive response was viewed as a sign of weakness, it was criticized by analysts and competitors alike. An immediate loss of $13.4 billion in the company's value showed that investors, too, reacted negatively to the cut in the price of Marlboros.[43] Procter & Gamble (P&G) announced plans to close 20 percent of its factories and eliminate 13,000 jobs (12 percent of the firm's worldwide work force) partly in response to the success of the private-label products competing against P&G's offerings.

A group of familiar brand-name products is presented in Figure 3–4. Predictions of the future for these items, along with the reasoning for each prediction, are included in the figure.

Different strategic challenges are suggested for the firms producing the products included in Figure 3–4. For those companies predicted to have a brand name that will remain a source of competitive advantage (e.g., Oil of Olay and Frito-Lay), there is a need to continue nurturing and exploiting that advantage competitively. At the opposite extreme, for companies that are producing products with brand names that no longer yield a competitive advantage (e.g., Subaru and Borden), the challenge is to form and exploit other core competencies to develop a different competitive advantage.

As a source of capabilities, resources are a critical part of the pathway to development of sustainable competitive advantage (see Figure 3–2). But, individually, many resources have little value. It is through their *integration and combination* that resources contribute to the selection of a firm's competitive actions and the

**FIGURE 3–4** **Products with Famous Brand Names**

# RATING THE BIG LABELS

| ↑ Thriving | ↓ Troubled | → Under Fire |

**→ Marlboro**
Goodbye steep price hikes and 50% operating margins.

**↑ Compaq**
Will weather the computer price wars. A continuous stream of smart, new products keep it humming.

**↑ Absolut**
Why pay nearly twice the price of Smirnoff? Those clever ads drive you to drink it.

**↑ Big G**
General Mills stems storebrand competition better than king Kellogg.

**↓ Dell Computer**
A marketing master that forgot about product development. Everybody's invading its mail-order niche.

**↑ Nike**
CEO Phil Knight: "Try running a marathon in $9.99 shoes from Wal-Mart."

**↑ Oil of Olay**
P&G's emerging megabrand worldwide. It doesn't hurt that women are aging. The new bar soap is cleaning up.

**↑ Wrigley**
Global giant with a 50% U.S. market share. Five sticks for a quarter, as in 1987.

**→ Kellogg**
Private labels are eating into Corn Flakes, Raisin Bran. Global power.

**↑ Taco Bell**
PepsiCo's ringer. Same-store sales, a prime indicator of restaurant health, have risen 19 consecutive quarters.

**↑ Campbell Soup**
Sales are stirring. Raises prices more easily than most others.

**↓ Subaru**
What not to drive. The automaker's upscaling strategy hit the skids. Its ad agency just lost the account.

**↓ Fab**
Colgate-Palmolive's a loser in suds. The company's U.S. growth bubble burst.

**→ Budweiser**
Nothing beats a Bud? Wrong. Sales slip as Anheuser's own lower-priced beers steal drinkers.

**↓ Tambrands**
A Marlboro-like disaster. Raised prices, and consumers fled.

**↑ Gillette**
Mighty like Coke globally. Quality bar rises constantly.

**→ Hershey**
Smart pricer. Copped U.S. candy crown from Mars. Weak abroad.

**↑ Hanes**
Sara Lee sells 'em cheap—T-shirts, hosiery, bras, socks, gloves, hats—and converts store-brand consumers.

**↓ Heinz**
50% share, but private label controls 22%. Back on TV after two-year hiatus.

**↑ President's Choice**
The original brand-buster has sales of $750 million. Canada's Loblaw puts the label on soup to nuts.

**↑ Swatch**
New models multiply. The basic Swatch's retail price barely ticks ahead.

**↑ Equate**
Wal-Mart's private-label drug line, made by Perrigo, underprices famous brands like Tylenol and Nyquil.

**↓ Purina**
Ralston Purina underspent and missed the gourmet trend.

**↓ Gleem**
A toothpaste with less than 1% U.S. market share and no reason for being. Our bet to be the brand P&G kills next.

**↑ Intel**
King of microprocessors. Brilliant "Intel Inside" ads create a brand preference for what's in a computer.

**↑ Frito-Lay**
Gains 6% in volume annually. Low prices and constant innovation are key.

**↑ Jeep**
Sales have revved 56% so far this year. Baby-boomers are buying the Chrysler Grand Cherokee.

**→ Diet Coke**
Fizzzzzzzzzzzz. Drinkers are switching to waters and teas.

**↑ Rubbermaid**
Unit sales bounce ahead 7% to 9% yearly as management raises prices below inflation. Launches one new product per day.

**→ Gerber**
Poor pricing and marketing, even with no private-label threat. Needs to build international franchise.

**↓ Crystal Pepsi**
A dud, despite $40 million in marketing spending. PepsiCo should drop this ill-flavored drink.

**↓ MasterCard**
Antiglitz ads are helping to lift U.S. market share following a 14-year rut. They hope you'll use it in the supermarket.

**→ Gatorade**
Coke and Pepsi are aiming to douse Quaker Oats' best brand.

**↓ Mattel**
Forever-young Barbie brings in about $1 billion in annual sales. Should be one hot Christmas product. Again.

**↓ Borden**
Who can manage 3,200 snack varieties? Not these guys, who are now in the process of simplifying.

**↓ Keebler**
A weak No. 2, crushed by Nabisco in a cookie war.

SOURCE: P. Sellers, 1993, Brands: It's thrive or die, *FORTUNE*, August 23: 53, © Time Inc. All rights reserved.

achievement of strategic competitiveness. Defined in Chapter 1, **capability** is the capacity for a set of resources to integratively perform a task or an activity. Capabilities are unique combinations of a firm's information-based, tangible resources (see Table 3–1) or intangible resources (see Table 3–2) and are what a firm can do as a result of teams of resources working together.

▲ **Capability** is the capacity for a set of resources to integratively perform a task or an activity.

## Capabilities

As suggested above, capabilities represent a firm's capacity to deploy *integrated* resources to achieve a desired end state.[44] The glue that binds an organization together,[45] capabilities emerge over time through complex interactions between and among tangible and intangible resources. They are based on developing, carrying, and exchanging information and knowledge through the firm's human capital. Thus, a firm's knowledge base is embedded in and reflected by its capabilities and is a key source of sustainable competitive advantage in the global economy.[46]

Because the primary basis for a firm's capabilities is the skills and knowledge of its employees, the value of human capital in the development and use of capabilities and core competencies cannot be overstated.[47] For example, Wal-Mart concluded that its people play a significant role in satisfying customer needs.[48] Wal-Mart's CEO believes that maintenance of an organization of compulsive overachievers, "constantly challenging them to listen and learn and accomplish more than they do currently," is one key to the company's growth and success.[49]

The set of knowledge possessed by a firm's human capital is among the most significant of an organization's capabilities and ultimately may be at the root of all competitive advantages.[50] Some even view knowledge as "the sum of everything everybody in [a] company knows that gives [the firm] a competitive edge in the marketplace."[51] Moreover, the *rate* at which firms acquire new knowledge and develop the skills necessary to apply it in the marketplace is a key source of sustainable competitive advantage in the global economy.[52]

The importance of human capital to a firm's success, and the need to provide continuous learning opportunities for it, was highlighted by Robert Reich, secretary of labor for the Clinton administration. In response to some executives' view that they cannot afford to train their workers, Secretary Reich offered the following: "You can't afford not to train your workers. Any competitor can come in and use precisely the same machines, the same equipment. The only thing you have that's unique is the commitment and skills of your work force."[53] Today, some companies are striving to better integrate and coordinate their training programs to provide people with the set of *competencies* required to complete their work efficiently and effectively.[54]

How many capabilities are required for a firm to develop a sustainable competitive advantage? Responses to this question vary. McKinsey & Co., for example, recommends that clients identify three or four capabilities that are core competencies for their firm. Once identified, a firm's strategic actions should be framed around the core competencies.[55]

Capabilities are often developed in functional areas (e.g., manufacturing, R&D, marketing, etc.).[56] Shown in Table 3–3 is a grouping of organizational functions and the capabilities certain companies are thought to possess in terms of those functions. PepsiCo, for example, is respected for its organization structure. The company's structure, which includes, among other components, its formal and

Wal-Mart stores, such as the one shown here, have been successful. Several capabilities have contributed to Wal-Mart's strategic competitiveness. However, the firm's human capital—its people—may be the most important capability of all. Through their knowledge and skill, Wal-Mart's associates appear to be able to uniquely combine the firm's resources in ways that result in sustainable competitive advantages.

▼ **TABLE 3–3**

### Examples of Firm Capabilities

| Functional Areas | Capabilities | Examples |
|---|---|---|
| Corporate philosophy | Viewing the firm as a collection of capabilities rather than products | NEC |
| Management | Effective strategic alliances | Corning<br>Toshiba |
| | Effective organization structure | PepsiCo |
| | Effective market-driven links with suppliers and customers | NCR |
| Management information systems | Data processing skills | Banc One<br>American Airlines |
| Marketing | Effective promotion of brand-name products | Gillette<br>McKinsey Consulting |
| Human resources | Effective and extensive training programs | Motorola |
| Research and development | Rapid product innovations | Honda<br>Intel |
| | Extensive applications of knowledge | 3M |
| | Extensive applications of fiber skills | DuPont |
| | Basic research capabilities | Sony<br>AT&T |
| Manufacturing | Rapid manufacture of trendy goods | Benetton |
| | Efficient production of small electric motors | Black & Decker |
| | Miniaturization of components and products | Sony |
| | Introduction of technologically sophisticated engines | Mazda |
| Distribution | Effective use of "cross-docking" | Wal-Mart |
| | Efficient distribution of products | The Limited |

*Source:* Adapted from R.M. Grant, 1991, *Contemporary Strategy Analysis* (Cambridge, England: Blackwell Business), 106.

informal planning, coordinating, and controlling mechanisms, is the product of uniquely combining and integrating PepsiCo's resources. Notice that each of the capabilities shown in Table 3–3, as is true for all capabilities, is a firm-specific set of work processes. Capabilities, then, are a firm's way of completing various tasks that are often associated with individual organizational functions.

How one company has been able to retain and nurture the competitive advantage provided by its capability in manufacturing is described in the following Strategic Focus.

Gillette has brand-name products that appear to provide superior value to customers. However, the competitive advantage earned through the Sensor razor will eventually be eliminated through imitation. Because of this, Gillette is committed to using its capability to continuously design and manufacture new products. Through these actions, Gillette seeks to sustain existing competitive advantages or, as necessary, to develop different ones.

## S T R A T E G I C    F O C U S

### Gillette's Manufacturing Capability Helps to Maintain Its Brand Name

An advertising slogan used by Gillette—"the best a man can get"—seems to describe accurately customers' perceptions of the company's products. At the close of a recent year, Gillette had captured 65 percent of blade and razor sales in the United States and an even larger percentage in Europe and Latin America. Other than in disposable razors, Gillette faces very little competition from private-label merchandisers. On sales of $5.2 billion in 1992, the company earned $513.4 million (Gillette's margin is much higher than those earned by many packaged-goods manufacturers). Analysts anticipated that the Sensor Excel razor, which was introduced into the European market in late 1993 and the U.S. market in early 1994, would be instrumental in keeping Gillette's earnings growing at a steady 16 percent annually.

What is the source of Gillette's competitive advantage? How does this company continue to perform well, while some other brand-name manufacturers (see Figure 3–4) encounter serious competitive problems?

The key to Gillette's performance and its competitive advantage is embedded in its resources and capabilities. An analysis of Gillette's operations shows that the firm's resources have been combined in ways that have created valuable capabilities. The Sensor razor is an interesting example of a product designed and manufactured through the use of Gillette's valuable core competencies.

Launched in 1990, the Sensor appears to be a simple device with twin blades mounted on tiny springs. But the product is more high-tech than is apparent because of the manufacturing process. All the equipment used to manufacture the Sensor razor has been designed and built by Gillette. According to analysts, this equipment is "exceptionally complicated gear," making it impossible for competitors to "clone it." Although Schick, one of Gillette's major competitors, won the rights to the Sensor patent, the company lacks the resources and capabilities needed to manufacture the laser welding machines that would be necessary to produce a look-alike product. Thus, even though Schick was able to circumvent a patent barrier, the firm does not possess the resources and capabilities needed to design and produce the complicated equipment used to manufacture high-tech razors, such as the Sensor.

*One way restaurants can improve their performance is to use space effectively and efficiently when serving customers. To increase its understanding of capabilities needed to successfully serve customers in its new, but smaller restaurants, TGI Friday's executives decided to study the practices of an extremely efficient food handler—the U.S. Navy. By learning how to uniquely combine its resources to form capabilities, it is possible that TGI Friday's could develop a competitive advantage through the preparation and distribution of food products.*

For example, the next generation of the Sensor razor, the Excel, retains all the features of its predecessor, but has additional performance characteristics that provide value to customers. Specifically, it has five rubbery strips in front of the blade. These strips stretch a person's skin and hence add value by making the shave both smoother and more comfortable. As with earlier versions of the Sensor, the Excel is manufactured using sophisticated equipment updates that come through Gillette's unique core competencies.

When an organization's capability is believed to be a core competence, others may seek to understand how resources were combined to develop it. For example, because TGI Friday's thought the Navy was an extremely efficient food handler, perhaps more efficient than for-profit companies, the firm wanted to understand the sources of that efficiency. Friday's executives concluded that successful imitation of the Navy's food-handling operations might help the firm learn a capability and gain a competitive advantage. This matter was of particular interest to Friday's because the firm is building smaller restaurants with almost the same number of seats as were included in the older designs (5,700 square feet with 210 seats compared to 9,200 square feet with 240 seats). These smaller designs place a premium on handling food products efficiently.

To study the Navy's food-based work processes, Friday's CEO spent a day aboard the nuclear submarine USS West Virginia. His visit occurred when a crew of 155 was engaged in a 70-day underwater voyage. Because the submarine had a crew on duty 24 hours per day, the Navy served four meals daily in an extremely confined space. A quick calculation shows that 4 daily meals, for 70 days, for 155 people, is over 43,000 meals.

The Navy was willing to let Friday's study its techniques. According to a Navy official, "These aren't things we want to keep secret. All of our food service research and development is funded by American tax dollars."[57] Thus, in this instance, one company may have identified an interesting way to learn how to combine its resources in strategically relevant ways to develop a competitive advantage. However, other firms could similarly study the Navy's operations to overcome Friday's competitive advantage.

In the next section, we discuss another framework companies use to identify and evaluate their resources and capabilities. Value chain analysis allows a firm to understand the parts of its operations that create value (recall our earlier definition of value) and those that do not. Understanding these issues is important because a company earns above-average profits only when the value it creates is greater than the costs incurred to create that value.[58]

## Value Chain Analysis

▲ **Primary activities** are involved with a product's physical creation, its sale and distribution to buyers, and its service after the sale.

▲ **Support activities** provide the support necessary for the primary activities to take place.

As shown in Figure 3–5, a firm's value chain can be segmented into primary and support activities. **Primary activities** are involved with a product's physical creation, its sale and distribution to buyers, and its service after the sale. Inbound logistics, operations, outbound logistics, marketing and sales, and service are the five categories of primary activities. **Support activities** provide the support necessary for the primary activities to take place. Included as support activities are firm infrastructure, human resource management, technology development, and procurement.

Presented in Table 3–4 are the items to be studied in order to identify and assess the value-creating potential of a firm's primary activities. In Table 3–5, we present the items to consider when studying the firm's support activities. As with

**FIGURE 3–5  The Basic Value Chain**

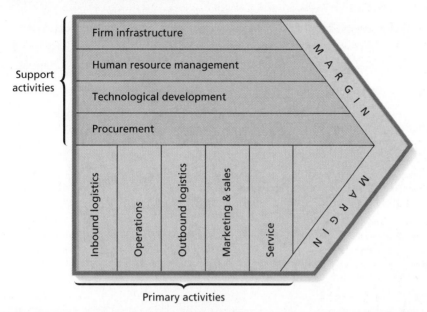

SOURCE: Adapted and reprinted with the permission of The Free Press, an imprint of Simon & Schuster from COMPETITIVE ADVANTAGE: Creating and Sustaining Superior Performance by Michael E. Porter, Fig. 2–2, p. 37. Copyright © 1985 by Michael E. Porter.

the analysis of primary activities, the intent in examining these items is to determine areas where firms have the potential to create value.

When using value chain analysis, managers seek to study a firm's resources and capabilities in relationship to the activities in which it engages to design, manufacture, and distribute products. All the items included in Tables 3–4 and 3–5 are to be assessed with competitors' capabilities in mind. To be a source of competitive advantage, a capability must allow a firm to (1) perform a particular primary or support activity in a manner that is *superior* to the manner in which competing companies perform it or (2) perform a value-creating activity that no competitor can perform. Only under these conditions can a firm create superior value for customers and earn a sustainable competitive advantage. Often this means reconfiguring or recombining value chain activities in unique ways. Federal Express changed the nature of the delivery business by reconfiguring both the primary and the support activities to create the overnight delivery business. Many new competitors have sought to dislodge Federal Express from the advantage it created through reconfiguring the value chain.

Rating a firm's capacities to execute the primary and the support activities is difficult and challenging. Earlier in the chapter, we noted that identifying and assessing the value of a firm's resources and capabilities requires judgment. Judgment is equally necessary when using value chain analysis to examine a firm's resources and capabilities. The reason for this is that there is no *obviously* correct model or rule available to help in this process. Moreover, the data that can be accessed for these evaluations are sometimes unreliable and/or incomplete.

Because of the potential impact of these model and data constraints, managers must identify and evaluate their firm's relative advantages and disadvantages, in terms of primary and support activities, as objectively as possible. Past performances and accomplishments should not be accepted as current indicators of

▼ **TABLE 3–4**

### Examining the Value-Creating Potential of Primary Activities

*Inbound logistics*

Activities, such as materials handling, warehousing, and inventory control, used to receive, store, and disseminate inputs to a product.

*Operations*

Activities necessary to convert the inputs provided by inbound logistics into final product form. Machining, packaging, assembly, and equipment maintenance are examples of operations activities.

*Outbound logistics*

Activities involved with collecting, storing, and physically distributing the final product to customers. Examples of these activities include finished goods warehousing, material handling, and order processing.

*Market and sales*

Activities completed to provide means through which customers can purchase products and to induce them to do so. To effectively market and sell products, firms develop advertising and promotional campaigns, select appropriate distribution channels, and select, develop, and support their sales force.

*Service*

Activities designed to enhance or maintain a product's value. Firms engage in a range of service-related activities, including installation, repair, training, and adjustment.

Each activity should be examined relative to competitors' abilities. Accordingly, firms rate each activity as *superior, equivalent,* or *inferior.*

*Source:* Adapted and reprinted with the permission of The Free Press, an imprint of Simon & Schuster from COMPETITIVE ADVANTAGE: Creating and Sustaining Superior Performance by Michael E. Porter, pp. 39–40. Copyright © 1985 by Michael E. Porter.

value creation potential. A firm that fails to conduct accurate and complete appraisals of primary and support activities may become complacent, and complacency is a forerunner of disaster in the highly competitive global economy.[59]

Known for its historic success, and its value-creating abilities in terms of product standardization, McDonald's may have become too satisfied, comfortable, and complacent during the first part of the 1990s. A McDonald's top-level manager seemed to suggest that this was the case when he stated that "We got spoiled by our success. For a while, [we thought] we didn't have competition."[60] Following a thorough appraisal of how it could use its core competencies to create superior value for customers, McDonald's took several actions intended to enhance the value of its products. Among these actions were the introduction of "Extra Value Meals" and the decision to establish its operations in different locations. By the end of 1993, McDonald's had units inside 30 Wal-Marts and 2 Sears stores and was negotiating to open restaurants in Home Depot stores.

An outcome of an effective value chain analysis is the identification of new ways to perform activities to create value. Because these types of innovations are firm-specific—that is, they are grounded in a company's unique way of combining its resources and capabilities—they are difficult for competitors to recognize, understand, and imitate. The greater the time necessary for competitors to understand how a firm is creating value through its execution of different primary and support activities, the more sustainable the competitive advantage gained by the innovating company.

R, C, C

> ▼ **TABLE 3–5**
>
> ### Examining the Value-Creating Potential of Support Activities
>
> *Procurement*
> Activities completed to *purchase* the inputs needed to produce a firm's products. Purchased inputs include items fully consumed during the manufacture of products (e.g., raw materials and supplies) as well as fixed assets—machinery, laboratory equipment, office equipment, and buildings.
>
> *Technological development*
> Activities completed to improve a firm's product and the processes used to manufacture it. Technology development takes many forms, such as process equipment design, both basic research and product design, and servicing procedures.
>
> *Human Resource Management*
> Activities involved with recruiting, hiring, training, developing, and compensating all personnel.
>
> *Firm Infrastructure*
> Firm infrastructure includes activities, such as general management, planning, finance, accounting, legal support, and governmental relations, that are required to support the work of the entire value chain. Through its infrastructure, the firm strives to effectively and consistently identify external opportunities and threats, identify resources and capabilities, and support core competencies.
>
> Each activity should be examined relative to competitors' abilities. Accordingly, firms rate each activity as *superior, equivalent,* or *inferior.*
>
> *Source:* Adapted and reprinted with the permission of The Free Press, an imprint of Simon & Schuster from COMPETITIVE ADVANTAGE: Creating and Sustaining Superior Performance by Michael E. Porter, pp. 40–43. Copyright © 1985 by Michael E. Porter.

But what should a firm do with respect to those primary and support activities in which its resources and capabilities are not a source of competence and sustainable competitive advantage? As we discuss in the next section, firms should examine the possibility of outsourcing the work associated with primary and support activities in which they cannot create value (as compared to competitors).

## Outsourcing

**Outsourcing** is the purchase of a value-creating activity from an external supplier. When discussing the prevalence of outsourcing, an executive from Rockwell International expressed his opinion that "Without a doubt, focusing on a core competence—and outsourcing the rest—is a major trend of the 1990s."[61] An indication of the increasing scope of outsourcing is suggested by the prediction that by mid-1995, more than 50 percent of the major commercial and government enterprises competing or working in the global environment are expected to be involved, to varying degrees, with outsourcing.[62]

The major reason outsourcing is being used prominently is that few, if any, firms possess the resources and capabilities required to achieve competitive superiority in all primary and support activities. By nurturing a few core competencies, a firm increases its probability of developing a sustainable competitive advantage. Moreover, outsourcing activities in which it lacks the competence necessary to create value allows a firm to concentrate fully on those areas in which it can.[63]

▲ **Outsourcing** is the purchase of a value-creating activity from an external supplier.

Rolls-Royce Motor Cars engages in outsourcing. The manufacturer of some of the world's most expensive automobiles, including the $319,300 (1993 price) Silver Spur II Touring Limousine, lost a total of $150 million in 1991 and 1992. One of the decisions made in order to return the firm to profitability was to engage in outsourcing. Today the company outsources a number of peripheral items such as car bodies and fasteners so it can concentrate "on its core competencies—engines, paint, leather, [and] wood."[64]

When engaged in outsourcing, a firm seeks the greatest value. Some advise that to maximize the value gained, a company must scan the entire global economy to locate the source that is the "best producer in the world" of the activity being outsourced.[65]

However, one successful company, The Gap, prefers to outsource to domestic firms. Speed to market is the key reason for this decision. Imports typically add three weeks to the time required to deliver goods to The Gap's locations. The strategy being implemented by The Gap calls for products to reach customers as quickly as possible. In this case, domestic sources appear to be able to provide more value to The Gap as compared to the value achieved through the use of global sources.[66] In contrast, Gitano, acquired by Fruit of the Loom in 1994, outsources to a large number of firms operating in Third World countries. To assure it creates value through its outsourcing, Gitano brings equipment to selected sites, trains the work force, and supports development of the infrastructure necessary for its products to be produced successfully.[67]

Critical to outsourcing is the ability to identify and evaluate a firm's resources and capabilities. A firm that is incapable of doing this might outsource activities or areas in which it possesses core competencies.[68] Moreover, a firm should be careful not to outsource primary and support activities that are used to neutralize environmental threats. Occasionally, a firm discovers that areas in which conventional wisdom holds it should possess competence can be outsourced. For example, many believe that banks should develop a core competence in the area of information technology (IT). However, following careful analysis, Continental Bank's top-level executives concluded that the bank did not have a competence in terms of information technology. As a result, a decision was made to outsource the IT activities so the bank could "focus on its true core competencies—intimate knowledge of customers' needs and relationships with customers."[69]

Armed with knowledge about resources and capabilities, strategists are prepared to select the firm's core competencies. Defined in Chapter 1, **core competencies** are resources and capabilities that serve as a source of competitive advantage over a firm's rivals. As explained in the next section, all resources and capabilities are not core competencies.

▲ **Core competencies** are resources and capabilities that serve as a source of competitive advantage over a firm's rivals.

## Core Competencies

Resources and capabilities provide the foundation a firm requires to formulate and implement strategies. The purpose of implementing value-creating strategies is to improve the firm's efficiency and effectiveness as it seeks to achieve strategic competitiveness and earn above-average profits.[70] In a sense, a value-creating strategy describes how the firm "defines its business and links together the only two resources that really matter in today's economy: knowledge and relationships or an organization's competencies and its customers."[71]

Not all of a firm's resources and capabilities are critical strategic assets. In fact, some resources and capabilities may result in incompetence because they represent competitive areas in which the firm is weak compared to competitors. Thus, some resources or capabilities can either stifle or prevent the development of a core competence. Firms with insufficient financial capital, for example, may be unable to purchase facilities or hire the skilled workers required to manufacture products that yield superior customer value. In this situation, financial capital (tangible resources) would be a weakness. Armed with in-depth understandings of their firm's resources and capabilities, strategists are challenged to find external environmental opportunities that can be exploited through the firm's capabilities while avoiding competition in areas of weakness.

Selecting capabilities that are a core competence for a firm, and, as such, a source of sustainable competitive advantage, requires analysis of customers and competitors. Capabilities become core competencies when they help the firm produce distinctive products. **Distinctive products** are goods or services with features and characteristics that are valued by customers. Only capabilities that allow a firm to provide such superior value to customers are recognized as core competencies.[72]

▲ **Distinctive products** are goods or services with features and characteristics that are valued by customers.

We have described general attributes of a firm's capabilities. Next we discuss four specific criteria managers use to decide which of their firm's capabilities are core competencies. The capabilities shown in Table 3–3 are core competencies for the firms possessing them. Thus, the firm-specific capabilities included in Table 3–3 have satisfied the four criteria of sustainable competitive advantage.

## Criteria of Sustainable Competitive Advantage

Capabilities that are valuable, rare, imperfectly imitable, and nonsubstitutable are a source of sustainable competitive advantage.[73] Capabilities failing to satisfy these criteria are not core competencies. Thus, as shown in Figure 3–6, every core competence is a capability, but every capability is not a core competence.

**FIGURE 3–6  Core Competence as a Strategic Capability**

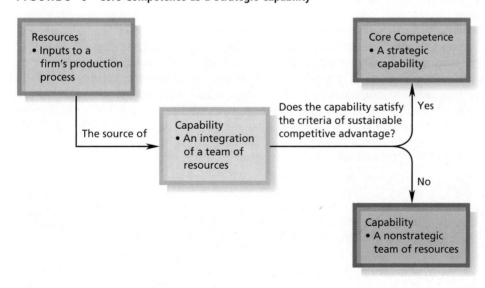

Capabilities are core competencies when they satisfy the four criteria of sustainable competitive advantage. A sustained competitive advantage is achieved only when competitors have tried, without success, to duplicate the benefits of a firm's strategy or when competitors lack the confidence to attempt imitation. However, in the short run, a firm may earn a competitive advantage through the use of capabilities that are, for example, valuable and rare, but highly subject to imitability. In such an instance, the length of time a firm can expect to retain its competitive advantage is a function of how quickly competitors can successfully imitate a product, service, or process. It is only through the combination of conditions represented by the four criteria that a firm's capabilities are identified as core competencies.

▲ **Valuable capabilities** are those that help a firm exploit opportunities and/or neutralize threats in its external environment.

**Valuable**   **Valuable capabilities** are those that help a firm exploit opportunities and/or neutralize threats in its external environment. Valuable capabilities enable a firm to formulate and implement strategies that create value for specific groups of customers.

▲ **Rare capabilities** are those possessed by few, if any, current or potential competitors.

**Rare**   **Rare capabilities** are those possessed by few, if any, current or potential competitors. Capabilities possessed by many rival firms can be exploited in the same ways in the pursuit of competitive advantage. In other words, firms with the same capabilities select the same strategy to implement them. Implementation of a strategy common across firms prevents any single firm from earning a sustainable competitive advantage.

▲ **Imperfectly imitable capabilities** are those that other firms cannot develop easily.

**Imperfectly Imitable**   **Imperfectly imitable capabilities** are those that other firms cannot develop easily. Imperfect imitability can occur because of one or a combination of three reasons.

First, a firm sometimes is able to develop capabilities because of *unique historical conditions*. Some capabilities are acquired or developed as a result of a firm's location in time and space. For example, a company that establishes its facilities at a location that turns out to be more valuable than originally expected possesses an imperfectly imitable resource (notice that this is an example of how an individual tangible resource can be the source of competence and sustained competitive advantage). Parking facilities located around a college or university campus that were established before the institution experienced explosive growth cannot be imitated easily. In these instances, the cost of land that remains around the educational institution is beyond the economic value the owner could expect to receive from its use as a parking facility. A firm with a unique organizational culture, one that emerged during the early stages of the company's life, can have an imperfectly imitable advantage over a competitor with a culture developed during a subsequent historical period.[74]

On the other hand, a firm's unique culture can become a source of competitive disadvantage. Cultures steeped in individual company histories probably contributed to the competitive problems encountered at General Motors and IBM during the 1980s and 1990s. Originally, decision processes grounded in multiple checks allowed these companies to control their costs efficiently while dominating their markets. When operating in *relatively* stable environments, such as those that existed when the firms were founded and during many of the succeeding decades, culturally based attributes of relying on formal organizational controls to dictate decisions and actions were appropriate. However, in a fast-paced global economy, cultures preventing rapid decision-making processes and product introductions often are sources of competitive disadvantage.

An example of a firm with a unique culture as a source of sustainable competitive advantage is presented in the Strategic Focus concerned with McKinsey & Co. Because it is a source of sustained competitive advantage, it is vital that McKinsey nurture and reinforce its culture. Continuing to hire people with attributes believed to be linked with adherence to the principles articulated long ago by the firm's founder, Marvin Bower, is one way the uniqueness and the effectiveness of McKinsey's culture are maintained. Thus, the sustained competitive advantage provided by McKinsey's organizational culture is probably grounded in a historical place and time. To date, other consulting firms, many with cultures that were framed in a time period subsequent to the one in which McKinsey's was developed, have not been able to *precisely* duplicate the benefits of McKinsey's value-creating culture.

A second condition of imperfect imitability occurs when the link between a firm's competencies and its competitive advantage is *causally ambiguous*. In these instances, competitors are unable to clearly understand how a firm is using its competencies as the foundation for sustainable competitive advantage. As a result, competitors are uncertain about the competencies they should develop in order to duplicate the value-creating benefits of a competitor's strategy.

*Social complexity* is the third reason that capabilities can be imperfectly imitable. Social complexity means that at least some, and in some instances, many, capabilities are the product of complex social phenomena. Examples of socially complex capabilities include interpersonal relationships among managers and a company's reputation with suppliers and customers.

**Nonsubstitutable**  **Nonsubstitutable capabilities** are those that do not have strategic equivalents. In general, the strategic value of capabilities increases the more difficult they are to substitute.[75] The more invisible capabilities are, the more difficult it is for firms to find substitutes and the greater the challenge is to competitors trying to imitate a firm's value-creating strategy. Firm-specific knowledge and trust-based working relationships between managers and nonmanagerial personnel are examples of capabilities that are difficult to identify and for which finding substitutes is challenging.

▲ **Nonsubstitutable capabilities** are those that do not have strategic equivalents.

## Core Competencies—Cautions and Reminders

An attractive attribute of the capabilities that are a firm's core competencies is that, unlike physical assets, they tend to become more valuable through additional use. A key reason for this is that they are largely knowledge-based. Sharing knowledge, across people, jobs, and organizational functions, often results in an expansion of that knowledge in competitively relevant ways.[76] Gaining these positive outcomes, however, requires effort. Core competencies should never be taken for granted. To maximize profits, a firm should invest continuously in core competencies to upgrade their quality.[77]

Finally, managers must never allow competencies to become a source of rigidity. Competencies that become core rigidities prevent a firm from changing when change is appropriate. Firms that have achieved strategic competitiveness and have earned above-average profits for extended periods of time are sometimes

## McKinsey & Co.'s Organizational Culture

Over the years, McKinsey & Co. has been called the "most secretive, most prestigious, most consistently successful, most envied, most trusted, and most disliked management consulting firm on earth." Although the company does not discuss its prices, both competing firms and its clients agree that McKinsey is the most expensive general management consulting firm in the world. Also recognized as the world's most *powerful* consulting firm, McKinsey & Co. (or "The Firm," as its members have long called it) is a brand name that contributes significantly to the firm's sustainable competitive advantage.

As measured by sales volume growth, McKinsey's performance remained strong toward the end of 1993. In fact, its sales doubled between 1989 and 1993, to a total of $1.2 billion. Committed to the importance of competing successfully in the global economy, McKinsey is truly a global company. Operating from 58 offices located throughout the world, McKinsey derives 60 percent of its revenues from outside the United States. Markets in Russia, Eastern Europe, China, and India were identified as areas critical to the company's future growth and profitability.

How does McKinsey retain its sustainable competitive advantage in what is an increasingly fragmented and competitive marketplace for consulting services? Or, phrasing the question in a slightly different way, one might ask the following: In a business where the only constants seem to be upheaval, transience, faddism, and customer suspicion of snake oil, how does McKinsey inspire such a high level of trust?

Competitors, clients, and analysts alike agree that McKinsey's *culture* is the source of its sustainable competitive advantage. As testimony to the intangibility of culture, even to some of those familiar with it, consider the following description of culture as McKinsey's source of advantage: "It is that culture,

*continued*

hesitant to change what they are doing. However, capabilities are core competencies *only* when they are strategically relevant, that is, when their use permits exploitation of opportunities in the external environment. Rapid and significant changes in the global economy prevent firms from permanently exploiting the same competencies. Firms failing to recognize this reality may quickly find themselves at a competitive disadvantage. Thus, executives are challenged to strike a balance between nurturing and supporting *existing* core competencies while simultaneously encouraging the type of forthright appraisals that will cause the development of *new* core competencies.[78]

## Strategic Inputs and Strategic Actions

As shown in Figure 1–1, the results gained through analyses of the external and the internal environments provide the strategic inputs a firm needs to develop its strategic intent and strategic mission. The value of intent and mission is that they describe what a firm would like to achieve in light of its internal competencies and its external opportunities. With the beginning of the next chapter, the focus of our discussion shifts—from examining strategic inputs to studying actions completed unique to McKinsey and eccentric, which sets the firm apart from virtually any other business organization and which often mystifies even those who engage [its] services."

The foundation for McKinsey's culture was established by Marvin Bower, the company's founding father. In fact, "much of what McKinsey *is* today harks back to the early 1930s" when Bower entered the consulting business. Bower's concept of how his consulting firm would operate was that it should provide advice about effective managerial practices to top-level executives.

As guidance for McKinsey's consultants, Bower developed a set of principles. Cited frequently and with intensity, these principles actually define what McKinsey was and is today. As such, they are the backbone of the company's unique, and what some think is an enigmatic, culture. According to Bower's principles, a McKinsey consultant should (1) put the interests of the client ahead of increasing the company's revenues, (2) remain silent about the client's business operations, (3) be truthful and not fear challenging a client's opinion, and (4) perform only work that he/she believes is in the client's best interests and is something McKinsey can do well.

Supporting and nurturing McKinsey's culture are its people. The company is famous for the quality of its people and for hiring "the same people over and over." As compared to other consulting firms, McKinsey has much less diversity among its personnel. The majority of the company's top-level managers are men who graduated near the top of their class from one of a small set of famous business schools. However, given the increasing number of women entering the professional work force and the large number of entrepreneurial businesses headed by women, the firm may need to promote more women into its managerial ranks.

What kind of people does McKinsey want to hire? According to the company's former managing director, McKinsey strives to employ people who are, "first, very smart; second, insecure and thus driven by their insecurity; and third, competitive."

to select and implement different types of strategies. Business-level strategies are considered in Chapters 4 and 5, while corporate-level strategies are described in Chapter 6.

To close our discussion of strategic inputs, we offer a few final comments about intent and mission. Defined in Chapter 1, **strategic intent** is the leveraging of a firm's internal resources, capabilities, and core competencies to accomplish what may at first appear to be unattainable goals in the competitive environment.[79] Managers are challenged to stimulate development of strategic intent among employees, even when some in a firm do not understand its importance. When employees are motivated by a well-articulated vision, such strategic intent stretches a firm's competencies[80] and suggests a new reality that may create future success.[81]

To establish strategic intent among employees, managers must have a clear understanding of their firm's core competencies and how these competencies allow achievement of sustainable competitive advantage.[82] In addition, developing intent requires analysis of (1) an industry's history and structure, (2) the challenges associated with an industry's possible futures, and (3) competitors' core competencies.[83] Framed in global terms, strategic intent is informed through answers to questions such as the following: Where is this firm going in the long term? What

▲ **Strategic intent** is the leveraging of a firm's internal resources, capabilities, and core competencies to accomplish what may at first appear to be unattainable goals in the competitive environment.

businesses should we be in? What businesses are we in currently, and should we remain in them, and why? What new markets can we establish through the use of our core competencies? What is the range of possibilities suggested by our current core competencies? How could our resources be combined differently to form new, strategically relevant capabilities?[84]

Answers to these questions, and to others, suggest how firms can leverage their competencies through strategic intent. Wal-Mart's actions and decisions are an example of this. Recently the firm opened a huge store (240,000 square feet of space) in Mexico City. When opened, this store was the largest in the firm's chain of 1,971 outlets. Selling everything from nails to cars, this unit is very successful. Encouraged by these results, Wal-Mart's executives began evaluations of the possibility of opening stores in Eastern Europe.[85] Considering this type of stretch—that is, operating in additional global markets—is possible because of the firm's core competencies in logistics, information technology, and communications, among others. Wal-Mart executives expect sales to grow by 18 percent annually through 1998. If this growth is achieved, Wal-Mart's sale volume will be $150 billion by 1999.[86]

Andersen Consulting is another firm leveraging its competencies to achieve what may at first appear to be unattainable goals in its competitive environment. As part of an effort to reinvent itself, Andersen recently indicated that its intention is to become the world's first and foremost full-service consulting emporium, capable of serving clients by rewiring computer systems, recrafting strategies, reeducating employees, and reengineering work processes.[87] Although this goal is challenging, Andersen appears to possess the competencies that can be stretched to achieve this intent.

Strategic intent defines the framework for a firm's strategic mission. The **strategic mission** is a statement of a firm's unique purpose and the scope of its operations in product and market terms.[88] Because it specifies the products a firm will offer in particular markets, the strategic mission is an application of strategic intent. Once formulated, the strategic intent and strategic mission form the basis for the development of corporate- and business-level strategies.

▲ **Strategic mission** is a statement of a firm's unique purpose and the scope of its operations in product and market terms.

## Summary

- Because of the global economy, traditional sources of competitive advantage, including labor costs, capital costs, and raw materials, have become relatively ineffective. In the 1990s, managers are evaluated in terms of their ability to identify, nurture, and exploit their firm's core competencies. Both the external and the internal environments influence a firm's attempts to achieve strategic competitiveness and earn above-average profits. However, in the global economy, it may be that core competencies, rather than the nature of the general, industry, and competitive environments, should be viewed as the primary foundation for strategy formulation and implementation. But no competitive advantage can be sustained permanently. Eventually, competitors learn how to duplicate the benefits of a firm's strategy. Thus, every firm is challenged to exploit its current competitive advantage while simultaneously using its resources, capabilities, and competencies to develop advantages that will be relevant in the future.

- Effective management of core competencies requires careful analysis of a firm's resources (inputs to a firm's production process) and capabilities (capacities for teams of resources to integratively perform a task or an activity). Resources are the source of capabilities, which are the source of core competencies, that are the foundation for sustainable competitive advantage (see Figure 3–2). Among other characteristics, managers must be willing to hold people accountable for their work and use proper judgment when identifying and evaluating a firm's resources and capabilities.

- Individually, resources are usually not sources of *sustainable* competitive advantage. Capabilities, which result from groupings of different tangible and intangible resources, are more likely to yield a sustainable advantage. A key reason for this is that how a company forms, nurtures, and exploits its capabilities is less visible to competitors and hence more difficult to understand and imitate.
- On a comparative basis, intangible resources are a more likely source of core competencies than tangible resources. A brand name is an intangible resource that historically has been an important source of capability. But firms must nurture a brand name carefully if it is to be a source of competence and, in turn, part of a foundation for sustainable competitive advantage.
- The skills and knowledge of a firm's human capital may be the primary basis for all of its capabilities. Capabilities emerge by developing human capital and sharing information regarding how tangible and intangible resources can be combined in strategically relevant ways. Because of its link with attempts to develop a sustainable competitive advantage, firms are challenged to nurture and develop their human capital.
- Value chain analysis is a technique used to identify and evaluate a firm's resources and capabilities. By studying their primary and support activities, firms determine those areas that are sources of competitive advantage. When such a capability allows a firm to complete a strategically relevant activity that competitors cannot or to complete relevant activities better than competitors can, it becomes a source of competitive advantage.
- In the cases of primary and support activities in which a firm cannot create value, the possibility of outsourcing is considered. Used frequently today, outsourcing occurs when a firm purchases a value-creating activity from an external supplier. When engaged in this process, the firm is cautioned to outsource only to companies possessing sustainable competitive advantages in terms of the activities being outsourced. Moreover, managers must be certain that areas in which their firm does possess competence are not outsourced. Achieving this objective requires managers to fully understand which of their firm's capabilities are, in fact, core competencies.
- Not all of a firm's capabilities are core competencies. Only capabilities that are valuable, rare, imperfectly imitable, and nonsubstitutable are sources of sustainable competitive advantage and, as such, can be called core competencies. Over time, managers are challenged to nurture their firm's competencies. However, core competencies should not be allowed to become core rigidities. Competencies are a source of sustainable competitive advantage *only* when they allow the firm to create value by exploiting external environmental opportunities. When this is no longer the case, a firm's attention must be shifted to other capabilities that are a source of competitive advantage.
- Strategic intent and strategic mission are grounded in the results obtained through analyses of a firm's external and internal environments. Intent and mission create value for a firm by specifying how its resources and capabilities can be leveraged to create value through offering goods or services to particular markets. Taken together, the results of environmental analyses and a firm's intent and mission provide information needed to formulate and implement both business-unit and corporate-level strategies.

## Review Questions

1. What factors and conditions do firms examine in analyzing their internal environment? Why is an effective analysis of these factors critical to achieving strategic competitiveness?
2. What is value? How do firms earn value?
3. What are the differences between tangible and intangible resources? Which of these two categories of resources do you believe typically contributes more to the development of a sustainable competitive advantage, and why?
4. What are capabilities? Why is a firm's human capital so critical to the development and use of its capabilities?
5. For what purpose would you use value chain analysis in an organization? Is there any subjectivity involved with value chain analysis? If so, in what respect(s)?
6. What is outsourcing? Why is it valuable to companies competing in the global economy?
7. Describe the criteria used to determine which of a firm's capabilities are its core competencies. Why is it important for managers to use these criteria?

## Application Discussion Questions

1. Strategic actions being taken by JCPenney and Woolworth Corp. during 1993 and 1994 are described in the opening parts of the chapter. Obtain from your library, daily newspapers, and/or business magazines the information necessary to study these firms' current financial performances. Through your analysis, determine if either or both of these firms still have sustainable competitive advantages and, if so, what they are.

2. Select a store in your local community from which you purchase items. Talk to the store's top manager to ask what value that store provides to customers. Write a paragraph or two describing the answer you received to this question. In general, do you agree with the answer you received? Is the value the manager believes the store is providing the value you believe you receive when purchasing goods or services from the store? If there is a difference of opinion between the two of you, what is the meaning of that difference for the store's top manager?

3. Choose an organization or club in which you currently hold membership. Prepare a list of what you believe are its tangible and intangible resources. Use the resource categories shown in Tables 3–1 and 3–2 to group your organization's resources. Show your lists to other members of the selected organization and ask for their reactions. Did they agree with the contents of your lists? If not, what do you believe might account for the different opinions?

4. Refer to the third question. Was it more difficult for you to list the intangible resources as compared to the tangible resources? If so, why?

5. Select one of the products included in Figure 3–4 for which the prediction is that the brand name may no longer be a source of sustained competitive advantage. As the manager charged to turn the competitive situation around for that product, what actions would you take to increase the value provided by the product to customers? Be prepared to justify the actions you select.

6. Prepare an argument to support your acceptance or rejection of the following statement: "I believe, without a doubt, that a firm's human capital is ultimately the source of all sustainable competitive advantages."

7. Use value chain analysis to identify your university's or college's primary and support activities. Select those activities in which your institution creates value. Be prepared to justify your selections during classroom discussions.

8. According to information presented in the final Strategic Focus, McKinsey & Co. uses three primary criteria when selecting personnel. What are these criteria? In your opinion, are these valid selection criteria? Why or why not?

9. Assume you overheard the following statement: "In my opinion, there is no difference between a firm's strategic intent and its strategic mission." Do you agree or disagree with this statement, and why?

## Ethics Questions

1. Can an emphasis on obtaining competitive advantage result in unethical practices such as insider trading?

2. Can ethical practices facilitate development of a brand-name and a corporate reputation? If so, explain how.

3. What is the difference between exploiting human capital and nurturing human capital to arrive at competitive advantage? Can exploitation of human capital lead to sustainable competitive advantage? If so, how?

4. The restructuring of the 1980s and 1990s has lead to significant layoffs of personnel. What are the ethical considerations to this approach to improving competitive advantage?

5. How can a firm use its strategic mission to guard against unethical practices that employees may be tempted to use to help a firm fulfill its strategic intent to gain competitive advantage?

6. Is there a potential danger that certain classes of people may be exploited through outsourcing because regulations regarding workers (e.g., child labor laws) differ among countries and regions? What about differences in regulations regarding the environment (such as those enforced by the U.S. Environmental Protection Agency) or product safety (such as those enforced by the U.S. Food and Drug Administration)?

## Notes

1. M. Moukheiber, 1993, Our competitive advantage, *Forbes,* April 12; 59–60.

2. Ibid; *Value Line.* 1994. Penney (JC). February 25, 1647.

3. R. Amit and P.J.H. Schoemaker, 1993, Strategic assets and organizational rent, *Strategic Management Journal* 14: 33–46.

4. M. Halkias, 1993, Filling the catalog void, *Dallas Morning News,* January 13, H1, H8.

5. M. Halkias, 1993, Penney to open catalog sales to Mexican shoppers, *Dallas Morning News,* October 29, D1, D10.

6. I.C. MacMillan, 1988, Controlling competitive dynamics by taking strategic initiative, *Academy of Management Executive* 2, no. 2: 111–118.

7. G. Hamel and C.K. Prahalad, 1989, Strategic intent, *Harvard Business Review* 67, no. 3: 69.

8. L.T. Perry, 1990, *Offensive Strategy: Forging a New Competitiveness in the Fires of Head-to-Head Competition* (New York: Harper Business).

9. M.E. Porter, 1990, Have we lost our faith in competition? *Across the Board,* December, 37–46.

10. C.K. Prahalad and G. Hamel, 1990, The core competence of the corporation, *Harvard Business Review* 68, no. 3: 79–91.

11. G. Hamel and C.K. Prahalad, 1993, Strategy as stretch and leverage, *Harvard Business Review* 71, no. 2: 75–84; The future for strategy: An interview with Gary Hamel, 1993, *European Management Journal* 11, no. 2: 150–157.

12. M.A. Peteraf, 1993, The cornerstones of competitive strategy: A resource-based view, *Strategic Management Journal* 14: 179–191.

13. A.A. Lado, N.G. Boyd, and P. Wright, 1992, A competency based model of sustainable competitive advantage: Toward a conceptual integration, *Journal of Management*: 18: 77–91.

14. Prahalad and Hamel, The core competence; J.A. Klein, G. Edge, and T. Kass, 1991, Skill-based competition, *Journal of General Management* 16, no. 4: 1–15.

15. D. Ulrich and M.F. Wiersema, 1989, Gaining strategic and organizational capability in a turbulent business environment, *Academy of Management Executive* 3, no. 2: 115–122.

16. Prahalad and Hamel, The core competence.

17. Jack Welch's lessons for success, 1993, *Fortune,* January 25, 86–93.

18. R. Normann and R. Ramirez, 1993, From value chain to value constellation: Designing interactive strategy, *Harvard Business Review* 71, no. 4: 65–77.

19. T.C. Powell, 1992, Organizational alignment as competitive advantage, *Strategic Management Journal* 13: 119–134.

20. J.B. Barney, 1986, Strategic factor markets: Expectations, luck, and business strategy, *Management Science*: 32: 1231–1241; I. Dierickx and K. Cool, 1989, Asset stock accumulation and sustainability of competitive advantage, *Management Science* 35: 1504–1514.

21. Amit and Schoemaker, Strategic assets.

22. B. Wernerfelt and C.A. Montgomery, 1986, What is an attractive industry? *Management Science* 32: 1223–1230.

23. Amit and Schoemaker, Strategic assets.

24. Lado, Boyd, and Wright, A competency based model;

25. R.P. Castanias and C.E. Helfat, 1991, Managerial resources and rents, *Journal of Management* 17: 155–171.

25. M. Loeb, 1993, Making sense of the chaos, *Fortune,* April 5, 6.

26. N. Kawamoto, 1993, Comment regarding Honda Motor Company, *Fortune,* February 22, 16.

27. Five hot ideas for today's economy, 1993, *Fortune,* October 18, 112–121.

28. A. Taylor, 1992, What's ahead for GM's new team, *Fortune,* November 30, 58–61.

29. W. Kiechel, 1993, Facing up to denial, *Fortune,* October 18, 163–165.

30. Lado, Boyd, and Wright, A competency based model, 84.

31. Amit and Schoemaker, Strategic assets, 35.

32. R.M. Grant, 1991, The resource-based theory of competitive advantage: Implications for strategy formulation, *California Management Review* 33, Spring: 114–135; A.D. Meyer, 1991, What is strategy's distinctive competence? *Journal of Management* 17: 821–833.

33. Meyer, What is strategy's distinctive competence? 823.

34. R. Hall, 1991, The contribution of intangible resources to business success, *Journal of General Management* 16, no. 4: 41–52.

35. R.M. Grant, 1991, *Contemporary Strategy Analysis* (Cambridge, England: Blackwell Business), 94.

36. R. Hall, 1993, A framework linking intangible resources and capabilities to sustainable competitive advantage, *Strategic Management Journal* 14: 607–618; R. Hall, 1992, The strategic analysis of intangible resources, *Strategic Management Journal* 13: 135–144.

37. D.A. Aaker, 1989, Managing assets and skills: The key to sustainable competitive advantage, *California Management Review* 31, no. 2: 91–106.

38. Hall, The strategic analysis, 140.

39. Grant, *Contemporary Strategy Analysis,* 102.

40. P. Baldwin, 1993, Penney ads take new focus, *Dallas Morning News,* October 28, D1, D13.

41. A. Taylor, 1993, Making up for lost time, *Fortune,* October 18, 78–80.

42. P. Sellers, 1993, Brands: It's thrive or die, *Fortune,* August 23, 52–55.

43. Business milestones, 1994, *Fortune,* January 10, 14–15.

44. Amit and Schoemaker, Strategic assets, 35–37.

45. Prahalad and Hamel, The core competence, 82.

46. J.B. Quinn, 1993, Managing the intelligent enterprise: Knowledge and service-based strategies, *Planning Review* 21, no. 5: 13–16.

47. Prahalad and Hamel, The core competence, 90.

48. G. Talk, P. Evans, and L.E. Shulman, 1992, Competing on capabilities: The new rules of corporate strategy, *Harvard Business Review* 70, no. 3: 57–69.

49. B. Soporito, 1993, David Glass won't crack under fire, *Fortune,* February 8, 80.

50. J.-C. Spender, 1993, Workplace knowledge as a competitive advantage: Tracing the roots of the organization's idiosyncratic knowledge assets (working paper, Rutgers University); M.J. Kiernan, 1993, The new strategic architecture: Learning to compete in the twenty-first century, *Academy of Management Executive* 7, no. 1: 7–21.

51. T.A. Steward, 1991, Brainpower, *Fortune,* June 3, 44.

52. Hamel and Prahalad, Strategic intent, 69; Porter, Have we lost our faith? 37; P.M. Senge, 1990, The leader's new work: Building learning organizations, *Sloan Management Review* 33, no. 1: 7–23.

53. R. Henkoff, 1993, The labor secretary speaks out on training and the two-tier work force, *Fortune,* March 8, 13.

54. R. Henkoff, 1993, Companies that train best, *Fortune,* March 22, 62–74.

55. S. Fatsis, 1993, Bigger is not necessarily better, *Waco Tribune-Herald,* January 17, B1, B6.

56. M.A. Hitt, and R.D. Ireland, 1986, Relationships among corporate level distinctive competencies, diversification strategy, corporate strategy and performance, *Journal of Management Studies* 23: 401–416; M.A. Hitt and R.D. Ireland, 1985, Corporate distinctive competence, strategy, industry and performance, *Strategic Management Journal* 6: 273–293.

57. M. Zimmerman, 1993, Deep 6 the mayo, *Dallas Morning News,* September 29, D1.

58. M.E. Porter, 1985, *Competitive Advantage* (New York: Free Press), 33–61.

59. D.W. Cravens and S.H. Shipp, 1991, Market-driven strategies for competitive advantage, *Business Horizons* 34, no. 1: 53–61.

60. P. Sellers, 1993, Look who learned about value, *Fortune,* October 18, 76.

61. S. Tully, 1993, the modular corporation, *Fortune,* February 8, 106.

62. J.R. Oltman, 1990, 21st century outsourcing, *Computerworld* 24, no. 16: 77–79.

63. J.A. Welch and P.R. Nayak, 1992, Strategic sourcing: A progressive approach to the make-or-buy decision, *Academy of Management Executive* 6, no. 1: 23–31.

64. A. Taylor, 1993, Shaking up Jaguar, *Fortune,* September 6, 66.

65. M.L. Fagan, 1991, A guide to global sourcing, *Journal of Business Strategy* 12, no. 2: 21–25.

66. J. Ostroff, 1991, Gap: U.S. men's firms can compete with imports, *Daily News Record,* April 30, 2, 9.

67. Fagan, A guide to global sourcing, 23.

68. R.A. Bettis, S.P. Bradley, and G. Hamel, 1992, Outsourcing and industrial decline, *Academy of Management Executive* 6, no. 1: 7–22.

69. R.L. Huber, 1993, How Continental Bank outsourced its "crown jewels," *Harvard Business Review* 71, no. 1: 128.

70. J.B. Barney, 1991, Firm resources and sustained competitive advantage, *Journal of Management* 17: 99–120.

71. Normann and Ramirez, From value chain, 65.

72. Quinn, Managing the intelligent enterprise, 14.

73. This section is based primarily on Barney, Firm resources, 106–112.

74. J.B. Barney, 1986, Organization culture: Can it be a source of sustained competitive advantage, *Academy of Management Review* 11: 656–665.

75. Amit and Schoemaker, Strategic assets, 39.

76. Prahalad and Hamel, The core competence.

77. R.M. Kanter, 1990, How to compete, *Harvard Business Review,* 14, no. 6: 7–8.

78. D. Leonard-Barton, 1992, Core capabilities and core rigidities: A paradox in managing new product development, *Strategic Management Journal* 13 (Special Issue): 111–125.

79. Hamel and Prahalad, Strategic intent.

80. Hamel and Prahalad, Strategy as stretch.

81. M.S.S. El-Namaki, 1992, Creating a corporate vision, *Long Range Planning* 25, no. 6: 25–29.

82. M. Alexander, 1992, Brief case: Strategic fatigue, *Long Range Planning* 25, no. 2: 119–121.

83. P.J.H. Schoemaker, 1992, How to link strategic vision to core capabilities, *Sloan Management Review* 34, no. 1: 67–81.

84. G. Hamel and C.K. Prahalad, 1991, Corporate imagination and expeditionary marketing, *Harvard Business Review* 15, no. 4: 81–91; P. Sellers and D. Kirkpatrick, 1993, Can this man save IBM? *Fortune,* April 19, 63–67; P. Sellers, 1993, The new siege at RJR Nabisco, *Fortune,* February 8, 118–125.

85. T. Eaton, 1993, A shopper's heaven, *Dallas Morning News,* October 24, H1, H3.

86. R. Saporito, 1994. And the winner is still. . . . Wal-Mart, *Fortune,* May 2, 62–70.

87. R. Henkoff, 1993, Inside Andersen's army of advice, *Fortune,* October 4, 78–86.

88. R.D. Ireland and M.A. Hitt, 1992, Mission statements: Importance, challenge, and recommendations for development, *Business Horizons* 35, no. 3: 34–42.

# PART 2

# Strategic Actions: Strategy Formulation

# CHAPTER 4
# Business-Level Strategy

▼

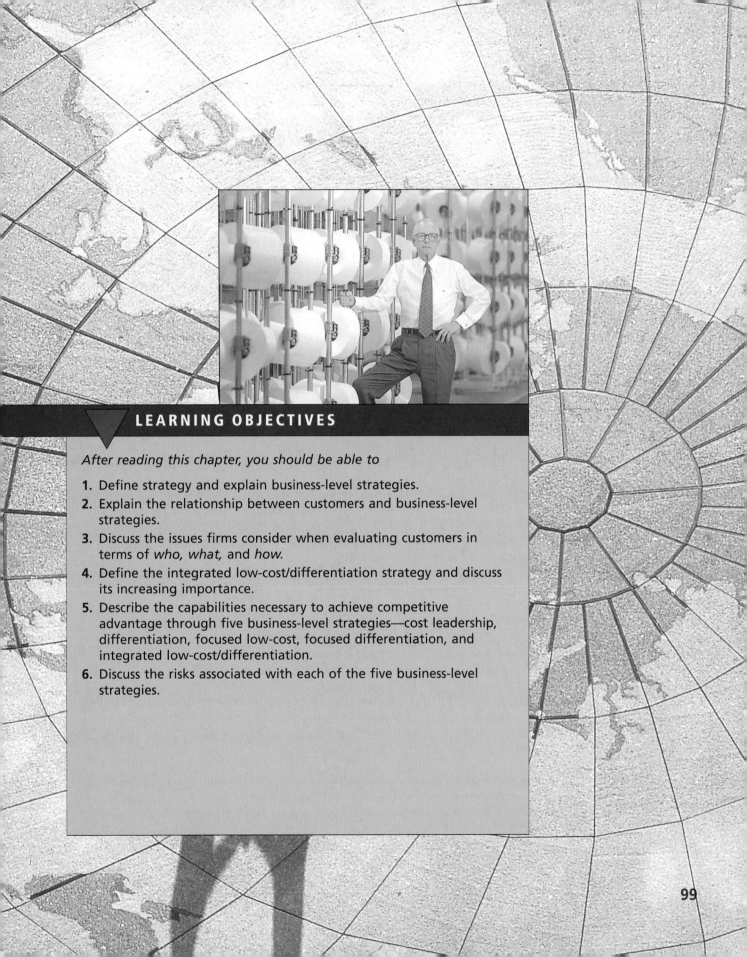

*After reading this chapter, you should be able to*

1. Define strategy and explain business-level strategies.
2. Explain the relationship between customers and business-level strategies.
3. Discuss the issues firms consider when evaluating customers in terms of *who, what,* and *how.*
4. Define the integrated low-cost/differentiation strategy and discuss its increasing importance.
5. Describe the capabilities necessary to achieve competitive advantage through five business-level strategies—cost leadership, differentiation, focused low-cost, focused differentiation, and integrated low-cost/differentiation.
6. Discuss the risks associated with each of the five business-level strategies.

## Achieving Strategic Competitiveness at Unifi

QUALITY THROUGH PRIDE

Unifi (the name rhymes with "superfly") is a North Carolina textile manufacturer. The firm's shareholders earned an attractive average annual return of 37 percent during a recent five-year period.

How Unifi achieved strategic competitiveness is an interesting story. The firm's primary product is a yarn called textured polyester. A fabric that has been the source of many jokes over the years, polyester's popularity peaked in the early 1970s. In fact, the demand for filament poly, the raw material used to make polyester yarn, fell from 1.4 billion pounds in 1975 to 650 million pounds in 1985. Unifi's founder and chairman (who has been described as opportunistic, shrewd, and aggressive) considered the reduction in demand for polyester yarn to be an environmental opportunity, rather than a threat.

Following a careful and thorough analysis, Unifi's chairman, Allen Mebane, (shown in the detail photo on page 99), concluded that only a few of the 50 or so U.S. manufacturers would survive the shrinking polyester demand. Mebane viewed this as an opportunity to consolidate what had been a fragmented industry. A **fragmented industry** is one in which no manufacturer is large enough to significantly influence the industry's characteristics in its own favor. Mebane decided that his firm should spend heavily to purchase state-of-the-art manufacturing equipment. Using a combination of internally generated cash, bank debt, and public offerings, the company purchased equipment that greatly improved its productivity and product quality.

Through its investments, Unifi became the low-cost producer in the industry. The company's success forced out a number of its competitors, particularly those for whom polyester was but one of many businesses. At the beginning of 1994, Unifi was the world's largest producer of textured polyester and held over 70 percent of the U.S. polyester market. Part of its success with polyester yarn occurred because Unifi found new customers for polyester in automobiles and home furnishings.

Based on the success of its low-cost strategy in the polyester market, Unifi decided to implement the same strategy to manufacture nylon. Accordingly, the firm invested heavily in new production technologies, pushed its costs much lower, and grabbed market share from competitors. After only a few years, Unifi held almost 70 percent of the hosiery market (Sara Lee, the maker of Hanes and L'eggs, was its largest customer).

In 1993, Unifi entered the supercompetitive cotton spun-yarn business. As before, the company believed strategic competitiveness could be achieved in this market through implementation of a low-cost strategy. To enter the cotton business, Unifi acquired two firms—Vintage and Pioneer. Both of these private companies were growing quickly and, between them, held a 15 percent market share.

Although the early results from operations in the cotton spun-yarn business were not as positive as desired, Unifi's chairman remains confident that his low-cost strategy will work in this market as it has in the polyester and nylon markets. To describe his company's plans, Mebane stated the following: "We'll continue to spend to build the cotton business no matter what. After all, it's not a bad time to go after market share when demand falls apart, is it?"  ▲

▲ A **fragmented industry** is one in which no manufacturer is large enough to significantly influence the industry's characteristics in its own favor.

To achieve strategic competitiveness and earn superior profits, a company must *analyze* its external environment, *identify* opportunities in that environment, *determine* which of its internal resources and capabilities are core competencies, and *choose* an appropriate strategy to implement.[1] A **strategy** is an integrated and coordinated set of actions taken to exploit core competencies and gain a competitive advantage. Recall from Chapter 1 that **core competencies** are the resources and capabilities that have been determined to be a source of competitive advantage for a firm over its rivals. Long-term strategic competitiveness and superior profitability hinge on a firm's ability to develop and exploit new core competencies faster than competitors can mimic the competitive advantages yielded by current ones.[2]

As explained in this chapter, successful firms use their core competencies to satisfy customers' needs and in the process earn superior profits. The relationship between appropriate strategic actions and the achievement of strategic competitiveness is increasingly important in today's turbulent and competitive environment.[3] These relationships are shown in Figure 1-1. As displayed in that figure, a firm's strategic inputs (gained through study of the external and the internal environments) are used to select the strategic actions (the formulation and implementation of value-creating strategies) that will yield desired strategic outcomes (strategic competitiveness and above-average profits).

Unifi exemplifies the relationships among strategic inputs, actions, and outcomes. Through examination of its external environment components (the general, industry, and competitor environments), Unifi identified an opportunity. What this firm viewed as an opportunity (the manufacture of polyester yarn) may have been considered a threat by its competitors.

Although it may seem unusual for competing firms to examine the same external environment and reach different conclusions, such differing perceptions are probably due to internal environments. Opportunities are chosen through a study of a firm's external *and* internal environments. Thus, Unifi determined that it had the core competencies necessary to implement a value-creating strategy in a particular market. For example, Unifi believed its resources and capabilities permitted the development of efficient and effective production technologies and that, as a core competence, these technologies were a source of competitive advantage.

The results gained through the study of its external and internal environments also indicate an appropriate strategic intent and strategic mission for Unifi. Because of its dominance in the textured polyester market, it appears that Unifi has established a strategic intent calling for leadership in this market. Its mission apparently called for applications of the strategic intent in the home furnishings and automobile markets, as well as traditional markets.

Business-level-strategy is the focus of this chapter. The other major type of strategy formulated and implemented by large firms—corporate-level strategy—is described in Chapter 6. A **business-level strategy** details actions taken to provide value to customers and gain a competitive advantage by exploiting core competencies in specific, individual product markets. Thus, business-level strategies are grounded in firm-specific core competencies[4] and indicate how an organization intends to compete in a particular product market and gain competitive advantage over its rivals.

To fulfill its strategic intent, Unifi decided to pursue a cost leadership strategy. A **cost leadership strategy** provides goods or services with features acceptable to customers at the lowest competitive price. In contrast, a **differentiation**

▲ A **strategy** is an integrated and coordinated set of actions taken to exploit core competencies and gain a competitive advantage.

▲ **Core competencies** are resources and capabilities that serve as a source of competitive advantage over a firm's rivals.

▲ A **business-level strategy** details actions taken to provide value to customers and gain a competitive advantage by exploiting core competencies in specific, individual product markets.

▲ A **cost leadership strategy** provides goods or services with features acceptable to customers at the lowest competitive price.

▲ A **differentiation strategy** provides products that customers perceive as being unique in ways that are important to them.

**strategy** provides products that customers perceive as being unique in ways that are important to them.[5] Because of their unique features, differentiated products offer value to customers for which they are often willing to pay a premium price. Comments about these two business-level strategies are provided in subsequent sections.

For an increasing number of companies, an important objective is to operate in environmentally sound and appropriate manners when competing in individual product markets. For example, Hanson PLC is a large, diversified firm operating companies in both the United Kingdom and the United States (more information about Hanson is provided in a Strategic Focus in Chapter 6). Hanson is committed to the position that a concern for the environment is an integral part of the formulation and implementation of its business-level strategies. To describe its commitment, Hanson developed an environmental policy. This policy, which was included in one of the company's recent annual reports, appears in Table 4-1. In reading the policy, notice the perceived relationship between concern for the environment and achievement of competitive advantage.

Firms' business-level strategies are not formulated and implemented in isolation. Competitors anticipate and react to actions, including those concerned with the environment, taken by those with which they compete. Chapter 5's analysis of the nature and effects of these competitive actions and responses adds important insights to the understanding of business-level strategies.

Strategic competitiveness and superior profitability are achieved when *customers* are the foundation for a firm's strategic actions. In the words of one CEO, "When you get people focused on customers, it has a very remarkable effect"[6] on the firm's performance. This chapter begins with a discussion of customers because of their strategic importance. Three issues—*who, what,* and *how*—are considered in this analysis. Each firm determines *who* it will serve, *what* needs the customers have that it will satisfy, and *how* those needs will be satisfied through its strategy. Although examined separately, decision makers evaluate the three issues simultaneously when selecting a business-level strategy.

---

▼ **TABLE 4-1**

### Environmental Policy of Hanson PLC

Our concern for the environment is an integral part of our everyday business strategy, providing an impetus to improve resource management, efficiency and competitive advantage. Our companies endeavor to achieve the highest standards of environmental performance throughout their broad range of industrial processes, with the primary goal of keeping any adverse impact to a minimum.

Each Hanson company has its own environmental plan and policy appropriate to its activities whereby it strives to:

• Respond to the needs and concerns of the community with a sympathetic attitude toward environmental interest groups.
• Comply with environmental legislation and plan ahead of future requirements.
• Develop management systems to eliminate problems at the source.
• Monitor, evaluate and review performance.
• Improve employee awareness by maximum exposure to environmental issues.
• Encourage the interaction of expertise between companies.

*Source:* Hanson Industries, 1992, *Annual Report,* 16.

Following the discussion on customers is a description of four generic business-level strategies. These strategies are called *generic* because they can be implemented in all industries—manufacturing, service, and not-for-profit.[7] Our analysis of the generic strategies includes descriptions of how each one allows a firm to address the five competitive forces discussed in Chapter 2. In addition, we use the value chain (see Chapter 3) to show examples of primary and support activities necessary to implement each generic strategy successfully. Organizational requirements for implementation are discussed in Chapter 10. Risks associated with implementing individual generic strategies are also presented in this chapter.

A fifth business-level strategy that firms are implementing more frequently in today's global economy in order to create value for customers is considered in the final section of this chapter. Some believe that this hybrid strategy (a combination of the cost leadership and the differentiation strategies called the *integrated strategy*) is essential to establishing and exploiting competitive advantages in global competitive environments.[8]

## Customers—Who, What, and How

Organizations operating in the manufacturing, service, and not-for-profit sectors must satisfy some group of customers' needs to survive and achieve strategic competitiveness. In the global economy, the challenge of identifying and determining how to satisfy customers' needs is increasingly difficult.[9] Although our discussion of customers is concerned primarily with manufacturing and service firms, the guidance it provides is also applicable in the not-for-profit sector. Not-for-profit organizations, too, must understand who their customers are, what needs their customers have that they are able to satisfy, and how the core competencies they possess can be used to satisfy those needs.

Strategically competitive organizations of the 1990s and the twenty-first century will think continuously about who their customers are[10] and how to use their core competencies in a way that competitors cannot imitate.[11] For example, the chairman of Allied-Signal, a manufacturer of aerospace equipment, auto parts, and a range of other products, recently observed that there is a near unanimous opinion in his firm that its businesses should be run primarily by customer-oriented processes.[12] Thus, decisions made in terms of the customer-based issues examined in the next three subsections strongly influence how a firm intends to compete. In fact, these issues, and the decisions made about them, are at the center of the selection of business-level strategies.

## Who: Determining the Customers to Serve

Customers can be divided into groups based on differences in their needs. Common dimensions on which customers' needs vary include life style, socioeconomic class, individual personality characteristics, industry structural characteristics, and organizational size.[13]

A company may decide that the differences in need preferences within a customer group are not significant. This conclusion causes a firm to offer its products with performance characteristics it believes will appeal to the "average" or "typical" customer. A classic example is Henry Ford's decision in the early 1900s to offer a single, standardized product to customers seeking transportation. Ford believed that there were few, if any, meaningful differences in preferences among customers interested in purchasing an automobile. Similarly, in years past, bicycles were designed for two basic customer groups—females and males. The "tract housing" approach used frequently in the 1950s and 1960s in the United States was based on the conviction that all customers within a certain socioeconomic status preferred virtually the same design and features in their homes. An alternative explanation, which also accounts for the decision to offer only a standardized product, is that the firm has chosen to ignore the differences in customers' needs or preferences.

Thus, in general, companies seeking to serve customers with a standardized product believe that the differences in customers' needs are not competitively significant, that their product cannot be easily altered to satisfy different needs, or that their commitment to producing a standardized product should not be changed. For these reasons, firms providing standardized, undifferentiated products typically strive to offer goods and services to customers at the lowest competitive prices as they implement the cost leadership strategy. As described in the opening case, Unifi achieved strategic competitiveness through implementation of the cost leadership strategy.

**Increasing Segmentation of Markets**   In the global economy, firms have become adept at identifying precise differences among customers' needs and preferences. Armed with these understandings, firms are able to segment customers into competitively relevant groups. **Competitively relevant groups** are those with unique needs or preferences.

▲ **Competitively relevant groups** are those with unique needs or preferences.

In the United States, it has been estimated that there are at least 62 distinct classes of citizens, each with its own beliefs, aspirations, tastes, and needs. Moreover, some believe that, if anything, the trend in the United States toward fragmentation into smaller classes and subgroups is accelerating.[14] Thus, the number of competitively relevant groups in the United States appears to be increasing. Accompanying this growth are significant competitive opportunities for companies capable of serving the specialized needs of the different customer groups.

Among other capabilities, sophisticated information-processing technologies allow firms to pinpoint the uniqueness of customers' needs. Once known, firms can produce products tailored to the specific needs of individual customer groups. For example, personal computers and software packages for them are designed for highly segmented customer groups. Wall Data Inc. develops software for business users *in large organizations*.[15] Other specialized software applications include those for use in homes, a wide array of not-for-profit organizations (e.g., government agencies, churches, community-service groups), and different sizes and types of educational institutions. The segmentation of markets for automobiles, bicycles, and housing provides additional examples of how customers' needs have been grouped in competitively relevant ways.

As our discussion indicates, global markets are becoming increasingly segmented. However, in some instances, because of the nature of the product or the industry's structural characteristics, it is difficult to segment markets. This is the case for Unifi's polyester yarn and for companies manufacturing cement and bulk chemicals, for example.[16]

Once a firm has identified *who* it will serve, it should focus its attention on that customer group or set of segments. Trying to "be all things to all people" typically results in less-than-satisfactory performance. For instance, Kmart's recent performance difficulties may be partly caused by the company's failure to focus on a key customer group. "Kmart tried to compete with Wal-Mart below and Sears above, and at the same time run [their] boutiques [boutiques at least partly owned by Kmart include Builders Square, Waldenbooks, OfficeMax, and Sports Authority]. Instead, they lost ground everywhere."[17]

How another company lost contact with the customers it intended to serve is described in the next Strategic Focus. The actions the firm is taking to become focused again on the needs of its primary customer group are also discussed.

## STRATEGIC FOCUS

### Liz Claiborne Inc. and Its Relationships with Customers

The largest women's apparel maker in the United States, Liz Claiborne Inc. has long had a strategy that called for the company to serve the needs of working women. But financial results recorded in 1993 suggested the firm had "found its passionate relationship with consumers on the rocks." Sales at the $2.2 billion company were flat in the first three quarters of 1993. Even more dangerous, earnings plunged 40 percent in the third quarter. This drop followed double-digit earnings declines in 1993's first and second quarters. For all of 1993, the firm expected profits to be off by at least 40 percent. The price of Claiborne's stock fell 44 percent from April to the end of 1993.

Viewing these results caused many to wonder "what soured [Claiborne's] dreamy love affair with consumers?" In the eyes of both company executives and market analysts, the answer was relatively simply—the wrong products, too many of them, and a loss of contact with the firm's primary customers.

By the end of the 1980s, Claiborne had expanded beyond its traditional clothing lines to include petites and large sizes, accessories, fragrances, and men's clothing (among still other lines). Asking Claiborne managers to handle such a diverse array of products caused them to lose their focus on the company's core merchandise for working women. Compounding the difficulty for Claiborne was the failure of top-level management. According to one former Claiborne executive, top managers failed to quickly recognize problems. "If the product didn't sell, it was always someone else's fault. The buyers didn't show it right, or it wasn't delivered the right way. They didn't allow themselves to think that maybe they just weren't listening to the consumer."

What can Claiborne do to change its fortunes? One of the most significant challenges may be to invigorate the company's $1.2 billion sportswear division. This division consists primarily of Collection, LizSport, and LizWear. The charge to these groups is to provide clothing for women to wear at the office, at jobs permitting more casual dress, and on weekends, respectively. The firm's new CEO is committed to the position that clear product identities that are highly visible to customers must be established. In describing his firm's intended relationship with the customer, the CEO stated, "It's up to us to make sure she sees the distinction and value in each brand."

To establish clear product identities, specific types of merchandise are being allocated to each line. The Collection line, for example, will be mainly career-oriented skirts, jackets, and tailored pants. LizSport will feature casual clothes such as cotton pants, sweaters, and vests. Basic products, including jeans, T-shirts, and turtlenecks, will be handled by LizWear.

*Rubbermaid is known for its ability to understand and respond successfully to its customers' needs. Rubbermaid is able to continuously improve its wide range of household products in ways that provide additional value to customers. Through the leadership of the firm's CEO, shown above, Rubbermaid's already strong commitment to product innovation was recently strengthened.*

Time will tell if Liz Claiborne's commitment to refocus on its primary customers will be successful. However, the desire to develop product lines with values that are easily recognized by working women may facilitate Claiborne's efforts to regain its strategic competitiveness.

## What: Determining the Customer Needs to Satisfy

The basic need all customers have is to purchase goods and services that provide value. Companies that continue to provide increasing value to customers often achieve strategic competitiveness and earn superior profits. In a recent year, for example, Rubbermaid was identified as America's most admired corporation in *Fortune* magazine's Corporate Reputations Survey. A key reason for Rubbermaid's success appears to be its ability to make incremental product changes that are valued by customers.[18]

As noted, customers' needs must be determined once a firm's customer group(s) has been selected. Top-level managers play a critical role in an organization's efforts to recognize and understand customers' needs. Their instinctive capacity to gain valuable insights from listening to customers influences product, technology, and distribution decisions. Thus, in strategically competitive firms, customer contact is a key responsibility for top-level managers as well as for marketing and sales personnel.[19]

By studying customers' needs, a firm shows that it wants to produce customer value, given its particular strategic approach. These needs can be satisfied through implementation of one of the five business-level strategies—cost leadership, differentiation, focused low-cost, focused differentiation, or a combination of cost leadership and differentiation. In a global economy, an additional competitive advantage accrues to firms capable of providing customers with unexpected value. This type of value is not related to a product's overall integrity or quality (high quality is viewed as a given—a necessary, but not sufficient, condition to achieve strategic competitiveness). Rather, unexpected value is providing customers with something they did not request, yet do value in terms of a product's performance capabilities.[20] To facilitate providing extra value, firms should listen carefully to their customers in order to *anticipate* their future needs.[21] Descriptions of customer firms' strategic intent, mission and operations may suggest their future product performance capabilities and needs. For example, in the latter part of the 1980s, Wall Data, in an attempt to better serve its customers, sought to discover the answer to the following question: "What would the [computer] business user in a large corporation need at her desktop in 1994?"[22] Similarly, people from Sony Medical spend significant amounts of time with doctors and health maintenance organizations in order to understand their current and future needs. A manufacturer of color printers and other peripherals for use with medical imaging equipment (such as ultrasound machines), Sony Medical scans the rest of Sony to find technologies that could be used to develop products capable of satisfying customers' future needs.[23]

## How: Determining Core Competencies to Use to Satisfy Customers' Needs

Firms use their core competencies to satisfy customers' needs. Individually, or in groups, core competencies are combined to implement a value-creating strategy. At IBM, the chief executive officer (CEO) believes that the firm must find ways to more quickly convert its technological competence into commercial products.[24] Similarly, at John Fluke Manufacturing, a manufacturer of voltmeters and other test and measurement devices, the CEO has stated that all new products must use the company's technological competence.[25] Honda's motorcycle, car, lawn mower, and generator businesses are all based on the company's core competence in engines and power trains. At Canon, core competencies in optics, imaging, and microprocessor controls are the foundation for the strategic success the firm has had in a range of product markets, including copiers, laser printers, cameras, and image scanners.[26]

Important as core competencies are, firms cannot blindly use them to produce new products and to implement business-level strategies. At John Fluke Manufacturing, for example, new products must "meet a market need" as well as be based on the firm's core competence in technology.[27] As obvious as this point seems, companies occasionally apply their core competencies to the development of products without understanding the value a product might provide to potential customers. As described in the next Strategic Focus, at one time Yamaha Corp. engaged in this ineffective practice.

As Yamaha Corp.'s experiences indicate, business-level strategies should be formulated and implemented through an integrated understanding of *who* is being served and *what* customer need is being satisfied. Failure to focus simultaneously on customer-based issues prevents successful implementation of a value-creating strategy.

## STRATEGIC FOCUS

### Yamaha's Short-Term Failure to Link Competencies With Customer Needs

Yamaha Corp. is the world's leading manufacturer of pianos, horns, and several other musical instruments. Primarily committed to the higher-end markets, the company implements a differentiation strategy. Its core competencies in manufacturing techniques and the acquisition and crafting of unique materials are two of the competencies that serve as a foundation for its strategy.

Yamaha's craftsmen have long been known for their superior ability to bend and laminate woods for piano cabinets. Originally, this competence was logically and appropriately extended to the manufacture of guitars and drums. However, Yamaha also used this competence to produce less-familiar products, including skis, tennis rackets, and furniture. In a similar manner, the company relied on its competencies to build electronic organs as well as to produce televisions, video cassette recorders, and audio equipment.

Unfortunately for Yamaha, the use of its core competencies to produce other products was not successful. Its obsession with applying its production skills to an increasing array of diverse products caused the company to lose touch with its primary customer groups. "Instead of just worrying whether they are building things right, they should be asking, 'Why are we building this product?'"

But Yamaha's top-level managers were quick to recognize and correct the problem. To describe the approach Yamaha Corp. uses today, the president states, "We are studying new markets very carefully now before introducing new products."

Next we discuss each of the different business-level strategies firms implement to provide *distinctive products* to customers and create competitive advantage.

## Types of Business-Level Strategy

Business-level strategies are concerned with a firm's position within an industry relative to competitors.[28] When favorably positioned in terms of the five forces of competition discussed in Chapter 2, firms achieve strategic competitiveness and earn above-average profits. Firms that have been able to establish favorable industry positions are better able to cope with the five forces than are their competitors. Thus, favorably positioned firms have a competitive advantage over their industry rivals.

There are four generic strategies—*cost leadership, differentiation, focused low-cost,* and *focused differentiation*—from which firms choose to establish and exploit a competitive advantage within an industry.[29] As shown in Figure 4-1, competitive advantage is sought by competing in many of an industry's customer segments when implementing either the cost leadership or the differentiation strategy. In contrast, through implementation of focus strategies, firms seek either a cost advantage or a differentiation advantage in a *narrow customer segment.* In combination, the structural characteristics of the five forces of competition make certain generic strategies feasible in some industries, but not in others.

### Cost Leadership Strategy

When implementing the cost leadership strategy, firms offer products with acceptable features to customers at the lowest competitive price. Thus, the principal

**FIGURE 4–1  Four Generic Strategies**

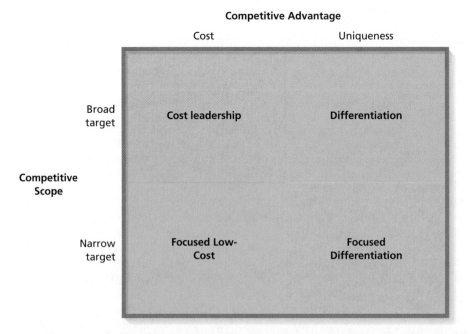

SOURCE: Adapted and reprinted with the permission of The Free Press, an imprint of Simon & Schuster from *COMPETITIVE ADVANTAGE: Creating and Sustaining Superior Performance* by Michael Porter, Fig. 1-3, 12. Copyright © 1985 by Michael E. Porter.

source of value provided to customers through implementation of this strategy is a product's low cost. Firms seeking competitive advantage by implementing the cost leadership strategy sell no-frills, standardized products to the most typical customers in the industry. As part of its global strategy, General Electric's appliance business unit has established a joint venture with Godrej to manufacture and sell low-cost ovens in India.[30] As described in the opening case, Unifi implements the cost leadership strategy to produce and sell three types of standardized products—polyester yarn, nylon, and cotton spun-yarn. Dollar General, a general variety store, also implements the cost leadership strategy. Founded in 1939, the chain's name derives from the fact that originally all of its products sold for less than one dollar. In the early 1990s, no product in the firm's 1,500 stores sold for more than $25 (an amount that is less than $2.50 in 1939 dollars).[31]

Successful implementation of the cost leadership strategy requires a consistent focus on driving costs lower, relative to competitors' costs. Emerson Electric Co., a U.S. manufacturing company that has earned superior profits during both favorable and unfavorable economic conditions, bases its operations on two principles—continuous cost reduction and open communication.[32] Often firms drive their costs lower through investments in efficient-scale facilities, tight cost and overhead control, and cost minimizations in various areas, including service, sales force, and R&D. Recall that Unifi made significant investments in its manufacturing technologies in order to drive its costs lower. Emerson Electric recently invested $250 million to retain its favorable cost positions in all of its major product lines.[33]

As described in Chapter 3, a firm's value chain determines the parts of its operations that create value and those that do not. Primary and support activities that allow a firm to create value through a cost leadership strategy are shown in Figure 4-2. Firms that cannot efficiently and effectively link the activities included in this figure lack the resources and capabilities (and hence the core competencies) required to successfully implement the cost leadership strategy.

When implementing the cost leadership strategy, firms must be careful not to completely ignore sources of differentiation (e.g., innovative designs, service after the sale, product quality, etc.) that customers value. In general, customers continue to purchase a cost leader's products as long as they have *acceptable* features that are close to or exceed those offered by competitors. For example, cost leader Emerson Electric will continue to satisfy customers as long as its products are at least similar in style and quality to those of competitors.

Implementation of a cost leadership strategy allows a firm to earn superior profits in spite of the presence of strong competitive forces.

**Rivalry with Existing Competitors**   Having the low-cost position serves as a valuable defense against rivals. Because of the cost leader's advantageous cost position, rivals hesitate to compete on the basis of price. However, if rivals do challenge the firm to compete on the basis of price, the low-cost firm can still earn profits after its competitors have competed theirs away.[34]

**Bargaining Power of Buyers (Customers)**   When powerful, customers can force the low-cost leader to reduce its prices. However, price will not be driven below the level at which the next most efficient competitor in the industry can earn average profits. While powerful customers could force the low-cost leader to reduce prices even below this level, they probably will choose not to do so. Still lower prices would prevent the next most efficient competitor from earning

**FIGURE 4–2**  **Examples of Value-Creating Activities Associated with the Cost Leadership Strategy**

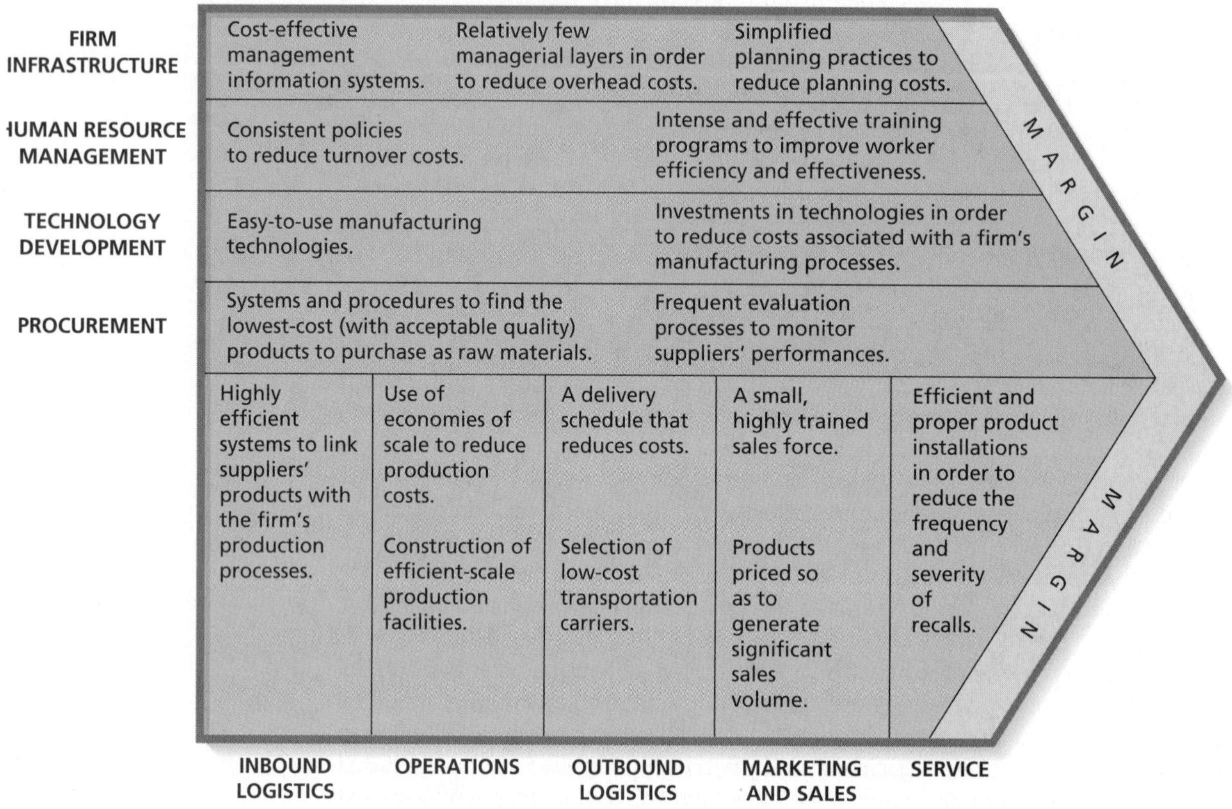

| FIRM INFRASTRUCTURE | Cost-effective management information systems. | Relatively few managerial layers in order to reduce overhead costs. | Simplified planning practices to reduce planning costs. | |
|---|---|---|---|---|
| HUMAN RESOURCE MANAGEMENT | Consistent policies to reduce turnover costs. | | Intense and effective training programs to improve worker efficiency and effectiveness. | |
| TECHNOLOGY DEVELOPMENT | Easy-to-use manufacturing technologies. | | Investments in technologies in order to reduce costs associated with a firm's manufacturing processes. | |
| PROCUREMENT | Systems and procedures to find the lowest-cost (with acceptable quality) products to purchase as raw materials. | | Frequent evaluation processes to monitor suppliers' performances. | |
| | Highly efficient systems to link suppliers' products with the firm's production processes. | Use of economies of scale to reduce production costs. Construction of efficient-scale production facilities. | A delivery schedule that reduces costs. Selection of low-cost transportation carriers. | A small, highly trained sales force. Products priced so as to generate significant sales volume. | Efficient and proper product installations in order to reduce the frequency and severity of recalls. |
| | INBOUND LOGISTICS | OPERATIONS | OUTBOUND LOGISTICS | MARKETING AND SALES | SERVICE |

*MARGIN* (shown along the right-side arrow of the value chain diagram)

SOURCE: Adapted with the permission of The Free Press, an imprint of Simon & Schuster from COMPETITIVE ADVANTAGE: Creating and Sustaining Superior Performance by Michael Porter. Copyright © 1985 by Michael E. Porter.

average profits, resulting in its exit from the market and leaving the low-cost leader in a monopoly position. Customers lose their power, and pay higher prices, when forced to buy from a firm operating in an industry without rivals.

**Bargaining Power of Suppliers**  A firm with the low-cost position in an industry operates with margins greater than those of its competitors. Among other benefits, these margins make it possible for the low-cost firm to absorb price increases from suppliers. When an industry is faced with substantial increases in the cost of its supplies, the low-cost leader may be the only one able to pay the higher prices and still earn above-average profits. Alternatively, powerful low-cost leaders (those with large market shares) may be able to force suppliers to hold down their prices, reducing their power in the process.

**Potential Entrants**  Because of their lower margins (relative to the margins earned by firms successfully implementing the differentiation strategy) low-cost leaders must sell large volumes of their product to achieve superior profitability. Recall, for example, that Unifi produces a quantity of polyester yarn that results in the firm holding a 70 percent market share. Through continuous investments to drive costs even lower, low-cost leaders become very efficient. Ever-improving levels of efficiency serve as a significant entry barrier to an industry. New entrants must be willing to accept no better than average profits until they gain the experience required to approach the efficiency of the low-cost leader. To earn even average profits, new entrants must have the competencies required to match the cost levels of all competitors other than the low-cost leader.

**Product Substitutes**   As compared to its industry rivals, the low-cost leader holds an attractive position in terms of product substitutes. When faced with the possibility of a substitute, the low-cost leader has more flexibility than does its competitors. For example, to retain customers, the low-cost leader can reduce the price of its product. With still lower prices and features of acceptable quality, the low-cost leader increases the probability that customers will prefer its product, rather than a substitute.

## Competitive Risks of the Cost Leadership Strategy

The cost leadership strategy is not without risks. For example, the low-cost leader's manufacturing equipment could become obsolete through technological innovations by competitors. These innovations may allow rivals to produce at costs lower than those of the original cost leader. Sometimes, because of their focus on continuously driving costs lower, firms implementing a cost leadership strategy fail to detect significant changes in customers' needs or in competitors' efforts to differentiate what has traditionally been a commodity-like product.

In a recent year, for example, MCI Communications turned a classic commodity business—common-carrier long-distance service—into a differentiated service. To customize its long-distance service, MCI developed a brand name to outpace AT&T, its primary rival. Called Friends and Family, this program provides customers with a 20 percent discount to as many as 22 other MCI users. As an extension of this brand name, MCI formed the Friends Around the World program for international calls. The positive responses to these programs suggest that MCI found a way to provide value to customers and that its efforts to differentiate a commodity product had the potential to enhance the firm's strategic competitiveness.[35] Also, even though AT&T's commitment to gaining global market share appeared to be succeeding in the mid 1990s (see the opening case in Chapter 1), the firm should verify that it simultaneously remains focused on its domestic U.S. market as well.

A final risk of the cost leadership strategy concerns imitation. Competitors sometimes learn how to successfully imitate the low-cost leader's strategy. When this occurs, the low-cost leader is challenged to find ways to increase the value provided by its good or service. Usually, value is increased by selling the current product at an even lower price or by adding features while maintaining price.

## Differentiation Strategy

When implementing the differentiation strategy, the *unique* attributes and characteristics of a firm's product (other than cost) provide value to customers. Because a differentiated product satisfies customers' unique needs, the firm can often charge a premium price. It is the ability to sell its differentiated product at a price that exceeds what was spent to create it that allows the firm to outperform its rivals and earn superior profits. As shown by two of this chapter's Strategic Focus segments, Liz Claiborne and Yamaha selected a differentiation strategy for some of their product lines.

The differentiator's premium price is typically greater than that of the cost leader. Accompanying highly differentiated products is the image of exclusivity. Thus, a firm implementing the differentiation strategy typically does not hold large shares of the markets it serves. While costs cannot be ignored, they are not the primary focus when implementing the differentiation strategy. The focus instead is on continuously investing in and developing features that differentiate products in ways that customers value.

The ways a product's features can be differentiated are almost endless. Superior quality, unusual features, responsive customer service, rapid product innovations and technological leadership, perceived prestige and status, different tastes, engineering design and performance are examples of approaches to differentiation. In fact, virtually anything a firm can do to create value for customers is a basis for differentiating a product. Arizona Iced Tea, for example, seems to provide value to customers primarily through its unique packaging. Chosen as one of 1993's "Products of the Year" by *Fortune* magazine, this product was introduced to the market by a small, privately held Brooklyn brewing company named Ferolito Vultaggio & Sons. This company was able to differentiate what is essentially a commodity product by packaging iced tea in cans with an attractive Southwestern look.[36] Overall, a firm using the differentiation strategy wants to be differentiated from competitors along as many dimensions as possible. The less the similarity between a firm's goods or services and those of its competitors is, the more buffered the firm is from its rivals.

Another dimension on which products have been differentiated is perceptual image orchestration. For example, because it has been able to give its products a prestigious image through advertising and other actions, the French cosmetics giant L'Oreal is able to charge more for its *everyday* cosmetics. The value of the prestige these products provide to customers appears to be significant, even during recessionary times. L'Oreal's sales records show that, even when faced with a difficult economic environment, customers are still willing to treat themselves to a $75 (and up) bottle of the firm's perfume.[37] Thus, seeking to manage the perceptual image of the product can create differentiation and customer loyalty.

Commonly recognized differentiated products include Toyota's Lexus ("the relentless pursuit of perfection"), Ralph Lauren's clothing lines (image), Caterpillar (a heavy-equipment manufacturing firm committed to providing rapid delivery of spare parts to any location in the world), Maytag appliances (product reliability), McKinsey & Co. (the most high priced and prestigious consulting firm in the world),[38] and Rolex watches (prestige and image). Less commonly known differentiated products include the wave of New Age beverages (e.g., Clearly Canadian, 2 Calorie Quest, and Welch's Sparkling Water Refresher),[39] Guiltless Gourmet's baked (not fried) tortilla chips,[40] and Pleasant Co.'s dolls.

To differentiate its products from competitors' offerings, Pleasant Co. manufactures and distributes a mail-order line of historical dolls—dolls intended to teach U.S. history, family values, and self-reliance. Even at a cost of $82 for one of the company's five basic dolls (this figure can be as high as $1,000 if all accessories are purchased), the firm's sales volume increased over 40 percent between 1992 and 1993.[41]

A firm's value chain can also be used to determine if a firm can effectively and efficiently link the activities required to create value through implementation of the differentiation strategy. Examples of primary and support activities that are commonly used to differentiate a product are shown in Figure 4-3. Companies without the core competencies required to link these activities cannot expect to successfully implement the differentiation strategy.

As with the cost leadership strategy, successful implementation of the differentiation strategy allows a firm to earn superior profits in spite of the presence of strong competitive forces.

**Rivalry with Existing Competitors** Customers tend to be loyal purchasers of products that are differentiated in ways meaningful to them. As their loyalty to a brand increases, their sensitivity to price increases lessens. This relationship between brand loyalty and price sensitivity insulates a firm from competitive rivalry. Thus, McKinsey & Co. is insulated from its competitors, even on the basis of price, as long as it continues to satisfy the differentiated needs of what appears to be a loyal customer group.

**Bargaining Power of Buyers (Customers)** Differentiated goods or services are considered unique. This uniqueness insulates the firm from competitive rivalry and reduces customers' sensitivity to price increases. Dolls manufactured by Pleasant Co., for example, satisfy customers' unique needs for a product that both

**FIGURE 4–3 Examples of Value-Creating Activities Associated with the Differentiation Strategy**

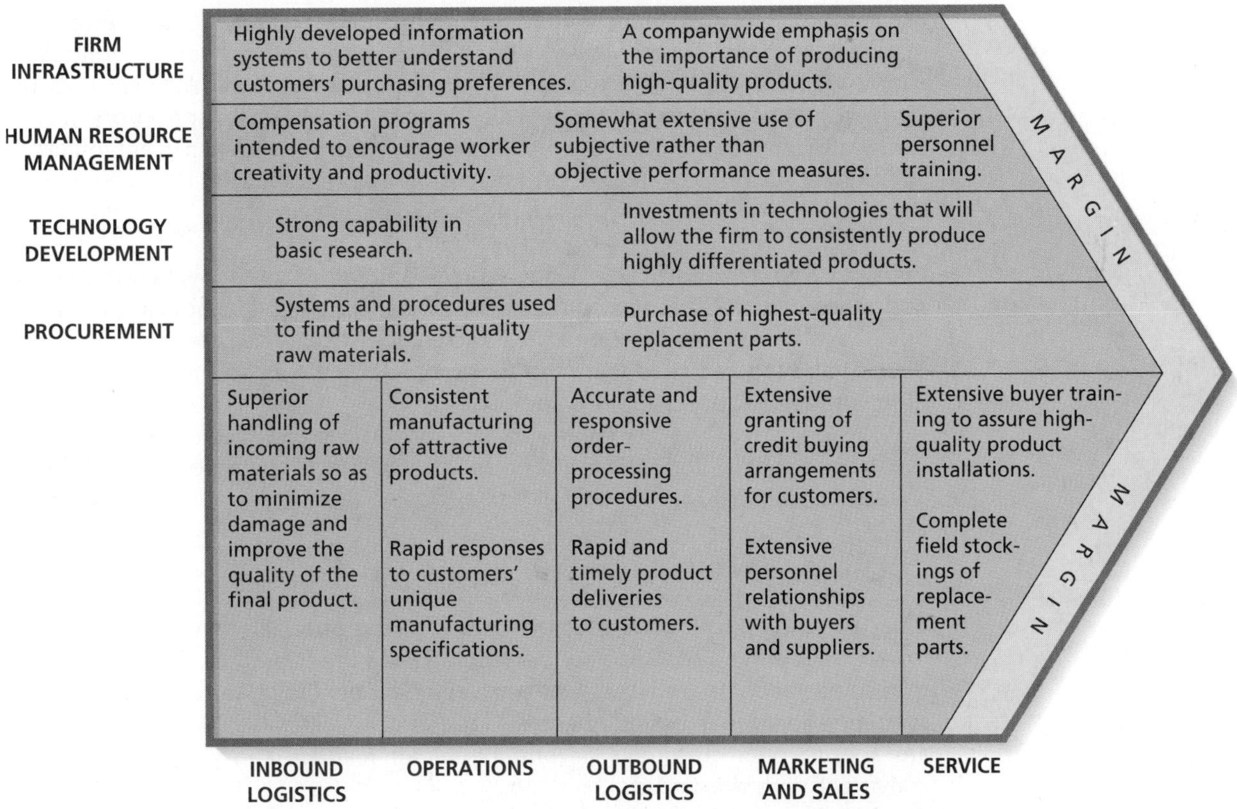
FIRM INFRASTRUCTURE
Highly developed information systems to better understand customers' purchasing preferences.
A companywide emphasis on the importance of producing high-quality products.
HUMAN RESOURCE MANAGEMENT
Compensation programs intended to encourage worker creativity and productivity.
Somewhat extensive use of subjective rather than objective performance measures.
Superior personnel training.
TECHNOLOGY DEVELOPMENT
Strong capability in basic research.
Investments in technologies that will allow the firm to consistently produce highly differentiated products.
PROCUREMENT
Systems and procedures used to find the highest-quality raw materials.
Purchase of highest-quality replacement parts.
Superior handling of incoming raw materials so as to minimize damage and improve the quality of the final product.
Consistent manufacturing of attractive products.
Rapid responses to customers' unique manufacturing specifications.
Accurate and responsive order-processing procedures.
Rapid and timely product deliveries to customers.
Extensive granting of credit buying arrangements for customers.
Extensive personnel relationships with buyers and suppliers.
Extensive buyer training to assure high-quality product installations.
Complete field stockings of replacement parts.
MARGIN
MARGIN
INBOUND LOGISTICS
OPERATIONS
OUTBOUND LOGISTICS
MARKETING AND SALES
SERVICE

*SOURCE: Adapted and reprinted with the permission of The Free Press, an imprint of Simon & Schuster from COMPETITIVE ADVANTAGE: Creating and Sustaining Superior Performance by Michael Porter, Fig. 4-1, 22. Copyright © 1985 by Michael E. Porter.*

entertains and educates their children. The following words of Pleasant Co.'s president describe her image of the firm's product: "We're in the little-girl business, not the doll business. We want to have a positive impact on their lives."[42] Thus, this firm's product seeks to satisfy customer needs that are not served by its competitors' offerings. A key reason buyers are willing to pay a premium price for these dolls is that there are no comparable product alternatives.

**Bargaining Power of Suppliers**   Because a firm implementing the differentiation strategy charges a premium price for its products, suppliers must provide it with high-quality parts. However, the high margins the firm earns when selling effectively differentiated products partially insulate it from the influence of suppliers. Typically, higher supplier costs can be paid through these margins. Alternatively, because of buyers' relative insensitivity to price increases, the differentiated firm might choose to pass the additional cost of supplies on to the customer by raising the price of its unique product.

**Potential Entrants**   Customers' loyalty and the need to overcome the uniqueness of a differentiated product are substantial entry barriers faced by potential entrants. Entering an industry under these conditions typically demands significant investments of resources and a willingness to be patient while seeking the loyalty of customers.

Interestingly, however, evidence suggests that Japanese manufacturers have been able to enter and compete effectively in the luxury segment of the automobile market long dominated by Mercedes-Benz, BMW, and a few other companies. This entry was successful for a number of reasons. A key reason may be that the Japanese luxury cars seem to provide differentiated features similar to those of their competitors, but at a substantially lower purchase price (up to 40 percent lower). In addition to providing value to current customers, this reduced cost allows new customers to enter the luxury automobile market.

**Product Substitutes**   Firms selling brand-name products to loyal customers are positioned effectively against product substitutes. In contrast, companies without brand loyalty are more subject to their customers switching either to products that offer similar differentiated features, but at a lower price, or to products that offer more attractive features at the same price.

As our discussion has shown, firms can gain competitive advantage through successful implementation of the differentiation strategy. Nonetheless, several risks are associated with this strategy.

## Competitive Risks of the Differentiation Strategy

One risk is that customers might decide that the price differential between the low-cost producer's product and the differentiated firm's product is too significant. In this instance, a firm may be providing differentiated features that exceed customers' needs. When this happens, the firm is vulnerable to competitors that are able to offer customers a combination of features and price that is more consistent with their needs.

Another risk of the differentiation strategy is that a firm's means of differentiation may no longer provide value to customers. As an example, consider that for some customers the prestige of purchasing L'Oreal perfume, as an everyday cosmetic, may no longer be worth the product's premium price. The need for differentiated features tends to decrease as buyers become more sophisticated.

A third risk of the differentiation strategy is that customer learning can narrow customers' perceptions of the value of a firm's differentiated features. The value of the IBM name on personal computers was a differentiated feature for which some customers were willing to pay as the product emerged. However, as customers familiarized themselves with the standard features and as a host of PC clones entered the market, IBM brand loyalty began to fail. Clones offered customers features similar to those of the IBM product at a substantially lower price, reducing the attractiveness of the IBM product.

## Focus Strategies

Through both the cost leadership and the differentiation strategies, a firm seeks to exploit its core competencies on an industrywide basis to gain competitive advantage. In contrast, a firm seeks to use its core competencies to serve the needs of a particular customer group in an industry when implementing a **focus strategy.** Thus, through successful implementation of a focus strategy, a firm can gain a competitive advantage in its chosen target segments even though it does not possess an industrywide competitive advantage.[43] The foundation of focus strategies is that a firm can serve a narrow industry segment more effectively or efficiently than can industrywide competitors. Success with a focus strategy rests on a firm's ability to either find segments where unique needs are so specialized that broad-based competitors choose not to serve them or locate a customer segment being served poorly by the broad-based competitors.[44] Value can be provided to customers through two types of focus strategies—focused low-cost and focused differentiation.

▲ A **focus strategy** is implemented when a firm seeks to use its core competencies to serve the needs of a particular customer group in an industry.

**Focused Low-Cost Strategy**   Liuski International, a wholesale distributor of personal computers, uses the focused low-cost strategy. Liuski targets the smallest buyers in the market. Typically, these customers spend approximately $700 per order. The firm sells 1,400 different personal computers (PCs) and accessories that are made by dozens of manufacturing companies, including Seagate, Samsung, and Toshiba.

Key to successful implementation of Liuski's focused low-cost strategy is the firm's decision to locate its distribution warehouses close to its customers. In late 1993, Liuski had eight warehouses in the United States, one in Canada, and another one planned for the United States. Through these well-placed outlets, the firm is able to deliver products to most of its customers within a single day.

Liuski also differs from other distributors in that it manufactures and distributes its own private-label, IBM-compatible PCs and components. Sold under the name Magitronic, these products are manufactured in Taiwan and assembled in the United States. Through this production method, Liuski keeps its costs low, while developing products suited specifically for small buyers' needs. Evidence suggests that its strategy allows Liuski to achieve strategic competitiveness. One of the fastest-growing companies in the industry, the firm's net income increased 41 percent in 1993 on a 29 percent increase in revenues.[45]

Rally's fast food restaurants also implement the focused low-cost strategy. Using a double-drive-through format, the restaurants have limited menus and do not have indoor seats for customers. According to the firm's CEO, Rally's serves

A Rally's restaurant focuses its efforts on a particular type of customer. People purchasing food items from Rally's seek low price, fast service, and product quality. The fact that Rally's is one of the fastest-growing restaurant chains in the United States suggests that the firm is achieving strategic competitiveness through implementation of a focused low-cost strategy.

"the little-spare-time-or-cash crowd that McDonald's and Burger King have all but abandoned." Concentrating on the basics of price and speed of service, the firm recently sold, and delivered to the customer in 45 seconds, a "fully-dressed" burger, a 16-ounce soft drink, and a good-sized fries for $1.97.[46]

How still another firm achieves strategic competitiveness and earns superior profits through implementation of the focused low-cost strategy is described in the next Strategic Focus on Cooper Tire & Rubber.

**Focused Differentiation Strategy**   Other firms use the focused differentiation strategy in the pursuit of strategic competitiveness. Competing on a global basis, Superior Industries is the world's largest manufacturer of aluminum wheels for the original equipment market. Although most of its wheels are sold to U.S. automakers (51 percent to Ford and 47 percent to General Motors in a recent year), Superior is expanding its shipments to Japanese automakers (Nissan, in particular). Primarily because of their weight advantage, compared to wheels made of steel, aluminum wheels improve both fuel efficiency and handling. However, they are also more expensive than steel wheels. As a result, Superior's product is still used by automobile manufacturers principally for their higher-priced car and truck models.[47]

Custom Chrome also implements the focused differentiation strategy. Focusing on the after-market (sales made to customers after their purchase of the original product), this company designs and distributes over 9,500 engine parts for only Harley-Davidson motorcycles. As a global competitor, the firm sells its products in the United States, Europe, and Japan. Selling under different brand names, including RevTech, C.C. Rider, and Premium, Custom Chrome can supply parts for Harley models built as long ago as 1936.[48]

Building a host of products from simple steel cabinets housing electrical and electronic components to complete canning lines, In-Land Technologies Services (ITS) is a global firm implementing the focused differentiation strategy. In only its third year of business, one-third of the company's sales were exported to markets outside the United States. Emerson Electric, PepsiCo, Miller Brewing, and Olin are some of ITS's customers. The source of the firm's competitive advantage is its

## STRATEGIC FOCUS

### Strategic Consistency and Profitability at Cooper Tire & Rubber

During the 1980s, Cooper Tire & Rubber's performance was outstanding. The stock price increased an impressive 6,800 percent over this decade. Between 1980 and 1992, the company ranked 28th in total returns to investors—stock appreciation plus dividends—on *Fortune's* 500 Industrials list. Cooper was able to achieve all of this while choosing not to compete in the original-equipment sales to automobile manufacturers (OEM) market. Cooper continues to be the only major tire maker not competing for OEM sales. The company focuses exclusively on the replacement market, which in the early 1990s was three times larger and growing faster than the OEM market. Because of its focus strategy, Cooper ranks ninth in sales volume among tire manufacturers (and behind large firms such as Goodyear, Michelin, and Bridgestone/Firestone).

Cooper provides value to customers through its focused low-cost strategy. All aspects of its operations are geared toward driving costs lower. Its corporate headquarters building, linoleum floors intact, is located in Findlay, Ohio. The building is similar in appearance to an elementary school. Cooper's annual report, which is very basic in its appearance and content, is printed in black and white to control costs. The firm does not have its own retail outlets (as do Goodyear and Bridgestone/Firestone). Instead, Cooper sells half of its production as private-label merchandise through oil companies, large independent distributors, and mass marketers such as Western Auto Supply and Pep Boys. The remaining half of its tires are sold to independent dealers, that account for 67 percent of total replacement tire sales. These dealers enjoy working with Cooper because it does not have its own retail outlets. As a result, unlike Goodyear and Bridgestone/Firestone, Cooper is not competing for retail sales with its distributors.

Over the years, Cooper's investments have been made with the objective of being an extremely efficient tire manufacturer. The efficiency levels it has achieved work to its dealers' advantage. Because of its efficiency, Cooper provides dealers with the highest gross profit margin in the industry—33 percent. This margin compares very favorably with the average of 28 percent allowed dealers by competing brands. But as should be the case with firms implementing the low-cost strategy, Cooper constantly seeks ways to become even more efficient in its manufacturing operations. In the words of the firm's chief financial officer, "If you are making 20 million tires a year and you can take ten seconds out of the curing process, just think how much capacity you free up." For example, because of changes made in materials flow and production scheduling processes, the inventory in Cooper's Texarkana, Arkansas, plant is now turned ten times a year instead of the more common turn of three to five times.

To further reduce costs, Cooper runs its plants at 100 percent capacity (the industry average is 80 percent). When it desires to add capacity, it does so cheaply. This is accomplished by purchasing old plants and retrofitting them. Recently, for example, Cooper purchased a defunct Mansfield Tire & Rubber plant in Tupelo, Mississippi. Following retrofitting, this facility now operates 24 hours a day, 7 days a week.

The company also saves on R&D expenditures. Cooper is not interested in pioneering tire designs; instead, the company typically waits to see what tires sell well as original equipment. In the opinion of the company's CEO, this approach works because all Cooper "has to do is produce the winners."

ability to custom manufacture many different products. ITS's market is an array of market niches—50 or so cabinets for one customer, a fully-equipped control room for another one. The firm handles jobs that are too specialized for individual customers to build for themselves and too small for industrywide competitors to handle economically.[49]

As with the cost leadership and the differentiation strategies, firms must be able to complete various primary and support activities in a competitively superior manner in order to achieve strategic competitiveness when implementing a focus strategy. The activities that must be completed for the focused low-cost strategy and the focused differentiation strategy are virtually identical to those shown in Figure 4-2 and 4-3, respectively. Similarly, the manners in which the two focus strategies allow a firm to deal successfully with the five competitive forces parallel those described with respect to the cost leadership and the differentiated strategies. The only difference is that the competitive scope changes from industrywide to a narrow segment of the industry. Thus, reviewing Figures 4-2 and 4-3 and the text regarding the five competitive forces provides the relationship between the focus strategies and competitive advantage.

## Competitive Risks of Focus Strategies

When implementing either type of focus strategy, a firm faces the same general risks as does the company pursuing either the cost leadership or the differentiation strategy on an industrywide basis. However, focus strategies have three additional risks beyond these general ones. First, a competitor may be able to focus on an even more narrowly defined segment and "outfocus" the focuser. Second, a firm competing on an industrywide basis may decide that the market segment being served by the focus strategy firm is attractive and worthy of competitive pursuit. Burger King, for example, has built stores with double-drive-throughs and walk-up windows in certain areas to serve the more narrow segment identified by Rally's and other focusers.[50] With its superior resource base, the larger firm may be able to better serve the needs of a narrow segment. Finally, the needs of customers within a narrow segment may become more similar to those of customers as a whole. When this occurs, the advantages of a focus strategy are either reduced or eliminated.

Next we describe a business-level strategy that may be used more frequently in the latter part of the 1990s and into the twenty-first century because of global competition.

## Integrated Low-Cost/Differentiation Strategy

Particularly in global markets, a firm's ability to blend the low-cost and the differentiation approaches may be critical to sustaining competitive advantages in the 1990s and into the twenty-first century.[51] Compared to firms relying on one dominant generic strategy for their success, a company capable of successfully implementing an integrated low-cost/differentiation strategy should be better positioned to adapt quickly to environmental changes, learn new skills and technologies more quickly, and effectively leverage their core competencies across business units and product lines.

Mercedes, Porsche, and Jaguar and, to an even greater extent, Rolls Royce are perceived to be high-value competitors that follow a differentiation strategy. On the other hand, Toyota, Ford, and Volkswagen can be described generally as competing on low delivered costs and associated pricing. The advent of a car such as the Lexus (Toyota) reveals there are opportunities to combine high perceived value through differentiation with the low-cost strategy.

Firms able to provide customers with products that have differentiated features they value at a relatively low cost can earn superior profits.[52] A key reason for this is that the benefits of the integrated strategy are additive—"differentiation leads to premium prices at the same time that cost leadership implies lower costs."[53] Thus, this strategy allows firms to gain competitive advantage by offering degrees of two types of value to customers—some differentiated features (but not as many as are provided by the product-differentiated firm) and a relatively low cost (but not as low as the products of the low-cost leader).

How Southwest Airlines is creating value and earning superior profits through use of the integrated low-cost/differentiation strategy is described in the Strategic Focus. How many companies employ a top-level manager to focus on customers' needs? Probably not too many. Nonetheless, this position reflects Southwest Airline's commitment to fully understanding customers' needs so the firm can simultaneously drive its costs lower, while offering valuable differentiated features to its customers.

In early 1994, Southwest used the industry's switch to digital telephone systems in the air as a means of further differentiating its distinctive service from that of competitors. Through use of new digital telephone systems, Southwest Airline's passengers were able to use the on-board phone system to transmit computer files or faxes from their laptops to computers on the ground. Southwest was the first carrier to offer this service, capturing first-mover advantages in the process (first-mover advantages are explained in Chapter 5). By the middle of 1995, however, the majority of jet fleets in the United States are expected to offer this service.[54] Thus, Southwest offered this convenience early in order to differentiate its service from that of competitors. Consistent with the demands of the integrated low-cost/differentiation strategy, Southwest's focus is on reducing its costs, while offering some valuable differentiated features to customers.

Following their study of Southwest Airlines, some analysts concluded that the firm's core competence is its culture—a culture that calls for the company to be committed to providing value to customers in terms of both low cost and differentiated features. To date, competitors have been unable to duplicate the benefits of this strategy.[55] As such, Southwest's integrated low-cost/differentiation strategy appears to be creating strategic competitiveness and superior profitability. Other firms recognized for their ability to achieve strategic competitiveness through this strategy include Toyota, Campbell Soup, Siemens, and Canon.

Several interrelated conditions make it possible for firms to gain competitive advantage and earn superior profits through implementation of the integrated low-cost/differentiation strategy.

**Flexible Manufacturing Systems**   A **flexible manufacturing system** (FMS) is a computer-controlled process used to produce a variety of products in moderate, flexible quantities.[56] The goal of FMS is to eliminate the low-cost versus product-variety trade-off inherent in traditional manufacturing technologies. When used properly, an FMS can help a firm become more flexible in response to changes in its customers' needs, while retaining low-cost advantages and consistent product quality. An FMS reduces the lot size needed to manufacture a firm's product

▲ A **flexible manufacturing system** (FMS) is a computer-controlled process used to produce a variety of products in moderate, flexible quantities.

## STRATEGIC FOCUS

### Keeping Promises at Southwest Airlines

During 1993, Southwest Airlines increased its passenger traffic 20 percent as it expanded from its Southwest base into eastern U.S. markets. Most airline carriers experienced net losses in 1993, but not Southwest. In fact, Southwest earned its highest profits ever in 1993 and was once again the most profitable carrier among major airlines.

What are the secrets to Southwest Airline's strategic competitiveness? Some analysts believe the answer to this question lies in the firm's ability to break company rules (when necessary) in order to keep promises to its customers. An incident described by the firm's executive vice president for customers shows what Southwest Airlines will do to serve customers.

As the door to a Boeing 737 closed so a flight could depart, a Southwest Airline's pilot noticed a ticket holder running down the jetway. Because the plane was pulling back from the jetway, the customer appeared to be too late. Having spotted the anguished look on the customer's face, however, the pilot returned to the gate to rescue the traveler from his predicament. In the words of Southwest's executive vice president for customers, "It broke every rule in the book, but we congratulated the pilot on a job well done."

Other actions contribute more consistently to Southwest Airline's strategic competitiveness. For example, surveys show, time and time again, that when given a choice, customers prefer lower fares. Southwest responds aggressively to this need—its fares are often one-third those of competitors. Not providing meals and assigned seating are among the many actions the company takes to drive its costs lower. Southwest also understands that customers want to be on time. Accordingly, the firm is the "pinnacle of punctuality." Part of the reason its planes are punctual is that their point-to-point routes bypass most congested hubs.

Competitors can duplicate Southwest Airline's prices, but not its personal marketing competence. Frequent fliers receive birthday cards. If a plane is delayed in takeoff or landing, customer service agents orchestrate games in efforts to relieve tension and keep customers satisfied. One of these is called "Guess the Gate Agent's Weight." Dissatisfied customers often receive something from the company to smooth their feathers—a stuffed bear, a T-shirt, or some other knickknack—in addition to a commitment to solve their concerns.

One of Southwest Airlines most important commitments to customer service is shown by the latitude provided its employees. When difficulties do arise, the firm's employees have the power to resolve them, more so than at other airlines. For example, "one customer—irate because his snarling, pony-size dog was not permitted aboard—discovered what service really means when a customer service agent took care of the beast for the duration of the flier's two-week vacation."

Because the service commitments and actions provided to Southwest customers are not standardized, they are difficult for competitors to duplicate. The culture is largely credited to the company's CEO, who believes that passengers want to be treated like human beings even though they may be paying a low price for the services they receive. The words of the firm's executive vice president for customers effectively capture the commitment to customers: "Rules are great, programs are great, but the bottom line is to do the right thing" for customers.

*Herb Kelleher, above, is the CEO of Southwest Airlines. Some analysts believe that the primary core competence this firm uses to achieve strategic competitiveness while operating in a highly competitive and turbulent environment is its culture. Organizational cultures are complex, and their development is difficult to understand. Nonetheless, Kelleher has played a major role in the evolution of what appears to be a unique organizational culture at Southwest Airlines.*

efficiently. Because of this, the firm's capacity to engage in niche marketing is increased. Thus, FMS technology is a significant technological advance that allows a firm to produce a large variety of products at a low cost.

**Information Networks Across Firms**   New information networks that link manufacturers with their suppliers and customers is another technological development that increases a firm's strategic flexibility and responsiveness. Ford Motor Co., Allen Bradley, Hitachi, Motorola, and Boeing all use information linkages to coordinate their product design and development activities. These computer-based information linkages substantially reduce the time needed to conceive and test new products and allow a firm to compete on the basis of fast delivery (a differentiated feature) and low cost. Campbell Soup is making significant investments in modern integrated networks. These networks also facilitate just-in-time (JIT) inventory control systems. Such systems allow for more product variety, while keeping cost lower. Through these linkages, the firm has been able to produce a greater variety and mix of products at a lower cost.

**Total Quality Management Systems**   Many firms have established total quality management (TQM) systems for improving product value and productivity.[57] Improved quality focuses the attention of customers on improvements in product performance, feature utility, and reliability. This allows a firm to achieve differentiation and ultimately higher prices and market share. Emphasis on quality in production techniques lowers manufacturing and service costs through savings in rework, scrap, and warranty expenses. This provides a cost advantage. Thus, TQM programs integrate aspects of differentiation and cost leadership. TQM techniques are described in more detail in Chapter 5.

Schlitz Brewing Co. discovered the cost of not maintaining quality.[58] In the early 1970s, Schlitz was the second largest brewer next to Anheuser-Busch. It then started a program that focused on cost cutting. For instance, it reduced the quality of its ingredients by switching to corn syrup and hop pellets and shortened the brewing cycle by 50 percent. In the short term, this change improved the firm's financial performance as measured by return on assets. Over time, however, customers recognized the inferior product, and Schlitz lost market share. By 1980, its sales had declined 40 percent, and its stock price fell from $69 to $5. The company was eventually sold.

As with the other business-level strategies, there are risks associated with use of the integrated low-cost/differentiation strategy.

**Competitive Risks of the Integrated Low-Cost/Differentiation Strategy**
The potential of the integrated strategy, in terms of superior profitability, is significant. However, this potential is accompanied by high risk. Selecting a business-level strategy calls for firms to make choices about how they intend to compete. Achieving the low-cost position in an industry, or a segment of an industry in the case of a focus strategy, demands that the firm strive consistently to reduce its costs. Use of the differentiation strategy, with either an industrywide or a focused competitive scope (see Figure 4-1), results in superior profitability only when the firm provides customers with differentiated products which they value and for which they are willing to pay a premium price.

## Continental Ag and Pirelli Experience Difficulties With Their U.S. Tire Ventures

Unlike Cooper Tire, Germany's Continental AG and Italy's Pirelli SpA are finding the U.S. market agonizing as they try to compete across all market segments in the United States—"from high-performance, name-brand tires to the low-cost private-label ones that stores sell under their own brand names." They are experiencing tough competition from big rivals such as Michelin and Goodyear, which can withstand slim profit margins. They are also getting squeezed by chain stores that dominate sales and pressure for lower prices.

Both firms purchased U.S. tire manufacturers in the late 1980s and have had repeated restructuring changes in trying to turn around their U.S. brands. Continental, the world's fourth largest tire manufacturer, bought General Tire, Inc., for $628 million and has sunk an additional $750 million into the operation. Pirelli bought Armstrong Tire Corp. for $196 million and added another $120 million to improve results. However, both U.S. operations continue to lose money.

Some have suggested that these two units merge to solve their difficulties. However, a big impediment to such a merger is the memory of an unfriendly takeover of Continental by Pirelli in 1990 that failed. Furthermore, neither firm has reason to think that increased size will cure its difficulties. Guiseppe Bencisni, head of Pirelli's tire business, says that "Pirelli's tire business has got a more than sufficient critical mass" worldwide. Also, Continental is profitable worldwide, and its "prime goal" now is to reform its U.S. unit. Thus, there is little felt need for the two firms to merge or form a cooperative strategic alliance.

Continental's lack of consistent strategy for General has added to General's difficulties. In 1988, Continental pushed General away from manufacturing private-label products. Later it reversed course. Now Continental is pushing to use General's facilities to make and sell Continental-brand tires. Associated with the shifting strategic emphases has been a high level of turnover of key personnel. Alan Okene is the third U.S. president of General since 1987. Between August 1993 and March 1994, the company replaced or eliminated 8 of its 19 vice presidents and reorganized sales and management. There is definitely a "communication problem" between the U.S. unit and Continental's German headquarters.

With these management difficulties and resulting production problems, a poor quality image has hurt General. Although Okene indicated that quality has improved, an image of poor quality changes slowly. In fact, quality complaints provoked Big O Tires, a large tire store chain in the Southwest, to drop General as a producer of its private-label brand. Hot roads in the Southwest are hard on tires, and this was costly for Big O because tire returns on its warranty increased. Although Big O had noticed improved tire quality, it was too late to save the relationship. In regard to Continental's difficulties, one analyst suggested, "Continental needs to choose, worldwide, between becoming a market giant, through merger, or shrinking to become a niche player" like Cooper.

A firm failing to consistently establish a leadership position in its industry, as the low-cost producer or as a differentiator, risks becoming "stuck-in-the-middle."[59] Such an unattractive position in the industry prevents the firm from dealing successfully with the five competitive forces and from earning above-average profits. Moreover, the firm stuck in the middle can earn average profits only when an industry's structure is highly favorable or when the firm is competing against others that are also stuck in the middle.[60] This unattractive position typically results when a firm fails to make consistent choices in terms of the demands of the business-level strategy it has chosen to use in the pursuit of strategic competitiveness. The Strategic Focus on page 122 illustrates the difficulty of trying to implement an integrated strategy on a global basis.

The Continental and Pirelli examples illustrate the major risk of the integrated low-cost/differentiation strategy. These firms, in their efforts to provide a product with some differentiated features that customers value at a relatively low cost, are failing in their efforts. When this happens, the firm finds itself producing a product without features valued by any customer. The firm's products are too expensive to compete with the low-cost producer's product and too undifferentiated to provide the value offered by the differentiated firms' goods or services. The difficulty of pursuing the dual strategy in global markets only increases, especially in a very competitive industry such as tires. Cooper Tire has been much more successful pursuing its OEM replacement (focus) strategy.

Once a firm has selected its business-level strategy, it must both anticipate and be prepared to respond to competitors' actions and responses. The dynamics of competition that occur as firms implement business-level strategies are examined in the next chapter.

## Summary

- A strategy is an integrated and coordinated set of actions taken to exploit core competencies and gain a competitive advantage. A firm's success, as measured by strategic competitiveness and superior profitability, is a function of its ability to develop and exploit new core competencies faster than competitors can mimic the competitive advantages yielded by current ones.

- Business-level strategies, which are coordinated actions taken in specific product markets, are the focus of this chapter. Cost leadership, differentiation, focused low-cost, focused differentiation, and integrated low-cost/differentiation are the five business-level strategies examined in the chapter. The cost leadership strategy calls for firms to provide products with features acceptable to customers at the lowest competitive price. In contrast, the differentiation strategy calls for firms to provide products that customers perceive as being unique in ways that are important to them. For both of these strategies, a firm's targeted customer market is broad. Focus strategies call for firms to specialize—that is, to provide superior service to a narrow segment of a market through either cost leadership or differentiation. With the integrated low-cost/differentiation strategy, firms intend to provide products with differentiated features that customers value, but at a low cost.

- Successful business-level strategies are founded on customers' needs. When considering customers, a firm simultaneously examines three issues—*who, what,* and *how.* Respectively, these issues cause the firm to determine the customer groups it will serve, the needs those customers have that it seeks to satisfy, and the core competencies it possesses that can be used to satisfy customers' needs. The increasing segmentation of markets occurring throughout the world creates multiple opportunities for a firm to identify unique customer needs. Satisfying these needs effectively helps a firm achieve strategic competitiveness.

- Firms seeking competitive advantage through the cost leadership strategy typically produce and sell no-frill, standardized products to an industry's average or typical customer. Superior profitability is earned through this strategy when firms continuously drive their costs lower than those of their competitors, while providing customers with acceptable levels of differentiated features in their products.

- Competitive risks associated with the cost leadership strategy include (1) a loss of competitive advantage to newer technologies purchased or developed by competitors, (2) a failure to detect changes in customers' needs (usually this is caused by a firm's singular focus on driving its costs lower), and (3) the ability of competitors to imitate the low-cost leader's competitive advantages through their own unique strategic actions.

- The differentiation strategy calls for firms to provide customers with products that have unique (and valued) attributes and characteristics. Because of their uniqueness, differentiated products are sold at a premium price. Thus, the value offered to customers by differentiated products is something other than cost. Products can be differentiated along any dimension that some group of customers values. These dimensions include quality, service, technological sophistication, engineering design and performance, and rapid product innovations. Firms using this strategy want to be differentiated from competitors along as many dimensions as possible. The less the similarity with competitors, the more buffered a firm is from competition with its rivals.

- Risks associated with the differentiation strategy include (1) a customer group's decision that the differences between the differentiated product and the standardized product (as provided by the low-cost producer) are not worth the differentiated product's premium price, (2) the inability of a differentiated product to create the type of value for which customers are willing to pay a premium price (this tends to happen as buyers become more sophisticated), and (3) the ability of competitors to provide customers with products that have features similar to those associated with the differentiated product, but at a lower cost.

- Unlike with the cost leadership and the differentiation strategies, firms use a focus strategy to serve the specialized needs of a narrow segment of a market. This strategy is successful when firms have the core competencies required to provide value to a particular customer group that exceeds the value available from firms serving the typical customer in an entire industry. This value can be provided through either a product's low cost or its differentiated features.

- As with the other business-level strategies, focus strategies have competitive risks. These risks include (1) a competitor's ability to use its core competencies to "outfocus" the focuser by serving an even more narrowly defined segment of the market (2) decisions by industrywide competitors to use their resources to serve the customers' specialized needs that the focuser has been serving, and (3) a reduction in differences of the needs between customers in a narrow market segment and the total market.

- Firms using the integrated low-cost/differentiation strategy strive to provide customers with relatively low cost products that have some differentiated features they value. This business-level strategy may become increasingly appropriate for use in the global economy—an economy in which a growing number of firms have developed the core competencies required to produce a large variety of products at relatively low costs.

- The primary risk of the integrated low-cost/differentiation strategy is that firms will produce products that do not offer sufficient value—in terms of either low cost or differentiation. Although this is a difficult business-level strategy to implement successfully, the rewards accompanying its effective use, in terms of strategic competitiveness and superior profitability, are attractive.

## Review Questions

1. How is strategy defined in this chapter? What are business-level strategies?

2. What is the relationship between a firm's customers and its business-level strategy, and why is this relationship important?

3. When studying customers in terms of *who, what,* and *how,* what questions are firms trying to answer?
4. What is the integrated low-cost/differentiation strategy? Why is the value of this business-level strategy increasing?
5. How is competitive advantage achieved through successful implementation of the cost leadership strategy? The differentiation strategy? The focused low-cost strategy? The focused differentiation strategy? The integrated low-cost/differentiation strategy?
6. What are the risks associated with selecting and implementing each of the five strategies mentioned in question 5?

## Application Discussion Questions

1. You are a customer of your university or college. In your opinion, what actions does your school take to understand *what* your needs are and to use the best technologies to satisfy those needs? Be prepared to discuss your views.
2. Choose a firm in your local community that is of interest to you. Based on your interactions with this company, which business-level strategy do you believe the firm is implementing? What evidence can you provide to support your belief?
3. Assume that you have decided to establish and operate a restaurant in your local community. Who are the customers you would serve? What needs do these customers have that you could satisfy through your restaurant? What technologies would you use to satisfy those needs? Be prepared to discuss your responses.
4. As discussed in a Strategic Focus segment, Liz Claiborne Inc. did not perform well during 1993. An important indicator of its ineffective performance is a 44 percent decline in the value of its stock over a nine-month period. Using library materials, determine this firm's performance during the most recent year. Is the firm's performance better than it was in 1993? If so, what strategic actions do you believe accounted for the improvement? If its performance has not improved, what strategic actions do you believe prevented the firm from improving?
5. What business-level strategy is your school implementing? What core competencies are being used to implement this strategy?
6. As described in a Strategic Focus segment in this chapter, Cooper Tire & Rubber has historically earned superior profits through implementation of a focused low-cost strategy, while General Tire (Continental) and Pirelli have had difficulties. Using library materials, describe actions these or other firms in the tire industry have taken to realize favorable or unfavorable positions in different segments of the automobile tire industry.
7. Assume you overheard the following comment: "It is impossible for a firm to produce a low-cost, highly differentiated product." Accept or reject this statement, and be prepared to provide evidence supporting your opinion.

## Ethics Questions

1. Can an image of good ethical conduct on issues such as the environment, commitment to product quality, and living up to contractual agreements affect competitive advantage?
2. If a firm is involved in an ethical dilemma that becomes public, does a firm pursuing a differentiation strategy suffer more than a low-cost leader? Explain your answer.
3. Is there more incentive for differentiators or low-cost leaders to pursue stronger ethical conduct? Think of an example to support your answer.
4. Can an overemphasis on low-cost leadership or differentiation lead to ethical problems (such as poor product design and manufacturing) that create costly problems such as product liability lawsuits?
5. Many questions are currently being raised about the effect brand images have on behavior. For instance, there is considerable concern about brand images that are managed by tobacco firms and their effect on teenage smoking habits. Should firms be concerned about how they form and use brand images? Why or why not?
6. The model of competition associated with the five business-level strategies deals with "power" to overcome the five competitive forces. If, in fact, differentiation or low-cost leadership effectively deals with these competitive forces, does this give the implementor of such a strategy monopoly power? Should the government restrict such success through the Federal Trade Commission as it does when it considers the situation "anti-competitive"?

## Notes

1. J.T. Mahoney and J.R. Pandian, 1992, The resource-based view within the conversation of strategic management, *Strategic Management Journal* 13: 363–380.

2. G. Hamel and C.K. Prahalad, 1989, Strategic intent, *Harvard Business Review* 67, no. 3: 63–76.

3. R.H. Hayes and G.P. Pisano, 1994, Beyond world-class: The new manufacturing strategy, *Harvard Business Review* 72, no. 1: 77–86.

4. M.A. Peteraf, 1993, The cornerstones of competitive advantage: a resource based view, *Strategic Management Journal* 14: 179–191.

5. M.E. Porter, 1980, *Competitive Strategy* (New York: Free Press), 35–40.

6. B. Saporito, 1993, How to revive a fading firm, *Fortune,* March 22, 80.

7. Porter, 1980, *Competitive Strategy.*

8. D.F. Abell, 1993, *Managing with Dual Strategies: Mastering the Present, Preempting the Future* (New York: Free Press); D. Lei, M.A. Hitt, and J.D. Goldhar, 1993, Generic strategies, complementarities and organization design in global manufacturing firms (Working Paper Series, Texas A & M University).

9. R.C. Whiteley, 1991, Why customer focus strategies often fail, *Journal of Business Strategy* 12, no. 5: 34–37.

10. R. Randall, 1993, Mass customization redefines many businesses, *Planning Review* 22, no. 4: 2.

11. J. Kurtzman, 1994, Real strategy, *Harvard Business Review* 72, no. 1: 12.

12. A master class in radical change, 1993, *Fortune,* December 13, 82–90.

13. D.F. Abell, 1980, *Defining the Business: The Starting Point of Strategic Planning* (Englewood Cliffs, N.J.: Prentice-Hall).

14. K. Labich, 1994, Class in America, *Fortune,* February 7, 114–126.

15. C. Burck, 1993, How to care for your customers, *Fortune,* December 13, 200.

16. Porter, *Competitive Strategy.*

17. B. Saporito, 1994, Bloody new year for retailers, *Fortune,* February 7, 16, 20.

18. M. Loeb, 1994, Making the best better, *Fortune,* February 7, 6.

19. F.J. Gouillart, and F.D. Sturdivant 1994, Spend a day in the life of your customers, *Harvard Business Review 72,* no. 1: 116–225; B. Dumaine, 1993, The new non-manager managers, *Fortune,* February 22, 80–84.

20. The future for strategy: An interview with Gary Hamel, 1993, *European Management Journal* 14: 179–191.

21. C.K. Prahalad, 1993, The role of core competencies in the corporation, *Research-Technology Management* 36, no. 6: 40–47.

22. C. Burck, 1993, Learning from a master, *Fortune,* December 27, 144.

23. B. Dumaine, The new non-manager managers.

24. D. Kirkpatrick, 1993, Gerstner's new vision for IBM, *Fortune,* November 15, 119–126.

25. Saporito, How to revive a fading firm.

26. C.K. Prahalad and G. Hamel, 1990, The core competence of the corporation, *Harvard Business Review* 68, no. 3: 79–91.

27. Saporito, How to revive a fading firm.

28. M.E. Porter, 1985, *Competitive Advantage* (New York: Free Press), 26.

29. Porter, *Competitive Strategy;* Porter, *Competitive Advantage.*

30. T. Smart, P. Engardio, and G. Smith, 1993, GE's brave new world, *Business Week* November 8, 64–70.

31. Dollar General, 1991, *Fortune,* August 26, 98.

32. C.F. Knight, 1992, Emerson Electric: Consistent profits, consistently, *Harvard Business Review* 70, no. 1: 57–70.

33. Knight, Emerson Electric.

34. Porter, *Competitive Strategy,* 36.

35. P. Sellers, 1994, Yes, brands can still work magic, *Fortune,* February 7, 133–134.

36. R. Sookdeo, 1993, Oh, baby! What a year for products, *Fortune,* December 27, 90–95.

37. W. Echikson, 1993, Aiming at high and low markets, *Fortune,* March 22, 89.

38. J. Huey, 1993, How McKinsey does it, *Fortune,* November 1, 56–81.

39. M. Magiera, 1993, New Age beverages try new tricks, *Advertising Age* 64, no. 20: 8.

40. Guiltless Gourmet founder's fast success cost him big, big company, 1993, *Dallas Morning News,* October 15, 1D, 11D.

41. B. Dumaine, 1994, How to compete with a champ, *Fortune,* January 10, 106.

42. Ibid.

43. Porter, *Competitive Advantage, 15.*

44. Ibid.

45. J. Labate, 1993, Liuski International, *Fortune,* September 6, 81.

46. N.J. Perry, 1992, Hit 'em where they used to be, *Fortune,* October 19, 112–113.

47. J. Labate, 1993, Superior Industries International, *Fortune,* June 14, 121.

48. J. Labate, 1993, Custom Chrome, *Fortune,* May 31, 99.

49. C. Burck, 1993, The real world of the entrepreneur, *Fortune,* April 5, 62–80.

50. Perry, Hit 'em where they used to be.

51. Abell, *Managing the Dual Strategies;* Lei, Hitt, and Goldhar, Generic strategies.

52. C.W.L. Hill, 1988, Differentiation versus low cost or differentiation and low cost: A contingency framework, *Academy of Management Review* 13: 401–412.

53. Porter, *Competitive Advantage, 18.*

54. T. Maxon, 1994, Live on the air, *Dallas Morning News,* January 18, 1D, 19D.

55. R.S. Teitelbaum, 1993, Keeping promises, *Fortune* (Special Issue, Winter/Autumn), 32–34.

56. E.E. Adam, Jr., and R. Ebert, 1992, *Production and Operations Management,* 5th ed. (Englewood Cliffs, N.J.: Prentice-Hall).

57. J.W. Dean and J.R. Evans, 1994, *Total Quality Management, Organization and Strategy* (St. Paul: West).

58. B.T. Gale, 1992, Quality comes first when hatching power brands, *Planning Review* 21, no. 4: 4–9.

59. Porter, *Competitive Advantage,* 16.

60. Ibid, 17.

# CHAPTER 5
## Competitive Dynamics

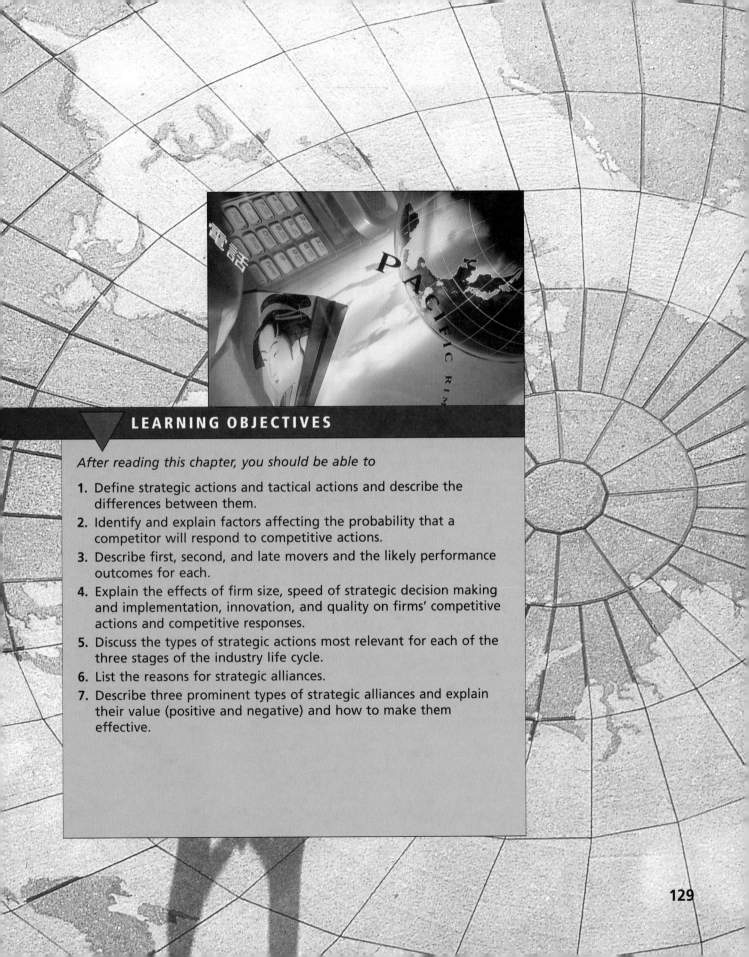

## LEARNING OBJECTIVES

*After reading this chapter, you should be able to*

1. Define strategic actions and tactical actions and describe the differences between them.
2. Identify and explain factors affecting the probability that a competitor will respond to competitive actions.
3. Describe first, second, and late movers and the likely performance outcomes for each.
4. Explain the effects of firm size, speed of strategic decision making and implementation, innovation, and quality on firms' competitive actions and competitive responses.
5. Discuss the types of strategic actions most relevant for each of the three stages of the industry life cycle.
6. List the reasons for strategic alliances.
7. Describe three prominent types of strategic alliances and explain their value (positive and negative) and how to make them effective.

## The Global Communications Market Heats Up for a Competitive Battle

In 1993, British Telecommunications (BT) faced a number of new competitors interested in its most profitable business, international telephone service. BT's most formidable competitor may be American Telephone and Telegraph Company (AT&T). In April 1993, AT&T applied for permission from the British government to begin telephone services in Great Britain. AT&T's action brings to 18 the total number of firms that have applied for various kinds of telephone service licenses in Great Britain. Because of these competitors' entries into the market, analysts have predicted that BT's share of the British telecommunications-service market will decrease from approximately 95 percent in 1993 to 83 percent in the later 1990s.

Similarly, in the United States, MCI and Sprint, two of the major competitors with AT&T for long-distance service, found it difficult to compete with AT&T in the international market. In fact, AT&T announced it would offer global service in combination with several international carriers, including Japan's Kokusai and Denshin Denwa and Singapore Telecom. AT&T also declared that it would build a network in Europe if it could not find a European partner to join its new service, called World Serve.

In response to AT&T's intended competitive actions, British Telecommunications and MCI began discussions about the formation of a strategic alliance to offer international services and to fend off AT&T's competitive actions. While the negotiations were arduous and lengthy, BT and MCI finally agreed on the formation of a strategic alliance. Although BT will own approximately 75 percent of the new venture, the companies announced that they would act as equal partners. MCI will manage the marketing of global voice and data services in North, South, and Central America, as well as the Caribbean. BT will market these services in other parts of the world, such as Western Europe and the Pacific Rim. Together, the two partners will invest more than $1 billion in the new venture to combine their efforts to provide voice and data services to multinational corporations. The objective of the new venture is to compete directly with AT&T in international services.

Analysts suggest that the BT–MCI alliance represents a direct competitive response to AT&T's plans to offer global services to multinational corporations. In fact, one analyst referred to this as AT&T's "worst nightmare" because BT is now a partner with its main U.S. competitor.

Neither BT nor MCI alone could mount a formidable challenge to AT&T's global telecommunications services. In 1993, AT&T was the largest provider of global telecommunications services, BT ranked fourth, and MCI ranked sixth. However, together, BT and MCI provide formidable competition for AT&T.

There are other possible competitive actions that could be taken by the BT–MCI alliance and/or by the two firms alone because of the strategic alliance. For example, MCI may move into cable television in the United States, as have many of the Baby Bell companies. The objective is to move into the emerging multimedia and interactive information and entertainment businesses. MCI is also examining alliances with software companies. Therefore, AT&T's competitors are responding strongly to its actions and may develop some independent competitive actions on their own as well. Undoubtedly, the communications industry and markets will be an exciting and competitive battlefield over the next decade. ▲

The global telecommunications industry, as described in the opening case, features the type of competitive landscape that probably will exist in many industries during the latter part of the 1990s and into the twenty-first century. This landscape is different from the one firms faced historically. Among other traits, this new landscape is more volatile, unpredictable and international in focus.

A changed competitive landscape requires firms to compete differently to achieve strategic competitiveness and earn superior profits. In the global automobile industry of the twenty-first century, for example, it may be necessary for companies to focus their resources and capabilities on better product designs, smarter marketing, and improved distribution practices—rather than manufacturing—to earn above-average profits.[1]

Several reasons account for the changes taking place in many industries' competitive landscape. First, in most industries, there is now a declining emphasis on a single domestic market and an increasing emphasis on international and global markets. As firms diversify internationally, their view of competition expands to multiple markets. Second, significant advances in communications technology allow more effective coordination across operations in multiple markets, along with faster decision making and competitive responses. Third, increasing technology and innovation, particularly in the computer industry, have changed competitive landscapes in ways that facilitate small and medium-sized businesses' efforts to compete more effectively. Peerless Saw Co., for example, worked with suppliers to create a new technology that allowed this small firm to design and manufacture customized saw blades. Through these efforts, Peerless created a new, high-margin, custom market. This market differed substantially from the high-volume, low-margin, standardized-products market in which the firm had been competing against larger companies. Because of its initial success, Peerless developed a new division to explore the possibility of applying its new technology in still other markets.[2] Finally, the increasing number of agreements to allow free trade across country borders (such as the 1993 North American Free Trade Agreement—NAFTA) is facilitating a growing international focus. The changing competitive landscape even has former competitors cooperating in such areas as new technology development and forming strategic alliances to compete against other competitors. An example is the strategic alliance between MCI and BT in response to a competitive action taken by AT&T.

The focus of this chapter is on competitive dynamics. The essence of this important topic is that a firm's strategic actions (see Figure 1–1) are dynamic in nature. Actions taken by one firm often elicit responses from competitors. These responses, in turn, typically result in responses from the firm that acted originally. The series of competitive actions and competitive responses among firms competing within a particular industry create **competitive dynamics.**

To discuss the part of the strategic management process called competitive dynamics, we examine the competitive actions and responses taken in markets with competitive rivalry. We also describe the importance of size, speed, innovation, and quality in competitive actions and responses. Following these descriptions is a discussion of the different types of competition that exist as an industry matures. The role of strategic alliances is emphasized in the final section of the chapter. This emphasis is provided through discussions of reasons for strategic alliances, different types of alliances, their value, and various means of making them successful.

▲ **Competitive dynamics** result from the series of competitive actions and competitive responses among firms competing within a particular industry.

## Competitive Rivalry and Competitive Dynamics

▲ **Competitive rivalry** exists when two or more firms jockey with one another in the pursuit of an advantageous market position.

Over time, in all industries, competing firms are involved with a number of competitive actions and competitive responses. **Competitive rivalry** exists when two or more firms jockey with one another in the pursuit of an advantageous market position. Competitive rivalry takes place between and among firms (in the form of actions and responses) because one or more competitors feel pressure or see opportunities to improve their market position. In most industries, a firm's competitive actions have observable effects on its competitors and may cause responses designed to counter the action.[3] KFC (the PepsiCo subsidiary known formerly as Kentucky Fried Chicken), for example, responded recently to the success of competitive actions taken by one of its competitors—Boston Chicken Inc.

Boston Chicken Inc.'s primary products are plump, rotisserie-roasted birds and home-style side dishes. The company went public in November 1993. The market's reaction to the stock offering was "frenzied." On its first day of trading, the stock, offered initially at $20 per share, rocketed to more than $50 a share. When it went public, Boston Chicken operated only 175 franchised and company-owned stores. By March 1994, the chain had grown to almost 250 stores. The company's top-level managers envisioned 450 outlets by the end of 1994, 1,500 by the year 2000, and, ultimately, a total of 3,000 units. Partly in response to Boston Chicken's success, KFC added and promoted heavily its own rotisserie chicken and home-style side dishes (e.g., corn bread, baked beans, and macaroni and cheese).[4]

As the example of competitive actions and competitive responses between Boston Chicken and KFC demonstrates, firms are mutually interdependent with their competitors.[5] Mutual interdependence among firms means that strategic competitiveness and superior profitability result only when companies recognize that their strategies are not implemented in isolation from their competitors'

*KFC and Boston Chicken Inc. are two firms jockeying with each other in the pursuit of competitive advantage. Because they are engaged in competitive rivalry, the actions of either one of these firms likely will generate a competitive response from the other firm. This pattern of competitive actions and responses affects the ability of each firm to achieve strategic competitiveness and earn above-average profits.*

actions and responses. Over time, KFC and Boston Chicken, along with their other competitors, will engage in a series of competitive actions and responses in efforts to establish sustainable competitive advantages. Thus, because it affects strategic competitiveness and profitability, firms are concerned about the pattern of competitive rivalry, and the competitive dynamics it creates, in the market or markets in which they compete.[6]

A **competitive action** is a significant competitive move taken by a firm that is designed to gain a competitive advantage in a market. Some competitive actions are large and significant; others are small and designed to help fine tune or implement a strategy.

There are two types of competitive actions—strategic and tactical. A **strategic action** represents a significant commitment of specific and distinctive organizational resources; it is difficult to implement and to reverse. A **tactical action** is taken to fine tune a strategy; it involves fewer and more general organizational resources and is relatively easy to implement and reverse, if necessary. AT&T's development of World Serve, a competitive action taken to offer global telecommunications services to multinational firms, is an example of a strategic action. This action requires a number of specific and distinctive organizational resources, will be difficult to implement, and will be complicated to reverse or eliminate. Because of these realities, AT&T has formed strategic alliances with companies in Japan and Singapore to implement this competitive action.[7]

A price increase in a particular market (e.g., in air fares) is an example of a tactical action. This action involves few organizational resources (e.g., communicating new prices/changing prices on products), its implementation is relatively easy, and it can be reversed (through a price reduction, for example) in a relatively short period of time. An announcement of a change in price could be used as a competitive weapon to capture a larger market share from competitors and could be one of several tactical moves designed to implement a particular strategy, such as either the low cost or the integrated low-cost/differentiation strategies, discussed in Chapter 4.

The likelihood of a response by a competitor to an action depends on the type of action taken (strategic or tactical), its probability of success, and its potential effect on competitors. A **competitive response** is a move taken to counter the effects of an action by a competitor. Not all competitive actions will elicit or require a response from competitors. On the whole, there are more competitive responses to tactical than to strategic actions.[8] It is easier to respond to tactical than to strategic actions and sometimes more necessary, at least in the short term.

The strategic alliance between MCI and British Telecommunications, however, is a prime example of a competitive response to a strategic action, the one taken by AT&T to offer global telecommunications services. BT was searching for a way to respond to AT&T's movement into its market and, in particular, to the threat of competition in the international telephone service market, one of the most profitable for British Telecommunications. Likewise, MCI wanted to move into global telecommunications services, but did not have the ability to do so alone and compete effectively against AT&T. Therefore, the strategic alliance between MCI and BT served the needs of both companies.

The type of competitive action taken is based on a firm's strategy (five business-level strategies were described in the previous chapter). Strategic actions are designed to help implement a business-level strategy; tactical actions are

▲ A **competitive action** is a significant competitive move taken by a firm that is designed to gain a competitive advantage in a market.

▲ A **strategic action** represents a significant commitment of specific and distinctive organizational resources; it is difficult to implement and to reverse.

▲ A **tactical action** is taken to fine tune a strategy; it involves fewer and more general organizational resources and is relatively easy to implement and reverse, if necessary.

▲ A **competitive response** is a move taken to counter the effects of an action by a competitor.

designed to fine tune that strategy. Once competitive actions have been taken, competitors must determine whether to respond and, if so, how.

## Likelihood of Response

Companies initiate more tactical than strategic actions and, as noted above, more competitive responses to tactical than to strategic actions. As explained below, the probability of a competitor response to a competitive action is based on the type of action, the reputation of the competitor taking the action, the competitor's dependence on the market, and the resources available to competitors.

**Type of Action**  Responses to a strategic action, as compared to a tactical action, are more difficult, require more organizational resources, and are more time consuming. For example, the BT and MCI strategic alliance discussions took place off and on for a period of three years. An agreement was not reached until after AT&T announced its move into Great Britain. Even then, arduous and lengthy negotiations (a full week of daily 15- and 16-hour sessions in London) were required to gain agreement on the alliance's provisions. Furthermore, the alliance could not be completed without regulatory and shareholder approvals. This was not a significant problem because at the time AT&T had not gained regulatory approval to move into the British market. Furthermore, its effort to establish World Serve is a part of a long-term strategy. Thus, British Telecommunications and MCI developed a competitive response approximately one and one-half months after AT&T announced its move into Great Britain. Because both the strategic action and the competitive response require long-term efforts for implementation, they are on relatively comparable time lines.

As compared to strategic actions, tactical actions usually have more immediate effects. For example, the announcement of a price increase in a price-sensitive market could have immediate effects on competitors. This is often true in low-cost goods and services markets. The strongly competitive airline industry, for example, is highly sensitive to price changes. As such, it is not uncommon to find airlines responding quickly to a competitor's price change, particularly if the announced change represents a price decrease, because without a response other airlines may lose market share.[9] Cash flow is critical in the industry, and consumers are price sensitive because there is relatively little differentiation in the services provided.

**Actor's Reputation**  An action (either strategic or tactical) taken by a market leader is likely to serve as a catalyst to a larger number of and faster responses from competitors and to a higher probability of imitation of the action. In other words, firms are more likely to imitate the actions of a competitor that is a market leader. Firms also often react quickly to imitate successful competitors' actions. Alternatively, firms that have a history as a strategic player that takes risky, complex, and unpredictable actions are less likely to solicit responses to and imitation of their actions.[10] Finally, firms that are known to be price predators (frequently cutting prices to hurt competitors and obtain market share, only to raise prices later) also do not elicit a large number of responses or imitation. In fact, there is less imitation and a much slower response to price predators than to either of the other two types of firms (market leader and strategic player).[11]

**Dependence on the Market**   Firms with a high dependency on a market in which a competitive action is taken are more likely to respond to that action. For example, firms with a large amount of total sales from one industry are more likely to respond to a particular competitive action taken in their primary industry than is a firm with businesses in multiple industries (e.g., a conglomerate). As described in Chapter 6, single and dominant business firms depend heavily on their success in the primary industry for their overall returns. Thus, if the type of action taken has a major effect on them, they are likely to respond, regardless of whether it is a strategic or a tactical action. Of course, a strategic action tends to require more time to respond effectively, assuming it had not been anticipated and a strategic response had not been planned. Swift action can be anticipated with tactical actions in these cases.

**Competitor Resources**   A competitive response to a strategic or a tactical action requires organizational resources. Firms with fewer resources are more likely to respond to tactical actions than to strategic ones because responses to tactical actions require fewer resources and are easier to implement. In addition, firm resources may dictate the type of response. For example, neither MCI nor British Telecommunications was in a position to respond individually to AT&T's strategic action to offer global telecommunications services.

They could not act alone because they did not have the resources necessary to mount a formidable challenge to a firm as large as AT&T. Although MCI and BT are large ($10 billion and $25 billion annual revenues, respectively), AT&T is huge by comparison ($65 billion annual revenues) and has significantly more resources to implement a global telecommunications service. Therefore, the strategic alliance between MCI and British Telecommunications allowed the firms to combine their resources and mount a substantive challenge to AT&T in the global telecommunications market. Moreover, the pooling of their resources may allow each partner to take other strategic actions, either alone or in concert, as described in the opening case.[12]

Small firms probably cannot compete effectively with any of these firms in the global telecommunications market. Other companies (both large and small) have applied for licenses for international telephone service in the British market. It is unlikely, however, that many will be able to compete successfully against AT&T and the alliance of MCI and British Telecommunications. Some even predict that Sprint, a major competitor of MCI and AT&T in the U.S. market, may be unable to compete with AT&T and the MCI–BT alliance in the global market. One analyst believes that AT&T and British Telecommunications represent the gorillas, and MCI's linkage with British Telecommunications suggests that Sprint is now in a different league. This analyst feels that Sprint represents a small fish in a big pond of whales. This suggestion is interesting, given that Sprint had revenues in 1992 of $10.4 billion. Therefore, it is not a small firm. On the other hand, relative to the resources available to AT&T and to the alliance between MCI and British Telecommunications, Sprint is a small fish.[13] It is possible that AT&T, MCI, and BT may earn above-average profits at the expense of Sprint and other smaller competitors with fewer resources. Competitors may wish to respond to the competitive actions taken by AT&T, MCI and BT; however, their inability to muster adequate resources may preclude them from doing so.[14]

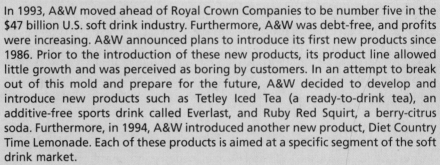

## A&W on the Warpath

In 1993, A&W moved ahead of Royal Crown Companies to be number five in the $47 billion U.S. soft drink industry. Furthermore, A&W was debt-free, and profits were increasing. A&W announced plans to introduce its first new products since 1986. Prior to the introduction of these new products, its product line allowed little growth and was perceived as boring by customers. In an attempt to break out of this mold and prepare for the future, A&W decided to develop and introduce new products such as Tetley Iced Tea (a ready-to-drink tea), an additive-free sports drink called Everlast, and Ruby Red Squirt, a berry-citrus soda. Furthermore, in 1994, A&W introduced another new product, Diet Country Time Lemonade. Each of these products is aimed at a specific segment of the soft drink market.

Interestingly, while the firm became number five in the market, earned at least average profits, and was debt-free, its stock price decreased sharply in 1993. This is because of the introduction of new products. A&W's growth in profits declined because of the new product development costs. In addition, A&W distributes 62 percent of its products through Coca-Cola and PepsiCo bottlers. Because A&W's new products compete directly with Coca-Cola and Pepsi products, their bottlers would not distribute A&W's new products. Therefore, A&W must rely on second-tier bottlers, with much less power relative to competitors, to market and distribute its new products.

Another competitive issue facing A&W is that its new sports drink competes directly with Gatorade, a leader in the sports drink market. Quaker Oats' Gatorade Division amassed a $70 million war chest to defend its share of the sports drink market (almost 90 percent when A&W introduced Everlast). In contrast, A&W had only $15 million to advertise all of its products in 1993. Therefore, A&W's new products compete directly with large and strong competitors that have significant resources to respond competitively. The stock market is concerned that A&W's new products, although perhaps appealing, will not be able to compete effectively in their individual markets. Evidently, current and potential shareholders are concerned that A&W lacks the resources to compete with Coca-Cola, PepsiCo, and Quaker Oats.

The competitive challenges facing A&W are recognized by its top executives. For example, A&W's CEO recently observed that "Our bottlers don't expect us to do the same thing that cola companies do, and the financial community doesn't expect us to have the volumes that cola companies have. They expect us to grow and be profitable, and that we will do well." Only time will tell if A&W's competitive actions will contribute to the firm's strategic competitiveness or not.

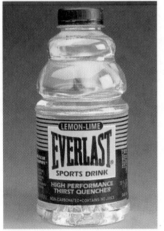

*A division of Quaker Oats, Gatorade has held as much as 90 percent of the sports drink market. Even though its drink may appeal to customers, A&W may lack the resources needed to compete successfully against its much larger rival, Quaker Oats. The differences in resource bases will affect the patterns of competition between these two firms.*

Competitive actions being taken by a smaller firm in an effort to compete successfully with its larger competitors are described in the Strategic Focus concerned with A&W.

A&W has been a profitable and successful company. It has been able to succeed by avoiding direct competition with its much larger and more powerful industry competitors. It is unclear whether A&W will be successful with its new products. It will be difficult for the firm to succeed in its attempt to compete against Coca-Cola and PepsiCo, as well as the Gatorade Division of Quaker Oats. It is possible that A&W's new products could be overpowered by heavy advertising from much larger and more powerful competitors.

As noted in Table 5–1, A&W's action is strategic, one that requires more organizational resources to initiate a competitive response. A&W's reputation is fine in niche markets, but does not match the strength of its competitors' reputations. Coca-Cola, PepsiCo, and Quaker Oats are diversified, lowering their dependence on the markets A&W has entered with new products. While all three of A&W's major competitors have the resources to respond, they are less likely to do so early. Instead, these firms are more likely to monitor closely A&W's new products and respond only if they expect these products to be successful and negatively affect their market share.

## Order of Actions and Responses

The order of each competitive action and response influences an industry's competitive dynamics. Of greatest importance are first movers, second movers, and late movers. The speed of decision and speed of change in a product market (a related and increasingly important topic) are addressed later in a separate subsection of the chapter.

A **first mover** is a firm that takes an initial competitive action (either strategic or tactical). First movers have the capabilities and core competencies required to take pioneering actions. Through these actions, first movers hope to gain a sustainable competitive advantage.

▲ A **first mover** is a firm that takes an initial competitive action (either strategic or tactical).

Several competitive advantages can accrue to the firm that is first to initiate a competitive action. Successful actions allow a firm to earn above-average profits (often referred to as monopolistic profits) until other competitors are able to respond effectively. In addition, first movers have the opportunity to gain customer loyalty, thereby making it difficult for responding firms to capture customers.

The advantages, and the length of time a firm receives them, vary by type of competitive action and industry. First-mover advantages also vary based on the ease with which competitors can imitate the action.[15] The more difficult an action is to imitate, the longer a firm may receive the benefits of being a first mover. When core competencies are the foundation of a competitive action, first-mover advantages tend to last for a longer period of time. Core competence–based competitive actions have a high probability of resulting in a sustainable competitive advantage.

There also are potential disadvantages of being the first firm to initiate a competitive action. Chief among these is the degree of risk taken by first movers. This is because it is not easy to predict the amount of success a particular competitive action will produce prior to its initiation.[16] Oftentimes, first movers

**TABLE 5–1**

**Comparison of A&W's Competitors on the Four Factors Affecting the Probability of Response**

|  | A&W | Coca-Cola | PepsiCo | Quaker Oats |
|---|---|---|---|---|
| Type of action | Strategic | — | — | — |
| Actor's reputation | Fair | Good | Good | Good |
| Dependence on market | High | Moderate | Moderate | Moderate |
| Competitor resources | — | High | High | High |

have high development costs. Second movers can avoid these costs through reverse engineering (taking apart a new product and then reassembling it to learn how it works). Another potential disadvantage of being a first mover is the extent the market in which the firm is competing is dynamic and uncertain. In other words, the extent and range of marketplace competition heighten the potential risk. In fact, in a highly uncertain market, it may be more appropriate to be a second or later mover.

▲ A **second mover** is a firm that responds to a first mover's competitive action, often through imitation or a move designed to counter the effects of the action.

A **second mover** is a firm that responds to a first mover's competitive action, often through imitation or a move designed to counter the effects of the action. When the second mover responds quickly, a short time after the first mover's competitive action, it may earn some of the first-mover advantages without experiencing the potential disadvantages. For example, a fast second mover may gain some of the profits and obtain a portion of the initial customers and thereby customer loyalty. However, it avoids some of the risks encountered by the first mover. In other words, the firm taking a second action as a competitive response to the first mover can do so after evaluating customers' reactions to the first-mover's action.[17] To be a successful first or fast second mover, a company must be able to analyze its markets and identify critical strategic issues.[18] Coke and Pepsi can more easily be a second mover to A&W new products than to new products introduced by the other (Coke or Pepsi).

In some instances, it may not be possible to move quickly in response to a first mover's action. For example, if the first mover introduces a sophisticated new product and competitors have not undertaken similar research and development, considerable time may be required to respond effectively, even with successful imitation of the first mover's product. Therefore, there are some risks involved in being a follower, as opposed to a leader, in the market. However, there are no blueprints for first-mover success. Followers may be able to respond without significant market development costs in that second movers can learn from a first mover's successes and mistakes. Thus, the actions and outcomes of the first firm to initiate a competitive action may provide a more effective blueprint for second and later movers.[19]

▲ A **late mover** is a firm that responds to a competitive action, but only when considerable time has elapsed after the first mover's action and the second mover's response.

A **late mover** is a firm that responds to a competitive action, but only after considerable time has elapsed after the first mover's action and the second mover's response. While some type of competitive response may be more effective than no response to effective actions, late movers tend to be poorer performers and often are weak competitors. In contrast, companies acting and responding promptly to competing firms' actions tend to be higher performers than those that do not initiate strategic or tactical actions and/or are late to respond. The relationship between timing of competitive actions/responses and average firm performance is shown in Figure 5–1.

## Other Factors Affecting Competitive Rivalry and Competitive Dynamics

In addition to the four conditions that affect the probability of a competitor's response to a competing firm's competitive actions, there are four more general factors that shape the character of competition within an industry. These factors are (1) firm size and the distribution of size within an industry, (2) the speed at which competitive actions and competitive responses are made, (3) the extent of innovation by firms in the industry, and (4) product quality.

**FIGURE 5-1**  **Timing and Performance Effects of Competitive Actions and Responses**

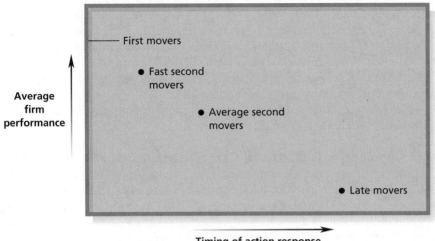

**Firm Size**    The size of a firm can have two important, but opposite, effects on an industry's competitive dynamics. First, the larger a firm, the greater its market power. Of course, the extent of any firm's market power is relative to the power of its competitors. In the U.S. auto industry, all competitors are large; however, no firm has relative and critical power over the others. Nonetheless, it is difficult for small firms to enter the market, since the sheer size of the larger firms creates substantial entry barriers to the industry.

Another example of market power is shown by the problems that A&W faces in introducing new products that are competitive with those of its much larger rivals—Coca-Cola, PepsiCo, and Quaker Oats. Many believe that A&W's new products will fail not because customers will deem them unattractive, but because of the potential responses by the firm's larger and more powerful competitors (e.g., Pepsi and Coke).

As firms grow larger, they often implement complicated structures and bureaucratic rules that inhibit their competitive abilities. In particular, these structures and rules stifle a firm's innovativeness. Without innovation, it is difficult for a firm to be a first mover and to respond quickly to competitors' actions. Even when a competitor takes a strategic action that could affect a large firm, a significant amount of time may be required for that firm to develop and implement an effective competitive response. The content of the response is important, but its timing could be more critical.

Problems created by firm size are demonstrated by events—both historical and current in nature—in the computer industry. While the giant in the industry, IBM, was highly successful, it did not invent or first introduce the microcomputer, which is the primary basis of the industry today. It took entrepreneurial ventures, such as Apple Computer, Dell Computer and Compaq, to introduce the innovations in products and services that revolutionized the industry. Small firms often do this by fostering what is referred to as creative destruction.[20] As Steven Jobs and his partner Steve Wozniak revolutionized the computer industry, Michael Dell, who was in high school when Apple introduced its computers, revolutionized the way computers were produced and distributed. As a result, small businesses, often stronger in lower technology industries (because of lower required capital investments), have become a force for change in high-technology industries.[21]

A quote attributed to Herbert Kelleher, co-founder and chief executive officer (CEO) of Southwest Airlines, best describes the approach needed by large firms. In Kelleher's words, "Think and act big and we'll get smaller. Think and act small and we'll get bigger."[22] This suggests that large firms should use their size to build market power, but that they must think and act like a small firm (e.g., move quickly and be innovative) in order to achieve strategic competitiveness and earn above-average profits over the long run.

**Speed of Competitive Actions and Competitive Responses**   Our world is one in which time and speed are important. We go to fast food restaurants and use microwave ovens. We regularly use overnight express mail (public and private) and fax machines. The same is true with competition. The speed with which a firm can initiate competitive actions and competitive responses may determine its success. In the global economy, speed in developing a new product and moving it to the marketplace is becoming critical to a firm's efforts to establish a sustainable competitive advantage and earn superior profits.

Under the leadership of former CEO Stanley C. Gault, Rubbermaid took actions necessary to speed up significantly its product development processes. These actions are thought to have played an important role in the firm's sterling performance during Gault's 11-year tenure as Rubbermaid's CEO (sales grew from $300 million to $1.5 billion, and net income grew from $27 million to $163 million during Gault's time at the helm).[23]

Speed to the marketplace is one of the problems U.S. automobile manufacturers have experienced in competing with Japanese firms. Some time ago, Japanese auto companies were able to design a new product and introduce it to the market within three years. In comparison, U.S. firms required between five and eight years to complete these activities. This time differential made it possible for Japanese firms to design and move to the market two or three new automobiles in the same time it took a U.S. automaker to do one.

The competitive actions one U.S. automobile manufacturer took to design and introduce a new product into the marketplace quickly are described in the next Strategic Focus.

The competitive actions initiated by Chrysler to design and introduce the Neon into the global marketplace were partly in response to the successful actions taken some time ago by its Japanese competitors. As this Strategic Focus suggests, Chrysler hopes that its experiences with the Neon will facilitate elimination of the speed-based competitive advantages enjoyed recently by its Japanese competitors. Eliminating this advantage is important because some believe that in a global economy, firms must think in terms of speed to market in order to earn superior profits.[24]

In a global economy, then, time may be the new and critical source of sustainable competitive advantage. However, managing for speed requires more than attempting to have employees work faster. Essentially, it requires working smarter, using different types of organizational structures, and having the time required for completion as a primary work-related goal.

Research has shown that the pace of strategic decision making may be affected by an executive's cognitive ability, use of intuition, tolerance for risk, and

## STRATEGIC FOCUS

### The Rapid Development of Chrysler's Neon

In April 1990, Chrysler's top-level managers approved the preliminary investigation into the development of a new subcompact automobile. The group charged with investigating and possibly developing such an automobile included 600 engineers and 289 suppliers. In the same month that Chrysler began investigation of a new subcompact, Ford introduced the new Escort, jointly engineered with Mazda. Shortly thereafter, Chrysler made a decision to pull out of a proposed joint venture with Fiat to develop a new car. In January 1991, General Motors introduced the Saturn automobile, and, a short time later, Chrysler's top management team approved the development of the Neon. During its period of development, other competitors introduced new small cars, such as the Nissan Sentra as well as restyled versions of the Honda Civic and Toyota Corolla.

The Neon was developed in a total of 42 months, a new U.S. record for the development of a small automobile, and for a fraction of the development costs of most automobiles. Furthermore, the newly developed Neon is expected to cost $500 less to build than any competing subcompact, allowing it to be marketed at an attractive price for customers. The development cost was $1.3 billion. In contrast, the Ford Escort took five years to develop at a cost of $2 billion. Ford's new Mondeo compact cost $6 billion to develop, and General Motors' Saturn required seven years and $5 billion for development. At least partly because of its lower development costs, Chrysler believed the Neon quickly would become a highly profitable product.

Chrysler was able to develop the Neon at a lower cost in a shorter period of time using cross-functional teams. Organizational structure also contributed to this project's success. As compared to some of its competitors, including Ford and General Motors, Chrysler is less bureaucratic. Moreover, the company's style is informal and proactive. Words spoken by Chrysler President Robert Lutz seem to capture the essence of the reductions in the firm's bureaucratic rules: "We don't have premeetings, and we don't get predigestion by the finance or strategy staff. We've gotten rid of the ritualistic B.S. that does nothing but increase response time, add cost, and result in compromise solutions that are the lowest common denominator."

The Neon was introduced into the U.S. market in January 1994. To capitalize on what it hoped would be worldwide popularity, Chrysler intended to make the Neon available in the Pacific Basin region as early as the spring of 1995.

Chrysler's expectations for the Neon were significant. Members of the team that developed the car hoped for worldwide popularity to rival that of Volkswagen's famous Beetle. In admitting that in his view a Beetle phenomenon was not out of the question, Lutz did little to downplay his firm's rather strong belief that the Neon would be a competitive product in the global automobile market. Another indicator of Chrysler's optimism was the projection that 370,000 units would be sold annually beginning in 1996 (a mere two years after Neon's introduction into the automobile marketplace).

propensity to act.[25] Executives who use intuition, have a greater tolerance for risk, and are predisposed to take actions make faster strategic decisions than do those without such characteristics. It is also known that decisions are likely to occur faster in centralized organizations because they will not have to go through as many levels or get approval from as many people. More formalized and bureaucratic organizations, however, may find it difficult to make fast strategic decisions.[26] These organizations require more layers of approval for such decisions.

John F. Welch, chairman and CEO of General Electric, states that speed is the driver sought by all of today's organizations.[27] He suggests that companies are striving to develop products faster, speed up production cycles in moving them to the market, and improve response time to customers. In Welch's opinion, having faster communications and moving with agility are critical to competitive success.

Welch's comments tend to agree with the suggestion of Herbert Kelleher (Southwest Airlines' CEO) that you have to think small in order to become large. Welch believes that you have to act as though you are small in order to obtain the speed necessary to achieve strategic competitiveness and earn above-average profits in the global economy.

*Cross-Functional Teams*   One of the primary structural devices used to manage the time-to-market concern is the cross-functional team. Mentioned briefly in Chapter 1 and considered more fully in Chapter 12, a **cross-functional team** is one in which members from different functions work together to resolve a major organizational problem or accomplish an important organizational goal. In some ways, because of the need to consider all inputs, cross-functional teams can increase the time required to make decisions. As explained below, however, they can reduce the total time needed in that they change the way an organization reaches and implements decisions.

Historically, most firms organized for product development and the introduction of new products into the marketplace with sequential movements through individual functions. Typically, a product idea was developed in R&D laboratories. The product idea was then moved to the design function for development and refinements. Once designed, product specifications were sent to manufacturing. After it was produced, a product was sent to the marketing function, where decisions were made regarding how it was to be distributed to the marketplace and serviced after the sale.

Unfortunately, few interactions occurred among functions through this sequential process. Because of the time needed to rework and redesign a product and the processes used to produce and distribute it, the lack of interaction and integration associated with the sequential process created multiple delays. For example, after a product was designed, it might be discovered that it was too expensive to manufacture. At that point, the product would have to be returned to the design function for changes so that it could be manufactured within appropriate cost and quality standards. After the manufacturing process was designed, the marketing function might determine that the new product needed changes to satisfy customer needs. This could necessitate product redesign, and, in turn, require changes in the manufacturing process.

The historically lengthy process required by General Motors (GM) to design a new automobile and move it to the marketplace (e.g., Saturn) demonstrates the delays that sequential product design and distribution processes can create. Length of time is noteworthy in that the longer the time a product is in the development sequence, the greater is the development cost. Therefore, the example of Chrysler's Neon is an important one in the industry (recall that as compared to the Neon, GM's Saturn cost $3.7 billion dollars more and required three and one-half additional years to develop and introduce to the marketplace).

▲ A **cross-functional team** is one in which members from different functions work together to resolve a major organizational problem or accomplish an important organizational goal.

A key reason that less time and fewer financial resources were required to design and introduce the Neon was Chrysler's use of cross-functional teams (at Chrysler, cross-functional teams are called platform teams). Thought by some to be a structure that could become a model for other companies, Chrysler's structural innovation was "to put all the engineers and designers assigned to a specific project together on a single floor, along with representatives of marketing, finance, purchasing, and even outside suppliers—hundreds of people in all, and grant them considerable autonomy."[28] In the early part of the 1990s, Chrysler's structural innovation (its platform teams) proved to be instrumental in the firm's ability to introduce three successful vehicles—the Jeep Grand Cherokee, the Dodge Intrepid and other LH sedans, and the Dodge Ram pickup truck—to the marketplace.

As a competitive action, Chrysler's platform teams will generate responses from the firm's competitors, which, in turn, will stimulate other actions and responses from Chrysler. This series of competitive actions and responses—that is, the industry's competitive dynamics—continues to influence companies' efforts to establish sustainable competitive advantages and earn superior profits.

The pace of strategic decision making may affect a firm's ability to gain and sustain a competitive advantage. Obviously, a firm that is able to take a strategic action and/or respond quickly to a critical strategic action taken by a competitor may be able to gain a competitive advantage or forestall such an advantage by a competitor.[29] Therefore, the speed with which strategic decisions are made can affect a firm's ability to earn above-average profits.

As a part of an organization's structure, cross-functional teams do not automatically enhance a firm's strategic competitiveness. In fact, cross-functional teams require effective management to improve a firm's performance.[30] These teams are difficult to manage because the individuals who are a part of them have different backgrounds and decision premises. The different skills and information that individual team members want to contribute to a decision process sometimes make it more difficult for teams to reach decision consensus. As a result, careful management is important in order for cross-functional teams to reduce the time required, as well as to increase the quality of the design and development of the new product.

**Innovation**   A third general factor, innovation, has long been known in some industries, such as pharmaceuticals and computers, to have a strong influence on firm performance. The strategic importance of innovation is explored further in Chapter 12. In today's global economy, research suggests that innovation (both product innovation and process innovation) is becoming linked with superior profitability in a growing number of industries. One study, for example, found that companies with the highest performance also invested the most in research and development. In 1960, U.S. firms held over two-thirds of the world market in 10 of the top 15 major industries. By 1970, the United States continued to dominate 9 of those 15 industries. However, by 1980, U.S. domination was limited to only 3 of the 15 industries. The study found that this was due largely to changes in innovation. Firms from other countries were more innovative than U.S. firms in many of the industries.[31] In fact, a contributing factor to the productivity and technology problems experienced by U.S. firms has been managers' unwillingness to bear the costs and risks of long-term development of product and process innovations.[32]

An integral part of developing and sustaining a competitive advantage is to deny competitors access to proprietary technology. Thus, firms need to innovate to be market leaders and then deny access to the technology in order to sustain the competitive advantage created.[33] However, as explained next, one firm was able to build a competitive advantage and sustain it for a considerable period of time by sharing its technology with others in the industry.

Sun Microsystems operated as an open system with regard to its workstation products. It was able to gain market share and transform the market with its unique strategy. In 1983, Sun held approximately 15 percent of the workstation market; Apollo, a competing firm, commanded approximately 43 percent of the market. However, Sun Microsystems' unique open-system strategy of sharing technology allowed it to gain market share equal to almost 30 percent by 1989. In contrast, Apollo's market share decreased markedly during this time period (to under 15 percent). Others in the industry, such as Hewlett Packard (HP) and Digital Equipment Co. (DEC), achieved marginal gains in market share. Sun's revenues increased by almost $1.8 billion during this time; Apollo's revenues increased by only $300 million.

Essentially, the strategy Sun implemented between 1983 and 1989 called for the firm to share its technology with rivals in order to build a consensus on industry standards and a network of systems in support of customers' needs. With this strategy, Sun avoided investing large amounts of dollars in R&D to develop products for specific market segments. Because Sun allowed competitors to develop unique products that were compatible with its own workstations, it did not have to invest heavily in its own R&D.

In contrast to Sun Microsystems' competitive actions and strategy, some competitors, including IBM and DEC, chose not to share their technology with others, preferring instead to develop noncompatible systems. While this was a positive short-term strategy, eventually the Sun strategy began to erode IBM's and DEC's shares of the workstation market. Sun's strategy of sharing technology and allowing a consensus to develop on standards transformed the workstation part of the computer industry, providing valued products to customers in the process. Sun's strategy allowed the firm to achieve strategic competitiveness during the 1980s.[34]

By 1992, Sun owned a 38.3 percent share of the workstation market. In comparison, HP had a 17.1 percent share, DEC had a 12.1 percent share, and IBM had a 7.3 percent share (HP, IBM, and DEC were Sun's major competitors). Sun's revenues reached $3.5 billion in the same year. But these positive indicators did not mask the fact that Sun faces serious competitive challenges. Its profits have fallen, and there is potential competition from personal computer makers, such as Apple Computer, on the horizon. With the new operating systems and powerful microprocessors that have been developed recently, Sun's technological edge in workstations may be deteriorating.[35] As Sun's experiences show, competitive advantages are rarely sustainable in perpetuity, particularly in high-technology industries with frequent innovation. The competitive actions and responses occurring in the workstation market create an interesting set of competitive dynamics. Firms competing in this market are challenged continuously in their efforts to establish sustainable competitive advantages and earn superior profits.

One firm's reliance on its innovative ability to achieve strategic competiveness in its industry is described in the next Strategic Focus.

## STRATEGIC FOCUS

### An Innovative Company Reaches the Top

Merck and Co., Inc., develops, manufactures, and markets human and animal health products and specialty chemicals. It also places primary effort and resources in the internal research and development of new products. Merck has been one of the leaders in the pharmaceutical industry not only in the United States, but also throughout the world, for an extended period of time.

Merck followed a strong internal development strategy during the 1980s and early 1990s when it was not in vogue. Many of its sister firms, even competitors, were investing heavily in mergers and acquisitions and acquiring significant debt.

Merck's success during this period of time was not duplicated by any of its competitors. In the five years from 1987 to 1991, for example, Merck had an annual growth rate in sales of 14.1 percent, for a total 70 percent increase. Its net income grew at an annual rate of 23.6 percent, for a total 134 percent increase, and its earnings per share increased over 100 percent during that five-year period. Merck invested slightly more than 10 percent of its revenues (over $1 billion) in research and development annually. It had a debt-to-equity ratio of approximately .10, extremely low among large U.S. corporations. The diversification undertaken by Merck was not into new product lines, but across geographic boundaries, globally. Through its diversification efforts, Merck built a global network and market.

As noted above, Merck's operating results were phenomenal during this period. The firm's performance earned it recognition by others. In a survey of 750 independent pharmacists, Merck was rated number one out of 42 pharmaceutical manufacturers in six different categories, including product quality. Even more impressive, perhaps, is the fact that Merck was rated the most admired corporation in the United States for six consecutive years in *Fortune's* Reputation Survey. During this time period, then, Merck exemplified extremely effective management and was one of the most successful corporations in the world. There are many reasons for its success; one was its emphasis on innovation.

Our discussion of factors influencing an industry's competitive dynamics suggests that large firms with significant market power that act like small firms—making strategic decisions and implementing them with speed—and that are innovative are strong competitors and are likely to earn superior profits. Merck is an example of one of these firms. Interestingly, however, in 1993, Merck completed a major multibillion-dollar acquisition in response to increased price competition in the industry. Only time will tell if its fundamental change in strategy will continue or limit its success.

No matter how large, fast, and innovative organizations are, there is a final factor that affects an industry's competitive dynamics and influences firms' ability to achieve strategic competitiveness in global markets—product quality.

**Quality**   Product quality has become a universal theme in the global economy and continues to shape the competitive dynamics in many industries. Today product quality is important in all industry settings and is a necessary, but not sufficient, condition to successful implementation of the low-cost, differentiation, focus, and integrated low-cost/differentiation strategies.

Without quality goods or services, strategic competitiveness cannot be achieved. Quality alone, however, does not guarantee that a firm will achieve strategic competitiveness or earn superior profits. In the words of the president of the National Center for Manufacturing Sciences, a nonprofit research consortium, "Quality used to be a competitive issue out there, but now it's just the basic denominator to being in the market."[36] To have an *opportunity* to compete successfully, for example, Ford Motor Co. had to first improve the quality of Jaguar's two primary models to the levels of competitors' offerings (Ford paid $2.5 billion in 1989 to buy Jaguar).[37]

In the global economy, ISO 9000 (International Organization for Standardization) standards are rapidly becoming important in establishing the quality levels as a basic denominator of effective competition in worldwide markets. As observed recently by the vice president and general manager of Caterpillar's engine division, "Today, having ISO 9000 is a competitive advantage. Tomorrow, it will be the ante to the global poker game."[38]

Detailed in a slender paperback volume and available from the American National Standards Institute, among other sources, ISO 9000 standards do not tell firms how to design and manufacture their products (either goods or services) more effectively and efficiently. But the standards do "provide a framework for showing customers how [a firm committed to quality management practices] tests products, trains [its] employees, keeps records, and fixes defects."[39] ISO 9000 standards are formally described as "the refinement of all the most practical and generally applicable principles of quality systems and the culmination of agreement between the world's most advanced authorities on these standards as the basis of a new era of quality management."[40] Firms earning an ISO-based certificate (certificates are awarded by one of many independent auditors) have demonstrated that their factory, office, or laboratory has satisfied the quality management requirements determined by the International Organization for Standardization.

Nowhere is the lesson of quality more vivid than among the U.S. automakers. At one time, the Big Three U.S. automakers—GM, Ford, and Chrysler—dominated the huge U.S. auto market. However, Japanese automakers—in particular, Toyota, Nissan, and Honda—took advantage of the fuel-efficiency emphasis in the U.S. market by introducing small automobiles. The critical issue, however, was that their products were of higher quality than those produced by U.S. automakers. In a relatively short period of time, product quality became a source of competitive advantage, strategic competitiveness, and superior profitability for many Japanese automakers.

By the early to middle part of the 1990s, Ford, GM, and Chrysler were producing cars with quality levels similar to those manufactured by Japanese companies. Thus, after a number of years, the Big Three appeared to be responding successfully to the challenge of product quality. The loss of quality as a consistent source of competitive advantage, coupled with the effects of a deep recession in their home market, was creating unfavorable conditions for Japanese automakers. Headlines in late 1993 and early 1994 described these firms' plight: "Sales fall 11.3% in October; Excess plants, workers, bedevil Japan; Nissan, Mazda, Isuzu to furlough workers for product cuts; and Mitsubishi Motors posts profit drop."[41]

Although they looked vulnerable in the early to middle part of the 1990s, some analysts believed Japanese automakers would rebound quickly from their slump. In an industry where firms are known widely for their competitive actions and competitive responses, it is reasonable to expect Japanese car manufacturers to initiate competitive responses intended to reverse what they hope would be a short-lived decline in their strategic competitiveness. In the words of an executive speaking to the U.S. Society of Automotive Analysts, "We continually underestimate Japan's ability to adapt and remain competitive. The smart money says Japan's trouble will be only temporary. They will become leaner and meaner."[42] Thus, Japanese automakers can be expected to use their core competencies to develop a source of competitive advantage other than product quality. The competitive actions taken to establish that competitive advantage—whatever it may be—will, of course, stimulate competitive responses from the world's other car manufacturers.

**Quality** involves meeting or exceeding customer expectations in the products and/or services offered.[43] The quality dimensions of products and services are shown in Table 5–2. As a competitive dimension, quality is as important in the service sector as it is in the manufacturing sector.[44]

While there are multiple dimensions of product and service quality, quality begins at the top of the organization. Top management must create values for quality that permeate the entire organization.[45] These values should be built into strategies that reflect long-term commitments to customers, stockholders, and other important stakeholders.[46] In so doing, a process of total quality management pervades the firm in all activities and processes.

Quality and total quality management are closely associated with the philosophies and teachings of W. Edwards Deming (and, to a lesser extent, Joseph Juran). Simple, yet powerful in its value, these individuals' contribution to the practice of management is based on the understanding that "it costs less to make quality products than defect-ridden ones. . . ."[47]

**Total quality management (TQM)** is a "total, company-wide effort that includes all employees, suppliers, and customers, and that seeks continuously to

▲ **Quality** involves meeting or exceeding customer expectations in the products and/or services offered.

▲ **Total quality management (TQM)** is a "total, company-wide effort that includes all employees, suppliers, and customers, and that seeks continuously to improve the quality of products and processes to meet the needs and expectations of customers."

**TABLE 5–2**

**Product and Service Quality Dimensions**

| Product Quality Dimensions | Service Quality Dimensions |
|---|---|
| 1. *Performance*—Operating characteristics | 1. *Timeliness*—Performed in promised time period |
| 2. *Features*—Important special characteristics | 2. *Courtesy*—Performed cheerfully |
| 3. *Reliability*—Meeting operating specifications over some time period | 3. *Consistency*—All customers have similar experiences each time |
| 4. *Durability*—Amount of use before performance deteriorates | 4. *Convenience*—Accessible to customers |
| 5. *Conformance*—Match with preestablished standards | 5. *Completeness*—Fully serviced, as required |
| 6. *Serviceability*—Ease and speed of repair or normal service | 6. *Accuracy*—Performed correctly each time |
| 7. *Aesthetics*—How a product looks and feels | |
| 8. *Perceived quality*—Subjective assessment of characteristics (product image) | |

*Sources:* Adapted from J. W. Dean, Jr., and J. R. Evans, 1994, *Total Quality: Management, Organization and Society* (St. Paul: West); D. Garvin, 1988, *Managed Quality: The Strategic and Competitive Edge* (New York: Free Press); H. V. Roberts and B. F. Sergesketter, 1993, *Quality Is Personal* (New York: Free Press).

improve the quality of products and processes to meet the needs and expectations of customers."[48] Actually a philosophy about how to manage, TQM "combines the teachings of Deming and Juran on statistical process control and group problem-solving processes with Japanese values concerned with quality and continuous improvement."[49] Statistical process control (SPC) is a technique used to continually upgrade the quality of the goods or services a firm produces.[50] SPC benefits the firm through the detection and elimination of variations in processes used to manufacture a good or service.[51]

Although there are skeptics, when applied properly, the principles of total quality management can help firms achieve strategic competitiveness and earn superior profits.[52] Three principal goals sought when practicing total quality management are boosting customer satisfaction, reducing product introduction time, and cutting costs. As discussed in this chapter, achievement of these goals can be expected to have a positive effect on a firm's performance. To reach these goals, firms must provide their employees and leaders with effective TQM training.[53]

Ironically, Deming's and Juran's ideas on quality and continuous improvement were adapted and implemented by Japanese firms long before many U.S. firms acknowledged their importance. For this reason, a host of Japanese firms developed a competitive advantage in product quality that has been difficult for U.S. firms to overcome.[54] Deming's 14 points for managing and achieving quality (see Table 5–3) have become a watchword in many current businesses globally.

Embedded within Deming's 14 points for management is the importance of striving continuously to improve how a firm operates and the quality of its goods or services. In fact, Deming did not support use of the TQM term, arguing that he did not know what total quality was and that it is impossible for firms to reach a

---

### ▽ TABLE 5–3

**Deming's 14 Points for Management**

1. Create and publish to all employees a statement of the aims and purposes of the company or other organization. The management must demonstrate constantly their commitment to this statement.
2. Learn the new philosophy, top management and everybody.
3. Understand the purpose of inspection, for improvement of processes and reduction of cost.
4. End the practice of awarding business on the basis of price tag alone.
5. Improve constantly and forever the system of production and service.
6. Institute training.
7. Teach and institute leadership.
8. Drive out fear. Create trust. Create a climate for innovation.
9. Optimize toward the aims and purposes of the company the efforts of teams, groups, staff areas.
10. Eliminate exhortations for the work force.
11. (a) Eliminate numerical quotas for production. Instead, learn and institute methods for improvement.
    (b) Eliminate Management by Objective. Instead, learn the capabilities of processes and how to improve them.
12. Remove barriers that rob people of pride of workmanship.
13. Encourage education and self-improvement for everyone.
14. Take action to accomplish the transformation.

*Source:* Reprinted from *Out of the Crisis* by W. Edwards Deming by permission of MIT and The W. Edwards Deming Institute. Published by MIT, Center for Advanced Engineering Study, Cambridge, MA 02139. Copyright 1986 by W. Edwards Deming.

goal of "total quality." The pursuit of quality improvements, Deming believed, should be a never-ending process.

As advocated by Deming and Juran, quality is a critical component of achieving competitive advantage or of disallowing competitors such an advantage. For example, research conducted by the Strategic Planning Institute (from a database of 1,200 companies) found the following:

- Firms with high-quality goods and services often have large market shares.
- Quality is related positively to high returns on investment.
- Firms with higher-quality products can usually charge higher prices than competitors.[55]

Because of the importance of product and service quality in achieving competitive parity or a competitive advantage, many firms in the United States and around the world are emphasizing total quality management and integrating it with their strategies. For example, Xerox achieved a critical turnaround in its performance in the 1980s that was largely attributed to its Leadership Through Quality program. Between 1986 and 1990, Xerox's annual revenues increased from $9.42 billion to $12.69 billion, and its return on assets increased from 7.8 percent to 14.6 percent. In 1989, Xerox won the prestigious Malcolm Baldridge National Quality Award.[56]

As our discussions have indicated, there are relationships between each of the four general factors (size, speed, innovation, and quality) that influence an industry's competitive dynamics and a firm's performance. These relationships are shown in Figure 5–2. Those responsible for selecting a firm's strategy should understand these relationships and anticipate that competitors will take competitive actions and competitive responses designed to exploit the positive relationships depicted in Figure 5–2.

In the next section, we describe different sets of competitive dynamics that are a part of the three general stages of an industry's life cycle.

**FIGURE 5–2  Effects of Firm Size, Order of Decisions/Actions, Innovation, and Quality on Firm Performance***

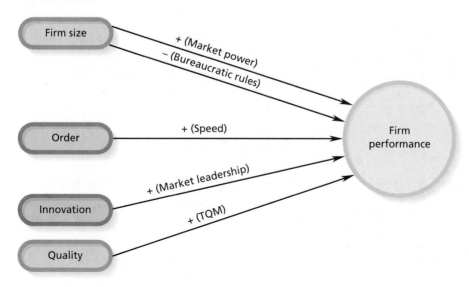

*plus and minus signs indicate effects on performance.*

## Competition and Industry Life Cycle

Because industry structure differs based on the life cycle of each industry, the competitive dynamics and competitive strategies necessary for success also differ. There are three general stages of the industry life cycle relevant to our study of competitive dynamics: new emerging industries, growth industries, and mature industries. These are shown in Figure 5–3.

Firms entering new emerging industries attempt to establish a niche or a form of dominance within an industry. There is strong competitive rivalry for the loyalty of customers. In these industries, depending upon the types of products, firms often attempt to establish product quality, technology, and/or advantageous relationships with suppliers in order to develop a sustainable competitive advantage in the pursuit of strategic competitiveness. These firms are striving to build their reputation. As a result, a variety of different competitive strategies may be employed in such an industry. Such diversity can be beneficial to many of the firms in the industry. The diversity of competitive strategies may avoid direct competition and help firms gain dominance in market niches.[57] While speed may be important in new emerging industries, access to capital is often the critical issue. Therefore, it is not uncommon to have strategic alliances develop between a new firm entering the market and a more established firm that wishes to gain a foothold in the new industry.[58]

Growth industries contain the survivors from the emerging industry stage. Thus, many of these firms are more established, but no less competitive. In fact, as the industry begins to mature, the variety of strategies being implemented tends to decrease.[59] Oftentimes there will be groups of firms that follow a similar strategy and thus are directly competitive. However, the rivalry between groups may be more indirect.[60] In industries where there is considerable within-strategic-group rivalry and competitive rivalry between firms in separate strategic groups, there is often less profitability among most firms.[61] Some of these industries may also be fragmented. Fragmented markets, such as fast food restaurants, tend to offer standardized facilities and products, but decentralized decision making to the local

**FIGURE 5–3  Industry Life Cycle**

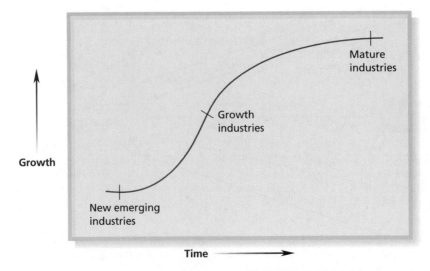

units. The standardization allows for low-cost competition. The primary value added comes from services provided. These markets offer a prime opportunity for franchising because of the ability to standardize facilities, operations, and products.

In nonfragmented industries, the speed of new product development and introduction to the marketplace becomes an important competitive weapon. Consumers tend to be more sophisticated and expect not only quality products, but also product designs that meet their needs. Firms that have the capability to move new products that better meet consumers' needs to the market more quickly are likely to gain a major competitive advantage.

In mature industries, there are usually fewer surviving competitors, and surviving companies tend to be larger. Furthermore, emphasis is placed on offering product lines that are profitable and producing those products in an efficient manner. New product innovation is deemphasized, while process innovation is emphasized. Process innovation helps to maintain cost efficiencies and the quality of the product manufactured and provided to customers.[62] Finally, firms in mature industries frequently seek international expansion or an increasing emphasis on their international operations and sales, a move that often extends the product life cycle (as explained in Chapter 8).

Firms in many industries have sought alternative means of attempting to manage and/or deal with strong competition in their pursuit of strategic competitiveness and above-average profits. One means that has become popular in the 1990s is that of strategic alliances.

## Managing Competition Through Strategic Alliances

**Strategic alliances** are partnerships between firms whereby resources, capabilities, and core competencies are combined to pursue mutual interests.[63] Sometimes strategic alliances are formed to achieve competitive parity, rather than competitive advantage (strategic alliances to achieve competitive advantage through innovation are discussed in Chapter 12). For example, while the BT–MCI strategic alliance may help these two firms achieve a competitive advantage over Sprint, it is designed primarily to help achieve competitive parity with AT&T in global markets. Strategic alliances may help some firms to move from below-average profits to average profits (industry average) by achieving competitive parity.

▲ **Strategic alliances** are partnerships between firms whereby resources, capabilities, and core competencies are combined to pursue mutual interests.

There are several distinct reasons for the formation of strategic alliances. In some manner, each reason relates to a firm's efforts to initiate competitive actions and competitive responses that will increase its strategic competitiveness.

### Reasons for Strategic Alliances

In addition to stiff competition, firms may be forced to undertake strategic alliances because of rapidly advancing technology and the shorter product and process life cycles. To enter some international markets, they may be required legally to form a strategic alliance and/or may need the knowledge necessary to operate effectively within that market.[64] Although these requirements may be reduced by the 1993 NAFTA and GATT agreements, there are multiple contingency factors that may form the basis for the formation of strategic alliances. However, one rationale for strategic alliances is to develop a sustainable competitive advantage.

▼ **TABLE 5–4**

### Reasons for Strategic Alliances

- Gain access to new markets
- Enter new businesses
- Introduce new products
- Overcome trade barriers
- Avoid predatory competition
- Gain access to complementary resources
- Pool resources, skills, and risk capital
- Share risk
- Share R&D expenses

Strategic alliances may be formed to enter new businesses or gain access to new markets. Many of the strategic alliances formed by U.S. companies with Chinese firms are developed to gain access to the Chinese market. In countries that have legal restrictions creating trade barriers (e.g., China) strategic alliances with firms in that country may help overcome those trade barriers to gain entry to the market. In addition, strategic alliances may be utilized to introduce new products in existing markets faster than new start-up ventures can.[65]

Oftentimes strategic alliances may avoid predator and/or wasteful competition within a particular market. In addition, they give firms an opportunity to gain access to resources complementary to their own and to spread the risk. A strategic alliance may be undertaken to share heavy research and development expenses in a high-technology industry. This pooling of resources and skills, along with access to risk capital, should help firms retain or regain strategic competitiveness.[66] In so doing, strategic alliances can help fill gaps in current market and technological bases, turn excess manufacturing capacity into profits by producing economies of scale, accelerate new product introductions, and reduce costs for entering new markets.[67] Research has shown that strategic alliances are often used to reduce market demand uncertainty and problems of competitive rivalry.[68] One way they do so is to create the opportunity for cooperation among competitors. Therefore, they cooperate, rather than compete. The primary reasons for strategic alliances are summarized in Table 5–4.

## Types of Strategic Alliances

Strategic alliances can take many forms. They can be short term or long term and may include partial or contractual ownership.[69] Rosabeth Moss Kanter of the Harvard Business School refers to strategic alliances as PALs—Pooling, Allying, and Linking—across companies. In her view, alliances provide a way for a firm to change from being an adversary to being an ally.

Kanter also proposes that there are three general types of alliances: service alliances, opportunistic alliances, and stakeholder alliances. **Service alliances** occur where a group of organizations with a similar need (often in the same industry) creates a new venture to satisfy that need. A common example of this alliance type is an industry research consortium. In a research consortium, firms pool their resources in order to perform research and development in search of new products and processes that have the potential to benefit all parties. The National Cooperative Research Act of 1984 allowed the formation of joint research and development consortia. Within a year, at least 40 R&D consortia were organized.[70]

**Opportunistic alliances** are those in which organizations see an opportunity to gain a competitive advantage, perhaps temporary, through the formation of a strategic alliance. The goal in this type of alliance is to form a new venture and create opportunities that did not exist for either partner acting alone. These types of alliances are normally referred to as joint ventures.

The third type of alliance is referred to as a stakeholder alliance because it creates complementary coalitions among stakeholders. A **stakeholder alliance** occurs when a firm forms an alliance with its suppliers, customers, employees, or other important stakeholders. Depending on the stakeholder, each of these alliances has a potentially different goal. For example, an alliance with a supplier may be used to outsource the development and manufacture of a particular product or part.[71]

▲ **Service alliances** occur where a group of organizations with a similar need (often in the same industry) creates a new venture to satisfy that need.

▲ **Opportunistic alliances** are those in which organizations see an opportunity to gain a competitive advantage, perhaps temporary, through the formation of a strategic alliance.

▲ A **stakeholder alliance** occurs when a firm forms an alliance with its suppliers, customers, employees, or other important stakeholders.

The type and number of alliances may be affected by culture and idiosyncratic country laws. For example, in countries where there is a strong emphasis on the family unit (leading to many family businesses), where labor contract law creates employment inflexibility, and there is a lack of capital to build larger businesses, large networks of alliances between smaller businesses develop. In effect, the networks of alliances substitute for larger organizations. Such networks are common in Italy's packaging and package machinery industry, for example.[72]

## Benefits of Strategic Alliances

Strategic alliances represent cooperative strategies that are becoming more common in domestic and international markets. Strategic alliances provide benefits to firms that they cannot obtain when acting alone. In fact, the reasons for strategic alliances shown in Table 5–3 largely represent the benefits that can be achieved through strategic alliances. It is not uncommon to see large corporations aligned with smaller corporations in an effort to develop a leading-edge technology. Furthermore, global strategic alliances have become particularly popular in the 1990s. Companies in the United States have aligned with foreign firms to enter international markets. General Electric has formed approximately 100 strategic alliances, and IBM has joined as a partner in over 400 strategic alliances. AT&T has formed strategic alliances with partners from the Netherlands, Italy, Spain, South Korea, Taiwan, and Japan, among others.[73]

Corning Glass Works uses alliances as a centerpiece of its corporate-level strategy. As such, the firm defines itself as a network of organizations. Over 50 percent of its corporate earnings come from joint ventures, suggesting the possibility that Corning may be the most successful practitioner of strategic alliances in the United States and the world.[74] Thus, firms may be successful with alliances by cooperating with a partner to facilitate the achievement of their own long-range goals. Strategic alliances enable firms to push the limits of technology by combining technological and creative resources and by providing access to more capital and to greater management capabilities. When managed properly, strategic alliances can increase the probability a firm can be successful.[75]

Alliances may be used by one or both partners to develop new capabilities (described in more detail in Chapter 12). However, not all firms are equally adept at developing and managing strategic alliances. Moreover, firms must be wary of the strategic intent of their partners. As suggested by the actions described in the next Strategic Focus, some firms have competitive as well as collaborative goals for the strategic alliance.[76]

As described in this Strategic Focus, a partner's strategic intent does not have to be malicious or intentionally competitive to lead to failure. In the GM-Daewoo joint venture, neither party understood the strategic orientation or the strategic intent of the other. As a result, they had much conflict, and multiple operational problems that could not be resolved. Thus, the joint venture ended in failure. We may conclude that while strategic alliances can be beneficial, they offer no panacea to competitive problems. They provide a potentially beneficial approach to cooperative strategies that can eliminate or avoid costly competition. Alternatively, they also have their own costs.[77]

The need for understanding partners' strategic orientation and intent in order to facilitate cooperation between them is displayed in Figure 5–4.

## Understanding a Partner's Strategic Intent

Komatsu, a Japanese firm, entered into licensing agreements with three U.S. companies—International Harvester, Bucyrus-Erie, and Cummins Engine—to manufacture and sell earthmoving equipment in Japan. These licensing agreements represented a first step toward the goal of Komatsu to become a global competitor in the earthmoving equipment business. However, its licensing partners were probably unaware of Komatsu's strategic intent. By the early 1980s, Komatsu had gained the knowledge necessary from the licensing agreements to become a full-line manufacturer and supplier of earthmoving equipment. It appealed to Japan's fair trade commission to support objections to contractual terms restricting the export of new products using the Bucyrus-Erie technology. The Japanese government agency agreed with Komatsu and allowed it to buy out the contract with Bucyrus-Erie. Soon thereafter it did the same with International Harvester. Essentially, Komatsu had digested the licensed technology and established its own. Therefore, it wanted out of the licensing agreements as another step toward becoming a major global competitor in this market.

However, not all partnerships fail because of the competitive strategic intent of one or more partners. In other cases, one partner may not understand the other's strategic orientation and intent, which may not be compatible. This is exemplified by the joint venture of General Motors (GM) and Daewoo, a Korean firm. In 1984, GM and Daewoo signed an agreement to build a factory in Korea to produce the Pontiac LeMans subcompact car. This automobile would utilize GM's German-based technology used in the Opel Kadett. The alliance would also provide GM with a manufacturing base in the Asian market. On the surface, the joint venture seemed to be a positive one for both partners. Daewoo did not have the expertise to design and manufacture a car such as the LeMans. Alternatively, GM did not have the ability to produce the LeMans in numbers that were needed to be profitable. There were other extensions of this venture, such as into auto parts. In fact, Daewoo was hoping to take advantage of this joint venture to gain market share from one of its chief Korean competitors, Hyundai.

However, multiple problems developed, and sales of the LeMans fell dramatically short of projected goals. The strategic orientations and intents of the two partners were quite different, which created multiple problems, including conflict between the managers of the two firms. For example, Daewoo wanted to invest aggressively in order to take advantage of Korea's booming domestic market in the late 1980s, but General Motors was not interested in making additional investments to take advantage of this market. There were numerous management clashes and operational disputes. Daewoo wanted to make decisions and move quickly, and GM's methodical approach prolonged decision making and created conflict. The partners did not understand each other's strategic goals or each other's strengths and weaknesses. The strategic orientation and intent of each partner differed from those of the other, and this was not known to either party prior to forming the venture. This led to production problems and multiple other obstacles. In fact, in Korea the LeMans was referred to as the Pontiac Lemons. One executive suggested that the two partners never learned to walk together before trying to run together. Unfortunately, the venture was dissolved.

**FIGURE 5–4**  Successful Strategic Alliances

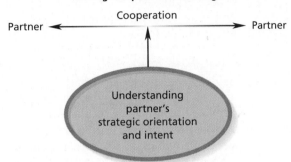

**Gaining competitive advantage**

## Summary

- Competitive rivalry entails actions and responses to competitive actions taken by other firms. There are two types of competitive actions, strategic and tactical. Strategic actions are more long term in nature, require many specific resources, and are difficult to reverse. Alternatively, tactical actions tend to be more short term in orientation, require fewer and more general resources, and be more easily reversed.

- The probability of a response by a competitor to a competitive action is based partially on the extent to which the competitor is dependent on the particular market in which the action was taken. In addition, the probability of response is based on the type of action, the reputation of the firm taking the strategic action (the expectation of success), and the resources available to the competitor contemplating response.

- There are more tactical than strategic actions taken, and there are more responses to tactical than to strategic actions. It is easier to respond to a tactical action, partly because it requires fewer resources. In addition, a tactical action is likely to have a shorter-term effect than a strategic action. Responses to strategic actions are more difficult, require more resources, and require a longer-term investment.

- The highest probability of a response comes when an action is taken by a market leader. Furthermore, when an action is taken by a market leader, it is more likely that a competitor will imitate the action taken. Alternatively, if the firm has a reputation as a strategic player (a firm that takes more complex and risky actions), there is a lower probability of re-

sponse. A price predator is also less likely to elicit a response from competitors.

- When competitors are highly dependent on a market in which competitive actions are taken, there is a high probability that they will respond to such actions. However, firms that are more diversified across markets are less likely to respond to any particular action that affects only one of the markets in which they compete.

- One of the critical characteristics affecting the probability of response is the level of resources available to competitors. Those with more resources are more likely to respond than are those with fewer resources. Also, those with more resources are more likely to respond to strategic actions than are those with fewer resources. Furthermore, the probability of response is determined not only by the amount of resources, but also by the types of resources available and needed to respond to particular actions.

- Other important characteristics in competitive actions and responses include the size of the acting and responding firms, the function of speed in the industry, the importance of innovation in competitive moves and product quality.

- First movers can gain a competitive advantage and customer loyalty by being the first in the market. First movers also take more risk. However, first movers often are higher performers. Second movers, particularly those that are fast, can also gain a competitive advantage and/or be profitable because they imitate, but do not take some of the risks that first movers do. The longer the time required to respond, the higher the probability that the first mover will enjoy strong performance gains. Late movers (those that respond a long time after the original action was taken) tend to be lower performers and much less effective.

- Large firms often have strong market power. Alternatively, as firms grow larger, they often institute bureaucratic rules, procedures, and structures. These have the effect of reducing the probability that a firm will take actions and respond to others' actions. In addition, they reduce the speed with which a firm may be able to implement an action or respond to competitors' actions.

- Speed is becoming increasingly important in many industries in order to gain and hold a competitive advantage. In fact, many large firms must act like small firms (flexible and agile) in order to be competitive. This may require that they decentralize many responsibilities and decisions and that they create cross-functional teams in order to speed multiple processes (e.g., the innovation process) in the firms.

- Both product and process innovation are becoming more important in the competitive posture of may industries. Some research has shown that firms that invest more in R&D and that are more innovative tend to have higher performance in multiple industries. Product innovation tends to be more important in new emerging and growth industries. However, mature industries may emphasize process innovation.

- Product quality has become critical in order to maintain competitive parity in most industries. Total quality management (TQM) must be infused throughout the organization by top management and integrated with firm strategies.

- The industry life cycle is important in determining the type of competition and the type of competitive actions that are the most effective. For example, in new emerging industries, firms are attempting to establish a reputation and develop dominance in a market niche and/or in the technology or quality of products provided. In growth industries, special emphasis may be placed on innovation and speed of actions taken. Whereas, in mature industries with fewer competitors, special emphasis is placed on the most profitable product lines and process innovation in order to produce and distribute those products with the greatest efficiency (lowest cost).

- As a way of responding to the strong competitive pressures in many industries, firms have begun to develop cooperative strategies; chief among them is strategic alliances. There are multiple reasons for the formation of strategic alliances, including gaining access to new materials, entering new businesses, introducing new products, overcoming trade barriers, avoiding predatory competition, gaining access to complementary resources, sharing risk, and pooling resources, skills, and risk capital, as well as sharing R&D expenses.

- Strategic alliances can produce significant benefits, but they are also not without costs. In addition to having to share the profits, firms must understand partners' strategic orientations and intents. It is not uncommon for some firms to enter strategic alliances in order to appropriate technological knowledge that will give them future competitive advantage over their partners and others in the industry.

## Review Questions

1. What are the differences between strategic and tactical actions?
2. On what four factors is the likelihood of a response to a competitive action based?
3. What is the likelihood of response to a tactical action, a strategic action, and actions taken by market leaders? Explain why.
4. What are the advantages and the disadvantages of size regarding strategic actions and responses thereto?
5. Why is speed important in many industries? What can firms do to increase the speed at which they make and implement strategic decisions?
6. In what types of industries is innovation important for competitive advantage? Explain the importance of different types of innovation (product and process) for success in different industries.
7. How do industry life cycles affect competition? Identify three stages of the industry life cycle, and briefly explain the types of competitive actions most important in those stages.
8. What are the reasons for the formation of strategic alliances? Describe the different types of strategic alliances firms might undertake. Explain the advantages and the disadvantages of each type and how they might be used.

## Application Discussion Questions

1. Read the popular business press (e.g., *Business Week, Fortune*), and identify a strategic action and a tactical action taken by firms approximately two years ago. Next read the popular business press to see if, and how, competitors responded to those actions. Explain the actions and the responses, linking your findings to the discussion in this chapter.
2. Why would a firm regularly use a second-mover strategy? Likewise, why would a firm purposefully be a late mover?
3. Explain how Sun Microsystems' strategic actions affected its primary competitors (e.g., IBM).
4. Choose a large firm and examine the popular business press to identify how its size, speed of actions, level of innovation, and quality of goods or services have affected its competitive position in its industry. Explain your findings.
5. Identify three strategic alliances in different industries. After reading the business press's descriptions of these alliances and/or the firms' annual reports, explain the reasons for these strategic alliances, describe their type, and estimate their value to the firms involved.
6. Identify a new emerging industry, a growth industry, and a mature industry. Describe the type of competition that exists within each of these industries, using the concepts communicated in this chapter.

## Ethics Questions

1. In your opinion, are some industries known for ethical practices, while others are not? If so, name industries thought to be ethical and those that are evaluated less favorably in terms of ethics. How might the competitive actions and competitive responses differ between an "ethical" and an "unethical" industry?
2. When engaging in competitive rivalry, firms jockey for a market position that is advantageous, relative to competitors. Would it be unethical for a firm to take a competitive action simply to observe its chief competitor's response to that action? Why or why not?
3. A second mover is a firm that responds to a first mover's competitive actions, often through imitation. Is there anything unethical about how a second mover engages in competition? Why or why not?
4. Standards for competitive rivalry differ in countries throughout the world. What should firms do to cope with these differences?
5. Can cross-functional teams be used to foster ethical practices in the design, production, and distribution of a firm's products? If so, how?
6. Is it possible that total quality management practices could result in firms operating more ethically than before such practices were implemented? If this is possible, what might account for an increase in the ethic behavior of a firm and when using TQM principles?
7. What ethical issues are involved with the formation of a strategic alliance? Are there certain industries in which you believe alliances might be less effective? If so, what industries, and for what reasons?

## Notes

1. A. Taylor III, 1994, The new golden age of autos, *Fortune*, April 4, 51–66.
2. J. Meredith, 1987, The strategic advantages of new manufacturing technologies for small firms, *Strategic Management Journal*, 8: 249–258.
3. M. E. Porter, 1980, *Competitive Strategy* (New York: Free Press), 17.
4. Associated Press, 1994, Hot management team helps put sizzle in Boston Chicken, *Dallas Morning News*, March 13, 14H.
5. Porter, *Competitive Strategy*, 17.
6. M. Chen and D. Miller, 1994, Competitive attack, retaliation and performance: An expectancy-valence framework, *Strategic Management Journal* 15: 85–102.
7. K. G. Smith, C. M. Grimm, and M. J. Gannon, 1992, *Dynamics of Competitive Strategy* Newberry Park, Calif.: Sage).
8. Ibid.
9. K. Labich, 1994, Air wars over Asia, *Fortune*, April 4, 93–98.
10. Smith, Grimm, and Gannon, *Dynamics of Competitive Strategy*.
11. Ibid.
12. J. J. Keller and M. L. Carnevale, 1993, MCI–BT tie is seen setting off a battle in communications, *Wall Street Journal*, June 3, A1, A6.
13. J. J. Keller, 1993, Sprint hangs back as its rivals forge global alliances, *Wall Street Journal*, June 4, B4.

14. K. G. Smith, C. M. Grimm, M. J. Gannon and M. J. Chen, 1991, Organizational information-processing, competitive responses and performance in the U.S. domestic airline industry, *Academy of Management Journal* 34: 60–85.

15. R. R. Nelson and S. G. Winter, 1982, *An Evolutionary Theory of Economic Change* (Cambridge: Harvard University Press).

16. M. B. Lieberman and D. B. Montgomery, 1988, First-mover advantages, *Strategic Management Journal* 9: 41–58.

17. Smith, Grimm, and Gannon, *Dynamics of Competitive Strategy.*

18. A. Ginsberg and N. Venkatraman, 1992, Investing in new information technology: The role of competitive posture and issue diagnosis, *Strategic Management Journal* 13 (Special Issue): 37–53.

19. Smith, Grimm, and Gannon, *Dynamics of Competitive Strategy.*

20. J. A. Schumpeter, 1961, *Theory of Economic Development* (New York: Oxford University Press).

21. H. Gleckman, 1993, Meet the giant-killers. *Business Week* (Special Issue), 68–73.

22. R. A. Melcher, 1993, How Goliaths can act like Davids, *Business Week* (Special Issue), 193.

23. P. Nulty, 1994, Hall of fame, *Fortune,* April 4, 118–128.

24. J. T. Vessey, 1991, The new competitors: They think in terms of "speed to market," *Academy of Management Executive* 5, no. 2: 23–33.

25. S. Wally and J. R. Baum, 1994, Personal and structural determinants of the pace of strategic decision-making, *Academy of Management Journal,* in press.

26. Ibid.

27. T. Smart and J. H. Dobrzynski, 1993, Jack Welch on the art of thinking small, *Business Week* (Special Enterprise Issue), 212–216.

28. Taylor, Will success spoil Chrysler?

29. K. M. Eisenhardt, 1989, Making fast strategic decisions in high-velocity environments, *Academy of Management Journal* 32: 543–576; K. M. Eisenhardt and J. Bourgeois, 1988, Politics of strategic decision making in high-velocity environments: Toward a midrange theory, *Academy of Management Journal* 31: 737–770.

30. M. A. Hitt, R. E. Hoskisson, and R. Nixon, 1993, A mid-range theory of interfunctional integration, its antecedents and outcomes, *Journal of Engineering and Technology Management* 10: 161–185.

31. L. G. Franko, 1989, Global corporate competition: Who's winning, who's losing, and the R&D factor as one reason why, *Strategic Management Journal* 10: 449–474.

32. R. E. Hoskisson and M. A. Hitt, 1994, *Downscoping: How to Tame the Diversified Firm* (New York: Oxford University Press).

33. P. Ghemawat, 1986, Sustainable advantage, *Harvard Business Review* 64, no. 5: 53–58.

34. R. Garud and A. Kumaraswamy, 1993, Changing competitive dynamics in network industries: An exploration of Sun Microsystems' open systems strategy, *Strategic Management Journal,* 14: 351–369.

35. M. Chase, 1993, Sun Microsystems juggles new strategies and old rivals, *Wall Street Journal,* May 19, B2.

36. J. Aley, 1994, Manufacturers grade themselves, *Fortune,* March 21, 26.

37. A. Taylor III, 1993, Shaking up Jaguar, *Fortune,* September 6, 65–68.

38. R. Henkoff, 1993, The hot new seal of quality, *Fortune,* June 28, 117.

39. Ibid., 116.

40. B. Rothery, 1993, *ISO 9000,* 2nd ed. (Brookfield, Vt.: Gower Press), 19.

41. A. Taylor III, 1993, Here comes Japan's carmakers—again, *Fortune,* December 13, 129.

42. Ibid.

43. J. W. Dean, Jr., and J. R. Evans, 1994, *Total Quality: Management, Organization and Society* (St. Paul: West).

44. T. F. Rienzo, 1993, Planning Deming management for service organizations, *Business Horizons* 36, no. 3: 19–29.

45. S. Chatterjee and M. Yilmaz, 1993, Quality confusion: Too many gurus, not enough disciples, *Business Horizons* 36, no. 3: 15–18.

46. Dean and Evans, *Total Quality.*

47. Nulty, Hall of fame, 118.

48. Dean and Evans, *Total Quality,* 12.

49. E. E. Lawler III, Total quality management and employee involvement: Are they compatible? *Academy of Management Executive* 8, no. 1: 68.

50. Nulty, Hall of fame.

51. E. Adam, Jr., and R. J. Ebert, 1992, *Production and Operations Management,* 5th ed. (Englewood Cliffs, N.J.: Prentice-Hall), 634–641.

52. R. Jacob, 1993, TQM: More than a dying fad? *Fortune,* October 18, 66–72; R. Krishnan, A. B. Shani and G. R. Baer, 1993, In search of quality improvement: Problems of design and implementation, *Academy of Management Executive* 7, no. 4: 7–20.

53. R. Blackburn and B. Rosen, 1993, Total quality and human resources management: Lessons learned from Baldridge award-winning companies, *Academy of Management Executive* 7, no. 3: 49–66.

54. H. V. Roberts and B. F. Sergesketter, 1993, *Quality Is Personal* (New York: Free Press).

55. Dean & Evans, *Total Quality.*

56. Ibid.

57. M. A. Hitt, B. B. Tyler, C. Hardee, and D. Park, 1994, Understanding strategic intent in the global marketplace, *Academy of Management Executive,* in press.

58. G. Miles, C. Snow, and M. P. Sharfman, 1993, Industry variety and performance, *Strategic Management Journal* 14: 163–177.

59. D. Lei, 1989, Strategies for global competition, *Long-Range Planning* 22:102–109.

60. Miles, Snow, and Sharfman, Industry variety.

61. K. Cool and I. Dierickx, 1993, Rivalry, strategic groups and firm profitability, *Strategic Management Journal* 14: 47–59.

62. D. M. Schroeder, 1990, A dynamic perspective on the impact of process innovation upon competitive strategies, *Strategic Management Journal* 11: 25–41.

63. B. Borys and D. B. Jemison, 1989, Hybrid arrangements as strategic alliances: Theoretical issues in organizational combinations, *Academy of Management Review* 14: 234–249; J. E. Forrest, 1992, Management aspects of strategic partnering, *Journal of General Management* 17, no. 4: 25–40.

64. D. B. Merrifield, 1992, Global strategic alliances among firms, *International Journal of Technology Management* 7: 77–83.

65. M. Selwyn and L. Valigra, 1991, Making marriages of convenience; Fuji-Xerox: Example worth copying, *Asian Business,* January, 26–29; J. C. Mason, 1993, Strategic alliances among firms: Partnering for success, *Management Review* 82, no. 5: 10–11.

66. R. Peterson, 1992, Strategic alliances can also aid small businesses, *Marketing News,* May 24, 3.

67. P. Flanagan, 1993, Strategic alliances keep customers plugged in, *Management Review* 82, no. 3: 24–26.

68. W. P. Burgers, C. W. L. Hill, and W. C. Kim, 1993, The theory of global strategic alliances: The case of the global auto industry, *Strategic Management Journal* 14: 419–432.

69. Forrest, Management aspects.

70. R. M. Kanter, 1989, Becoming PALs: Pooling, allying, and linking across companies, *Academy of Management Executive* 3: 183–193.

71. Ibid. J. Lorinc, 1990, Alliances: Going global made simple, *Canadian Business* 63 (November): 126–137; M. Robert, 1992, The do's and don'ts of strategic alliances, *Journal of Business Strategy* 13 (March/April): 50–53.

72. G. Lorenzoni and O. Ornati, 1988, Constellations of firms and new ventures, *Journal of Business Venturing,* 3, 41–57; A. Lipparini and M. Sobrero, 1994, The glue and the pieces: Entrepreneurship and innovation in small-firm networks, *Journal of Business Venturing,* 9, 125–140.

73. Hitt, Tyler, Hardee, and Park, Understanding strategic intent.

74. J. D. Lewis, 1991, Competitive alliances redefine companies, *Management Review* 80, no. 4: 14–18; S. Sherman, 1992, Are strategic alliances working? *Fortune,* September 21, 76–78.

75. D. Lei, and J. W. Slocum, Jr., 1992, Global strategy, competence-building and strategic alliances, *California Management Review,* 35 (Fall): 81–97.

76. G. Hamel, 1991, Competition for competence and inter-partner learning within international strategic alliances, *Strategic Management Journal* 12: 83–103.

77. Hitt, Tyler, Hardee, and Park, Understanding strategic intent.

# CHAPTER 6
## Corporate-Level Strategy

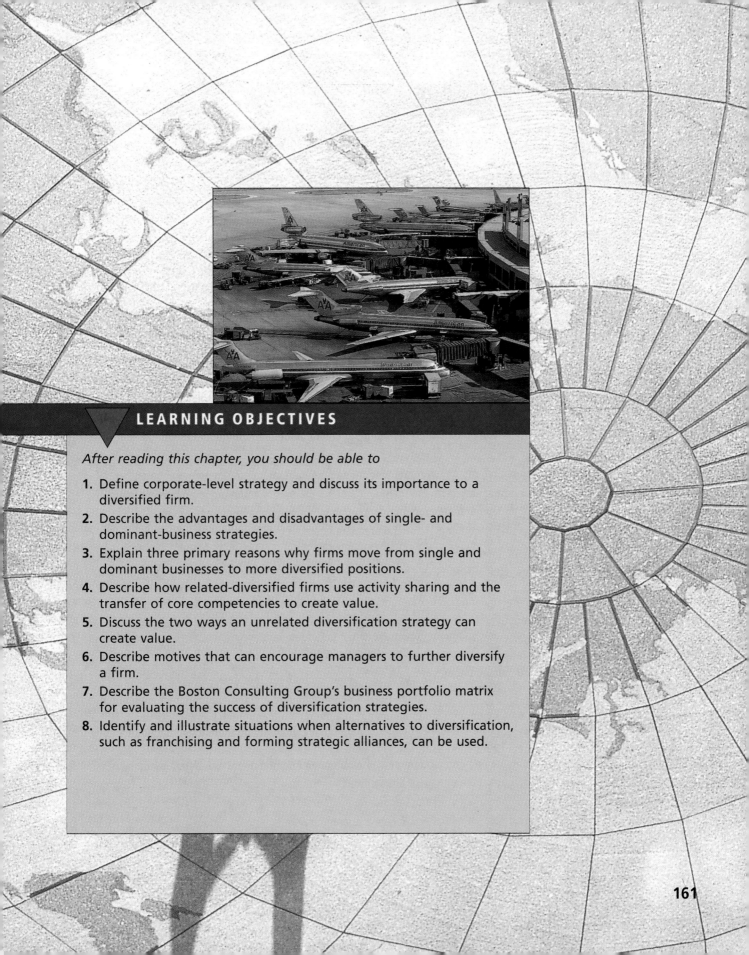

*After reading this chapter, you should be able to*

1. Define corporate-level strategy and discuss its importance to a diversified firm.
2. Describe the advantages and disadvantages of single- and dominant-business strategies.
3. Explain three primary reasons why firms move from single and dominant businesses to more diversified positions.
4. Describe how related-diversified firms use activity sharing and the transfer of core competencies to create value.
5. Discuss the two ways an unrelated diversification strategy can create value.
6. Describe motives that can encourage managers to further diversify a firm.
7. Describe the Boston Consulting Group's business portfolio matrix for evaluating the success of diversification strategies.
8. Identify and illustrate situations when alternatives to diversification, such as franchising and forming strategic alliances, can be used.

## Tired of Losses in Its Airline Business, AMR Corp. Seeks More Diversification

In recent years, AMR Corporation has suffered significant losses. The primary reason for this is that the firm's main business, American Airlines, has been unprofitable. Between 1990 and 1992, AMR lost $1.2 billion, with additional losses incurred in 1993, but without American Airlines, AMR would have been profitable. The airline industry has been hounded by a global recession, vicious fare wars, and volatile fuel prices. In addition, because of new entrants and expansion by other airlines, the industry suffers from overcapacity.

Unlike its airline company, AMR's other businesses, including Sabre Travel Information Network, AMR Services, AMR Information Services, American Airlines Decision Technologies, AMR Investment Services, and AMR Consulting Group, were profitable in the early 1990s. Losses from its airline unit underscore the importance of expanding AMR's diversified businesses, while reducing its focus on American Airlines. Recently, the company earned 91 percent of its sales from the airline unit.

In the 1980s, part of AMR's corporate-level strategy called for growth in the American Airlines business unit. This growth was achieved through the purchase and use of more planes to establish additional hubs and routes and offering more flights. However, these growth plans were abandoned. The problem encountered in implementing the airline's strategy was that virtually all airlines throughout the world were initiating the same competitive actions. Because its actions were not based on core competencies, American Airlines was not able to establish a sustainable competitive advantage.

To reduce its overcapacity, and to gain a competitive advantage in the process, American Airlines attempted to simplify fares in 1992. This tactical competitive action did not yield the results sought, causing Robert L. Crandall, AMR Corp.'s CEO, to suggest that many of the airline industry's problems are intractable.

AMR has initiated many competitive actions to deal with its challenges. Since November 1992, the firm has laid off 1,000 airline management employees, with additional layoffs planned for airline operations personnel. The firm is also attempting to apply some of the airline unit's resources, capabilities, and core competencies in its other businesses. For instance, ticket processors from American's keypunch center are being retrained to handle medical and dental insurance claims for Blue Cross/Blue Shield. AMR Information Services is building a computerized reservations system for a French high-speed rail network, and a similar system is planned for the tunnel under the English Channel. This business unit is also providing Canadian Airlines with an information-services system, including computerized reservations, accounting, data processing, and pricing services. The Polish government has contracted with AMR Corp. to manage the Warsaw Airport in Poland. AMR also publishes in-flight magazines for other airlines, such as Southwest and Delta. With all these efforts, the nonairline units earned $216.3 million in 1992 and $240 million in 1993. In contrast, the American Airlines unit recorded a $237.8 million net loss in 1992 alone. Without its diversification strategy, AMR would have little choice but to cut costs and suffer continuing losses in its airline business. ▲

As do all firms, AMR Corp. seeks to formulate and implement strategies through which its core competencies are used to gain a sustainable competitive advantage. At least partly because its American Airlines unit operates in one of the world's most cyclical and competitive industries,[1] AMR's top-level managers are challenged to manage the firm's corporate-level strategy effectively. As indicated by information in the opening case, one way AMR's managers are dealing with this challenge is to expand beyond the firm's core business of flying passengers and cargo into nonairline businesses.[2] Furthermore, AMR indicated recently that it would "make ongoing determinations as to the appropriate degree of reallocation of resources from the airline operations to its other businesses, which may include, if the airline cannot be run profitably, the disposition or termination, over the long term, of a substantial part or all of the airline operations."[3]

In Chapters 4 and 5, our discussions focused on the selection and use of business-level strategies. In essence, a business-level strategy is a competitive strategy; that is, it is a strategy indicating the actions a firm will take to compete in a particular industry or product market.[4] Thus, our discussions of different business-level strategies (Chapter 4) and the competitive dynamics associated with their use (Chapter 5) were concerned primarily with firms competing in a single industry or product market.

When a firm chooses to diversify its operations beyond a single industry and to operate businesses in several industries, a corporate-level strategy is required. A diversified company, then, has two levels of strategy: a business-level (or competitive) strategy and a corporate-level (or company-wide) strategy.[5] In diversified firms, each business unit chooses the business-level strategy it will implement to achieve strategic competitiveness and earn above-average profits. But diversified firms must also choose a strategy that is concerned with the selection and management of its businesses. Defined formally, a **corporate-level strategy** is action taken to gain a competitive advantage through the selection and management of a mix of businesses competing in several industries or product markets. In essence, a corporate-level strategy is what makes "the corporate whole add up to more than the sum of its business unit parts."[6] Corporate-level strategy is concerned with two key questions: what businesses the firm should be in and how the corporate office should manage its group of businesses.[7] In the current complex global environment, top-level managers should view their firm's businesses as a portfolio of core competencies when seeking answers to these critical questions.[8]

▲ A **corporate-level strategy** is action taken to gain a competitive advantage through the selection and management of a mix of businesses competing in several industries or product markets.

As with business-level strategies, corporate-level strategies are expected to create value for a firm.[9] In the early 1990s, some suggested that few corporate-level strategies actually create value.[10] In the final analysis, the value of a corporate-level strategy "must be that the businesses in the portfolio are worth more under the management of the company in question than they would be under any other ownership."[11] When managed effectively, then, corporate-level strategies enhance a firm's strategic competitiveness and contribute to its profitability.[12] In the latter part of the 1990s and into the twenty-first century, corporate-level strategies will be managed in a global business environment characterized by high degrees of risk, complexity, uncertainty, and ambiguity.[13]

A primary approach to corporate-level strategy is diversification. A corporate diversification strategy requires that corporate executives craft a multibusiness strategy. An argument supporting use of a diversification strategy is that managers of diversified firms possess unique, general management skills that can be used to craft multibusiness strategies and enhance a firm's strategic competitiveness.[14] The essence of the prevailing theory of diversification is that firms diversify when they have excess resources, capabilities, and core competencies that have multiple uses.[15] A multibusiness strategy often encompasses many different industry environments, and, as is discussed in Chapter 10, this type of strategy requires a unique organizational structure.

This chapter begins by addressing the history of diversification. Included in this discussion are descriptions of the advantages and disadvantages of single- and dominant-business strategies. We next describe different levels of diversification (from low to high) and reasons firms pursue a corporate-level strategy of diversification. Two types of diversification strategy—related and unrelated—are then examined.

Large diversified firms often compete against each other in several markets. This is called multipoint competition. For instance, RJR Nabisco competes against Philip Morris in both cigarettes and consumer foods. Vertical integration strategies designed to exploit market share and gain power over competitors are also explored. To help understand strategic allocations of resources among a firm's portfolio of businesses, a technique for evaluating diversification strategies, the Boston Consulting Group portfolio matrix, is discussed. We selected this particular matrix for analysis because it is the most widely known approach.

Of course, there are alternatives to diversification. These approaches entail long-term contracts, such as strategic alliances and franchising. Closing the chapter are discussions of these diversification alternatives.

## History of Diversification

In 1950, only 38.1 percent of the *Fortune* 500 U.S. industrial companies generated more than 25 percent of their revenues from diversified activities. By 1974, this figure had risen to 63 percent. In 1950, then, over 60 percent of the largest *Fortune* 500 industrial companies were either single-business or dominant-business firms; by 1974, this had dropped to 37 percent.[16]

Beginning in the late 1970s, and especially through the middle part of the 1980s, a significant trend of refocusing and divestiture of business units unrelated to core business activities took place in many firms. As a result, by 1988, the percentage of single- or dominant-business firms on the *Fortune* 500 list of industrial companies had increased to 53 percent.[17] Although many diversified firms have returned to a more specialized approach, this is somewhat masked because there has been extensive market and international diversification (compared to product diversification) that would not be encompassed in these statistics. As Chapter 8's discussion reveals, international strategy has been increasing in importance and has led to increased financial performance relative to product diversification.[18]

The trend toward product diversification of business organizations has been most significant among U.S. firms. Nonetheless, large business organizations in Europe, Asia, and other parts of the industrialized world have also implemented diversification strategies. In the United Kingdom, the number of single- or dominant-business firms fell from 60 percent in 1960 to 37 percent in 1980. A similar, yet less dramatic trend toward more diversification occurred in Japan. Among the largest Japanese firms, 60 percent were dominant- or single-business firms in 1958, although this percentage fell only to 53 percent in 1973.

These trends toward more diversification, which have been partially reversed due to restructuring, indicate that learning has taken place regarding corporate diversification strategies. The main lesson learned is that firms performing well in their dominant business may not want to diversify. Moreover, firms that diversify should do so cautiously, choosing to focus on a relatively few, rather than many, businesses.[19] However, there are risks to limited diversification, as AMR's historical focus on American Airlines suggests.

Other firms, such as the Wm. Wrigley Jr. Co., with its focus on chewing gum, have become very successful by emphasizing a dominant business.[20] In addition to increasing its share of the U.S. chewing gum market, Wrigley's sales were expanding rapidly in international markets in 1994. Because of dramatic sales volume growth in Poland, Central Europe, and Russia, Wrigley held discussions with Polish officials about the possibility of building a chewing gum plant in Poznan.[21]

Other information about Wrigley is presented in the next Strategic Focus.

## Levels of Diversification

Diversified firms vary according to the level of diversification and connection between and among their businesses. Figure 6–1 lists and defines five categories of businesses according to increasing levels of diversification. Besides single- and dominant-business categories, more fully diversified firms are classified into related and unrelated categories. A firm is related through its diversification when there are several links between business units. Through these links, units share products or services, technologies, and/or distribution channels. The more linkages among businesses, the more "constrained" the relatedness of diversification. Unrelatedness refers to a lack of direct linkages between businesses.

### Low Levels of Diversification

A firm pursuing a low level of diversification focuses its efforts on a single or a dominant business. The Wm. Wrigley Jr. Co. is an example of a firm with little diversification. A firm is classified as a single business when revenues generated by the dominant business are greater than 95 percent of the total sales.[22] Dominant businesses are firms that generate between 70 percent and 95 percent of their total sales within a single category. Because of the sales it generates from breakfast cereals, Kellogg is an example of a dominant-business firm. Often dominant-business firms have some level of vertical integration. In an evolutionary sense, many firms (such as Texaco in petroleum) started as single businesses and evolved to dominant businesses through vertical integration.

### Moderate to High Levels of Diversification

When a firm earns more than 30 percent of its sales volume outside a dominant business, and when its businesses are related to each other in some manner, the

## STRATEGIC FOCUS

### Achieving Strategic Competitiveness in a Nondiversified Firm

Since its beginning, Wm. Wrigley Jr. Co. has held the largest share of the U.S. chewing gum market. Early in its life, however, the firm was challenged to promote its product and gain market acceptance. In 1915, as a method of product promotion, Wrigley mailed one stick of chewing gum to every person listed in a telephone book in the United States. Today Wrigley is the world's largest manufacturer and seller of chewing gum, specialty gums, and gum base. Its principal brands of chewing gum are Wrigley's Spearmint, Doublemint, Juicy Fruit, Big Red, Extra, and Freedent.

The Wrigley Co. has not diversified extensively, even into related products (although it acquired the Reed Candy Co. in 1989). Recently Wrigley held 48 percent of the $2.4 billion U.S. market for chewing gum. Its chief competitors, RJR Nabisco (Beechnut and Carefree) and Warner-Lambert (Trident and Dentyne), had much smaller market shares. Wrigley's strategic focus has obviously paid off relative to its more diversified competitors (RJR Nabisco and Warner-Lambert). Its only market share decline in recent times occurred in the late 1970s when other firms first introduced sugar-free gum. Wrigley responded to this competitive action by quickly introducing its own sugar-free gum, Extra, which now owns the largest share of this market.

Wrigley is one of the few large and well-known firms that has maintained a strategic focus on one product line and has not diversified to any significant extent. Its success has been aided by a relatively constant demand for chewing gum. In fact, the demand for chewing gum may increase slightly during recessions. While Wrigley has avoided the trend to diversify, many U.S., European, and other firms throughout the world have diversified their product lines, some significantly so. Unfortunately, the performance of many of these diversified firms has not matched that of the Wrigley Co.

The Wm. Wrigley Jr. Co. has avoided costly diversification. A continuous and strong focus on the firm's core business, chewing gum, allows the executives to maintain strategic control of the business. Family members were not concerned about employment risk and, in fact, desired to maintain strategic control. The result was a clear strategic focus and a highly competitive firm in its primary market.

company is classified as a related-diversified firm. With more constrained linkages between the businesses, the firm is defined as related constrained. Examples of related-constrained firms include Campbell's Soup Co., Procter & Gamble, Xerox, Boise Cascade, and Merck & Co. If there are relatively few linkages between businesses, the firm is defined as a mixed related and unrelated business, or a related-linked firm (see Figure 6–1). Johnson and Johnson, Westinghouse, General Electric, General Mills, Schlumberger, and USX Corp. are examples of related-linked firms. Related-constrained firms share a number of resources and activities between businesses. However, related-linked firms have less sharing of actual resources and assets and relatively more transfers of knowledge and competencies between businesses. Highly diversified firms, which have no relationships between businesses, are called unrelated-diversified firms. There are more unrelated-diversified firms in the U.S. than in other (e.g., European or Asian) countries. Firms that have

**FIGURE 6–1** Levels and Types of Diversification

**Low levels of diversification**

Single-business:    Over 95% of revenues come from a single business.

Dominant-business:    Between 70% and 95% of revenues come from a single business.

**Moderate to high levels of diversification**

Related-constrained:    Less than 70% of revenues comes from the dominant business, and all businesses share product, technological, and distribution linkages.

Mixed related and    Less than 70% of revenues comes from
unrelated (related-linked):    the dominant business, and there are only limited links between businesses.

**Very high levels of diversification**

Unrelated diversification:    Less than 70% of revenues come from the dominant business, and there are no common links between businesses.

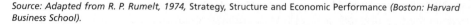

*Source: Adapted from R. P. Rumelt, 1974,* Strategy, Structure and Economic Performance *(Boston: Harvard Business School).*

pursued unrelated diversification in past years include Tenneco, Textron, ITT, TRW, LTV, and Hanson Trust (a British firm).

Consistent with a global trend of refocusing, at least some firms pursuing a strategy of unrelated diversification are now concentrating on fewer lines of business. Textron, for example, has sold 24 businesses since 1985. In the process of

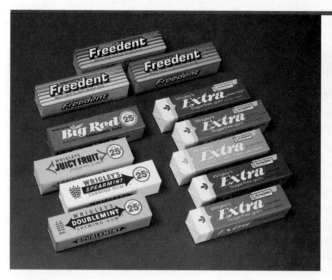

*To achieve strategic competitiveness, some firms concentrate on a single or a dominant business line. Wrigley, for example, earns at least 95 percent of its sales revenues from chewing gum products. Concentrating primarily on cereals, Kellogg earns at least 70 percent of its sales from a product category called breakfast cereals. Both of these firms have been successful in their implementation of strategies with low levels of diversification.*

doing so, the company has deemphasized financial services to focus on its manufacturing operations. Since 1979, ITT has sold over 240 businesses. With relatively few business units remaining, ITT earned $913 million in 1993. In early 1994, the firm's stock was up 207 percent from its 1990 low. Although refocused, both Textron and ITT are still unrelated-diversified firms.[23]

## Reasons for Diversification

There are many reasons firms implement a diversification strategy as their corporate-level strategy. A partial list of these is shown in Table 6–1. These reasons are discussed throughout the remainder of this chapter in relationship to specific diversification strategies.

Most firms implement a diversification strategy to enhance the strategic competitiveness of the entire corporation. When this is accomplished, the total value of the firm is increased. Value is created through either related diversification or unrelated diversification when those strategies allow a corporation's business units to increase revenues and/or reduce costs while implementing their business-level strategies. Another reason for diversification is to gain market power relative to competitors.

Other reasons for implementing diversification may not create value, but may be value neutral or may actually increase costs or decrease a firm's revenues. These reasons include diversification (1) to neutralize a competitor's market power (e.g., to neutralize the advantage of another firm by acquiring a distribution outlet similar to those of the competitors) or (2) to expand a firm's portfolio in order to reduce managerial employment risk (e.g., if a single business fails, a top-level manager remains employed in a diversified firm). Because diversification can increase firm size, managers may have motives to diversify a firm. This type of diversification may decrease shareholder wealth and firm value.

## Related Diversification

▲ **Economies of scope** are cost savings attributed to transferring the capabilities and competencies developed in one business to a new business without significant additional costs.

Firms that have selected related diversification as their corporate-level strategy seek to exploit economies of scope between business units. Available to firms operating in multiple industries or product markets,[24] **economies of scope** are cost savings attributed to transferring the capabilities and competencies developed in one business to a new business without significant additional costs.

There are two basic kinds of operational economies through which firms seek to create value from economies of scope: sharing activities and transferring core competencies. The difference between sharing activities and transferring competencies is based on how different resources are used jointly to create economies of scope. Tangible resources, such as plant and equipment or other business-unit physical assets, often must be shared to create economies of scope. Less tangible resources, such as sales forces, also can be shared. However, know-how, an intangible resource, is the essence of competence transfer. When know-how is transferred between separate activities and there is no physical or tangible resource involved, transferring competencies, as opposed to sharing activities, is the main source of value creation.

## Sharing Activities

Activity sharing is quite common, especially among related-constrained firms. At Procter & Gamble, a paper towels business and a baby diapers business both use paper products as a primary input to the manufacturing process. Having a joint paper production plant that produces inputs for both divisions is an example of a potential shared activity. In addition, these businesses are likely to share distribution sales networks because they both produce consumer products.

In Chapter 3, primary and support value chain activities were discussed. In general, primary activities, such as inbound logistics, operations, and outbound logistics, might have multiple shared activities. Through effective and efficient sharing of these activities, firms may be able to create core competencies that result in competitive advantages. In terms of inbound logistics, the business units may share common inventory delivery systems, warehousing facilities, and quality assurance practices. Operations might share common assembly facilities, quality control systems, or maintenance operations. With respect to outbound logistics, two business units might share a common sales force and sales service desk. Support activities could include the sharing of procurement and technology development efforts. For example, Otis Elevator has a number of different businesses, all of which are combined through the firm's electrical engine utilization technology. Today many large automobile firms use the standard platform around which many of their vehicles are designed, thus saving costs on engineering design.[25]

Although activity sharing may reduce costs through economies of scope, the savings must overcome other costs that are created by such sharing. Because separate business units are required to coordinate thoroughly their activities to achieve sharing, overcoming the costs of coordination is an expense that has to be reconciled. Business-unit leaders may also have to compromise their separate business-unit strategies in order to accommodate the coordination of shared activities. This is often not a simple problem because in the United States, division managers usually have an individualistic ethic, relative to other countries. That is, individual business-unit managers seek to control their own strategic destiny. Sharing activities requires sharing business-unit strategic control. Moreover, one business-unit manager may feel that another business-unit manager is receiving more benefit from the activity sharing. If, for instance, a manager in a Procter & Gamble plant focusing on baby diapers receives higher-quality cost inputs from the sharing of activities than does the paper towels manager, the paper towels manager may feel that sharing benefits the baby diaper division manager more through the allocation of annual bonuses. Such a perception could create conflicts between division managers. Activity sharing is also risky because business-unit ties create linkages between outcomes. If demand for the product of one business is reduced, there may not be sufficient revenues to cover the fixed costs of running the joint paper plant. Shared activities create interrelationships that affect the ability of both businesses to achieve strategic competitiveness. Activity sharing may be ineffective if these costs are not taken into consideration.

## Transferring Core Competencies

Over time, a strategically competitive firm develops intangible resources, such as know-how, that become the foundation for competitively valuable capabilities and core competencies. Marketing expertise is an example of a core competence that

---

▼ **TABLE 6–1**

### Reasons for Diversification

Value-Enhancing Motives
  *Economies of scope
    —Sharing of activities
    —Transferring of core competencies
  *Market power
    —Blocking competitors through multipoint competition
    —Vertical integration
  *Financial economies
    —Efficient internal capital allocation
    —Risk reduction among businesses
    —Business restructuring

Value-Neutral Motives
  *Tax incentives
  *Anti-trust regulation
  *Poor performance
  *Uncertain future cash flows
  *Firm risk reduction

Devaluation Motives
  *Diversifying managerial employment risk
  *Increasing managerial compensation

could be developed this way. Because the expense of developing such a competence has already been incurred, and because competencies based on intangible resources are less visible and more difficult for competitors to understand and imitate, transferring these types of competencies from an original business unit to another one may reduce costs and enhance an entire firm's strategic competitiveness.[26] A key reason Philip Morris decided to acquire Miller Brewing Company was that by transferring its marketing core competence to Miller, it believed a competitive advantage could be achieved.

As a cigarette company, Philip Morris developed a particular expertise in marketing. When Philip Morris purchased Miller Brewing, the beer industry had efficient operations. However, it seemed that no firm in the industry had established marketing competence as a source of sustainable competitive advantage. The marketing competence transferred from Philip Morris to Miller resulted in the introduction of improved marketing practices to the brewing industry. These practices, especially in terms of advertising, proved to be the source of competitive advantage that allowed Miller Brewing to earn above-average profits for a period of time. In fact, several years passed before Anheuser-Busch, the largest firm in the brewing industry, developed the capabilities required to duplicate the benefits of Miller's strategy. A strong competitive response from Anheuser Busch could be predicted, however, in that beer is the firm's core business.[27]

Service firms may also seek to transfer competencies among related businesses. Many large financial service firms, such as Sears and American Express, have sought to do this. However, as described in the next Strategic Focus, they have not been as successful with this strategy as has Merrill Lynch.

As the Strategic Focus suggests, Merrill Lynch's attempt to create economies across clients appears to be successful. In the near future, however, Merrill could face another interesting competitor. General Electric (GE) continues to expand its presence in financial services. In 1993, 44 percent of GE's revenues were produced by its service businesses. Revenues from the firm's main service businesses—GE Capital, Kidder Peabody, and NBC—grew from $14.3 billion in 1988 to $25.2 billion in 1993. Continuation of this 12 percent annual growth rate would result in over one-half of GE's revenues being earned through service businesses by 1996. In the middle of the 1990s, GE examined carefully additional financial services GE Capital could provide to continue its positive contributions to the parent corporation's strategic competitiveness and profitability.[28]

Unlike Merrill Lynch, some firms discover that they either are unable to transfer competencies or seek to transfer competencies that do not help a business unit establish a competitive advantage. One way managers facilitate the transfer of competencies is to move key people into new management positions. Philip Morris accomplished competence transfer to Miller Brewing in this way. However, a business-unit manager of an older division may be reluctant to transfer key people that have accumulated the wisdom necessary to transfer the competencies. Thus, managers with the ability to facilitate the transfer of a core competence may come at a premium or may not want to transfer, and the top-level managers from the transferring division may not want them to be transferred to a new division to fulfill the diversification objective.

Some related-diversified firms are using their core competencies to attempt to establish sustainable competitive advantages in markets that are new to them. For instance, the communications giant AT&T has sought to create a joint business in

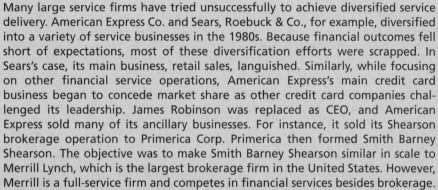

## Successful Transfer of Core Competencies at Merrill Lynch

Many large service firms have tried unsuccessfully to achieve diversified service delivery. American Express Co. and Sears, Roebuck & Co., for example, diversified into a variety of service businesses in the 1980s. Because financial outcomes fell short of expectations, most of these diversification efforts were scrapped. In Sears's case, its main business, retail sales, languished. Similarly, while focusing on other financial service operations, American Express's main credit card business began to concede market share as other credit card companies challenged its leadership. James Robinson was replaced as CEO, and American Express sold many of its ancillary businesses. For instance, it sold its Shearson brokerage operation to Primerica Corp. Primerica then formed Smith Barney Shearson. The objective was to make Smith Barney Shearson similar in scale to Merrill Lynch, which is the largest brokerage firm in the United States. However, Merrill is a full-service firm and competes in financial services besides brokerage.

Merrill Lynch had $500 billion in client assets in 1993, 2.5 percent of all U.S. assets. It is the largest brokerage firm, with 12,000 brokers and 6.2 million clients. It is the second largest mutual fund company. It brings to market one in five new stock and bond issues. It has even surpassed Goldman, Sachs & Co. as a stock underwriter. When it got into this business in the 1970s, it served primarily small investors. It is now the 24th largest insurer and services $5.2 billion in home mortgage loans. But some of its diversification forays have not been successful. It sold its poorly performing real estate brokerage and telecommunications operations. Also, its small business lending operation has suffered loan losses.

Merrill Lynch's pursuit of diversified financial services, however, is not extensive. It uses its diversified operations as a link to its core brokerage operations. Although it provides home mortgages because of the high earnings from fees, it does not pursue consumer loans on cars and boats. Rather, it encourages clients to use their brokerage accounts to borrow against assets Merrill holds. Also, its main insurance line of business is in annuities.

Merrill could push further into lending, and some clients are pleased with its services. Banks have been strapped recently with strong regulatory loan provisions. This situation is advantageous for investment banks such as Merrill because they can respond with more flexibility to clients' needs. Its services beyond brokerage create income through fees that support the cyclical brokerage business. Merrill plans to cover its fixed costs by fee services by the end of the decade, which may allow it to be profitable in any market.

Merrill Lynch is a rare example of a successful diversified service company. It has maintained strategic competitiveness by using its knowledge-based core competencies to deliver several types of financial services. Because a service business's main source of competitive advantage often is its sales force (in addition to financial assets that often are mobile), acquisitions become risky (because sales personnel may decide to change companies and take key clients with them). Merrill has maintained the dedication of its sales personnel because they see themselves as financial consultants, not only as stockbrokers. The additional financial services provide a greater number of opportunities for the sales force to create value for customers, increasing its own compensation as a result.

communications and computers because many office products will require their combined application in the future. To implement this part of its corporate-level diversification strategy, AT&T purchased NCR Corp. Furthermore, Bell Labs continued to provide shared research and development activities for all of AT&T's diverse communications and computer businesses. The successful application of core competencies in new businesses often requires the use of cross-functional teams. The importance of these teams is recognized in many of today's related-diversified firms, including Rockwell International. At Rockwell, teams of employees from all disciplines focus their collective efforts on meeting the specific challenges of applying core competencies to new businesses.[29] Sometimes, however, the use of cross-functional teams can be costly, suggesting that the costs and benefits of their use should be evaluated carefully.[30]

## Market Power

▲ **Market power** exists when a firm is able to sell its products above the existing competitive level or decrease the costs of its primary activities below the competitive level, or both.

▲ **Multipoint competition** is present when two or more diversified firms compete in the same product areas or geographic markets.

▲ **Mutual forbearance** is a relationship between two or more firms in which excessive competition leads to a situation where all firms in the competitive set see that such competition is self-destructive and, without formal agreement, cease the self-destructive competitive actions and responses.

Related diversification can also be used to gain market power. **Market power** exists when a firm is able to sell its products above the existing competitive level or decrease the costs of its primary activities below the competitive level, or both.[31]

One approach to gaining market power by diversification is multipoint competition. **Multipoint competition** is present when two or more diversified firms compete in the same product areas or geographic markets. For example, with its ROLM subsidiary, IBM seeks to compete in both computer and telecommunication markets. AT&T, a communication company, with its acquisition of NCR, intends to compete in both communication and computer markets. The rivalry between these two companies is an example of multipoint competition. When Philip Morris moved into foods by buying General Foods and Kraft, RJR's competitive response was the acquisition of another foods company, Nabisco.

If these firms compete head to head in each market, multipoint competition will not create potential gains, but rather will generate excessive competitive activity. However, over time, if these firms refrain from competition and in effect realize mutual forbearance, this may be classified as a form of related diversification that creates value for each firm through less competitive activity. **Mutual forbearance** is a relationship between two or more firms in which excessive competition leads to a situation where all firms in the competitive set see that such competition is self-destructive and, without formal agreement, cease the self-destructive competitive actions and responses.

Walt Disney and Time Warner operate in similar businesses—theme parks, movie and television production, and broadcasting activities. Disney spent considerable amounts of money ($40 million) from 1988 through 1993 advertising its theme parks in Time Warner magazines. Time Warner, however, began an aggressive advertising campaign aimed at taking Disney's theme park customers. Disney retaliated by canceling its advertising in Time Warner's publications. Time Warner responded by canceling corporate meetings in Florida at a Disney resort. Disney responded by canceling Time Warner advertisements of its theme parks on a Los Angeles television station owned by Disney.[32] This illustrates the potential negative side of multipoint competition.

Alternatively, the three large U.S. automobile manufacturers, competing with Japanese companies in a number of markets, considered lobbying the federal government for tighter import restrictions on their Japanese competitors. However, because of joint ownership arrangements and strategic alliances with Japanese firms (Ford with Mazda, General Motors with Toyota, and Chrysler with Mitsubishi), excessive restrictions were not pursued. The U.S. firms were concerned that higher Japanese import quotas would hamper relationships with their Japanese partners. This is an example of mutual forbearance.

Another approach to creating value by gaining market power is the strategy of vertical integration. **Vertical integration** exists when a company is producing its own inputs (backward integration) or owns its own source of distribution of outputs (forward integration). It is also possible to have partial vertical integration where some inputs and some outputs are sold by company units, while other inputs and outputs are produced or sold by outside firms.

A company pursuing vertical integration is usually motivated to strengthen its position in its core business by gaining market power over competitors. This is done through savings on operations costs, avoidance of market costs, better control to establish quality, and, possibly, protection of technology. If a steel mill takes raw steel, hot from the furnace, and refines it into rolled steel and other refined products through rolling mills, this saves reheating and, in turn, production costs. By purchasing and selling its own inputs and outputs internally, the firm saves transaction costs and markups from potential suppliers or wholesale distributors.

Vertical integration can also enable a company to protect product quality. The opening of McDonald's first restaurant in Moscow provides a good example. To protect product quality, McDonald's vertically integrated backward into sources. This strategy allowed the company to prepare its products in the same way it does in locations throughout the world. Ownership of its input and output sources protects the firm's core technology from information diffusion to other competitors through buyer and supplier sources. Vertical integration therefore is a way to protect core technology from imitation.

▲ **Vertical integration** exists when a company is producing its own inputs (backward integration) or owns its own source of distribution of outputs (forward integration).

*Across its global operations, McDonald's is committed to protecting the quality of its products. To provide quality products to customers in its Moscow unit, the firm decided to vertically integrate its operations. By integrating backward, McDonald's is able to obtain the items it requires to produce products that satisfy its food preparation standards. As shown above, McDonald's strategy is apparently being implemented successfully in Moscow.*

Of course, there are limits to vertical integration. For example, an outside supplier may produce the product at a lower cost. As a result, internal transactions from vertical integration may be expensive and reduce profitability. Also, bureaucratic costs are incurred when implementing this strategy. Because it requires that substantial sums of capital be invested in specific technologies, vertical integration can be problematic when technology changes quickly. Changes in demand also create capacity balance and coordination problems. If one division is building a part, but realization of state-of-the-art economies of scale requires the division to build it at a scale beyond the capacity of the internal buyer to absorb demand, this would compel sales outside the company. However, if demand slackens, there would be overcapacity, because the internal users cannot absorb total demand. This problem led General Motors to have many unnecessary expansions and contractions in employment. Japanese firms, instead, have developed a network of suppliers. Often Japanese firms have more than one supplier for each part.[33] In summary, although vertical integration can create value and contribute to strategic competitiveness, especially in gaining market power over competitors, it is not without risks and costs.

## Unrelated Diversification

▲ **Financial economies** are cost savings realized through improved allocations of financial resources based on investments inside or outside the firm.

An unrelated diversification strategy can create value through two types of financial economies. **Financial economies** are cost savings realized through improved allocations of financial resources based on investments inside or outside the firm.

The first type of financial economy involves efficient internal capital allocations. This type also seeks to reduce risks among the firm's business units. This can be achieved, for example, through development of a portfolio of businesses that have different risk profiles, thereby reducing business risk for the total corporation. A second approach of financial economies is concerned with purchasing other corporations and restructuring their assets. This approach allows a firm to buy and sell businesses in the external market with the intent of increasing its total value.

### Valuable Internal Capital Market Allocation

Capital allocation is usually distributed efficiently in a market economy by capital markets. Efficient distribution of capital is induced because investors seek to purchase shares of firm equity (ownership) that have high future cash-flow values. Capital is allocated not only through equity, but also through debt, where shareholders and debtholders seek to improve the value of their investment by investing in businesses with high growth prospects. In large diversified firms, however, the corporate office distributes capital to divisions to create value for the overall company. Such an approach may provide potential gains from internal capital market allocation, relative to the external capital market.[34] The corporate office, through managing a particular set of businesses, may have access to more detailed and accurate information as well as actual business and performance prospects.

Textron Corporation continues to manage a *diverse* set of businesses using this approach (although, as noted earlier, the *total number* of businesses owned by Textron has been reduced). Compared to Textron's corporate office personnel, investors would have relatively limited access to internal information and can only estimate actual divisional performance and future business prospects. Although businesses seeking capital must provide information to capital providers (e.g., banks, insurance firms), firms with internal capital markets may have at least two informational advantages. First, information put out to capital markets through annual reports and other sources may not include negative information, but rather only positive prospects and outcomes. External sources of capital have limited ability to know *specifically* what is taking place inside large organizations. Although owners have access to information, they have no guarantee of full and complete disclosure.

Second, although a firm must disseminate information, this information then becomes available to potential competitors simultaneously. With insights gained by studying this information, competitors might attempt to duplicate a firm's competitive advantage. Without having to reveal internal information, a firm may protect its competitive advantage through an internal capital market.

If intervention from outside the firm is required to make corrections, only significant changes are possible, such as forcing the firm into bankruptcy or changing the dominant leadership coalition (e.g., the top-management team described in Chapter 11). Alternatively, in an internal capital market, the corporate office may choose to adjust managerial incentives or suggest strategic changes in the division to make fine-tuned corrections. Thus, capital allocation can be adjusted according to more specific criteria than is possible with external market allocation. The external capital market may fail therefore to allocate resources adequately to high-potential investments, compared to corporate office investments, because it has less accurate information. The head office of a diversified company can more effectively perform such tasks as disciplining underperforming management teams and allocating resources.

A firm can also reduce its overall risk by allocating resources among a set of diversified businesses. However, such risk reduction strategies may not be valuable to all firms' stakeholders. Shareholders and debtholders have lower-cost ways of reducing their risk through diversification of their own investment portfolios. Successful implementation of an unrelated diversification strategy requires that a firm incur fewer costs to reduce an individual investor's risks as compared to the costs that investor would experience to diversify his or her own portfolio.[35]

## Restructuring

Another alternative, similar to the internal capital market approach, focuses exclusively on buying and selling other firm assets in the external market. It is similar to the real estate business, where profits are earned by buying assets low, restructuring them, and selling them as high as possible. The restructuring approach usually entails buying the firm, selling off assets such as corporate headquarters, and terminating corporate staff members.

Selling underperforming divisions and placing the remaining divisions under the discipline of rigorous financial controls are other restructuring actions initiated frequently. Rigorous controls require divisions to follow strict budgets and account regularly for cash inflows and outflows to corporate headquarters. A firm pursuing this approach may have to use hostile takeovers or tender offers. Hostile takeovers have the potential to increase the resistance of the target firm's top-level managers. Diversification would be difficult under these circumstances because of the need to decentralize operating responsibility to division managers where business-level expertise is required. However, in the restructuring alternative, corporate-level managers are dismissed, often while division managers are retained.

As explained in the next Strategic Focus, Hanson PLC uses the restructuring approach successfully to create value through an unrelated diversification strategy. Dedicated to its unrelated diversification strategy, Hanson continuously reviews acquisition opportunities for growth in the United Kingdom, United States, and Europe.[36] But, for any firm, including Hanson, implementing an unrelated diversification strategy requires an understanding of significant trade-offs.

First, success usually requires a focus on mature, low-technology businesses. Otherwise, resource allocation decisions become too complex because the uncertainty of demand for high-technology products requires information-processing capacities beyond the smaller corporate staffs of unrelated-restructuring firms. Service businesses are also difficult to buy and sell in this way because of their client or sales orientation. Sales staffs of service businesses are more mobile than those of manufacturing-oriented businesses and may seek jobs with a competitor, taking their clients with them. This is true in professional service businesses such as accounting, law, and investment banking. As such, these businesses probably would not create value if acquired by an unrelated-restructuring firm such as Hanson.

# Diversification: Incentives and Resources

The economic reasons given above summarize the conditions under which diversification strategies increase a firm's value. However, diversification is often undertaken with the expectation that doing so will prevent a firm from decreasing its value. Thus, there are reasons to diversify that are value neutral. AMR Corp.'s situation is a case in point. As we explain in the next section, several incentives may lead a firm to pursue further diversification.[37]

## Incentives to Diversify

Incentives provide reasons to diversify; they come from both the external environment and a firm's internal environment. The term *incentive* implies that managers have some choice whether to pursue the incentive or not. Incentives external to the firm include anti-trust policies and tax laws. Internal firm incentives include low performance, uncertain future cash flows, and overall firm risk reduction.

**Anti-Trust Policies and Tax Laws**   Anti-trust policies and tax laws are government policies that provided incentives for U.S. firms to diversify in the 1960s and 1970s. Applications of anti-trust laws regarding mergers that create increased market power (vertical and horizontal integration) were stringent in the 1960s and 1970s. As a result, many of the mergers during this time were unrelated—that is, they involved companies pursuing different lines of business. Thus, the merger wave of the 1960s was "conglomerate" in character. Merger activity leading to conglomerate diversification was encouraged primarily by the Celler-Kefauver Act (which discouraged horizontal and vertical mergers). For example, in the 1973–1977 period, 79.1 percent of all mergers were conglomerate.[38]

The mergers of the 1980s, however, were different. Anti-trust enforcement ebbed, permitting more and larger horizontal mergers (acquisition of the same line of business, such as the Texaco-Getty merger between two oil firms). In addition, investment bankers became more freewheeling in the kinds of mergers they would

### STRATEGIC FOCUS

## Unrelated Diversification at Hanson PLC

Hanson PLC is one of the ten biggest companies in Britain, and its U.S. arm, Hanson Industries, is among the 60 largest U.S. industrial concerns. Hanson PLC has grown primarily through acquisitions of other businesses—as evidenced by over 150 different businesses in its portfolio. The firm's unrelated diversification strategy has gained Hanson a reputation for being one of the most successful takeover machines in the world.

Hanson's acquisition philosophy involves an intricate set of values. Target firms usually have high-profile businesses with low-level technologies where commodities are involved. Thus, there is substantial cash flow available. Research is undertaken to locate these firms and assess their potential. Funding considerations are also undertaken, and usually stock swaps are suggested. In the process, debt is reduced or eliminated.

The approach Hanson takes often results in the firm being labeled an "asset stripper." Such a firm is known to eliminate excess overhead in the acquired firm. Typically, this is accomplished by selling corporate headquarters and other unnecessary assets. Divisions that are retained or created through restructuring are brought under an elaborate system of financial controls. Division managers are given distinct incentives for improving their unit's performance. Operational synergy between businesses is deemphasized, and decentralization to division managers is critical.

Current Hanson holdings in the United States include Jacuzzi, makers of whirlpools and other swimming apparatus; Farberware, makers of pots and pans; Peabody Cole; and Tommy Armour golf equipment. In Britain, Hanson is the largest cement and building products producer. It has substantial holdings in tobacco, chemicals, and forest products. Firms Hanson owns in the United Kingdom include the London and Butterley Brick companies, Beazer Homes, ARC Crushed Stone Products, Crabtree Electrical, and Imperial Tobacco. Recently Hanson purchased the largest U.S. producer of polypropylene, a base product used in the making of commodities such as plastic bags and other packaging plastics.

try to facilitate; as a consequence, hostile takeovers rose to unprecedented prominence.[39] The conglomerates or highly diversified firms of the 1960s and 1970s became more "focused" in the 1980s, as merger constraints were relaxed and restructuring implemented.[40]

Tax effects on diversification stem not only from individual tax rates, but also from corporate tax changes. Some companies (especially mature companies) may have activities generating more cash than they can reinvest profitably. Michael Jensen (a prominent financial economist) believes that such "free cash flows" (liquid financial assets for which investments in current businesses are no longer economically viable) should be redistributed to shareholders in the form of dividends.[41] However, in the 1960s and 1970s, dividends were taxed more heavily than ordinary personal income. As a result, in the pre-1980s, shareholders preferred that companies retain these funds for use in buying and building companies in high-performance industries. If the stock value appreciated over the long term, shareholders might receive a better return for these funds than through dividends because they would be taxed more lightly under capital gains rules.

In 1986, however, the top ordinary individual income tax rate was reduced from 50 percent to 28 percent, and the special capital gains tax was changed, causing capital gains to be treated as ordinary income. These changes suggested that shareholders would no longer encourage firms to retain funds for purposes of diversification. Moreover, the elimination of personal interest deductions, as well as the lower attractiveness of retained earnings to shareholders, has prompted the use of more leverage by firms (interest expense is tax deductible for firms). These tax law changes likely influenced an increase in divestitures of unrelated business units after 1984. Thus, individual tax rates for capital gains and dividends may have created a shareholder incentive for increased diversification before 1986, but an incentive for reduced diversification after 1986, unless funded by debt (which is tax deductible).

Regarding corporate taxation, acquisitions typically increase a firm's depreciable asset allowances. Increased depreciation (non–cash flow expense) produces lower taxable income, thereby providing additional incentive for acquisitions. Before 1986, acquisitions may have been the most attractive means for securing tax benefits.[42] The tax incentives are particularly important because acquisitions represent the primary means of firm diversification. However, the 1986 Tax Reform Act reduced some of the corporate tax advantages of diversification.[43] Over the years, then, government policy has provided incentives that vie for both increased and decreased levels of diversification. In addition to these external incentives, there are incentives internal to the firm that increase the likelihood that diversification will be pursued.

**Low Performance**   It has been proposed that "high performance eliminates the need for greater diversification,"[44] as in the example of the Wm. Wrigley Jr. Co. Conversely, as the AMR example suggests, low performance may provide an incentive for diversification. Often firms plagued by poor performance seek to take higher risks.[45] Interestingly, though, some researchers have found that low returns are related to greater levels of diversification.[46] Poor performance may lead to increased diversification, especially if resources exist to pursue additional diversification. Continued poor returns following additional diversification, however, may slow the pace of diversification and even lead to restructuring divestitures. Thus, an overall curvilinear relationship, as illustrated in Figure 6–2, may exist between diversification and performance. In the AMR example, it is likely that diversification will continue until mistaken diversification begins to reduce performance. The relationship illustrated in Figure 6–2, however, only applies to firms that have already diversified. Firms that have effectively focused on a single business, such as Wrigley (chewing gum) and Kellogg (breakfast cereals), have not sought to diversify (because they continue to achieve strategic competitiveness and earn superior profits).

**Uncertain Future Cash Flows**   As a firm's product line matures and/or is threatened, diversification may be perceived as an important defensive strategy. Firms in mature or maturing industries sometimes find it necessary to diversify to survive over the long term. Certainly, this has been one of the dominant reasons for the 1960s' and 1970s' diversification among railroad firms. Railroads diversified primarily because the trucking industry was perceived to be significantly reducing demand for rail transportation. However, uncertainty can be derived from both supply and demand sources.

**FIGURE 6–2   The Curvilinear Relationship Between Diversification and Performance**

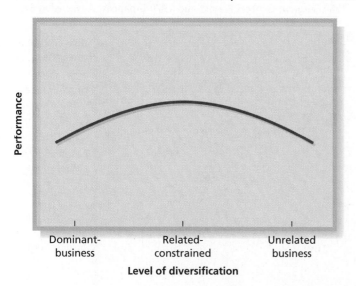

Diversification among tobacco firms is another example of a demand uncertainty incentive. Most large tobacco firms anticipated decreasing cash flows from lower demand for their main product. As the external threat to health was flagged repeatedly by successive Surgeon General reports and bans on television advertising, all major tobacco firms increased their level of diversification. Figure 6–3 illustrates how the largest tobacco firms pursued a program of diversification after the first Surgeon General report in 1964 and the ban on advertising in 1970. This process continued into the 1980s with the purchase of General Foods and Kraft by Philip Morris and Nabisco by RJR.

This argument also pertains to firms in industries where foreign competitors with lower average costs have penetrated domestic markets. The 1970s' diversification in the steel industry exemplifies this type of supply side uncertainty as an incentive. To reduce its dependence on steel, U.S. Steel bought Marathon Oil and Texas Oil and Gas. This competitive action was taken because international integrated steel makers (such as Nippon Steel) were able to produce steel at a lower cost due to lower labor costs and newer, more efficient production facilities. After these acquisitions, U.S. Steel was renamed USX to signal that it was more than just a steel manufacturer.

Also, petroleum firms in the middle to late 1970s experienced exceptionally high oil prices and expectations of increasing demand, while forecasted reserves (supply) were expected to be rapidly depleted. Because of possible competition from predicted alternative energy sources, fewer available revenues were expected from their dominant business, thereby creating uncertainty about future profits. In order to preserve present capital, most petroleum firms with excess liquid capital pursued a diversification strategy. For example, Atlantic Richfield and SOHIO bought mining operations (Anaconda and Kennecott, respectively), while Mobil purchased Montgomery Ward. Thus, both supply and demand uncertainties about expected future cash flows affected oil firm diversification strategies. Although diversification may increase shareholder wealth in selected instances, the evidence indicates generally that it may decrease the uncertainty of future cash flows, but often at the expense of profitability.

**FIGURE 6–3**  Illustration of Increase in Percentage of Sales in Tobacco versus Other Diversified Businesses After 1964 Surgeon General Report and 1970 Broadcast Advertising Ban

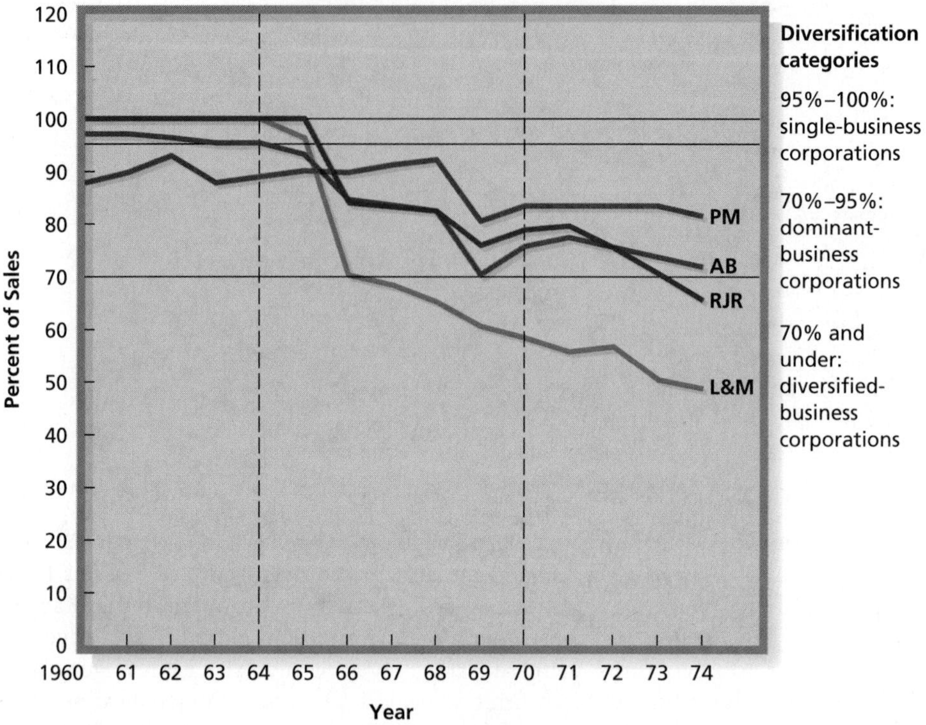

**Diversification categories**

95%–100%: single-business corporations

70%–95%: dominant-business corporations

70% and under: diversified-business corporations

**PM** = Phillip Morris    **RJR** = R. J. Reynolds
**AB** = American Brands    **L&M** = Liggett & Meyers

*Source: Reprinted with permission from Robert H. Miles,* Coffin Nails and Corporate Strategies, *1982 (Englewood Cliffs, N.J.: Prentice-Hall).*

▲ **Synergy** exists when the value created by business units working together exceeds the value the units create when working independently.

**Overall Firm Risk Reduction**    Because diversified firms pursuing economies of scope often have investments that are too inflexible to realize synergy between business units, several potential problems exist. **Synergy** exists when the value created by business units working together exceeds the value the units create when working independently. For example, as a firm increases its relatedness between business units, it increases its risk of corporate failure because synergy produces joint profitability between business units and the firm's flexibility of response is constrained. This threat may force two basic decisions.

First, the firm may reduce the level of technological change by operating in more certain environments. This may make the firm risk averse and thus uninterested in pursuing new product lines that have potential, but are not proven. Alternatively, the firm may constrain the level of activity sharing and forego the benefits of synergy. Either or both decisions may lead to further diversification. The former would lead to related diversification into industries where more certainty exists. The latter result may produce further, but unrelated, diversification.[47]

## Resources and Diversification

Besides incentives to diversify, a firm must possess resources required to make diversification economically feasible. As mentioned above, tangible, intangible, and financial resources may facilitate diversification. Resources vary in their utility for value creation, however, because of differences in rarity and mobility; that is, some resources are easier for competitors to duplicate because they are not rare, valuable, imperfectly imitable, and non-substitutable. For instance, free cash flows may be used to diversify the firm. Because financial resources such as free cash flows are more flexible and common, they are less likely to create value as compared to other types of resources.[48] The diversification mentioned above for tobacco and oil firms was facilitated significantly by the presence of free cash flows. Tobacco firms have been cash rich traditionally because of significant cash flows from tobacco products. In the 1970s, oil firms, too, were cash rich. For instance, SOHIO used cash generated from oil reserves in Alaska to purchase Kennecott Copper Corp. Thus, these assets were simply purchased at market prices by liquid assets and were not likely to result in above-average profits.

Tangible firm resources usually include the plant and equipment necessary to produce a product, and, therefore, such assets may be less flexible. Any excess capacity of these resources (plant and equipment) often can be used only for very closely related products, especially those requiring highly similar manufacturing technologies. Excess capacity of other tangible resources, such as a sales force, can be used to diversify more easily. Again, excess capacity in a sales force would be more effective with related diversification because it may be utilized to sell similar products. The sales force would be more knowledgeable of related product characteristics, customers, and distribution channels. Tangible resources may create resource interrelationships in production, marketing, procurement, and technology, defined above as activity sharing.

Intangible resources would, of course, be more flexible than actual tangible physical assets in facilitating diversification. Although the sharing of tangible resources may induce diversification, other intangible resources could encourage more diversification.

## Extent of Diversification

If a firm has incentives and resources to diversify, the extent of diversification will be greater than if it just has incentives or resources alone. The more flexible, the more likely the resources will be used for unrelated diversification; the less flexible, the more likely the resources will be used for related diversification. Thus, flexible resources are likely to lead to relatively greater levels of diversification. Also, because related diversification requires more information processing to manage linkages between businesses, more unrelated units can be managed by a small corporate office. To the extent a firm has incentives and resources to diversify, it will increase the level of diversification to the optimal level of firm performance. However, because many of the incentives listed above suggest that diversification is needed due to low or expected lower performance, the optimal level of firm performance may not be the same as that of a more formidable competitor.

## Managerial Motives to Diversify

Managerial motives for diversification may exist independent of incentives and resources. These motives include managerial risk reduction and a desire for increased compensation. For instance, diversification may reduce top-level managers' employment risk (risk of job loss or income reduction). That is, corporate executives may diversify a firm in order to diversify their employment risk, as long as profitability does not suffer excessively.[49] Diversification also provides an additional benefit to managers that shareholders do not enjoy. Diversification and firm size are highly correlated, and as size increases, so does executive compensation.[50] Large firms are more complex and harder to manage, and, thus, managers of larger firms are compensated more highly. As a result, diversification provides an avenue for increased compensation and therefore may serve as a motive for increased diversification. Governance mechanisms, such as the board of directors, ownership monitoring, executive compensation, and the market for corporate control may limit managerial tendencies to overdiversify. These governance mechanisms are discussed in more detail in Chapter 9.

Governance mechanisms may not be strong, and, in some instances, managers may diversify the firm to the point that it fails to earn even average profits.[51] Resources employed to pursue such diversification are most likely to include financial assets (e.g., free cash flows), but may also involve intangible assets. Thus, this type of diversification is not likely to lead to improved performance. The loss of adequate internal governance may result in poor relative performance, thereby triggering a threat of takeover. Although external controls, such as the threat of takeover, may create improved efficiency by replacing ineffective managerial teams, managers may avoid takeovers through defensive tactics (golden parachutes, poison pills, etc.). Therefore, an external governance threat, although having a restraining influence on managers, does not provide flawless control of managerial motives for diversification.[52]

The majority of large, publicly held firms are profitable because managers are positive agents and many of their strategic actions (e.g., diversification moves) contribute to this success. As mentioned above, governance devices are designed to deal with exceptions to the norms of achieving strategic competitiveness and increasing shareholder wealth in the process. It is overly pessimistic to assume that managers will usually act in their own self-interest as opposed to their firm's interest.

Managers may also be held in check by concerns for their reputation in the labor market. If reputation facilitates power, poor reputation may also reduce power. Likewise, a market for managerial talent may also constrain managerial abuse of power to pursue suboptimal diversification.[53] In addition, some diversified firms also provide policing of other diversified firms. Large, highly diversified firms such as Hanson Trust seek out poorly managed diversified firms for acquisition in order to restructure the target firm's asset base. Knowledge that their firms could be acquired, if not managed successfully, encourages managers to find ways to achieve strategic competitiveness.

Even with the likelihood of negative reputation effects and self-regulation among diversified firms, managers still may continue to abuse their positions. For example, top-level managers in firms owning railroad assets were criticized for taking capital from their railroad subsidiaries to invest in other businesses.[54]

In summary, although managers may be motivated to increase diversification, there are governance mechanisms in place to discourage such action merely for managerial gain. However, this governance is imperfect and may not always produce the intended consequences. Even when governance mechanisms cause managers to correct a problem of overdiversification, these moves are not without trade-offs. For instance, spin-off firms may not realize productivity gains, although it is in the best interest of the divesting firm.[55] As such, the assumption that managers need disciplining may not be entirely correct, and sometimes governance may create consequences that are worse than those resulting from overdiversification. Therefore, the diversification level of firms must be based on optimal levels indicated by market and strategic characteristics (resources) peculiar to each firm. Optimality may be judged by the factors discussed in this chapter (resources, incentives, and managerial motives) and included in the model in Figure 6–4.

For instance, diversification level will be based partly on how the interaction of resources and incentives affects the adoption of particular diversification strategies. As indicated above, it is expected that the greater the incentives and the more flexible the resources, the higher the level of expected diversification. Financial resources (the most flexible) should have a stronger relationship to the extent of diversification than either tangible or intangible resources. Tangible resources (the most inflexible) would be useful primarily for related diversification.

The model suggests that implementation issues are important to whether diversification creates value or not. It also suggests that governance mechanisms are important to the level and type of diversification implemented.

## Techniques for Analyzing Diversified Companies' Portfolios

Once a firm has a set of diversified businesses, three issues confront corporate-level strategic decision makers. First, the attractiveness of the current group of businesses must be determined. Second, assuming the current set of businesses is attractive, an

**FIGURE 6–4** Summary Model of the Relationship Between Firm Performance and Diversification

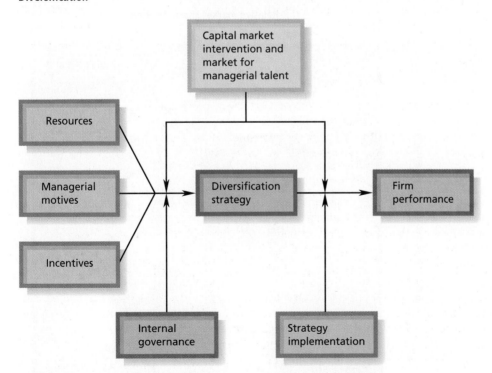

Source: R. E. Hoskisson and M. A. Hitt, 1990, Antecedents and performance outcomes of diversification: A review and critique of theoretical perspectives, Journal of Management, 16: 498.

estimate of each unit's future potential must be developed. Finally, if these answers are not satisfactory, top-level managers must decide which businesses to divest and which ones to develop.

There are several techniques managers can use to manage portfolios by seeking to answer these three basic questions. The most famous portfolio matrix is a four-square grid devised by the Boston Consulting Group (BCG), a leading management consulting firm (see Figure 6–5). The matrix is composed of two different dimensions: relative industry growth rate and relative market share position. Each dimension represents one of the two basic questions above. The relative industry growth rate dimension suggests future attractiveness of the business. The relative market share dimension represents current attractiveness and market and future staying power. **Relative market share** is the ratio of a business's market share to the market share held by the most significant, comparable rival firms in the industry. This dimension is measured in unit volume, not dollars. The standard border between high and low relative market share is 1. Businesses with a ratio above 1 are in a strong position relative to rivals. Firms trailing rivals in market share have a ratio below 1.0. The original BCG matrix arbitrarily placed the dividing line between high- and low-growth industry rates at around twice the original GNP growth rate. However, individual users can raise or lower the desired growth rate to suit their preferences.

Next, we discuss the strategic meaning of each quadrant shown in Figure 6–5.

▲ **Relative market share** is the ratio of a business's market share to the market share held by the most significant, comparable rival firms in the industry.

**FIGURE 6–5**  **Boston Consulting Group Growth-Share Business Portfolio Matrix**

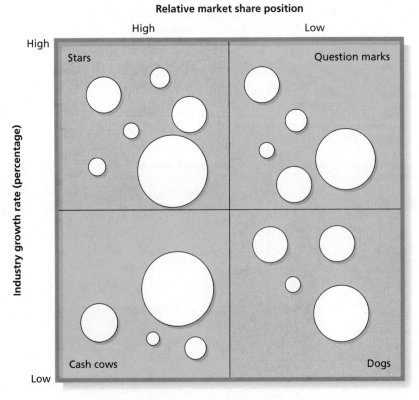

**Question Marks**  Businesses falling within the **question mark** quadrant have high growth, but low relative market share. These fast-growing businesses may require large infusions of cash to maintain pace with the market's growth rate. However, the reason for the question mark label is that there is a question whether the parent corporation will decide this business is a cash hog or a worthwhile investment because of the amount of cash necessary to fund market share growth, which may not lead to market leadership.

▲ Businesses falling within the **question mark** quadrant have high growth, but low relative market share.

**Stars**  On the other hand, **star** businesses have high growth with relatively high market share positions. Although they require large cash investments to expand production facilities, they have relatively strong market positions and thus strong future prospects for stable growth. However, these businesses often require substantial capital investment beyond what they can generate on their own and may require significant amounts of cash from corporate headquarters.

▲ **Star** businesses have high growth with relatively high market share positions.

**Cash Cows**  **Cash cow businesses** generate substantial surpluses over what is needed for reinvestment and growth. These businesses, having relatively high market share and an industry leadership position, are usually mature and have sales volumes and reputations that earn substantial profits. Because the industry growth rate is slow and the business is mature, the cash requirements to sustain market position are not as great. As a consequence, these businesses generate a lot of cash that may be used for resource allocations elsewhere.

▲ **Cash cow businesses** generate substantial surpluses over what is needed for reinvestment and growth.

**Dogs**  **Dogs** are businesses that trail market share leaders in slow-growth industries and thus may be considered dim prospects for growth. The logic is to divest businesses with poor prospects because they may not be able to develop a strategy to defend their positions relative to market share leaders.

▲ **Dogs** are businesses that trail market share leaders in slow-growth industries and thus may be considered dim prospects for growth.

## Pitfalls of Matrix Techniques

There are two disaster sequences in the BCG matrix that highlight misallocation. First, a star's position may erode, so that, over time, it loses relative market share and its industry growth rate slows. Ultimately, a star business experiencing these realities becomes a dog. Second, a cash cow may lose market leadership and become a dog. Also, there may be overinvestment and underinvestment strategies. Overinvesting in a safe cash cow or underinvesting in a question mark can be a mistake, resulting in negative outcomes.

The BCG matrix and other similar matrices have been criticized because of their lack of emphasis on strategic considerations and their use of historical data (regarding industry growth rates and market share positions).[56] Heavy reliance on these matrices has produced poor performance.[57] If an unrelated diversified firm is using such a matrix, it may overinvest in new growth businesses, given the logic of the BCG matrix. The high-performing, unrelated firms have been shown to buy and sell strong cash cows (as shown in the Strategic Focus on Hanson PLC).

The example in Figure 6–5 illustrates a balanced portfolio. A balanced portfolio contains businesses in each quadrant. The logic of portfolio matrices draws attention to the cash flow and investment characteristics of various types of businesses and has implications for resource allocations among businesses. Thus, to pursue a balanced portfolio, given the logic of the BCG matrix, would be a mistake for an unrelated firm because this would force it to invest in uncertain growth businesses. This strategy goes against the nature of the successful unrelated strategy, which requires investment in low-growth, mature businesses.

A firm pursuing a related diversification strategy needs to aim at industries where there is a strategic fit with its core competencies. Because the BCG and other matrices focus on cash flow for resource allocation, they emphasize separation between divisions and do not account for strategic interconnectedness. Thus, these matrices have fallen out of favor, as they do not take into consideration the nature of unrelated strategies or the underlying nature of related strategies. Moreover, firms following the proposed guidelines usually underinvest in innovation.[58]

Because of these problems, fewer firms now use portfolio matrices as a decision tool when selecting corporate-level strategies. Experience has shown that adhering strictly to the guidelines of portfolio matrices is unlikely to help a firm develop core competencies and, in turn, sustainable competitive advantages. In fact, strict adherence to the guidelines might even result in a competitive disadvantage. Portfolio guidelines are well known throughout the executive community. Because of this, their use signals competitively relevant information to competitors. One senior executive, for example, stated that "We're glad to find a competitor managing by the portfolio concept—we can almost predict how much share we'll have to take away to put the business on the CEO's sell list."[59] But, on a positive note, these matrices can assist top-level managers to determine the *attractiveness* of the businesses currently in their firm's portfolio.

## Alternatives to Diversification

As noted earlier, economies of scope are a primary goal of diversified companies. But methods other than pursuing economies between different businesses internal to the firm can be used by diversified firms. For example, a firm may substitute a low-cost leadership strategy emphasizing economies of scale in a single business and thus obtain the economies required to be successful. Therefore, growing the independent business is a substitute for economies of scope in several businesses.

Another alternative for exploiting economies of scope may be strategic alliances. By forming alliances, two or more firms may gain economies of scope that would not have been obtained otherwise. Two firms might, for example, create a joint research or manufacturing facility that they both use to their advantage and thus obtain economies without necessarily having relationships between two businesses internal to the firm.

As explained in the next Strategic Focus, Sony Corporation is willing to share its know-how with small firms. A key reason Sony forms these strategic alliances is to acquire commercially useful economies of scope without incurring the range of costs associated with diversifying through the acquisition of other companies.

Strategic alliances create conditions through which one firm can be exploited by the opportunistic behavior of its partner. When a strategic alliance lacks a significant threat of opportunistic behavior, it may be a low-cost alternative for diversification. However, it is unlikely that a firm could organize this type of alliance without the experience of developing internal relationships among two or more business units. The main reason for this difficulty is that the experiences

## STRATEGIC FOCUS

### Sony's Alliances with Small Firms

Japan's Sony Corporation may be the world's most innovative and respected consumer electronics company. In recent years, Sony has developed a significant presence in the United States through its acquisition of Columbia Pictures Entertainment, Incorporated, and CBS Records Group. Its U.S. acquisitions are critical to the firm's efforts to develop synergy across its diverse product lines. To assist in this effort, Sony has formed a number of strategic alliances with small firms. Sony's top-level managers believe that by sharing its research and development skills, production facilities, and other competencies with these small companies, the firm is able to effectively enter new markets with new products.

Sony is working with Panavision, Inc., to develop a lens for high-definition television cameras. It is collaborating with Compression Labs, Inc., to create a commercially successful video-conferencing machine and with Alphatronics, Inc., to develop a rewritable optical-disc storage system for computers.

While many large companies have avoided untested, small companies, Sony has been willing to take a chance and deal with entrepreneurs. It seeks to quiet fears that it is out to take over the small firm's market. Rather, Sony's success with small companies is due to the selection of partners based on business strategies that complement its own. This approach allows Sony to validate if a market exists for a particular product. If the strategic alliance is successful, Sony knows that a market does, in fact, exist for the alliance's product. Furthermore, small entrepreneurial companies can commercialize new products more effectively than corporate giants.

Effective collaborative relationships of this type require time, serious commitments, and mutual trust. Experiences between Sony and Alphatronics illustrate this matter. During one meeting, Alphatronics demonstrated its storage optical system to Sony. At a subsequent meeting, Sony showed prototypes of its hardware to Alphatronics' CEO. In turn, the CEO agreed to let Sony's scientists test the system in his firm's laboratory. In exchange, Sony permitted closer examination of its prototypes by Alphatronics' personnel. Alphatronics now purchases the optical disc drives that it uses in its data storage system from Sony. Because of the products resulting from their strategic alliance, Sony and Alphatronics are viewed as leaders in this field.

critical to successful strategic alliances are socially complex and difficult to duplicate.

Franchising is another alternative to diversification, primarily for service firms. Firms often diversify because focus on a single business is risky. Service firms may diversify some of the financial risk by creating a franchise system. Many hotels and fast food restaurants (e.g., Hilton Hotels and McDonald's) use this diversification alternative. Real estate firms, such as Century 21, also create nationwide chains through franchising. Franchising reduces financial risk because franchisers invest their own capital to expand the service. Due to their capital investment, franchisers are also motivated to succeed by perpetuating the quality, standards, and reputation of the original business. As such, franchising may allow growth (undiversified) at less risk. Of course, the franchising firm loses some control, but the franchise contract usually allows for performance and quality auditing.

## Summary

- Pursuing a single- or dominant-business corporate-level strategy may be preferable to a diversified-business strategy, unless a corporation can develop economies of scope or financial economies, or obtain market power between businesses through additional levels of diversification. These economies are the main sources of value creation for firm diversification.
- The primary reasons for a firm to pursue increased diversification are value creation through economies of scope, financial economies, or market power; actions because of government policy, performance problems, or uncertainties about future cash flow; and managerial motivations (e.g., to increase their compensation).
- Related diversification can be obtained by sharing activities or transferring core competencies.
- Activity sharing usually involves sharing tangible assets between businesses. Competence transfer involves transferring the core competencies developed

in one business, but applicable in another. It also may involve transferring competencies between the corporate office and a business unit.
- Activity sharing is usually associated with related-constrained diversification. Activity sharing is costly to implement and coordinate, may create unequal benefits for the divisions involved in sharing, and may induce reduced risk-taking behaviors.
- Successful unrelated diversification is accomplished by efficiently allocating resources or restructuring a target firm's assets and placing them under rigorous financial controls.
- The BCG matrix is an example of a technique used to evaluate diversification strategies. However, such techniques have fallen out of favor recently and do not facilitate strategic specialization in related or unrelated businesses.
- Strategic alliances and franchising are alternatives to the diversification strategies discussed in this chapter.

## Review Questions

1. What is corporate-level strategy? What is its importance to the diversified firm?
2. Identify the advantages and disadvantages of single and dominant businesses as compared to businesses with higher levels of diversification.
3. What are three reasons that explain why firms choose to move from either a single- or a dominant-business position to a more diversified position?
4. Explain how sharing activities and transferring core competencies are used to obtain economies of scope, while pursuing a related diversification strategy.

5. Describe the two ways to obtain financial economies when pursuing an unrelated diversification strategy.
6. What motives might encourage managers to push a firm toward a more diversified position?
7. Discuss the problems of portfolio matrices such as the BCG matrix.
8. Why would firms choose to use strategic alliances or franchising as an alternative to diversification? What risk does a firm accept when it engages in a strategic alliance as an alternative to diversification?

## Application Discussion Questions

1. This chapter suggests that there is a curvilinear relationship between diversification and performance. How can this relationship be modified so that the negative relationship between performance and diversification is lessened

and the downward curve has less slope or begins at a higher level of diversification?
2. *Fortune* 500 firms are very large, and many of them have significant product diversification. Are these large indus-

trial firms overdiversified currently and experiencing a negative relationship to performance over and above that which they should? Explain.

3. Discuss whether overdiversification is due to industrial policies, such as taxes and anti-trust regulation, or whether managers have overdiversified to pursue self-interest, increased compensation, and reduced risk of job loss.

4. Discuss the situations when portfolio analysis techniques might be applicable and when they might harm corporate performance.

5. One rationale for pursuing related diversification is to obtain market power. In the United States, too much market power, however, may result in a challenge by the Justice Department (because it may be perceived as anti-competitive). Under what situations might related diversification be considered unfair competition?

6. AMR Corp. is the subject of this chapter's opening case. In early 1994, the firm was monitoring carefully the performance of its American Airlines business unit. What is the status of American Airlines currently? Is it profitable, or does it continue to reduce AMR Corp.'s earnings? Given the information you have acquired, what recommendations do you have for AMR's CEO and why?

7. Assume you have received two job offers—one from a dominant-business firm and one from an unrelated-diversified firm (the beginning salaries are virtually identical). Which offer would you accept and why?

8. By the year 2010, do you believe large firms will be more or less diversified than they are today? Why? Will the trends regarding diversification be identical in Europe, the United States, and Japan? If not, why?

## Ethics Questions

1. Assume you overheard the following statement: "Those managing an unrelated-diversified firm face far more difficult ethical challenges than do those managing a dominant-business firm." Based on your reading of this chapter, do you accept or reject this statement and why?

2. Is it ethical for managers to diversify a firm rather than return excess earnings to shareholders? Be prepared to provide reasoning in support of your answer.

3. What unethical practices might occur when a firm restructures its operations? Explain.

4. Is it harder to ethically manage a "dog" business unit as compared to a "star" unit? If so, why? What ethical advice would you offer to someone asked to manage a diversified firm's most unattractive business unit?

5. Do you believe ethical managers are unaffected by the managerial motives to diversify discussed in this chapter? If so, why? In addition, do you believe ethical managers should help their peers learn how to avoid making diversification decisions on the basis of the managerial motives to diversify? Why or why not?

6. What guidelines and procedures would you establish to encourage the display of ethical behaviors among all parties involved with a strategic alliance?

## Notes

1. *Value Line,* 1993, Edition 2 (December 24): 252.

2. T. Maxon, 1994, Tunnel vision: Channel train to use AMR technology, *Dallas Morning News,* March 23, 1D, 2D.

3. T. Maxon, 1994, AMR may spin off tech groups, *Dallas Morning News,* April 1, 1D, 14D.

4. M. E. Porter, 1980, *Competitive Strategy* (New York: Free Press), xvi.

5. M. E. Porter, 1987, From competitive advantage to corporate strategy, *Harvard Business Review* 65, no. 3: 43–59.

6. Ibid., 43.

7. Ibid.

8. C. K. Prahalad and G. Hamel, 1990, The core competence of the corporation, *Harvard Business Review* 68, no. 3: 79–91.

9. B. C. Reimann, 1987, *Managing for Value: A Guide to Value-Based Strategic Management* (Oxford, Ohio: The Planning Forum), 50.

10. M. Goold and K. Luchs, 1993, Why diversify? Four decades of management thinking, *Academy of Management Executive* 7, no. 3: 7–25.

11. Ibid., 22.

12. A. A. Lado, N. G. Boyd, and P. Wright, 1992, A competency based model of sustainable competitive advantage: Toward a conceptual integration, *Journal of Management* 18: 77–91.

13. N. A. Nichols, 1994, Scientific management at Merck: An interview with CFO Judy Lewent, *Harvard Business Review* 72, no. 1: 88–99.

14. Goold and Luchs, Why diversify? 8.

15. M. A. Peteraf, 1993, The cornerstones of competitive advantage: A resource-based view, *Strategic Management Journal* 14: 179–191.

16. R. P. Rumelt, 1974, *Strategy, Structure and Economic Performance* (Cambridge, Mass.: Harvard University Press).

17. R. E. Hoskisson, M. A. Hitt, R. A. Johnson, and D. S. Moesel, 1993, Construct validity of an objective (entropy) categorical measure of diversification strategy, *Strategic Management Journal* 14: 215–235.

18. M. A. Hitt, R. E. Hoskisson, and R. D. Ireland, 1994, A mid-range theory of the interactive effects of international and product diversification on innovation and performance, *Journal of Management,* 20:297–326.

19. W. M. Bulkeley, 1994, Conglomerates make a surprising comeback—with a '90s twist, *Wall Street Journal,* March 1, 1A, 6A.

20. *Value Line,* 1994, Edition 10 (February 18): 1494.

21. Ibid.

22. Rumelt, *Strategy, Structure, and Economic Performance;* L. Wrigley, 1970, Divisional autonomy and diversification (Ph.D. diss., Harvard Business School).

23. Bulkeley, Conglomerates.

24. M. E. Porter, 1985, *Competitive Advantage* (New York: Free Press), 328.

25. A. Taylor III, 1994, Will success spoil Chrysler? *Fortune,* January 10, 88–92.

26. R. M. Grant, 1991, The resource-based theory of competitive advantage: Implications for strategy formulation, *California Management Review* (Spring): 114–135.

27. Anheuser-Busch Companies, Inc., 1992, *Annual Report,* 6.

28. T. P. Pare, 1994, GE as a service company, *Fortune,* April 18, 16.

29. Rockwell International, 1993, *Annual Report,* 4.

30. M. A. Hitt, R. E. Hoskisson, and R. D. Nixon, 1993, A mid-range theory of interfunctional integration: Its antecedents and outcomes, *Journal of Engineering and Technology Management* 10: 161–185.

31. W. G. Shepherd, 1986, On the core concepts of industrial economics, in H. W. deJong and W. G. Shepherd (eds), *Mainstreams in Industrial Organization* (Boston: Kluwer Publications).

32. L. Landro, P. M. Reilly, and R. Turney, 1993, Disney relationship with Time Warner is a strained one, *Wall Street Journal,* April 14: 1A, 9A.

33. J. Richardson, 1993, Parallel sourcing and supplier performance in the Japanese automobile industry, *Strategic Management Journal* 14: 339–350.

34. O. E. Williamson, 1975, *Markets and Hierarchies: Analysis and Antitrust Implications* (New York: Macmillan Free Press).

35. R. Amit and J. Livnat, 1988, A concept of conglomerate diversification, *Journal of Management* 14: 593–604.

36. Hanson, 1992, *Annual Report,* 4.

37. R. E. Hoskisson and M. A. Hitt, 1990, Antecedents and performance outcomes of diversification: A review and critique of theoretical perspectives, *Journal of Management* 16: 461–509.

38. R. M. Scherer, 1980, *Industrial Market Structure and Economic Performance* (Chicago: Rand McNally).

39. D. J. Ravenscraft and R. M. Scherer, 1987, *Mergers, Sell-Offs and Economic Efficiency* (Washington, D.C.: Brookings Institution), 22.

40. J. R. Williams, B. L. Paez, and L. Sanders, 1988, Conglomerates revisited, *Strategic Management Journal* 9: 403–414.

41. M. C. Jensen, 1986, Agency costs of free cash flow, corporate finance, and takeovers, *American Economic Review* 76: 323–329.

42. R. Gilson, M. Scholes, and M. Wolfson, 1988, Taxation and the dynamics of corporate control: The uncertain case for tax motivated acquisitions, in J. C. Coffee, L. Lowenstein, and S. Rose-Ackerman (eds.), *Knights, Raiders, and Targets: The Impact of the Hostile Takeover,* 271–299 (New York: Oxford University Press).

43. C. Steindel, 1986, Tax reform and the merger and acquisition market: The repeal of the general utilities, *Federal Reserve Bank of New York Quarterly Review* 11, no. 3: 31–35.

44. Rumelt, *Strategy, Structure and Economic Performance,* 125.

45. E. H. Bowman, 1982, Risk seeking by troubled firms. *Sloan Management Review* 23: 33–42.

46. Y. Chang and H. Thomas, 1989, The impact of diversification strategy on risk-return performance, *Strategic Management Journal* 10: 271–284; R. M. Grant, A. P. Jammine, and H. Thomas, 1988, Diversity, diversification, and profitability among British manufacturing companies, 1972–1984, *Academy of Management Journal* 31: 771–801.

47. N. M. Kay and A. Diamantopoulos, 1987, Uncertainty and synergy: Towards a formal model of corporate strategy, *Managerial and Decision Economics* 8: 121–130.

48. Jensen, Agency costs.

49. Y. Amihud and B. Lev, 1981, Risk reduction as a managerial motive for conglomerate mergers, *Bell Journal of Economics* 12: 605–617.

50. H. Tosi and L. Gomez-Mejia, 1989, The decoupling of CEO pay and performance: An agency theory perspective, *Administrative Science Quarterly* 34: 169–189.

51. R. E. Hoskisson and T. Turk, 1990, Corporate restructuring: Governance and control limits of the internal market, *Academy of Management Review* 15: 459–477.

52. J. P. Walsh and J. K. Seward, 1990, On the efficiency of internal and external corporate control mechanisms, *Academy of Management Review* 15: 421–458.

53. E. F. Fama, 1980, Agency problems and the theory of the firm, *Journal of Political Economy* 88: 288–307.

54. C. R. Loderer and D. P. Sheehan, 1989, Corporate bankruptcy and managers' self-serving behavior, *Journal of Finance,* 44: 1059–1075.

55. C. Y. Woo, G. E. Willard, and U. S. Dallenbach, 1992, Spin-off performance: A case of overstated expectations? *Strategic Management Journal* 13: 433–448.

56. S. F. Slater and T. J. Zwirlein, 1992, Shareholder value and investment strategy using the general portfolio model, *Journal of Management* 18: 717–732.

57. R. G. Hamermesh, 1986, *Making Strategy Work* (New York: John Wiley and Sons).

58. R. E. Hoskisson, M. A. Hitt, and C. W. L. Hill, 1991, Managerial risk taking in diversified firms: An evolutionary perspective, *Organization Science* 2: 296–313.

59. G. Hamel and C. K. Prahalad, 1989, Strategic intent, *Harvard Business Review* 67, no. 3: 63–76.

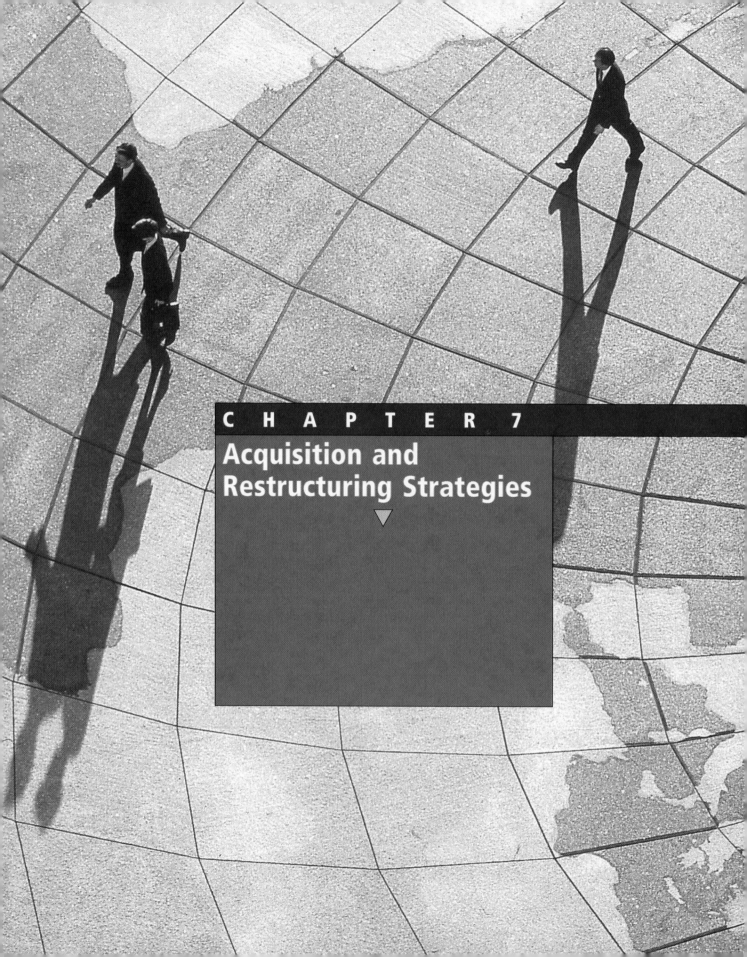

# CHAPTER 7
# Acquisition and Restructuring Strategies

▽

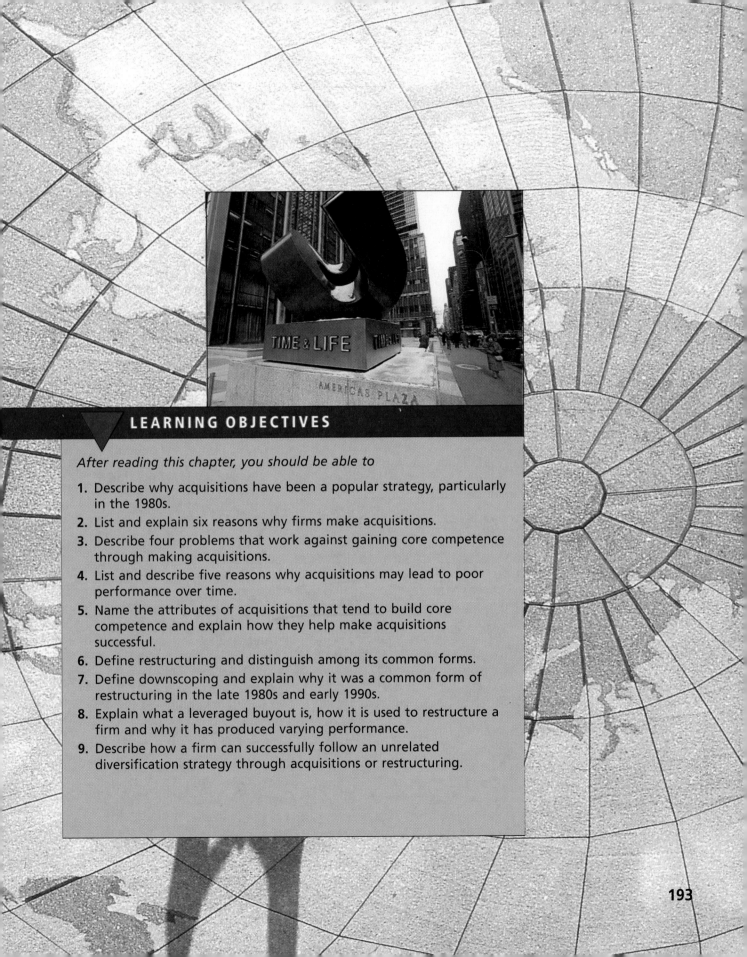

## LEARNING OBJECTIVES

*After reading this chapter, you should be able to*

1. Describe why acquisitions have been a popular strategy, particularly in the 1980s.
2. List and explain six reasons why firms make acquisitions.
3. Describe four problems that work against gaining core competence through making acquisitions.
4. List and describe five reasons why acquisitions may lead to poor performance over time.
5. Name the attributes of acquisitions that tend to build core competence and explain how they help make acquisitions successful.
6. Define restructuring and distinguish among its common forms.
7. Define downscoping and explain why it was a common form of restructuring in the late 1980s and early 1990s.
8. Explain what a leveraged buyout is, how it is used to restructure a firm and why it has produced varying performance.
9. Describe how a firm can successfully follow an unrelated diversification strategy through acquisitions or restructuring.

193

## Bold and Risky Merger Between Time and Warner

# TIME WARNER

In 1989, Time, Inc., and Warner Communications completed a merger that ended a takeover battle, one of the most bitter of the 1980s. To complete the $8.1 billion merger, Time had to fend off a rival bid from Paramount Communications Corp., itself a recent acquisition target, creating a situation that eventually had to be settled in the courts. In fact, the court ruled that public corporations did not have to accept takeover offers if their own strategic plans predict enhanced shareholder value over a longer time period. This ruling became a precedent for firms defending against unwanted takeover bids.

Of greater importance was the potential that the merger between Time and Warner provided. Merging the two firms allowed for the opportunity to merge print and visual media into a "multimedia" firm. However, from 1989 to 1993, the shareholders did not realize the promise provided by the merger. There were several reasons for this outcome. First, a massive amount of debt was required to finance the transaction. The Time-Warner Co. (the merged firm) ended up with almost $20 billion of debt. As a result, the Standard and Poor's Corporation rated Time-Warner's debt load as excessive. In addition, there were significant problems in merging the two cultures. Warner executives stated that the Time culture was antithetical to their fast-paced entrepreneurial style. They suggested that new ideas had to go through multiple managers, meetings, and committees before a decision could be made to move forward, whereas, at Warner, when somebody had a good idea, the chief executive officer (CEO), then Steven Ross, was the only person required to approve it, and he generally did. Therefore, the Time-Warner merger took considerable time to realize its potential.

Recently, its new CEO, Gerald Levin, announced a $2.5 billion strategic alliance with U.S. West, Inc. This has been labeled as a bold and risky move as well because Time is making available a large portion of its most prized assets and mortgaging its future cash flow. However, one reason for this alliance is to utilize the funds from U.S. West to reduce its huge debt load. Therefore, it is still paying for the merger in 1989. The announcement of the alliance suggested that U.S. West would acquire a 25.5 percent interest in Time-Warner Entertainment L.P., which includes all cable television and filmed entertainment operations. The primary purpose of the new strategic alliance is to build a full-service multimedia network that carries communications, entertainment, and information on Time-Warner cable TV systems to millions of subscribers. Because Time-Warner sold a 12.5 percent interest in Time-Warner Entertainment for $1 billion to two Japanese firms in 1992, Time-Warner now owns approximately 62 percent of Time-Warner Entertainment. U.S. West also obtained an option to acquire an additional 8.5 percent of the unit if certain conditions are met. While this looks to be an investment with much potential, there is also significant risk for Time-Warner. It is losing valuable ownership of and future income from the unit. However, it needs the cash flow from U.S. West to reduce its significant debt load and invest for the future. In other words, the firm's debt load forced it to seek an alliance in order to move forward to develop a new electronic superhighway for the transmission of all forms of information to multiple people in the United States and, potentially, worldwide. ▲

The Time-Warner merger was highly publicized. It came at the end of a decade, the 1980s, and was the result of a bitter takeover battle. Furthermore, a precedent-setting court case was required before the Time-Warner merger could be consummated. In addition, the $15 billion in debt necessary to finance the merger was quite controversial. However, the market power and the communication expertise in the combined firm were significant and, with these resources, produced strong potential for the development of new opportunities in communication markets. Therefore, the Time-Warner merger demonstrates both the positive and the negative attributes of the stream of acquisitions in the 1980s.

Chapter 6 examined corporate-level strategy and, in particular, discussed types and levels of product and market diversification that can build core competencies. The dominant means for fashioning a diversification strategy is through acquisitions. While making acquisitions has been a popular strategy among U.S. firms for many years, the decade of the 1980s was labeled by some as "merger mania." In fact, depending on whether only whole firm acquisitions are counted or partial (ownership) acquisitions are included, the number of acquisitions completed in the United States during the 1980s varies from slightly over 31,000 to as many as 55,000. The total value of these acquisitions exceeded $1.3 trillion, with 1988 representing the peak year with $246.9 billion invested in acquisitions.[1] This investment in acquisitions is even more significant because it accounted for almost 40 percent of U.S. firms' 1988 capital expenditures.[2] Therefore, it is clear that acquisitions represented a popular strategy in the 1980s. In fact, it has been described as the most prolific, sustained merger and acquisition wave in history.

With the large amount of acquisition activity evidenced in the 1980s and the substantial capital investment required to support this activity, one would expect strong positive returns to shareholders of the acquiring firms. However, the outcomes evidenced from acquisitions do not fully support this belief. For example, research has shown that *shareholders of acquired firms* derive significant value from the acquisition, but that *shareholders of acquiring firms* are less likely to gain such value. In fact, the average return to shareholders of acquiring firms was close to zero.[3] The significant negative returns earned from some acquisition activity and the overdiversification of some firms, as described in Chapter 6, have produced a trend toward restructuring activities. Restructuring involves firms divesting businesses (often ones that they acquired in earlier years) to strategically refocus their operations and develop effective core competencies.[4]

The purpose of this chapter is to explore the rationale for mergers and acquisitions and the potential problems firms encounter in attempting to obtain strategic competitiveness through an acquisition strategy. We also examine the primary reasons for the lack of strategic competitiveness among acquiring firms, along with the attributes of acquisitions that create a competitive advantage. Thereafter, we explore the phenomenon of restructuring (often reversing the diversification attained through acquisitions), the reasons for its use, and the restructuring alternatives that create strategic competitiveness. Finally, we explain how a few unique firms are able to create core competence through unrelated diversification. These firms may obtain a core competence of continually acquiring other firms, restructuring them, and retaining certain firm assets, while divesting others.

## Mergers and Acquisitions

▲ A **merger** is a transaction where two firms agree to integrate their operations on a relatively coequal basis because they have resources and capabilities that together may create a stronger competitive advantage.

▲ An **acquisition** is a transaction where one firm buys a controlling or 100 percent interest in another firm with the intent of more effectively using a core competence by making the acquired firm a subsidiary business within its portfolio of businesses.

▲ A **takeover** is an acquisition where the target firm did not solicit the bid of the acquiring firm.

A **merger** is a transaction where two firms agree to integrate their operations on a relatively coequal basis because they have resources and capabilities that together may create a stronger competitive advantage. Alternatively, an **acquisition** is a transaction where one firm buys controlling or 100 percent interest in another firm with the intent of more effectively using a core competence by making the acquired firm a subsidiary business within its portfolio of businesses. Usually, the management of the acquired firm reports to the management of the acquiring firm. Most mergers represent friendly agreements between the two firms, whereas acquisitions often (but not always) are unfriendly takeovers. A **takeover** is an acquisition where the target firm did not solicit the bid of the acquiring firm. Only a small minority of these transactions are mergers; most are acquisitions. Therefore, the primary focus in this chapter is on acquisitions.

### Reasons for Acquistions

There are several potential reasons that firms follow an acquisition strategy and/or make selected acquisitions. Among them are achieving a competitive advantage through greater market power, overcoming significant barriers to entry, and increasing the speed of market entry. Associated reasons include avoiding the significant costs involved in developing new products, avoiding the risks of new product development, achieving diversification (either related or unrelated), and, finally, avoiding competition. These reasons are described more fully below.

**Market Power**　A primary reason for acquisitions is to achieve greater market power. Many firms may have core competence, but lack the size to exercise their resources and capabilities. Market power usually is derived from the size of the firm and the firm's resources and capabilities to compete in the marketplace through its market share. Therefore, most acquisitions designed to achieve greater market power entail buying a competitor or a business in a highly related industry to allow exercise of a core competence and gain competitive advantage in the acquiring firm's primary market. Acquisition of a competing firm is referred to as a **horizontal acquisition.** Acquisition of a firm in a highly related industry is referred to as a **related acquisition.**

▲ A **horizontal acquisition** is an acquisition of a competing firm.

▲ A **related acquisition** is an acquisition of a firm in a highly related industry.

　　The opportunity to make horizontal acquisitions was enhanced by changes in the interpretation and enforcement of anti-trust laws in the early 1980s.[5] Prior to that time, very few acquisitions of direct competitors were allowed by the U.S. government. Of course, this action by the federal government represented a major impetus to an acquisition strategy. Firms that gain greater market share and/or have more resources for gaining competitive advantage have more power to use against competitors in their markets. The Time-Warner transaction represented a related acquisition designed to create synergy that would afford greater market power in domestic and global markets. For example, Time-Warner may be better able to compete with Paramount Pictures and CBS Records, which were acquired and supported by Sony Corp.

　　Similarly, the acquisition of Ashton-Tate in 1981 by Borland International was designed to significantly enhance Borland's market power in the software industry. The $440 million acquisition of the database market leader was applauded by many software analysts, with some predicting that Borland might gain a competitive advantage over Microsoft. However, Borland was unable to exploit this new acquisition to gain such a competitive advantage, at least in the short term. Problems were experienced in managing the larger and more complex firm, along with other decisions made by the CEO, Philippe Kahn. As a result, Borland International suffered a significant net loss of over $80 million in 1992. However, through some swift strategic actions (e.g., price reductions), it seems to be making a comeback. Microsoft recognized Borland's move into databases to gain a competitive advantage and also bought a small database supplier that developed a clone of the Ashton-Tate primary dBase program. Therefore, Microsoft moved to offset any advantage gained by Borland in its acquisition of Ashton-Tate.[6]

More recently, as competition continued, Novell, the long-time leader in software for networking personal computers, agreed to purchase WordPerfect Corp., which was privately held, for $1.4 billion. Furthermore, it bought Borland International's spreadsheet business for $145 million.[7] While still half the size of Microsoft, the new Novell will have an impressive range of key businesses. It will have the leading network software as well as the traditional leader in word-processing programs. Borland's Quatro Pro spreadsheet software holds a distant third place behind Lotus Development's and Microsoft's spreadsheet software. In some ways, the merger represents a rescue of Borland's spreadsheet business and, to a lesser extent, a rescue of WordPerfect, which hesitated to move to the Windows format and lost market share to Microsoft. Of course, the current challenge is to integrate the disparate operations. But without the increased size and potential capabilities, it is unlikely that the merged firm will be able to maintain its success against Microsoft's market power. Also at issue will be the competitive response from Microsoft. These competitive actions and responses represent the competitive dynamics discussed in Chapter 5 and were labeled multipoint competition in Chapter 6.

**Barriers to Entry**   **Barriers to entry** (introduced in Chapter 2) represent factors associated with the market and/or firms currently operating in the market that make it more expensive and difficult for a new firm to enter that market. For example, it may be difficult to develop a new venture in a market with large and established competitors. Such an entry may require substantial investments in a large manufacturing facility and in massive advertising and promotion to produce adequate sales in order for the manufacturer to achieve economies of scale and offer goods at a competitive price. Market entry also requires the firm to have an efficient distribution system and outlets to reach the ultimate consumer. If consumers have loyalty to brands already in the market, even these actions may not be adequate to produce a successful new venture. In this case, a firm may find it easier to enter the market by acquiring an established firm already operating in that market. While the acquisition can be costly, the acquiring firm can achieve immediate access to the market and can do so with an established product that may have consumer loyalty. In fact, the higher the barriers to entry are, the more likely it is that acquisitions will be used to enter a particular market.

Whirlpool holds the dominant position in the white-goods appliance business in North America. However, it lacked a strong presence in Europe at a time when a more united Europe seemed imminent. Therefore, Whirlpool sought and completed an acquisition of the appliance business of Philips Electronics NV.[8] The acquisition was initiated with a 53 percent stake in 1989, and the business was

▲ **Barriers to entry** represent factors associated with the market and/or firms currently operating in the market that make it more expensive and difficult for a new firm to enter that market.

wholly owned by 1991. Whirlpool simplified its European organization by replacing 17 separate country units with four regional offices. It is also trying to exploit the "value gap" between U.S. and European markets. European consumers pay up to twice as much for major appliances as their U.S. counterparts. Although the acquisition allowed stronger entry in Europe, Whirlpool is third in market share. The leader, Sweden's Electrolux AB, has also made several acquisitions. For instance, earlier it acquired the large Italian firm Zanussi, building its presence in southern Europe.[9] The number two appliance business in Europe, Bosch-Siemens Hausgerate GmbH, also has an agreement with a strong U.S. competitor of Whirlpool, Maytag. Whirlpool intends to build strong pan-European brands as country barriers are reduced. Philips had a strong brand name, and Whirlpool hopes to build on that and on its own reputation for quality.

**Cost and Speed**   Oftentimes, developing new products internally and starting new ventures can be quite costly and require significant time to develop the products and achieve a profitable return. For example, new ventures require an average of 8 years to achieve profitability and 12 years to generate adequate cash flows.[10] In addition, it has been estimated that almost 88 percent of innovations fail to achieve adequate returns on investment.[11] Furthermore, about 60 percent of innovations are effectively imitated within four years after patents are obtained. Therefore, internal development is often perceived by managers as entailing high risk.[12] The basic problem is that the costs of developing and bringing a new product to market can be substantial. As a result, managers may prefer other means of market entry that are much quicker and less risky. Acquiring an established firm, while sometimes costly, is less risky because there is a track record on which that firm can be evaluated. Furthermore, an acquisition offers immediate access to the market with an established sales volume and customer base. This is one reason AT&T bought NCR Corp. The acquisition provided AT&T with an immediate presence in the computer market and an opportunity to build the joint networking market (requiring both communication and computer technology and knowledge). The Whirlpool example shows that speed can be increased, but also that integration is difficult. Whirlpool's operating margins improved to 5.6 percent in Europe, but it has not realized its goal of 10 percent. However, new ventures often have to build their sales volume over time, working hard to develop a relationship with customers. Therefore, acquisition of an established firm provides a significant presence in the market and can provide profitability in the short term. This is one of the reasons that acquisition has been such a popular strategy, as shown in the Strategic Focus on BMW.

**Risk**   As noted in the Strategic Focus on BMW-Rover, internally developed new ventures can be quite risky, as Mercedes-Benz may experience. New ventures have high failure rates and take longer to achieve adequate cash flows and profitability. Alternatively, acquisitions provide outcomes that are more certain and can be estimated (forecasted) more accurately. This is because the target firms (e.g., Rover) have a track record that can be carefully analyzed and forecasts of future revenues and costs can be based on historical records. No such records exist for newly developed products.[13]

It has been suggested that acquisitions have become a common means of avoiding risky internal ventures (and therefore risky R&D investments). In fact, acquisition may become a substitute for innovation.[14] This is because firms may

## STRATEGIC FOCUS

### BMW Acquires Rover Cars to Gain an Immediate Presence in the Sport Utility Vehicle Market

To enter the popular U.S. market for sport utility vehicles, BMW acquired 80 percent of Rover Cars from parent British Aerospace PLC for $1.2 billion. Honda passed up the chance to buy, having held 20 percent of Rover Cars for four years. BMW wanted to maintain the alliance agreement between Rover Cars and Honda, which included product sharing. Both BMW and Rover were strong among European car companies, even though Europe has been experiencing the worst slump since World War II. BMW was still in the black, while competitor Mercedes-Benz experienced losses in 1993. Rover essentially broke even in 1993 on increased sales after several years of losses.

With the deal, BMW could immediately have three sport utility vehicles to sell from $50,000 to below $30,000. The Range Rover is on the high end, and the new Discovery was introduced in April 1994 for under $30,000. The Discovery could take sales from Ford's Explorer and Chrysler's Grand Cherokee, the two volume leaders. Even more promising for BMW is the fact that the Discovery could upstage Daimler-Benz AG (the parent of Mercedes-Benz), which is not expected to sell its first sports utility vehicle in the United States until 1997. Mercedes-Benz is currently building a $300 million plant in Tuscaloosa, Alabama, to produce its sports utility vehicles. Helmut Panke, CEO of BMW, said, "We are on the fast track into this segment" through this acquisition.

Rover has 84 U.S. dealerships, many of which will become "Land Rover Centres," for four-wheel-drive vehicles. In addition, BMW's 350 U.S. dealerships could offer Land Rover vehicles, although Panke indicated that the dealers would have to be consulted on this issue. Also, BMW and Rover will both be strengthened in Europe by the acquisition because Rover is strong in market niches and countries where BMW is weak. Furthermore, the combination of Rover and BMW could offer a full range of vehicles from tiny subcompacts such as Rover's Mini to BMW's luxury models. Rover also has trucks and owns such well-loved British names as Triumph, MG, Morris Minor, and Austin Mini. All these product offerings come with no additional research and development expense. Thus, this may provide a huge advantage relative to Mercedes-Benz, which is trying to enter the same market niches by developing its own products. The Mercedes approach may not be timely, and it is not clear how successful Mercedes will be in the sport utility vehicle segment, given its luxury image.

The market reacted positively to the announcement of the acquisition. BMW's stock price increased 8.3 percent in Frankfurt, while British Aerospace increased 13 percent in London. However, to complete the acquisition, BMW will have to take on substantial debt. As a result, Standard and Poors downgraded the debt ratings of BMW and signaled concern about the potential high debt load.

want to avoid the risk of internal ventures and/or because firms have constraints on their resources and capabilities and have to decide whether to invest their scarce resources in developing new products or in making acquisitions. Of course, acquisitions are not riskless ventures. The risks of making an acquisition are discussed later in the chapter.

*The 7 Series is important to BMW's success in the luxury automobile segment. However, until it acquired 80 percent of Rover Cars, BMW did not have an entry in the fast-growing sport utility vehicle market. This acquisition allowed BMW to quickly enter the sports utility vehicle market with offerings in different price ranges. Introduced in April of 1994 at a price below $30,000, the Discovery is one of the sports utility vehicles BMW hopes will help it to achieve a competitive advantage in a fast-growing segment of the U.S. automobile market.*

**Diversification**   One of the most common means of diversifying is through acquisition. In fact, a firm may find it easier to develop new products and new ventures within its current market because its managers better understand the products and the market. However, it is often more difficult for a firm to develop new products that are quite different from its existing set of products and to enter new markets because its managers may have less understanding of such markets. Thus, it is uncommon for a firm to develop new products and ventures internally as a means of diversifying its product line.[15]

In addition, until the early 1980s, the U.S. government frowned on horizontal acquisitions and often precluded them through the enforcement of anti-trust laws. However, as noted in Chapter 6, changes in the interpretation and enforcement of such laws led to a substantial number of horizontal acquisitions within the same market and acquisitions of firms in related businesses. Therefore, acquisitions have become a popular means of expanding market share and/or moving into related markets (and thus achieving related diversification) as well as making unrelated diversification moves.

**Avoiding Competition**   A number of firms, particularly in the United States, used acquisitions to move into related and unrelated markets to decrease dependence on markets with substantial competitive pressure, frequently from foreign firms (e.g., Japan and Germany). It is common knowledge that U.S. firms in many industries experienced problems in maintaining their competitiveness in markets where Japanese, German, and other foreign firms had a strong presence. This is probably best exemplified by the U.S. automobile market. At the start of the 1980s, General Motors had approximately a 50 percent share of the U.S. automobile market. However, by the early 1990s, General Motors' share of the U.S. automobile market was below 30 percent. Much of the lost market share went to Japanese firms. During the mid-1980s, General Motors acquired Electronic Data Systems (EDS) and Hughes Aerospace.

U.S. Steel's mergers with Marathon Oil and Texas Oil and Gas were, in part, an attempt to avoid competition with imported steel from Japan. The Japanese do not have a strong industrial sector in petroleum and natural gas. Therefore, many U.S. firms attempted to spread their risks and diversify into other industries because of significant foreign competition. This has not been an effective strategy because it did not help U.S. firms gain strategic competitiveness or earn above-average profits, although, in some cases, it prevented below-average profits.

The Japanese have been much less active in acquisitions than have U.S. firms, and many of the earlier acquisitions in Japan, such as the merger to create Nippon Steel, were designed primarily to increase the market power of firms within Japanese markets.[16] However, as Sony's acquisition of CBS Records and Bridgestone's acquisition of Firestone Tire and Rubber Co. illustrate, the Japanese became important players in the international market for acquisitions in the 1980s. (See the Strategic Focus). The increase in Japanese acquisitions at this time was partly motivated by the lower value of the dollar relative to the yen; as the yen appreciates in value relative to the dollar, U.S. assets can be bought with yen that are worth more dollars.

There were multiple reasons for these acquisitions. In both the Sony and the Bridgestone cases, the acquisitions provided the acquiring firms with significant footholds in the market. Sony's acquisitions of CBS Records and Columbia Pictures provided vertical integration and outlets for some of Sony's new technology and products. Also, these acquisitions helped both Sony and Bridgestone overcome significant barriers to entry in those U.S. markets, were completed rapidly, and entailed less risk because of the known markets and past performance of each firm.

The Bridgestone acquisition of Firestone Tire and Rubber Co. was a horizontal acquisition. Therefore, while it did not represent product diversification, it did represent international diversification, an important topic covered in Chapter 8. Alternatively, Sony's acquisitions of CBS Records and Columbia Pictures represented related diversification moves. As such, neither entailed significant risk because of potential increased capabilities and synergies from these acquisitions. These and other primary reasons for making acquisitions are depicted in Figure 7–1.

Many of these same reasons were used to describe the benefits for pursuing strategic alliances in Chapter 5. Strategic alliances may also be used to diversify as Corning, Inc. has done (see Strategic Focus on Corning in Chapter 12). However, usually strategic alliances are not used to implement a corporate diversification strategy. Strategic alliances are commonly used to gain market power to counter competitive moves at the business-unit level. Because strategic alliances can have multiple purposes, they are also discussed in Chapter 8 on international strategy and in Chapter 12 on corporate entrepreneurship.

While there are advantages to be gained from acquisitions, there are also some potentially significant problems that can accrue. Sometimes, these problems may equal or exceed the benefits gained. As a result, the average returns on acquisitions have varied closely around zero, as noted earlier in this chapter. Next, we examine some of the potential problems of acquisitions.

## Acquisition Problems

Among the potential problems of an acquisition strategy are paying too much for the target firm, overestimating capability and synergy gains, paying the high cost of financing and arranging the acquisition, and integrating the acquired firm into

## Japanese Firms' Acquisitions of CBS Records and Firestone Tire and Rubber Company

The Sony Corp. acquired the CBS Records Division in 1987 for $2 billion. At the time, CBS was attempting to reduce its expenses, refocus on its core business of broadcasting, and divest lower-performing businesses.

Sony and CBS had been partners in a joint venture in Tokyo since 1967. The joint venture, designed to manufacture and sell records and music tapes, was quite successful, with a return on sales of approximately 20 percent in 1987. Furthermore, Sony was concerned that if CBS Records was sold to another firm, it might lose valuable options for future growth in its digital audio tape recorder (DAT). Therefore, the CBS Records Division represented a major opportunity for Sony to gain a primary foothold in the U.S. market. Interestingly, Sony obtained the CBS Records Division by paying a 28 percent premium (over the assumed value of the business), but this was well below the 60 percent premium that was relatively common for similar acquisitions at this point in time. In fact, Sony paid a 60 percent premium in 1989 when it acquired another major U.S. business, Columbia Pictures, for $3.45 billion. That acquisition was designed as a vertical integration move into entertainment software that could be combined with Sony's video hardware. Therefore, Sony's acquisitions of major U.S. businesses were expected to produce positive synergies.

Likewise, Japan's largest tire company, Bridgestone Corp., acquired Firestone Tire and Rubber Co., the third largest tire manufacturer in the United States at the time, for $2.6 billion in 1988. Prior to this acquisition, Bridgestone had only a minor presence in the U.S. and European tire markets, although it controlled over 50 percent of the tire market in Japan. This acquisition increased Bridgestone's share of the global tire market to just below the two largest global competitors, Goodyear and Michelin. The largest single tire market in the world is in the U.S., which accounts for approximately 38 percent of the total global demand for tires.

Bridgestone executives weighed the options (building a new plant or acquiring an established firm) for several years before entering the U.S. market. However, consolidation of the auto industry in the United States during the middle and late 1980s lessened the opportunities for foreign producers to obtain attractive plant locations without building expensive new plants. This was problematic because the industry already had substantial overcapacity. In order to purchase Firestone, Bridgestone had to overcome a tender offer from the Pirelli Group of Italy. Bridgestone made an offer that was 38 percent above the Pirelli bid and therefore won the competition to acquire Firestone.

the acquiring firm after the acquisition is completed. In fact, integration of the two firms, after acquisition, has long been a significant problem. These problems are also shown in Figure 7–1.

**Integration**    Several problems can accrue, making integration difficult after the acquisition has been completed.[17] Among these are melding two disparate corporate cultures,[18] linking different financial and control systems, building effective working relationships (particularly when management styles differ), and resolving

**FIGURE 7–1   Reasons for Acquisitions and Problems in Achieving Success**

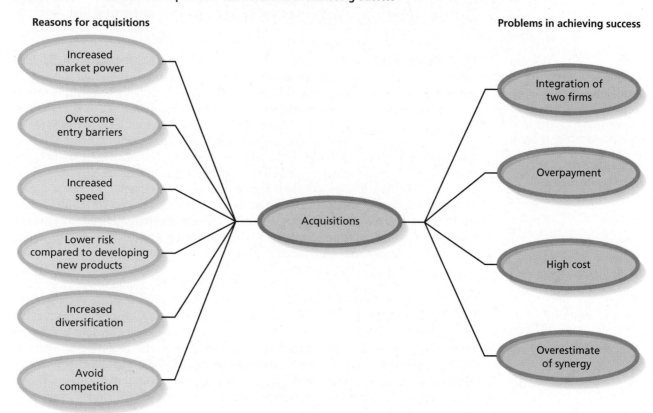

problems regarding the differing status of acquired firm executives.[19] The problem of melding different corporate cultures is exemplified in the merging of Time and Warner Communications. It was noted that approval of new ideas within Time was difficult to obtain because of the multiple levels and people involved in the approval process. However, new ideas within Warner Communications oftentimes had to be approved only by Steven Ross, former CEO. While there may be some idiosyncrasies involved in allowing one person to approve or disapprove new ideas/innovations, such a firm is more likely to be innovative and to implement innovations more quickly. Warner Communications executives were frustrated because of the bureaucratic procedures required by Time executives to gain approval of new ideas. These issues are often not discussed in negotiations to arrive at a price.[20]

**Overpayment**   One potential problem is that a firm may pay too much for the target firm. If a firm does not thoroughly analyze the target firm and does not develop adequate knowledge of its market value, it is possible to offer too much money to acquire the target firm. In addition, current shareholders in the target firm must be enticed to sell their stock. To do so, they often require a premium over the current stock price. These premiums frequently are between 40 and 60 percent. You may recall the example of Sony's purchase of CBS Records in which a 28 percent premium was paid. However, Sony paid a 60 percent premium for Columbia

Pictures, and Bridgestone paid approximately a 60 percent premium for Firestone Tire and Rubber Co. Premiums may be even greater when there are multiple bidders in the process.[21]

**High Cost**   Many of the acquisitions completed in the 1980s were financed with significant debt. In fact, the 1980s produced an innovation called junk bonds.[22] **Junk bonds** represented a new financing option in which risky acquisitions were financed with money (debt) that provided a high return to the lenders (often referred to as the bondholders). Some of the interest rates on junk bonds were as high as 18 and 20 percent because they are unsecured (not tied to specific assets as collateral) and thus are risky. Furthermore, firms were encouraged to take on significant debt because debt was believed to create positive managerial discipline. Some well-known finance scholars argued that debt disciplines managers not to misuse funds, and, therefore, executives were often encouraged to utilize significant leverage to complete large acquisitions.[23] There are dramatic and unfortunate examples of the significant costs entailed in financing acquisitions. For example, Campeau Corp. of Canada acquired Federated Department Stores for $6.5 billion in a heavily leveraged acquisition in 1988. Campeau intended to integrate Federated's major stores with those of Allied Stores, acquired in 1986. The long-run strategy of Campeau was to create a merchandising and real estate empire in the development of shopping malls. However, the leverage acquired by Campeau stretched its repayment capability to the maximum, when combined with the debt utilized to finance the acquisition of Allied Stores. Unfortunately, the recession in the late 1980s reduced the cash flow from retail operations and created problems in paying the interest and repaying the debt. As a result, the U.S. retailing units declared bankruptcy, and Campeau encountered significant financial problems.[24]

**Overestimate of Synergy**   Another significant problem in achieving success with acquisitions is overestimating the synergy involved and/or the benefits of such synergy. To achieve a sustained competitive advantage through an acquisition, a firm must realize private synergy and core competence that cannot be easily imitated by competitors. **Private synergy** refers to the benefit from merging the acquiring and the target firms that is due to a unique resource or a capability (set of resources) that is complementary between the two firms and not available among other potential bidders for that target firm.[25] Unfortunately, private synergy that is not easily imitated by competitors is uncommon. Perhaps this is one of the primary reasons that acquisitions rarely provide significant positive returns to acquiring firms' shareholders. RJR Nabisco had merged to create a larger consumer products company to compete with the merger between Philip Morris and General Foods. However, the merger ran into difficulties and became the subject of a leveraged buyout. In fact, the much-hailed $25 billion buyout of RJR Nabisco by Kohlberg Kravis Roberts and Co. (KKR) in 1989 turned sour in 1993. The paper profits realized by KKR and the pool of pension fund investors in the 1989 buyout were erased in 1993 when the stock price of RJR decreased by 36 percent. KKR is well known for buying significant assets and selling them later at a premium. In this case, it will be difficult to do. Multiple problems beset RJR Nabisco. It lost its chairman, Louis V. Gerstner, Jr., to IBM. The tobacco business has been tarnished because of the health-related problems created by its product. Finally, the threatened sin tax on tobacco products to help pay for a new national healthcare plan helped to dampen interest in RJR Nabisco stock.[26]

▲ **Junk bonds** represented a new financing option in which risky acquisitions were financed with money (debt) that provided a high return to the lenders (often referred to as the bondholders).

▲ **Private synergy** refers to the benefit from merging the acquiring and the target firms that is due to a unique resource or a capability (set of resources) that is complementary between the two firms and not available among other potential bidders for that target firm.

In addition to these general problems that may be encountered in making acquisitions, there may be other reasons for the long-term poor performance of acquisitions. Some of the reasons for long-term poor performance may lead to the problems noted above.

## Long-Term Performance of Acquisitions

As noted earlier in this chapter, the performance of acquisitions may be questioned. The research suggests that the long-term performance of many acquisitions is not positive. It is not uncommon for prior acquisitions to be divested several years thereafter, primarily because of poor performance.[27] Long-term poor performance may be attributed to several factors, including overdiversification, managerial energy absorption in the acquisition process, too much debt, too large a size, and the decline in innovation.

**Overdiversification**   One of the outcomes of the trend of acquisitions over the 1960s, 1970s, and 1980s was that firms became overdiversified. As noted earlier, acquisition has been used as a primary means of diversifying a firm's product line. When a firm becomes overdiversified, it is difficult to manage effectively. The level at which a firm becomes overdiversified differs for each firm. This is because the type of diversification and managerial expertise determines when a firm reaches a point of diversification that is too complex and unmanageable. Because related diversification requires more information processing than unrelated diversification, overdiversification is reached with fewer business units than with unrelated diversification.[28] When this occurs, firm performance usually suffers.[29]

In addition, high diversification often is accompanied by other attributes that can produce lower long-term performance. For example, when a firm becomes more diversified, top executives often have to emphasize financial controls over strategic controls in the evaluation of divisional performance.[30] Strategic and financial controls are defined and explained in Chapter 10. The change in emphasis comes about because the top executives do not have adequate knowledge of the various businesses to effectively evaluate the strategies and strategic actions taken by division general managers. For example, in the early 1980s, General Electric had 40 separate businesses. Its CEO suggested that it was difficult to even name all of the businesses, much less understand the products and markets of each. In these circumstances, top executives are forced to emphasize the financial outcomes of the businesses, rather than evaluating strategic actions. As a result, the division general managers become short-term oriented. Oftentimes their compensation is tied to the achievement of certain financial outcomes. As a result, they may reduce long-term investments (e.g., R&D, capital investment) that entail some risk in order to boost short-term profits.[31] When they do so, long-term performance may suffer. An example of the problem of overdiversification is shown in the Strategic Focus on Imperial Chemical Industries PLC.

The overdiversification experienced by ICI led to poor performance (e.g., lower sales and net loss in 1992). The overdiversification created significant problems for the management of the firm. Top-level managers could not effectively manage each of the businesses and maintain strategic competitiveness. Over time, this resulted in lower performance in those businesses. The problems exemplified in ICI did not allow the managers to focus on developing the core competencies in each of their businesses.

## ICI Divides into Two Separate Businesses

For several years, Imperial Chemical Industries PLC (ICI) of Great Britain followed a diversification strategy similar to that of several of the major U.S. chemical firms, such as Dupont, Dow Chemical, and Monsanto. ICI had been building its diverse portfolio of businesses since the 1940s. While a number of the businesses under ICI's umbrella share related attributes, their markets differ considerably. Furthermore, ICI had a large global expansion in the 1980s, adding thousands of employees in multiple locations throughout the world. As a result, the organization grew unwieldy, both in diversity and in size. The managers were unable to provide adequate attention and resources to many of the firm's rapidly growing businesses, particularly the pharmaceuticals unit. Therefore, ICI decided to downsize and significantly reduce its costs.

The firm laid off approximately 21,000 employees in 1990. However, downsizing did not adequately deal with the problem. The top executives were still attempting to deal with many different businesses, and they could not adequately understand and make effective decisions regarding the diverse markets and competitors. Therefore, top management decided to split the firm into two separate units and spin off one of those businesses, renamed Zeneca. Zeneca retained the pharmaceutical, pesticide, and specialty chemical businesses. ICI has the paints, materials, explosives, industrial chemicals, and other regional businesses within its portfolio. ICI may still be too broadly diversified. As a result, the firm will search for parties interested in acquiring or working on a joint venture with several of its major businesses where the firm is earning below average profits. These businesses' profits do not warrant further investment, according to company management.

This change is intended to reverse the performance problems experienced by ICI. The firm lost $866 million on sales of $18.33 billion in 1992. The 1992 performance was considerably below the net income of $824 million on sales of $18.98 billion in 1991. Analysts predict that the chemical business may rebound, and ICI could produce significant competition for the major U.S. chemical firms as a result of this change. In addition, there is an expectation that Zeneca will facilitate the pharmaceutical business, the largest one in its portfolio.

**Managerial Energy Absorption** An active acquisitive growth strategy often requires much managerial time and energy. For example, the process of making acquisitions requires extensive preparation and sometimes lengthy negotiations. Searches for viable acquisition candidates must be conducted, and these involve extensive data gathering and analyses. While executives are rarely involved in the data gathering and analyses, they must review the results and select the best candidate from the alternatives. After selecting the acquisition candidate, an effective acquisition strategy must be formulated and implemented. Negotiations with target-firm representatives can consume considerable time, particularly if the acquisition is an unfriendly takeover. Therefore, the process involves much time and energy on the part of executives from both the acquiring and the acquired firms. Such focused energy can divert their attention from other important matters within the firm, particularly those that are long term and require significant time and attention.[32] Furthermore, these negotiations often do not consider potential post-merger integration problems.[33]

Target-firm executives also may spend substantial amounts of time and energy on the acquisition. In fact, operations in target firms being pursued for acquisition have been described as being in a state of virtual suspended animation.[34] While day-to-day operations continue, albeit sometimes at a slower pace, most target-firm executives are unwilling to make long-term commitments. Commitments are frequently postponed until the negotiation process has been completed. Therefore, the acquisition process can create a short-term perspective and greater risk aversion among top executives in the target firm.[35]

After Phillips Petroleum had successfully fought off two takeover attempts (the most feared was that by T. Boone Pickens), anxiety remained high. It affected Phillips' ability to retain and motivate its top employees. As a result, it took the unprecedented step of adopting a corporate bylaw whereby a raider had to buy the house of any employee fired after the acquisition. Similarly, RJR Nabisco employees were distracted during talks regarding a buyout by Kohlberg Kravis Roberts. The greatest distraction and fear existed at RJR corporate headquarters because executives there were the most likely to be laid off if the buyout occurred.[36]

Given the large amount of turnover in the executive ranks of acquired firms, it is not surprising that many executives are reluctant to make major decisions for fear that they may be evaluated negatively by acquiring firm executives and laid off after the acquisition is completed.[37] This loss of managerial personnel can be problematic in other ways. In addition to losing significant managerial experience and expertise, those championing new products may leave (as at Phillips Petroleum and RJR Nabisco), and, therefore, the development and transfer of those new products to the market may be postponed or eliminated.

**Debt** As noted previously, many U.S. corporations significantly increased their use of debt during the 1980s. The use of debt is often referred to as leverage. Operationally, **leverage** is the ratio of total debt to total equity. The use of leverage is designed to increase the amount of financial gains firms can accrue from the equity employed by using borrowed resources to help finance business activities. Debt can be a valuable tool for businesses and help them to increase the size of their activities and the return on the equity invested. However, debt must be used carefully and with much forethought.

▲ **Leverage** is the ratio of total debt to total equity.

The heavy use of debt in the 1980s has not always produced positive outcomes. A study conducted by Dun and Bradstreet showed that a total of $108.8 billion worth of liabilities was associated with 87,266 bankruptcies in 1991. Furthermore, bankruptcies were not limited to small and intermediate-sized firms. A number of large firms, such as Macy's, USG Corp., and Zales Corp., also filed for bankruptcy. A great deal of the increased number and dollar value of bankruptcies has been attributed to the use of excess leverage, the cost of such debt, and the reduced managerial flexibility resulting from high leverage.[38] For example, Macy's bankruptcy was attributed to poor retail sales and too much debt. Zales' problems stemmed from a $1.2 billion debt created by two takeovers financed with junk bonds.[39] Also, as the BMW acquisition of Rover indicates, the increased debt load for BMW may be the Achilles heel of an otherwise promising combination.

Some of the use of leverage was fueled by the sale of junk bonds, described earlier, and by the notion that the use of high levels of debt constrains managers from taking opportunistic actions in their own interest and forces them to act more in shareholders' interest.[40] While this is an accurate characterization of the effects of debt, it fails to recognize the potential trade-offs that firms may have to make when large amounts of debt are used, particularly when the costs of debt are high. Obviously, there are finite resources, and when payments for interest and principal on the debt are high, those dollars cannot be invested in other opportunities. A significant amount of evidence suggests that when a firm has significant debt, managers forego investments that are likely to have long-term payoffs. These investments may include research and development and capital equipment. In both cases, these types of investments appear to be important for long-term firm competitiveness.[41]

USG Corp., burdened with a $2.66 billion debt, had to reduce its work force by one-third and its capital investments by 25 percent to meet the debt payments and avoid bankruptcy. Moreover, USG had to forego participation in favorable expansion opportunities. Unfortunately, even these moves were not enough to keep USG from considering bankruptcy.[42]

Therefore, we conclude that the use of debt has "Jekyll and Hyde" effects. On the one hand, leverage can be a positive force in the development of a firm, allowing it to take advantage of attractive expansion opportunities. However, the use of too much leverage (e.g., extraordinary debt) can lead to negative outcomes, such as postponing or eliminating investments necessary to maintain strategic competitiveness.

**Size**  Most acquisitions create a larger firm. The only circumstance in which this would not be the case is if the acquiring firm sells off assets equal to or greater than the size of the acquired firm. While it's not unusual for the acquiring firm to sell some of the acquired firm's assets, it is rare that 100 percent of the acquired assets are sold shortly after the acquisition.

In theory, increased size should help the firm gain economies of scale and therefore develop more efficient operations. This would be true, for example, in research and development operations, and, thus, larger firms should, over time, produce greater amounts of innovation (in theory). However, it has been found that increases in size create efficiencies only when the acquiring firm is not too large. After some level of size is reached, the problems created by large size outweigh the benefits gained from increased size. For example, larger firms can become unwieldy to manage. If too many levels of managers are between the bottom and the top, approval for the development and implementation of innovations can become lengthy and burdensome. Furthermore, to manage the increased size, firms often increase bureaucratic controls. **Bureaucratic controls** are formalized supervisory and behavioral rules and policies that are designed to ensure consistency across different units' decisions and actions. While these more formalized rules and policies can be beneficial to the organization, they sometimes produce more rigid and standardized behavior among managers.

It is not uncommon for the acquiring firm to adopt and implement centralized controls within the acquired firm in order to facilitate integration. This reduces flexibility and, in the long run, may produce less innovation and less creative decision making. Therefore, long-term firm performance can be harmed.[43]

▲ **Bureaucratic controls** are formalized supervisory and behavioral rules and policies that are designed to ensure consistency across different units' decisions and actions.

In the 1990s, firms have been attempting to solve this problem by downsizing. Downsizing not only reduces the number of employees, but often shrinks the number of management levels as well. Middle managers have been particularly vulnerable to downsizing changes. Downsizing can make firms more efficient. Downsizing is becoming more common in Japan and Germany as well, as described in a Strategic Focus later in this chapter.

**Substitute for Innovation**   If acquisitions produce greater diversification, absorb the time and energy of managers, are financed by a large amount of debt, and create larger-sized organizations, they are likely to have a negative effect on investments in and outcomes from research and development (e.g., patents).[44] Unless an industry is mature and requires little innovation to remain competitive, competitors are likely to gain an advantage over firms that rely heavily on an acquisitive growth strategy over time.

Firms following an acquisition strategy may begin to use acquisition as a substitute for innovation. They become locked into a self-reinforcing cycle. They make several acquisitions that produce less innovation over time. As they encounter significantly stronger competition and lose their competitive advantage in certain markets, they may seek to acquire firms in other markets. This reinforces the cycle. As a result, if firms use acquisitions as a substitute for innovation, they are likely to eventually encounter performance problems.[45] Reasons for the poor long-term performance of many acquisitions are presented in Figure 7–2.

While much of the discussion above suggests that acquisitions may have negative outcomes and lead to long-term performance difficulties, they can create benefits and improved capabilities. Below we explore the characteristics of effective acquisitions.

## Effective Acquisitions

As noted, the evidence suggests that acquisition strategies rarely produce positive returns for the acquiring firm's shareholders. Furthermore, we identified a number of potential problems with acquisitions and reasons they may lead to long-term performance difficulties. However, an acquisition strategy can have positive outcomes, as the Whirlpool example illustrates. There are some specific attributes of acquisitions that are more likely to produce positive outcomes and therefore may require the careful attention of top executives considering an acquisitions strategy.

Recent research identified some potentially important attributes of successful acquisitions.[46] The research suggested that successful acquirers often conducted a deliberate and careful selection of target firms and also considered the ensuing negotiations. Oftentimes targets were selected and "groomed" by establishing a working relationship sometime prior to the acquisition (e.g., through strategic alliances or joint ventures). In addition, the acquiring and frequently the target firms had considerable financial slack. The slack may be in the form of cash and/or debt capacity. A significant attribute was that the merged firm continued to maintain a low or moderate debt position, even if a substantial amount of leverage was used to finance the acquisition. Where substantial debt was used to finance the acquisition, it was quickly reduced by selling off assets from the acquired firm. Often the assets sold were not complementary to the acquiring firm's businesses or

**FIGURE 7–2**    Reasons for Acquisitions' Poor Performance

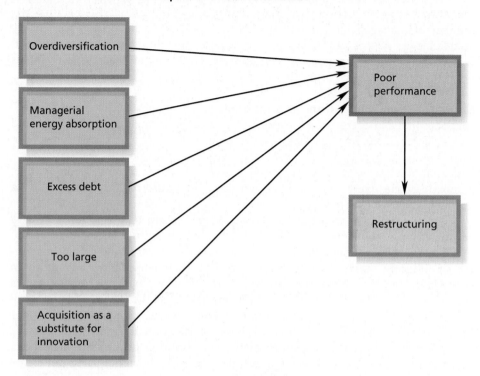

they were performing poorly. Also, the acquiring firm would sometimes sell its own lower-performing businesses after making an acquisition. In this way, high debt and debt costs were avoided. Therefore, the debt cost did not prevent long-term investments, and managerial discretion on cash flow due to debt payments was relatively flexible.

In most cases, the successful acquisitions entailed target firms that had complementary assets or resources for the acquiring firm. As a result, when the acquired firm was integrated into the acquiring firm, positive synergy and capability were created. In fact, the integration of the two firms frequently produced unique resources, a requirement to build strategic competitiveness, as described earlier.[47] Thus, the acquisitions were generally highly related to the acquiring firm's businesses. In fact, the acquiring firm maintained its focus on core businesses and leveraged those core businesses with the complementary assets and resources from the acquired firm.

The Strategic Focus on Gillette exemplifies many of the characteristics of a successful acquisition. Clearly, it has chosen acquisitions that provide complementary assets or resources. In addition, the Parker Pen acquisition increases its market power and reduces its competition. This acquisition helps build capability in one of its core businesses and uses the resources of Parker Pen to increase the market power of that core business globally. Also, the acquisition of majority control of the Chinese razor blade manufacturing firm, in addition to the one purchased in India and the new plant opened in Russia, establishes a significant presence for one of its other core businesses, razor blades, in large and expanding international markets. It provides a base for strategic competitiveness and above-average profits over the

## Gillette Is Sharpening Its Competitive Edge

In August of 1992, the Gillette Company acquired majority control of the largest razor blade manufacturer in China. This established access to a large market in the country with the largest population in the world. One month later, the company acquired Parker Pen Holdings Ltd. (a U.K. firm). When integrated with its Paper Mate and Waterman brands, Gillette became the largest manufacturer of writing instruments in the world. This acquisition gained approval from analysts who felt that it was a strategically sound move and helped Gillette expand a business in which it already had a global presence.

In addition to its horizontal acquisition of Parker Pen and its joint venture with the Chinese razor blade manufacturer, Gillette continued to bring innovative new products to the market. Gillette has a majority equity share and management control of the joint venture. For example, in 1992, Gillette first marketed its Sensor for Women razor, an attempt to replicate the success of the Sensor razor for men, introduced two years earlier. In addition, Gillette began a related diversification move into men's toiletries. While this represented some risk, Gillette had strength in products for men, and the new line included 14 items, such as pre- and after-shave lotions, as well as a gel shaving cream. It also included a gel-based deodorant and antiperspirant that rolls on using a new patented grid delivery system.

Many are crediting the CEO, Alfred M. Zeien, for seizing opportunities for long-term growth and profitable operations. In fact, during the first six months of 1992, the net income of Gillette increased by 20 percent to $249.9 million. Sales were $2.4 billion, an increase of only 9 percent over the same time period in 1991. Therefore, Gillette seems to be making acquisitions work to its advantage.

One of its primary core businesses, razors and blades, accounted for 37 percent of its sales and 62 percent of its profits in 1991. In the early 1990s, Gillette had a 50 percent share of the world's razor and blade market. But, by the end of 1992, it had captured 65 percent of the market in the United States and even more in Europe and Latin America. In order to maintain its healthy growth, Gillette is focusing on international sales. In addition to the Chinese joint venture noted above, it has also obtained control of a large razor blade manufacturer in India and has recently opened a new manufacturing plant in Russia. Gillette feels that it has razor and blade products that are technologically superior to anything in the world that can be produced at low cost. Furthermore, its sophisticated and difficult-to-clone manufacturing equipment (as mentioned in the Strategic Focus on Gillette in Chapter 3) has allowed it to stay ahead of the competition such as Schick. Gillette ended 1993 on a strong note with an annual gain in share value of about 15 percent. Also, it has a reservoir of new products. Therefore, Gillette is poised for success in the twenty-first century.

next decade. As explained in Chapter 8, one of the major modes of moving into international markets is through acquisitions. International moves can have multiple positive effects, both on the performance of the firm and on its continuing innovation. This is shown by Gillette in that it continues to introduce and manufacture new products, even though it is also following an acquisitions strategy.

*Recently, Gillette formed a joint venture with China's leading blade manufacturer, the Shanghai Razor Blade Company. Shown in this picture is a facility that is a part of the company, officially called Gillette Shanghai Ltd. It was formed as a result of the joint venture. According to company officials, this joint venture represents another step in carrying out Gillette's strategy for global expansion of the blade and razor business.*

Another characteristic of firms that launch successful acquisitions is that they emphasize innovation and continue to invest in research and development as a part of their overall strategy. As a result, they maintain a high managerial commitment to innovation. This is clearly evidenced in Gillette, which introduced a new razor for women and a new line of toiletries in the same year it completed two major acquisitions.

The final two characteristics of firms that are able to implement acquisitions successfully are flexibility and adaptation skills, along with an emphasis on friendly acquisitions, as opposed to hostile takeovers. When both the acquiring and the target firms have experience in managing change, they are more skilled in adapting their capabilities to new environments. As a result, they are more adept at integrating the two organizations, particularly important when they have disparate cultures. Adaptation skills allow the two firms to more quickly, efficiently, and effectively integrate the two firms' assets. As a result, the merged firm begins to produce the positive synergy and capabilities envisioned more quickly. In addition, friendly acquisitions normally facilitate integration of the two firms. The two parties work together to find ways to integrate their firms and achieve positive synergy. Under conditions of hostile takeovers, oftentimes there is animosity between the two top management teams, which can permeate the new joint organization. As a result, there may be more loss of key personnel in the acquired firm, and those who remain may resist the changes necessary to integrate the two firms and create synergy.[48]

The attributes of a successful acquisition and their results are summarized in Table 7–1. As shown, an effective acquisition is usually achieved when the target firm is deliberately and carefully selected, the firms have an established working relationship, the firms have considerable financial slack, a low to moderate debt position is maintained, the target firm has complementary assets or resources, those assets are leveraged to emphasize and strengthen the firms' core competence, the merged firm emphasizes innovation, the two firms have adaptation skills, and

**▼ TABLE 7-1**

### Attributes of Successful Acquisitions

| Attributes | Results |
|---|---|
| 1. Careful and deliberate selection of target firms and conduct of negotiations | Selects most appropriate target firms to achieve synergy and avoid overpayment |
| 2. Preselection of targets and established working relationship before acquisition | Facilitates integration speed and effectiveness |
| 3. Financial slack in acquiring and target firms | Allows easier and less costly financing of acquisition |
| 4. Low to moderate debt position of merged firm | Lowers cost, avoids trade-offs of high debt and lower risk (e.g., of bankruptcy) |
| 5. Acquired firm with complementary assets and/or resources to those in the acquiring firm | Provides high probability of positive synergy and gaining competitive advantage |
| 6. Continued investment in R&D and emphasis on innovation | Maintains competitive advantage in markets |
| 7. Skills of flexibility and adaptation to change | Facilitates integration speed and development of positive synergy |
| 8. Friendly acquisition | Facilitates integration speed and effectiveness |

the acquisition is friendly in orientation.[49] While firms can make successful acquisitions, the majority of acquisitions completed over the last three decades have not been highly successful. Because of their lack of success and the growth of some firms to unmanageable size and diversity, a number of firms, in the United States and internationally, have begun to restructure.

## Restructuring

Restructuring, a significant wave in the late 1980s and early 1990s, changed the composition of many U.S. and international firms. While it was a common strategy among many U.S. firms during this period, it has spread internationally to countries such as Japan and Germany. (See Strategic Focus on international restructuring).
**Restructuring** refers to changes in the composition of a firm's set of businesses and/or financial structure.[50] Much restructuring has entailed downsizing and the divestiture of businesses.[51] During this time period, there was a significant reduction in the number of acquisitions being made, as firms attempted to "get their houses in order." The primary impetus for restructuring was poor performance, along with correcting for overdiversification.[52] For example, Sears, Roebuck and Co. has gone through a painful downsizing and divestiture of some of its diversified businesses. These changes have been quite difficult not only for the firm, but sometimes for the communities in which it operated. For example, the closing of Sears' catalog business and 113 retail stores in 1993 meant the loss of jobs for 50,000 employees. This is not the end of the story, however. A number of others with ties to Sears and/or to the communities in which it closed operations will lose business and their jobs, because of the substantial multiplier effect.[53]

▲ **Restructuring** refers to changes in the composition of a firm's set of businesses and/or financial structure.

While the restructuring has been worldwide, some of the most significant restructuring has taken place in U.S. firms. Below we examine some of the more common means of restructuring.

## International Restructuring of Japanese and German Firms

The worldwide recession in the early 1990s prompted Japanese firms to take actions, some of which are considered radical in Japan. For example, Nissan Motor Co. experienced significant reductions in sales and profits because of the recession. The firm decided to close one of its automobile manufacturing plants, the first time such a plant had been closed in Japan. Furthermore, it reduced employment by 5,000, albeit through attrition. As an example of its problems, Nissan experienced a net loss in fiscal year 1993, the first since 1946. Other major Japanese firms, such as Matsushita Electric Industrial Co. and Nippon Telegraph and Telephone Corp. (NTT), Japan's largest firm, have experienced significant financial problems as well. NTT announced a plan to reduce its work force by 30,000 people and close 1,300 sales outlets between 1993 and 1995.

German firms have also experienced multiple economic problems in recent years. While Germany had enjoyed significant success in the 1980s, it also experienced high interest rates, significant global competition, substantive labor conflict, and an economic recession in the 1990s. As a result, some German firms lost their international market leadership. However, many German firms are fighting back, although some refer to it as a revolution. For example, there have been significant corporate restructurings that have included the layoff of approximately 500,000 workers in 1992 and early 1993. In addition, many German firms are opening manufacturing facilities in other countries, including Eastern Europe, China, and the United States. The purpose is to access cheaper labor and serve fast-growing international markets with local operations. Like many U.S. firms, they are also flattening the management hierarchy to increase the speed of decision making in the design, production, and market processes.

Some well-known German firms have experienced significant problems. For example, Volkswagen, a manufacturer of 3.5 million vehicles in 1993, reduced its work force by 36,000 employees and its spending on plants and equipment by $3.8 billion annually. Similarly, Mercedes-Benz experienced a reduction of its profits by 45 percent in 1992. Competition from luxury automobiles manufactured by Japanese firms, which had production costs 35 percent below those of Mercedes-Benz, captured a significant share of Mercedes-Benz's market. As a result, Mercedes-Benz is developing a new automobile to compete with the Japanese. Also, Mercedes is building a new plant in the United States to produce high-visibility sport utility vehicles.

Some of the restructuring among German firms has paid off. For example, Siemens flattened its management structure and created a large number of profit centers to which authority was decentralized. In so doing, it reduced product development time by 30 percent and became closer to its customers, and more cost efficient as well. One result is that it is receiving significant orders from Asia, a large market that is growing at the rate of 10 percent annually.

▲ **Downsizing** is a reduction in the number of employees, and sometimes in the number of operating units, but may or may not change the composition of businesses in the corporation's portfolio.

## Downsizing

One of the most common means of making changes among U.S. firms has been that of downsizing. **Downsizing** is a reduction in the number of employees, and sometimes in the number of operating units, but may or may not change the composition of businesses in the corporation's portfolio. The late 1980s and early

1990s evidenced the loss of thousands of jobs in private and public organizations throughout the United States. This includes work force reductions of 74,000 employees at General Motors, along with the closing of 21 plants over a four-year period. There have also been significant work force reductions at IBM, Kodak, Procter & Gamble, TRW, UNISYS, and Xerox, among many others. The intent of these downsizings was to become "lean and mean."[54] However, results of a survey published in the *Wall Street Journal* suggested that many of the firms that downsized did not meet their goals. Eighty-nine percent of the firms surveyed suggested that the downsizing had a goal of reducing expenses, but only 46 percent achieved this goal. Another 71 percent suggested that their goal was to improve productivity, but only 22 percent of the respondents said that they met their goal for increasing productivity. Finally, 67 percent stated a goal of increasing competitive advantage, but only 19 percent noted that this goal was achieved.[55] Thus, downsizing has not been nearly as successful as intended. Furthermore, it has other unintended and potentially negative consequences. For instance, it is often problematic because corporations do not have total control of which employees stay and which seek new positions elsewhere. Often the best employees take advantage of separation payments during layoffs because they have other employment options.

## Downscoping

Other firms have downscoped and met more success.[56] **Downscoping** refers to divestiture, spin-off, or some other means of eliminating businesses that are unrelated to a firm's core businesses. This is often referred to as strategically refocusing on the firm's core businesses. A firm that downscopes often also downsizes. However, it does not eliminate key employees from its primary businesses, which could lead to loss of core competence. The firm reduces its size by reducing the diversity of businesses in its portfolio. When accomplished, the top

▲ **Downscoping** refers to divestiture, spin-off, or some other means of eliminating businesses that are unrelated to a firm's core businesses.

management team can more effectively manage the firm. This is because the firm becomes less diversified, and the top management team can better understand and manage the remaining businesses, primarily the core businesses and other related businesses.[57] Strategic leadership exercised by the top management team is the focus of Chapter 11.

One example of downscoping is shown in Ball Corporation's spin-off of its noncore businesses. In the 1980s, Ball purchased two large former joint ventures, acquired additional glass-container capacity, upgraded its plants, and gained a substantial presence in the U.S. food-can business through acquisition of Heekin Can, Inc. The spin-off includes the home canning business and other relatively small operations. The total of the businesses spun off included $269 million in revenue in 1992, compared to $2.18 billion in revenue for the other remaining businesses. However, the primary reason for the spin-off, according to Ball's CEO, was that each of the small operations still required a fair amount of resources in capital and management time. After the spin-off, Ball may begin making acquisitions of other food-can operations in order to expand its geographic reach. It will remain focused on its core businesses, but intends to expand those businesses through internal development and acquisitions. Furthermore, while Ball has some international operations, it intends to increase those over the next several years. Thus, Ball is downscoping in order to increase its strategic focus and improve its expansion opportunities and performance through the focus of management time, effort, and resources on its core businesses.[58]

## Leveraged Buyouts

▲ A **leveraged buyout** (LBO) is a restructuring action whereby the managers of the firm and/or an external party buys all of the assets of the business, largely financed with debt, and takes the firm private.

While downscoping is a prominent and generally successful restructuring strategy, another restructuring strategy, leveraged buyouts, has received significant attention in the popular press. A **leveraged buyout** (LBO) is a restructuring action whereby the managers of the firm and/or an external party buys all of the assets of the business, largely financed with debt, and takes the firm private. The firm is bought by a few owners, primarily by obtaining significant amounts of debt, and the stock is no longer traded publicly. This form of restructuring was predicted by a prominent finance scholar to be the corporate form of the future.[59] Oftentimes the new owners of the LBO firm also sell a significant number of assets after the purchase and, in so doing, downscope the firm. Some of these assets are sold to help reduce the significant debt costs. In addition, it is frequently the intent of the new owners to increase the efficiency of the firm and sell it within a period of five to eight years.

While this has been hailed as a significant innovation in the financial restructuring of firms, there are potentially negative trade-offs. First, the large debt increases the financial risk of the firm. This has been evidenced by the number of LBO firms that have had to file for bankruptcy in the 1990s. Several were mentioned earlier in the chapter in our discussion of problems with debt. In addition, Northwest Airlines bordered on bankruptcy in 1993, the primary result of a $4 billion LBO a few years earlier. The firm had significant problems in its cash flow during the recession and was unable to repay its debt costs, as required in its agreement to obtain the debt financing.

The intent of owners to increase the efficiency of the firm and sell it within five to eight years sometimes creates a short-term and risk-averse managerial focus. As a result, many of these firms failed to invest in research and development and take other major actions designed to maintain or improve the core competence of the firm.[60] The effects of these actions may not be known for several years to come. However, such an approach is likely to have negative effects on these firms' strategic competitiveness relative to domestic and international competitors.

Research has shown that LBOs are most successful with mature businesses that have been relatively inefficient and do not require large investments in R&D or other actions to maintain strategic competitiveness.[61] In these cases, improvements in operating efficiency may improve the performance of the firm, and the short-term orientation is less of a problem because R&D is less necessary in mature product industries to maintain strategic competitiveness.

## Restructuring Outcomes

The restructuring alternatives, along with typical short- and long-term outcomes, are presented in Figure 7–3. As shown in the figure, the most successful restructuring actions are those that help top management regain strategic control of the firm's operations. Thus, downscoping has been the most successful because it refocuses the firm on its core business(es). Executives can control the strategic actions of the businesses because they are fewer, are less diverse, and deal with operations with which top management is more knowledgeable. However, some firms are able to manage highly unrelated diversified businesses successfully, as discussed in Chapter 6. While they clearly represent a minority, we briefly review how they are able to do so.

We have suggested that most unrelated diversification strategies are unsuccessful and require firms to restructure and downscope in pursuit of higher performance. However, some firms may actually become more unrelated because

**FIGURE 7–3  Restructuring and Outcomes**

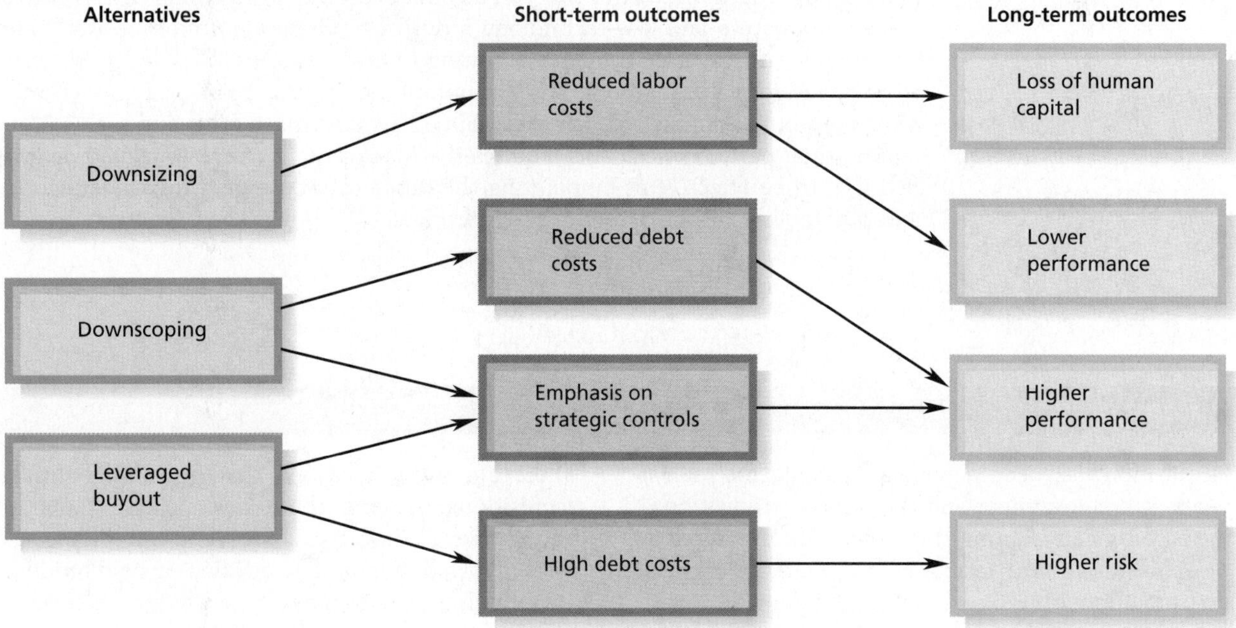

they divest related businesses. In addition, some firms that initiate restructuring by divesting unrelated businesses continue to be unrelated diversified businesses or are classified as conglomerates. This is partly because they may continue to make acquisitions of other unrelated businesses. In other words, they are restructuring their portfolio of businesses, but not with the purpose of changing their overall level of diversification.[62] It has been shown that under some circumstances unrelated acquisitions can produce higher performance for shareholders.[63]

As introduced in Chapter 6, Hansen PLC is one of the best-known examples of a firm that has successfully employed an unrelated diversification strategy. Hansen's annual sales place it among the top 100 industrial firms in the world. It had $13.8 billion in sales in 1991 and divested approximately 50 whole businesses or parts of businesses between 1989 and 1990. While this number of divestitures suggests significant restructuring, Hansen has remained an unrelated diversified firm. It continually restructures by selling and acquiring businesses; in fact, its primary core competence is its ability to buy, restructure, and sell businesses at appropriate times. Hansen buys mature businesses (often ones that are performing poorly), improves their efficiency and performance, keeps the parts of those businesses that are the most effective, and sells the rest. This type of firm fulfills a policing function often discussed in relationship to improved corporate governance (see Chapter 9 for a discussion of the governance function of unrelated diversified firms). As such, conglomerates such as Hansen are seen as corporate raiders.

This type of firm often makes large acquisitions in low-technology industries.[64] Because Hansen owns businesses, primarily in low-technology and mature industries, its top management can institute tight financial controls, avoid long-term and risky investments (e.g., R&D), and turn around the performance of the acquired firms.[65] To be successful with an unrelated diversification strategy, most firms are likely to employ a strategy similar to that of Hansen PLC. These types of firms do not employ strategic controls that emphasize a strong understanding of their operations in each industry. As a result, to be successful, they must have a portfolio of firms in industries that can be effectively managed by financial controls. Therefore, mature and low-technology industries, where investment in R&D and other long-term or risky activities requiring industry-specific knowledge is generally unnecessary, compose the list of appropriate targets. Such an approach may also allow firms such as Hansen to acquire low-performing firms and seek to turn around their performance. This requires the management of the unrelated diversified firm to be effective at pinpointing the problems and enhancing the efficiency and profitability of poorly performing businesses.[66]

## Summary

- Acquisition has been a popular strategy for many years, but the number and the size of acquisitions increased greatly during the 1980s. The popularity of acquisitions was facilitated by a change in the interpretation of U.S. anti-trust laws and innovations in the financing of large acquisitions (i.e., junk bonds).

- There are several reasons that firms might make acquisitions. Among these are increasing market power, overcoming barriers to entry, avoiding the costs involved in internally developing new products and bringing them to market, increasing the speed at which the firm can have a new business, reducing the risk of entering a new business, diversifying the firm more easily, and avoiding severe competition, often from foreign firms.

- Acquisitions produce their share of problems for the acquiring firm as well. It is often difficult to achieve effective integration between the acquiring and the acquired firms. Firms sometimes pay too much for the acquired firm because of the bidding process. In addition, firms can overestimate the potential capabilities and synergy that can be created between the acquiring and the acquired firms. Finally, the costs of acquisition can be significant. These include the costs of obtaining financing and arranging for the acquisition of another firm, as well as the specific costs of restructuring the merged firm.

- A number of acquiring firms have not been too successful. Some research has shown that as many as one-third of acquired firms are eventually divested. Reasons for poor performance include over-diversification, high managerial energy absorption (which precludes appropriate managerial oversight over other firm operations and time to make long-term investment decisions), high levels of debt, too large a size (which makes the firm more difficult to manage), and the use of acquisition as a substitute for innovation (which may result in the loss of core competence).

- However, acquisitions can be successful. Successful acquisitions often require deliberate and careful selection of target and firm negotiations. In addition, both the acquiring and the target firms in successful mergers frequently have considerable slack in the form of cash and/or debt capacity. Successful acquiring firms often maintain a low or moderate debt position. Even if significant leverage is used to finance the acquisition, the firm quickly reduces the debt and debt costs by selling off portions of the acquired firm or some of its own lower-performing businesses. Successful acquisitions involve firms with complementary assets/resources, and those complementary resources are used to leverage the core competence of the joint firm. Acquisitions also tend to be more successful when both the acquiring and the target firms have experience in adapting to change and therefore are better able to achieve effective integration. Finally, many of the successful acquiring firms maintain an emphasis on innovation and R&D as a part of their overall strategy.

- In the late 1980s and early 1990s, restructuring became a common and important strategic action. Oftentimes this restructuring is undertaken to downsize the firm. The approach requires employee layoffs and also seeks to reduce the number of hierarchical levels in an organization. Although it does reduce formal behavioral controls, it is problematic because corporations do not have total control of which employees stay and which seek new positions elsewhere. Therefore, a firm may lose many high-performing employees.

- Another approach to restructuring is downscoping. The goal of downscoping is to reduce the level of a firm's diversification. This form of restructuring is often accomplished by divesting unrelated businesses, whereby the firm's top executives can strategically refocus on the firm's core business. It is often accompanied by downsizing as well. This approach has been more successful than downsizing alone.

- Another popular form of restructuring is known as the leveraged buyout (LBO). In a leveraged buyout, the management or an external party buys 100 percent of the firm's stock, largely financed with debt, and takes the firm private. This form of restructuring has met with mixed success. Oftentimes the intent is to improve the firm's efficiency and performance and to sell the firm (or take it public) within five to eight years after the leveraged buyout. Some LBO firms have been successful, but in recent years many have experienced performance problems, primarily because of the high debt and debt costs.

- The primary goal of corporate restructuring, in most cases, is to gain or regain strategic control of the firm. Downscoping and strategic refocusing on core businesses reduce the pressure for processing information to manage a wider diversity of businesses and allow the top executives to control the businesses by evaluating strategic actions, as opposed to an emphasis on financial outcomes. This generally produces higher performance and achieve strategic competitiveness over the long term.

- While most restructuring is designed to reduce the level of diversification, some firms may restructure and remain unrelated diversified. A few of these firms are able to do so and perform quite well. Generally they can do so if they focus on mature and low-technology industries, which they can manage using financial controls, as opposed to strategic controls. In addition, if they can acquire under-performing businesses and turn around their performance, they may be able to enhance the value of those firms and either maintain or resell them at a profit.

## Review Questions

1. Why were acquisitions so popular in the 1980s?
2. What are the reasons that firms might follow an acquisition strategy?
3. What problems might be encountered by firms following an acquisition strategy?
4. Why might firms following an acquisition strategy eventually begin performing poorly?

5. What are some of the attributes of firms that employ an acquisition strategy successfully?
6. Why did restructuring become popular in the late 1980s and early 1990s? What are some of the popular forms of restructuring and their goals?
7. How can some firms achieve success with an unrelated diversification strategy?

## Application Discussion Questions

1. Given the evidence that the shareholders of many acquiring firms gain little or nothing in value from acquisitions, why do so many firms follow such a strategy?
2. Of the reasons for following an acquisition strategy described in the chapter, which are positive, and which are more negative and likely to create performance problems over the long term?
3. After reading popular press accounts of large acquisitions, choose a recent one and detail the important characteristics of the acquiring and the acquired firms. Based on these characteristics and other information, do you think this acquisition will succeed in achieving high performance? Explain why or why not.
4. Search popular press accounts to find an acquisition that has the attributes necessary for success. Why do you feel

this acquisition has a high probability of success over the long term?
5. What is meant by the term *synergy*? Explain how the merger of two separate businesses can create synergy. How can firms create private synergy that cannot be easily imitated by other companies?
6. How can top executives in a firm know the most appropriate level of diversification and thereby avoid becoming overdiversified? How can they know the appropriate level of debt/leverage to utilize?
7. Why have LBOs not become the organization of the future, as proposed by a prominent finance scholar?
8. In comparing acquiring a business with developing a new product/business internally, what are the risks and the advantages and disadvantages of each?

## Ethics Questions

1. If there is a relationship between the size of the firm and a top executive's compensation, is there an inducement for top executives to engage in mergers and acquisitions in order to increase their compensation? What is the board of directors' role in maintaining the integrity of the compensation system?
2. When a manager seeks to restructure (acquire or divest firm assets), are there incentives to do it in a way that builds the manager's power relative to shareholders or other stakeholders such as employees, rather than the firm's power relative to the market in order to achieve strategic competitiveness? Could this motive be related to the lack of success among acquiring firms?
3. If shareholders increase their wealth through a downsizing, does this come at the expense of employees who have invested a considerable portion of their life in the firm or at the expense of whole communities dependent on employment from the downsizing firm?

4. Do "corporate raiders" always target firms that are performing poorly and thus have a rational reason for pursuing the restructuring due to mismanagement, or is there also an incentive to pursue firms that have resources to "buy off" hostile suitors ("green mail")?
5. When a leveraged buyout is attempted, shareholders often increase their wealth (e.g., stock price increases), but debtholders may find their investment at risk because bond ratings are often downgraded. Are there any ethical issues associated with the transfer of wealth from debtholders to shareholders?
6. Should a manager reveal information about planned new products before the LBO that might bring personal gain (e.g. the manager becomes an owner through the LBO) once the firm is private, rather than gain to public shareholders?

## Notes

1. M. A. Hitt, R. E. Hoskisson, R. D. Ireland, and J. S. Harrison, 1991, Effects of acquisitions on R&D inputs and outputs, *Academy of Management Journal* 34: 693–706; J. F. Weston and K. S. Chung, 1990, Takeovers and corporate restructuring: An overview, *Business Economics* 25 (no. 2): 6–11; M. Sikora, 1990, The M&A bonanza of the '80s and its legacy, *Mergers and Acquisitions* (March/April): 90–95.

2. L. Weiner, 1989, No slowdown in mergers foreseen, *American Banker* 154 (no.222): 8.

3. M. C. Jensen, 1988, Takeovers: Their causes and consequences, *Journal of Economic Perspectives* 2: 21–48.

4. M. E. Porter, 1987, From competitive advantage to corporate strategy, *Harvard Business Review* 65, no. 3: 43–59.

5. R. W. Reagan, 1990, *An American Life* (New York: Simon and Schuster).

6. G. P. Zachary, 1993, Borland defies expectations and posts a healthy profit, *Wall Street Journal,* April 28, B4.

7. G. P. Zachary, 1994, Novell to buy WordPerfect, Lines of Borland, *Wall Street Journal,* March 22, A3, A6.

8. R. L. Rose, 1994, Whirlpool is expanding in Europe despite the slump, *Wall Street Journal,* January 27, B4.

9. D. Anderson, N. De Sanctis, B. Finzi, and J. Franzan, 1992, Electrolux: The acquisition and integration of Zanussi, in C. A. Barlett and S. Ghoshal (eds.), *Transnational Management: Text, Cases, and Readings in Cross-Border Management* (Homewood, Ill.: Irwin), 462–482.

10. R. Biggadike, 1979, The risky business of diversification, *Harvard Business Review* 57(3): 103–111.

11. E. Mansfield, 1969, *Industrial Research and Technological Innovation* (New York: Norton).

12. E. Mansfield, M. Schwartz, and S. Wagner, 1981, Imitation costs and patents: An empirical study, *Economic Journal* 91: 907–918; L. H. Clark, Jr., and A. L. Malabre, Jr., 1988, Slow rise in outlays for research imperils U.S. competitive edge, *Wall Street Journal,* November 16, A1, A5.

13. M. A. Hitt, R. E. Hoskisson, and R. D. Ireland, 1990, Mergers and acquisitions and managerial commitment to innovation in M-form firms, *Strategic Management Journal* 11 (Special Issue): 29–47.

14. J. Constable, 1986, Diversification as a factor in U.K. industrial strategy, *Long Range Planning* 19: 52–60; R. Burgelman, 1986, Managing corporate entrepreneurship: New structures for implementing technological innovation, in M. Horwitch (ed.), *Technology in the Modern Corporation* New York:

Pergamon Press; Hitt, Hoskisson, and Ireland, 1990, Mergers and acquisitions.

15. Hitt et al., 1991, Effects of acquisitions; Hitt, Hoskisson, and Ireland, 1990, Mergers and acquisitions.

16. W. C. Kester, 1991, *Japanese Takeovers: The Global Contest for Corporate Control* (Boston: Harvard Business School Press), 94–95.

17. D. K. Datta, 1991, Organizational fit and acquisition performance: Effects of post-acquisition integration, *Strategic Management Journal* 12: 281–297; J. Kitching, 1967, Why do mergers miscarry? *Harvard Business Review* 45, no. 6: 84–101.

18. A. F. Buono, J. L. Bowditch, and J. W. Lewis, 1985, When cultures collide: The anatomy of a merger, *Human Relations* 38, no. 5: 477–500.

19. A. F. Buono and J. L. Bowditch, 1989, *The Human Side of Mergers and Acquisitions* (San Francisco: Jossey-Bass).

20. D. B. Jemison and S. B. Sitkin, 1986, Corporate acquisitions: A process perspective, *Academy of Management Review* 11: 145–163.

21. J. B. Barney, 1988, Returns to bidding firms in mergers and acquisitions: Reconsidering the relatedness hypothesis, *Strategic Management Journal* 9 (Special Issue): 71–78.

22. G. Yago, 1991, *Junk Bonds: How High Yield Securities Restructured Corporate America* (New York: Oxford University Press), 146–148.

23. M. C. Jensen, 1986, Agency costs of free cash flow, corporate finance, and takeovers, *American Economic Review* 76: 323–329; M. C. Jensen, 1987, A helping hand for entrenched managers, *Wall Street Journal,* November 4, A6.

24. M. Sikora, 1990, Deals and misdeals: Mergers and acquisitions as agents of great change, *Mergers and Acquisitions,* (March/April): 104–119.

25. Barney, 1988, Returns to bidding firms; Hitt et al., 1991, Effects of acquisitions.

26. R. Smith and E. Shapiro, 1993, KKR's luster dims as fall in RJR stock hurts investors' take, *Wall Street Journal,* April 26, A1, A6.

27. Porter, 1988, From competitive advantage; D. J. Ravenscraft and R. M. Scherer, 1987, *Mergers, Sell Offs and Economic Efficiency* (Washington, D.C.: Brookings Institution).

28. C. W. L. Hill and R. E. Hoskisson, 1987, Strategy and structure in the multiproduct firm, *Academy of Management Review* 12: 331–341.

29. C. C. Markides, 1992, Consequences of corporate refocusing: Ex ante evidence, *Academy of Management*

*Journal* 35: 398–412; R. A. Johnson, R. E. Hoskisson, and M. A. Hitt, 1993, Board of director involvement in restructuring: The effects of board versus managerial controls and characteristics, *Strategic Management Journal* 14 (Special Issue): 33–50.

30. Hill and Hoskisson, 1987, Strategy and structure.
31. Hitt, Hoskisson, and Ireland, 1990, Mergers and acquisitions.
32. Ibid.
33. Jemison and Sitkin, 1986, Corporate acquisitions.
34. Hitt et al., 1990, Effects of acquisitions.
35. R. E. Hoskisson, M. A. Hitt, and R. D. Ireland, 1994, The effects of acquisitions and restructuring (strategic refocusing) strategies on innovation, in G. von Krogh, A. Sinatra, and H. Singh (eds.), *Managing Corporate Acquisitions* (London: Macmillan Press), 144–169.
36. C. Solomon, 1989, Takeover raids leave Phillips employees fearing new assaults, *Wall Street Journal,* January 1: A1; J. Helyar, 1988, RJR employees fight distraction amid buyout talks, *Wall Street Journal,* November 1, A8.
37. J. P. Walsh, 1988, Top management team turnover following mergers and acquisitions, *Strategic Management Journal* 9: 173–183.
38. M. A. Hitt and D. L. Smart, 1994, Debt: A disciplining force for managers or a debilitating force for organizations? *Journal of Management Inquiry.* 3:144–152.
39. D. A. Depke, 1992, Macys: Blame Harvard Business School, *Business Week,* February 10: 34; G. Hassell, 1991, Zales to shut 400 jewelry stores: Debt-plagued company also stops payments, *Houston Chronicle,* December 31, C-1.
40. Jensen, 1987, A helping hand; M. C. Jensen, 1989, Is leverage an invitation to bankruptcy? On the contrary—it keeps shaky firms out of court, *Wall Street Journal,* February 1, A14.
41. B. Baysinger and R. E. Hoskisson 1989, Diversification strategy and R&D intensity in multi-product firms, *Academy of Management Journal* 32: 310–332; B. H. Hall, 1990, The impact of corporate restructuring on industrial research and development, in M.N. Baily and C. Winston (eds.), *Brookings Papers on Economic Activity* 3: 85–135.
42. C. Duff, 1992, Costly recapitalization drives USG to the wall, *Wall Street Journal,* June 3, B4.
43. Hitt, Hoskisson, and Ireland, 1990, Mergers and acquisitions.
44. Hitt et al., 1991, Effects of acquisitions.
45. Hoskisson, Hitt, and Ireland, 1993, The effects of acquisitions.
46. M. A. Hitt, J. S. Harrison, R. D. Ireland, and A. Best,

1993, Lifting the veil of success in mergers and acquisitions. (Paper presented at the Strategic Management Society Conference, Chicago).
47. Barney, 1988, Returns to bidding firms; J. S. Harrison, M. A. Hitt, R. E. Hoskisson, and R. D. Ireland, 1991, Synergies and post acquisition performance: Differences versus similarities in resource allocations, *Journal of Management* 17: 173–190.
48. J. P. Walsh, 1989, Doing a deal: Merger and acquisition negotiations and their impact upon target company top management turnover, *Strategic Management Journal* 10: 307–322.
49. Hitt, et al., 1993, Lifting the veil.
50. J. E. Bethel and J. Liebeskind 1993, The effects of ownership structure on corporate restructuring, *Strategic Management Journal* 14 (Special Issue): 15–31.
51. E. Bowman and H. Singh, 1990, Overview of corporate restructuring: Trends and consequences, in L. Rock and R. H. Rock (eds.), *Corporate Restructuring* (New York: McGraw-Hill).
52. R. E. Hoskisson, R. A. Johnson, and D. D. Moesel, 1994, Divestment intensity of restructuring firms: Effects of governance, strategy and performance, *Academy of Management Journal,* forthcoming.
53. J. Valente and C. Duff, 1993, Trickle down pain: Demise of the catalog hurts small businesses that counted on Sears, *Wall Street Journal,* March 2, A1, A6.
54. R. E. Hoskisson and M. A. Hitt, 1994, *Downscoping: How to Tame the Diversified Firm* (New York: Oxford University Press).
55. A. Bennet, 1991, Downsizing doesn't necessarily bring an upswing in corporate profitability, *Wall Street Journal,* June 4, B1, B4.
56. Hoskisson and Hitt, 1994, Downscoping.
57. R. E. Hoskisson and M. A. Hitt, 1990, Antecedents and performance outcomes of diversification: A review and critique of theoretical perspectives, *Journal of Management* 16: 461–509; Johnson, Hoskisson, and Hitt, 1993, Board of directors involvement.
58. J. P. Miller, 1993, Ball is preparing to clean out its corporate cupboard, *Wall Street Journal,* February 24, B3.
59. M. C. Jensen, 1989, Eclipse of the public corporation, *Harvard Business Review* 67, no. 5: 61–74.
60. W. F. Long and D. J. Ravenscraft, 1993, LBOs, debt, and R&D intensity, *Strategic Management Journal* 14 (Special Issue): 119–135.
61. Ibid.
62. R. E. Hoskisson and R. A. Johnson, 1992, Corporate restructuring and strategic change: The effect on diversification strategy and R&D intensity, *Strategic Management Journal* 13: 625–634.

63. W. B. Lee and E. S. Cooperman, 1989, Conglomerates in the 1980s: A performance appraisal, *Financial Management* 18, no. 2: 45–54; J. R. Williams, B. L. Paez, and L. Sanders, 1988, Conglomerates revisited, *Strategic Management Journal* 9: 403–414.

64. K. N. M. Dundas and P. R. Richardson, 1982, Implementing the unrelated product strategy, *Strategic Management Journal* 3: 287–301.

65. Hoskisson and Hitt, 1994, Downscoping.

66. Dundas and Richardson, 1982, Implementing the unrelated product strategy.

# CHAPTER 8
# International Strategy
▼

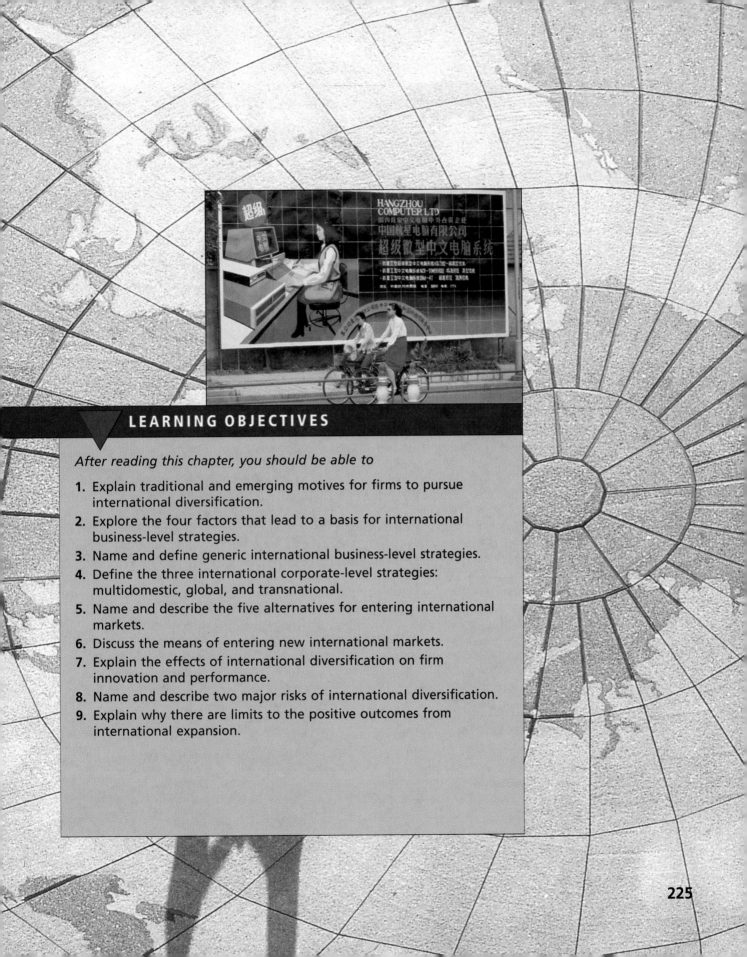

*After reading this chapter, you should be able to*

1. Explain traditional and emerging motives for firms to pursue international diversification.

2. Explore the four factors that lead to a basis for international business-level strategies.

3. Name and define generic international business-level strategies.

4. Define the three international corporate-level strategies: multidomestic, global, and transnational.

5. Name and describe the five alternatives for entering international markets.

6. Discuss the means of entering new international markets.

7. Explain the effects of international diversification on firm innovation and performance.

8. Name and describe two major risks of international diversification.

9. Explain why there are limits to the positive outcomes from international expansion.

## China: The Next Global Frontier

China is experiencing an economic boom. For example, in Changan, a city with a population of 30,000 people, approximately an hour north of the Hong Kong border, there are almost 700 factories, employing approximately 100,000 employees from other parts of China. The city of Changan earned approximately $40 million in 1993 by renting the plants to foreign joint ventures. The city has four-lane expressways, office towers, a new cultural center, public recreation facilities (golf course, Olympic-size swimming pool), and multiple modern townhouses. One city official predicted that by the year 2010, Changan would have a population of over 1 million. This is only one example of many within China. Currently, the economy is growing at an annual rate of 12 percent, despite its many problems. In 1993, it exported approximately $100 billion dollars worth of finished goods and components, up from approximately $50 billion in 1989. Furthermore, foreign investment reached approximately $60 billion in 1993, up from slightly over $5 billion in 1989.

China is being transformed into a more capitalistic marketplace through decentralization. Some of the less strategic government ministries are being given free rein to develop their products. For instance, the textile monopoly has been divided into separate units. The central government headquarters no longer has control of the local manufacturing facilities. Government officials have to use their expertise and national and international connections in the market to provide distribution for local manufacturing. In effect, they are becoming trading companies. The local manufacturing plants controlled by cities are now free to sell their products to whom they will, but they lack marketing experience. As such, they can use the headquarters trading experience, but they are not constrained to do so. Thus, both entities are forced into a market situation where they have to prove their worth by enticing manufacturers to work with them (headquarters) and finding sources of distribution (local manufacturing).

However, managers at this point may have extraordinary freedom. For instance, Shougang Corp., a Beijing-based steel maker, does not have to justify its strategy to the stock market. On the other hand, like a state-owned steel maker in Europe, it is not being questioned by politicians. Its managers report directly to the country's powerful State Council, rather than to bureaucrats at the Ministry of Metallurgical Industry, as other Chinese steel makers do. Therefore, Shougang can count on government support in a crisis.

Also, some of the local operators are selling factories to foreign companies. Many international investors—for example, U.S. multinational firms—are beginning to invest heavily in China. In fact, China is expected to become one of the world's top five economic powers; the world's largest manufacturing region; the largest market for critical industries, such as telecommunications and aerospace; and one of the largest users of capital. However, the investment climate for foreign firms could change quickly. Often U.S. businesses are caught in the middle as the U.S. government pushes for more human rights and a more open political climate. This is usually done by threatening not to approve most favored nation status, which would mean higher tariffs for Chinese products. As one U.S. businessman put it, "It just grows the business of our competition."

China's strengths, at first, will not be in technology-based industries, but rather in light manufacturing and low-technology industries. Unlike Japanese firms, Chinese corporations will probably be more open to foreign participation. Furthermore, some Chinese corporations are growing dramatically, partly through acquisitions of national and international competitors. For example, Shougang Corp. intends to double its steel-manufacturing capacity to 10 million tons by 1995. It is doing so partly by acquisitions, such as the $120 million iron mine in Peru and a Fontana, California, steel plant that it plans to dismantle and ship home to China. Thus, China represents a new global market for international firms, as well as potential competitors in certain manufacturing and low-technology industries. Its huge market is enticing to many international firms. ▲

The dramatic success of Japanese firms and products in the United States and other international markets provided a powerful jolt to U.S. managers and awakened them to the importance of international competition and global markets. China represents a potential major international market opportunity for firms from many countries, including the United States, Japan, Korea, and Europe. It also represents a potential formidable competitor, particularly in manufacturing and low-technology industries. Therefore, the international arena affords many potential opportunities, but also a number of potential threats. Given the success of the Japanese and other international firms in domestic U.S. markets, U.S. firms are now well aware of those threats. However, U.S. firms are also awakening to the major opportunities provided by international markets. These opportunities are exemplified in the opening of China's huge market (1.2 billion people). This chapter focuses not only on the opportunities to develop capabilities and core competence through diversifying into international markets, but also on the problems and complexities of managing such operations.[1]

In this chapter, we discuss the importance of international strategy based on the incentives and opportunities to internationalize. Once a firm decides to internationalize, it must select its strategy. Furthermore, it must choose a mode of entry. For instance, it may enter international markets by exporting from domestic-based operations, licensing, forming joint ventures with international partners, acquiring a foreign-based firm, or establishing a new subsidiary. Such international diversification can produce higher performance and more innovation. However, this is tempered by political and economic risks and the problems of managing a complex international firm with operations in multiple countries. Figure 8–1 provides an overview of these choices and outcomes. The relationships among international opportunities, exploration of resources and capabilities that result in strategies, and ultimate modes of entry based on core competence and strategic competitiveness outcomes are explored in this chapter.

**FIGURE 8–1** Opportunities and Outcomes of International Strategy

| Identify international opportunities | Explore resources and capabilities | Use core competence | | Achieve strategic competitiveness |
|---|---|---|---|---|
| | International strategies | Modes of entry | | |
| Increase market size | International business-level strategy | Exporting | Management problems and risk | Higher performance |
| Return on investment | Multidomestic strategy | Licensing | | |
| Economies of scale and learning | Global strategy | Strategic alliances | | Innovation |
| Location advantage | Transnational strategy | Acquisitions | Management problems and risk | |
| | | Establishment of new subsidiary | | |

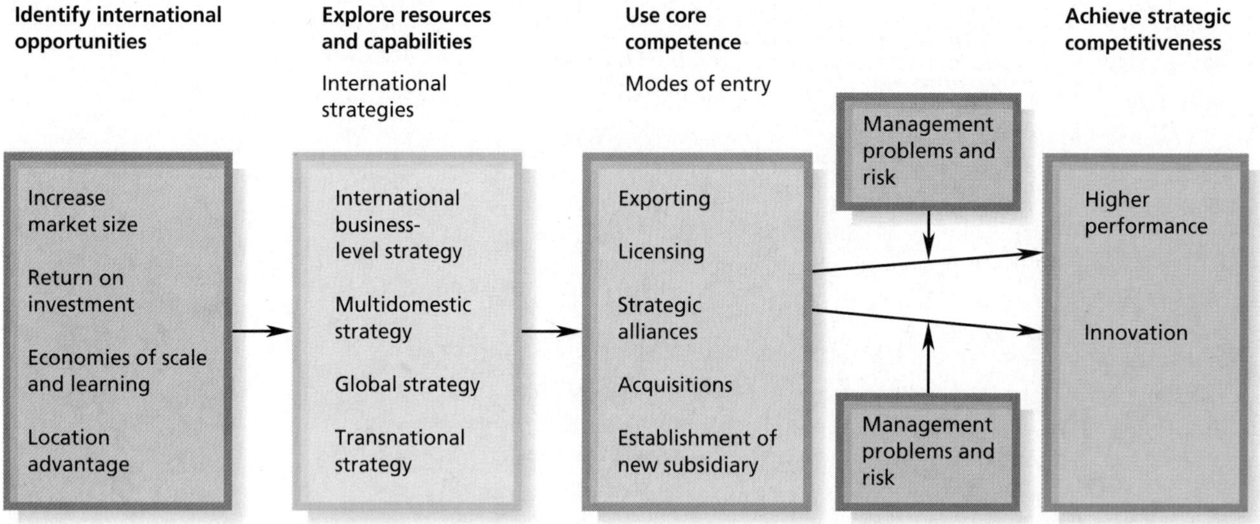

## Identifying International Opportunities: The Incentive to Pursue International Strategy

▲ An **international strategy** refers to selling products in markets outside the firm's domestic market.

An **international strategy** refers to selling products in markets outside the firm's domestic market. One of the primary reasons for implementing an international strategy (as opposed to a strategy focused on the domestic market) is that international markets yield potential new opportunities to expand the market. Raymond Vernon captured the classic rationale for international diversification.[2] He suggested that typically a firm discovers an innovation in its home country market, especially in advanced economies such as that found in the United States. However, some demand for the product may develop in other countries, and, thus, exports are provided by domestic operations. Increased demand in foreign countries justifies foreign direct investment in production capacity abroad, especially as foreign competitors also organize to meet increasing demand. As the product becomes standardized, the firm may rationalize its operations by moving production to a region where production costs are low. Vernon therefore suggested that firms pursue international diversification according to the product life cycle introduced in Chapter 5.

Another traditional motive for firms to become multinational is to secure key resources. Key supplies of raw material, especially minerals and energy, are important in some industries. For instance, aluminum producers need a supply of bauxite, tire firms need rubber, and oil companies scour the world to find new petroleum reserves. Others seek to secure access to low-cost factors of production. Clothing, electronics, watchmaking, and many other industries have moved portions of their operations to foreign locations in pursuit of lower-cost labor or capital (possibly government subsidized). Many international firms such as Daimler Benz have moved into the United States because of local government subsidies and incentives.[3] For example, Alabama outbid North and South Carolina for the first U.S. Mercedes Benz car plant. The state provided land and training wages for new workers and made commitments that government and utilities would buy large quantities of the four-wheel-drive recreational vehicles the plant will produce.

Although these traditional motives continue to operate, as the Mercedes example illustrates, there are emerging motivations that have been driving international expansion (see Chapter 1). For instance, there has been increased pressure for global integration of operations, mostly driven by more universal product demand. As nations industrialize, demand for commodity products appears to become more similar.[4] This nationless or borderless demand for products may be due to life-style similarities in developed nations. Also, increases in global communication (especially television) facilitate the ability of people in different countries to visualize and model life styles in disparate cultures.[5] In some industries, technology is driving globalization because economies of scale necessary to reduce costs to the lowest level often require efficient scale investment greater than the size of domestic market demand. There is also pressure for cost reduction in purchasing from the lowest-cost global supplier. For instance, R&D expertise for the next product extension may not be found in the domestic market. Furthermore, the emergence of large-scale markets, such as Russia, China, and India, provide a strong incentive because of potential demand. And, because of currency fluctuations, firms may want to have their operations distributed in many countries to reduce the risk of currency devaluation in one country.

On the other hand, there has been increased pressure for local country or regional responsiveness, especially where products require customization because of cultural differences. Most products require local repair and service. For large products, such as heavy earthmoving equipment, transportation costs become significant. Employee contracts and labor forces differ significantly. It is much harder to negotiate employee layoffs in Europe than in the United States because of employment contract differences. Often host governments demand joint ownership in order to avoid tariffs. Also, host governments often require a high percentage of local procurement, manufacturing, and research and development. These issues increase the need for local investment and responsiveness.

Given the traditional and emerging motivations for expanding into international markets, there are four basic opportunities that firms may achieve through international diversification: to increase the size of their potential markets; to enjoy greater returns on major capital investments and/or investments in new product and process developments; to gain economies of scale, scope, and/or experience; and/or to gain a competitive advantage through location (e.g., access to low-cost labor, critical resources, or customers).

## Increased Market Size

Firms can expand the size of their potential market, sometimes dramatically, by moving into international markets. Moving into international markets is a particularly attractive strategy to firms with domestic markets that are limited in growth opportunities. For example, the soft drink industry in the United States is saturated. Most changes in market share for any single firm must come at the expense of competitors' market share. As a result, there is fierce competition to maintain, as well as to increase, market share. The two major soft drink manufacturers, Coca-Cola and PepsiCo, moved into international markets several years ago

*Shown in this photo are cans of Pepsi that are sold in different countries. By offering its products in multiple nations, PepsiCo hopes to increase the size of its total market. Expanding market share by entering other international markets is especially attractive to firms, such as PepsiCo, who are facing saturated domestic markets.*

because of the limited growth opportunities in the U.S. market. Pepsi Cola moved into the Soviet Union many years ago, and later Coca-Cola moved into China. Originally each obtained an exclusive franchise in those countries. However, recently these two potentially huge markets are beginning to open to other competitors. Coca-Cola is currently planning to build plants in Moscow and St. Petersburg in an aggressive attempt to expand sales in Russia and other parts of the former Soviet Union. Interestingly, while PepsiCo controls approximately twice as much of the soft drink market in Russia as does Coca-Cola, the numbers are small. PepsiCo has a 4 percent market share, whereas Coca-Cola has only 2 percent. As a result, the potential market for the two firms is substantial. There are many other firms attempting to exploit the emerging Russian market, including McDonald's, Microsoft, Sun Microsystems, Philip Morris, Upjohn Company, Lockheed Corporation, and United Technology Corporation's Otis Elevator Division.[6]

## Return on Investment

Large markets may be crucial for earning a return on large investments, such as plant and capital equipment and/or research and development. Therefore, most R&D-intensive industries (those requiring heavy investment in R&D) are international. For example, the aerospace industry requires heavy investments in order to develop new aircraft. To recoup this investment may require selling the new aircraft in both the domestic market (e.g., United States for Boeing and McDonnell Douglas) and international markets. The Chinese market for aircraft is experiencing significant growth. Passenger traffic is growing by approximately 25 percent per year, and, therefore, China needs increased airline capacity. As a result, China Southern Airlines recently ordered six Boeing 777s, in addition to fourteen 737s and four 757s. Boeing also expects other large orders. In fact, China is expected to purchase $40 billion worth of commercial jets from U.S. and Western European firms over the next 20 years. China will rank second to Japan as the largest export market for Boeing, Airbus, and McDonnell Douglas.[7]

In addition to the need for a large market to recoup heavy investment in research and development, the pace of new technology development is increasing. As a result, new product obsolescence occurs more rapidly. Therefore, there is a need to recoup the investment more quickly before a product is made obsolete by another new product brought into the market. Once the existing product is obsolete, its sales will decrease rapidly. In addition to rapid obsolescence, abilities to develop new technologies are expanding, and because of different patent laws across country borders, competitor imitation is more likely. In fact, through reverse engineering, competitors are able to take apart a competitive product, learn the new technology, and develop a similar product that imitates the new technology (see Chapter 12). Because of competitors' abilities to do this relatively quickly, the need to recoup new product development costs rapidly is increasing. Therefore, the larger markets provided by international expansion are particularly attractive in many industries (e.g., computer hardware) because they expand the opportunity to recoup large capital investment and large-scale R&D expenditures.[8]

## Economies of Scale and Learning

When firms expand their markets, they may be able to enjoy economies of scale, particularly in their manufacturing operations. In other words, they are able to spread their fixed costs over a larger sales base and therefore enjoy a higher profit margin on each product sold. Thus, to the extent that firms are able to standardize products across country borders and use the same or similar production facilities, coordinating critical resource functions, they are likely to achieve optimal economic scale.[9] This is the goal of many firms in Europe as the common market continues to evolve.

Firms may also be able to exploit core competencies or distinctive firm capabilities. Firms with strong core competencies, which are often product or industry specific, can apply them across international markets. This allows resource sharing between units across country borders. It produces synergy and helps the firm produce higher-quality goods or services at lower cost.

## Location Advantages

Firms may locate facilities in other countries in order to lower the basic costs of the goods and/or services provided. For example, they may have easier access to lower-cost labor, energy, and other natural resources. Other location advantages include access to critical supplies/resources and to customers. In both cases, certain resources and/or customers may not be accessible without operations in particular countries where they exist. For example, U.S. retailers are finding that Mexican markets provide a boon to their retail sales. As shown in the next Strategic Focus, some U.S. firms have larger sales per outlet in Mexico than in any other location. As a result, firms such as Dillard's Department Stores and JCPenney must locate operations in Mexico to have access to Mexican customers.

Motorola is another firm that has entered the Chinese market. In 1992, Motorola built a makeshift plant in the northern port city of Tianjin to manufacture paging devices for Chinese and export markets. In 1993, Motorola sold 10,000 units in China. Demand for pagers in China has increased dramatically from 1 million in 1991 to 4 million in 1993. As a result, Motorola is now planning the largest manufacturing venture in China by any U.S. firm. In 1993, it completed a $120 million first-phase plan to make pagers, simple integrated circuits, and cellular phones. Currently it plans to build a second plant to manufacture automotive electronics, advanced microprocessors, and walkie-talkie systems within three more years. Finally, Motorola is considering building a plant to fabricate silicon wafers. In all, Motorola's total investment in the three plants would be more than $400 million. Motorola's commitment is indicative of the potential significance of the Chinese market.[10]

We have explored why international strategies may be important and some of their advantages. Next we describe the types and content of international strategy that might be utilized.

## International Strategy

An international strategy may be one of two basic types, business or corporate level. At the business level, firms follow generic strategy types: low cost, differentiation, focused low-cost, focused differentiation, or integrated low cost/differentiation. At the corporate level, firms follow three types: multidomestic, global, or transnational (a combination of multidomestic and global).

### U.S. Retailers Find Gold Mine in Mexico

Mall developer Mel Simon, who created Minneapolis's huge Mall of America, is about to undertake the development of multiple malls in Mexico City. He plans to develop three million-square-foot shopping centers, each anchored by U.S. retailers Dillard's Department Stores and JCPenney. Access to the Mexican market is particularly important for U.S. retailers because of the stagnating sales in the United States. In contrast, Mexico's retail sales have been growing at twice the rate of its economy. Expectations are that the Mexican market will increase even more rapidly with the finalization of the North American Free Trade Agreement.

The prospects for such growth have attracted major retailers such as Kmart, Domino's Pizza, and Wal-Mart and others such as Arby's. In one section of Mexico City, a Sam's Club store (part of Wal-Mart Stores' joint venture with Mexican retailer Cyfra SA) has achieved higher sales per square foot than any other Sam's outlet in the world. In addition, an Arby's restaurant outlet has achieved $2 million a year in sales and is the leader in that chain.

The potential is great, exemplified by the fact that the population of Sao Paulo, Brazil, is only 20 percent of that of Mexico City, but it has 12,000 pizza restaurants, while Mexico City has only a few hundred. Fifty percent of Mexico's population is under the age of 20. While the per capita income is relatively low, the richest 10 to 15 percent of Mexicans are wealthier than most Americans. Therefore, the opportunities for U.S. retailers in the Mexican markets are significant.

## Business-Level International Strategy

Each business must develop a competitive strategy focused on its own domestic market. We discussed business-level generic strategies in Chapter 4 and competitive dynamics in Chapter 5. However, there are some unique features to international business-level strategies. In pursuing an international business-level strategy, the home country of operation is often the most important source of competitive advantage. The resources and capabilities established in the home country often allow the firm to pursue the strategy beyond the national boundary. Michael Porter developed a model that describes the factors contributing to the advantage of firms in a dominant global industry and associated with a specific country or regional environment.[11] His model is illustrated in Figure 8–2.

The first dimension in the model, termed **factors of production,** refers to the inputs necessary to compete in any industry, such as labor, land, natural resources, capital, and infrastructure (such as highway, postal, and communication systems). Of course, there are basic (e.g., natural and labor resources) and advanced (e.g., digital communication systems and highly educated work forces) factors. There are also generalized (highway systems, supply of debt capital) and specialized factors (skilled personnel in a specific industry, such as a port specialized in handling bulk chemicals). If a country has both advanced and specialized production factors, it is likely that this will serve an industry well in spawning strong competitors at the business level. Ironically, countries often develop advanced and specialized factor capabilities because they lack critical basic resources. Some Asian

▲ **Factors of production** refer to the inputs necessary to compete in any industry, such as labor, land, natural resources, capital, and infrastructure (such as highway, postal, and communication systems).

**FIGURE 8–2**  **Determinants of National Advantage**

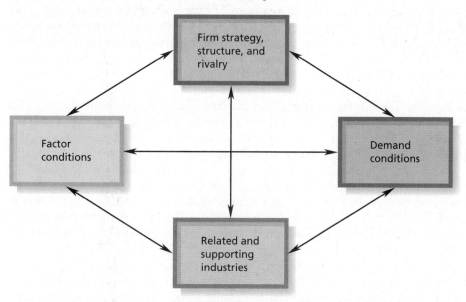

*SOURCE: Adapted and reprinted with the permission of The Free Press, an imprint of Simon & Schuster from* THE COMPETITIVE ADVANTAGE OF NATIONS *by Michael E. Porter, p. 72. Copyright © 1990 by Michael E. Porter.*

countries, such as Korea, lack abundant natural resources, but the strong work ethic and abundant numbers of engineers as well as the system of large firms have created an expertise in manufacturing. Germany developed a strong chemical industry, partially because Hoechst and BASF spent years developing a synthetic indigo dye to reduce their dependence on imports. This was not the case in Britain because large supplies of natural indigo were available in the colonies.[12]

The second dimension, *demand conditions,* is characterized by the nature and size of the buyers' needs in the home market for the industry's goods or services. The sheer size of a sales segment could produce the demand necessary to create scale-efficient facilities. This efficiency could also lead to domination of the industry in other countries. However, specialized demand may also create opportunities beyond national boundaries. For example, Swiss firms have long led the world in tunneling equipment, because of the need to tunnel through mountains for rail and highway passage. Japanese firms have created a niche market for compact, quiet air conditioner units. Small, but quiet units are required because homes are often small and packed tightly together. Under these conditions, large, noisy units would be unacceptable.[13]

*Related and supporting industries* are the third dimension in the model. Italy has become the leader in the shoe industry because of related and supporting industries. The leather supplies necessary to build shoes are furnished by a well-established industry in leather processing. Also, many people travel to Italy to purchase leather goods from fine shops. Thus, there is support in distribution. In addition, supporting industries in leather-working machinery and design services contribute to the success of the shoe industry. In fact, the design services industry supports many related industries, such as ski boots, fashion apparel, and furniture. In Japan, cameras and copiers have been related industries. In Denmark, the dairy products industry is related to an industry focused on food enzymes.

*Firm strategy, structure, and rivalry,* the final country dimension, also foster the growth of certain industries. The pattern of firm strategy, structure, and rivalry among firms varies greatly from nation to nation. Earlier much attention was placed on examining U.S. enterprise managers; more recently the Japanese have been scrutinized and emulated. In Germany, because of the excellent technical training system, there is strong inclination toward methodological product and process improvement. In Japan, unusual cooperative and competitive systems have facilitated cross-function management of complex assembly operations. In Italy, the national pride of its designers has spawned strong industries in sports cars, fashion apparel, and furniture. In the United States, competition among computer manufacturers and software producers has favored the development of these industries.

The four basic dimensions of the "diamond" model (see Figure 8–2) emphasize the environmental or structural attributes of a national economy that may contribute to national advantage. One could therefore conclude that chance or luck has led to the competitive advantage of individual firms in these industries. To a degree this is true. Also, government policy has contributed to the success and failure of firms and industries. This is certainly the case in Japan, where the Ministry of International Trade and Investment (MITI) has contributed significantly to the corporate strategies followed. However, each firm must create its own success. Not all firms have survived to become global competitors, given the same country factors that spawned the successful firms. Therefore, the actual strategic choices managers make are likely to be the most compelling reason for success or failure. The factors illustrated in Figure 8–2 therefore are likely to lead to firm competitive advantages only when an appropriate strategy is applied, taking advantage of distinct country factors. We therefore reiterate examples of low-cost, differential, focused low-cost, focused differentiation, and integrated low-cost/differentiation generic strategies discussed in Chapter 4, but also pursued in international markets.

**International Low-Cost Strategy**   The international low-cost strategy is likely to develop in a country with a large demand. Usually the operations of such an industry are centralized in a home country, and obtaining economies of scale is the primary goal. Outsourcing of low value-added operations may take place, but high value-added operations are retained in the home country. As such, products are often exported from the home country.

However, as with any other strategy, there are risks associated with pursuing this one. Often the risks have to do with the underlying factors supporting the strategy. In the late 1970s, Korea was the dominant manufacturer in the sport shoe industry. In the 1980s, the Korean conglomerate HS Corporation had a plant employing 9,000, and Kukje Corporation had the largest shoe factory in the world, with 24 lines and 20,000 employees. In Pusan, the Korean shoe hub, these and other Korean firms manufactured sport shoes for Nike, Reebok, and other well-known brands. In 1990, there were approximately 130,000 shoe workers in 302 factories, but by 1993, there were just over 80,000 workers in 244 factories, most employing less than 100 people. Of course, the large corporations, even the Korean ones, are still in the shoe business. However, they are manufacturing them in China and Indonesia where the wages are $40 versus the current $800 per month in Pusan. The industry has moved from the United States to Taiwan and from Korea to China and Indonesia. However, the Koreans have built a level of expertise and have moved to manufacturing specialty shoes, such as high-technology hiking boots. They also have strong supporting industries, such as petrochemicals (synthetic fabrics) and leather tanneries. However, their strategy must change to differentiation because they can no longer compete on wage differentials with other Asian countries.[14]

**International Differentiation Strategy**   A country with advanced and specialized factor endowments is likely to develop an international differentiation strategy. Germany has a number of world-class chemical firms. The differentiation strategy followed by many of these firms to develop specialized chemicals was possible because of the factor conditions surrounding the development of this industry. The Kaiser Wilhelm (later Max Planck) Institutes and university chemistry programs were superior in research and also produced the best chemistry education in the world. Also, Germany's emphasis on vocational education fostered strong apprenticeship programs for workers. This environment nurtured many strong chemical firms.[15] However, not all German chemical firms have been successful. The most successful have often followed a strategy of international differentiation.

The Japanese capabilities in consumer electronics have led to their advantage in memory chips and integrated circuits, which are the dominant component in this industry. Toshiba is an example of a producer of memory chips that has differentiated its products. However, the United States is the leader in logic chips, which are the main components of computers, telecommunications equipment, and defense electronics. Intel is the world's leading producer of computer logic chips, and its products are differentiated worldwide by the slogan "Intel inside."

**International Focus Strategies**   The ceramic tile industry in Italy contains a number of medium and small fragmented firms that produce approximately 50 percent of the world's tile.[16] These tile firms, clustered in the Sassuolo area of Italy, have formed a number of different focus strategies. Firms such as Marazzi, Iris, Cisa-Cerdisa, and Flor Gres invest heavily in technology to improve product quality and aesthetics as well as to improve productivity. These firms have close relationships with equipment manufacturers. They tend to emphasize the focused low-cost strategy, while maintaining a quality image. Another group, including Piemme and Atlas Concorde, attempts to compete more on image and design. They invest heavily in advertising and showroom expositions. Because they try to appeal to selected customer tastes, they emphasize the focused differentiation strategy. A larger group of smaller firms competes largely on price. They try to rapidly imitate the technology leaders (low cost) and design-sensitive firms (differentiation).

**International Integrated Low-Cost/Differentiation Strategy**   The integrated strategy has become more popular because of flexible manufacturing systems, improved information networks within and across firms, and total quality management systems. Because of the wide diversity of markets and competitors, following an integrated strategy (combined low cost and differentiation) may be the most effective in global markets.[17] Therefore, competing in global markets requires sophisticated and effective management. The Strategic Focus on Komatsu illustrates the pursuit of this strategy. Komatsu was able to gain on a strong competitor, Caterpillar, by pursuing the integrated low-cost/differentiation strategy. Caterpillar had a very strong brand image in world markets, but Komatsu was able

## STRATEGIC FOCUS

### Komatsu's Strategy to Copy and Surpass Caterpillar in the Earthmoving Equipment Industry

In the late 1970s and early 1980s, Caterpillar Tractor Company (Cat) had just over 50 percent of the world's market share in the earthmoving equipment (EME) industry. Komatsu, a Japanese competitor had about 14 percent by the late 1970s. However, by 1984, Cat's share had dropped to 43 percent, while Komatsu's had risen to 25 percent. How had Komatsu been able to gain on the world's leader in EME?

In the 1950s, Komatsu produced products that were half the quality of international standards in terms of durability. In 1963, Japan's Ministry of International Trade and Investment (MITI) opened the EME industry to foreign investment as a quid pro quo opportunity for not opening the auto and electronic industries. MITI did not feel that Japan possessed a long-run competitive advantage in the EME industry. Thus, Cat sought a joint venture with Mitsubishi. However, Komatsu opposed the venture and won a two-year reprieve. Almost immediately Komatsu launched a program to improve its product quality. It entered into costly licensing agreements with International Harvester, Bucyrus-Erie, and Cummins Engine in the United States. Komatsu also initiated one of the first total quality management (TQM) programs, which was an adaptation of the well-known Japanese quality-control circles in manufacturing. They won the highly coveted 1964 Deming Prize for quality control within three years of launching the program. The first phase focused on quality at any price, while the next phase, called Project A, concentrated on cost reduction. Every aspect of Komatsu's business from design to final assembly was subject to scrutiny. As a result, between 1965 and 1970, domestic market share increased from 50 percent to 65 percent, despite the creation of the Mitsubishi-Caterpillar joint venture.

*continued on next page*

to overcome this differentiation advantage by improving its image and reducing its costs. It was initially able to do this because of lower labor costs and steel prices. Furthermore, in the 1970s, the dollar was strong, and this allowed a successful export strategy. Although Komatsu has remained very competitive, it faces critical challenges today due to a resurging Caterpillar and the strong yen.

## International Corporate-Level Strategy

The business-level strategies discussed above depend, to a degree, on the type of international corporate strategy the firm is following. Some corporate strategies give individual country units the authority to develop their own strategies, while other corporate strategies require that country business-level strategies be compromised because of dictates from the home office and that there be coordination across units to accomplish standardization of products and sharing of resources. International corporate-level strategy is distinguished from international business-level strategy by the scope of the operations in both product and geographic diversification. International corporate-level strategy is required when the level of

In 1972, Komatsu launched Project B, which focused on developing overseas markets, primarily through export. In the 1970s, Komatsu aggressively sought emerging markets. It sent company representatives to China, Africa, Australia, Russia, and Latin America and developed these markets through presales service on large projects. It often adapted its products to local conditions, such as the difficulties of mining in Australia. These also tended to be markets where Cat did not have a strong dealer presence. At the same time these markets were emerging, Cat's traditional markets were curtailing growth because major development projects, such as the interstate highway system in the United States, were being completed. However, Komatsu realized that its distribution system (mostly through independent dealers who also sold other brands) could not match that of Cat for service and delivery. Therefore, it sought to make its product more desirable through better product performance and price. One dealer commented, "We tell contractors we can give them 10% more machine for 10% less money." Komatsu also tried to extend its quality commitment to its dealers and suppliers. As a result, in 1981, it won the Japan Quality Prize. Much of Komatsu's success was inspired by the idea of beating Cat some day. In fact, the dominant company slogan was "Maru-C," which roughly translates into "Encircle Caterpillar."

Komatsu's success was also a driving force for change at Caterpillar. Cat had to formulate a strategy that dealt with the declining importance of large machines relative to smaller and more versatile machines. This change also coincided with Komatsu's emergence in the new dominant segment. Cat had to use its strengths in this new segment, where cost/quality criteria were fundamentally different, and at the same time solicit dealers to focus on this new segment. In addition, it had to change its organizational and manufacturing processes. Strategic and organizational changes have been dramatic, especially considering that the firm had to build new capabilities to maintain its strategic competitiveness.

product complexity increases to multiple industries and multiple countries or regions. Corporate strategy is guided by headquarters, rather than by business or country managers (see Chapter 10).

**Multidomestic Strategy**     A **multidomestic strategy** is one where strategic and operating decisions are decentralized to the strategic business unit in each country in order to tailor products to the local market. A multidomestic strategy focuses on competition within each country. It assumes that the markets differ and therefore are segmented by country boundaries. In other words, consumer needs and desires, industry conditions (e.g., number and type of competitors), political and legal structures, and social norms vary by country. Multidomestic strategies allow for the customization of products to meet the specific needs and preferences of local customers. Therefore, they should be able to maximize competitive response to the idiosyncratic requirements of each market. However, multidomestic strategies do not allow for the achievement of economies of scale and thus can be more costly. Firms employing a multidomestic strategy decentralize strategic and operating decisions to the strategic business units operating in each country. As a result,

▲ A **multidomestic strategy** is one where strategic and operating decisions are decentralized to the strategic business unit in each country in order to tailor products to the local market.

each strategic business unit tailors its products or services to the market it serves. The multidomestic strategy has been more prominent among European multinational firms because of the varieties of cultures and markets found in Europe.

**Global Strategy**   Alternatively, a global strategy assumes more standardization of products across country markets. As a result, competitive strategy is centralized and controlled by the home office. The strategic business units operating in each country are assumed to be interdependent, and the home office attempts to achieve integration across these businesses. Therefore, a **global strategy** is one where standardized products are offered across country markets and competitive strategy is dictated by the home office. Thus, a global strategy emphasizes economies of scale and offers greater opportunities to utilize innovations developed at the home office or in one country in other markets. However, a global strategy often lacks responsiveness to local markets and is difficult to manage because of the need to coordinate strategies and operating decisions across country borders. Therefore, achieving efficient operations with a global strategy requires the sharing of resources and an emphasis on coordination and cooperation across country boundaries. This requires more centralization and central headquarters control. The Japanese have often pursued this strategy with success.

▲ A **global strategy** is one where standardized products are offered across country markets and competitive strategy is dictated by the home office.

**Transnational Strategy**   A **transnational strategy** is a corporate strategy that seeks to achieve both global efficiency and local responsiveness. Realizing the diverse goals of the transnational strategy is difficult because one goal requires close global coordination, while the other requires local flexibility. Thus, "flexible coordination" is required to implement the transnational strategy. It requires building a shared vision and individual commitment through an integrated network. In reality, it is difficult to achieve a pure transnational strategy because of the conflicting objectives. If the appropriate structure and culture can be developed, however, they are likely to result in strategic competitiveness because it would be hard for competitors to duplicate them. The three strategies are depicted in Figure 8-3.

▲ A **transnational strategy** is a corporate strategy that seeks to achieve both global efficiency and local responsiveness.

## Environmental Trends

Although the transnational strategy is difficult to achieve, there is an increasing emphasis on the need for global efficiency as more industries begin to experience global competition as well as an increased emphasis on local requirements. For example, even global products often require some customization to meet government regulations within particular countries and/or tailoring to fit customer tastes and preferences. In addition, most multinational firms desire to achieve some coordination and sharing of resources across country markets to hold down costs. Furthermore, some products and industries may be better suited for standardization across country borders than others. As a result, most large multinational firms with multiple diverse products may employ a partial multidomestic strategy with certain product lines and global strategies with others.

These trends are exemplified among international automobile manufacturers. While large U.S. manufacturers General Motors and Ford have followed a multidomestic strategy, many Japanese and European automobile manufacturers have followed a global strategy. For example, General Motors and Ford have large separate and decentralized automobile businesses in Europe and North America.

**FIGURE 8–3** **International Corporate Strategies**

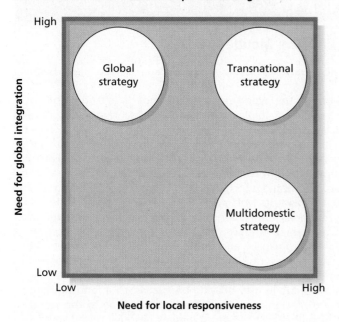

Each of these separate operations had independent design, manufacturing, and marketing functions. Alternatively, the top Japanese and European manufacturers have often developed automobiles in their home markets and sold them, with only minor variations, in markets around the world. While European automobile manufacturers often employ a global strategy, many other European firms use a multidomestic strategy, similar to U.S. firms. However, as explained in the next Strategic Focus, Ford is attempting to break out of the mold with its new world car, the Mondeo.

As noted above, global strategies require integration across units, whereas multidomestic strategies emphasize local responsiveness. Firms must find ways to balance the need for local responsiveness and the need for global integration. Integration allows the achievement of economies and therefore efficiency, but local responsiveness provides the opportunity to more effectively meet consumer needs. Therefore, integration should facilitate competition on costs, and local responsiveness should facilitate competition on differentiation. As noted earlier, however, it is rare to achieve a pure transnational strategy. For example, even Ford's new world car (evidence of a global strategy) is adapted somewhat for the local markets. While the Mondeo will have 75 percent common parts, the U.S. version will be slightly longer and will have more chrome. The interiors of the two automobiles will also differ slightly.

In addition, achieving global integration to produce a world product that is acceptable to consumers in multiple international markets is no easy task. Ford's original plan was to coordinate the design of the Escort between the North American and the European divisions. However, the problems of coordinating that design were so great that two distinct models were developed. When the Escort finally was introduced to both markets, the North American and the European versions shared only one part, a water pump seal.

## STRATEGIC FOCUS

### Ford's New World Car: The Mondeo

Ford has long envied the Japanese and European automakers that have been able to reduce costs by designing automobiles in their home markets and selling them in markets throughout the world. Its first attempt to change from a multidomestic strategy entailed a joint venture with Mazda Motor Corp., in which it owns a 25 percent stock interest. However, the discussions and cooperation on producing a small automobile in Europe by the mid-1990s did not succeed. The problems centered around Mazda's financial woes and Ford's concern that the new product might compete with its Escort automobile.

However, Ford has attempted to change its style by coordinating the design of a new automobile with its North American and European subsidiary operations. In fact, the European and American designers worked together to design the new world car, named the Mondeo. The intent was to design an automobile that could be manufactured and sold both in the United States and in Europe. While this was no easy task and was expensive, the Mondeo was introduced in Europe in the spring of 1993 and in North America in mid-1994. At the very least, this new automobile may provide an answer to a longstanding controversy over the idea of designing a single product to suit all of the world markets. Of course, its $6 billion cost for development has also raised several eyebrows. It is two to three times competitors' costs in developing a new automobile. Furthermore, the Mondeo took five years to develop, which is well past the current industry standard of three years.

While it is a costly program that took longer than competitors' programs to develop, Ford will gain two new families of modern high-technology engines, a new line of automatic transmissions, and a capacity to produce as many as 700,000 Mondeos per year in Europe and North America. Therefore, there will be multiple spin-off benefits from this new automobile. In fact, Ford spent considerable time attempting to name the new automobile. Mondeo is based on the word for *world* in the Romance languages of French, Spanish, and Italian. Therefore, it is truly designed to be a world automobile.

## Regionalization

Another issue on which firms must decide is whether to compete in all (or many) world markets or to focus on a particular region. The advantage of attempting to compete in all markets relates to the economies that can be achieved because of the size of the combined markets. However, if the firm is competing in industries where the international markets differ greatly (e.g., it must employ a multidomestic strategy), it may wish to narrow its focus to a particular region of the world. In so doing, it can better understand the cultures, legal and social norms, and other factors important in effective competition in those markets. Therefore, a firm may focus on Far East markets, rather than attempting to compete in the Middle East, Europe, and the Far East. It may choose a region of the world where the markets are more similar and thus where some coordination and sharing of resources may be possible. In this way, the firm may be able not only to understand the markets better, but also to achieve some economies, even though it may have to employ a multidomestic strategy.

Regional strategies may be promoted by countries that develop trade agreements to increase the economic power of a region. For example, the European Community (EC) and the Organization of American States (OAS-South America) are collections of countries that developed trade agreements to promote the flow of trade across country boundaries within the region. As described in Chapter 7, Whirlpool has been acquiring and integrating appliance businesses in Europe to better rationalize pan-European brands as the EC creates more unity in European markets. The North American Free Trade Agreement (NAFTA), signed by the United States, Canada, and Mexico, is designed to facilitate free trade across country borders in North America and may be expanded to include other countries in South America, such as Argentina, Brazil, and Chile.[18] These agreements loosen restrictions on international strategies within a region and provide greater opportunity to realize the advantages of international strategies. This does not mean solely that U.S. businesses will go south. Bernardo Dominguez, a Mexican businessman, arranged to purchase Westin Hotels Group in North America, South America, and Europe for $708 million from Aoki Corp. of Japan.[19] Cementos de Mexico, the largest cement company in Mexico, has been buying cement makers in California, Arizona, and New Mexico in order to extend its market share after the NAFTA agreement was confirmed. It is likely that such rationalization will continue.

After firms decide on their international strategies and whether to employ them in regional or world markets, they must decide how to accomplish such international expansion. Therefore, the next section discusses how to enter new international markets.

## Choice of International Entry Mode

The means of international expansion include exporting, licensing, strategic alliances, acquisitions, and wholly owned subsidiaries. These means of entering

> **TABLE 8–1**
>
> **Global Market Entry:**
> **Choice of Entry Mode**
>
> | Type of Entry | Characteristics |
> | --- | --- |
> | Exporting | High cost, low control |
> | Licensing | Low cost, low risk, little control, less profit |
> | Strategic alliances | Shared costs, shared resources, shared risks, problems of integration (e.g., two corporate cultures) |
> | Acquisition | Quick access to new market, high cost, complex negotiations, problems of merging with domestic operations |
> | New, wholly owned subsidiary | Complex, often costly, time consuming, high risk, maximum control, potential high profit |

international markets and their characteristics are depicted in Table 8–1. Each has its advantages and disadvantages, and they are described below.

## Exporting

Many industrial firms initially begin international expansion by exporting their goods or services into other countries. While exporting does not require the cost of establishing operations in the host countries, exporters must establish means of distribution and outlets for their products. In so doing, exporting firms must develop contractual arrangements with host country firms to distribute and sell their products in that country. Its disadvantages include the often high costs of transportation and possible tariffs placed on incoming goods. Furthermore, the exporter has less control over the marketing and distribution of its products in the host country and must pay the distributor and/or allow the distributor to add to the price to recoup its costs and make a profit. As a result, it may be difficult to market a competitive product through exporting. Clearly, it is difficult to provide a product that is customized to each international market through exporting. However, many Japanese firms have been successful at doing this, as the Komatsu example illustrates.

## Licensing

A licensing arrangement allows a foreign firm to purchase the right to manufacture and sell the firm's products within a host country or set of countries. The licenser is normally paid a royalty on each unit produced and sold. The licensee takes the risks and makes the monetary investments in facilities for manufacturing and in marketing and distributing the goods or services. As a result, licensing is possibly the least costly form of international expansion. Before Komatsu had its own R&D operation, it acquired licenses from International Harvester, Bucyrus-Erie, and Cummins Engine in the United States to build better-quality earthmoving equipment.

Molson Breweries signed an agreement with Miller Brewing to be the exclusive licensee to market Molson brand beers in the United States. This agreement with Miller solved a dilemma for Molson on how to finance a large marketing effort in the United States, estimated to cost approximately $100 million per year. The agreement with Miller was a natural for Molson because it already brews and markets Miller beers in Canada. Miller views this agreement as rounding out its product lines to help compete with Anheuser-Busch. Miller pays a royalty to Molson for each product sold, and Miller is expected to turn Molson into a major brand in the U.S. domestic market.[20]

Of course, there are costs involved in licensing as well. For example, this approach to international expansion provides the firm very little control over the manufacture and marketing of its products in other countries. In addition, licensing provides the least potential profit because profits must be shared between the licenser and the licensee. It is also the least costly and therefore the least risky (the firm does not have to make major capital investments in a foreign country). However, the international firm may learn the technology and, after the license expires, produce and sell a similar competitive product, as shown in the Strategic Focus on Komatsu.

## Strategic Alliances

Strategic alliances have enjoyed popularity in recent years as a primary means of international expansion. As discussed in Chapter 5, strategic alliances allow firms to share the risks and the resources required to enter international markets. In addition, most strategic alliances are with a host country firm that has knowledge of the competitive conditions, legal and social norms, and cultural idiosyncrasies that should help the firm manufacture and market a competitive product. Alternatively, the host firm may find access to technology and new products attractive. Therefore, each alliance partner brings knowledge and/or resources to the partnership.

An example of an international strategic alliance is that being negotiated by Electronic Data Systems (EDS), a subsidiary of General Motors, and British Telecommunications PLC. EDS is a large computer-services company that wants to expand internationally, but its parent corporation, General Motors, does not have adequate cash flow to finance such an expansion. British Telecom has a worldwide network and contracts with multinationals in a fast-growing market, but needs a computer-services partner for state-of-the-art technology. Such a venture would provide access to international markets for EDS and allow British Telecom to broaden its services beyond the telephone business.[21] British Telecom also developed a major strategic alliance with MCI in 1993 to counter AT&T's competitive actions in global long-distance markets.

Strategic alliances are not without problems and risks, however. For example, often these new ventures formed by cooperating parties encounter difficulties in merging the separate corporate cultures (a predicted problem for EDS and British Telecom). In addition, one must be aware of the strategic intent of alliance partners, as we discussed in Chapter 5. The venture could be complicated by partners' incompatibility or divergent goals, strategic orientation, or other different processes (e.g., decision making, marketing). Sometimes a partner's strategic intent may be to gain specific knowledge about a technology or market that will allow it to eventually become a competitor in the same and other markets.[22]

In 1984, General Motors and Daewoo Motor Company signed an agreement to jointly build a factory to produce the Pontiac LeMans subcompact automobile. The new automobile would utilize General Motors' German-based technology, responsible for the successful Opel Kadette, and provide General Motors a manufacturing base in the Asian market. Unfortunately, the venture did not work, and General Motors and Daewoo have gone through a bitter divorce. Each had different strategies for the venture. Daewoo officials wanted to expand rapidly, while General Motors executives wanted to focus on building better automobiles. Furthermore, each used different accounting methods, such that Daewoo reported a profit for the venture of $13.6 million in 1991 and General Motors reported a loss for the same time period of $1.3 million. The partners did not understand one another before or during the alliance, and the venture failed.[23]

## Acquisitions

As explained in Chapter 7, acquisitions can provide quick access to a new market. In fact, acquisitions may provide the fastest and oftentimes the largest initial international expansion of any of the alternatives. This was the case with BMW's acquisition of Rover Cars in order to enter the sport utility vehicle market. Therefore, international acquisitions have become a popular mode of entering international markets. They are not without their costs, however. International acquisitions carry some of the same disadvantages for domestic acquisitions discussed in Chapter 7. In addition, they can be expensive and often require debt financing (which also carries an extra cost). International negotiations for acquisitions can be exceedingly complex, generally more complicated than in domestic acquisitions. Dealing with the legal and regulatory requirements in the foreign host country of the target firm and obtaining appropriate information for effective negotiation of the agreement frequently present a significant problem. Finally, the problems of merging the new firm into the acquiring firm often are more complex than for domestic acquisitions. The acquiring firm must deal not only with different corporate cultures, but also with potentially different social cultures and practices. Therefore, while international acquisitions have been popular because of the rapid access to new markets they provide, they also carry with them important costs and multiple risks.

Interestingly, Japanese acquisitions of firms in other countries grew from less than 50 in 1981 to almost 450 in 1989. However, Japan ranked only fifth in the number of U.S. firms acquired during this period. Firms from the United Kingdom, Canada, West Germany, and France (listed in order of the number of acquisitions) acquired more U.S. firms than did Japanese firms during the 1980s.[24]

## New, Wholly Owned Subsidiary

▲ A **greenfield venture** is the establishment of a new, wholly owned subsidiary.

The establishment of a new, wholly owned subsidiary is referred to as a **greenfield venture.** This is often a complex and potentially costly process. This alternative has the advantage of providing maximum control for the firm, and, therefore, if successful, it is potentially the most profitable. However, because of the costs involved in establishing a new business operation in a new country, the risks are also great. The firm may have to acquire the knowledge and expertise of the existing market by hiring host country nationals, possibly from competitive firms, and/or consultants (which is likely costly). It maintains control over the technology, marketing, and distribution of its products through this process. Alternatively, it must build new manufacturing facilities, establish distribution networks, and learn and implement appropriate marketing strategies to compete in the new market.

The establishment of a new, wholly owned subsidiary in a host country, such as the Mercedes Benz plant in Alabama, may be a lengthy process, more time consuming than the alternative modes of entering international markets. Therefore, the firm must decide the importance of protecting its technology and controlling its manufacturing and marketing versus the costs of establishing the new operation. Oftentimes, firms will choose this alternative only after expanding into markets through other alternatives, such as exporting and forming strategic alliances. In addition, this means of international market entry may be attractive in high-technology industries where the protection and control of a technological competence are critical to gaining and/or maintaining a competitive advantage in the market.

## Dynamics of Mode of Entry

Choice of mode of entry will be determined by a number of factors. However, initial market entry will often be through export because this requires no foreign manufacturing expertise and investment only in distribution. Licensing can also facilitate the product improvement necessary to enter foreign markets, as in the Komatsu example. In addition, licensing can facilitate direct market entry, as in the Molson contract with Miller. Strategic alliances have been popular because they allow partnering with an experienced player already in the market targeted. Strategic alliances also reduce risk through the sharing of costs. These modes therefore are best for early market development tactics.

However, to secure a stronger presence, acquisitions or greenfield ventures may be required. The Philips acquisition by Whirlpool has allowed Whirlpool to challenge Electrolux and Siemens in the European appliance market. Merck has gained a significant presence in Japan's pharmaceutical market through its acquisition of Banyu. Alternatively, many Japanese automobile manufacturers, such as Honda, Nissan, and Toyota, have gained presence in the United States through a greenfield venture in addition to joint ventures. The new Mercedes Benz plant in Alabama is an example of a risky greenfield venture. Both acquisitions and greenfield ventures are likely to come at later stages in the development of an international diversification strategy. However, Wal-Mart is building many new stores throughout Mexico after experimenting with stores on the U.S. side of the border with Mexico. Many consider this risky, as Disney has recently found with its Euro Disney operation.

Euro Disney found that there were cultural differences in Europe that were not encountered in its successful U.S. and Japanese operations. Just because a number of visitors come from Europe each year to visit Disney World in Florida does not mean that a Disney operation will be successful in Europe. The troubled resort was losing $1 million a day. Its park entry prices, emphasis on American

*To enhance strategic competitiveness, firms may decide to internationalize their operations. Based on previous successes, the Walt Disney Company decided to operate an amusement park, shown here in Europe. Called Euro Disney, this venture was troubled from its beginning. Disney's experiences in Europe highlight the difficulty companies may encounter in their efforts to implement an international strategy.*

culture, and lack of European ethnic and convenience foods in its restaurants contributed to the alienation of European tour operators.[25] Therefore, there are multiple means of entering new markets, and firms may employ some or all of these alternatives in sequential fashion or use different modes with different products and in different markets.

## Strategic Competitiveness Outcomes

Once the strategy and mode of entry have been established, firms need to be concerned about overall success. However, international expansion can be risky and may not result in a competitive advantage. Thus, the following strategic competitiveness issues are discussed, as suggested in Figure 8–1.

### International Diversification and Performance

▲ **International diversification** is the manufacture and sale of the firm's product lines across country boundaries (in multiple international markets).

The primary international corporate-level strategy may be referred to as international diversification. In Chapter 6, we discussed the corporate-level strategy of product diversification, in which a firm engages in the manufacture and sale of multiple diverse products. In contrast, **international diversification** is the manufacture and sale of the firm's product lines across country boundaries (in multiple international markets).

As noted earlier, there are multiple reasons for firms to diversify internationally. Because of its potential advantages, international diversification should be positively related to firm performance. Research has shown that as international diversification increases, firm performance increases, whereas domestic product diversification is often negatively related to firm performance.[26] There are multiple reasons for the positive effects of international diversification, such as the potential economies of scale and experience, location advantages, increased market size, and potential to stabilize returns. The stabilization of returns helps reduce a firm's overall risk.[27]

In addition to these common advantages, international diversification may allow a firm to better exploit its core competencies. Therefore, the sharing of knowledge resources can produce synergy among the operations in different countries/international markets.[28] On the other hand, firm performance may affect international diversification as well. For example, profitability in a domestic market may encourage a firm to expand internationally in order to enhance its profit potential. Furthermore, resources are necessary to finance international expansion, and, therefore, it is unlikely that poorly performing firms will be able to expand internationally.[29] In addition, internationally diversified firms (multinationals) may, in turn, have access to more efficient labor and benefit from global scanning for competition and market opportunities.[30] As a result, multinational firms with efficient and competitive operations are more likely to produce higher returns for their investors and better products for their customers than are solely domestic firms.[31]

### International Diversification and Innovation

In Chapter 1, we noted that the development of new technology is at the heart of strategic competitiveness. Michael Porter stated that a nation's competitiveness depends on the capacity of its industry to innovate and suggested that firms achieve competitive advantage in international markets through innovation. Competitors eventually and inevitably outperform firms that fail to innovate and improve their operations and products. Therefore, the only way to sustain a competitive advantage is to continually upgrade it.[32]

International diversification provides the potential for firms to achieve greater returns on their innovations (through larger and/or more numerous markets) and thus lowers the often substantial risks of R&D investments. Therefore, international diversification provides incentives for firms to innovate. In addition, international diversification may be necessary to generate the resources required to sustain a large-scale R&D operation. An environment of rapid technological obsolescence makes it difficult to invest in new technology and the capital intensive operations required to take advantage of it. Firms operating solely in domestic markets may find such investments difficult because of the length of time required to recoup the original investment. Furthermore, if the time is extended, it may not be possible to recover the investment before the technology becomes obsolete.[33] As a result, international diversification improves the firm's ability to appropriate additional and necessary returns from innovation before competitors can overcome the initial competitive advantage created by the innovation (e.g., through reverse engineering).

Therefore, there is a complex relationship among international diversification, innovation, and performance. Some level of performance is necessary to provide the resources to generate international diversification. International diversification provides incentives and resources to invest in research and development. Research and development, if appropriately done, should enhance the performance of the firm, which, in turn, provides more resources for continued international diversification and investment in R&D. An example of this complex relationship is discussed in the next Strategic Focus on the global software market.

Obviously, U.S. software firms enjoyed enhanced performance because of their international diversification. In fact, their diversification into the European and the Japanese markets gave them market leadership from which they have earned profits over the years. Those profits gave them incentives and resources to continue developing new software that could be used not only in the domestic U.S. market, but also in the European, Japanese, and other international markets. In so doing, their global strategy has helped them remain the market leaders in the global software market.

Because of the potential positive effects of international diversification on performance and innovation, some have argued that such diversification may even enhance performance in product-diversified firms. International diversification would increase market potential in each of the product lines. However, the complexity of managing a product-diversified and international-diversified firm is significant. Therefore, it is likely that international diversification can enhance the performance of a firm that is highly product diversified, but only when it is well managed.[34]

In recent years, Anheuser-Busch has begun to increase its international diversification. In 1993, Anheuser-Busch acquired 18 percent of Grupo Modelo SA, Mexico's biggest brewer and formed a strategic alliance with Japan's largest brewer, Kirin Brewery Co. The intent of the strategic alliance is to distribute Budweiser beer in Japan, with the goal of transforming an important imported beer into a mainstream beer in that country. Also, Anheuser-Busch is seeking international alliances with other firms outside of Mexico and Japan. The editor of a leading industry trade publication suggests that a new era of globalization has begun in the beer business.

## S T R A T E G I C   F O C U S

### U.S. Firms Finds Riches in Global Software Market

The global software market was estimated to be approximately $25 billion in 1991 and has only grown since that time. The two biggest markets outside of the United States are Europe and Japan. Current figures put the European software market at approximately $9.5 billion annually. Furthermore, U.S. firms, particularly Microsoft Corp. and Lotus Development Corp., have enjoyed major profits from being leaders in the global software market.

Until recently, these two firms have experienced very little competition in the global software market, particularly for personal computers. Without meaningful competition, these two U.S. firms were able to charge premium prices for their software. However, they have been reducing prices in both the European and the Japanese markets. The primary reason for their price reductions in the European market is new competition from Borland International, which won a contract to supply Peugeot with 14,000 copies of its electronic spreadsheet software. The bid by Borland International included a price that was more than 95 percent below its normal price on the electronic spreadsheet. As a result, Microsoft and Lotus Development are offering price discounts in order to maintain their 40 percent market share in Europe.

A new competitor may emerge with the acquisition of WordPerfect by Novell, the dominant leader in network software. Such consolidation may spell trouble for small firms that do not have the market pricing clout and bundling strategies with hardware companies.

Interestingly, Microsoft and Lotus have also reduced prices on several of their major software packages by 26 percent to 41 percent in the Japanese market. This was done even though there are no Japanese competitors large enough to pose a significant threat in the Japanese software market. The price reductions may be designed to erect barriers to entry into this market by Japanese and other competitors. Japan failed to develop a strong software business, and this has had important effects on its electronic business sector. Because of increased competition and soft demand, computer hardware prices have been dramatically lowered. As a result, much of the profit in the computer industry is now coming from software businesses, an area in which Japanese firms have not competed effectively.

One reason that Japanese firms have not been effective competitors in the software market is that they emphasized hardware systems and often subcontracted the software development to go along with these hardware systems. Therefore, they did not see the importance or the potential for the software market and did not develop appropriate competencies in software development.

However, while Anheuser-Busch has been making important moves internationally in its primary core business, beer, some of its related diversified products have not performed well. For example, its strategic alliance to build a theme park and resort near Barcelona, Spain, has encountered major problems. The theme park has been stalled while the primary developer, Tibidabo SA, sought additional financing. Therefore, the international diversification in Anheuser-Busch's core business seems to be successful and to have high potential to produce positive returns. Alternatively, its diversified product lines outside of its core business are encountering performance difficulties in both the domestic and the international markets.[35] Thus, there are limits to the positive contributions of international diversification.

## Complexity of Managing Multinational Firms

While there are many potential benefits of implementing an international strategy, there are also problems and complexities in doing so. For example, there are multiple risks involved in operating in several different countries and there are limits to international expansion. Firms can become only so big and so diverse before they become unmanageable or the costs of managing them exceed their benefits. There are other complexities, including the highly competitive nature of global markets, multiple cultural environments, potentially rapid shifts in the value of different currencies, and the potential instability of some national governments. Therefore, managing in an international environment produces a number of unique managerial challenges.

### Risks in an International Environment

International diversification carries with it multiple risks. International expansion is difficult to implement and manage after implementation because of these risks. Primary among these are the political and economic risks. Specific examples of political and economic risks are shown in Figure 8–4.

**Political Risks**   **Political risks** are related to instability in national governments and to war, civil or international. Instability in a national government creates multiple potential problems. Among these are economic risks, as well as the uncertainty created in terms of government regulation, legal authority, and potential nationalization of private firm assets. For example, foreign firms that are investing in Russia may have concerns about the stability of the national government and what might happen to their investments/assets in Russia should there be a major change in government. Different concerns exist with foreign firms investing in China. They are less worried about the potential for major changes in China's national government than about the uncertainty of China's regulation of foreign business investments in that country.

▲ **Political risks** are related to instability in national governments and to war, civil or international.

     Uncertainties are exemplified by events and actions such as civil war in Bosnia (formerly part of Yugoslavia), the Persian Gulf War and tensions in the Middle East, frequent coups in South American countries, tensions between North and South Korea, and internal strife in Ireland. Furthermore, it is not uncommon in many countries to require that profits from investments in that country be reinvested only in that country.

**Economic Risks**   Economic risks are interdependent with political risks, as noted above. However, there are other economic risks associated with international diversification. Chief among these are the differences and fluctuations in the value of different currencies. For example, with U.S. firms, the value of the dollar relative to other currencies determines the value of their international assets and earnings. An increase in the value of the dollar can reduce the value of international assets

**FIGURE 8–4   International Environment—Risks**

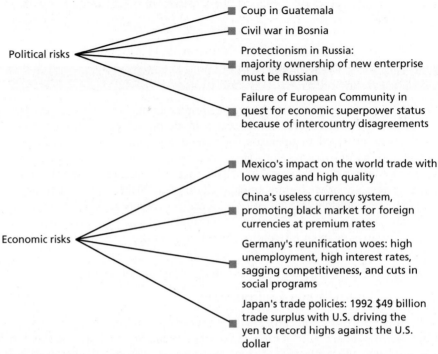

Political risks
- Coup in Guatemala
- Civil war in Bosnia
- Protectionism in Russia: majority ownership of new enterprise must be Russian
- Failure of European Community in quest for economic superpower status because of intercountry disagreements

Economic risks
- Mexico's impact on the world trade with low wages and high quality
- China's useless currency system, promoting black market for foreign currencies at premium rates
- Germany's reunification woes: high unemployment, high interest rates, sagging competitiveness, and cuts in social programs
- Japan's trade policies: 1992 $49 billion trade surplus with U.S. driving the yen to record highs against the U.S. dollar

*SOURCE: L. Holyoke and S. Reed, 1993, Why the soaring yen won't shrink Japan's trade surplus,* Business Week, *May 3, 47; G. E. Schares, D. Wise, and B. Javetski, 1993, Kohl prods the giant,* Business Week, *January 25, 52–54; Global wrap-up: Russia, 1993,* Business Week, *February 1, 43; B. Javetski, R. A. Melcher, and P. Oster, 1993, Who can put Europe's humpty-dumpty together again,* Business Week, *May 31, 55; S. Baker, G. Smith, and E. Weiner, 1993, The Mexican worker,* Business Week, *April 19, 84–92; What's news, 1993,* Wall Street Journal, *June 2, A1; J. McGregor, Reform in China adds to currency woes,* Wall Street Journal, *June 2, A10.*

and the earnings of U.S. multinational firms with substantial investments in other countries. Furthermore, the value of different currencies can, at times, dramatically affect a firm's competitiveness in global markets because of its effect on the prices of goods manufactured in different countries.[36] For example, an increase in the value of the dollar can harm U.S. firms' exports to international markets because of the price differential of the products.

Another economic risk is the different inflation rates across country borders. In actuality, the United States and many of the Western industrialized countries enjoy low inflation rates relative to many countries throughout the world. The U.S. inflation rate over the last several years has been less than 5 percent annually. There have been many countries, including South American and Eastern European countries, that have experienced annual inflation rates of several hundred percent. Of course, the inflation rate is interdependent with the value of the currency because high inflation rates lower the value of the currency relative to the currencies in other countries with lower inflation rates.

## Limits to International Expansion: Management Problems

Research has shown that there are positive returns to early international diversification, but they tend to level off and become negative as the diversification increases past some point.[37] There are multiple reasons for the limits to the positive effects of international diversification. For example, greater geographic dispersion across country borders increases the costs of coordination between units and distribution of products. Also, different government regulations and trade laws across countries create significant barriers to coordination.

The problems experienced in international diversification are shown by entrepreneur Dean Butler's venture into Russia. Butler is an entrepreneur who started and built the LensCrafters optical chain. He and Yuri Fainstein, a native of Russia who fled the country in 1979 to avoid persecution of Soviet Jews, formed a partnership to sell designer eyeglasses and prescription swimming goggles to Russians and Latvians. However, when they first flew to Russia, they discovered that poor quality glass was used in lenses, store clerks did calculations on abacuses, and the ruble was weak relative to the value of the dollar. In fact, the amount a worker might be able to spend on a pair of glasses oftentimes would not cover the wholesale price of those glasses. However, they opened their first store in St. Petersburg in 1992 and began selling U.S.-made lens-making machines to clinics across the country. They also recruited another partner, a former Latvian director of Optika, a state-owned supplier of optical and health care equipment, for which Fainstein had worked during his time in the old Soviet Union. The new partner, Valery Solovyov, capitalized on his government contacts to arrange for the store to obtain a tax-free status for two years and avoid a 15 percent import duty. This helped the store hold down prices and also earn a more reasonable profit. While it remains to be seen whether this will be a long-term profitable venture, in the short term the business seems to be surviving well. Nevertheless, they still have to train employees to be more customer oriented, and they have to deal with the Russian government bureaucracy. For example, to order supplies, an agreement must be established for review by the Russian customs agency. Each subsequent order represents an amendment to the original agreement. Translating contracts into both Russian and English can be a frustrating experience, and checking accounts do not exist in Russia.[38]

Trade barriers, logistical costs, cultural diversity, and other differences by country (e.g., access to raw materials, different employee skill levels) greatly complicate the implementation of international diversification for managers.[39] There are often institutional and cultural factors that represent strong barriers to the transfer of a firm's competitive advantages from one country to another. Many times, marketing programs have to be redesigned and new distribution networks established when firms expand into new countries. In addition, they may encounter different labor costs and capital charges. Therefore, it is difficult to effectively implement, manage, and control international operations.[40]

Scholars have argued that it is necessary for most internationally diversified firms to establish a global integration of international operations, while at the same time allowing local operations the autonomy to respond to local markets. This is extremely difficult because it requires firms to be managed as if they are simultaneously centralized and decentralized.[41] This is because organization structures that allow autonomy in each geographic operation so that it can respond to the local market often sacrifice strategic coordination among units in different countries. Likewise, centralized structures, designed to achieve highly coordinated and integrated international operations, often sacrifice the ability to respond effectively and efficiently to local market changes. While there may be some mixed structures that can partially facilitate both centralization and decentralization, there is not one that allows both needs (global integration and coordination and local business autonomy) to be completely satisfied simultaneously.[42]

The amount of international diversification that can be managed will vary by firm and the abilities of the managers. The problems of central coordination and integration are reduced if the firm diversifies into more friendly countries that have similar cultures. In so doing, there are fewer trade barriers, a better understanding of the laws and customs, and it is easier to adapt the product for local markets. For example, U.S. firms may find it less difficult to expand their operations into Canada and Western European countries (e.g., Great Britain, France) than into Asian countries (e.g., Japan, Korea).[43]

## Other Management Problems

One critical concern is that the global marketplace is highly competitive. Firms accustomed to a highly competitive domestic market experience more complexities in international markets. That is caused not only by the number of competitors encountered, but also by the differences of those competitors. A U.S. firm expanding operations into a Western European country may encounter competitors not only from Great Britain, Germany, France, and Spain, but also from countries outside of Europe, such as Hong Kong, Japan, Korea, Taiwan, Canada, and possibly even South America. Firms from each of these countries may enjoy different strategic advantages. Some may have low labor costs, while others have easy access to financing and low capital costs and still others may have access to new high technology. Finally, attempting to understand the strategic intent of a competitor is more complex because of the different cultures and mindsets.

Another problem focuses on the relationships between the host government and the multinational corporation. For example, while Japanese firms face few trade barriers in competing in U.S. markets, U.S. firms often encounter many barriers to selling their products and operating in Japanese markets. This is exemplified by International Game Technology, a Reno, Nevada, firm that sells slot machines, which has faced its strongest competition in the U.S. market from three Japanese firms. As a result, the firm decided to compete in Japan as well. However, the company encountered severe problems in attempting to gain access to Japanese markets. For four years, the company lobbied the Japanese government for the opportunity to sell its goods to Japanese firms. International Game Technology encountered problems not with tariffs, but with other complex and oftentimes challenging rules, spoken and unspoken. The firm's CEO suggested that Japan has a different mindset and it requires much patience and persistence to move into the Japanese market. An example is shown by comparison of the regulations for slot machines in the United States, which are about 30 pages long, and in Japan, where they represent three thick volumes. Regulators in Japan scrutinize every part of the machine, even individual screws. When the firm first filed, regulators rejected the application because it was on the wrong size paper. Finally, after four years, the firm gained approval to export its first slot machine to Japan.[44]

Even given these problems, many firms continue to see opportunities in global markets. This is exemplified by the goals and international diversification being implemented by Hong Kong and Shanghai Banking Corp. Its CEO, William Purves, is attempting to remake the $258 billion banking organization and turn it into a global banking firm that rivals Citicorp. Currently, it is ranked 12th in total assets among world banks. It has holdings in North and South America, Europe, the Middle East and India, Hong Kong, and the Asia-Pacific region. Its most profitable operation is in Hong Kong, its home base. It is using the huge profits earned in Hong Kong to pursue international expansion. In 1992, Hong Kong and Shanghai Banking Corp.'s profits were $2.6 billion, with $1.7 billion coming from its Hong Kong operations. The banking corporation has established a management boot camp that seeks to develop managers of different races, sexes, and nationalities into cohesive groups. The intent is to build a global operation where managers with different cultures and nationalities can work together in a coordinated fashion in the best interests of the banking corporation.[45]

## Summary

- International diversification is increasing not only because of traditional motivations, but also due to emerging reasons. Traditional motives include extending the product life cycle, securing key resources, and having access to low-cost labor. Emerging motivations focus on increased pressure for global integration as the demand for commodity products becomes borderless, and yet pressure for local country responsiveness is increasing.

- An international strategy usually attempts to capitalize on four important opportunities: potential increased market size; opportunity to earn a return on large investments, such as plant and capital equipment and/or research and development; economies of scale and learning; and potential location advantages.

- International business-level strategies are similar to the generic business strategy types: international low cost, international differentiation, international focus, and international integrated low cost/differentiation. However, each of these strategies is usually grounded is some home country advantage, as Porter's diamond model suggests. The diamond model emphasizes four determinants: factors of production, demand conditions, related and supporting industries, and patterns of strategy, structure, and rivalry.

- International corporate-level strategies are classified into three types. A multidomestic strategy focuses on competition within each country in which the firm operates. Firms employing a multidomestic strategy decentralize strategic and operating decisions to the strategic business units operating in each country so each can tailor its products and services to the local market. A global strategy assumes more standardization of products across country boundaries. Therefore, competitive strategy is centralized and controlled by the home office. A

transnational strategy seeks to combine aspects of both multidomestic and global strategies in order to emphasize both local responsiveness and global integration and coordination. The strategy is difficult to implement, requiring an integrated network where a culture of individual commitment is necessary.

- Although the transnational strategy is difficult to implement, environmental trends are causing all multinational firms to consider the needs for both global efficiencies and local responsiveness. Most large multinational firms, particularly those with multiple diverse products, may use a multidomestic strategy with some product lines and a global strategy with others.

- Some firms decide to compete only in certain regions of the world, as opposed to viewing all markets in the world as potential opportunities. Competing in regional markets allows firms and managers to focus their learning on specific markets, cultures, location resources, etc.

- Firms may enter international markets in one of several different ways, including exporting, licensing, forming strategic alliances, making acquisitions, and establishing new, wholly owned subsidiaries, often referred to as greenfield ventures. Most firms begin with exporting and/or licensing because of their lower costs and risks, but later may expand to strategic alliances and acquisitions. The most expensive and risky means of entering a new international market is through the establishment of a new, wholly owned subsidiary. Alternatively, it provides the advantages of maximum control for the firm and, if successful, potentially the most profit as well.

- International diversification facilitates innovation in the firm. It provides a bigger market to gain more and faster returns from investments in innovation. In addition, international diversification may generate the resources necessary to sustain a large-scale R&D program.

- In general, international diversification is related to higher performance. However, this assumes effective implementation of international diversification and management of international operations. International diversification provides greater economies of scope and learning. These, along with the greater innovation, help produce higher performance.

- There are several risks involved in managing multinational operations. Among these are political risks (e.g., instability of national governments) and economic risks (e.g., currency value fluctuations).

- There are also limits to the ability to effectively manage international expansion. International diversification increases coordination and distribution costs, and management problems are exacerbated by trade barriers, logistical costs, and cultural diversity, among other factors.

- Other important considerations for managers include the fact that international markets are highly competitive and the importance of maintaining an effective working relationship with the host government.

## Review Questions

1. What are the traditional motives and emerging trends causing firms to expand internationally?
2. What are the main opportunities from which multinational firms seek to benefit in their pursuit of international diversification?
3. What are the factors that serve as a foundation for an international business-level strategy?
4. How do the types of international business-level strategies described in the chapter differ?
5. What are the differences among the following corporate-level international strategies: multidomestic, global, and transnational?
6. What modes of international expansion are available, and what is the normal sequence of their use?
7. What is the relationship between international diversification and innovation? How does international diversification affect innovation?
8. What is the effect of international diversification on firm performance?
9. What are the risks involved in expanding internationally and managing multinational firms?
10. What are the factors that create limits to the positive outcomes of international expansion?

## Application Discussion Questions

1. Given the advantages of international diversification, why do some firms not expand internationally?
2. How do firms choose among the alternative modes for expanding internationally and moving into new markets (e.g., forming a strategic alliance versus establishing a wholly owned subsidiary)?
3. Should international diversification affect innovation similarly in all industries? Why or why not?
4. What is an example of political risk in expanding operations into China or Russia?
5. Why do some firms gain competitive advantages in international markets? Explain.
6. Why is it important to understand the strategic intent of strategic alliance partners and competitors in international markets?
7. What are the challenges in pursuing the transnational strategy? Explain.

## Ethics Questions

1. As firms attempt to internationalize, there may be a temptation to locate where product liability laws are lax to test new products. Are there examples where this motivation is the driving force behind international expansion?
2. Regulation and laws regarding the sale and distribution of tobacco products are stringent in the U.S. market. Undertake a study of selected U.S. tobacco firms to see if sales are increasing in foreign markets compared to domestic markets. In what countries are sales increasing and why?

3. Some firms may outsource production to foreign countries. Although the presumed rationale for such outsourcing is to reduce labor costs, examine the liberality of labor laws (for instance, the strictness of child labor laws) and laws on environmental protection in another country.

4. Fair trade is an increasingly prominent issue in newspapers and the popular press. Discuss whether the Japanese markets are closed or open and whether the United States or other nations should attempt more protectionist policies in an effort to force the Japanese government to make its markets more accessible.

5. Are there markets that the U.S. government protects through subsidy and tariff? If so, which ones and why?

6. Should the United States seek to impose trade sanctions on other countries such as China because of human rights violations?

7. Latin America has been experiencing a significant change in both political orientation and economic development. Describe these changes. What strategies should foreign international businesses implement, if any, to influence government policy in these countries? Is there a chance these political changes will reverse? How would business strategy change if Latin American politics reverses its current course?

## Notes

1. C. A. Bartlett and S. Ghoshal, 1991, Global strategic management: Impact on the new frontiers of strategy research, *Strategic Management Journal* 12: 5–16.

2. R. Vernon, 1966, International investment and international trade in the product cycle, *Quarterly Journal of Economics* 80: 190–207.

3. E. S. Browning and H. Cooper, 1993, States bidding war over Mercedes plant made for costly chase, *Wall Street Journal,* September 24, A1, A6.

4. N. J. Adler, R. Doktor, and S. G. Redding, 1986, From the Atlantic to the Pacific century: Cross-cultural management review, *Journal of Management* 12: 295–318.

5. K. Sera, 1992, Corporate globalization: A new trend. *Academy of Management Executive* 6, no. 1: 89–96.

6. L. Hayes, 1993, Amid Russian turmoil, Coca Cola is placing a bet on the future, *Wall Street Journal,* April 6, A1, A5.

7. J. Barnathan and D. G. Yang, 1993, Look up in the sky: A swarm of Chinese airplanes, *Business Week,* May 17, 60.

8. M. Kotabe, 1990, The relationship between offshore sourcing and innovativeness of U.S. multinational firms: An empirical investigation. *Journal of International Business Studies* 21: 623–638.

9. S. J. Kobrin, 1991, An empirical analysis of the determinants of global integration, *Strategic Management Journal* 12 (Special Issue): 17–37.

10. P. Engardio, 1993, Motorola in China: A great leap forward, *Business Week,* May 17, 58–59.

11. M. E. Porter, 1990, *The Competitive Advantage of Nations* (New York: Free Press).

12. Ibid., 84.

13. Ibid., 89.

14. S. Gain, 1993, Korea is overthrown as sneaker champ, *Wall Street Journal,* October 7, A14.

15. Porter, *The Competitive Advantage,* 133.

16. Ibid., 210–225.

17. D. Lei, M. A. Hitt, and J. D. Goldhar, 1993, Generic strategies, complementarities, and organization design in global manufacturing firms (unpublished working paper, Southern Methodist University).

18. J.I. Martinez, J.A. Quelch, and J. Ganitsky, 1992, Don't forget Latin America, *Sloan Management Review,* 33 (Winter): 78–92.

19. P. B. Carroll, 1994, Buyer of Westin deal may represent new breed of Mexican businessman, *Wall Street Journal,* March 1, A15.

20. L. M. Greenberg, 1993, Canada's top brewers draft ways to fight new rivals, *Wall Street Journal,* March 16, B4.

21. P. Dwyer and W. Zellner, 1993, This splice could be golden, *Business Week,* February 8, 36–37.

22. W. A. Dymsza, 1988, Successes and failures of joint ventures in developing countries: Lessons from experience, in F. J. Contractor and P. Lorange (eds.), *Cooperative Strategies in International Business,* 403–424 Lexington, Mass.: Lexington Books).

23. D. Darlin and J. B. White, 1992, Failed marriage: GM venture in Korea nears end, betraying firms' fond hopes, *Wall Street Journal,* January 16, A1, A12.

24. M. Mason, 1992, United States direct investment in Japan: Trends and prospects, *California Management Review* 35, no. 1: 98–115; W. C. Kester, 1991, *Japanese Takeovers: The Global Contest for Corporate Control* (Boston: Harvard Business School Press).

25. P. Gumbel, 1994, Euro Disney calls in Mary Poppins to tidy up the mess at resort in France, *Wall Street Journal,* February 22, A17.

26. R. Buhner, 1987, Assessing international diversification of West German corporations, *Strategic Management Journal* 8: 25–37.

27. A. M. Rugman, 1979, *International Diversification and the Multinational Enterprise* (Lexington, Mass.: Lexington Books); R. E. Caves, 1982, *Multinational Enterprise and*

*Economic Analysis* (Cambridge: Cambridge University Press); J. M. Geringer, P. W. Beamish, and R. C. daCosta, 1989, Diversification strategy and internationalization: Implications for MNE performance, *Strategic Management Journal,* 10: 109–119.

28. G. Hamel, 1991, Competition for competence and inter-partner learning within international strategic alliances, *Strategic Management Journal* 12: 83–103.

29. R. M. Grant, A. P. Jammine, and H. Thomas, 1988, Diversity, diversification, and profitability among British manufacturing companies, 1972–1984, *Academy of Management Journal* 31: 771–801.

30. Kobrin, An empirical analysis.

31. M. Kotabe, 1989, Hollowing-out of U.S. multinationals and their global competitiveness, *Journal of Business Research* 19: 1–15.

32. Porter, *The Competitive Advantage.*

33. Kotabe, The relationship.

34. M. A. Hitt, R. E. Hoskisson, and R. D. Ireland, 1994, A mid-range theory of the interactive effects of international and product diversification on innovation and performance, *Journal of Management,* 20: 297–326.

35. R. Gibson, 1993, Anheuser-Busch to buy 18% stake in Mexican brewer, *Wall Street Journal,* March 23, B3.

36. A. K. Sundaram and J. S. Black, 1992, The environment and internal organization of multinational enterprises, *Academy of Management Review,* 17: 729–757.

37. Geringer, Beamish, and daCosta, Diversification strategy; Hitt, Hoskisson, and Ireland, The interactive effects.

38. V. Reitman, 1993, To succeed in Russia, U.S. retailer employs patience and a local ally, *Wall Street Journal,* May 27, A1, A7.

39. Porter, *The Competitive Advantage.*

40. B. Kogut, 1985, Designing global strategies: Comparative and competitive value added change (Part I), *Sloan Management Review* 27: 15–28.

41. C. A. Bartlett and S. Ghoshal, 1987, Managing across borders: New strategic requirements, *Sloan Management Review* 28: 7–17; C. A. Bartlett and S. Ghoshal, 1988, Organizing for a worldwide effectiveness. The transnational solution, *California Management Review* 30: 54–74; C. A. Bartlett and S. Ghoshal, 1989, *Managing Across Borders: The Transnational Solution* (Boston: Harvard Business School Press).

42. C. K. Prahalad and Y. L. Doz, 1987, *The Multinational Mission: Balancing Local Demands and Global Vision* (New York: Free Press).

43. C. Horng, 1991, Cultural variability: Managing headquarters-subsidiary relations (Ph.D. diss., Texas A&M University).

44. J. M. Schlesinger, 1993, A slot machine maker trying to sell in Japan hits countless barriers, *Wall Street Journal,* May 11, A1, A5.

45. P. Engardio, P. Dwyer, and W. Glasgall, 1993, Global banker: Willie Purves is racing to remake Hong Kong's big bank, *Business Week,* May 24, 50–52.

# Strategic Actions: Strategy Implementation

# CHAPTER 9
# Corporate Governance
▼

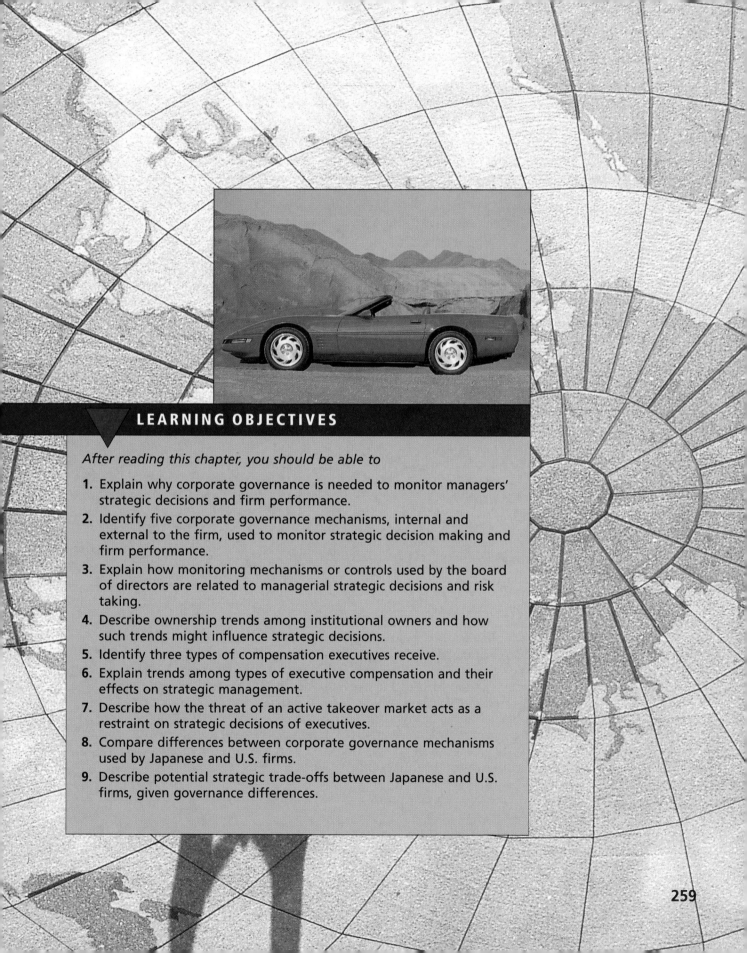

## LEARNING OBJECTIVES

*After reading this chapter, you should be able to*

1. Explain why corporate governance is needed to monitor managers' strategic decisions and firm performance.
2. Identify five corporate governance mechanisms, internal and external to the firm, used to monitor strategic decision making and firm performance.
3. Explain how monitoring mechanisms or controls used by the board of directors are related to managerial strategic decisions and risk taking.
4. Describe ownership trends among institutional owners and how such trends might influence strategic decisions.
5. Identify three types of compensation executives receive.
6. Explain trends among types of executive compensation and their effects on strategic management.
7. Describe how the threat of an active takeover market acts as a restraint on strategic decisions of executives.
8. Compare differences between corporate governance mechanisms used by Japanese and U.S. firms.
9. Describe potential strategic trade-offs between Japanese and U.S. firms, given governance differences.

## Change of the Guard at General Motors

Late in 1991, CEO Robert C. Stempel announced a major restructuring of General Motors (GM). By 1994, GM expected to close 21 plants and lay off approximately 74,000 employees. Many of these plant closings and layoffs were planned for the company's domestic U.S. auto operations. However, the outside members of the board of directors became restless with the slow pace of reform and continued huge net losses, particularly in the North American operations. In 1992, GM reported the largest one-year net loss in U.S. corporate history, $23.5 billion, although mostly due to a noncash charge for future health care. As a result, the board of directors, led by the outside board members, removed CEO Stempel as the chair of the executive committee of the board. While he remained on the executive committee of the board, he no longer had the power to control that committee. Furthermore, they pressured Stempel into replacing Lloyd Reuss, president of General Motors, with John F. Smith and to replace the chief financial officer as well. Stempel eventually resigned and was replaced as CEO by Smith. One institutional owner of GM stock noted that "with the plant closings, they shook up the troops, but with this board action, they shook up the generals."

These actions were stimulated by concern among the outside directors that General Motors needed to make some major changes in its management and operations to become more competitive and stem the tide of net losses. They were not opposed to Stempel's plan, but rather to the pace with which the plan was to be implemented. There was a belief that the CEO created concern on the part of the outside directors when he failed to deliver a visionary long-term plan. Instead, he presented a plan to help the company reach the breakeven point. Many felt that the General Motors action was long overdue. Others referred to it as a watershed event among large corporations and suspected that it may provide the impetus for other boards to become more proactive.

Substantial restructuring as announced by GM requires significant resources and a changed mindset. The new president, John Smith, is dealing with both. First, he sold $2.15 billion of common stock to provide the resources to implement the restructuring plan. Considerable effort by top GM executives was put into marketing the stock across the globe. In addition, Smith charged the corporate purchasing manager with helping to reduce costs and change the GM mindset. This manager challenged employees to change their diets in a manifesto entitled "Feeding the Warrior Spirit." In addition, he encouraged GM executives to change their watches to their right arms to show that times have changed. He met with major suppliers and asked for double-digit price reductions and promised to send teams from GM to suppliers' plants to identify waste. Finally, he held meetings to charge his employees to make changes and become competitive. Therefore, the change in CEO made by the board of directors is filtering down throughout the organization. ▲

The General Motors example shows that those responsible for firm governance (the board of directors) can have a significant impact on strategic direction. Removal of the CEO and/or other top executives of a firm is an extreme action uncommon among top U.S. corporations. However, since the GM action, boards of other firms have taken similar actions where performance was unsatisfactory. Most U.S. companies treat shareholders as the central stakeholders because they are the companies' legal owners. This chapter analyzes the various mechanisms used by owners to govern managers and ensure that they comply with their responsibility to maximize shareholder wealth. We examine how owners and boards of directors, who govern public and private firms, affect the strategies formulated by their top executives. The chapter explains the reasons for increasing board activism and its potential positive and negative outcomes for firm strategy and control.[1]

The governance mechanisms examined are types of shareholders and their incentives to monitor managers, boards of directors, executive compensation, and the market for corporate control (potential owners who are looking to "raid" undervalued firms and replace ineffective management teams). Among large firms, the multidivisional (M-form) structure is used as a governance mechanism to help manage large businesses with many shareholders. The characteristics of this structure and their effects on governance are described. Finally, the U.S. system of governance is compared to that of Japan. The Japanese approach to corporate governance is different from that in the United States and may have different effects on corporate strategy and managerial risk taking. This comparative discussion highlights how corporate governance can create competitive advantages and disadvantages for firms. Thus, this chapter addresses corporate governance, such as forms of ownership, intended to direct executives toward preferred stakeholder objectives. However, the primary purpose of governance is to prevent severe problems, not to provide strategic direction. The General Motors example indicates, however, that corporate governance can have an effect on CEOs and the strategies they implement.

In the 1980s and early 1990s, chief executive compensation increased faster than inflation and profits, and, as a result, a significant protest has been reported in the media. CEO pay at *Standard and Poors* 500 companies has risen more rapidly than factory workers', teachers', or engineers' pay.[2] Because a CEO is often chairman of the board of directors, the board may provide ineffective corporate governance. The compensation committee of the board of directors, often composed of other CEOs, surveys the pay of executives from other firms and often increases the current CEO's pay when it falls below the second quartile of other CEOs' pay. However, shareholders are protesting because this approach is not related to performance. For instance, the California Public Employee Retirement System (CALPERS) pursued discussions with 12 targeted companies in which it has a significant ownership position because of poor performance, excessive pay, and board problems. Although most of these companies have been red-flagged because of pay problems, CALPERS also made suggestions regarding leadership and strategy. CALPERS, for instance, was concerned about the successor to Lee Iacocca. Dale Hansen, chief executive at CALPERS, indicated, "we had no preference, but we want to make sure that a totally independent committee is doing the job, that this isn't just Lee choosing his successor." It apparently had an effect because long board deliberations preceded the March 16, 1992, announcement of Chrysler's CEO-designate, Robert J. Eaton.[3]

## Separation of Ownership and Managerial Control

The modern public corporation is based on the efficient separation of ownership and managerial control. Shareholders purchase stock, which entitles them to income (residual profits) from firm operations after expenses have been paid. This privilege, however, requires that they also take risk; the firm's expenses may be greater than its revenues. To manage this investment risk, shareholders seek to maintain a diversified investment portfolio (to invest in several firms to balance the risk). In small firms, managers often are the owners, so there is no separation between ownership and managerial control. As firms grow and require more capital, managerial owners may not have enough capital to meet the requirements of the business. Alternatively, in the large publicly traded corporations, managers primarily contract to oversee decision making and receive compensation for services rendered. Thus, the contractual nature of the publicly held corporation reserves the risk bearing for shareholders, while the managers specialize in strategy development and decision making.[4]

Shareholders can diversify their risk by owning shares in several firms. As owners diversify their investments over a number of firms, their risk declines (the poor performance or failure of any one firm in which they invest has less overall effect). Shareholders thus specialize in managing their investment risk. Managers in large firms specialize in decision making. Without management specialization in decision making and owner specialization in risk bearing, a firm probably would be limited by the abilities of its owners to manage. Therefore, the separation and specialization of ownership (risk bearing) and managerial control (decision making) is economically efficient.

The separation between owners and managers, however, creates some potential costs for owners. Delegation of management responsibilities creates the opportunity for conflicts of interest. Managers may take actions not always in the best interests of the owners. Thus, managers may select strategic alternatives that do not necessarily serve the interests of shareholders. Major deviations from owner expectations, such as poor performance, may be partially controlled by an active external takeover market (referred to as the market for corporate control). Generally, control of decisions appropriate to maximize firm value for shareholders rests with the internal firm governance mechanisms, especially with high-percentage-ownership shareholders and the board of directors. For example, product diversification can be beneficial for both shareholders and managers. Managers, however, may prefer more product diversification than do shareholders. To prevent more diversification than desired by shareholders, increased monitoring by the owners of large blocks of the firm's stock (see the earlier CALPERS example) and the board of directors may be necessary.

▲ **Managerial employment risk** is the risk of job loss, loss of compensation, or loss of managerial reputation.

▲ **Free cash flows** are resources generated after investment in all projects that have positive net present values within the firm's current product lines.

Product diversification provides two benefits to managers that shareholders do not enjoy. First, diversification and firm size are positively related, as are firm size and executive compensation. Thus, increased diversification provides an opportunity for higher managerial compensation through growth in firm size.[5] Second, diversification can reduce managerial employment risk. **Managerial employment risk** is the risk of job loss, loss of compensation, or loss of managerial reputation. These risks are reduced with increased diversification because the firm (and the manager) is less vulnerable to reduction in demand (or failure) for one product line. Furthermore, large firms may have free cash flows (slack resources) over which managers have discretion. **Free cash flows** are resources generated after investment in all projects that have positive net present values within the firm's current product lines.[6] Managers may use these funds to invest in products that are not current lines of business where they anticipate good investment opportunities. However, the addition of these new product lines may increase firm diversification. Shareholders may prefer that these funds be returned to them as dividends so that they will have control over reinvestment.[7]

Managers who want to avoid risk may desire to invest resources in unrelated diversification beyond the point where the expected rate of return from the new business equals the estimated cost because such diversification reduces their employment risk. AMR Corp., the parent firm of American Airlines, signaled the need to diversify its line of businesses because of losses in its dominant business. Robert L. Crandall, AMR chairman and chief executive officer, stated, "our diversification strategy has been to try to make the most of those things we have learned how to do in being an airline."[8]

Although a certain amount of diversification may be good for shareholders (as in the case of AMR Corp.), too much diversification may become a liability for them. Shareholders diversify their risk over a portfolio of investments and thus generally do not prefer product diversification, particularly where the returns are negative. Shareholders prefer the amount of diversification that maximizes firm value, but managers want to maximize firm value plus increase their risk-adjusted compensation. However, managers cannot work for a diverse portfolio of firms to balance their employment risk. To the extent that increasing product diversification also increases size and reduces employment risk, managers may prefer more diversification than shareholders.

Curve S in Figure 9-1 depicts the optimal firm diversification position for owners versus that desired by managers. Owners desire appropriate levels of diversification to reduce the risk of total business failure and increase the value of the firm through economies of scope and/or synergy. Out of the four strategy

**FIGURE 9-1   Manager and Shareholder Risk and Diversification**

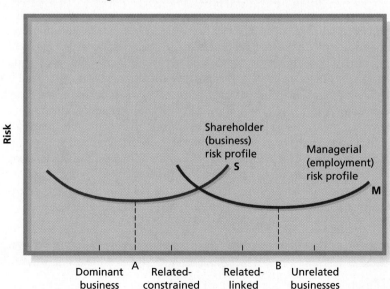

types, curve *S* depicts this position somewhere between the dominant-business and the related-business strategies, the less diversified position. The optimum level of diversification will, of course, vary by firm.

Like shareholders, managers generally do not prefer unlimited diversification because it may produce poor performance. Declining performance increases the probability of being acquired by another firm, and being acquired dramatically increases the target firm managers' employment risk. Furthermore, a manager's employment opportunities (in the managerial labor market) may be harmed by poor firm performance. Therefore, managers will prefer diversification, but not to the point that the firm experiences poor performance that produces higher employment risk and difficulty in obtaining a new job.

Curve *M*, however, suggests that managers prefer relatively higher levels of diversification compared to shareholders (curve S). Shareholders prefer riskier strategies with more focused diversification, while managers prefer more diversification in order to maximize firm size and executive compensation and reduce employment risk.

At one time, Goodyear was the best tire manufacturer in the world. In 1960, it had 50 percent of the U.S. domestic tire market. Goodyear reached a point where it could not obtain an adequate return on increases in market share (these increases cost too much to achieve). The firm had an accumulation of cash with limited reinvestment opportunities in its core business. Rather than deciding to remain the best tire company in the world and pay handsome dividends to shareholders, Robert Mercer, CEO and chairman of the board, decided to use the cash to invest in other businesses. Thus, Goodyear first acquired an oil company, outbidding all firms in the oil industry (the nearest bidder offered $400 million less). Next Goodyear acquired an aerospace firm, followed by investments in the real estate business only a short time before real estate values crashed. Ralph Whitworth, president of the United Shareholders Association, felt the decision to diversify, the businesses chosen for acquisition, and the amount paid for the acquisitions were all bad decisions, particularly for Goodyear's shareholders.[9] By the middle of the 1990s and after restructuring, Goodyear again became successful with focused leadership from Stanley Gault, CEO.

Given the potential conflict of interests between shareholders and managers over the optimal amount of diversification, managers' preferences will probably prevail if the internal governance is weak and management is allowed much autonomy in making strategic decisions. If management autonomy is controlled by the board of directors, or if other strong governance mechanisms are used, however, firm diversification is likely to approach the shareholders' optimum.

The governance mechanisms designed to monitor and encourage managers to make strategic decisions that serve the best interests of shareholders are: ownership concentration in large blocks, institutional shareholders, managerial stock ownership, the board of directors, executive compensation, and organizational structure. The next sections explain the effects of various means of governance on managerial decisions to implement strategies such as product diversity.

## Ownership Concentration

As more shareholders own fewer shares of stock, their incentive to monitor managerial decisions in any one firm declines. All shareholders bear the cost of monitoring, but they benefit from monitoring in proportion to their percentage of ownership in a firm. Owners of large blocks of stock (those with a higher percentage of ownership) are more interested in monitoring managerial decisions, especially if their wealth is not widely diversified in other investments, while shareholders with smaller holdings and more diversified portfolios are less interested in monitoring because their risk is dispersed among their diversified investments. This depends on the percentage of an individual's wealth invested in a particular firm. In general, diffuse ownership (a large number of shareholders with small holdings and no large-block shareholders) may produce weak monitoring of managerial decisions and actions. For example, higher levels of monitoring may encourage managers to avoid inefficient levels of diversification. Therefore, such monitoring may also disallow excessive compensation paid to managers by holding down diversification and thereby the size of the firm as well. In support of these conclusions, research has found that ownership concentration is associated with lower levels of diversification.[10] **Ownership concentration** is defined by both the number of large-block owners (usually those holding five percent or more of the shares issued) and the total percentage held by these large-block owners.

Shareholders usually monitor a firm through the board of directors. The shareholders elect members to the board to oversee managers and to ensure that the firm is operated in the shareholders' best interests. Obviously, owners with large blocks of stock have greater influence on the election of directors, whereas, with diffuse ownership, shareholders often have less knowledge of particular directors nominated by managers and less influence on the election of such directors. As such, directors are more likely to respond to large-block shareholders than to shareholders who have smaller ownership positions.[11]

An example of such pressure on the board of directors occurred at Digital Equipment Company (DEC). While DEC was one of the industry leaders and high performers, in recent years its performance has suffered. One reason for the poor performance is that the firm avoided the lucrative personal computer market. As a result, the board of directors stepped up pressure and ultimately replaced Kenneth H. Olsen as the CEO. While Olsen was the only DEC executive on the board, many of the outside directors on DEC's board were closely allied with Olsen. This made it difficult for the board to act in a timely fashion. However, the poor performance of the firm increased the pressure on the board to take action, and Olsen was forced to retire.[12]

Although large-block ownership by individuals has decreased in recent years, concentration of ownership positions by institutional owners has increased. **Institutional owners** are financial institutions, such as stock mutual funds and pension funds, that control large-block shareholder positions. CALPERS, mentioned earlier, is such a financial institution. These institutions now own over 50 percent of the stock in large U.S. corporations. This recent trend in institutional ownership affects managerial strategic decisions.[13] In the 1930s, a classic work by Adolph Berle and Gardiner Means suggested that the "modern" corporation was characterized by a separation of ownership and control.[14] However, this view of diffuse ownership has become somewhat outdated. Over the last several decades, major changes in the nature of the capital market have had far-reaching implications.

As the CALPERS example indicates, shareholders, especially institutional investors, are becoming more aggressive in taking action against CEOs who receive excessive pay or perks while tolerating poor firm performance. Furthermore, outside directors are becoming more common on boards relative to inside directors and also are becoming more assertive. The ratio of outside to inside directors of

▲ **Ownership concentration** is defined by both the number of large-block owners (usually those holding five percent or more of the shares issued) and the total percentage held by these large-block owners.

▲ **Institutional owners** are financial institutions, such as stock mutual funds and pension funds, that control large-block shareholder positions.

large firms is now 3 to 1 compared to 2 to 1 in 1980. These outside directors often run important board committees and outnumber insiders at over 95 percent of large U.S. companies, up from 81 percent a decade ago. Because of the aggressive stance of many outside directors, some argue that poorly performing CEOs may be replaced or "pursue other interests" on an involuntary basis.[15]

Individual ownership by CEOs and other top executives may affect strategic decisions differently than institutional ownership. However, it is difficult for a single manager, or even a coalition of managers, to assemble a significant owner-ship position in a large corporation, even if one is a member of a wealthy family. The following institutions hold the greatest bulk of wealth in the form of stock, by descending portfolio size: banks, insurance funds, pension funds, and mutual funds.[16] Manager-owners and individual outside owners hold far less wealth. However, institutional owners, except for investment banks, are restricted as to how they manipulate the ownership positions (portfolios) in firms in which they invest client assets. These restrictions are designed to prevent coalitions of individuals and banks from exercising too much power over industrial firms (and their wealth).

Ralph Whitworth, president of the United Shareholders Association, told the following story regarding institutional investors and managerial ownership. In a recent meeting between a group of institutional investors and a CEO, there was considerable rancor. The firm's stock price had fallen from $125 to $20 per share. The institutional investors angrily described a series of poor strategic decisions, such as spending $100 million to acquire a professional baseball team that was now worth about $50 million. When they finished, the CEO replied that it could have been worse. They asked how, and he replied, "It could have been my money."[17]

When individual managers have high levels of ownership in the firm they manage and also have a diversified portfolio of personal investments, they are more likely to exercise strategic risk in their decisions for the firm. For instance, firms managed by such owner-managers tend to have higher R&D expenditures and to be less diversified. However, relative to institutional investors, owner-managers who have great deal of individual wealth invested in the firm without portfolio diversification may still prefer higher levels of firm diversification than other shareholders. Other strategically risky expenditures, such as R&D, likely will also be lower.

While many institutional investors have remained largely passive, some have become more active in monitoring executive actions. For example, CALPERS, the nation's largest public fund (at $68 billion), first worked for changes at 12 companies in which it owned stock. It threatened a proxy war on directors at eight of those companies that have refused to meet its terms. Similarly, Colorado's employee pension fund hired a proxy consultant and withheld votes for directors at American Express, Westinghouse Electric Corp., and Travelers Corp. Because the shareholders vote on directors, and not on managers, boards are feeling increased pressure. On the other hand, the primary targets are firms' top executives.[18]

The Securities and Exchange Commission has given shareholders a boost by easing its rule on communications among shareholders. Previously, shareholders could not communicate as a group except through a cumbersome and expensive filing process. However, under the new rules, shareholders can meet to discuss the company's direction with a simple notification to the SEC. If they agree, they can also vote as a block. For example, the 20 largest shareholders at Philip Morris own approximately 25 percent of the firm. A 25 percent vote against a management proposal or a director would send a powerful message. Some refer to this as shareholder empowerment. Others argue that there should be even fewer restrictions on mutual funds and other institutional owners and managers allowing them to sit on boards of directors.[19] Therefore, it is possible that institutional owners may soon be able to exercise more of their potential power against dissident managers.

This increased action by shareholders and outside directors may provoke reactions from CEOs. One CEO was quoted as saying, "It begins to smack of micro-managing the company," which is not a board's job.[20] In this situation, managers may become risk averse and implement low-risk strategies (low risk for the CEO), such as increased diversification. Therefore, managers may attempt to protect themselves against employment risks when there are large institutional shareholders. They may foresee institutional shareholders as willing to vote in favor of an acquiring firm. As a result, they may desire takeover protection, such as golden parachutes that pay a guaranteed salary for a specified period of time (e.g., three years) in the event there is a takeover and the CEO is replaced.[21] However, it is questionable whether institutional shareholders, who own shares in hundreds of companies, can monitor all of these firms effectively. For instance, CALPERS targets only 12 companies at a time. The New York Teachers Retirement Fund, another active investor, focuses on only 25 of the 1,300 companies in its portfolio. Realistically, given limited resources, institutional investors can only focus on large companies.[22] Therefore, although shareholder activism has increased, institutional investors face legal and informational barriers to their exercise of governance.

## Boards of Directors

Notwithstanding the increase in concentrated institutional ownership, dispersed ownership remains the most common among U.S. firms. Therefore, there is limited monitoring of managers by individual shareholders in large U.S. corporations. Furthermore, large financial institutions that control much wealth are prevented from directly owning firms and from having representatives on boards of directors. This highlights the importance of the board of directors for corporate governance. The primary role of the **board of directors** is to monitor and ratify major managerial decisions to protect the interests of owners. The objectivity, expertise, and motivation of the board largely determines its ability to perform this function. Some have argued that boards are not honoring their primary fiduciary duty to protect shareholders.[23] They believe that managers dominate boards and exploit their personal ties with them. Those who question the current effectiveness of boards advocate reforms to ensure that independent outside directors represent a significant majority.[24]

To date, board reforms have focused largely on the primary role, protecting owners from powerful managers. These reforms have generally increased the number of outside directors on the board. For example, in 1984, the New York Stock Exchange started requiring that listed firms have board audit committees composed solely of outside directors.[25] As a result of the external pressure, more boards of large corporations are dominated by outsiders, as indicated in the GM example. With fewer inside (management) directors on the board, managers' concerns may not be adequately represented, and there are strategic implications of this change.

▲ The **board of directors** monitors and ratifies major managerial decisions to protect the interests of owners. Boards of directors also have a secondary role: to protect the contractual relationship between the firm and its managers, including hiring, disciplining, and setting pay policies for top executives.

The central function of outside directors is to safeguard the shareholders' investment in the firm against potential managerial opportunism or ineffectiveness. Outsiders fulfill this obligation by reviewing and approving management initiatives and monitoring the quality of managerial decisions as these initiatives are implemented. Outside directors, however, do not have contact with the firm's day-to-day operations. Therefore, to effectively evaluate strategic initiatives, they often need rich information about the quality of management and management decisions. This type of information is best obtained through frequent interactions, developed over time, with inside directors during board meetings. Alternatively, inside board members have rich information by virtue of their positions. Thus, boards with a critical mass of insiders can be more effectively informed. Without this type of information, outsider-dominated boards may emphasize financial, as opposed to strategic, evaluations. They evaluate managers based on financial outcomes, rather than their strategic actions (because they do not have the necessary information to evaluate the appropriateness of those actions). This shifts risk to managers, who, in turn, may seek to reduce their risk by lowering R&D expenditures, diversifying the firm's product line, and/or increasing their compensation (to compensate themselves for the increased risk).[26]

In the General Motors example at the beginning of this chapter, the outside board members are becoming a more dominant force. This is likely to have both positive and potentially negative outcomes, as noted above. Outside board members are likely to be more objective and less tied to internal political issues. As representatives of the stockholders and with no other specific ties to the corporation, their objectivity should have an impact on strategic actions and their outcomes. However, General Motors may become more profitable in the short term, but may emphasize short-term performance over long-term strategic actions (because of the emphasis on financial controls over strategic controls). The actions taken by General Motors are mixed in this regard. The announcement of John Smith as the new chief executive officer suggests a stronger focus on the bottom line, an emphasis for which he was known in his previous position as chief operating officer (COO). His initial actions as CEO support this notion. For example, he reorganized the headquarters staff and began reducing the number of models in GM's product lines. The intent was to focus on fewer and more profitable models. His reorganization of the headquarters staff produced significant staff reductions.[27] These actions were appropriate and needed, but they also emphasize bottom-line results. On the other hand, GM's overall reorganization plan suggested that the firm was willing to sell off units unrelated to its automobile operations. Thus, the firm may reduce its level of diversification (downscope).[28]

While boards of directors are playing an increasingly important governance role for large firms like GM, they also are growing in importance at small firms, as explained in the next Strategic Focus. Small firms also must deal with unhappy shareholders. A recent survey showed that approximately 17 percent of publicly traded small businesses had been the subject of shareholder lawsuits. On average, each of these suits had cost the firm an average of $692,000 in legal fees and 1,055 hours of managers' time.[29] Thus, it is not surprising that small firms are seeking help by adding more outside board members.

Research provides some mixed signals on the effects of board involvement in strategic decisions. For example, research has shown that the board is more likely to be involved in strategic decisions in firms with less diversification.[30] In large, diversified firms, they are less likely to be active. In diversified firms, it is difficult for board members, particularly outside members, to have the appropriate rich

## More Small Firms are Employing Outside Directors

More small firms are employing outside directors to help them cope with an increasingly hostile environment, according to the National Association of Corporate Directors, based in Washington, D.C. During the recession and due to increased competition, many small firms decided that they could not manage without additional help. Furthermore, bankers are demanding more accountability for funds lent to smaller enterprises. Also, investment bankers are demanding outside directors to protect shareholders when small firms go public.

Why should the owner of a privately held or closely held firm want an active board? The answer is simple: A board serves as a think tank for strategic issues. The main objective then is to create a board that facilitates better strategic direction and resolves conflict. Suggestions include the following:

1. Have at least three outside directors who can bring a fresh perspective.
2. Do not include people that you already have access to, such as a lawyer, an accountant, or an insurance agent.
3. Rule out friends, employees, competitors, customers, and suppliers because they have self-interested opinions.
4. Keep family representation to a minimum, although it may be wise to have at least one other family owner to assure the other family owners that the board works well.
5. Keep board terms to a year, and extend terms only for those who make a contribution.

Boards can be costly to operate, and board size may depend on firm size. Also, boards take time to orient. It will require time to develop a company synopsis including the history, an organization chart, a family tree, a financial summary, biographies of other directors and top managers, and a list of main suppliers and customers. This exercise, however, may be useful in summarizing accomplishments and may set the stage for richer discussions of future strategic action. Apparently, the costs are increasingly worthwhile because many smaller firms are turning to outside directors for help.

information necessary to evaluate the strategic actions (because of the large number of different businesses that require evaluation). Rather, they are often limited to evaluating the financial outcomes of such actions. Alternatively, in firms that are relatively smaller (as in the example highlighted in the Strategic Focus) and nondiversified, it is possible to have more rich information on the appropriateness of strategic actions. Firms are likely to perform better when boards are involved in strategic actions. Thus, boards of directors are more likely to play a significant role in the success of small businesses.

▲ **Executive compensation** is a governance mechanism that seeks to align managers' and owners' interests through salary, bonuses, and especially long-term incentive compensation, such as stock options.

## Executive Compensation

**Executive compensation** is a governance mechanism that seeks to align managers' and owners' interests through salary, bonuses, and especially long-term incentive compensation, such as stock options. Executive compensation can help to align managers' and owners' interests by tying managerial pay to firm performance. As the Strategic Focus on executive compensation indicates, between the late 1970s and the 1990s, there has been a significant increase in long-term incentive compensation based on stock options, compared to salary-based compensation.

Incentive compensation is complicated. First, the strategic decisions made by top executives are typically complex and nonroutine; thus, direct supervision of top executives is inappropriate for judging the quality of their decisions. As such, there is a tendency to link compensation to measurable outcomes, such as financial performance (e.g., return on investment). Second, management decisions often affect firm financial outcomes over extended periods of time, making it difficult to assess the effect of current decisions on firm performance. In fact, strategic decisions are more likely to have long-term, rather than short-term, effects on firm performance. Third, a number of variables intervene between management behavior and firm performance. Unpredictable economic, social, or legal changes mentioned in Chapter 2 make it difficult before implementation to discern the effects of strategic decisions that may become unfavorable after implementation. Thus, although performance-based compensation may provide incentives to managers to make decisions benefiting shareholders, such compensation plans alone are imperfect in their ability to produce optimal strategies.

While incentive compensation plans may increase firm value in line with shareholder expectations, they are subject to managerial manipulation. For instance, annual bonuses may provide incentives to pursue short-run objectives at the expense of the firm's long-term viability. Supporting this conclusion, some research has found that bonuses, based on annual performance, were negatively related to investments in R&D, which may affect the long-term competitiveness of the firm.[31] Although long-term performance-based incentives may reduce the temptation to underinvest in the short term, they increase executive exposure to risks associated with uncontrollable events, such as market fluctuations and industry decline.[32] The longer the focus of incentive compensation, the greater the long-term risks borne by the executive. Annual incentive compensation plans shift risk to managers and therefore may enhance biases against investments with long-term potential payoffs.

One way managers can compensate for increases in their risk is to propose higher levels of compensation or longer-term employment contract guarantees. In addition, research has shown that incentive compensation is positively related to diversification.[33] Diversification is a way managers can reduce their risk, as described earlier. The evidence suggests that short-term incentive compensation schemes encourage managers to diversify the firm because these plans shift risk to managers (in large publicly held firms that do not have concentrated ownership).

In recent times, stockholders have become angered about executive pay. This suggests that boards of directors may not have been effective in developing and implementing executive incentive compensation plans. The increases in incentive compensation approved by boards are largely responsible for the huge increases in total executive compensation. Boards may have overly relied on this form of governance, and managers may be implementing strategies to take advantage of the incentives provided. However, the large sums have attracted much attention. Without aggressive and outspoken stockholders, however, it is not likely that boards will create a better balance among governance mechanisms. Because of their significant holdings, institutional inventors' outspoken dissatisfaction has received the attention of a number of executives and boards of directors.[34]

S T R A T E G I C   F O C U S

## Large Increases in Executive Compensation Due to Stock Options

In the 1980s, average compensation for chief executive officers increased by 212 percent. During the same time period, factory workers received pay increases of 53 percent, engineers 73 percent, and teachers 95 percent. The average earnings per share of the Standard & Poors top 500 companies increased by only 78 percent during the 1980s. Thus, unless top executives were significantly under-paid prior to the 1980s, the increase in pay during this decade does not seem deserved, either relative to other employees or based on increases in earnings. But some changes occurred in the early 1990s. For example, the average CEO's salary and bonus fell by 7 percent in 1991. Undoubtedly, the decline occurred during a recessionary period in which corporate profits fell by 18 percent and thousands of managers were laid off. However, when long-term compensation, to include stock options, is added to the CEO's compensation, the chief executives' total pay increased by 26 percent during 1990.

Executive compensation influences managerial action and has been studied for a number of years. Over the years, the emphasis in executive compensation has changed from primarily salary-based to increasingly incentive-based. In particular, in recent years, executive compensation has emphasized stock ownership and stock option plans. In 1978, 15 percent of top executive compensation was composed of long-term incentive compensation (stock ownership and option plans). By 1988, this percentage had increased to 42 percent. In 1992, base executive compensation continued to fall by 2 percent, while total compensation increased 42 percent for large firms (this excludes the 1992 sweepstakes winner Thomas Frist, Hospital Corporation of America, at $127 million). In 1993, Michael D. Eisner, CEO of Disney, exercised options worth $197 million.

*Some believe that the compensation received recently by Disney CEO Michael Eisner was appropriate because he is an important source of corporate governance and a possible source of sustainable competitive advantage for the firm.*

## The Multidivisional Structure

Oliver Williamson argues that organization structure, particularly the multidivisional (M-form) structure, serves as a governance mechanism. Williamson suggests that the M-form structure effectively deals with the problems of managerial opportunism in large firms.[35] The **M-form structure** serves as a governance mechanism through the corporate office, which, in addition to the board of directors, monitors strategy and performance of division managers. This suggests that managers, specifically division managers in firms with this type of structure, are more interested in profit maximization than are managers in firms with other types of structure (e.g., functional). While the M-form structure may limit division managers' opportunistic actions, it may not limit corporate-level managers' self-interested actions. In fact, the other governance mechanisms (e.g., boards of directors) aimed at corporate-level executives in M-form firms are similar to those used in firms with other structures (e.g., functional). Thus, the M-form, without additional means of governance, may not appropriately monitor and control corporate managerial decisions. For example, research has found that firms using the M-form structure are more likely to continue further diversification.[36] If the

▲ The **M-form structure** serves as a governance mechanism through the corporate office, which, in addition to the board of directors, monitors strategy and performance of division managers.

firm becomes highly diversified, corporate executives may be forced to change from strategic to financial controls of divisional performance. The overuse of financial outcomes to evaluate strategic decisions often focuses division managers' attention on short-term, as opposed to long-term, investments.

In addition, a depth-for-breadth trade-off often occurs in an extensively diversified firm with an M-form structure. Because of the diversification of product lines (breadth of businesses), top executives do not have adequate information to evaluate strategic actions. They must wait for the outcomes, but the delay may allow inefficient or opportunistic behavior in the interim.[37] Where internal controls are limited because of extensive diversification, only the external market for corporate control and the external managerial labor markets provide controls on managers pursuing strategic actions in their own best interests (e.g., pursuing acquisitions to increase the size of firms, their compensation and power). Because external markets lack access to internal information on the firm, they tend to be less efficient than internal systems for monitoring corporate executive performance. While the market for corporate control may become active, the cost of executing takeovers makes this threat feasible only where a firm is significantly undervalued. Therefore, firms with an M-form structure require additional, strong internal governance mechanisms for effective control of corporate managers. Without additional effective governance mechanisms, the M-form structure may actually facilitate overdiversification and inappropriately high compensation for corporate executives and may lead division managers to overemphasize short-term performance.[38]

## Market for Corporate Control

▲ The **market for corporate control** is composed of individuals and firms that buy ownership positions in (or take over) potentially undervalued firms so they can form new divisions in established diversified firms or merge two previously separate firms; they usually displace the target firm's management team to revise the strategy that caused low firm performance.

The market for corporate control serves as a means of governance, usually after internal controls have failed. The **market for corporate control** is composed of individuals and firms that buy ownership positions in (or take over) potentially undervalued firms so they can form new divisions in established diversified firms or merge two previously separate firms; they usually displace the target firm's management team to revise the strategy that caused low firm performance. The market for corporate control should be activated by poor performance relative to competitors in the same industry. Poor or inadequate internal governance may result in poor relative performance, thereby triggering a threat of takeover. Thus, declining performance increases the probability of being acquired, and this, in turn, often dramatically increases the probability of dismissal of the top executives after the acquisition.

It is important to note that as the market for corporate control became more active in the 1980s, it was accompanied by an increase in the sophistication and variety of managerial defense tactics against hostile takeovers.[39] Some tactics require asset restructuring, such as divesting a business (division), while others only require financial structure changes, such as repurchasing shares of stock. Still other tactics, such as a change in the state of incorporation, require shareholder approval, while others, such as targeted shareholder repurchase agreements (greenmail—money paid to repurchase stock from a raider to avoid the takeover), do not.

Activist shareholders can play a role in the market for corporate control as well. For example, the Wisconsin Retirement Fund, an institutional investor, has become an activist. It led a proxy campaign against key board members of Paramount Communications because of the firm's poor performance. Fliers were sent to other Paramount shareholders arguing that the large bonuses received by Chairman Martin Davis were not consistent with the firm's poor performance. Shortly thereafter, Wisconsin's concerns were supported by takeover bids for the company. Paramount was eventually acquired after a bidding war, and Wisconsin earned a healthy return on its investment. This investor also filed a suit challenging the price paid by Marvel Entertainment to acquire Fleer Corp., in which Wisconsin had a sizable ownership stake. Wisconsin won the suit and obtained a 23 percent increase in the price, giving it an extra $6 million.[40]

Interestingly, managerial defenses do not always reduce a firm's stock prices. One study found that adoption of golden parachutes (contingency contracts that pay managers significant extra compensation, but only if the firm is taken over) can have a positive effect on shareholder returns.[41] Golden parachutes can have a positive effect on stock prices because they may reduce top managers' resistance to being acquired (because of the extra compensation). On the other hand, if the cost of golden parachutes is too high, it may reduce potential acquirers' interest. However, in this case, the stock price should fall.

There are other potential problems in the market for corporate control. It may not be as efficient as assumed. A study of several of the most active corporate raiders in the 1980s showed that approximately 50 percent of their takeover attempts targeted firms with above-average performance in their industry.[42] In these cases, the firms were neither undervalued nor poorly managed. Such targeting of high-performance businesses may lead to acquisitions at premium prices or force managers of high-performing firms to take actions to avoid the takeover and protect their shareholders' value. These actions, however, may be costly. Thus, external controls do not always create effective change by replacing poorly functioning managerial teams, and defensive managerial tactics do not always result in reductions in stockholder returns. Therefore, external governance, although providing a restraining influence on managers, does not provide flawless control of inappropriate or ineffective managerial strategies. There must be internal governance mechanisms as well.

Although defensive tactics have increased, the 1980s showed that large firms reduced their focus on diversified businesses and increasingly focused on core businesses, as Figure 9-2 demonstrates. This evidence is confirmed by research showing that when firms reduced their scope of businesses (downscoped), they experienced an increase in stock price.[43] Although external governance often produces imperfect changes (because it lacks the precision possible with internal governance mechanisms), the market for corporate control has been responsible for significant changes in the corporate strategy of many firms.

## Corporate Governance: Japan Versus the United States

Comparison of governance mechanisms used in another economic system, such as in Japan, with those used in the United States provides interesting insights. Such a comparison must consider more than the particular mechanisms, such as the board of directors. Boards and other means of governance represent only part of a set of safeguards and incentives that affect the activities of corporations and their stakeholders. The effectiveness of the Japanese system of governance is demonstrated by the limited market for corporate control in Japan.

**FIGURE 9-2**   **Reduced Diversification among Large Businesses in the 1980s**

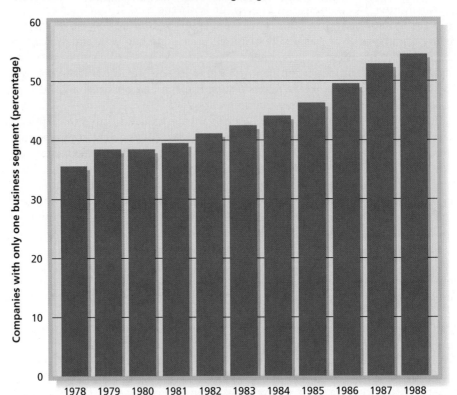

SOURCE: G. Jarrell, 1991, For a higher share price, focus your business, Wall Street Journal, May 13, A14.
Reprinted by permission of Wall Street Journal, © 1991 Dow Jones & Company, Inc. All Rights Reserved
Worldwide.

The most significant differences exist between the U.S. and Japanese financial systems. In the United States, individual shareholders in the external capital market provide much of the financing for large firms. In the 1980s in the United States, over 58 percent of equities were held by individuals, while approximately 38 percent were held by corporations (including financial institutions). In Japan, about 27 percent were held by individuals, while over 67 percent were held by corporations.[44] Although these figures are changing in both countries, the relative balance should be maintained well into the twenty-first century. In the United States, owners as well as boards of directors play a significant monitoring role, as described earlier. Alternatively, banks play a more important role in financing and monitoring large public firms in Japan. Among the Japanese banks holding stock in a firm, the bank that typically owns the largest share of stocks and debt, called the main bank, has the closest relationship with the management of the firm. The main bank not only provides financial advice to the firm, but also is responsible for closely monitoring the management. Thus, Japan has a bank-based financial and governance system, while the United States has a market-based financial and governance system.

Aside from lending money (debt), a Japanese bank can hold up to 5 percent of the total stock in a firm, and a group of financial institutions can hold up to 40 percent of the firm's total stock. In many cases, main bank relationships are part of a keiretsu, an industrial group of firms that interacts with the same main bank.

Often firms in the keiretsu develop interrelationships and become interdependent. A number of keiretsu groups exist in Japan, such as Mitsui, Mitsubishi, Sumitomo, Fuji, and Dai-Ichi Kangyo. These industrial groups are both diversified and vertically integrated to such an extent that they include one or more firms in almost all important industrial sectors.

The main bank maintains the largest share of loans extended to the firm by all financial institutions. It has been estimated that, on average, loans from main banks accounted for approximately 25 percent of bank loans to firms listed in the first section (i.e., the largest firms) of the Tokyo Stock Exchange in 1980. Also, the main bank is typically a major shareholder in the firm. For instance, main banks were among the top five shareholders for 72 percent of the firms listed in the first section of the Tokyo Stock Exchange in 1980.[45]

Firms borrow from other banks as well as their main bank, and the main bank lends to firms in other keiretsus. There is an implicit agreement among banks that the main bank is responsible for monitoring the firm and helping it in times of trouble. In fact, the main bank often bears a large responsibility to produce the necessary financial assistance to turn around a firm in trouble. The main bank is willing to do so because maintaining its reputation as a responsible monitor is important for effective relationships with other banks. As a result, the main bank has strong incentives to actively monitor firms. It has significant stakes in firms within its keiretsu as major shareholder and debtholder. Therefore, actively monitoring a firm can help the main bank not only safeguard its investment, but also gain significant returns from firm profit.

Banks often have their representatives on the boards of firms for which they serve as main bank, which facilitates the monitoring of firm management. For instance, about half of the large firms have main bank representatives on their boards. In addition, industrial groups have regular meetings for affiliated firms and financial institutions. Participating firms typically have a common main bank relationship and significant interlocking shareholdings. Although these meetings do not result in formal decisions, they are mechanisms whereby participating financial institutions and firms can exchange information and coordinate decision making. Therefore, these meetings help main banks keep informed of firms' strategic

*As suggested by this picture, many fast-paced transactions take place at the Tokyo Stock Exchange. Given the nature of corporate governance in Japan, different keiretsus are key players in a large number of these transactions.*

actions and interim financial outcomes. Main bank relationships are typically stable, which helps main banks accumulate a large amount of information specific to firms.

In summary, main banks have the incentives and processes to actively monitor firms in their industrial groups. Main banks primarily monitor large firms in Japan, while shareholders primarily monitor firms in the United States. However, main banks in Japan are likely to have better information about firm strategy and better opportunities to influence firm strategy than shareholders in the United States (especially if the firm is in financial distress). As discussed earlier, to the extent that U.S. shareholders have information and control disadvantages regarding firm strategy, corporate managers of U.S. firms have latitude to pursue strategies that may not maximize firm performance. Given that main banks are likely to efficiently monitor large firms, Japanese firms are less likely to pursue ineffective unrelated diversification. Therefore, Japanese firms may focus on achieving sound performance with related diversification through cooperation and synergistic economies within the firm and within the keiretsu. This efficient monitoring does not require that boards rely on incentive compensation, which has produced excessive compensation for U.S. executives. Thus, executive compensation for comparative firms, as noted in the next Strategic Focus, is lower in Japan than in the United States. Finally, time horizons may be longer in Japan than in the United States because the monitors and owners have a strategic understanding of the businesses operated by the firm. Governance focuses on the executives' strategic intent as well as on the businesses' financial outcomes. In the United States, governance is more dependent on financial outcomes, which shifts risk to managers, as discussed earlier.

Emphasis on financial outcomes often focuses executives on the short term. This is exacerbated by incentive compensation plans that emphasize annual performance targets. In fact, some argue that one of the advantages Japanese businesses enjoy is their executives' articulation of a clear long-term vision for the firm.[46] It is interesting that U.S. executives seem less concerned about the long term, they are paid considerably more (see Strategic Focus), and their firms have performed less well compared to those run by Japanese executives. Given that executive compensation is used as a means of governance in the United States, it should be focused on the appropriate goals. The heavier emphasis on stock options in U.S. executive compensation in recent years represents an attempt to focus U.S. executives on the achievement of long-term goals.

The Japanese system of governance is not without trade-offs. Centralized financial systems like those of the Japanese have limitations. An innovation project is evaluated by a smaller number of sources in centralized financial systems than in decentralized financial systems, such as those in the United States. Accordingly, a project has a lower chance of getting funded in centralized financial systems than in decentralized financial systems because there is more chance in the decentralized system to reduce the project's uncertainty. In particular, an innovation project, which entails a high amount of uncertainty by nature, would have a much lower chance of getting funded in centralized financial systems compared to decentralized financial systems.[47] As such, Japanese managers pursue research projects that lead to incremental changes in the product and the manufacturing process, while the incentives in the United States allow more radical introductions of new products and processes. Until recently, most Japanese firms emphasized the development of process innovations and incremental product improvements, whereas the R&D

## STRATEGIC FOCUS

### U.S. and Japanese Executive Compensation Compared

The U.S. recession in the early 1990s did not lead to a reduction in total compensation for U.S. executives. In 1992 and 1993, the Japanese economy experienced a deep recession, and leading companies cut executive pay substantially. "When company results are down, managers have to take responsibility and accept such cuts," says Takahiko Shinohoara, a managing director of Hitachi. Even the highest-paid CEOs in Japan make a fraction of the compensation of their U.S. counterparts. Hiroshi Yamauchi of Nintendo and Shoichire Toyoda of Toyota received $6.3 and $4.8 million in 1991, respectively. This is high relative to the average of $872,646 in 1991, which is about 25 percent of the U.S. average. In Japan, CEO pay is less than 17 times the average factory worker's salary and 26 times what the typical school teacher makes. In the United States, the gap is considerably wider: roughly 157 and 113 times for factory workers and teachers, respectively. The perks of Japanese and U.S. CEOs are roughly the same, even though American CEOs have claimed that Japan's top executives receive more than meets the eye in the form of hidden expense accounts, expensive golf-club memberships, chauffeured limousines, and company-provided houses.

However, few Japanese CEOs are held individually responsible for overall company performance. American CEOs carry more individual responsibility for decision making than their Japanese counterparts. In Japan, much of the burden of decision making is distributed among capital providers (banks), keiretsu partners, and subordinates. Furthermore, stock options, the main component of incentive compensation for U.S. CEOs in recent years, are not used in Japan. Also, there is no external market for managerial talent that helps to bid up pay for CEOs in Japan. That is because there is very little movement of Japanese managers between firms. The Japanese tradition has been lifelong employment.

In sum, Japanese CEOs are paid substantially less than their U.S. counterparts. This is primarily due to the system of governance where managers are nurtured from within the system. Thus, there is no external market of CEO talent. CEO monitoring is accomplished primarily by the main bank and keiretsu partners, who are not only lenders, but also significant and committed owners. The cooperative system in which Japanese CEOs are placed requires less individual responsibility for decisions and thereby less individual incentive pay, such as stock options. For these reasons, CEO pay is lower in Japan and has led Akio Morita, chairman of Sony Corp., to say, "American top management must adjust and restrain themselves." In addition, Makoto Utsumi, Japan's vice finance minister for international affairs, questioned the productivity of the U.S. system of top executive compensation.

investments in many U.S. firms emphasized product innovations and incremental process improvements. Although efficient in governing large firms, Japanese financial systems are not as effective in financing innovation-oriented projects.

Although the Japanese financial system may not be as effective in financing innovation-oriented projects, this has not posed a serious problem to date. Japanese firms have focused largely on the adaptation and improvement of existing technology, rather than on creating new technology. Also, Japanese firms have focused on process, rather than product, R&D.[48] Therefore, Japanese innovation projects entail a lower level of uncertainty than the U.S. innovation-oriented projects.

## Governance and Ethical Behavior

The governance mechanisms described in this chapter are designed to ensure that management is effective and that managers work to achieve stakeholders' goals. Of course, one of the most important stakeholders is the owner(s) (shareholders). However, there are other important stakeholders, as well. In the long term, these stakeholders (e.g., customers) must be satisfied in order for shareholders' wealth to be maximized. Therefore, it is important that governance mechanisms not focus managers too much on the short term. Short-term returns can be maximized, but often at the expense of other stakeholders in the long term. Therefore, the design and implementation of governance mechanisms (e.g., executive compensation) must take into consideration the interests of all of the firm's stakeholders.

As noted earlier, when internal governance mechanisms fail, performance may suffer, and the market for corporate control is likely to become active. However, this assumes that managers make poor strategic and operating decisions only in this situation. When governance fails, firm performance can sometimes be maintained, but through unethical decisions. Such was the case at Par Pharmaceuticals. Shortly after Kenneth Sawyer became CEO in 1989, he discovered that many unethical and unlawful managerial decisions had been made. For example, Quad Pharmaceuticals was one of the most profitable units of Par, but an audit ordered by Sawyer found that managers had submitted false drug-test data to the Food and Drug Administration (FDA) to gain approval for manufacturing and marketing them commercially. The audit results led to indictments of three managers of that unit. Sawyer also found that false data had been submitted to the FDA from Par's core business. Two managers, the head of R&D and the head of production, pleaded guilty to conspiracy to obstruct the regulatory functions of the FDA.

Obviously, governance failed at Par Pharmaceuticals. The firm's three outside directors were preoccupied with trying to fend off shareholder suits. The board of directors failed in its role to monitor management, and the incentive structure did not promote the appropriate type of behavior. Sawyer is now trying to put the company back on track. He voluntarily withdrew drugs from the market until he could ensure that proper testing was done. Furthermore, he implemented a number of strict policies to be followed in all such cases. He hired new executives and tried to repair the firm's corporate image. To do these things, Sawyer had to withstand death threats to him and his family.[49]

Fortunately, Par Pharmaceuticals is an extreme example of what can happen when governance mechanisms fail. However, it emphasizes the importance of having effective corporate governance.

## Summary

- Under limited or inadequate internal governance, corporate managers may control the firm without adequate oversight. As a result, they are likely to implement higher levels of diversification to increase firm size and their compensation and reduce their employment risk.

- Concentrated owners (large-block shareholders) usually prefer lower levels of product diversification than do managers, who have personal incentives (higher pay and lower risk) to pursue higher levels of diversification.

- Although once less assertive because they are different from typical owners and are prevented by law from having too much involvement with managers, institutional owners are becoming more aggressive and voicing concerns about internal governance issues, such as CEO pay.
- It is likely that financial controls will be emphasized because although outside directors are now in the majority on boards of large firms, they lack the ability and time, in general, to be informed completely about strategic matters. Without a balanced emphasis on strategic and financial controls, the focus on financial controls shifts risk to managers. Managers, in turn, seek to reduce that risk through further diversification or higher compensation (or both).
- A strong emphasis on incentive compensation as a means of governance has resulted in excessive managerial pay compared to others. Also, U.S. executives receive compensation in excess of that received by executives in comparable multinational firms, such as those in Japan.
- In general, even though owners and board members are becoming more vigilant, it does not appear that current governance mechanisms can effectively control extensive diversification in the United States without the help of external capital market intervention (the market for corporate control). Although external market intervention is an imperfect means of governance, it has been effective in causing firms to downscope (reduce diversification).
- It appears that the Japanese system of governance allows closer monitoring at a lower cost and provides lower executive compensation. Thus, not only has the U.S. governance system created strategies, such as extensive diversification, that hinder competitive advantage, but also the Japanese system of governance may have created other competitive advantages.
- There are significant trade-offs for the Japanese system of corporate governance, especially an emphasis on low-risk innovation projects that stress incremental process improvements.
- Corporate governance is important and must ensure that all critical stakeholders' interests are satisfied over time.

## Review Questions

1. Identify and briefly describe five means of corporate governance, at least four of which are internal to the firm.
2. Explain the different roles for owners and managers and how these roles create efficiency.
3. Explain what problems the efficient separation of ownership from control creates.
4. Discuss how the increasing number of outside directors on boards of large corporations may affect managerial behavior and strategy positively and/or negatively.
5. Discuss how the increased monitoring and aggressiveness of institutional owners are likely to affect the corporate strategy of large firms.
6. Total executive compensation has been increasing significantly, particularly over the past decade. Discuss why this happened and how executive compensation policies affect corporate strategy.
7. Explain how the M-form structure operates as a means of corporate governance.
8. Explain the effect of the market for corporate control on corporate strategy in the 1980s.
9. The Japanese system of corporate governance is significantly different from that found in the United States. Highlight the key differences and explain how they are likely to affect corporate strategy.

## Application Discussion Questions

1. Explain how various means of governance interact to create a governance system whereby one governance mechanism that is limited may require another governance mechanism to be stronger. For instance, how might ownership concentration be linked to the number of independent outside directors? Provide a business example.
2. The roles of managers and board of directors are different. The board has traditionally emphasized its role in monitoring managers, while managers have been in charge of strategy. Some have argued that the board should be more involved in strategy formulation. Provide an example where this was an advantage and an example where it was a disadvantage. Explain why.

3. Discuss whether you think U.S. firms have been overgoverned by some means of corporate governance and undergoverned by others. Provide a business example of each.

4. How can a system of corporate governance create "patient" capital, allowing managers to create a competitive advantage and focus on long-term performance? In the business press, find an example of a firm where this has occurred and describe it.

5. The Japanese system of corporate governance lacks means for external intervention (that is, the market for corporate control is not highly developed). Explain how this is both advantageous and disadvantageous.

## Ethics Questions

1. Is it ethical for managers to act in their own self-interest? Explain why or why not.

2. Is it ethical for owners to shift much of the risk to managers? Explain why or why not.

3. When the Wisconsin Retirement Fund sued Marvel Entertainment and obtained a judgment to increase the amount paid for its shares of Fleer Corp., no other stockholders benefited. What are the ethical issues involved in the activism of institutional investors?

4. What are the responsibilities of the board of directors to stakeholders other than shareholders?

5. What are the ethical issues involved in executive compensation? How can we determine if top executives are paid too much?

6. Are there ethical considerations when raiders complete a hostile takeover? If so, explain.

7. How can governance mechanisms be designed to ensure against managerial opportunism, ineffectiveness, and unethical behavior?

## Notes

1. Parts of this chapter are based on Chapters 3 and 6 from R. E. Hoskisson and M. A. Hitt, 1994, *Downscoping: How to Tame the Diversified Firm* (New York: Oxford University Press).

2. J. A. Byrne, 1993, Executive pay: The party ain't over yet, *Business Week*, April 26, 56–64.

3. J. H. Dobrzynski, 1992, CALPERS is ready to roar, but will CEOs listen? *Business Week*, March 30, 44–45.

4. E. F. Fama and M. C. Jensen, 1983, Separation of ownership and control, *Journal of Law and Economics* 26: 301–325.

5. S. Finkelstein and D. C. Hambrick, 1989, Chief executive compensation: A study of the intersection of markets and political processes, *Strategic Management Journal* 10: 121–134.

6. M. S. Jensen, 1986, Agency costs of free cash flow, corporate finance, and takeovers, *American Economic Review* 76: 323–329.

7. C. W. L. Hill and S. A. Snell, 1988, External control, corporate strategy, and firm performance in research intensive industries, *Strategic Management Journal* 9: 577–590.

8. B. O'Brian, 1993, Tired of airline losses, AMR pushes for its bid to diversify business, *Wall Street Journal*, February 18, A1.

9. R. V. Whitworth, 1993, The role of shareholders in corporate governance, in *Proceedings of the 1993 Emerson Electric Center for Business Ethics Conference*, (Emerson Electric Center: St. Louis University) April, 29–43.

10. R.E. Hoskisson, R.A. Johnson, and D.D. Moesel, 1994, Corporate divestiture intensity in restructuring firms: Effects of governance, strategy, and performance, *Academy of Management Journal*, in press.

11. Hoskisson and Hitt, *Downscoping*.

12. J. R. Wilke, 1992, On the spot: At Digital Equipment Company, Ken Olsen is feeling pressure to produce, *Wall Street Journal*, May 13, A1, A8; Byrne, Executive pay.

13. Hoskisson and Hitt, *Downscoping*.

14. A. Berle and G. Means, 1932, *The Modern Corporation and Private Property* (New York: Macmillan).

15. J. S. Lublin, 1991, More chief executives are being forced-out by tougher boards, *Wall Street Journal*, June 6, A1, A10.

16. M. Roe, 1990, Political and legal restraints on ownership and control of public companies, *Journal of Financial Economics* 27: 7–41.

17. Whitworth, The role of shareholders: 29.

18. K. G. Salwen and J. S. Lublin, 1992, Activist holders: Giant investors flex their muscles more at U.S. corporations, *Wall Street Journal*, April 27, A1, A5.

19. M. J. Roe, 1993, Mutual funds in the board room, *Journal of Applied Corporate Finance* 5, no. 4: 56–61.

20. S. Mieher, 1993, Weak force: Shareholder activism, despite hoopla, leaves most CEOs unscathed, *Wall Street Journal*, May 24, A1.

21. P. Mallette and K. L. Fowler, 1992, Effects of board composition and stock ownership on the adoption of poison pills, *Academy of Management Journal* 35: 1010–1035.

22. S. Mieher, Weak force.

23. T. M. Jones and L. D. Goldberg, 1982, Governing the large corporation: More arguments for public directors, *Academy of Management Review* 7: 603–611.

24. E. S. Herman, 1981, *Corporate Control, Corporate Power* (New York: Cambridge University Press); M. Eisenberg, 1986, *The Structure of the Corporation* (Boston: Little, Brown and Co.).

25. I. F. Kesner, 1988, Director characteristics in committee membership: An investigation of type, occupation, tenure and gender, *Academy of Management Journal* 31: 66–84.

26. B. D. Baysinger and R. E. Hoskisson, 1990, Board composition and strategic control: The effect on corporate strategy, *Academy of Management Review* 15: 72–87.

27. J. B. Treece, 1992, The board revolt: Business as usual won't cut it anymore at a humbled GM, *Business Week,* April 20, 30–34, 36; J. B. Treece, and J. Templeman, 1992, Jack Smith is already on a tear at GM, *Business Week,* May 11, 37.

28. Hoskisson and Hitt, *Downscoping.*

29. B. Bowers, 1994, Shareholder suits beset more small companies, *Wall Street Journal,* March 9, B1–B2.

30. W. Q. Judge, Jr., and C. P. Zeithaml, 1992, Institutional and strategic choice perspectives on board involvement in the strategic decision process, *Academy of Management Journal* 35: 766–794.

31. R. E. Hoskisson, M. A. Hitt, and C. W. L. Hill, 1993, Managerial incentives and investment in R&D in large multiproduct firms, *Organization Science* 4: 325–341.

32. K. A. Merchant, 1989, *Rewarding Results: Motivating Profit Center Managers* (Boston: Harvard Business School Press); J. Eaton and H. Rosen, 1983, Agency, delayed compensation, and the structure of executive remuneration, *Journal of Finance* 38: 1489–1505.

33. J. Kerr, 1985, Diversification strategies and managerial rewards: An empirical study, *Academy of Management Journal* 28: 155–179; N. K. Napier and M. Smith, 1987, Product diversification, performance criteria, and compensation at the corporate manager level, *Strategic Management Journal* 8: 195–201.

34. Salwen and Lublin, Activist holders.

35. O. E. Williamson, 1985, *The Economic Institutions of Capitalism: Firms, Markets and Relational Contracting* (New York: Macmillan Free Press).

36. B. W. Keats and M. A. Hitt, 1988, A causal model of linkages among environmental dimensions, macro organizational characteristics, and performance, *Academy of Management Journal* 31: 570–598.

37. R. E. Hoskisson and M. A. Hitt, 1988, Strategic control and relative R&D investment in large multiproduct firms, *Strategic Management Journal* 9: 605–621.

38. M. A. Hitt, R. E. Hoskisson, and R. D. Ireland, 1990, Mergers and acquisitions and managerial commitment to innovation in M-form firms, *Strategic Management Journal* 11 (Special Issue): 29–47.

39. J. P. Walsh and J. K. Seward, 1990, On the efficiency of internal and external corporate control mechanisms, *Academy of Management Review* 15: 421–458.

40. L. Scism, 1994, Wisconsin Pension Fund is activist hawk, *Wall Street Journal,* March 18, C1, C16.

41. R. A. Lambert and D. F. Larcker, 1985, Golden parachutes, executive compensation, and shareholder wealth: A review of the evidence, *Journal of Accounting and Economics* 7: 179–203.

42. J. P. Walsh and R. Kosnik, 1993, Corporate raiders and their disciplinary role in the market for corporate control, *Academy of Management Journal* 36: 671–700.

43. C. C. Markides, 1992, Consequences of corporate refocusing: Ex ante evidence, *Academy of Management Journal* 35: 398–412.

44. S. D. Prowse, 1990, Institutional investment patterns and corporate financial behavior in the United States and Japan, *Journal of Financial Economics* 27: 43–66.

45. P. Sheard, 1989, The main bank system and corporate monitoring and control in Japan, *Journal of Economic Behavior and Organization* 11: 399–422.

46. M. C. Lauenstein, 1993, Strategic planning in Japan, in S. Durlabhji and N. E. Marks (eds.), *Japanese Business* (Albany: State University of New York Press), 239–252.

47. R. K. Sah, 1991, Fallibility in human organizations and political systems, *Journal of Economic Perspectives* 5, no. 2: 67–88.

48. E. Mansfield, 1988, Industrial R&D in Japan and the United States: A comparative study, *American Economic Review* 78, no. 2: 223–228.

49. R. Stodgill, 1994, Red ink, wiretaps and death threats, *Business Week,* February 21, 80–82.

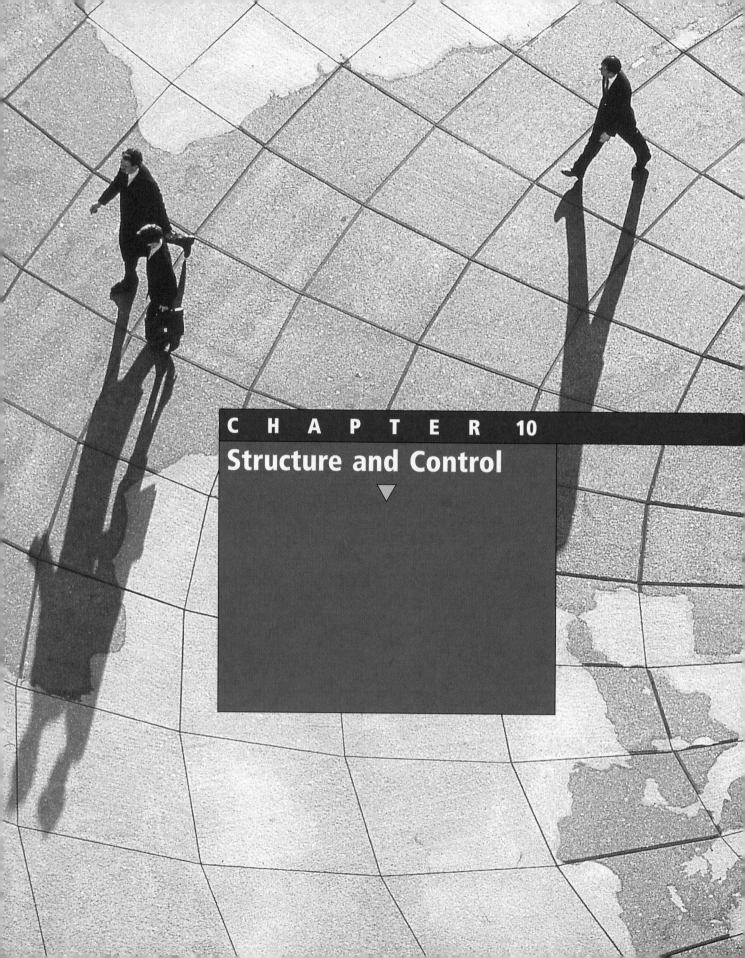

CHAPTER 10
Structure and Control

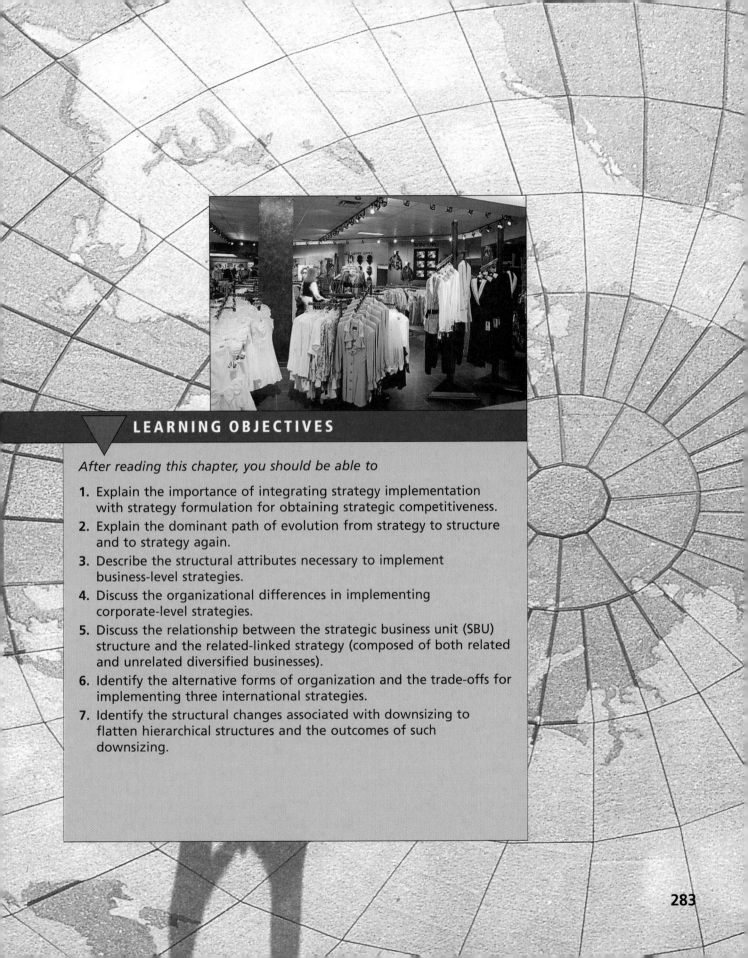

*After reading this chapter, you should be able to*

1. Explain the importance of integrating strategy implementation with strategy formulation for obtaining strategic competitiveness.

2. Explain the dominant path of evolution from strategy to structure and to strategy again.

3. Describe the structural attributes necessary to implement business-level strategies.

4. Discuss the organizational differences in implementing corporate-level strategies.

5. Discuss the relationship between the strategic business unit (SBU) structure and the related-linked strategy (composed of both related and unrelated diversified businesses).

6. Identify the alternative forms of organization and the trade-offs for implementing three international strategies.

7. Identify the structural changes associated with downsizing to flatten hierarchical structures and the outcomes of such downsizing.

## Sears Restructures Its "Socks and Stocks" Strategy

Sears, Roebuck and Co. abandoned its financial supermarket strategy in the last quarter of 1992. Directors approved a program to spin off Sears's Dean Witter Financial Services Group, most of its Coldwell Banker real estate holdings, and 20 percent of its Allstate Insurance unit. Furthermore, in the first quarter of 1993, Sears closed its catalog business, the original business of the company. Sears now plans to focus on its retailing business (its core business) again, reversing the strategy formulated in 1981. Edward Brennan, the chairman of Sears, is abandoning his dream of developing a financial services supermarket. Sears has steadily lost market share in retailing, dropping from the number one to the number three position, behind discounters Wal-Mart Stores, Inc., and Kmart Corp. In 1992, Moody's Investment Services lowered Sears's credit rating. Some say the announcement to unravel the strategy was made to overcome the credit-rating reduction.

In recent years, many of the separate financial services have done well. The Dean Witter Financial Services Group, including the Discover credit card operation, has been quite successful, contributing as much as 70 percent of Sears's overall profit. Although the Allstate Insurance unit was a drain in 1992 due to the losses associated with Hurricane Andrew, Allstate has been profitable in past years. However, now the retail business must stand alone and, as a consequence, will be pressured to produce.

Why did Sears reverse its decision to diversify and undertake this restructuring? Chairman Brennan enthusiastically diversified business operations, and Sears's senior executives were interested in the new ventures and their potential for synergy. The basic business of Sears's retail stores, however, accounted for half of Sears's overall sales. While Sears expanded in real estate and launched the Discover credit card, managers seemed to be largely ignoring the retail stores. In large, diversified firms, the corporate office often becomes highly separated from the divisional operating units. In this way, corporate officers, not being able to focus on all businesses, lose the strategic understanding of the basic businesses and the competitive dynamics in their markets. A number of specialty businesses began to capture significant market shares. For example, Toys-R-Us and Kids-R-Us grabbed a large portion of the toy and children's clothing market. The Limited, Inc., and other chains did the same in apparel, as did several shoe chains. At the same time, Wal-Mart and Kmart undercut the Sears strategy by developing a stronger cost leadership position. Thus, Sears was hurt by both low-cost leaders and firms with strong focused differentiation strategies.

The basic problem is that Sears lost strategic control of its core business and thus managed its retailing business by financial control. Resource allocation to its diversified growth businesses requiring money, such as Sears's Discover card, left inadequate funds for its core retailing business. The operation of Sears's multidivisional structure created a problem whereby managers spent too much time and energy dealing with the diversified businesses and lost operational understanding of its core business. Now Sears will be playing catch-up with its new structure. The managers, although pressured, are hopeful that they will be able to regain Sears's number one position and return to profitability in the retail industry. ▲

Although the Sears diversification strategy may have been poorly conceived, implementation is critical even for an appropriate strategy to create above-average profits. Many strategies have failed because structure, control systems, and rewards were not adequately designed to implement them. Also, a strategy that is formulated and implemented may affect future strategy and structure. Thus, the intended strategy affects structural implementation, and, in turn, structure affects strategy. For instance, a diversification strategy requires the multidivisional structure for effective implementation. This structure, as explained below, facilitates management of diversified operations. In turn, the multidivisional structure facilitates further diversification. In some instances, the multidivisional structure has fostered overdiversification, and overdiversification may lead to below-average profits. To avoid this type of problem, strategy formulation and strategy implementation should be integrated. Far too often the separation of formulation from implementation leads to frequent reformulation and restructuring. The relationship between formulation and implementation is shown by a horizontal arrow in Figure 1–1 (see Chapter 1).

Hewlett Packard (HP) had its origin in the electrical instruments business, as represented by its digital voltmeters and ultimately its highly successful calculator line. These businesses required a technically sophisticated sales force, usually marketing to engineers who used its sophisticated instruments. The organization structure that evolved was highly decentralized, with each instrument having a separate business division and a specialized sales force. However, when HP decided to manufacture and market computers, a different structure became necessary. Selling computers requires significant coordination. To be profitable in computers requires that the separate divisions marketing computers, workstations (often with microcomputers), peripherals (e.g., printers, disk drives), communication networks, and software work together to sell an integrated computer system. Each of the separate products needs to be compatible with other system components. By the mid 1980s, approximately 50 percent of HP's sales was in computers and 50 percent in independent instruments. The computer businesses required an organization that centrally coordinated the fabrication and selling of computer systems. The instruments businesses continued to use independent, decentralized divisions. To instrument managers, the organization required by the computer business threatened the "HP Way," where decentralization is equated with divisional entrepre-

*Shown in this picture is HP's Apollo 9000 VRX workstation family. Applications for this product include computer-aided software engineering, electrical and mechanical engineering, technical publishing, scientific visualization and industrial design. Computers remain an important product line for Hewlett-Packard.*

neurship. The computer business, following this system, had difficulty in coordinating separate division operations. The conflict between these two approaches led to frequent attempts to make organizational adjustments and restructure.[1] Although HP continues to be successful, its top executives did not realize ahead of time the organizational difficulties of entering the computer business. To avoid such problems, firms must not only formulate strategies based on internal capabilities and environmental opportunities, but also consider implementation difficulties that may arise and design effective implementation approaches that match their strategy.

This chapter addresses implementation issues of structure and control. The first section emphasizes the evolution of strategic growth, followed by structural adjustment, which, in turn, affects future strategy formulation. For instance, Sears diversified into financial services from retail sales. In so doing, it developed a multidivisional structure, wherein each division was represented by a different service business. However, the corporate managers were not in full strategic control of each of these businesses. That is, they did not fully understand nor comprehend each business equally. As the example indicates, they spent considerable time examining new ventures in which their understanding was not as great as in retail sales. In the implementation of their diversification strategy, they neglected the core business, retail sales. Because implementation was poorly executed, Sears had to restructure and refocus its business portfolio. Thus, the evolutionary sequence of strategy, structure, strategy occurred and is explored more fully in this chapter.

The second section discusses the means for implementing business-level strategy. The dominant structures, control systems, and structural characteristics associated with these strategies are explained.

Corporate-level strategy implementation is then discussed. The transition from the functional to the multidivisional structure is highlighted in this section. This major change evolved from the implementation of the innovative multidivisional structures at DuPont and General Motors in the 1920s. Specific variations of the multidivisional structure are described in relationship to implementing the related and unrelated strategies. Related diversification requires cooperation, whereas the unrelated strategy requires resource allocation among divisions on a competitive basis.

Implementing an international strategy is discussed next. A discussion of the structure and control characteristics of the multidomestic strategy is followed by a similar discussion of the global strategy. The transnational strategy, emphasizing both local responsiveness and global integration, is examined next, along with the variations in structure necessary to implement this strategy.

Finally, recent patterns of restructuring—in particular, patterns of downsizing and downscoping—are explained. The strategies resulting from this restructuring activity, along with structure, control, and reward patterns, are discussed. Implications of this activity for strategic competitiveness are explored.

## Evolutionary Patterns of Strategy and Structure Implementation

All organizations require some form of organization structure to implement and manage the strategy formulated. As firms change their strategies and grow in sales and diversification, often new structural arrangements are necessary. Figure 10–1 depicts two types of growth patterns explained next.

**FIGURE 10-1** Evolutionary Growth Patterns of Strategy and Structure Implementation

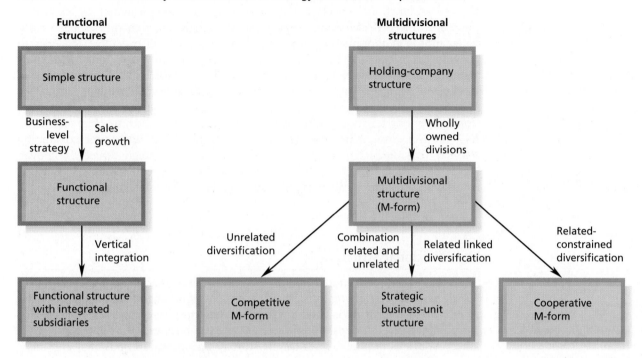

## Simple Structure

A small firm following a single-business strategy requires a **simple structure,** defined as an organizational form in which the owner-manager makes all major decisions directly and monitors all activities, while the staff merely serve as an extension of the manager's supervisory authority. This structure involves little specialization of tasks, few rules, and limited formalization. Information systems are unsophisticated, and owner-managers are directly involved in all phases of day-to-day operations.

Typically organizations using the simple structure are quite small. Such establishments might involve fast food restaurants, repair businesses, and other specialized enterprises that have limited complexity. The simple structure provides a great deal of flexibility. Communication is fast and direct, and new products can be introduced to the market (commercialized) quickly. Because of these characteristics, there are few of the coordination problems that are more common in larger firms. Thus, small firms with simple structures, in some instances, may be able to outmaneuver larger, more complex firms and earn above-average profits.

▲ A **simple structure** is an organization form in which the owner-manager makes all major decisions directly and monitors all activities, while the staff merely serves as an extension of the manager's supervisory authority.

## Functional Structure

As a firm grows larger, information-processing demands put pressure on owner-managers in the simple structure, who may not have sufficient skills to manage the specialized tasks required in production, accounting, marketing, and finance. The **functional structure** consists of a chief executive officer and limited corporate staff, with functional line managers in dominant functions such as production,

▲ The **functional structure** consists of a chief executive officer and limited corporate staff, with functional line managers in dominant functions such as production, accounting, marketing, R&D, engineering, and human resources.

accounting, marketing, R&D, engineering, and human resources. This structure allows for functional specialization, but is centrally coordinated by the chief executive officer. Because differences in functional orientation may impede communication and coordination, the central task of the chief executive officer is to integrate decisions and actions of the overall business across functions.[2] This organizational form also facilitates career paths and professional development in specialized functional areas. However, such specialists may develop a myopic perspective and language that overly focuses on a particular functional orientation. Conflicts among functional-area managers are often referred to the chief executive. As a consequence, chief executives may be inundated with time-consuming conflicts that distract their attention from important strategic issues. Moreover, functional-area managers may become isolated from overall company strategic issues and lose sight of the organization's overall mission and objectives.

## Multidivisional Structure

▲ The **multidivisional (M-form) structure** is composed of operating divisions where each division represents a separate business and the top corporate officer delegates responsibilities for day-to-day operations and business-unit strategy to the division manager; by such delegation, the corporate office becomes responsible for formulating and implementing overall corporate strategy and manages the divisions through strategic and financial controls.

▲ **Strategic control** refers to the operational understanding by corporate officers of the strategies being implemented within the firm's separate business units.

▲ **Financial control** refers to the ability of corporate officers to manage the cash flow of the divisions through budgets and an emphasis on profits from distinct businesses.

The chief executive's limited ability to process information and the isolation of functional managers are often cited as reasons for the change to the multidivisional structure. The **multidivisional (M-form) structure** is composed of operating divisions where each division represents a separate business and the top corporate officer delegates responsibilities for day-to-day operations and business-unit strategy to the division manager; by such delegation, the corporate office becomes responsible for formulating and implementing overall corporate strategy and manages the divisions through strategic and financial controls. **Strategic control** refers to the operational understanding by corporate officers of the strategies being implemented within the firm's separate business units. As diversification increases, strategic control can be strained.[3] **Financial control** refers to the ability of corporate officers to manage the cash flow of the divisions through budgets and an emphasis on profits from distinct businesses. As business units implement joint strategies, such as related-constrained diversification, financial control can be difficult. It may become difficult to attribute financial performance to one particular division. Therefore, extensive product diversification and implementation of joint business-unit strategic initiatives can compromise the internal controls of the multidivisional structure.[4]

Alfred Chandler, a noted business historian, examined the strategies and structures of large American firms.[5] He documented the development of the M-form structure as an innovative response to problems of coordination and control that arose in the functional structures of firms such as DuPont and General Motors in the 1920s. Firms such as DuPont began to grow significantly through diversified products. As a result, the functional departments, such as sales and production, found it difficult to deal with several distinct product lines and markets. These functional departments encountered difficulty in coordinating the conflicting priorities among different products. Because these firms were organized around functions and not businesses, and thus costs were not allocated to each product, it was difficult for top officers to identify the performance contribution of each separate product line. Top executives therefore experienced loss of control, making it difficult to optimally allocate the corporation's financial resources. Because of the coordination problems described above, top officers became heavily involved in solving short-run administrative problems and often neglected long-run strategic issues.

At General Motors, these problems were confronted by Alfred Sloan, Jr., who proposed to reorganize the firm on a divisional basis. He conceptualized separate divisions, each representing a distinct business, that would be self-contained and have their own functional hierarchies. Division managers were delegated day-to-day operating responsibilities. Sloan proposed the development of a corporate office with a small corporate staff. This general office would be responsible for determining long-term strategic direction for the corporation and for exercising overall financial control of the semi-autonomous divisions. Although each division made strategic decisions for its own business, these decisions could be superseded by the corporate office, which was looking at the interest of the whole corporation and not of one particular business segment. Also, the Sloan proposal offered market segmentation with Chevrolet, the low-priced product, up to Cadillac, the high-quality, high-priced product. This was the first time that market segmentation had been introduced into the automobile industry. It is an example of strong integration between strategy formulation and implementation.

The functional and multidivisional structures represent two different types. Each is required for separate strategies, and, thus, they represent alternative frames of reference for managers within those strategy and structural types. Functional structures perform well in managing single- and dominant-business strategies. However, once a firm becomes more diversified in either product or market, the multidivisional structure facilitates control, and, if not implemented, performance may suffer. Once the multidivisional (M-form) structure is in place, the firm is significantly changed, and it has the potential for more diversification. Research has shown that when the M-form is implemented, diversification often increases.[6] Of this structure, Oliver Williamson wrote that "The most significant organizational innovation of the 20th century was the development in the 1920s of the multidivisional structure."[7]

Figure 10–2 illustrates the occurrence of different diversification strategies in the U.S. economy. As this graph indicates, there are many single and dominant businesses. However, there are few firms that are in between the dominant-business and the diversified-business categories, suggesting that there is a chasm between the functional and the M-form structures. The evolutionary process described above suggests that two main structural types have evolved: the functional and the multidivisional structures. Figure 10–1, however, indicates that as other diversification strategies are implemented (e.g., related and unrelated strategies), additional structural types evolve.

As noted in Figure 10–2, there are a large number of single and dominant firms. While many of these firms are relatively small, a few are large. Wm. Wrigley Co. is one of the large and well-known firms that has maintained a strategic focus on one product line, with little diversification. It has almost 50 percent of the $2.4 billion U.S. chewing gum market and has had the largest share of this market since its inception.[8] Nondiversified firms, like Wrigley, use a functional structure, as described earlier. However, there are other, more fine-grained characteristics of their structures that are matched to the firm's strategy (e.g., low cost, differentiation). We examine next the structural characteristics that best fit specific business-level strategies.

**FIGURE 10–2**  Distribution of Large Firms Focusing on the Dominant-Business and Diversified-Business Approaches: Implications for Functional M-Form Structures

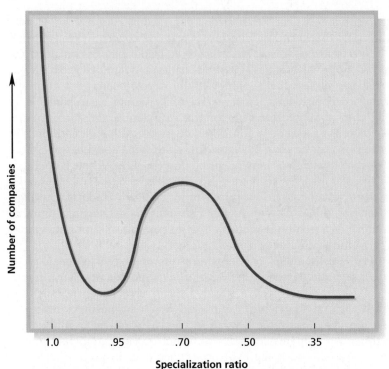

**Specialization ratio**
The specialization ratio of dominant business sales divided by total firm sales. Generally, the lower this ratio, the greater the level of diversification.

SOURCE: R. Reed, 1991, Bimodality in diversification: An efficiency and effectiveness rationale, *Managerial and Decision Economics 12: 59.*

## Implementing Business-Level Strategies: Structure and Controls

Organization structures are designed to allow effective use of resources, capabilities and core competencies to accomplish the strategic intent and mission. Structures help managers balance conflicting organizational forces. An organization usually has a division of labor and task specialization. However, specialized functions also need to be integrated to ensure effectiveness. Among business-level strategies, there are certain organizational attributes required to effectively implement specific strategies.

### Implementing Cost Leadership

To obtain competitive advantage with a cost leadership strategy, a firm must obtain optimal efficiency from its operations. Usually this strategic option includes producing a standardized product at a low cost per unit. Firms that are successful with this strategy often are large relative to competitors. These firms require access to resources that their competitors may not have. With these resources, they seek to establish economies of scale and incrementally increase efficient production capacities. Market share is important, especially when market demand increases with price concessions. It is difficult to create a sustainable competitive advantage with this strategy because many firms have implemented efficient forms of flexible manufacturing.

To implement the cost leadership strategy, there are distinct organizational requirements: a strong need for both specialization and centralization. **Specialization** is the extent to which tasks and roles required by a firm's technology can be divided into homogeneous subgroups. The basis for these subgroups is usually found in functional areas, products produced, or clients served. **Centralization** is the extent to which authority for decision making is retained at higher managerial levels in the organization. In the past, many of these centralized structures were tall (many layers of managers). However, with the significant restructuring occurring, many of these structures are becoming flatter as management layers are eliminated. Because the cost leadership strategy often emphasizes relatively standardized products manufactured in large quantities, a firm implementing this strategy may have substantial formalization. **Formalization** is the extent to which formal rules and procedures govern activities in an organization. The cost leadership strategy, then, requires strong specialization of tasks, centralization, and often formalization to allow for the emergence of a low-cost culture.

The structural characteristics of implementing the cost leadership strategy are illustrated in the functional structure shown in Figure 10–3. Typically firms implementing the cost leadership strategy focus on the production function. For production efficiency, production process engineering is emphasized, rather than

▲ **Specialization** is the extent to which tasks and roles required by a firm's technology can be divided into homogeneous subgroups.

▲ **Centralization** is the extent to which authority for decision making is retained at higher managerial levels in the organization.

▲ **Formalization** is the extent to which formal rules and procedures govern activities in an organization.

**FIGURE 10–3**  **Functional Structure for Implementation of a Cost Leadership Strategy**

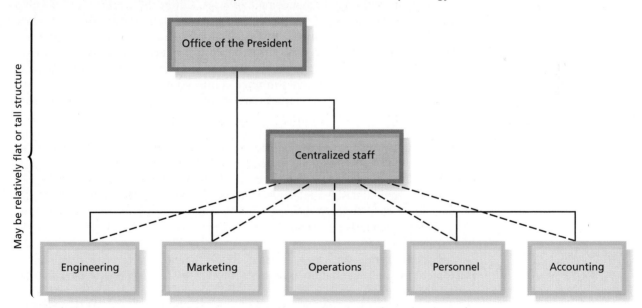

Notes:
• Operations is the main function
• Process engineering is emphasized, rather than new product R&D
• Relatively large centralized staff coordinates functions
• Formalized procedures allow for emergence of a low-cost culture
• Overall structure is mechanical; job roles are very structured

new product research and development. Frequent changes due to the introduction of new products often reduce efficiency in the production process. Because procedures are formalized, the overall structure is mechanical, resulting in highly structured job roles. These characteristics allow maintenance of the tight controls required to achieve the low-cost position.[9]

Quaker State Corp.'s position in motor oil and lubricants provides a case where managers decided to change the organization in a way that reduced the firm's competitive advantage. It attempted to implement a differentiation strategy without an appropriate structure, and it failed, as discussed in the next Strategic Focus. Thus, it shows that organization structure is extremely important in maintaining a strong market share position, especially in a commodity business such as motor oil.

## Implementing the Differentiation Strategy

A firm that decides to offer unique products is pursuing a differentiation strategy. As can be seen by the Quaker State example, great care needs to be taken when implementing a differentiation strategy if the firm wants to earn above-average profits. A firm seeking to differentiate particularly needs support from its manufacturing and marketing functions. These two functions allow for modification of existing production and quick response to changes in volume and demand. Efficient, flexible manufacturing systems are particularly valuable. If a firm is able to create the perception of product uniqueness among consumers, low costs become less crucial, but may still be important. The firm, however, usually has to bear higher costs for more frequent product modifications, packaging changes, and additional distribution and advertising expenses. Often the research and development function is important if differentiation is created by introducing new products or frequent product modifications. Implementation of a differentiation strategy can be accomplished in large or small firms because product uniqueness is the main distinguishing factor. The demand for unique products or services needs to be relatively unresponsive to changes in price. Thus, commodity-type products, such as motor oil, may not be as appropriate as other products for a differentiation strategy.

Decentralization of decision-making authority is paramount in implementing a differentiation strategy. To capitalize on emerging trends in key markets, the firm often must make rapid changes based on information received. This requires a relatively flat organizational structure. If there are multiple product offerings, managers should be designated to oversee specific products and new product lines. Because of quick changes, a differentiation strategy may suffer if the organization has extensive formalization. The overall structure needs to be flexible; job roles are less structured.

The marketing and new product R&D functions often are dominant in implementing a differentiation strategy. Although these functions, especially marketing, have decentralized components, each should have centralized staffs that work closely together. Integration of the two allows for more effective new product development and market introduction. To maintain control of new product development, a differentiator may have a centralized research facility. Also, to maintain efficiency, the manufacturing facility may need to be partially centralized. This allows integration of new products quickly, as well as maintaining the highest possible efficiency.[10] Alternatively, many firms are now using decentralized cross-functional teams composed of representatives from marketing, R&D, and manufac-

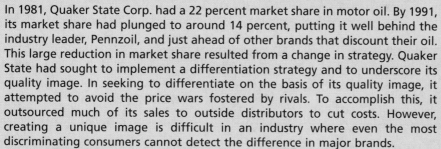

## Quaker State Slips in Pursuing Its Cost Leadership Strategy

In 1981, Quaker State Corp. had a 22 percent market share in motor oil. By 1991, its market share had plunged to around 14 percent, putting it well behind the industry leader, Pennzoil, and just ahead of other brands that discount their oil. This large reduction in market share resulted from a change in strategy. Quaker State had sought to implement a differentiation strategy and to underscore its quality image. In seeking to differentiate on the basis of its quality image, it attempted to avoid the price wars fostered by rivals. To accomplish this, it outsourced much of its sales to outside distributors to cut costs. However, creating a unique image is difficult in an industry where even the most discriminating consumers cannot detect the difference in major brands.

Jack W. Corn, chief executive, also sought to achieve higher margins without offering special deals and discounts. But at a Kmart auto center four miles south of Quaker State's corporate headquarters in Oil City, Pennsylvania, an auto manager indicated that many customers were changing to Quaker State's rivals, Pennzoil and Valvoline. This particular Kmart auto center had cut its use of Quaker State oil by 50 percent in the past year. Nationwide Auto Parts, a Columbus, Ohio, chain with 300 stores that buy millions of gallons of motor oil each year, slashed its orders of Quaker State by 50 percent in 1990 alone. Although the manager of Nationwide indicated that most oil companies provided lucrative advertising programs and incentives, Quaker State had not given distributors or retailers the opportunity to add value to their customers.

Critics suggest that Corn turned over sales responsibility to distributors who no longer had loyalty to the brand, despite Quaker's incentive programs. One estimate suggested that the direct sales force controlled by the company had been cut in half. A host of vice presidents and national and regional managers were fired, quit, or were demoted. Corn reduced costs by slashing the sales force. This eliminated much of the company's ability to win and service customers.

Without an appropriate organization in place, Quaker State lost its ability to control costs and its image. By 1991, it had lost much of its stock value and had not been able to cover its dividend in four years. Some workers hoped for a takeover in order to improve the situation.

turing to integrate these functions for new product design, manufacturing, and introduction to the market.[11] The characteristics of a functional structure implementing a differentiation strategy are shown in Figure 10–4.

## Implementing the Integrated Low Cost/Differentiation Strategy

Some firms, as Chapter 4 indicates, may seek to implement an integrated low cost/differentiation strategy. Firms that attempt this strategy are at risk of becoming stuck in the middle and may not be successful. Problems arise because implementation is difficult. Low cost normally requires an emphasis on production and manufacturing process engineering, with infrequent product changes. Differentiation requires an emphasis on marketing and new product R&D, with relatively

**FIGURE 10–4   Functional Structure for Implementation of a Differentiation Strategy**

*Notes:*
- Marketing is the main function for keeping track of new product ideas
- New product R&D is emphasized
- Most decentralized, but R&D and marketing may have centralized staffs that work closely with each other
- Formalization is limited so that new product ideas can emerge easily and change is more easily accomplished
- Overall structure is organic; job roles are less structured

frequent product changes to maintain perceptions of product uniqueness. These different functional emphases make implementation difficult. However, with the use of flexible manufacturing systems and horizontal coordination, such as cross-functional teams, more firms are effectively implementing an integrated low cost/differentiation strategy.[12] In addition, some firms have been able to do both by focusing on low-cost products, while creating other unique features, such as quality service. This has been the strategy of Crown, Cork and Seal in manufacturing metal cans that contain hard-to-hold products, such as beer and soft drinks.

Although the dual emphasis may be difficult to implement through structural characteristics alone, it may be possible by creating an appropriate organization culture. Crown, Cork and Seal functionally focuses on differentiation, but has established a low-cost culture where all employees seek to do things in low-cost ways. Also, cultures are difficult to imitate and thus may help create a sustainable competitive advantage.[13]

## Implementing a Focus Strategy

A firm implementing a focus strategy seeks to fulfill the needs of a particular buyer. Although the previous business-level strategies may require a functional structure, the focus strategy may be better managed with the simple structure. If the firm is large enough, however, it may also use the functional structure. The focus differentiation strategy revolves around smaller and more flexible production and possibly R&D functions. This strategy is best suited for making and responding to rapid technological advances and may also require support from the marketing function. It is important that the firm establish low levels of formalization to

*Successful implementation of the low cost/differentiation strategy requires coordination across a firm's functions (e.g., manufacturing, marketing, finance, etc.). Cross-functional teams, such as the one shown in this picture, include people from different parts of a firm. Working together, the team shown here tries to carefully coordinate all work necessary to produce and distribute its firm's products.*

respond quickly to marketplace changes. Depending on size and geographic distribution, it may be centralized or decentralized. For example, because of its small size and focus, Ryka is centralized.

Many firms that follow a focus strategy and target a market niche are relatively young and small, such as Ryka Inc. Ryka, founded by Sheri Poe, markets aerobic shoes for women.[14] However, others are medium-sized, such as Pier 1 Imports, or large for the industry, such as McKinsey & Co. in consulting services. Pier 1 provides unique home furnishings, imported from many countries. It follows a focused differentiation strategy. It now plans to have 250 stores operating outside of the United States and Canada by the year 2000. This will be no easy task because Pier 1 has succeeded in the U.S. market, but may have to change its product mix considerably to handle different cultures. This will require significant decentralization to allow local-unit autonomy.[15] Alternatively, executives at McKinsey & Co., a large U.S.-based management consulting firm, argue that strategic management is the firm's niche. However, critics suggest that the firm's significant growth has resulted in a bureaucratic organization that produces homogenized advice. As such, the structure is producing a standardized product/service that may not support its lofty image over time.[16]

Thus, we conclude that focus strategies are not easy to implement and that structure can have considerable effect on their success. As firms diversify, the simple and the functional structures are no longer effective. Next we discuss the type of structures necessary to implement strategies of greater diversification.

## Implementing Corporate-Level Strategies

Once a firm diversifies away from a dominant-product business strategy, implementation becomes more complex. As the earlier section described, evolution to a diversification strategy usually requires the implementation of the multidivisional structure. Multidivisional structures are organized around products or geographic markets. Each division has its own departments with specialists organized into their functional specialties. Divisions are relatively autonomous and governed by a central corporate office. The percentage of diversified firms in the *Fortune* 500 has increased from 30 percent in 1950 to approximately 75 percent in the late 1980s. Accordingly, the multidivisional structure has increased during the same period from under 20 percent to approximately 90 percent during the 1980s.[17]

Although the general reasons for adopting the M-form structure were described earlier, this section discusses how three variations of the M-form structure are required to implement different diversification strategies: related-constrained diversification, mixed related and unrelated diversification (called related-linked), and unrelated diversification. Business-level strategies can be quite successful, but when firms become more diversified, the functional structure has difficulties facilitating management and control of multiple businesses. When a firm operates in multiple related businesses, the potential for conflict among functional managers is high. More of the top management team's time and energy is required to resolve conflicts among functional executives. As conflict resolution demands more operational focus, it encroaches on the time for long-term strategy formulation. Thus, a functionally organized firm may overemphasize functional expertise to the detriment of the separate businesses in which the firm engages. These and other problems led to the implementation of the multidivisional structure, which became highly popular in the 1960s, 1970s, and 1980s. Variants of the M-form structure are necessary to implement each corporate-level strategy.

## Implementing the Related-Constrained Strategy

Linkages among business units are important in a related-constrained diversification strategy. Because of these linkages, top executives must encourage appropriate cooperation among divisions. Cooperation among these divisions is necessary to realize economies of scope or to facilitate the transferring of skills.[18] Some centralization is needed to achieve coordination between divisions. This coordination is managed by a central administrative office (headquarters) of the organization. This centralization is needed to ensure coordination between related divisions or between divisions that are vertically integrated. In this situation, capital investment decisions are more centralized in firms with a high degree of interdivision integration.[19]

Besides centralization, a number of structural integration mechanisms are necessary to foster the linkages between businesses in a related-constrained firm. As integrating mechanisms become more complex to foster the coordination between divisions, they are increasingly costly. Direct contact between division managers may be one way to foster coordination. As a secondary consideration, liaison roles may be designated in each division so that division managers do not spend as much time facilitating coordination. Temporary teams or task forces may also be formed around projects and may require multiple individuals from the separate divisions to facilitate coordination. Formal integration departments (facilitate coordination between divisions) might be used if these teams or task forces are needed on a continuing basis. Ultimately a **matrix organization** may evolve, where there is a dual structure combining both functional specialization and business products or projects specialization.[20]

▲ A **matrix organization** is a dual structure combining both functional specialization and business products or projects specialization.

To coordinate strategy between separate divisions requires guidelines and management of joint products. NEC Corp. has developed a unifying theme called C&C (computers and communications) for its businesses.[21] All businesses in NEC Corp. foster joint businesses between computers and communications, increasingly important in the office products market. This requires cross-business-unit committees and meetings, along with synergy champions that pursue joint projects between divisions. These teams and synergy champions are coordinated by the central office.

Human resource practices in firms implementing a related-constrained strategy are important. For example, job rotation among business units to foster coordination is common. However, this requires emphasis on promotion from within, and cooperation is facilitated by the way a manager is trained. Joint training between the corporate and the business units is also helpful to ensure that corporate objectives are instilled in both the business unit and the corporate levels. Joint business incentives that emphasize cooperation also facilitate implementation. Such incentives, however, often require the subjective evaluation of strategies and outcomes by corporate managers when cooperation is required. Because cooperation also includes the need to resolve conflict that may arise between sharing divisions, the tone of executive authority may be different than in other organizations with stronger vertical hierarchy. Thus, there is more authority sharing in a related-constrained firm, which necessitates frequent interaction and cooperation between division executives.

The **cooperative form,** a structure that employs a high number of integration devices and horizontal human resource practices to foster cooperation, may be the organization of the future.[22] It emphasizes horizontal organization more than either the functional structure or the other varieties of the M-form structure. As the Strategic Focus on corporate America's organizational revolution indicates, many firms are looking to these structural processes to prepare for the future, replacing vertical hierarchies emphasized in the past. The cooperative form is illustrated in Figure 10–5.

Reengineering the corporation into a horizontal organization as recommended by Michael Hammer or through the action steps promoted by McKinsey & Co. is not an easy process. A number of firms have attempted to reengineer their processes, but have failed to achieve the desired results. A recent examination of 100 companies that have attempted to reengineer pointed to critical success issues. In particular, reengineering efforts must have sufficient breadth and depth to be successful. Such efforts must include all units that are interdependent with the focal unit (breadth). Firms also must reengineer all key processes, roles, and values (depth). Even with sufficient breadth and depth, reengineering projects must have active involvement from top management if they are to succeed.[23] Unfortunately, some firms try to minimize disruption by choosing quick-fix approaches. However, such quick fixes rarely succeed.[24]

Achieving the cooperation described in the Strategic Focus is not without significant costs. As implied by the numerous horizontal procedures for coordination, information processing must increase dramatically to implement a related-constrained strategy. But from the business-level (division) executive's point of view, there may not be a compelling reason for such coordination. Cooperation between business units also implies a loss of division manager autonomy. In addition, coordination may create unequal benefits from synergy for each division manager. Decentralization, from the corporate point of view, often is seen as a means to induce division managers to take risks. Centralization may compromise increased risk taking, and corporate managers may not want to usurp the authority they have decentralized to a division manager.

▲ The **cooperative form** is a structure that employs a high number of integration devices and horizontal human resource practices to foster cooperation.

## Organizational Revolution for Corporate America

The predicted revolution in corporate America suggests that hierarchies of the future will be horizontal, rather than vertical. The CEOs of AT&T, Corning, and Xerox, among others, suggest that companies may need to be structured dramatically differently in the future. Eastman Kodak, Hallmark Cards, and General Electric are searching for a more effectively designed organization to compete in the twenty-first century. Although the organization of the future is not yet conceptually formalized, trends provide hints about what is emerging. First, the term "high-involvement work place" symbolizes the emergence of self-managing teams and other devices for empowering employees. Although self-managing teams were once novelties perceived as a participation fad, they have now been shown to produce strong efficiency gains, improve product quality, and increase job satisfaction. A second trend that has fostered horizontal organization is improved materials-handling processes. For instance, in Bayamon, outside San Juan, Puerto Rico, a new General Electric factory has been built. The plant makes arrestors, which are surge protectors that guard power stations and transmission lines against lightning strikes. The facility employs 172 hourly workers and just 15 salaried "advisors," plus manager R. Clayton Crum. It has just three layers of employees, no supervisors, and no staff. A comparable conventional plant would have about twice as many salaried people. Every hourly worker is on a team with about 10 others. The team meets weekly to plan and schedule the work of team members. The radical idea of horizontal organization is that the principal job of management is facilitating learning, rather than control.

The third driver of this revolution is information technology. Because of the microcomputer innovations, knowledge, accountability, and results can be distributed rapidly to most locations in the organization. Thus, workers do not need feedback from their bosses. It is readily available on their microcomputers. The current reorganization trend has been described as "reengineering" or "process innovation." Michael Hammer defines reengineering as the fundamental analysis and radical redesign of business processes in order to achieve dramatic improvements in critical measures of performance.

McKinsey & Co. has a 10-point blueprint for creating a horizontal structure: (1) Organize primarily around process, not task; (2) flatten the hierarchy by minimizing subdivision of processes; (3) give senior leaders charge of processes and process performance; (4) link performance objectives and evaluation of all activities to customer satisfaction; (5) make teams, not individuals, the focus of organization performance and design; (6) combine managerial and nonmanagerial activities as often as possible; (7) emphasize that each employee should develop several competencies; (8) inform and train people on a just-in-time, need-to-perform basis; (9) maximize buyer and customer contact with everyone in the organization; and (10) reward individual skill development and team performance instead of individual performance alone.

The horizontal organization will make companies more fluid. The growing number of strategic alliances supports this notion. Companies like Wal-Mart Stores and Procter & Gamble (P&G) have integrated their order and fulfillment process. When a Wal-Mart cash register indicates a box of Tide has been sold, a P&G warehouse receives an order to ship a new box of Tide to replace the one just bought. Thus, this type of horizontal organization may be increasingly important.

**FIGURE 10–5  Cooperative Form of the Multidivisional Structure for Implementation of a Related-Constrained Strategy**

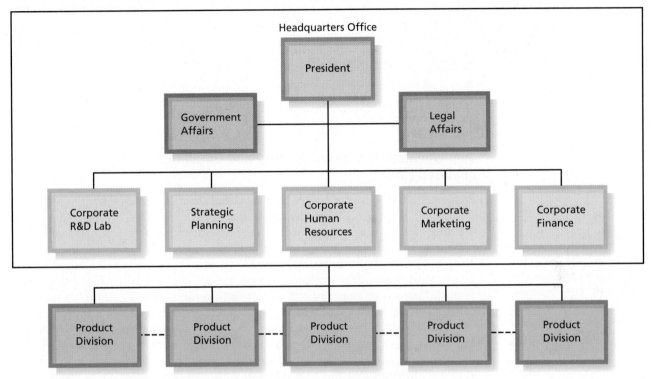

Notes:
- Structural integration devices create tight linkages among all divisions
- Corporate office emphasizes centralized strategic planning, human resources, and marketing to foster cooperation between divisions
- R&D is likely to be centralized
- Rewards are subjective and tend to emphasize overall corporate performance in addition to divisional performance
- Culture emphasizes cooperative sharing

Because cooperation requires subjective evaluation, equity in rewards becomes an issue. Division managers may perceive that their reward is unjust relative to the reward of another business-unit manager because cooperation between business units may be perceived as creating more cost savings for one division than another. Thus, corporate managers must be concerned with the perceptions and problems associated with subjective performance evaluations. These are not minor costs and have led many firms to eliminate divisional linkages, thus moving away from team cooperation between divisions because implementation to achieve economies of scope is costly. Alternatively, a firm might find team decision making so costly that it centralizes decisions that need to be made quickly.

Honda signaled that democracy may have gone too far. Honda's president, Nobuhiko Kawamoto, indicated, "We'd get the people from research, sales, and production together and everyone would say 'not this' and 'not that.'" Honda has found that being a larger organization creates difficulties, especially in trying to maintain a democratic cooperative culture. With more people on new product teams, agreement does not come easily. To reach agreement more quickly, the management team sought to increase centralization of decision making. Honda may have done too much team decision making.[25]

In the late 1970s and early 1980s, the corporate office of General Motors implemented a cost-sharing program among its divisions. Divisions shared the same basic car bodies and production lines. During this period of time, General Motors overemphasized its sharing strategies and in the process relinquished much of its product distinction between divisions. Top officers in the firm implemented a strategy where the products of each division began to imitate one another. One outcome of this process was the blurring of products between the Buick, Oldsmobile, and Pontiac divisions. This led to cannibalization of each division's sales by the other similar divisions. General Motors has now consolidated these separate product divisions.[26]

## Implementing the Mixed Related and Unrelated Strategy (Related-Linked)

▲ The **strategic business unit (SBU) structure** consists of at least three levels, with the top level, corporate headquarters; the next level, SBU groups; and, finally, divisions grouped by relatedness within each SBU.

Implementing the mixed related and unrelated (related-linked) strategy (defined in Chapter 6) requires a different structural form than the related-constrained strategy. Because the mixed strategy seeks to implement both related and unrelated divisions, the strategic business unit structure is needed for organizing its businesses. The **strategic business unit (SBU) structure** consists of at least three levels, with the top level, corporate headquarters; the next level, SBU groups; and, finally, divisions grouped by relatedness within each SBU. The firm organizes its portfolio of businesses into those related to one another within an SBU group and those unrelated in other SBU groups. Thus, divisions within groups are related, but groups are largely unrelated to each other. Large diversified corporations, such as Westinghouse and General Electric, have used this structure to organize their many different divisions. Within the SBU structure, divisions with similar products or technologies can be organized to achieve synergy. Each SBU becomes a profit center and is controlled by corporate headquarters. The SBU structure is illustrated in Figure 10–6. Such a structure provides a major benefit for the corporate headquarters staff in strategic planning and operational control. It allows individual divisions to react more quickly to environmental changes that would have previously required attention by the corporate office, but now can be handled by the SBU group executives.

With the addition of another hierarchical level, the top corporate officers are further removed from individual divisions and may be less aware of significant strategic changes that could affect the performance of the firm or a substantive part (e.g., SBU). Also, information coming from lower in the organization has more potential for distortion, as it has to go through an additional level to get to top management.

Often portfolio matrices, such as prescribed by the Boston Consulting Group, explained in Chapter 6, are implemented within SBU structures. However, implementation of the portfolio technique may lead to conflicting objectives between the SBU group and the headquarters office. For example, from the corporate perspective at General Electric, an appliance SBU might be considered a cash cow, while the jet engine SBU might be considered a star. The corporate office would want to allocate cash from the appliance division to fund the growth opportunities in the jet engine division. However, this may conflict with the SBU's own priority for using its cash. The appliance division may have its own star business and want to use its cash internally. For instance, toasters, a cash cow, may fund new businesses in electronic appliances, such as compact disc players. These problems

**FIGURE 10-6** SBU Form of the Multidivisional Structure for Implementation of a
Related-Linked Strategy

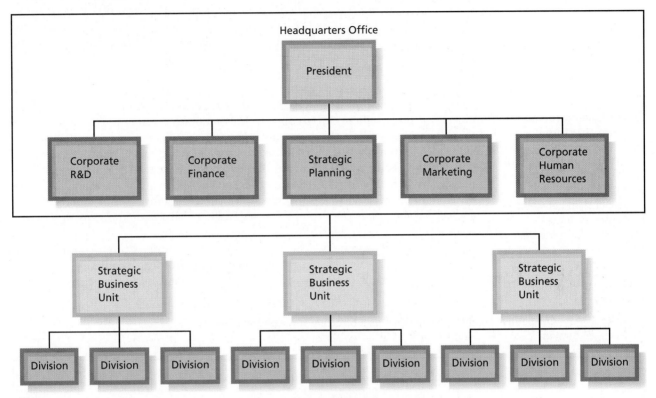

*Notes:*
- Structural integration among divisions within SBUs, but independence among SBUs
- Strategic planning may be the most prominent function in headquarters to manage the strategic planning approval process of SBUs for the president
- Each SBU may have its own budget for staff to foster immigration
- Corporate headquarters staff serve as consultants to SBUs and divisions, rather than having direct input to product strategy as in the cooperative form

may cause political conflict between the corporate office and the SBU group officers. Resolution of such conflict often requires political compromise that may delimit optimal strategy and resource allocation.[27] This type of difficulty led Jack Welch to restructure General Electric into fewer businesses and fewer hierarchical levels.

## Implementing the Unrelated Diversification Strategy

An unrelated firm can create value through efficient internal capital allocation or restructuring, buying, and selling businesses.[28] However, the appropriate organization for this strategy is different from those used when implementing a related diversification strategy.[29] The structure implemented in this situation is the **competitive form,** where the structure and controls emphasize competition between separate (usually unrelated) divisions for corporate capital. To realize benefits from efficient allocation of resources, divisions must have separate, identifiable profit performance and must be held accountable for such performance.

▲ The **competitive form** is where the structure and controls emphasize competition between separate (usually unrelated) divisions for corporate capital.

As such, the general office should have an arms-length relationship and not intervene in divisional affairs except to audit operations and discipline managers whose divisions perform poorly. In this situation, the general office sets rate-of-return targets and monitors the outcomes of divisional performance. It allocates cash flow on a competitive basis, rather than automatically returning cash to the division that produced it. The corporate culture in this case is explicitly competitive, rather than cooperative.[30]

The competitive form of the multidivisional structure is illustrated in Figure 10–7. The competitive culture created may also be found in related-linked diversified firms, where SBUs compete for corporate resources. The difference is that all business units in the competitive M-form are separate and no synergy exists as it does within SBUs in related-linked firms. Strategic business units at Hanson (an unrelated competitive-form firm discussed in Chapter 6) are in place only to reduce the span of control of the top officers and not to achieve synergy between divisions. Keeping divisions separate allows the corporate office flexibility to buy and sell businesses as opportunities arise. Frequent sales would disrupt synergistic relationships between divisions in a cooperative structure.

The holding-company structure used by some firms is often confused with the competitive structure described above. The **holding-company (H-form) structure** is a set of businesses that are often unrelated to each other, but it has

▲ The **holding-company (H-form) structure** is a set of businesses that are often unrelated to each other, but it has neither the system of controls fostering interconnection between businesses as in the cooperative form nor the strong internal resource allocation system as in the competitive form.

**FIGURE 10–7   Competitive Form of the Multidivisional Structure for Implementation of an Unrelated Strategy**

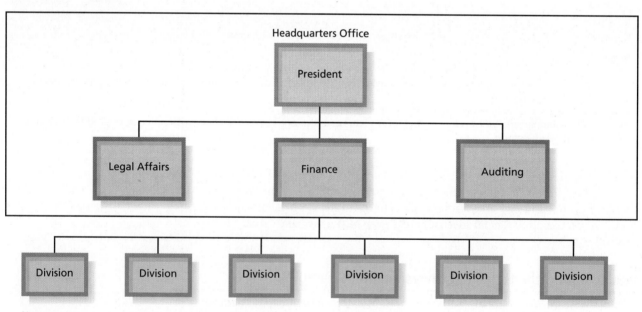

Notes:
- Corporate headquarters has small staff
- Finance and auditing are the most prominent functions in the headquarters to manage cash flow and assure accuracy of performance data coming from divisions
- Legal affairs function becomes important when acquiring and divesting assets
- Divisions are independent and separate for financial evaluation purposes
- Divisions retain strategic control, but cash is managed by corporate office
- Divisions compete for corporate resources

neither the system of controls fostering interconnection between businesses as in the cooperative form nor the strong internal resource allocation system as in the competitive form. The difference is that resources are not allocated between independent divisions in the H-form structure. The holding company manages a portfolio of businesses, but does not have complete control of cash flow, as in the unrelated, competitive M-form structure. Also, the competitive and the cooperative structures are not compatible. One of the differences between the cooperative and the competitive structures is that the competitive structure has a small corporate office. The cooperative form requires a larger corporate office to manage the interdependencies (ensure coordination). The small corporate staff in the competitive structure is possible because divisions are independent.

In summary, the above discussion described three main forms of organization, each associated with a different strategy. Table 10–1 illustrates the various characteristics of these three structures. As Table 10–1 indicates, there are differences in the degree of centralization, the focus of performance appraisal, the horizontal structures (integrating mechanisms), and the incentive compensation schemes necessary to implement these specific strategies. The most centralized and most costly organizational form is the cooperative structure. The least centralized, with the lowest bureaucratic costs, is the competitive structure. The SBU structure requires partial centralization and involves some of the mechanisms necessary to implement the relatedness between divisions. Also, the divisional incentive compensation awards are allocated according to both SBU and corporate performance. In the competitive structure, the most important criterion is divisional perfor-

### TABLE 10–1

#### Attributes of the Structures Necessary to Implement the Related-Constrained, Mixed Related and Unrelated, and Unrelated Strategies

| Structural Characteristics | Overall Structural Form | | |
|---|---|---|---|
| | Cooperative M-Form (Related-Constrained Strategy*) | SBU M-Form (Mixed Related and Unrelated Strategy*) | Competitive M-Form (Unrelated Strategy*) |
| Centralization of operation | Centralized at corporate office | Partially centralized (in SBUs) | Decentralized to division |
| Use of integrating mechanisms | Extensive | Moderate | Nonexistent |
| Divisional performance appraisal | Emphasizes subjective criteria | Uses a mixture of subjective and objective criteria | Emphasizes objective (financial or ROI) criteria |
| Divisional incentive compensation | Linked to overall corporate performance | Mixed linkage to corporate, SBU and divisional performance | Linked to divisional performance |

*Strategy implemented with structural form

mance. Although each of these structures has been successful when used with the appropriate strategy, increasingly the SBU form is being changed to either the cooperative or the competitive M-form. Research suggests that diversified firms are creating specialization among diversified businesses, and thus the mixed strategy implemented with the SBU multidivisional structure is being replaced by one of the more specialized (cooperative or competitive) forms.[31] This has been evidenced at Westinghouse, TRW, and many other firms, although some, such as General Electric, are continuing to try to do both.[32]

## Evolutionary Patterns of International Strategy and Structure

The previous discussion on implementing strategy and structure primarily pertains to domestic firms that pursue strategies such as domestic cost leadership (business level) or domestic product diversification (corporate level). However, strategies may be more complex, and so is the implementation. Many firms have diversified internationally and not only sell, but also manufacture their products worldwide.[33] Figure 10–8 depicts two types of growth patterns among internationally diversified firms. The first pattern illustrates firms with domestic functional structures that

**FIGURE 10–8**   **Evolution of International Strategy and Structure**

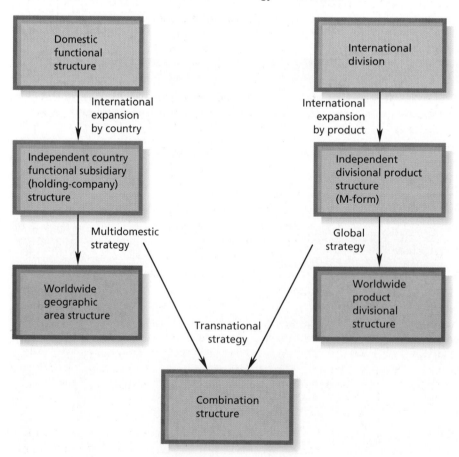

expand internationally by creating international functional subsidiaries in a holding-company structure. These functionally independent subsidiaries are usually decentralized from the headquarters of the domestic business. Historically, the multidomestic strategy developed from trying to duplicate successful domestic strategies in other countries where the resources and abilities were available to create products similar to those of the original domestic business. For example, Anderson-Clayton Corp. sought, in the 1930s, to replicate its vertically integrated operation producing cotton products in such countries as Mexico, Brazil, Argentina, and Egypt. Anderson-Clayton Corp. bought land and built cotton gins and seed mills that produced cotton fiber for textiles and cotton seed oil and animal feed. At one point, through these independent country subsidiary operations, Anderson-Clayton controlled 18 percent of the world's market share in cotton products.

Businesses employing a multidomestic strategy often attempt to isolate themselves from global competitive forces by establishing protected market positions or by competing in industry segments that are most affected by differences between the local countries. Firms employing multidomestic strategies often use worldwide geographic area structures. A **worldwide geographic area structure** is an organizational form in which national interests dominate and that facilitates management's ability to satisfy local or cultural differences.[34]

The global strategy emphasizes international scale and scope economies. In this strategy, competitive forces are perceived to span national boundaries. The business is linked across countries such that each function is sourced to the national market that has the lowest economies of scale or scope for developing the resources necessary to manufacture the product. This form of coordination is illustrated by how Procter & Gamble (P&G) manages its worldwide research and development function. Increased worldwide coordination of its R&D centers in the United States, Japan, and Europe allowed P&G to develop "world" liquid detergents that incorporated the best innovations from each location. The **worldwide product divisional structure** emphasizes managing the interdependencies created by pursuing a global strategy; extensive coordination of functional activities within global business units is used to implement this strategy.[35]

The final strategy in this evolutionary process is the transnational strategy. As firms compete in local markets, they seek not only to obtain national country-specific advantages by emphasizing local differences, but also to obtain the economies of scale and scope found in firms pursuing the global strategy. This is referred to as the transnational strategy. A **combination structure,** emphasizing both geographic and product structures, is used to implement the transnational strategy.[36] The fit between the multidomestic strategy and the worldwide geographic area structure and the global strategy and the worldwide product divisional structure is readily apparent. However, when a firm seeks to implement both the multidomestic and the global strategies simultaneously through a combination structure, the appropriate mechanisms for integrating the two structures are less clear. Some firms have developed a matrix structure, although it has not been as successful as other combination structures. The mixed structure, where some parts of the firm are organized along worldwide product divisions and other parts are organized along worldwide geographic areas, also has been used. Other firms have sought to implement the transnational strategy through a combination of structure and corporate culture. In this approach, the corporation seeks to instill in each employee a cultural orientation emphasizing the attributes of both strategies (multidomestic and global) through a socialization process. This has been labeled

▲ A **worldwide geographic area structure** is an organizational form in which national interests dominate and that facilitates management's ability to satisfy local or cultural differences.

▲ The **worldwide product divisional structure** emphasizes managing the interdependencies created by pursuing a global strategy; extensive coordination of functional activities within global business units is used to implement this strategy.

▲ A **combination structure,** emphasizing both geographic and product structures, is used to implement the transnational strategy.

the "matrix of the mind."[37] Because simultaneously implementing the two strategies composing the transnational strategy has been difficult, firms have sought to overcome the conflicting structural arrangements through cultural controls and socialization.

## Implementing International Strategies

### Implementing the Multidomestic Strategy

It has been argued previously that centralization of decision-making authority is a primary means of establishing coordination. Centralization can have the same outcomes in domestic and multinational corporations. Implementing the multidomestic strategy requires decentralization to specific country settings to differentiate approaches to each specific country market. Because pursuing a multidomestic strategy requires little coordination between different country markets, there is no need for integrating mechanisms among divisions in the worldwide geographic area structure. Also, because there is little need for integration across business units, formalization is low.

The coordination between units is often informal. The multinational corporations started in European countries exemplify this structure. This type of structure often was developed originally by friends and family members of the main business who were sent as expatriates into foreign countries to develop the independent country subsidiary. The relationship to corporate headquarters by divisions took place through informal communication among "family members."[38] Because each European country has a distinct culture, the multidomestic strategy and the associated worldwide geographic area structure were a natural outgrowth of the multicultural atmosphere. This structure is illustrated in Figure 10–9. Some U.S. firms, such as Bausch & Lomb, have also been successful in pursuing the multidomestic strategy. In particular, decentralization to local markets has allowed the firm to develop successful products adapted to the local cultures and markets, as indicated in the Strategic Focus on Bausch & Lomb.

The main pitfall of the multidomestic strategy and worldwide geographic area structure combination is the inability to create global efficiency. As the emphasis on lower-cost products has increased in international markets, the need for pursuing worldwide economies of scale and scope has increased. These changes have increased the use of the global strategy, which requires much more functional coordination and integration.

### Implementing the Global Strategy

Different from the multidomestic strategy, the global strategy requires more formal coordination, multiple integrating mechanisms, and stronger formalization to ensure the cooperation and coordination necessary. Bureaucratic costs increase with the coordination, integration, and formalization necessary with this strategy.

To implement the global strategy, centralization of decision-making authority is required. The **worldwide product divisional structure** centralizes decision-making authority in the worldwide division headquarters and establishes effective coordination and joint problem solving among disparate divisional subunits.[39] Integrating mechanisms also create effective coordination through mutual adjust-

**FIGURE 10–9**  **Worldwide Geographic Area Structure for Implementation of a Multidomestic Strategy**

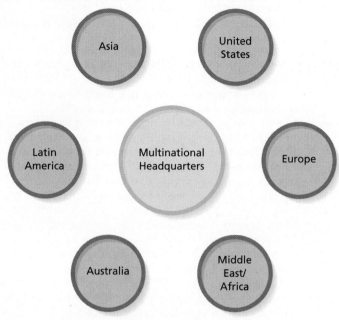

*Notes:*
- Shaded perimeter circles indicate decentralization of operations
- Emphasis is on differentiation by local demand to fit an area or country culture
- Corporate headquarters coordinates financial resources among independent subsidiaries
- The organization is like a decentralized federation

ment in personal interactions. Such integrating mechanisms include direct contact between managers, liaison roles between departments, temporary task forces or permanent teams, and integrating roles.[40] As managers make personal sacrifices in taking cross-country transfers, they are socialized in the philosophy of managing an integrated strategy through a worldwide product divisional structure. A shared vision of the firm's strategy and structure is developed through standardized policies and procedures (formalization) that facilitate implementation of the worldwide product divisional structure. Figure 10–10 illustrates the worldwide product divisional structure.

## Implementing the Transnational Strategy

Because of conflicting requirements to implement the transnational strategy, specific attributes of the structure are difficult to identify. The organization of the transnational must be centralized and decentralized, integrated and nonintegrated, and formalized and nonformalized. Thus, many firms have tried a number of different structural arrangements to implement the transnational strategy. The most popular is a variant of the combination structure called a network organization. In a network organization informal relationships develop between important managers where the performance of the whole organization takes precedence over the performance of any single part (e.g. division).[41] A network may evolve within a single firm, as in ABB (next Strategic Focus) or between firms as in a Japanese Keiretsu.

## STRATEGIC FOCUS

### Implementing the Multidomestic Strategy at Bausch & Lomb

Bausch & Lomb has been successful in pursuing the multidomestic strategy. Its international sales increased 25 percent from 1984 through 1992. While operating margins in its international business have more than doubled, Bausch & Lomb's key to success has been empowering local managers to develop their strategic goals and foster advantage and nuances in local markets.

In Japan, Bausch & Lomb was not successful in its attempts to market rigid gas-permeable contact lens through ophthalmologists, as it did in the United States. Japan insisted on a surface that goes well beyond clinical requirements. Rather than battling this demand, the company built a new plant in Korea in 1988 and developed the manufacturing process that met the desired requirements. By 1991, Bausch & Lomb had 11 percent of the Japanese market for those lenses.

It has also had to adapt its highly successful Ray-Ban sunglasses throughout the world. In Ray-Ban, Bausch & Lomb found that it had a marketable and recognizable brand throughout the world. In Europe, Ray-Bans tend to be flashier, more avant-garde, and costlier than in the United States. In Asia, the company redesigned them to suit the Asian face, and sales took off. The firm is now seeking to develop market positions in China and India for this product. In China, it is also seeking to develop a very low cost contact lens and to earn profits on a high volume of sales. China now ranks only behind the United States and Japan in unit sales of Bausch & Lomb's contact lenses.

Bausch & Lomb attributes its success to decentralization of authority to its local managers, allowing them to differentiate the product to meet specific market requirements.

A salient attribute for a transnational strategy is that of corporate cultural controls. Although many firms have sought to implement the transnational strategy, it has been very difficult to do in practice. Most firms end up emphasizing a global or multidomestic strategy, with a few aspects of the transnational strategy added where the firm has expertise or administrative heritage, as is the case of European multinational firms that are better at managing the multidomestic strategy.[42] Alternatively, Japanese multinational firms have been able to compete well with a global strategy, especially because their core competence is usually in manufacturing technology. With this expertise, Japanese firms have been able to expand and compete effectively when the global strategy is required. However, the Japanese have not been as effective with differentiation on a country-by-country basis. Their approach has been highly centralized and has provided a strong competitive advantage in industries moving toward a global strategy and its associated structure. As regionalization approaches reality in Europe and in North America (with the passage of NAFTA), however, the Japanese must more effectively deal with market differences in each region. This will be more difficult for them because of their centralized approach.[43]

A firm implementing the transnational strategy through structure and a distinctive corporate culture may be able to garner an advantage in the current environment because few firms will be able to achieve an effective fit. Thus, the transnational structure may be more in the "minds of theorists" than in the ability

**FIGURE 10–10** **Worldwide Product Divisional Structure for Implementation of a Global Strategy**

*Notes:*
• Shaded headquarters circle indicates centralization to coordinate information flows among worldwide products
• Corporate headquarters uses many intercoordination devices to facilitate global economies of scale and scope
• Corporate headquarters also allocates financial resources in a cooperative way
• The organization is like a centralized federation

of managers to implement. Some firms, such as ABB (a newly created, worldwide diversified competitor in electronics and manufacturing equipment that is larger than Westinghouse), are trying to implement a combination structure. ABB's efforts are described in the Strategic Focus.

ABB's diverse top management team may be a competitive advantage in identifying new international market opportunities. Such diversity may partially substitute for the learning required to enter new markets. However, this diversity represents a challenge to reach agreement on decisions.[44] Only time will tell if the ABB experiment will be successful. Other firms will continue trying to implement the network structure. Some firms may have to adjust their strategies to fit their structural arrangement. The next section discusses this issue.

## The Effect of Structure on Strategy

In the former Soviet Union, all enterprises were run by a highly centralized top-down system. Because of overcentralization, this system became so costly for the overall economy of the Soviet Union that it collapsed. It appears that many U.S. firms have also encountered problems because of excessive bureaucracy. In

## The Transnational Strategy at ABB

ABB, a Swiss-based electrical producer, was created from ASEA, a Swedish engineering group, and Brown Bover, a Swiss competitor in electrical equipment. The merger created an electrical equipment giant that is larger than Westinghouse and that can compete head to head with General Electric. It is a world leader in manufacturing high-speed trains, robotics, and environmental control equipment. It is a multinational without a national identity, although it has a mailing address in Zurich, Switzerland. Its top 13 managers have no common home-country language; only one is a natural English speaker, but ABB uses English in its management meetings. Although a European company, which usually approaches markets independently through decentralization, ABB has sought to integrate its operations throughout Europe. Its chief executive officer, Percy Barnevik, believes the best strategy against American and Japanese competitors is to break free of protected national markets. Furthermore, he feels the U.S. companies that have been bought by ABB were overly focused on the U.S. market. ABB has allowed its acquired U.S. subsidiaries the freedom to focus more on global markets.

ABB seeks to integrate globally and yet cater to local customs. It searches globally for its suppliers, which less internationally minded companies may shun. It recently bought a Polish firm, that had been state-owned, and makes turbines and other power-generation equipment. ABB has also acquired 20 other former state companies in Eastern Europe and the former Soviet Union. Barnevik believes that these countries do not lack technology and a work ethic; it is just a matter of providing pay and incentives and implementing a Western system.

All employees are given both a country manager and a business-sector manager. ABB therefore uses a matrix structure to integrate the two components. Although the matrix has experienced disfavor in U.S. business schools and has been abandoned by many multinational companies, Barnevik uses a loose, decentralized version to manage the many nationalities represented in ABB. ABB executives say the system facilitates interchange of technology and profits. Barnevik wants each of his systems to be run locally with intense local coordination. However, growing European integration may produce a surge of cross-border mergers. ABB is ahead of this wave and may be an example for many firms to facilitate not only decentralization and focus on local markets, but also global integration.

particular, those firms using one of the three types of the M-form structure have been restructuring and reformulating their strategies. Each structure is implemented to solve a strategic problem, but also may sow the seeds of the next strategy and possibly strategic revolution. The large corporations in the United States are becoming much more decentralized. For example, in November 1991, IBM announced it would organize into more autonomous operating units. In December 1991, General Motors announced that it was eliminating 74,000 jobs, closing 21 factories, and encouraging independent projects like the Saturn joint venture.[45] It appears that many of the major U.S. firms are becoming big-company/small-company hybrids. These firms are similar to the competitive M-form structure discussed earlier. Johnson & Johnson, Microsoft, Siemens, and others do not try to manage businesses, but rather provide capital and select the key people to run their separate businesses.

Many others are choosing to downsize their organizations. Similar patterns have been experienced by multinational corporations. For example, Procter & Gamble (P&G) recently indicated that it will lay off 10 percent of its work force.[46] P&G has found that its branded approach has been undercut by generic, lower-priced products. Apparently, the large cooperative structure can become too costly and allow opportunity for competitors to undercut firms that have used this approach. This development has forced many of these large firms to change their strategy. Also, firms with the SBU structure have repositioned themselves either with related-constrained diversification or unrelated diversification (such as Hanson Trust). They were undercut by firms more effective at implementing either related or unrelated diversification. Thus, the mixed strategy implemented with the SBU structure also has led to problems.

Many unrelated diversified firms have restructured to become related-constrained. Thus, many of the one-time conglomerates have become more narrowly scoped firms. Most unrelated diversified firms have not been able to achieve a reasonable return on investment. Each of the structures described in this chapter has weaknesses, given the costs of implementing structure and controls. This has led firms to reshape their strategy to overcome structural problems, suggesting that as managers formulate a strategy, they need to pay careful attention to the structure needed for implementation. When managers do this, a firm may be able to avoid the restructuring (e.g., upscoping and downscoping, upsizing and downsizing) that many firms have been through in the last decade. Therefore, managers must consider implementation requirements when formulating the firm's strategy. Likewise, after implementation, the firm must consider future problems for strategy formulation.

## Summary

- Implementation of business-level strategies usually requires the functional structure. However, each functional structure emphasizes different functions and organizational characteristics. For example, the cost leadership business strategy requires centralization and emphasis on manufacturing and process R&D. Alternatively, differentiation is implemented with decentralization throughout the organization (especially marketing), although certain functions, such as R&D, may require more centralization.

- The focus strategies, used in many small firms, may require a simple organization unless it moves beyond a specific geographic area. The focus strategies can be implemented with either the centralized functional structure for cost leadership or the partially decentralized functional structure for a differentiation strategy.

- The evolution from the functional to the multidivisional structure took place from the 1920s to the early 1970s. The multidivisional structure has evolved into three types: the cooperative M-form, the SBU M-form, and the competitive M-form. These structures are used to implement the related-constrained strategy, the mixed related and unrelated (related-linked) strategy, and the unrelated strategy, respectively.

- The cooperative M-form structure usually has a centralized corporate office and extensive integrating mechanisms and emphasizes subjective criteria in divisional performance evaluation. Divisional incentives are linked to overall corporate performance.

The competitive M-form structure is highly decentralized; integrating mechanisms are nonexistent, and objective financial criteria are used in appraising division manager performance. Incentive compensation is linked specifically to division, rather than corporate, performance.

- The SBU M-form structure has a partially centralized structure, with many functions centralized within the SBU group of divisions. It uses a moderate amount of integration within the SBU group, but not across SBU groups. The corporate office must use a mixture of subjective and objective financial criteria for evaluating group and division manager performance. Often there is negotiation between corporate headquarters and the SBU group managers regarding resource allocation. Divisional incentives are based on a mix of corporate, SBU, and divisional performance criteria.

- The evolution in international strategy and structure has followed patterns similar to the domestic functional and domestic M-form organizations. The functional structure evolved ultimately into a worldwide geographic area structure, used to implement the multidomestic strategy. The worldwide product divisional structure, emphasizing coordination to reduce cost through economies of scale and scope using worldwide resources, is used to implement the global strategy. The transnational strategy has evolved from both the multidomestic and the global strategies. The transnational strategy is implemented by a combination structure including the matrix, mixed geographic and product divisions, and corporate culture.

- The multidomestic strategy, implemented through the worldwide geographic area structure, emphasizes decentralization and locates all functional activities in the country or geographic area. This was illustrated in the Bausch & Lomb example.

- The global strategy is implemented through the worldwide product divisional structure and requires more centralization to coordinate and integrate functional departments and expertise to reduce economies of scale and increase economies of scope. This usually entails transferring knowledge from one department to another to facilitate implementation across geographic areas.

- The transnational strategy emphasizes both the local product differences between countries and geographic areas and the integration of product expertise globally. This strategy and its implementation were illustrated by ABB, a giant electronics equipment manufacturer. The difficulty in implementing this strategy is structural inconsistencies. Implementation therefore emphasizes processes and cultural controls to encourage cooperation among managers. Often the resulting network structure is difficult to implement. If accomplished, however, such a structure may create competitive advantage because few firms are able to effectively implement this strategy.

- Many firms are restructuring, downsizing, and changing their strategy due to problems with implementation. Firms must therefore pay careful attention not only to formulation, but also to implementation. Implementation can affect future strategy formulation. For example, the M-form, once implemented, allows for increased diversification. Increased diversification creates organizational problems of strategic control loss. Strategic control loss requires reformulation of strategy and structure in order to eliminate overdiversification. Firms therefore must concurrently consider formulation and implementation issues to avoid the constant restructuring many large firms experienced in the 1980s and 1990s.

## Review Questions

1. What are the differences in the functional structures required to implement the cost-leadership and the differentiation business-level strategies.

2. What are the problems created in the functional structure by diversification? How does the M-form structure solve these problems in large diversified firms?

3. What are three variants of the M-form structure and the structural and control attributes associated with implementing related-constrained diversification, mixed related and unrelated (related-linked) diversification, and unrelated diversification?

4. Describe the strategies leading to the three global structures: the worldwide geographic area structure, the worldwide product divisional structure, and the combination (e.g. network) structure.

5. Compare the structural characteristics of the worldwide geographic area structure with those of the worldwide product divisional structure.
6. Why does the combination structure creates conflicting

organizational attributes when trying to implement the transnational strategy?
7. How does structure affect strategy formulation?

## Application Discussion Questions

1. Explain why firms seem to go through evolutionary cycles where there is a fit between strategy and structure punctuated with short, revolutionary periods where structure and strategy are reorganized. Provide examples with a few prominent U.S. firms.
2. Compare and contrast the large M-form structures that evolved from the three different geographic areas. For instance, describe why you might expect that U.S. multinational firms that originally had an M-form structure would be different from structures that evolved from Asia (Japan) and Europe. How do the domestic administrative structures developed in these multinational corporations affect their strategies and ways of implementing these strategies?
3. How might the governance structures (e.g., ownership patterns) explained in Chapter 9 relate to both the formulation and the implementation described in this chapter?

4. Why does it seem that large firms have lost their competitive advantage and are being restructured into more flexible, independent units, as described in the last section of this chapter?
5. Examine the popular business press for examples of firms using the functional structure and firms using the M-form structure. Explain the differences in these firms that led to different structures.
6. Select three firms, one each with a domestic, a multidomestic, and a global strategy. Describe the structures employed by each firm.
7. Identify a firm (outside of the example in the chapter) using a transnational strategy. Describe its performance and the reasons for its success or lack thereof.

## Ethics Questions

1. When a firm makes major changes, such as moving from the functional to the M-form structure, what responsibilities does it have to the current employees?
2. Does a firm have special responsibilities to its customers when using a cost leadership or a differentiation strategy, outside of providing a low price or a unique product? Explain.
3. Are there ethical issues with which executives need to grapple in using strategic or financial controls? Explain.
4. Are there ethical issues involved in implementing the cooperative and the competitive M-form structures? Explain.

5. Multidomestic and global strategies imply different approaches to markets. What ethical concerns might surface when firms attempt to market standardized products globally or when they develop different products/approaches for each local market?
6. Are there potential ethical concerns when cultural controls are used? If so, describe them.

## Notes

1. S. K. Yoder, 1991, A 1990 reorganization at Hewlett-Packard already is paying off, *Wall Street Journal,* July 22, A1, A10.
2. P. Lawrence and J. W. Lorsch, 1967, *Organization and Environment* (Boston: Harvard Business School Press).
3. R. E. Hoskisson and M. A. Hitt, 1988, Strategic control and relative R&D investment in large multiproduct firms, *Strategic Management Journal* 9: 605–621.
4. M. A. Hitt, R. E. Hoskisson, and R. D. Ireland, 1990, Mergers and acquisitions and managerial commitment

to innovation in M-form firms, *Strategic Management Journal* 11 (Special Issue): 29–47.

5. A. D. Chandler, 1962, *Strategy and Structure: Chapters in the History of the American Industrial Enterprise* (Cambridge: MIT Press).

6. B. W. Keats and M. A. Hitt, 1988, A causal model of linkages among environmental dimensions, macro organizational characteristics and performance, *Academy of Management Journal* 31: 570–598.

7. O. E. Williamson, 1985, *The Economic Institutions of Capitalism: Firms, Markets and Relational Contracting* (New York: Macmillan Free Press), 279.

8. B. Pulley, 1991, Wrigley is thriving, despite the recession, in a resilient business, *Wall Street Journal,* May 29, A1, A8.

9. V. Govindarajan, 1988, A contingency approach to strategy implementation at the business-unit level: Integrating administrative mechanisms with strategy, *Academy of Management Journal* 31: 828–853.

10. Ibid.

11. M. A. Hitt, R. E. Hoskisson, and R. D. Nixon, 1993, A mid-range theory of interfunctional integration, its antecedents and outcomes, *Journal of Engineering and Technology Management* 10: 161–185.

12. D. Lee, M. A. Hitt, and J. D. Goldhar, 1993, Generic strategies, complementarities and organization design in global manufacturing firms (unpublished working paper, Southern Methodist University).

13. J. B. Barney, 1986, Organization culture: Can it be a source of sustained competitive advantage, *Academy of Management Review* 11: 656–665.

14. R. Stodgill, 1993, What makes Ryka run? Sheri Poe and her story, *Business Week,* June 14, 82–84.

15. S. Anderson and R. Golby, 1993, A Pier 1 in every port? *Business Week,* May 31, 88.

16. J. A. Byrne, 1993, The McKinsey mystique, *Business Week,* September 20, 66–74.

17. R. P. Rumelt, 1974, *Strategy, Structure and Economic Performance* (Boston: Division of Research, Harvard Business School); R. Reed, 1991, Bimodality in diversification: An efficiency and effectiveness rationale, *Managerial and Decision Economics* 12: 57–66.

18. C. W. L. Hill, M. A. Hitt, and R. E. Hoskisson, 1992, Cooperative versus competitive structures in related and unrelated diversified firms, *Organization Science* 3: 501–521.

19. R. W. Ackerman, 1970, Influences of integration and diversity on the investment process, *Administrative Science Quarterly* 15: 341–351.

20. J. R. Galbraith and R. K. Kazanjian, 1986, *Strategy Implementation: Structure, Systems and Process* (St. Paul: West).

21. M. A. Porter, 1985, *Competitive Advantage* (New York: Free Press), 412–413.

22. Hill, Hitt, and Hoskisson, Cooperative versus competitive structures.

23. G. Hall, J. Rosenthal, and J. Wade, 1993, How to make reengineering really work, *Harvard Business Review* 71, (November-December): 119–131.

24. M. A. Hitt and R. D. Ireland, 1987, Peters and Waterman revisited: The unended quest for excellence, *Academy of Management Executive* 1: 91–97.

25. C. Chandler and P. Ingrassia, 1991, Just as U.S. firms try Japanese management, Honda is centralizing, *Wall Street Journal,* April 1, A1, A10.

26. J. M. Schlesinger, 1988, GM seeks revival of Buick and Olds, *Wall Street Journal,* April 12, 37.

27. R. A. Bettis and W. K. Hall, 1983, The business portfolio approach—where it falls down in practice, *Long Range Planning* 12, no. 2: 95–104.

28. R. E. Hoskisson and M. A. Hitt, 1990, Antecedents and performance outcomes of diversification: A review and critique of theoretical perspectives, *Journal of Management* 16: 461–509.

29. C. W. L. Hill and R. E. Hoskisson, 1987, Strategy and structure in the multiproduct firm, *Academy of Management Review* 12: 331–341; R. E. Hoskisson, 1987, Multidivisional structure and performance: The contingency of diversification strategy, *Academy of Management Journal* 30: 625–644.

30. Hill, Hitt, and Hoskisson, Cooperative versus competitive structures.

31. R. E. Hoskisson and R. A. Johnson, 1992, Corporate restructuring and strategic change: Effect on diversification strategy and R&D intensity, *Strategic Management Journal* 13: 625–634.

32. K. W. Elderkin and C. A. Bartlett, 1991, General Electric: Jack Welch's second wave (A), Case #9-391-248 (Boston: Harvard Business School).

33. M. A. Hitt, R. E. Hoskisson, and R. D. Ireland, 1994, A mid-range theory of the interactive effects of international and product diversification on innovation and performance, *Journal of Management,* 20: 297–326.

34. J. D. Daniels, R. A. Pitts, and M. J. Tretter, 1985, Organizing for dual strategies of product diversity and international expansion, *Strategic Management Journal* 6: 223–238.

35. S. R. Gates and W. G. Egelhoff, 1984, Centralization in parent headquarters-subsidiary relationships, *Journal of International Business Studies* 15: 71–92.

36. C. A. Bartlett and S. Ghoshal, 1988, Organizing for worldwide effectiveness: The transnational solution, *California Management Review* 30: 54–74.

37. C. A. Bartlett and S. Ghoshal, 1989, *Managing Across Borders: The Transnational Solution* (Boston: Harvard Business School Press).

38. Bartlett and Ghoshal, *Managing Across Borders.*

39. Bartlett and Ghoshal, *Managing Across Borders.*

40. J. Galbraith, 1973, *Designing Complex Organizations* (Reading, Mass.: Addison-Wesley).

41. S. Ghoshal and C.A. Bartlett, 1990, The multinational corporation as an interorganizational network, *Academy of Management Review*, 15: 603–25.

42. Bartlett and Ghoshal, *Managing Across Borders.*

43. W. C. Kester, 1991, *Japanese Takeovers: The Global Contest for Corporate Control* (Boston: Harvard Business School Press).

44. G. E. Schares, 1993, Percy Barnevik's global crusade, *Business Week* (Special Enterprise Issue), 204–211.

45. B. Dumaine, 1992, Is big still good? *Fortune,* April 20, 50–60.

46. P. Zengerle, 1993, P&G plans to eliminate 13,000 jobs, *Houston Chronicle,* July 16, B1.

# CHAPTER 11
## Strategic Leadership

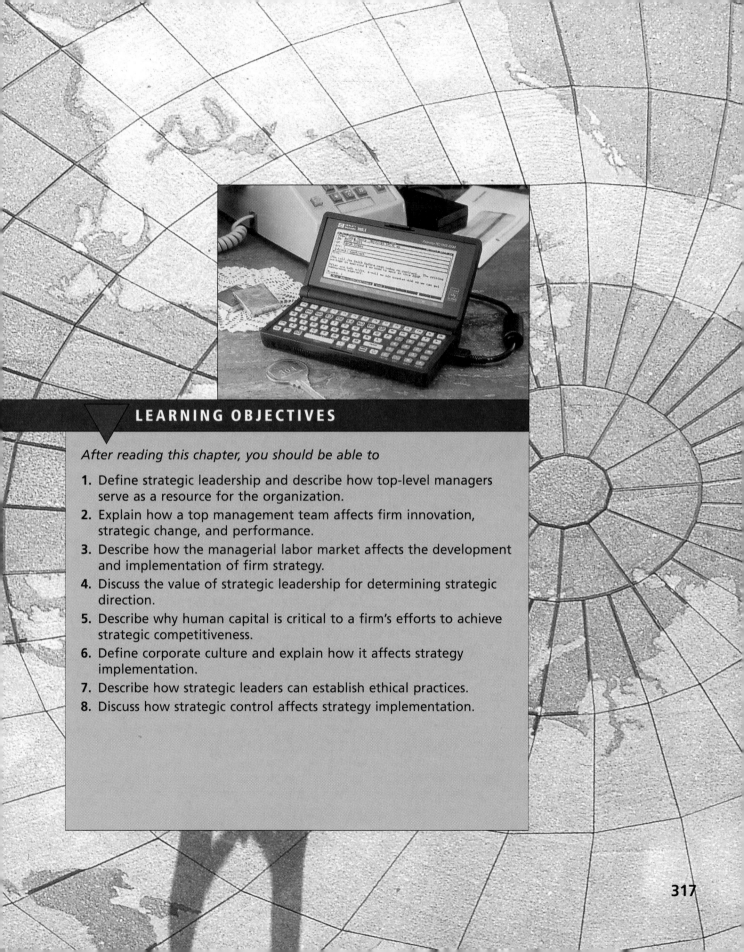

*After reading this chapter, you should be able to*

1. Define strategic leadership and describe how top-level managers serve as a resource for the organization.

2. Explain how a top management team affects firm innovation, strategic change, and performance.

3. Describe how the managerial labor market affects the development and implementation of firm strategy.

4. Discuss the value of strategic leadership for determining strategic direction.

5. Describe why human capital is critical to a firm's efforts to achieve strategic competitiveness.

6. Define corporate culture and explain how it affects strategy implementation.

7. Describe how strategic leaders can establish ethical practices.

8. Discuss how strategic control affects strategy implementation.

### Having the Right Top Management Team

In 1991, Oracle Corp.'s top management team met with upper-level executives from Hewlett Packard (HP). During this meeting, Oracle's CEO, Lawrence Ellison, observed how mature and knowledgeable the HP managers were compared to his own management team. In fact, Ellison commented to John Young, HP's CEO, that his company was managed by adolescents, including himself, compared to HP's managers. These differences in managerial maturity levels, Ellison thought, had something to do with the significant problems his firm has experienced.

In the early 1980s, Ellison adopted an innovative approach to retrieving data, referred to as structured query language. It was an instant commercial success, and IBM (at the top of its industry at the time) chose this approach as its standard, thereby ensuring Oracle's success. However, because of poor management practices, this success was short-lived. As the strategic leader, Ellison overlooked many important nontechnical details in which he was uninterested. The organization continued to grow, but Ellison paid relatively little attention to its development. As a result, a pattern of teamwork did not develop appropriately, and a poor organization culture evolved. One senior vice president referred to it as a culture of greed.

Because of Oracle's short-term success, Ellison largely ignored the chaotic conditions in the organization. However, performance began to suffer. Sales practices left customers complaining about bogus orders. Unethical accounting practices unduly inflated the stated profits (development costs were recorded as a capital investment, rather than as expenses). Programmers failed to meet customer orders, causing customers to rebel. In addition, the major shift from mainframe to smaller microcomputers caught Oracle unprepared. Financial controls were weak, and cash was low, making it necessary for Ellison to raise money quickly to keep the firm operating. He even considered selling part of the company, but eventually accepted a loan from Nippon Steel Corp. in exchange for an ownership position in Oracle's Japanese unit.

When Ellison realized that Oracle's problems were serious and that the root of those problems lay in the management of the organization, he made major changes. He used executive recruiters to help him build a new top management team. He drew on experienced managers from inside and outside the computer industry and delegated some of his authority to James Abrahamson, a retired general and former head of the federal government's Star Wars program. With this new top management team, Oracle's financial performance rebounded significantly. Even when troubled, Oracle had maintained a formidable position in software that manages large electronic databases. By renewing an emphasis on this competitive advantage, Oracle improved its performance. In 1993, Oracle's stock price increased by over 100 percent (as compared to one year earlier). Furthermore, the net income for the third quarter (1993) increased by 74 percent, despite a $25 million charge to settle shareholder lawsuits. Therefore, thanks to strong strategic leadership, Oracle was able to solve a number of significant problems and turn around its performance. ▲

The case of Oracle Corp. shows dramatically the potential impact and importance of top-level managers in a firm's attempts to achieve strategic competitiveness and earn above-average profits. Oracle's initial success was founded on the commercial worth of an innovation developed by Lawrence Ellison, the firm's CEO. For several years, the uniqueness of Oracle's primary product provided competitive advantage for the firm. But poor strategic leadership from top-level managers, coupled with ineffective management practices throughout the company, prevented the firm from sustaining its initial competitive advantage or developing another one. To correct its problems, Ellison restructured his top management team. Experienced managers, from corporations within and outside the computer industry, were a key part of the restructuring effort. Oracle's performance rebounded dramatically and projections for future performance were positive. Demand for the firm's database products was strong. Longer term, Oracle planned to expand its product line to work with pictures and sound. Oracle intended to establish a foothold in the emerging media services field.[1]

The example of Oracle emphasizes the importance of effective strategic leadership, the focus of this chapter. Strategic leadership is required to formulate and implement strategies successfully. Effective strategic actions, in the form of strategy formulation and implementation processes, are a prerequisite to developing a sustainable competitive advantage.[2]

This chapter begins with a definition of strategic leadership and a discussion of its importance. Next we examine top management teams and their effects on the strategy formulation and implementation processes. Included within this section is an analysis of the labor market for top-level managers. Following these discussions are descriptions of six key components of strategic leadership—determining strategic direction, exploiting and maintaining core competencies, developing human capital, sustaining an effective corporate culture, emphasizing ethical practices, and establishing strategic controls.

## Strategic Leadership

**Strategic leadership** entails the ability to anticipate, envision, maintain flexibility, and empower others to create strategic change as necessary.[3] It is multifunctional, largely involves managing through others,[4] and helps organizations cope with change[5] that seems to be increasing exponentially in today's globalized environment.[6] Strategic leadership requires an ability to accommodate and integrate both external and internal conditions and an ability to manage ambiguity and engage in complex information processing.[7] It is through effective strategic leadership that organizations are able to use the strategic management process successfully.

To be effective strategic leaders in the twenty-first century, managers must be willing to change their frames of reference, as appropriate, to deal with rapid changes in the global environment. A **managerial frame of reference** is the set of assumptions, premises, and accepted wisdom that bounds—or frames—a manager's understanding of a firm, the industry in which it competes, and the core competencies it uses in the pursuit of sustainable competitive advantages. For some top-level managers, changing their frame of reference is difficult, even when internal and external conditions indicate that such changes are required. Nonetheless, it is important for strategic leaders to be able to change because some researchers believe that a firm's "long-term competitiveness depends on managers' willingness to challenge continually their managerial frames" and that global

▲ **Strategic leadership** entails the ability to anticipate, envision, maintain flexibility, and empower others to create strategic change as necessary.

▲ A **managerial frame of reference** is the set of assumptions, premises, and accepted wisdom that bounds—or frames—a manager's understanding of a firm, the industry in which it competes, and the core competencies it uses in the pursuit of sustainable competitive advantages.

competition is more than product versus product or company versus company—it is also a case of "mind-set versus mind-set, managerial frame versus managerial frame."[8]

Effective strategic leaders are also willing to make courageous, yet pragmatic, decisions—decisions that are consistent with an organization's internal and external conditions.[9] Recently, for example, a manager at Briggs & Stratton suggested that his employer is thriving because the firm's leaders are willing to make tough decisions that are not always popular.[10] When making tough decisions, effective strategic leaders solicit corrective feedback from their peers and employees about the value of their decisions, often through face-to-face communications.[11]

As these conditions and realities suggest, strategic leadership is an extremely complex but critical form of leadership. Because it is a requirement of organizational success, and because some believe that organizations are relatively underled and overmanaged,[12] today's business schools, especially those offering Master of Business Administration degrees, are challenged to guide and counsel students with respect to strategic leadership and its effective practice.[13]

The primary responsibility for effective strategic leadership practices rests at the top of an organization—in particular, with the CEO. The CEO cannot delegate his or her strategic leadership *responsibility* to the manager of another function, regardless of how important that function may be.[14] However, strategic leadership must be exhibited, to some extent, by all managers throughout the organization in order to formulate and implement business-unit and corporate-level strategies effectively.

As discussed in Chapter 12, the exercise of strategic leadership influences corporate entrepreneurship, an important link to competitiveness in a global economy. In companies competing in the global marketplace, many strategic leaders attempt to champion innovations.[15] The management style of top-level managers can affect the performance level of new corporate ventures. In addition, middle-level managers must build effective coalitions among their peers and subordinates and with upper-level managers to gain their support for innovative new products.[16] Firms with more highly educated top management teams, and with more diverse functional expertise, tend to be more innovative.[17]

## Managers as an Organizational Resource

Top-level managers are an important resource for a firm seeking to develop a sustained competitive advantage. The critical element is having a top management team that has superior managerial skills.[18] Potentially important managerial resources (e.g., knowledge and skills) are shown in Figure 11–1.

Managers in organizations use their discretion when making strategic decisions.[19] As discussed in Chapters 5 and 6, managers make decisions regarding prices for products, their promotion and advertising, and many other competitive actions and competitive responses that are intended to help a firm gain a competitive advantage. Therefore, the way in which managers exercise discretion in determining appropriate strategic actions and in implementing them is critical to a firm's success.[20]

While they determine new strategic initiatives, top-level managers also design and implement the appropriate organizational structure of the firm, along with reward systems. In Chapter 10, we described how organizational structure and

**FIGURE 11–1**  **Managerial Resources**

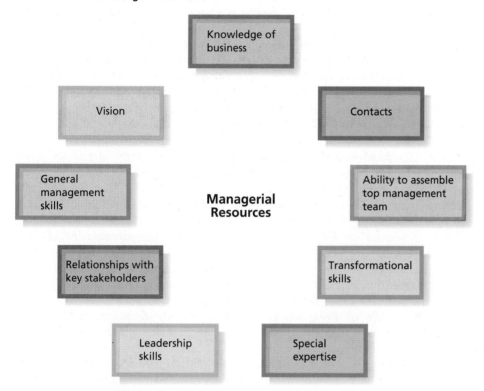

reward systems affect strategic actions taken to implement strategies effectively. Furthermore, top-level managers have a major impact on a firm's culture. Evidence suggests that managers' values are critical in shaping a firm's base cultural values.[21]

Top executives must not only know the right questions to ask subordinates, but also possess the knowledge necessary to evaluate answers to those questions.[22] However, in order for managerial resources to provide a sustained competitive advantage, they must also be valuable, rare, imperfectly imitable, and nonsubstitutable.[23] While many authors have described the characteristics of effective managers, identification of the most effective configuration of top-management-team skills for any one organization remains elusive. Of course, the most important strategic leaders are those at the top, especially the CEO. As described next, Harry C. Stonecipher, chairman and CEO of Sundstrand Corp., appears to exemplify the characteristics of an effective strategic leader—one who, through an ability to help a firm create needed strategic changes, can be a source of sustainable competitive advantage.

In 1987, Stonecipher left a managerial role at General Electric to join Sundstrand, an aerospace company, as an executive vice president. After Sundstrand pleaded guilty and paid $199 million in penalties for fraudulently inflating costs on defense contracts, Stonecipher was installed immediately as the firm's new CEO. One of Stonecipher's first actions was to begin reducing the company's reliance on defense contracts. He also informed both employees and various external stakeholder groups that under his leadership, Sundstrand's personnel would engage in only the highest ethical practices when conducting business.

To reduce the firm's dependence on the defense industry, Stonecipher decided that Sundstrand would no longer bid on fixed-price Pentagon contracts. Because of this decision, Sundstrand's 1993 military sales accounted for only 22 percent of total sales (this sales percentage was 42 percent just five years earlier). The goal is to reduce this volume to 15 percent of total sales by the end of 1995. Stonecipher's objective seems correct, given the significant projected reductions in military contracts and purchases in the 1990s. He believes that the commercial aerospace business, while depressed during the early part of the 1990s, will be a premier business over the next 20 years. Stonecipher bases this projection on the expected 4–6 percent annual growth in air travel. Increased travel may require airlines to purchase new, more technologically sophisticated planes to serve customers efficiently and safely.[24] Because of these projections, coupled with the firm's intended competitive actions, some analysts believed that Sundstrand's returns to investors would be above average during the years of 1996–1998.[25]

Another example of the importance of managerial resources is described in the Strategic Focus on Dell Computer Corporation. The experiences of Dell Computer suggest the importance of a top management team as a source of competitive advantage. To make the changes necessary for Dell to regain its strategic competitiveness, CEO Michael Dell had to form a new top management team with a different set of skills and knowledge bases.

By the middle of 1994, results from the strategic decisions and strategic changes made at Dell Computer were encouraging. Although the firm lost $36 million in 1993, its newly developed, build-to-order system of manufacturing personal computers (PCs) was the envy of the industry in early 1994 (recall from the Strategic Focus that development of its own manufacturing capabilities was a major change undertaken at Dell in 1993). In 1994, writers from a business periodical observed Dell employees physically use the firm's new capability to manufacture a single PC. Only 46 hours and 42 minutes were required to receive an order, custom-build a PC, and deliver it to Mr. Cozzette, the customer. As a competitive response to Dell's new manufacturing capability, Compaq Computer decided to restructure its entire logistics operations. Compaq hoped its actions would allow it to duplicate the marketplace success of Dell through the use of its flexible manufacturing system.[26]

Thus, it seems that Dell's new top management team, acting in concert with other stakeholders (e.g., employees, customers, suppliers), may be contributing positively to the firm's efforts to achieve strategic competitiveness and earn above-average profits. In this respect, it is interesting to note that some analysts feel that the additional experience gained by including industry veterans as members of its top management team "will help Dell more readily manage its growth going forward, as well as improve the development process for new products."[27]

*Dell Computer uses its unique core competencies in manufacturing its products. The firm hopes that these actions will result in the earning of above-average profits.*

▲ The **top management team** is composed of the key managers in the organization who are responsible for formulating and implementing the firm's strategy.

## Top Management Teams

The **top management team** is composed of the key managers in the organization who are responsible for formulating and implementing the firm's strategy. Typically, the top management team includes the officers of the corporation as defined by the title of vice president and above and/or service as an inside member of the board of directors.[28] The top management team shares a collective responsibility to shape a firm's strategic outcomes.[29] While strategy formulation may be driven to some extent by a formal strategic planning process, managers have considerable

## STRATEGIC FOCUS

### A New Top Management Team to Correct Problems at Dell Computer Corporation

A highly successful entrepreneurial venture, Dell Computer eventually rose to number four in the personal computer business. It developed into a $2 billion corporation with 5,600 employees selling personal computers in 95 countries. However, its growth was so dramatic that the management team did not keep up with the organization and it experienced problems. In 1993, Dell had a 48 percent decline in its first quarter earnings and lost another $75.7 million in the second quarter. Its stock price declined by almost 60 percent in the first six months of 1993. There were multiple problems, including a notebook computer product line that failed and poor inventory management systems. Part of the firm's strategic intent, formed under the leadership of the company's founder and CEO, Michael S. Dell, is to develop an organizational structure and capability that can direct Dell toward $10 billion in sales. This is problematic because Dell is short of cash and cannot obtain that from the public equity market, given the weakness of its stock price. Therefore, Michael Dell is relying strongly on a new management team. Beginning late in 1992, he almost completely rebuilt Dell's top management team.

In a period of approximately six months, Michael Dell hired four new top executives and ten other high-level managers from outside the corporation. Three of the new hires were executives with Compaq, a primary competitor. He has also added three new outside board members and, in the short term, planned to hire another dozen individuals for important management positions.

The newly hired executives are redesigning the company's processes, including product development and shipping. The goal is to grow by 50 percent in the short term to a total of $3 billion in sales. However, it is unclear whether the firm will be able to make such a dramatic change in the short term. One of the major changes under way at Dell is the development of its own manufacturing capabilities (previously, much of its manufacturing has been outsourced). In this way, it can better control the cost and quality of its products. It also must build new distribution channels for its products. Its primary distribution outlets have been mass merchandise retailers, but it has been difficult to obtain traditional dealers because Dell has been a primary competitor and "an enemy" of the dealers, in their eyes. One competitor suggested that Dell had not just burned its bridges behind it, but burned bridges in front of it as well. In fact, in July 1994, Dell announced that it was discontinuing its relationship with discount stores because the retail sales were disappointing.

The CEO is counting on the new management team to develop and lead the way for Dell in the future. How this new management team comes together and performs will dictate, to a large degree, Dell's future success.

impact on a firm's primary strategic direction.[30] As a result, the strategic actions formulated and implemented by the top management team may have a critical effect on a firm's strategic competitiveness.

Several studies have found a linkage between top-management-team characteristics and firm performance. Some research has shown the importance of fitting manager characteristics with particular strategies and the effect on firm performance.[31] Much of this research has emphasized the importance of particular functional skills for the implementation of specific types of strategy. For example, expertise in marketing and in research and development have been found important for effective implementation of growth-oriented strategies.[32] More recently, emphasis has been on the configuration of the top management team's skills and its importance for strategic change and firm performance.

**Top Management Team, Firm Performance, and Strategic Change**   The job of top executives is complex and requires a broad knowledge of firm operations, as well as the three key parts of a firm's external environment (general, industry, and competitor). Rarely can one person have all of the knowledge necessary to operate an organization effectively, while dealing simultaneously with all the important external stakeholders. This reality is particularly obvious for those managing large, diversified firms. Therefore, firms try to construct a top management team that has the appropriate knowledge and expertise to operate the internal organization, as well as deal with important external stakeholders. This normally requires a heterogeneous top management team. A **heterogeneous top management team** is composed of individuals with different functional backgrounds, experiences, and education. A more heterogeneous top management team, with varied expertise and knowledge, has the capacity to provide more effective strategic leadership.

▲ A **heterogeneous top management team** is composed of individuals with different functional backgrounds, experiences, and education.

It is also important that the top management team function effectively as a team. The more heterogeneous the team is, the more difficult it is to operate in a cohesive fashion. But, without cohesion, it is difficult for a heterogeneous top management team to operate effectively.[33] It is also important to have substantive expertise on the top management team in the functions and businesses that are considered core to the firm. In a high-technology industry, a firm may need to emphasize research and development and having R&D knowledge and expertise included on the top management team could be vital.[34]

The characteristics of top management teams are related to firm innovation and strategic change. One study found that more heterogeneous top management teams were associated positively with innovation. In addition, top-management-team heterogeneity has been found to be related positively to strategic change. In other words, firms that need to change their strategies are more likely to do so if they have top management teams with diverse backgrounds and expertise. It is possible that the diverse backgrounds of the new top management teams for Oracle Corp. and Dell Computer contributed to those firms' ability to change their strategies. Different sets of expertise allow the top management team to better evaluate different strategies and to change its firm's strategy as needed. A top management team with various areas of expertise is more likely to identify environmental changes (opportunities and threats) or changes within the firm that require a different strategic direction.[35]

**CEO and Top-Management-Team Power**   As suggested in Chapter 9, the board of directors is important for monitoring a firm's direction and for representing stockholders' interests. In fact, higher performance normally is achieved when the board of directors is involved more directly in shaping a firm's strategic direction.[36]

Alternatively, boards of directors may find it difficult to direct the strategic actions of powerful CEOs and top management teams. It is not uncommon for a powerful CEO to appoint a number of outside board members. In addition, the inside board members are also members of the top management team and report to the CEO. Therefore, the CEO may have significant control over the board's actions. Also, the top management team has a much stronger understanding of firm operations and provides information to the board of directors, particularly outside members.[37]

CEOs and top-management-team members can also achieve power in other ways. A CEO that holds the titles of chairman of the board and chief executive officer tends to have more power. In addition, the extent to which executives own stock in the firm often provides them more power. When executives own stock in the firm, it is likely that they will take strategic actions that are in the best interest of stockholders.[38]

Top management teams that have longer tenure—on the team and in the organization—also often have more power. As a result, the team may be able to forestall or avoid board involvement in strategic decisions. On the other hand, the top management team that employs strategic controls is less likely to have board interference in its strategic decisions. As we argued in Chapter 10, firms that employ strategic controls are more likely to be superior performers.[39]

There are potential problems when the board of directors is prevented from providing strategic direction and/or being involved in the strategic decisions of the firm, as shown by the example of Phar-Mor (a retail discount pharmaceuticals company).

At one time, Phar-Mor, Inc., was perceived to be an excellent firm. Unfortunately, some questionable actions were taken by the firm's top executives, who were indicated and accused of tampering with financial statements in order to hide large losses. In 1993, the former president and co-founder of the firm, Michael I. Monus, was indicted on 129 charges of fraud, embezzlement, and tax irregularities. The former chief financial officer, Patrick B. Finn, and former vice president of finance, Jeffrey C. Walley, pleaded guilty on lesser federal charges. The earnings and growth of the firm were inflated by the executives. One of the firm's other co-founders, David S. Shapira, formed a new management team and is reorganizing Phar-Mor under Chapter 11 of the bankruptcy law. Phar-Mor is expected to be a much smaller and less ambitious corporation when the reorganization and restructuring are completed.[40]

The Phar-Mor case represents a situation where top executives abused the power they had and the board of directors did not take appropriate action. Thus, while most strategic actions taken by top management teams are good-faith efforts intended to serve stockholders' best interests, there are examples where this is not the case. To have an effective top management team requires that managers be developed internally or attracted from other firms.

## Managerial Labor Market

Managers care about the performance of their firms because their associations with success and failure could affect their opportunities for better jobs in the managerial labor market. Managers want to avoid situations such as that at Phar-Mor for many reasons, but certainly because they have a negative effect on their future employment opportunities. Accordingly, managers must be concerned about the performance of their superiors and subordinates. Part of their responsibility is to develop those who work for them and to ensure they perform effectively. As a result, evaluation of a manager's performance is based partially on the performance of that manager's subordinates. In addition, a manager is concerned about his or her superior's performance because the manager is partially responsible for it and will be linked to it in the managerial labor market.[41] Thus, effective strategic leaders seek feedback from peers, subordinates, and their "boss."[42]

There are two types of managerial labor markets—internal and external. An **internal labor market** consists of the opportunities for managerial positions within a firm. An **external labor market** is the collection of career opportunities for managers in firms/organizations outside of the one for which they work currently.

▲ An **internal labor market** consists of the opportunities for managerial positions within a firm.

▲ An **external labor market** is the collection of career opportunities for managers in firms/ organizations outside of the one for which they work currently.

In past years, a promotion-from-within policy was emphasized in many organizations, including IBM and General Motors. In these instances, managers were most interested in understanding their organization's internal labor market. With the large number of downsizings, restructurings, and reductions of management layers in many firms (including IBM and General Motors), U.S. managers are becoming increasingly concerned about the external labor market. Interestingly, given the cultural and historical approach to employment in Japan, the internal labor market is the most crucial in Japanese firms, even though there is some evidence that this system may yield competitive disadvantages for Japanese firms competing globally.[43] In general, there has been greater emphasis on the external labor market in the United States; but effective strategic leaders recognize that the internal labor market is also critically important.[44]

The experiences of two firms that selected new CEOs are described in the following Strategic Focus on hiring CEOs from the outside. Michael H. Walsh was hired at Tenneco because of the firm's poor performance and the need to enhance its strategic competitiveness. Alternatively, C. Michael Armstrong was hired as CEO at Hughes Aircraft to change the company's strategic direction. In both cases, the new CEOs were from outside the firm. A number of Hughes' managers resented the hiring of Armstrong because they felt there were attractive inside candidates. However, the board of directors hired Armstrong not because of the lack of inside talent, but because it believed Hughes needed to pursue a different strategic direction.

Evidence reported by researchers may support Armstrong's selection. Recently tenure in an industry was found to be a strong determinant of executives' commitment to the status quo.[45] Recall that prior to his appointment as Hughes CEO, Armstrong spent 31 years at IBM—a company operating in a totally different industry. Thus, Armstrong's lack of knowledge about the aerospace industry may facilitate his efforts to establish a new strategic direction.

As our discussion has shown, there are both internal and external labor markets for upper-level managers and different reasons for using these markets in the hiring of new top executives. Firms that are doing well and that do not need changes in strategic direction more commonly promote individuals from inside the firm into top executive positions. However, in the cases of Tenneco and Hughes, the new leaders helped shape new strategic directions for the firms.

As shown in Figure 11–2, the composition of the top management team and the managerial labor market may interact to affect strategy. For example, when the top management team is homogeneous (e.g., members have similar functional experience and educational backgrounds) and a new CEO is selected from inside the firm, the current strategy is unlikely to change. On the other hand, when a new CEO is selected from outside the firm and the top management team is heterogeneous, there is a high probability of a change in strategy. When the new CEO is from inside the firm, the strategy may not change, but with a heterogeneous top

## STRATEGIC FOCUS

### Hiring A CEO from the Outside

For many reasons, most CEOs are developed and promoted from within an organization. CEOs that come from within are more knowledgeable about firm operations and the objectives of external stakeholders. Because of this knowledge, fewer changes should be necessary when a new CEO is named from within a firm. Furthermore, the selection of a CEO from inside the firm emphasizes the importance of the internal labor market and provides incentives to current managers. Even in light of these positive features, firms sometimes believe it is best that a new CEO be hired from the external labor market. In fact, it is relatively common to hire a new CEO from outside when a company has not been performing well or when the board of directors feels that a change in strategic direction may be necessary. This was the case in the hiring of Michael H. Walsh in 1991 to be Tenneco's CEO. Walsh was hired because he had completed a successful turnaround of Union Pacific Railroad. However, Tenneco appeared to be a more significant challenge.

At the time Walsh assumed the position of CEO, Tenneco was a $13.4 billion firm and ranked 27th among the *Fortune* 500. After reviewing much information, Walsh decided to make major changes to turn around Tenneco's performance and improve its strategic competitiveness. He implemented new quality teams that were designed to reengineer manufacturing processes and to improve productivity and profit margins. He made other, seemingly less significant changes, too. For example, he submitted an article on his changes to the company magazine, but was told by the editor that publication would require a clearance from three different layers of management within Tenneco. Walsh informed the editor that such approval would no longer be required in that he *was* the new approval person.

The situation, and the decision Walsh made to deal with it, captured the essence of the streamlining needed within Tenneco. He implemented divisional reviews in which peer managers were encouraged to question openly and critique one another's performance. Managers noted that this practice encouraged them to work hard to meet their objectives. Although Walsh recently passed away, significant progress was made during his term as CEO.

C. Michael Armstrong was appointed as the CEO at Hughes Aircraft Co. in 1992. Armstrong was a 31-year IBM Corp. executive prior to his appointment at Hughes. There were concerns that Armstrong did not know enough about missiles, aircraft, and defense contracts, the prime business of Hughes Aircraft. However, Hughes needed to make strategic changes because of the significant downsizing of the defense industry. Armstrong's primary task was to effect the strategic changes suggested by the defense industry downsizing.

One of Armstrong's first actions was to attempt to assure top executives that he respected their talents and wanted them to be a part of this team. He emphasized strongly the need to create a clear vision of a radically different organization. Executives were given a short period of time to either accept Armstrong and his intended actions or to exit the firm.

Armstrong was successful in cultivating a positive feeling of teamwork among his top executives. As a result, the shift from defense work to the development of new businesses (e.g., satellite distribution of entertainment programs) has been successful. Operating profits increased by 48 percent in the year after he became CEO. Armstrong suggested that new outside CEOs are better able to make changes in the corporate culture and in the strategic direction of the firm.

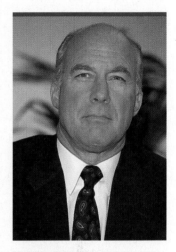

*C. Michael Armstrong, shown here, was selected from the external managerial labor market to be Hughes Aircraft's CEO. A key reason to select a CEO from outside is to facilitate the development of a new strategic direction for a firm.*

**FIGURE 11–2   Effects of CEO Succession and Top-Management-Team-Composition on Strategy**

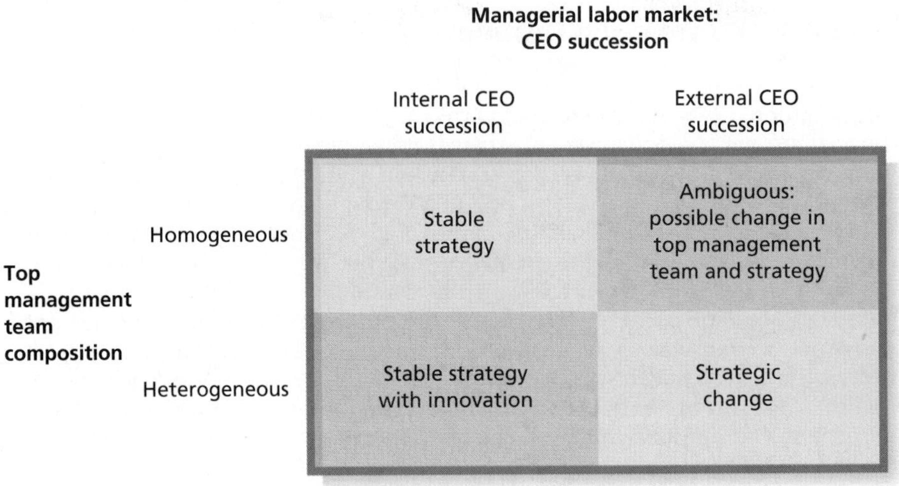

Managerial labor market:
CEO succession

|                          | Internal CEO succession | External CEO succession |
|--------------------------|-------------------------|-------------------------|
| **Homogeneous**          | Stable strategy         | Ambiguous: possible change in top management team and strategy |
| **Heterogeneous**        | Stable strategy with innovation | Strategic change |

Top management team composition

management team, innovation is likely to continue. An external CEO succession with a homogeneous team creates a more ambiguous situation. For example, C. Michael Armstrong invited existing members of the top management team to join him or to leave. After Armstrong won them over, the top management team combined its skills to change Hughes's strategy.

As noted earlier in the chapter, the exercise of strategic leadership is exemplified by several actions. The six most critical of these are shown in Figure 11–3. The remainder of this chapter is devoted to explaining each action.

## Determining Strategic Direction

▲ **Determining the strategic direction of the firm** refers to the development of a long-term vision of a firm's strategic intent.

**Determining the strategic direction of the firm** refers to the development of a long-term vision of a firm's strategic intent. As a mental image, a long-term vision of a firm's strategic intent normally entails a view of the firm at least 5 to 10 years in the future. This would encompass its strategy, organizational design, and subsystems, to include planning, and the information and control system.[46] For example, Boeing is attempting to maintain its market leadership by teaching a new generation of managers to embrace strategic change and look to the future. In fact, Boeing top executives suggest that their focus is 15 to 20 years in the future. As part of its efforts, Boeing has adopted a team-oriented, cost-conscious approach to designing, building, selling, and maintaining its planes. An early outcome from its new approach was the development of the 777 jetliner. This plane was the first commercial jetliner designed entirely on a computer.[47] The fact that Toyota has a 100-year plan suggests that it looks even further into the future to determine its strategic direction.[48]

The words of Whirlpool Corp.'s CEO, David Whitwam, demonstrate the strategic direction he has in mind for his firm. While reading the comments of Whitwam, notice the intention of leveraging the organization's capabilities to gain competitive advantages in the global marketplace:

**FIGURE 11–3**   **Exercise of Strategic Leadership**

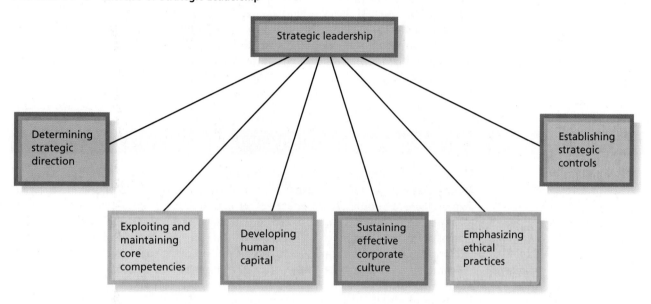

"Our vision at Whirlpool is to integrate our geographical businesses wherever possible, so that our most advanced expertise in any given area—whether it's refrigeration technology, financial reporting systems, or distribution strategy—isn't confined to one location or one division. We want to be able to take the best capabilities we have and leverage them in all of our operations worldwide."[49]

As these examples show, the determining-strategic-direction dimension of strategic leadership entails the anticipation, vision, and flexibility referred to earlier. It also requires the ability to create strategic change. For example, co-CEOs Robin Wilson and Glen Zander are attempting to devise a plan to move TWA from bankruptcy to a successful corporation with a long-term future. In 1988, TWA had revenues of $4.9 billion, profits of almost $250 million, 214 jets with an average age of 14.3 years, and 30,800 employees. In 1993, total revenues were approximately $3.6 billion, with a $318 million loss. It had 168 jets with an average age of 17.8 years and 25,000 employees. Carl Icahn took over TWA in 1988. However, his tenure at TWA was not successful, as it moved from a profitable firm to bankruptcy. After Icahn left, Wilson and Zander took over the firm. Interestingly, the month after Carl Icahn left, TWA posted the best on-time performance of any U.S. air carrier. This accomplishment may represent the reaction of the employees to the loss of Icahn and their alienation from him.

Wilson and Zander have a significant task in front of them. TWA has a $943 million debt, with only $81 million in equity and cash reserves of about $150 million. Its route structure is not a positive asset, with significant competition in some of its major hubs. The fleet of jets is aging and is not fuel efficient. However, Wilson and Zander are developing a means of operating the airline efficiently, attracting customers, and looking for strategic alliances to help revitalize the airline. Robert Crandall, CEO of American Airlines, one of TWA's primary competitors, believes that TWA will make it.[50]

You may recall that C. Michael Armstrong, the new CEO at Hughes Aircraft, helped create a clear vision of a new organization while emphasizing the firm's existing strengths. It is important not to lose continuity with the strengths of the organization when preparing the firm to deal successfully with needed strategic changes. Achieving this objective requires balancing the short-term needs of a firm with its long-term growth and survival. This suggests the need to emphasize and nurture an organization's core competencies.

## Exploiting and Maintaining Core Competencies

Examined in both Chapters 1 and 3, core competencies are the resources and capabilities that serve as a firm's source of competitive advantage over its rivals. Typically, core competencies relate to an organization's functional skills, such as manufacturing, finance, marketing, and research and development. Core competencies allow organizations to provide goods and services that have unique benefits and companies are able to produce and deliver products that have unique value for customers.[51] Merck has developed a core competence in its research and development function; Philip Morris has developed a core competence in its marketing function, especially in terms of its promotion skills.[52] Each of these firms uses its core competencies as a source of competitive advantage over its rivals.

As strategic leaders, top-level managers make decisions intended to help their firm develop, maintain, strengthen, leverage, and exploit core competencies. In the words of Whirlpool's CEO, "the only way to gain lasting competitive advantage is to leverage your capabilities around the world so that the company as a whole is greater than the sum of its parts."[53]

In many large firms, and certainly in diversified ones, core competencies are exploited when they are developed and applied across different units in the organization (economies of scope) in an attempt to create a competitive advantage. This is shown by Philip Morris applying its marketing and promotion competencies across its multiple businesses. Its well-known rejuvenation of Miller Beer by applying its marketing expertise is considered a classic example. As in the case of Whirlpool, competencies can also be emphasized across country borders. In fact, some argue that the development, nurturing, and application of core competencies within multinational firms facilitates managing the complex relationships across businesses operating in different international markets.[54]

Essentially, exploiting core competencies within organizations involves sharing resources across units. Generally the most effective core competencies are based on intangible resources. Because intangible resources relate to knowledge or skills, they are less visible to competitors. Effective strategic leaders promote the sharing of intangible resources across business units. If they can identify and nurture core competencies, they can build linkages across diverse units throughout the organization. Applying core competencies across business units helps firms achieve economies of scale and scope. In addition, systematic applications of core competencies usually are difficult for competitors to learn how to duplicate. Firms such as 3M, Nestle, Procter & Gamble, and Heinz have established competitive advantages in multiple product markets by emphasizing their core competencies.[55] Core competencies, however, cannot be developed or exploited effectively without appropriate human capital.

## Developing Human Capital

**Human capital** refers to the knowledge and skills of the firm's work force. In other words, employees are viewed as a capital resource. Much of the development of U.S. industry can be attributed to human capital. One-third of the growth in the U.S. gross national product from 1948 to 1982 was attributed to increases in the education level of the work force. Fifty percent of this growth resulted from technical innovations and knowledge that also are based strongly on education. Only 15 percent of the growth of gross national product during this time was attributed to investment in capital equipment.[56] In the view of many top-level executives, employees are the key source of the firm's competitive advantage.[57]

One means of developing human capital is through training and development programs. Management development programs can help build skills and inculcate core values and a systematic view of the organization. Development programs facilitate communication among employees by providing a common language, building employee networks, and constructing a common vision of the firm. Because development programs socialize and help inculcate a common set of core values, they promote cohesion among the employees. Furthermore, they should help employees improve skills critical to the firm's primary operations, core competencies, and customers.[58]

The efforts at Federal-Mogul, GE, and Procter & Gamble exemplify an emphasis on human capital. While it is important to continue the development of human capital and to utilize that capital once developed, as suggested in the next Strategic Focus, a large number of firms have been restructuring and downsizing. In these circumstances, it is critical to ensure that firms retain their best talent.

It has been estimated that as many as 1 million managers lost their jobs in the 1980s.[59] This represents a significant loss of potential human capital. Because of this loss, many firms are operating with little slack in their human capital. It is also not uncommon for restructuring firms to reduce their expenditures/investments in training and development programs. However, it can be argued that restructuring is an important time to increase investment in such development. These firms have less slack and cannot absorb as many errors; moreover, many employees may be placed into positions without all of the skills or knowledge necessary to effectively perform required tasks.[60] Effective strategic leaders view employees as a resource to be maximized, rather than a cost to be minimized.

General managerial skills are important, but so is knowledge of the industry and of the firm itself. Earlier, we referred to two examples where CEOs were brought in from the outside and were successful (Tenneco and Hughes Aircraft). However, lack of industry- and firm-specific knowledge can be problematic to the success of top executives. Such is the case where Gerald Grinstein, a former airline executive, was hired to head Burlington Northern, a railroad.

While airlines and railroads are both in the transportation business, the industries and the firms differ considerably. Grinstein has experienced several problems since coming to Burlington Northern. For example, he appointed a retired Air Force general as head of the Burlington Northern operating department, but had to reassign him after only 16 months on the job. The major problem was that he did not fully understand the firm's operations. Because of his lack of knowledge, employees had trouble interacting with him. But, Grinstein argues that he has

▲ **Human capital** refers to the knowledge and skills of the firm's work force.

## STRATEGIC FOCUS

### Implementing Techniques That Utilize Human Capital as Opposed to Capital Equipment

In the 1980s, many companies tried to duplicate the successes of some Japanese manufacturing firms. This duplication attempt found firms emphasizing capital equipment, rather than human capital, to produce products. The 1990s are finding many of these firms changing their operations again, choosing now to emphasize people power. A number of U.S. companies have decided that they went too far in their attempts to imitate Japanese manufacturers.

For example, Federal-Mogul Corp. has removed much of its automated equipment at its auto parts plant and is now emphasizing human capital more than capital equipment to produce products. A key reason for this is that after making changes to emphasize automation, Federal-Mogul discovered that its auto parts plant could, in fact, manufacture goods much faster than before; however, it could not change quickly from producing one product to producing another one. To change from manufacturing a small clutch bearing to a larger one required multiple changes, including readjusting parts and realigning mechanisms that hold parts in place while they are being machined. In addition, the complex automated machinery required extensive maintenance. For these reasons, automation did not lower costs, and it created a situation where the firm could not respond quickly to changes in customers' needs.

After the change from automation to an emphasis on employee power, the plant was able to manufacture almost three times as many different varieties of products as previously, but in the same amount of time. The plant can now switch from one part to another much more quickly and make smaller batches (e.g., 250 to 500 versus 5,000 to 10,000) of products.

Efforts to emphasize human capital are also under way at General Electric (GE). GE's home appliance division has replaced quality circles with work-out. The work-out system utilizes periodic town-hall-type meetings between workers and managers that are designed to encourage employees to offer new ideas. Workers propose ideas that may require significant changes and investment. This differs from quality circles, whereby a dozen or so workers in a group suggest multiple ways to make minor improvements. Managers are required to respond to workers' suggestions and have approved almost 90 percent of the ideas.

One of Procter & Gamble's plants in Lima, Ohio, is operated almost totally by workers. Approximately 200 workers have the authority to sign a purchase order up to $500 without further authorization. Time clocks were eliminated, and only one job classification was created, with 1 manager for each 60 employees. Each employee is trained to handle as many as 15 different jobs. The firm decided against using robots because of the desire for feedback from the employees. The plant manager suggests that the firm is trying to tap the potential of the human mind. The manager also believes that humans adapt where robots do not, even in repetitive jobs. The plant increased its annual productivity by approximately 25 percent and was profitable in its first year of operation.

reduced Burlington Northern's debt by 45 percent. Observers note, though, that he has done so by raising rates for the transportation of certain commodities. In a business known for fierce price competition, using this tactical strategic action may not yield the long-term results Grinstein seeks. In fact, one of the firm's primary competitors suggests that Burlington may have lost touch with the market. It has lost some of its business because it was outmarketed, according to a Boise Cascade executive who took his firm's business to a competitor. One major industry observer suggested that the basic mistake made by Grinstein was in bringing outsiders without railroad experience to senior management positions.[61] Thus, effective strategic leadership requires general management skills, as well as adequate knowledge of the firm's operations and its industry.

In comparison, GE Capital Services, Inc. (a subsidiary of GE), has flourished largely because it has built the human capital of its managerial work force. Observers suggest that because of its efforts, GE Capital now has enormous breadth and skill among its management team. CEO Gary Wendt selects and develops managers to expect and meet high standards. The strategic intent of this GE unit is to make strategic moves more quickly and service customers more effectively than competitors.

Managers at GE Capital deal with problems as they arise. One way the firm develops managers is to have four meetings a year to engage in what may be referred to as war games. In these meetings, three-year strategies are developed, and operating plans for the current year are examined and changed as necessary. There is an emphasis on searching for new opportunities and promoting new ideas from employees during the meetings.

GE Capital has grown dramatically over the last decade—in both size and profitability. From 1988 to 1992, this unit experienced a doubling of its profits and virtually a doubling of its total assets as well.[62] As the experiences at GE Capital show, developing, emphasizing, and nurturing human capital can facilitate strategic leaders' efforts to help firms cope successfully with strategic change and achieve strategic competitiveness.

## Sustaining an Effective Corporate Culture

A **corporate culture** consists of a complex set of ideologies, symbols, and values that are shared throughout the organization and that influence the way the firm conducts its business. Corporate culture helps regulate and control employee behavior.[63] Of course, strategic leaders must develop and nurture an appropriate corporate culture, one that promotes focused learning and human development, the sharing of skills and resources among units in the firm, and the entrepreneurial spirit important for innovativeness and competitiveness.[64] This type of culture is often referred to as a clan culture.[65] An appropriate corporate culture can encourage an entrepreneurial spirit, foster and facilitate a long-term vision, and create an emphasis on strategic actions linked with the manufacture of high-quality goods and services.[66]

▲ **Corporate culture** consists of a complex set of ideologies, symbols, and values that are shared throughout the organization and that influence the way the firm conducts its business.

## Entrepreneurial Spirit

Encouragement (or discouragement) to pursue entrepreneurial opportunities, especially in large firms, is often affected by the firm's culture. Pursuit of these opportunities must be rewarded and the penalty for failure minimized. Strong rule-

and structure-oriented control systems for approval of new projects can discourage entrepreneurial efforts. To nurture an entrepreneurial spirit, new product champions should be identified, supported, and rewarded.

Promotion of quality products and services can be affected by corporate culture, based on values emphasizing human resource development and cooperation. Obviously, it is important for firms to invest capital in new plants and equipment and new manufacturing technologies in order to improve or maintain quality. However, well-trained and knowledgeable/skilled employees may be critical to operate the new equipment and technology in order to produce high-quality goods or services. In addition, cooperation among functional units (interfunctional integration) can help facilitate product quality.[67]

An entrepreneurial culture must also promote individuality and diversity (as opposed to conformity). It should promote risk taking, rather than risk aversion; rewards should be based on long-term, as opposed to short-term, performance. Reward systems are critical in helping to maintain a corporate culture and to focus employees on entrepreneurial activities and a firm's long-term strategic competitiveness.[68] Of course, strategic leaders (the top management team) determine the reward system and have an impact on the value system of the firm. Developing strategic intent and infusing the vision it portrays throughout the organization clearly affect the value set emphasized in the corporation.

Firms with an effective corporate culture are reluctant to make major changes with strategic leaders. As a result, there may be sensitivities to bringing top executives from outside the firm. In 1993, new top executives at Exxon and Mobil were chosen from inside the firms. These individuals fit their corporate cultures. Lee R. Raymond, current president of Exxon, was chosen to become chairman and chief executive officer to succeed Lawrence Rawl upon his retirement at age 65. Raymond has served as president of Exxon since 1987 and has been with the firm for his whole career. He also held positions in Exxon's international operations and other important managerial positions with domestic operations. At Mobil, Lucio A. Noto, vice president and chief financial officer, was named president and chief operating officer. His new position makes him the number one heir to the position of chairman and chief executive officer, currently held by Allen E. Murray. Noto is an inside director at Mobil and has held several domestic and international management positions for the firm. One external analyst described Noto and Murray as coming from the same school of thought, being street smart and self-reliant.[69] These are examples of cultural continuity. Often a different approach to leadership succession is taken when change in the culture is needed.

## Changing Corporate Culture

Changing culture is more difficult than sustaining it. But effective strategic leadership also involves recognizing the need for changing the corporate culture and implementing the needed changes. Without a crisis or major cataclysmic event, changes in corporate culture are likely to be more incremental. Restructuring may provide an appropriate time to effect a change in a firm's culture. This may require creating a new strategic intent for the firm and infusing it throughout the organization, as noted above. The shaping and reinforcing of a new culture will require effective communication and problem solving, along with the selection of the right people (those who have the values managers wish to infuse in the organization), effective performance appraisals (establishing goals and measuring individual performance toward those goals that fit with the new core values), and appropriate reward systems (rewarding the desired behaviors that reflect the new core values).[70]

In the 1980s, Lee Iacocca was successful in creating a new strategic intent at Chrysler and in implementing major changes in the firm's corporate culture. He organized a top management team that helped develop and implement the strategic intent. In so doing, they were able to inculcate and reinforce new core values at Chrysler.[71]

One catalyst for change in corporate culture can be a new chief executive officer from outside the corporation. As noted above, the new top officers at Exxon and Mobil were chosen to fit the current corporate culture and for the explicit purpose of not making changes in those cultures. Alternatively, some firms may need changes in the corporate culture and see the choice of external top executives as facilitating the process of changing that culture.

An example of this intent is shown in the choice of Louis V. Gerstner, Jr., to be the new CEO of IBM. Gerstner has a reputation for being an inspirational manager who makes high demands on his subordinates, but who also wins their trust. His major executive roles at American Express and RJR Nabisco provided a base to enter IBM with the intent of making changes in its culture. Certainly, making changes in IBM's corporate culture, which has often been described as "awesomely thick," may be quite difficult. IBM is highly in-bred, partly because of its past success; thus, executives are rarely brought in from the outside. Gerstner will have to transform IBM's "thick" corporate culture and inspire the employees to make changes. He also will have to rebuild shareholder confidence in the firm and attempt to revive the potentially successful businesses, while eliminating the unsuccessful ones. Only time will tell if he can achieve success because it will be a formidable task.[72]

Unlike Gerstner at IBM, Jack Welch, CEO of GE, does not have to turn around his firm's performance. In the last 12 years, GE's annual revenues have doubled to $62.2 billion in 1992, while total employment was reduced from 412,000 to 229,000 employees. In the 1980s, GE was known to have a rather autocratic culture. However, Welch is in the process of transforming GE's culture to one that fits a "boundaryless" organization. That is, he is attempting to institute a culture that focuses on openness, candor, and teamwork. He admits that it is not an easy task. A system called work-out, described in an earlier Strategic Focus, is being used to encourage employees to take responsibility and become deeply involved in changing the organization.

Welch has discussed an example where hourly workers rearranged a factory through a work-out session. They determined that a part traveled three miles through the factory when it should only go 30 feet. The layout of the factory was changed to make it much more efficient. He also noted that everyone in the organization had to make changes, including management. There had to be a rethinking of the roles to cut back on the bureaucratic procedures, tear down the barriers/walls, and promote openness and teamwork. Welch has tried to make the boundaryless corporation a core value at GE. Individuals who are turf-oriented and self-centered, do not share ideas with others, and do not value new ideas are less accepted at GE.

To support its core values, GE employees are evaluated by their manager, their peers, and all subordinates in areas such as team building and quality. There is no attempt to punish people for falling short of targets because they are encouraged to set high targets. The firm attempts to reward individual and team progress toward their goals. Welch also notes that the process has not been easy and that there are still some autocratic managers in GE. In fact, he suggests that you may even have to fire some managers and employees who do not accept or fit with the new culture. However, he is determined to develop a boundaryless culture. Given his track record, there is every reason to believe that he will be successful.[73]

## Emphasizing Ethical Practices

Effective strategic leadership ensures ethical practices within an organization. One of the means of promoting ethical practices is to infuse ethical values through the organization's culture.[74] The ethics that guide individuals' actions are based on principles formed by long-term influences that extend beyond the organization. Nonetheless, organizations can to some extent shape and/or control managers' and employees' behavior within the organizational context. This can be done through formalized rules, economic rewards and sanctions, and the values and norms that represent corporate culture.

To the extent that employees and managers share a common set of values that includes ethical principles, there is a strong likelihood that ethical practices will be observed. Top executives at Johnson & Johnson, the pharmaceutical firm, suggest that a major source of their success has been their organizational culture, which emphasizes ethical conduct, even across international boundaries.[75]

Surveys conducted by the Center for Business Ethics at Bentley College provide an interesting snapshot of corporate actions that promote ethical practices. The center administered a survey in the middle 1980s and again at the end of the decade, with feedback from 244 major corporations. Survey results showed that at the end of the decade more corporations were focusing on promoting ethical practices than was the case in the middle 1980s. Their more recent survey found that 93 percent of the firms were taking active steps to incorporate ethical values into their daily operations. This has been accomplished by developing codes of ethics, by implementing ethics training programs for managers and employees, and, to some extent, by developing ethics committees. An overwhelming percentage of the responding firms (96 percent) felt that they had made satisfactory progress toward achieving their goals. However, only 18 percent of the respondents felt significant public pressure to develop ethical policies and practices. Fifty-seven percent of the respondents felt no or very little such pressure. This seems to suggest that managers are cognizant of the importance of ethical practices and are implementing them without feeling pressure from external sources (e.g., customers, government agencies, etc.).[76] Promoting ethical practices makes good business sense for many reasons, not the least of which is that it promotes a positive reputation with stakeholders.

While a number of firms have instituted training programs in ethics and have developed codes of ethics, potential problems remain. For example, some have questioned the potential exploitation of management buyouts (often in the form of leveraged buyouts, described in Chapter 7). The concern is managerial opportunism.

**Managerial opportunism** occurs when managers take actions that are in their own best interest, but not in the best interest of the firm. In other words, managers take advantage of their positions and therefore make decisions that benefit themselves to the detriment of the owners (shareholders). Problems with individual opportunism are well documented by the Wall Street insider trading scandals and other actions taken by those who financed large leveraged buyouts and acquisitions, such as Michael Milkin.[77] Other potential problems that have been documented include questionable hiring practices and sexual harassment in the workplace.[78]

Another recent set of studies sheds some light on these issues. Studies examining managers' ethical values and beliefs in the middle 1980s and again in the early 1990s showed little change. Managers at both times emphasized utilitarian goals, that is, the achievement of economic gains for the organization. In fact, the earlier survey found that one of the primary reasons managers emphasized ethical practices was to achieve greater profits. Some argue that the two go hand in hand. In other words, the firms that establish and maintain ethical practices are more likely to achieve strategic competitiveness and earn above-average profits. A key reason for this is that their reputation for ethical practices will attract loyal customers.[79]

Managers can take some actions to establish and maintain ethical practices. First, as noted earlier, the infusion of ethical values into the core cultural values of the firm can help control employee behavior and promote ethical practices. In addition, managers become role models, reinforcing to employees the importance of ethical practices. Managers can attempt to hire employees that have ethical values matching those of the firm. In so doing, they are more likely to have employees who engage in ethical practices. Finally, managers can and should reward behavior that parallels ethical practices. In these ways, managers establish and maintain ethical practices. In Jack Welch's attempt to change GE's culture, he emphasized a value that represents an important ethical principle. Welch said that integrity is the most important value for the organization and its employees.

Determining strategic direction, exploiting and maintaining core competencies, developing human capital, sustaining an effective corporate culture, and emphasizing ethical practices are all affected by the establishment and exercise of strategic controls by top executives.

▲ **Managerial opportunism** occurs when managers take actions that are in their own best interest, but not in the best interest of the firm.

## Establishing Strategic Controls

Earlier in this book we discussed the establishment and use of different control systems. In large corporations, financial controls are oftentimes emphasized. Financial controls focus on shorter-term financial outcomes, as opposed to the strategic actions employed. In contrast, strategic control focuses on the *content* of strategic actions, rather than their *outcomes*. Because there are multiple effects on financial outcomes, some strategic actions can be correct, but result in poor financial outcomes (e.g., caused by recessionary economic problems, unexpected domestic or foreign government actions, and natural disasters). Therefore, an emphasis on financial control often produces more short-term and risk-averse managerial decisions. Alternatively, strategic control encourages lower-level managers to make decisions that incorporate moderate and acceptable levels of risk.

Effective strategic leadership attempts to balance strategic control and financial control (not eliminate financial control) with the intent of achieving more positive long-term returns.[80] In fact, most corporate restructuring action is designed to refocus the firm on its core businesses, thereby allowing top executives to reestablish strategic control of their separate business units.[81]

Effective use of strategic controls by corporate managers is integrated frequently with appropriate autonomy for the various subunits so that they can better gain competitive advantage in their respective markets. Strategic controls can be used to promote the sharing of both tangible and intangible resources among interdependent businesses within a firm's portfolio. In addition, the autonomy provided allows the flexibility and innovation necessary to take advantage of specific marketplace opportunities. As a result, strategic leadership promotes the simultaneous use of strategic controls and autonomy.[82]

Interestingly, Louis Gerstner, CEO of IBM, did not apply strategic controls effectively with RJR's tobacco business when he was CEO of RJR Nabisco. He did not provide the strategic direction for the tobacco business largely because he lacked effective operating knowledge of that business. In fact, he purposefully maintained a distance from the tobacco business, possibly because he did not want to be identified too closely with the product because of its social stigma. As a result, the tobacco business performed poorly in 1992. This performance was reinforced with ineffective strategic decisions made at the business level. Competitors introduced new low-priced brands that stole business from the higher-priced RJR Winston and Salem brands. First, RJR reacted by heavily promoting these higher-priced brands, but enjoyed little success. As a result, it offered its own brands of low-priced cigarettes, but, in so doing, it undercut its own premium brands. Earnings for RJR's tobacco business were hurt. Some feel that Gerstner did not appropriately urge caution with these strategic decisions. However, this may have been difficult for Gerstner to do because he did not fully understand the tobacco business. Understanding the business is necessary in order to exercise effective strategic control. Therefore, he probably allowed too much autonomy and did not exercise appropriate strategic control in this case.[83]

## Summary

- Effective strategic leadership is required to formulate and implement strategies successfully. Strategic leadership entails the ability to anticipate, envision, maintain flexibility, and empower others to create strategic change. It has important effects on a firm's attempts to achieve strategic competitiveness and earn above-average profits.

- Top-level managers are an important resource necessary to obtain a sustained competitive advantage. Superior managerial skills are a prerequisite to attaining such an advantage. Top executives exercise discretion in making critical strategic decisions (e.g., determining new strategic initiatives). In addition, they develop and implement organizational struc-

tures and reward systems designed to help implement the firm's strategy.

- The top management team is composed of key managers who formulate and implement firm strategy. Generally, they are officers of the corporation and/or inside members of the board of directors. They determine a firm's strategic direction and, as such, affect its strategic competitiveness and ability to earn above-average profits.

- There is a relationship between the fit of top management team characteristics with firm strategy and subsequent performance. For example, a top management team that has significant marketing and research and development knowledge and/or expertise often enhances the firm's effectiveness as the team steers the firm toward implementation of growth-oriented strategies.

- Top executives' positions are complex. Top-level executives must understand firm operations and the external environment. Rarely can one person (e.g., the CEO) possess all the knowledge needed to deal with the critical strategic issues. Because of this, a top management team is required to lead many organizations. Most top management teams are more effective when they have diverse and heterogeneous skills. However, more heterogeneous top management teams are difficult to manage because of the need to achieve cohesiveness.

- Characteristics of top management teams have been found to be related to innovation and strategic change. More heterogeneous top management teams often are better able to produce firm innovation and strategic change.

- When boards of directors are involved in shaping strategic direction, firms generally improve their strategic competitiveness. Alternatively, boards may be less involved in strategic decisions when the CEOs have more power. CEOs obtain power by appointing board members, and they have authority over inside members who generally are on the top management team.

- The managerial labor market is importance for the top management team and strategic leadership. The internal labor market is composed of the opportunities provided for individuals within the firm to develop their knowledge and skill bases and to achieve higher-level and more responsible positions within the firm. There is also an external managerial labor market, represented by the competitive market for managers' services in other firms and organizations. It is used less commonly than the internal labor market, although it is more important in the United States than in Japan, due to culture differences.

- Strategic leadership entails determining strategic direction, exploiting and maintaining core competencies, developing human capital, sustaining an effective corporate culture, emphasizing ethical practices, and establishing strategic controls.

- Determining strategic direction requires vision and the ability to infuse it throughout the firm.

- Core competencies are the resources and capabilities that serve as a firm's source of competitive advantage over rivals. To achieve more resource sharing and economies of scale in resource use, the development, exploitation, and maintenance of core competencies by strategic leaders become important in establishing sustainable competitive advantages.

- A critical element of strategic leadership is the ability to develop human capital. While firms have often emphasized investments in capital equipment, the primary opportunity to improve productivity comes from investments in human capital. Many firms are now deemphasizing automation and robotics and emphasizing employee skills and problem solving instead.

- Corporate culture can be important for developing and managing human behavior in an organization. Top-level managers can infuse the organization with their vision and thereby affect the core values emphasized throughout it. Appropriate corporate cultures can embody entrepreneurial spirit.

- Strategic leadership also entails an emphasis on ethical practices. Ethical practices help build a positive reputation; they can be promoted through fostering a corporate culture that emphasizes ethical values, having managers serve as role models, hiring employees who share the firm's ethical values, and rewarding ethical behavior.

- Strategic leadership includes the establishment and maintenance of strategic controls. Strategic controls emphasize balancing an evaluation of strategic actions with the financial outcomes of such actions.

## Review Questions

1. In what ways can top-level managers be considered important resources for an organization?
2. What is a top management team, and how does it affect a firm's strategy?
3. How does the heterogeneity of the top management team and the different expertise on the team affect innovation, strategic change, and firm performance?
4. How does the managerial labor market affect the formulation and implementation of a firm's strategy?
5. What is strategic leadership? How does it affect determination of a firm's strategic direction?

6. What is the importance of human capital and its development for strategic competitiveness?
7. Define corporate culture, and explain how it can affect the implementation of strategy.
8. Describe four ways strategic leaders can establish and promote ethical practices.
9. What is strategic control, and how does it affect a firm's strategic competitiveness?

## Application Discussion Questions

1. Choose a CEO of a prominent firm you believe exemplifies the positive aspects of strategic leadership. Describe how this CEO exhibits strategic leadership and the effects of such leadership on his/her firm.
2. Select a CEO of a prominent firm you believe does not exemplify the positive aspects of strategic leadership. Describe the actions of this leader, and explain why they do not fit the definition of strategic leadership presented in this chapter.
3. What are managerial resources, and how do they relate to the strategic competitiveness of a firm?
4. By examining popular press articles, select a firm that has recently gone through a significant strategic change. Collect information on the top management team, and see if there are linkages between the characteristics of the top management team and the type of change the firm has undergone.
5. Examine popular press articles, and identify two new CEOs, one that was promoted from inside the corporation and one that was hired from the outside. Based on your reading, why do you believe these individuals were selected? What do they bring to the

job, and what strategy do you think they will employ in the future? Try to relate your findings to issues discussed in this chapter.

6. Based on your reading of this chapter and popular press accounts, select a CEO that you feel has exhibited vision, and describe how that vision has been realized.
7. Choose a firm and try to identify its core competence and the effects of that core competence on its performance.
8. Identify a firm with strategic leaders that have emphasized the importance of human capital and describe how that has affected its performance.
9. Identify a firm where strategic leaders have, in your opinion, fostered a unique corporate culture. Describe that culture and its potential effects on the firm's strategy and the implementation of it.
10. Why is the strategic control exercised by a firm's executives important for long-term competitiveness? How do strategic controls differ from financial controls and their effect on firm strategy?

## Ethics Questions

1. As discussed in this chapter, effective strategic leadership occasionally requires managers to make difficult decisions. In your opinion, is it ethical for managers to make these types of decisions without being willing to receive feedback from employees about the effects of those decisions? Be prepared to justify your response.
2. As an employee with less than one year of experience in a company, what course or courses of action would you pursue if you were to encounter unethical practices by one of your firm's strategic leaders?
3. In your opinion, are firms obligated ethically to promote from within, rather than relying on the external labor market to select strategic leaders? What is the reasoning that supports your position?

4. What are the ethical issues involved, if any, with a firm's ability to develop and exploit a core competence in the manufacture of goods that may be harmful to consumers (e.g., cigarettes)? Be prepared to discuss the reasons for your response.
5. As a strategic leader, would you feel ethically responsible to develop the human capital? Why or why not?
6. Describe the culture of an organization, social group, or volunteer agency in which you hold membership that you believe should be classified as "ethical." What are the factors that allowed this culture to be ethical?

## Notes

1. Oracle, *Value Line,* 1994, March 2, 122.
2. A. A. Lado, N. G. Boyd, and P. Wright, 1992, A competency based model of sustainable competitive advantage: Toward a conceptual integration, *Journal of Management* 18, no. 1: 77–91.
3. R. E. Byrd, 1987, Corporate leadership skills: A new synthesis, *Organizational Dynamics* 16, no. 1: 34–43.
4. D. C. Hambrick, 1989, Guest editor's introduction: Putting top managers back in the strategy picture, *Strategic Management Journal* 10: 5–16.
5. J. P. Kotter, 1990, What leaders really do, *Harvard Business Review* 68, no. 3: 103–111.
6. C. J. Fombrun, 1992, *Turning Points: Creating Strategic Change in Corporations* (New York: McGraw-Hill); J. Huey, 1994, The new post-heroic leadership, *Fortune,* February 21, 42–50.
7. M. A. Hitt and B. W. Keats, 1992, Strategic leadership and restructuring: A reciprocal interdependence, in R. L. Phillips and J. G. Hunt (eds.), *Strategic Leadership: A Multiorganizational-Level Perspective* (Westport, Conn.: Quorum Books), 45–61.
8. G. Hamel and C. K. Prahalad, 1993, Strategy as stretch and leverage, *Harvard Business Review* 71, no. 2: 75–84.
9. N. Nohria and J. D. Berkley, 1994, Whatever happened to the take-charge manager? *Harvard Business Review* 72, no. 1: 128–137.
10. J. Treffert, 1994, Post-heroic leadership—a comment, *Fortune,* April 4, 45–46.
11. D. L. Bradford and A. R. Cohen, 1994, Post-heroic leadership—a comment, *Fortune,* March 21, 29.
12. Kotter, What leaders really do.
13. B. O'Reilly, 1994, Reengineering the MBA, *Fortune,* January 24, 38–47.
14. J. Hagel III, 1993, The CEO as chief performance officer, *McKinsey Quarterly* 1993, no. 4: 16–28.
15. R. C. Hoffman and W. H. Hegarty, 1993, Top management influence on innovations: Effects of executive characteristics and social culture, *Journal of Management* 19: 549–574.
16. W. D. Guth and I. C. MacMillan, 1986, Strategy implementation versus middle management self-interest, *Strategic Management Journal* 7: 313–327.
17. W. D. Guth and A. Ginsberg, 1990, Guest editors' introduction: Corporate entrepreneurship, *Strategic Management Journal* 11 (Special Issue): 5–15.
18. R. P. Castanias and C. E. Helfat, 1991, Managerial resources and rents, *Journal of Management* 17: 155–171.
19. N. Rajagopalan, A. M. A. Rasheed, and D. K. Datta, 1993, Strategic decision processes: Critical review and future directions, *Journal of Management* 19: 349–384.
20. D. C. Hambrick and S. Finkelstein, 1987, Managerial discretion: A bridge between polar views of organizational outcomes, in B. Staw and L. L. Cummings (eds.), *Research in Organizational Behavior* (Greenwich, Conn.: JAI Press), 369–406.
21. N. Wernerfelt, 1989, From critical resources to corporate strategy, *Journal of General Management* 14: 4–12.
22. R. L. Katz, 1974, Skills of an effective administrator, *Harvard Business Review* 55, no. 5: 90–103; T. Levitt, 1991, *Thinking About Management* (New York: Free Press).
23. J. B. Barney, 1991, Firm resources and sustained competitive advantage, *Journal of Management* 17: 99–120.
24. J. P. Miller, 1993, Sundstrand aggressively waits out storm in industry: Aerospace concern moves corporate pieces to reposition itself for upturn, *Wall Street Journal,* April 21, B4.
25. Sundstrand Corp., *Value Line,* 1994, January 7, 582.
26. S. Losee, 1994, Mr. Cozzette buys a computer, *Fortune,* April 18, 113–116.
27. Dell Computer, *Value Line,* 1994, January 28, 1088.
28. J. G. Michel and D. C. Hambrick, 1992, Diversification posture and top management team characteristics, *Academy of Management Journal* 35: 9–37.
29. M. F. Wiersema and K. A. Bantel, 1993, Top management team turnover, *Strategic Management Journal* 14: 458–504.
30. D. C. Hambrick and P. A. Mason, 1984, Upper echelons: The organization as a reflection of its top managers, *Academy of Management Review* 9: 193–206; M. A. Hitt and B. B. Tyler, 1991, Strategic decision models: Integrating different perspectives, *Strategic Management Journal* 12: 327–352.
31. D. Norburn and S. Birley, 1988, The top management team and corporate performance, *Strategic Management Journal* 9: 225–238; A. M. Pettigrew, 1992, The character and significance of strategy process research, *Strategic Management Journal* 13 (Special Issue): 5–16; A. S. Thomas, R. J. Litschert, and K. Ramaswamy, 1991, The performance impact of strategy-manager coalignment: An empirical examination, *Strategic Management Journal* 12: 509–522.
32. Thomas, Litschert, and Ramaswamy, The performance impact.
33. Michel and Hambrick, Diversification posture.
34. M. A. Hitt, R. D. Ireland, and K. A. Palia, 1982, Industrial firms' grand strategy and functional importance: Moderating effects of technology and uncertainty, *Academy of Management Journal* 25:

265–298; M. A. Hitt and R. D. Ireland, 1985, Corporate distinctive competence, strategy, industry, and performance, *Strategic Management Journal* 6: 273–293; M. A. Hitt and R. D. Ireland, 1986, Relationships among corporate-level distinctive competencies, diversification strategy, corporate structure, and performance, *Journal of Management Studies* 23: 401–416.

35. K. Bantel and S. Jackson, 1989, Top management and innovations in banking: Does the composition of the top team make a difference? *Strategic Management Journal* 10: 107–124; M. F. Wiersema and K. Bantel, 1992, Top management team demography and corporate strategic change, *Academy of Management Journal* 35: 91–121.

36. J. A. Pearce II and S. A. Zahra, 1991, The relative power of CEOs and boards of directors: Associations with corporate performance, *Strategic Management Journal* 12: 135–154; W. Q. Judge, Jr., and C. P. Zeithaml, 1992, Institutional and strategic choice perspectives on board involvement in the strategic decision process, *Academy of Management Journal* 35: 766–794.

37. B. D. Baysinger and R. E. Hoskisson, 1990, The composition of boards of directors and strategic control: Effects on corporate strategy, *Academy of Management Review* 15: 72–87.

38. S. Finkelstein, 1992, Power in top management teams: Dimensions, measurement, and validation, *Academy of Management Journal* 35: 505–538.

39. R. A. Johnson, R. E. Hoskisson, and M. A. Hitt, 1993, Board of director involvement in restructuring: The effects of board versus managerial controls and characteristics, *Strategic Management Journal* 14 (Special Issue): 33–50.

40. G. Stern, 1993, Phar-Mor forges stronger ties with manufacturers: Suppliers gain in-store clout as discounter seeks narrower, profitable mix, *Wall Street Journal,* March 8, B4.

41. E. F. Fama, 1980, Agency problems and the theory of the firm, *Journal of Political Economy* 88: 288–307.

42. N. M. Tichy, 1993, Revolutionize your company, *Fortune,* December 13: 114–118.

43. E. Thornton, 1994, Revolution in Japanese retailing, *Fortune,* February 7, 143–146.

44. H. Kim and R. E. Hoskisson, 1993, U.S. and Japanese M-form firms: Effects of financial system and managerial labor market differences (paper presented at the Strategic Management Society Conference, Chicago).

45. D. C. Hambrick, M. A. Geletkanycz, and J. W. Fredrickson, 1993, Top executive commitment to the status quo: Some tests of its determinants, *Strategic Management Journal* 14: 401–418.

46. J. G. Hunt, 1991, *Leadership: A New Synthesis* (Newbury Park, Calif.: Sage).

47. K. West, 1994, The new jet set, *Dallas Morning News,* April 9, 1F, 2F.

48. D. J. Yang and A. Rothman, 1993, Reinventing Boeing: Radical changes and crisis, *Business Week,* March 1, 60–67.

49. R. F. Maruca, 1994, The right way to go global: An interview with Whirlpool CEO David Whitwam, *Harvard Business Review* 72, no. 2: 136.

50. K. Kelly and A. Rothman, 1993, Can a labor of love end TWA's tailspin? *Business Week,* April 19, 80–82.

51. The future for strategy: An interview with Gary Hamel, 1993, *European Management Journal* 11, no. 2: 150–157.

52. Hitt and Keats, Strategic leadership.

53. Maruca, The right way, 136.

54. D. Lei, M. A. Hitt, and R. A. Bettis, 1990, Core competencies and the global firm (unpublished working paper, Southern Methodist University).

55. Hitt and Keats, Strategic leadership.

56. B. Nussbaum, 1988, Needed: Human capital, *Business Week,* September 19, 100–102.

57. K. Chilton, 1994, *The Global Challenge of American Manufacturers* (St. Louis: Washington University, Center for the Study of American Business).

58. J. Kerr and E. Jackofsky, 1989, Aligning managers with strategies: Management development versus selection, *Strategic Management Journal* 10: 157–170.

59. P. Hirsch, 1988, *Pack Your Own Parachute* (Reading, Mass.: Addison-Wesley).

60. C. R. Greer and T. C. Ireland, 1992, Organizational and financial correlates of a contrarian human resource investment strategy, *Academy of Management Journal* 35: 956–984; M. A. Hitt, R. E. Hoskisson, J. S. Harrison, and B. Summers, 1994, Human capital and strategic competitiveness in the 1990s *Journal of Management Development,* 13, no. 1: 35–46.

61. D. Machalaba, 1993, Burlington Northern shows risks of hiring an outsider as CEO, *Wall Street Journal,* April 6, A1, A4.

62. T. Smart, 1993, G.E.'s money machine: How its emphasis on performance built a colossus of finance, *Business Week,* March 8, 62–67.

63. J. B. Barney, 1986, Organizational culture: Can it be a source of sustained competitive advantage? *Academy of Management Review* 11: 656–665; R. H. Kilmann, M. J. Saxton, and R. Serpa, 1986, Issues in understanding and changing culture, *California Management Review* 27: 209–224.

64. Lei, Hitt, and Bettis, Core competencies.

65. W. G. Ouchi, 1980, Markets, bureaucracies and clans, *Administrative Science Quarterly* 25: 129–141.

66. M. A. Hitt, R. E. Hoskisson, and J. S. Harrison, 1991, Strategic competitiveness in the 1990s: Challenges and opportunities for U.S. executives, *Academy of Management Executive* 5: 7–22.

67. M. A. Hitt, R. E. Hoskisson, and R. Nixon, 1993, A mid-range theory of interfunctional integration, its antecedents and outcomes, *Journal of Engineering and Technology Management* 10: 161–185.

68. J. Kerr and J. W. Slocum, 1987, Managing corporate culture through reward systems, *Academy of Management Executive* 1: 99–107.

69. A. de Rouffignac, 1993, Exxon, Mobil pick new top officers, men who fit their corporations' culture, *Wall Street Journal,* February 4, B5.

70. Hitt and Keats, Strategic leadership.

71. F. Westley and H. Mintzberg, 1989, Visionary leadership and strategic management, *Strategic Management Journal* 10: 17–32.

72. G. Anders, E. Shapiro, M. W. Miller and L. Hooper, 1993, Assessing Gestner: IBM's pick is talented but some see flaws in his record at RJR, *Wall Street Journal,* March 25, A1, A9.

73. J. Hillkirk, 1993, Tearing down walls builds G.E.: CEO Welch shapes a culture of openness, teamwork, *USA Today,* July 26, B5.

74. A. Sinclair, 1993, Approaches to organizational culture and ethics, *Journal of Business Ethics* 12: 63–73.

75. Ibid.

76. Center for Business Ethics, 1992, Instilling ethical values in large corporations, *Journal of Business Ethics* 11: 863–867.

77. M. Zey, 1993, *Banking on Fraud* (New York: Aldine De Gruyter).

78. G. Miles, 1993, In search of ethical profits: Insights from strategic management, *Journal of Business Ethics* 12: 219–225.

79. S. R. Premeaux and R. W. Mondy, 1993, Linking management behavior to ethical philosophy, *Journal of Business Ethics* 12: 349–357.

80. M. A. Hitt, R. E. Hoskisson, and R. D. Ireland, 1990, Mergers and acquisitions and the managerial commitment to innovation in M-form firms, *Strategic Management Journal* 11 (Special Issue): 29–47.

81. R. E. Hoskisson and R. A. Johnson, 1992, Corporate restructuring and strategic change: The effect on diversification strategy and R&D intensity, *Strategic Management Journal* 13: 625–634.

82. Hitt and Keats, Strategic leadership.

83. Anders, Shapiro, Miller and Hooper, Assessing Gerstner.

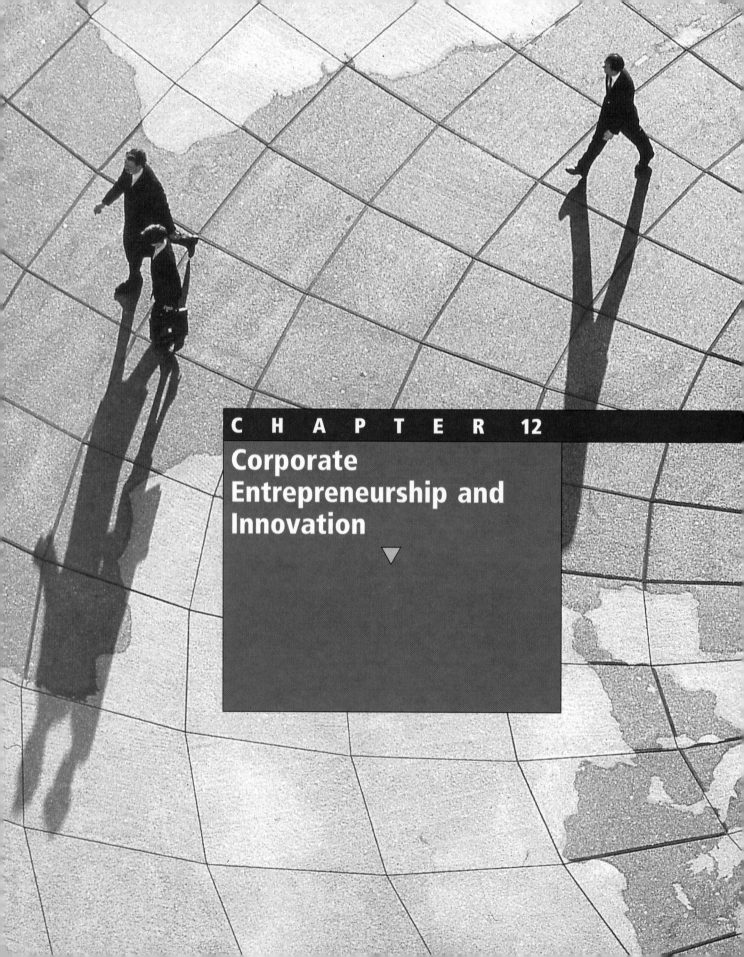

# Corporate Entrepreneurship and Innovation

▽

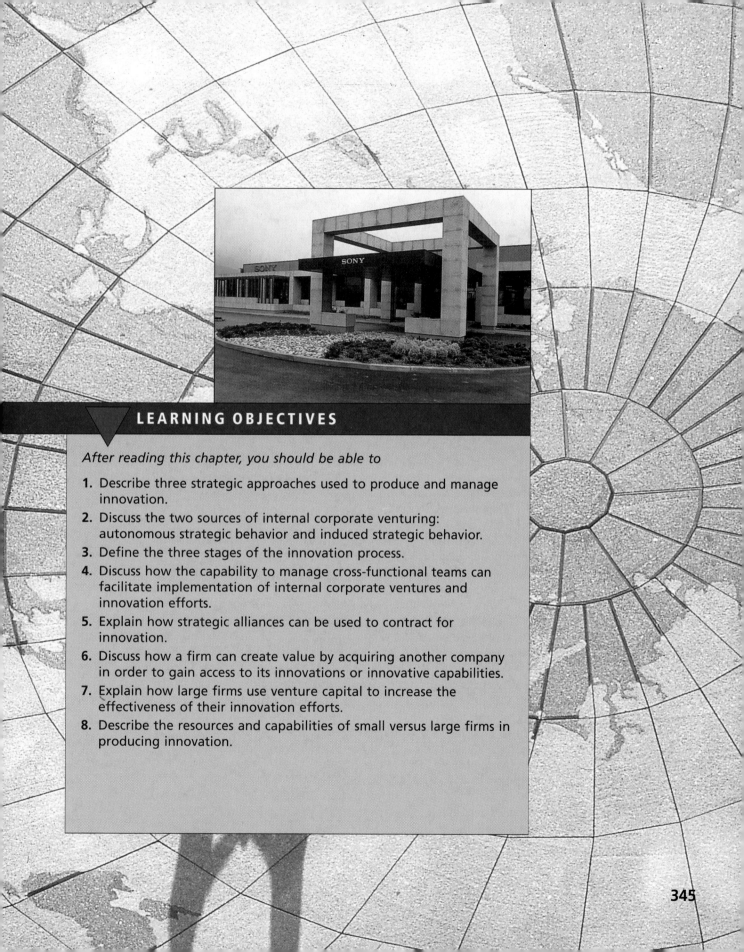

*After reading this chapter, you should be able to*

1. Describe three strategic approaches used to produce and manage innovation.
2. Discuss the two sources of internal corporate venturing: autonomous strategic behavior and induced strategic behavior.
3. Define the three stages of the innovation process.
4. Discuss how the capability to manage cross-functional teams can facilitate implementation of internal corporate ventures and innovation efforts.
5. Explain how strategic alliances can be used to contract for innovation.
6. Discuss how a firm can create value by acquiring another company in order to gain access to its innovations or innovative capabilities.
7. Explain how large firms use venture capital to increase the effectiveness of their innovation efforts.
8. Describe the resources and capabilities of small versus large firms in producing innovation.

## Corporate Entrepreneurship at Sony Corporation

**SONY**® Some consumer electronics firms strive to imitate product ideas from market leaders, turning out nearly indistinguishable calculators, VCRs, microwave ovens, stereos, televisions, and other electronic equipment. In contrast, Sony Corp. strives to be a market leader. Its successes have earned Sony recognition as the most innovative consumer electronics company in the world. Among the firm's many product innovations are the pocket-sized transistor radio, the battery-powered television set, the VCR, the 8mm camcorder, the compact disc player and most recently, the Mini Disc. Even the company's most celebrated innovation setback, the Betamax video cassette recorder, remains a profitable business because of commercial users of Betacam videotape equipment. This success has been achieved despite the overwhelming dominance of the VHS format in the consumer market. Sony's innovative capabilities also helped the firm introduce and standardize the 8 mm camcorder. This technology allowed for smaller camcorders and higher-quality videos simultaneously. Thus, even though it appeared to fail with the original video format, Sony learned from its mistakes and ultimately succeeded.

In 1993, Sony spent $2 billion (5.8 percent of total revenues) to support its research and development efforts. On an annual basis, Sony develops approximately 1,000 new products, an average of 4 for every business day in a year. Roughly 800 of these are improved versions of existing products; the remaining 200 or so are aimed at creating entirely new markets. While Sony has produced computer workstations for years, a major goal of the 1990s is to minimize the technology for workstations. This objective is identical to what the firm accomplished previously with its hi-fi equipment. The company seeks to package its latest technology into small products that anyone can understand and use.

Some believe that Sony's innovative ability results from use of a product-development capability employees call "Sony's way." As is the practice for other Japanese electronics companies, Sony hires new employees from engineering schools of major Japanese universities. The firm also trains engineers to be optimistic and open-minded and to pursue wide-ranging interests. Sony is committed to the position that the best technicians are those who are willing to move among product groups, trying their hand at technologies that may not have been studied formally at the university.

As effective as its internal development processes are, Sony also uses other strategic approaches to develop innovative products. As shown by its purchase of Columbia Pictures and CBS Records, the firm is also willing to acquire other companies' innovations and innovative capabilities. In addition, the purchase of firms provides Sony with opportunities to experiment in marketplaces where it expects to sell many of its future standardized products. The firm also has committed some of its resources to the development of strategic alliances with large and, in particular, small, high-tech firms.

Sony may be the quintessential entrepreneurial large firm. It uses every means available to develop innovative products and technologies through an emphasis on internal ventures. The firm does not hesitate to invest in or cooperate with other companies to gain access to their innovations. Through a system of strategic alliances, it tracks others' innovative ideas and shapes new product and process innovations in concert with its corporate partners. In total, the evidence suggests that Sony's core capabilities center on producing and managing innovation. ▲

This opening case illustrates three different strategic approaches through which innovation can be produced and managed, particularly in large firms. The first approach, called internal corporate venturing, focuses on producing innovation inside the organization. Sony Corp., for example, used an 8 mm technology that it developed within the firm as the basis for its miniaturization of the camcorder technology. The second approach is one in which firms contract for innovation through strategic alliances and/or joint ventures. This approach requires contracting and sharing innovation and complementary relationships between or among firms. Sony has done this through a network of strategic alliances. The third approach focuses on investing in good ideas outside the organization, or acquiring innovation. An example of this approach is Sony's purchase of Columbia Pictures and CBS Records.

This chapter examines the resources and skills required to use these three strategic approaches to produce and manage innovation. In addition, the pitfalls and trade-offs associated with each approach are described. This chapter emphasizes innovation in large companies. However, evidence shows that large firms are not the sole generators of product and process innovations. Many small and medium-sized firms are also effective innovators. Moreover, as demonstrated by Sony's actions, large companies often develop relationships with smaller firms to help them produce innovations. Because of the importance of their innovative abilities, the chapter's final section addresses the relative capabilities of small versus large firms in producing and managing innovation.

The chapter begins with brief discussions of a few of the basic terms associated with innovation.

## Innovation and Corporate Entrepreneurship

Some evidence suggests that effective innovation results in sustainable competitive advantage. More specifically, innovations that are (1) difficult for competitors to imitate, (2) able to provide significant value to customers, (3) timely, and (4) capable of being exploited commercially through existing capabilities and core competencies help firms develop competitive advantages.[1] Because of the apparent link with the development of competitive advantages and the earning of above-average profits, many companies, especially those active in the global marketplace, are interested in learning how to produce innovations and effectively manage the innovation process.

Corporate entrepreneurship includes the commitments, mindsets, and actions firms take to develop and manage innovations. Formally, **corporate entrepre-**

▲ **Corporate entrepreneurship** is the set of capabilities possessed by a firm to produce or acquire new products (goods and services) and manage the innovation process.

neurship is the set of capabilities possessed by a firm to produce or acquire new products (goods or services) and manage the innovation process. Corporate entrepreneurship is based on effective product design and successful commercialization. Because it is a set of capabilities that results in the effective *and* efficient design and manufacture of products, corporate entrepreneurship can be a basis for strategic competitiveness.

For U.S. companies, the role of corporate entrepreneurship in both effectiveness and efficiency has been recognized only somewhat recently. After World War II, for example, U.S. manufacturers sought to satisfy worldwide demand for their goods and services by focusing on mass-production techniques that allowed them to produce products in large quantities. This focus resulted in an opportunity for other producers (e.g., those in Japan and what was then West Germany) to use a different set of strategic actions.[2] The focus of U.S. firms on quantity allowed inefficiencies, which the Japanese and the Germans exploited commercially with high levels of product quality. By the 1970s, Japanese manufacturers were outcompeting their U.S. rivals through development and use of a host of product, process, and managerial innovations. Workers in Japanese factories, for example, were allowed to exercise a degree of responsibility unheard of in U.S. factories. Toyota Motor Co. pioneered what became known as lean production methods.

▲ **Lean production methods** combine the activities of everyone from top-level managers to line workers to suppliers into a tightly integrated whole.

**Lean production methods** combine the activities of everyone from top-level managers to line workers to suppliers into a tightly integrated whole. Firms committed to these methods set their sights on perfection: "continually declining costs, zero defects, zero inventories, and endless product variety."[3] Through its lean production methods, Toyota has been able to manufacture high-quality, low-cost automobiles.

Joseph Schumpeter's classic work on management of the innovation process suggests that firms engage in three types of innovative activity.[4] **Invention** is the act of creating or developing a new product (good or service) or process idea. **Innovation** is the process of creating a commercializable product from invention. Finally, **imitation** is adoption of the innovation by a population of similar firms. Resulting typically from imitation is standardization of the product or process idea. Particularly in the United States, the most critical of these activities has been innovation. Many firms are able to create ideas that lead to invention. However, commercializing those inventions through innovation has, at times, proved to be difficult.

▲ **Invention** is the act of creating or developing a new product (good or service) or process idea.

▲ **Innovation** is the process of creating a commercializable product from invention.

▲ **Imitation** is adoption of the innovation by a population of similar firms.

Strategic leaders, managers, and entrepreneurs all have roles that are critical to effective corporate entrepreneurship.[5] Especially with regard to corporate entrepreneurship, the strategic leader's role is to inspire an organization's members to work together in the pursuit of meaningful outcomes. Leaders and their words assume symbolic value to inspire organizational members to accomplish a firm's strategic intent and strategic mission. Lee Iacocca, for example, facilitated the return of Chrysler Corp. to profitability. During the firm's darkest days, Iacocca provided strong leadership and a sense of urgency about the actions the firm had to take to survive.[6] Of course, Chrysler's turnaround was a team effort, but, without Iacocca's inspiration, it is likely that the firm would have been forced to file for bankruptcy.[7]

Similarly, as CEO of Goodyear Tire & Rubber, Stanley Gault pushed for the implementation of a different strategic focus. Through his leadership, this tire manufacturer became committed to finding (and/or creating) the industry's fastest-growing, highest-margin markets. Once found, Goodyear Tire & Rubber intended to serve the specialty niches with innovative products. An example of these products is one for free-spending sports car owners. For these customers, the firm developed sets of tires "in which each tire, slightly different, is designed for a specific wheel, so consumers buy them four at a time, not one by one."[8] In a recent two-year period, Goodyear Tire & Rubber introduced 22 products into the marketplace. This number of product introductions far exceeded that of any other two-year period in the firm's history.

Managers are promoters and caretakers of organizational efficiency. Their work is especially important once a product idea has been commercialized and the organization necessary to support and promote it has been formed.[9] At Chrysler, the work of managers was instrumental in creating the turnaround Iacocca had inspired. In particular, these managers became more flexible and labored intensively to eliminate the barriers between workers and themselves that had developed over many years.[10]

Entrepreneurs are people who are the first to see an economic opportunity and seek to take advantage of it. Many times, entrepreneurs' commercial insights are not shared initially by others, forcing them to live with the social burden of not being accepted until the economic value of their insights is confirmed. Inside large organizations, entrepreneurs' activities have been labeled "intrapreneurship."[11]

The most effective entrepreneurs and intrapreneurs often are those that work against existing product standards by behaving as if they do not exist. This mindset seems to facilitate creativity and innovation. However, within large organizations, effective corporate entrepreneurship can be difficult to establish and support. In large organizations, people engaged in entrepreneurial practices must fully understand the corporate mindset that currently drives the firm's innovation process and the attributes of the structure, controls, and reward systems within which organizational work is completed.

## Internal Corporate Venturing

Composed of two processes, **internal corporate venturing** is the set of activities used to create inventions and innovations within a single organization.[12] Internal corporate venturing's two processes are shown in Figure 12-1.

The first internal corporate venturing process involves a bottom-up approach to the creation of product and process innovations. **Autonomous strategic behavior** is a bottom-up process in which product champions pursue new product ideas, often through a political process, whereby they develop and coordinate the commercialization of a new good or service until it achieves marketplace success. A **product champion** is a member of an organization who has an entrepreneurial vision of a new good or service and seeks to create support for its commercialization.

The autonomous strategic behavior of a product champion sometimes alters a firm's strategic intent and strategic mission and thereby its corporate- or business-level strategy. For example, Sears's original catalog (mail-order) business ultimately became dominated by its retail strategy through experimenting with retailing outlets at its catalog warehouses.[13] To support its commitment to innovation, Hewlett Packard encourages its workers to serve as product champions. The firm's employees are challenged continuously to strive for innovativeness, speed, and efficiency. Although a firm with over 96,000 employees and more than $21 billion in sales, Hewlett Packard recently earned 70 percent of its annual sales

▲ **Internal corporate venturing** is the set of activities used to create inventions and innovations within a single organization.

▲ **Autonomous strategic behavior** is a bottom-up process in which product champions pursue new product ideas, often through a political process, whereby they develop and coordinate the commercialization of a new good or service until it achieves marketplace success.

▲ A **product champion** is a member of an organization who has an entrepreneurial vision of a new good or service and seeks to create support for its commercialization.

**FIGURE 12–1**    **Model of Internal Corporate Venturing**

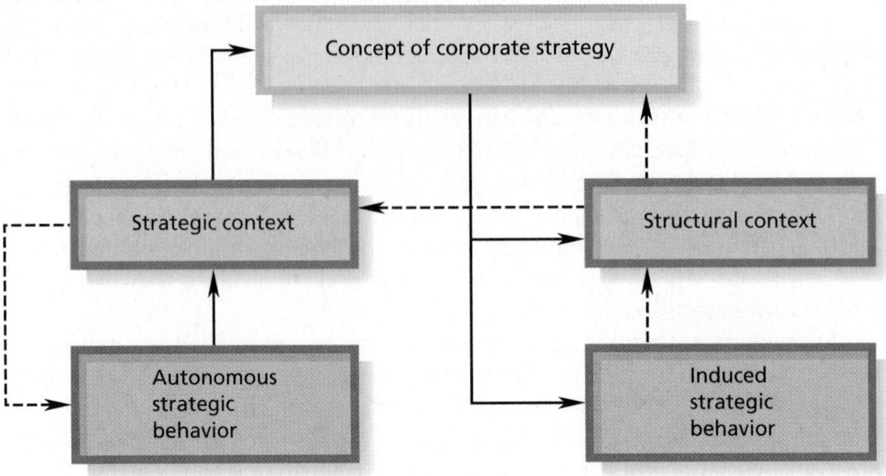

SOURCE: Adapted from, R. A. Burgelman, 1983, A model of the interactions of strategic behavior, corporate context, and the concept of strategy, Academy of Management Review 8:65.

from products that were introduced or revamped within the previous two years.[14] Product champions are also encouraged at Rubbermaid (this company was selected as America's most admired corporation in *Fortune* magazine's 1993 survey). Rubbermaid's CEO has challenged the firm's employees to innovate in ways that would allow the company to enter a new product category every 12 to 18 months, earn 33 percent of sales from products introduced within the past five years, and, by the year 2000, derive 25 percent of its total revenues from markets outside the United States.[15] Across time, the products Hewlett Packard and Rubbermaid introduce modify the implementation of some of the firms' business-level strategies.

Changing the concept of corporate-level strategy through autonomous strategic behavior, as was the case with Sears Roebuck & Co., results when product championing takes place within strategic and structural contexts (see Figure 12-1). The **strategic context** refers to the process used to arrive at strategic decisions. At Sears, the strategic context favored the mail-order business. Considerable amounts of product championing by a range of people ultimately led to the change in the firm's concept of its corporate strategy. The **structural context** refers to the hierarchical structure and reward system used to support the implementation of a corporate-level strategy. The structural context associated with Sears's commitment to the mail-order business also was a barrier to the emergence of a focus on a new retail strategy.

**Induced strategic behavior** is a top-down process where the current strategy and structure foster product innovations that are associated closely with the current strategy and structure. In this situation, the strategy in place is filtered through a matching structural hierarchy.

Outcomes achieved primarily through induced strategic behaviors are shown by study of one of the sterling successes in the U.S. economy, Intel Corp. Today, a dominant producer of logic chips for microcomputers, Intel was originally a

▲ **Strategic context** refers to the process used to arrive at strategic decisions.

▲ **Structural context** refers to the hierarchical structure and reward system used to support the implementation of a corporate-level strategy.

▲ **Induced strategic behavior** is a top-down process where the current strategy and structure foster product innovations that are associated closely with the current strategy and structure.

## STRATEGIC FOCUS

### Internal Corporate Venturing at Intel

A leading semiconductor manufacturer, Intel has survived more than 25 years as an independent company in an extremely dynamic industry. The firm grew from $1 million in sales in 1968, to $8.8 billion in 1993. Intel's strategy began with a focus on Dynamic Random-Access Memory (DRAM) chips. These chips were used as memory chips for all types of computers. In 1985, Intel was faced with a large cyclical downturn in the semiconductor industry and fierce Japanese price competition in DRAMs. Due to the downturn, the firm expected a loss of almost $200 million in 1986. Moreover, it needed to invest several hundred million dollars in new plant and equipment if it wanted to be competitive for the next generation of DRAMs. At the time, however, Intel's market share in DRAMs was only 3.4 percent. It ranked only ninth in the industry, behind a number of U.S. and Japanese memory producers.

Even though there was a push for more investment in DRAM chips from key engineers, by 1986, logic chips were becoming the firm's primary source of revenue. The push for investment in DRAM chips was related to the firm's image of itself as a memory company. The logic, or microprocessor business, following the development of the 8086, 286 and 386, and, ultimately, the 486 and Pentium processor chips, however, was established. The induced strategic processes, focusing on memory chips, caused the strategic initiative to continue building on existing organizational learning in DRAMs. However, Intel's small market share in memory chips as well as the greater profit margins in logic chips suggested a change was necessary. Although a major autonomous change in strategy was continually reducing the dollars and commitment to DRAMs, there was still momentum to invest in DRAMs.

The strategic shift to logic chips, outside the scope of the current strategy (DRAMs), was driven largely by operational-level managers seeking to use their skills in the firm's newly developing distinctive capability in logic chips. These lower-level managers, however, had to demonstrate viability through entrepreneurial activity. It took considerable effort on their part for the top management team to formally ratify the new corporate direction. Once ratified, the new direction became the new induced strategic initiative (strategic intent and mission). Thus, even though Intel's strategy of producing logic chips is recognized as one of the most successful ventures in the semiconductor industry, it took a significant amount of time for the firm's strategic leaders to recognize the change in strategy. The new strategic mission emerged by overcoming the previous induced strategic pattern and accepting the autonomous strategic processes that had created the success in logic chips.

manufacturer of memory chips. However, as the Strategic Focus on Intel shows, before the final strategic change was implemented fully and recognized formally by the firm's top-level managers, the change to the production of logic chips had followed *both* the induced and the autonomous internal venturing processes.

The Intel Corp. example is one of the most dramatic in U.S. economic history, particularly in the semiconductor industry. Intel's profits have soared because of the price competition in the microcomputer business, where Apple and

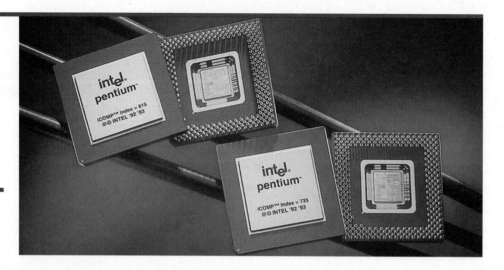

*Shown here is Intel's Pentium Processor chip. This product is another innovation in Intel's long line of successful microprocessor chips. The company uses what is now a well-known slogan—"Intel Inside"—as a part of the advertising campaign for its chips.*

IBM are competing with clone manufacturers and newer market entrants such as AST and Dell Corp. Fierce price competition has fostered increased demand for microcomputers and, in turn, the microprocessors produced by Intel. Moreover, software manufacturers continue to develop and market sophisticated applications that are of interest to a host of personal computer (PC) users. To operate these applications, users often must upgrade their PCs. Upgrades are accomplished through the purchase of more advanced microprocessing chips, such as those produced by Intel.[16]

Historically Intel has been able to maintain its margins by continuing to invent new, more efficient chips and to follow the learning curve with dexterity. In the middle of 1994, Intel's gross profit margin was 58 percent. The firm was supplying microprocessors for roughly 75 percent of all PCs sold. In 1993, Intel's net earnings of $2.3 billion (on sales of $8.8 billion) made it the most profitable company of its size in the world.[17] To continue supporting its internal innovation process, Intel allocated approximately 13 percent of its gross sales revenues to R&D in 1994.[18] Net revenues were expected to increase by about 20 percent during 1994. Contributing to this anticipated rise was an aggressive program of new product introductions, including the "ramping up of the Pentium microprocessor."[19]

Even the firm's dramatic success, however, does not overshadow the difficulty that Intel experienced when making the transition from memory chips to logic chips. There was substantial inertia in the firm's strategic context because of its image of itself as a memory chip company. Even years after it had changed to a logic company, it still saw itself as a memory company and continued to pour resources into the memory chip business. It was not until its outstanding success in logic chips and its recognition that it had fulfilled a need in the external environment that Intel recognized officially that its strategic intent and mission had changed.

Intel's experiences highlight the difficulty that large firms often encounter when striving to effectively pursue internal corporate ventures. The induced processes can dominate and create strategic and structural contexts or barriers to change. Effective internal corporate venturing processes are established only when both internal political processes and strategic and structural contexts have changed and a new strategic mission has emerged.

These difficulties regarding the development of effective internal corporate venturing processes appear to suggest that large firms may become more innovative through strategic alliances and external acquisitions of innovation than through attempts to foster internal innovation. New small firms, without a long corporate strategic history, may be better at initiating strategic change. Small firms, however, often lack the resources, capabilities, and core competencies necessary to commercialize a large volume of innovation-based projects. This point is discussed in greater detail later in the chapter. Nonetheless, with an appropriate culture, large firms can be entrepreneurial by encouraging new ideas through rewards and support for visible intrapreneurs.[20]

## Implementing Internal Corporate Ventures

Listed in Table 12-1 are companies that were recognized by *Fortune* magazine as the most innovative large firms in the United States in 1993. As shown in Table 12-1, Microsoft Corp. was voted by top-level U.S. executives as the nation's most innovative company. General Electric, second on the list, has long been recognized as an innovative company. Many of the remaining firms also may be recognized consistently as innovators in their respective industries. However, in the number 10 position, Chrysler Corp. may seem out of place. This ranking appears to suggest that the executives have given a lot of credit to Chrysler for the team concept the firm is now using to design and produce automobiles and trucks. The processes Chrysler Corp. is using to foster and support its internal corporate venturing capability are described in the next Strategic Focus.

Once a firm decides to produce a new good or service, problems of how to most effectively create it are encountered. The design and transfer of technology from engineering to manufacturing and ultimately to distribution and to the marketplace are critical. The design stage entails a high degree of integration among the various functions involved in the innovation process—from engineering to manufacturing, and ultimately to market distribution. Initial design efforts that do not consider down-line aspects in the production process (manufacturing, testing, marketing, service, etc.) may result in high product costs and low product quality. Such interfunctional integration facilitates reciprocal information flows among functions responsible for development, design, and implementation. Developing a capability to innovate rapidly using team processes as Chrysler has done, helps large firms overcome the difficulties they encounter when trying to be entrepreneurial. These matters are discussed in greater detail in the next subsection.

## Implementing Product Development Teams and Facilitating Interfunctional Integration

While the importance of interfunctional integration has been recognized for some time, it has not been practiced widely in industry until recently. However, because of an emerging emphasis on horizontal organization, firms are becoming more skilled at interfunctional integration. **Horizontal organization** refers to changes in organizational processes where managing across functional units becomes more critical than managing up and down functional hierarchies.[21] Therefore, instead of being built around vertical hierarchical functions or departments, the organization is built around core horizontal processes similar to Chrysler's platform teams. Also,

▼ **TABLE 12-1**

**Rankings of the Most Innovative Companies by Senior U.S. Executives**

1. Microsoft
2. General Electric
3. 3M
4. AT&T
5 Motorola
6. Apple Computer
7. Intel
8. Merck
9. Wal-Mart Stores
10. Chrysler

*Source:* J. Graves, 1993, Most innovative companies, *Fortune*, December 13, 11. ©1993 Time Inc. All rights reserved.

▲ **Horizontal organization** refers to changes in organizational processes where managing across functional units becomes more critical than managing up and down functional hierarchies.

## Chrysler Corporation's New Approach to Product Development

In the fall of 1991, Chrysler Corp. officially opened its $1 billion technical center, called the Chrysler Technology Center. Lee Iacocca, the firm's CEO in 1991, referred to the building as an "idea factory." The intent was to bring the best minds together—from product design, engineering, manufacturing, purchasing, and marketing. Having these people work together, Iacocca believed, would facilitate continuous interactions among the functions necessary to design and manufacture innovative and competitive products.

This innovation-based project, largely under the direction of then Chrysler President Robert Lutz, divided the organization into platform teams. The teams are cross-functional in nature. Representatives from all operating areas within the firm, as well as from key suppliers, are part of the teams. Each team is responsible for bringing a specific vehicle to the marketplace. Because it replaces the company's old in-sequence production with a concurrent production approach, this platform organization helps reduce the amount of time required to introduce innovative products into the marketplace.

This new approach is indicative of a larger change taking place at Chrysler Corp. The firm is now producing more products from its existing technological base, but with fewer people. In part, this is possible because cross-functional platform teams have empowered people working in the firm's facilities. At Chrysler, empowered teams have been able to increase productivity while using the same or a reduced amount of resources.

Thus, Chrysler Corp. has embarked on a dramatic cultural change from a traditional, bureaucratic, vertically structured organization to one organized into four nimble, cross-functional platform teams—one for small cars, one for large cars, one for minivans, and one for jeep vehicles and trucks. Within teams, everyone focuses not just on pieces of the car, but on the total vehicle. Communication flows are simultaneous and two-way—not sequential and one-way, as they used to be.

Underlying this change in culture was a study initiated by Iacocca. This study was intended to help Chrysler gain an understanding of the internal workings of Honda Motor Co. The final report indicated that Chrysler should scrap its traditional corporate structure. This structure was dominated by strong individual departments—engineering, manufacturing, marketing, purchasing, and styling, as examples. Each department protected its own interests above all else, so new vehicles were developed amid a series of compromises, with predictably mediocre results. Honda, in contrast, used a system similar to the lean production methods pioneered by Toyota Motor Co. to design and produce its automobiles. At Honda, members of all functional departments were assigned to work together simultaneously from the beginning of a new project. This approach allowed Honda to quickly introduce innovative vehicles to the marketplace.

Chrysler Corp.'s executives were able to implement this approach so successfully that other firms have begun to study Chrysler. A Lockheed Corp. top-level manager, for instance, suggested that "Chrysler executives are putting their money where their mouth is and are acting like a team." Chrysler Corp.'s stock price and financial performance have improved dramatically as a result of the strategic actions taken during the early 1990s. Moreover, as indicated above, executives outside of Chrysler are giving high marks to the firm for its capability to efficiently design and manufacture innovative products.

AT&T's Network Systems division reorganized all of its strategic actions around horizontal processes. General Electric used a horizontal design to reorganize its lighting business, abandoning its former vertical hierarchy in the process.

Evidence suggests that a key benefit that can be gained through successful application of horizontal organizational processes is effective utilization of sophisticated manufacturing technologies (e.g., the computer-aided design and manufacturing [CAD/CAM] system).[22] Thus, interfunctional integration can facilitate a firm's efforts to establish a sustainable competitive advantage.

## Barriers to Integration

There are barriers that can stifle attempts to effectively integrate functions within an organization. For example, an emphasis on functional specialization may affect interfunctional integration. Such specialization creates distancing of divergent functions and characteristically different roles for engineering, manufacturing, and marketing. Functional departments have been found to be differentiated along four dimensions: time orientation, interpersonal orientation, goal orientation, and formality of structure.[23] Although functional specialization may be damaging to the horizontal relationships necessary for implementing innovation, such specialization does have an important purpose in creating an efficient organization. Therefore, eliminating such task specialization to overcome barriers to interfunctional integration may do more harm than good to the organization. Methods must be found through which interfunctional integration can be promoted without concurrently changing the basic structural characteristics necessary for task specialization and efficiency.

## Facilitating Integration

There are three methods firms can use to achieve effective interfunctional integration.[24] The first of these methods utilizes shared values. Shared values, when linked clearly with a firm's strategic intent and strategic mission, become the glue that promotes coupling between and among functional units. Hewlett Packard has remained an accomplished technological leader because it has established the "HP way." In essence, the HP way refers to the firm's esteemed organizational culture that promotes internal innovation.

Leadership is a second method of achieving interfunctional integration. Effective strategic leaders remind organizational members continuously of the value that product innovations create for the company. In the most desirable situations, this value-creating potential becomes the basis for the integration and management of functional department activities. At General Electric, Jack Welch frequently highlights the importance of integrated work, among both business units and different functions. To frame this message consistently, Welch has been instrumental in establishing and operating a managerial training center that focuses on these relationships among all levels of the company's management structure.

A third method of achieving interfunctional integration is concerned with goals and budgets. This method calls for firms to formulate goals and allocate the budgetary resources necessary to accomplish them. These goals are specific targets for the integrated design and production of new goods and services. Chrysler Corp.'s reorganization to focus on platform teams, for example, has effectively reinforced in employees' minds the importance of team processes. S. C. Johnson & Son (a company commonly known as Johnson Wax) recently overhauled its factories and consolidated its international operations. A key objective of these actions was to reduce costs and focus the firm's resources in order to "recast itself more clearly as a provider of products that clean, shine, and debug the home."[25] Critical to these efforts was the company's commitment to step up innovation through the use of self-directed work teams.

## Appropriating (Extracting) Value from Innovation

Interfunctional integration, when implemented properly, may also facilitate decreased time to market, improve product quality, and create value for customers. Especially for firms competing globally, increasing attention is being paid to the amount of time required to transfer products from the lab to the consumer.[26] A firm can gain a competitive advantage if it is able to develop a product idea and transfer it to the market sooner than competitors, especially in high-tech environments such as biotechnology.[27] If the product has wide consumer appeal, this gives an advantage to the first mover.[28] While there is inherent risk in being a pioneer, a first mover may be able to establish a dominant position from which to build future market share and earn above-average profits. Research evidence suggests that firms with long development cycles typically are outperformed by companies with short ones.[29] Although shorter time-to-market cycles can help firms appropriate value from their innovations, poor design can lead to expensive recalls, higher production costs, low product performance, and product liability exposure.

Because product design teams often are composed of many different players, each of whom possesses critical knowledge and skills, interfunctional integration may reduce uncertainty and facilitate the successful introduction of innovative goods or services. In fact, research indicates that the simultaneous evaluation of multiple alternatives, as would be the case with cross-functional teams, increases decision speed.[30] Hewlett Packard, for example, is divided into global, cross-functional teams that are capable of making decisions quickly to deal with rapidly changing market conditions.[31] However, it is essential that design teams be managed effectively. If implementation is not effective in a complex situation, uncertainty may be increased.

In summary, the model presented in Figure 12-2 shows how value may be appropriated from internal innovation processes. As our discussion has indicated, the internal innovation process must be managed to facilitate interfunctional integration in order to appropriate the greatest amount of value from product design and commercialization efforts. Effective management of internal innovation processes can reduce both the time required to introduce innovations into the marketplace and the degree of decision uncertainty associated with the design of an innovative product and the demand for it. These desirable outcomes were achieved by Chrysler Corp. in the early 1990s through the effective management of the firm's internal innovation processes.[32]

## Strategic Alliances: Cooperating to Produce and Manage Innovation

It is virtually impossible for most firms to possess all the knowledge required to compete successfully in their product areas over the long term. Thus, internal innovation may contribute to the development of a sustainable competitive advantage when a firm possesses the capabilities and core competencies required to

**FIGURE 12–2**  **Appropriating Value from Internal Firm Innovation**

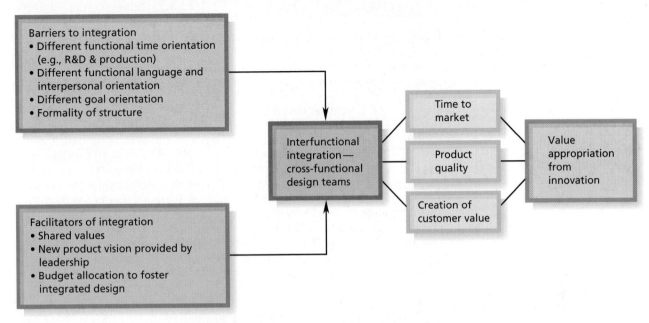

*SOURCE: Adapted from M. A. Hitt, R. E. Hoskisson, and R. D. Nixon, 1993. A mid-range theory of interfunctional integration, its antecedents and outcomes,* Journal of Engineering and Technology Management *10: 161–185.*

innovate effectively and efficiently. But because the stock of human knowledge is large and increasing at an accelerated pace, many single firms, regardless of their size, cannot keep up to date on this vast pool of knowledge by themselves. Complicating this matter is the fact that the knowledge base confronting today's organizations is not only vast, but also increasingly more specialized. As such, the knowledge needed to commercialize goods and services is frequently embedded within different corporations and countries that have the ability to create specialized products. For instance, the Japanese have special abilities to manufacture DRAMs or memory computer chips.

In Chapter 5, we discussed why and how firms use strategic alliances (strategic alliances are partnerships between firms whereby resources, capabilities, and core competencies are combined to pursue common interests and goals[33]) to gain either competitive parity or competitive advantage relative to rivals. Moreover, one of the specific reasons to enter into a strategic alliance is to introduce innovative goods or services. Strategic alliances are used often, especially by large firms, to innovate by sharing two or more firms' knowledge and skill bases.[34] Recently, Texas Instruments, Inc., and Microsoft Corp. formed a strategic alliance to develop tools tying personal computers with large central computers. Through this alliance, the firms intend to use their knowledge and skills to "develop a common approach to producing components for executing different functions, such as retrieving data that can be stored in electronic libraries."[35] Once functions are stored, software writers can access copies from a central source and use them to build programs quickly.

As described in the next Strategic Focus, Corning Inc. (known until recently as Corning Glass Works) takes advantage of knowledge links through strategic

## STRATEGIC FOCUS

### Corning Inc.'s Use of Strategic Alliances and Joint Ventures

Over the years, Corning Inc. has been involved with a number of successful strategic alliances and joint ventures. Most joint ventures have only a 46 percent success rate and an average life span of 3.5 years. In contrast, one-half of Corning Inc.'s joint ventures have existed for at least 10 years.

Apparently contributing to this success is the firm's unpretentious corporate culture. The culture allows Corning to learn from the alliances and ventures with which it has been involved. Moreover, each activity developed through an alliance is given significant amounts of autonomy. The management of projects that are a part of various alliances is a picture of diplomatic compromise and give-and-take. Apparently, trust and the ability to share are key capabilities in successful alliances.

Strategic alliances and joint ventures have helped transform Corning Inc.'s old-line manufacturing base into a modern variety of products with strong potential growth. In addition, its alliances and ventures with foreign companies, such as South Korea's Samsung Electronics Corp. and Germany's Siemens AG, have created political advantage as the firm expands into Europe, South America, and Asia. In this way, strategic alliances and joint ventures have become a form of political leverage, creating easier entry for Corning Inc. into the global marketplace.

Corning Inc. has formed joint ventures and strategic alliances since 1880 when the fledgling maker of decorative glass and dinnerware helped Thomas Edison develop the light bulb. Owens-Corning Fiberglass was formed in 1938 as a joint venture with Owens-Illinois Corp. This operation grew into the nation's largest maker of glass fiber. In 1943, Dow-Corning, with Dow Chemical Co. as a partner, became the leading producer of silicone. In 1985, Corning developed a partnership with Ciba-Geigy, then the world's second largest pharmaceutical maker. Ciba-Geigy possessed a highly regarded laboratory, and Corning Inc. had what Ciba-Geigy needed—a foothold in the medical-diagnostics business. Although two years were required for this strategic alliance to be formed and for a trusting relationship to evolve, Ciba-Corning Diagnostics Corp. has been successful in developing a new generation of blood and urine analyzers.

James Houghton, Corning Inc.'s chairman and CEO, believes that "the world has become too complicated for companies to enter new markets and form new businesses on their own." This conviction may explain why Corning Inc. chooses to innovate largely through the formation, use, and nurturing of a number of strategic alliances and joint ventures.

alliances and joint ventures with other companies (joint ventures are new business ventures that were not part of either partner's portfolio of businesses before the ventures began).

As described in this Strategic Focus, Corning Inc. has historically been successful with strategic alliances and joint ventures. Recently, however, some of the firm's alliances and ventures have been troubled. For example, in the middle of 1994, Dow-Corning, a joint venture in which Corning Inc. has a 50 percent stake, remained involved with consolidated federal multidistrict litigation over silicone-gel breast implants. At the same time, the firm was trying to change the nature of its strategic alliance with Vitro, a diversified Mexican company.[36]

Corning Inc.'s more recent experiences appear to suggest that, across time, the successful management of strategic alliances and joint ventures, in an attempt to produce innovations, is challenging. Alternatively, it is possible that a firm can become too dependent on strategic alliances and joint ventures—as a means both of innovating and of achieving strategic competitiveness and earning above-average profits. In 1992, Corning Inc.'s more than 20 joint ventures alone provided 14 percent of the firm's net income.[37]

In a more general sense, some argue that strategic alliances can be dangerous. Supporting this argument is the contention that strategic alliances allow partner firms to gain knowledge and resources that make them stronger competitors.[38] If true, the long-run effect of strategic alliances could very well be to create stronger competitors and ultimately lower profitability for an industry's leading firms. Thus, organizations are challenged to evaluate carefully all the risks associated with strategic alliances that might be formed in the pursuit of strategic competitiveness and superior profitability.

Two types of strategic alliances are used to foster innovation: product-link alliances and knowledge-link alliances. **Product-link alliances** are used to fill gaps in product lines; often such an alliance is part of a desire to outsource to global areas where a product can be made at low-cost production sites. **Knowledge-link alliances** are formed to help a company learn specialized capabilities from another firm, with the intention being that both partners will gain skills and capabilities that, in turn, will benefit future endeavors. Corning Inc.'s primary focus on knowledge links has contributed to the success of its strategic alliances.

Successful product-link alliances help firms cut costs, reduce risks, accelerate the introduction of innovative goods or services to the marketplace, build flexibility, and monitor and neutralize competitors' skills. Japanese automobile manufacturers are known for their ability to use product links with other low-cost producers in Asia to gain at least some of these positive outcomes, establishing competitive advantages in the process. In contrast, some U.S. firms may have used product-link alliances ineffectively—as a substitute for changes that they need to make and as an alternative to more effective management of current operations.

Mentioned briefly in Chapter 5, the strategic alliance between General Motors (GM) and South Korea's Daewoo Corp. is an example of an ineffective product-link alliance. This alliance was formed in 1986 to build small cars in Korea for sale in the U.S. market.[39] The alliance was troubled from the start. Neither firm understood the other's strengths and weaknesses, and the companies failed to jointly assess their goals and strategic intents. In essence, GM sought to use this strategic alliance only as a finger in the dike to prevent the rising tide of small-car competition from sweeping over it in the short run. Because it failed, innovative products were not produced by the GM-Daewoo alliance.

Across time, strategic alliances can slowly deskill a partner that does not understand their inherent risks. Collaboration within alliances can lead to competition, both in learning new skills and in refining new capabilities and core competencies that can be used to design and produce other innovative products and processes.

Japanese corporations, for example, appear to be expert in learning new technologies through strategic alliances. This skill has been instrumental in helping these firms learn how to compete in markets where they were locked out previously.[40] For instance, all electronics products sold under the Eastman Kodak, General Electric, RCA, Zenith, and Westinghouse brand names are made by their foreign alliance partners and imported into the United States. Moreover, General

▲ **Product-link alliances** are used to fill gaps in product lines; often such an alliance is part of a desire to outsource to global areas where a product can be made at low-cost production sites.

▲ **Knowledge-link alliances** are formed to help a company learn specialized capabilities from another firm, with the intention being that both partners will gain skills and capabilities that, in turn, will benefit future endeavors.

Electric (GE) and Westinghouse, firms that once dominated the world in the manufacture of products for the power-distribution industry, were becoming, in the early 1990s, only distributors of other companies' products. This change for GE and Westinghouse was especially noticeable in the small motor and turbine markets that utilize a high level of microelectronics and precision manufacturing. A similar trend was observed in the factory-automation and numerical-controls industry at the beginning of the 1990s.[41]

As our discussion has suggested, product-link alliances may reduce a firm's innovative ability. Moreover, these alliances can lead to a company's dependence on partners through outsourcing to obtain low-cost components and inexpensive assembly. Often manufacturing skills and knowledge related to upgrading precision manufacturing and testing are lost, while such skills are gained by competitors to which the firm is outsourcing. Ultimately, then, a firm may lose its core competence through product-link alliances.

Forming knowledge-link alliances may allow a firm to gain the initiative. To form a knowledge link, a firm must first be fully aware of its capabilities and competencies. It must also develop human resource practices that allow it to retain its most effective personnel. Many alliance partners believe that if they own 51 percent of the shareholding position, they have control. Legal control may be important, but legal control does not necessarily curtail the flow of knowledge and the rate of partner learning. Implementing horizontal organizational structures may facilitate knowledge development. The functional structure is created for efficiency. The horizontal structure is formed for learning and creates linkages among employees. Such an organization would facilitate learning in alliances.

In summary, building successful strategic alliances requires focusing on knowledge, identifying core competencies, and developing strong human resources to manage these core competencies. Expecting to gain financial benefits in the short run through product linkages may lead to unintended consequences in the long run. Firms establishing product linkages may not view their collaboration with other firms as an indirect form of competition for knowledge.[42]

## Buying Innovation: Acquisitions and Venture Capital

In this section, we focus on the third approach firms use to produce and manage innovation. The intent of this approach is to acquire innovation, and innovative capabilities, from outside the organization. An example of this approach is AT&T's acquisition of NCR Corp. This acquisition was completed to facilitate AT&T's efforts to shore up its developmental ability in computers. AT&T executives believed this ability was needed in light of rapid growth in the joint communication and computer market.

As approaches to producing and managing innovation, both strategic alliances and acquisitions appear to be increasing in popularity, especially among large firms. One reason for this is that the innovation prowess of other countries is growing at a rapid pace. A number of indicators suggest that Japanese firms, for instance, have progressed during the post-war period from borrowing, magnifying, and successfully commercializing foreign technologies to operating at the technological frontier especially in process innovation. The National Science Foundation reported in 1988 that Japanese firms accounted for the largest single share of foreign-origin patents.[43] Even in light of this type of evidence, it is possible that too many firms (including U.S.-based ones) competing in the global economy still view Japanese

R&D operations as oriented largely toward the Japanese market. However, Japanese companies are becoming skilled at transferring technologies from Japan into their global R&D networks. One way for companies from the world's other nations to gain competitive parity or perhaps competitive advantage when facing this situation is to gain more access to Japanese technology. Acquiring other companies is a method through which they can access such technology.

## Acquisitions

Acquiring other firms as a method of producing and managing innovation is not without risks. A key risk of this method is that a firm may substitute the ability to buy innovations for the ability to produce innovations internally. There is some research theory supporting this suggested trade-off and its negative effect on the processes a firm uses to produce innovations internally.[44]

Figure 12-3 shows that firms gaining access to innovations through the acquisition of other companies risk reductions in both R&D inputs (as measured by investments in R&D) and R&D outputs (as measured by the number of patents). Evidence in Figure 12-3 suggests that the R&D-to-sales ratio drops after acquisitions are completed and that the patent-to-sales ratio drops significantly after companies are involved with large acquisitions. These relationships indicate that firms substitute acquisitions for their internal innovation process. This may result

**FIGURE 12–3** Evidence of R&D Inputs (Expenditures) and Outputs (Number of Patents) per Dollar of Sales Before and After Large Acquisitions

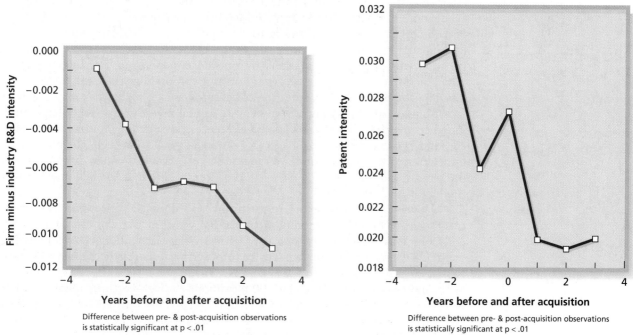

Difference between pre- & post-acquisition observations is statistically significant at p < .01

Difference between pre- & post-acquisition observations is statistically significant at p < .01

*SOURCE: M. A. Hitt, R. E. Hoskisson, R. D. Ireland, and J. S. Harrison, 1991, Are acquisitions a poison pill of innovation?* Academy of Management Executive 5, 4:24–25.

because firms lose strategic control and emphasize financial control of original, and especially of acquired, business units.[45] Although reduced innovation may not always result, acquiring firms should be aware of this potential outcome.

## Venture Capital

Another approach used to acquire innovations is concerned with venture capital. In some instances, firms choose to establish their own venture capital divisions. The charge to these divisions is to carefully evaluate other companies to identify those with innovations or innovative capabilities that, if acquired, would help the firm develop a sustainable competitive advantage. In other instances, firms decide to serve as an internal source of venture capital for innovative product ideas that can be spun off as independent or affiliate firms.

Historically the venture capital business has been associated primarily with independent venture capital firms. Recently, however, both domestic and foreign corporations have discovered that investing in venture capital adds a new dimension to their corporate development strategies and can produce an attractive return on their investments.[46] The strategic benefits to a corporation include the ability to invest early and observe what happens to the new venture. This may lead to subsequent acquisitions, technology licensing, product marketing rights, and possibly the development of international opportunities. Large firms often view venture capital as a window on future technological development. Participation by corporations can take many forms, but usually begins with investment in several venture capital funds as a limited partner and evolves into direct investments in new business ventures. Many firms begin this strategy by forming a venture development division. If financial returns are the only objective, usually a stand-alone venture fund is the best vehicle. Lubrizol Enterprises operates as an independent subsidiary of Lubrizol Corp. It uses venture capital to complete acquisitions and form partnerships, among other strategic actions. A key objective of Lubrizol Enterprises' actions is to develop strategic business units based on leading-edge technologies.

Disdain of large corporations by outside entrepreneurs can be a potential pitfall. Entrepreneurs may be very wary of large corporations that seek to dominate fledgling companies. The syndication of venture funds to reduce risk may also be a factor limiting potential gains from venture capital investments. Other large firms may become part of the syndication and reduce the potential returns for the large corporate partner (through sharing of knowledge).[47] Although there is some difficulty in obtaining corporate venture capital, the flow of venture capital to small firms nearly doubled in 1992, from $1.36 billion in 1991 to $2.63 billion. This was the first increase since 1987.

However, with corporate restructuring and downsizing continuing, executives seem willing to try more entrepreneurial ventures. Venture capital is apparently one way to participate and may be less risky than internal development.[48] Table 12-2 summarizes the main advice for fostering a successful corporate venture capital operation.

Another approach to producing innovations through venture capital is shown in the Strategic Focus on Thermo Electron Corp. This firm encourages internal entrepreneurship that can subsequently be spun off as an independent company.

▼ **TABLE 12–2**

## Issues in Managing a Corporate Venture Capital Division

A corporate venture should be established as an independent entity and should have access to a committed, separate pool of funds.

The funds should be managed by a skilled venture professional drawn from the independent venture community.

The corporate venture fund should be prepared to compensate its managers relative to top-quality managers' salaries throughout the venture capital industry. Thus, the comparison should be to other independent venture capitalists when setting compensation.

There can be strategic benefits when the new venture fits with the corporate strategy. This should not be overshadowed by the primary emphasis on realization of financial objectives (i.e., return on investment).

If the venture proposal fails on financial criteria, the potential venture might be referred to another part of the organization to explore an alternative relationship, such as a license or joint venture agreement.

A corporation should be willing to make a complete commitment of talent and capital if it seeks to establish its own corporate venture fund. Of course, this approach may significantly dilute potential strategic benefits.

*Source:* Reprinted with permission of the publisher from R. Siegel, E. Siegel, and I. C. MacMillian, 1988, Corporate venture capitalists: Autonomy, obstacles, and performance, *Journal of Business Venturing* 3: 233–47. Copyright 1988 by Elsevier Science Inc.

Research suggests that firms that reduce extensive diversification (overdiversification) through downscoping[49] have shown improvements in R&D expenditures relative to competitors.[50] Thus, it is important for a firm to maintain a level of new product or market entry (diversification) that allows proper strategic control of operations. Thermo Electron Corp. appears to have achieved an effective balance with respect to these issues. But if the company becomes too diversified, its efforts to provide strategic help to spin-off firms may be limited by its strategic expertise and information-processing capacities.

The venture capital spin-off network associated with Thermo Electron Corp. may be similar to the keiretsu found in Japan, although on a much smaller scale. Two types of keiretsu, horizontal and vertical, exist in Japan.[51] Horizontal keiretsus are currently organized into six major industrial groups: Mitsui, Mitsubishi, Sumitomo, Fuji, Sanwa, and Dai-Ichi Kangyo. Each firm in these groups is much larger than each firm that has been spun off by Thermo Electron Corp. In fact, each of the six major groups mentioned above includes one or more firms in almost all important industrial sectors in Japan. In contrast to horizontal keiretsus, vertical keiretsus focus on a particular product or industry and consist of a main manufacturer (e.g., Toyota Motor Co.) and its affiliated subcontractors.

As is the case with the horizontal keiretsu network, Thermo Electron Corp.'s ownership network may facilitate the monitoring of how effectively firms that have been spun off are being managed. Thermo Electron Corp.'s corporate officers may fill the role that a main bank in a keiretsu fills. The main bank in a keiretsu often has its representatives on the boards of firms with which it has a main bank relationship.[52] Similarly, Thermo Electron Corp. may have representatives on the boards of affiliate firms. Also, industrial groups in Japan have regular meetings for

## STRATEGIC FOCUS

### Thermo Electron's Use of Corporate Venture Capital

Thermo Electron Corp. manufactures high-tech devices. The firm's distinctive approach to producing and managing innovation is to spin off publicly traded independent offspring with new high-tech products. Thermo Electron Corp., however, creates products and spins them off into independent companies, often through an initial public offering of stock. It maintains a substantial position in each of the stock offerings. In a recent year, Thermo Electron Corp. owned 53 percent of Thermedics (biomedical materials and detection equipment), 81 percent of Thermo Instrument (analytic and environmental instruments and services), and 71 percent of Thermo Process Systems (incineration and heat-treating equipment, among many other ownership positions.

This innovation approach was introduced by George Hatsopoulos, the CEO. Hatsopoulos set out to build a company that would identify emerging societal problems and develop technological solutions to them. In the early 1980s, Hatsopoulos worried that his increasingly diversified corporation was losing its entrepreneurial edge. Equally troubling was the apparent failure of stock options to motivate managers as they had in the past. His key managers were exercising their options and then selling the company's stock. It was not because they were particularly greedy; they just did not feel part of a company that was getting so big. The second problem was that R&D outlays for new technology were dragging down earnings.

Hatsopoulos saw a single solution for both seemingly unrelated problems. "We recognized that there was a tremendous strength associated with smaller companies, so we came out with the idea of splitting the company into smaller pieces that would be cobbled together by some common culture." In 1983, Thermo Electronics sold 16 percent of Thermedics. The public offering solved the

*continued on next page*

affiliated firms and financial institutions. Participating firms typically have common main bank relationships and significant interlocking shareholdings (e.g., affiliate firms own each other's stock). This relationship is similar to Thermo Electron Corp.'s partial ownership of network firms. Although these meetings are not associated with formal decision-making authority, they are mechanisms whereby participating financial institutions and firms can exchange information and coordinate decision-making processes. Therefore, these meetings help main banks keep informed regarding firm strategy and performance. Thus, the venture capital network system developed by Thermo Electron Corp. may be improved by imitating, to the extent possible given legal restrictions in the United States,[53] the Japanese horizontal keiretsu system.

In summary, buying innovations through acquisitions requires careful execution. The fact that acquisitions offer immediate entrance to a new market may be attractive to mangers. While there are risks associated with acquisition activity, the outcomes may appear more certain to managers. The reason for this increased certainty is that forecasting the demand for acquired firms' established goods or first problem by giving Thermedics' managers better incentives to be involved. They initially obtained 3 percent of the shares, turning the managers into entrepreneurs. Today Thermedics' employees have options on 8 percent of the stock. The offering also addressed the second problem of raising capital for the firm. The public offering raised $5 million for Thermo Electron Corp.

Today the company continues to spin off divisions at the rate of one a year. Each time a spin-off has been completed, Thermo Electron Corp.'s stock has increased in value. Investors apparently believe that the firm is more valuable as an owner of 80 percent of a promising start-up company than as the owner of 100 percent of the start-up (as a wholly owned division).

Thermo Electron Corp.'s remaining divisions compete constantly to become the next spin-off. Because management will not cut a business loose unless it shows potential to grow 30 percent a year, candidates must perform exceptionally well. Since employees of high-tech companies are notorious for starting their own businesses, this gives Thermo Electron Corp. managers a payoff for remaining with the company and working hard.

Besides maintaining a majority interest in the spin-offs, Thermo Electron Corp. provides legal, accounting, and administrative help and offers advice. In return, the fledgling companies turn over 1 percent of their revenues to Thermo Electron Corp. and abide by a charter of broad guidelines governing cooperation among "family" businesses. Hatsopoulos predicts that the Thermo Electron Corp. family will include 20 publicly traded offspring by the year 2000.

Through its approach to producing and managing innovation, Thermo Electron Corp. has not only increased capital and provided a higher return for its shareholders, but also provided an incentive for managers to be more entrepreneurial in the high-tech sectors in which the firm competes. Some firms have reduced diversification because diversification has dampened the entrepreneurial spirit. Thermo Electron Corp., on the other hand, has restructured and spun off many firms in order to increase its entrepreneurial spirit.

services may be easier than forecasting the demand for new products created through a firm's internal innovation process. As managers complete acquisitions, their commitment to this approach to producing and managing innovations may increase over time. As acquisitions substitute for internally based innovation activity, managers may reduce their commitment to internal R&D activity. Over time, this reduction may lead to a substantial loss of internal innovative capability.

Of course, not all acquisitions affect internal innovation processes negatively. In fact, a targeted and well-planned acquisition may enhance firm innovation, growth, and value-creating potential. Acquisitions can be used to complement innovative capacity. Other acquisitions may be necessary to commercialize internally initiated R&D projects. The combination of Beecham and Smithkline (now called Smithkline and Beecham PLC) created one of the top five drugmakers worldwide and allowed for broader coverage. With Beecham strong in Europe and Smithkline strong in the United States, this newly created firm can focus on a larger number of research areas and, by doing so, increase the probability of discovering a new blockbuster drug.[54] Also, venture capital programs that intend to support new innovative product ideas can be profitable. As the Thermo Electron Corp. example indicates, innovative capability does not always have to come through direct R&D operations.

Up to this point, the focus of our discussion has been on corporate entrepreneurship in large firms. However, small firms may even be better at producing revolutionary innovations. Although large firms often possess the significant financial resources and organizational capabilities necessary to more fully exploit innovative product opportunities, small firms may have more flexibility to produce innovations.

## Entrepreneurship and the Small Firm

Individual entrepreneurs and small firms account for a significant amount of innovation. Much is being said about the "stateless corporation," suggesting that many large, multinational firms are becoming stateless due to the expanding base of knowledge created in countries outside their national boundaries. These large firms seek to obtain this knowledge by putting R&D labs in these foreign countries.[55] However, research suggests that small firms, based in the United States and other nations throughout the world, are awarded a large number of United States patents.[56] Although 80 percent of the world's R&D activities in developing nations are concentrated in firms with 10,000 or more employees, these same large firms account for under half of the world's technological activity, as measured by U.S. patenting. These facts show that while large firms are very important in technological advancement, small firms and private individuals account for more than their fair share of the innovative activity and technological progress. The fact that there now appears to be a significant shift to self-employment and entrepreneurial ventures in the United States[57] suggests that the ability of small firms to produce innovations that result in technological progress may be enhanced in the twenty first century.

Large firms are particularly effective at producing innovations in chemicals, motor vehicles, and electronic products. However, they account for very few of the innovations in capital goods sectors. Apparently, in industries where there is technological opportunity, where large firms can appropriate value from innovation, they tend to make substantial contributions to innovative activity. Because technology remains largely mechanical in capital goods industries, small firms and individuals can make important mechanical inventions and innovations without significant capital investments for specialized equipment and formal skills required in chemical and electronic technologies.[58] This discussion suggests that individual entrepreneurs in small firms, especially in capital goods sectors as discussed above, are extremely important to the innovation process.

Even in some of the areas where large firms are effective innovators, individual entrepreneurs and small firms still make significant contributions. This relationship is demonstrated by the interactions between small and large firms operating in the electronics industry (especially among firms located in the Silicone Valley in the United States). For instance, the semiconductor industry benefited significantly by the development of new technology-based firms. Most of these firms were spin-offs created by former employees of large firms.[59] Similarly, computer-aided design (CAD) benefited from small-firm entry. CAD was developed in four main phases: pre-1969 (industry origin), 1969–1974 (dynamic new firms); 1974–1980 (trend toward industry consolidation—larger firms); post-1980 (maturity). The industry was created in the late 1960s by a program (called "Design Augmented by Computers") initiated by General Motors. Most large firms used these programs to assist their in-house operations. However, the second phase benefited by small spin-off firms, which fostered rapid diffusion and industry growth. The third phase was characterized by the growth of some small firms and their ability to compete with their larger counterparts for market share. During this phase, some other small firms either were acquired or failed. Even in the maturity stage of this industry, there is ample room for small firms to produce and manage innovations. Today many small firms in the semiconductor industry offer specialized software to companies competing in different manufacturing sectors in an effort to achieve strategic competitiveness.

The balance of power between large and small companies appears to be shifting. In the United States, small and midsize companies were responsible for all of the 5.8 million new jobs created from 1987 to 1992—at a time when companies with 500 or more employees recorded a net loss of 2.3 million jobs.[60] The Davids have what the Goliaths so desperately want: agility, resourcefulness, and flexibility. Computers and communications technologies have been great levelers, giving individual entrepreneurs and small firms an enhanced ability to mobilize resources and hire qualified individuals. Small firms have created most of the new jobs in the U.S. economy in the 1990s because they have the flexibility provided by desktop computers, networks of small firms who have the ability to communicate with each other, vast computerized information databases, and computer-controlled machine tools that help small companies provide quality equal to that of large manufacturers.[61]

Although small firms do not have large safety nets and benefits for employees, there is a certain excitement in working for a small firm. In working at a small firm, employees feel a clear sense of purpose. The company knows what it is doing and where it is going. Lines of communication are short and direct; often the boss walks around the factory floor several times a day. Employees are dedicated and care and are given serious responsibility. They are trained in numerous jobs and typically are rewarded in ways that encourage their allegiance to their employer.[62]

Since the mid-1980s, large firms have been in chaos as they reengineered, restructured, transformed, flattened, downsized, and rightsized. These actions have likely contributed to the growing number of new firm startups as laid off managers and professionals start their own firms. In the main, firms initiated these actions to become more competitive in the global economy. Complacency, grounded in historic successes, contributed to the need for changes in many large firms. When a firm is successful, employees may forget to maintain the commitments and continuously take the types of actions that contributed to that initial effectiveness. In some instances, employees of historically successful firms lose their customer orientation and, with some arrogance, provide service that they think customers need without asking them. Bureaucratic hierarchies, which frequently develop in these kinds of firms, tend to suppress new ideas and make large firms risk averse.[63] Although there is a lot of nervousness in large corporations, cultures seem to be changing. However, such cultures are difficult to change; moreover, they are not likely to improve the innovativeness of large firms relative to small firms. These points are highlighted in the Strategic Focus on Minnesota Mining & Manufacturing (3M) Co.

## STRATEGIC FOCUS

### Innovation in a Large Firm: Post-It Notes, a 3M Innovation

In 1974, Art Fry, sitting through a church sermon, concocted the idea of the Post-It Note for use in his choir hymn books. "I don't know if it was a dull sermon or Divine inspiration, but my mind began to wander and suddenly I thought of an adhesive that had been discovered years earlier by another 3M scientist." In attempting to produce a strong glue, Spencer Silver—the 3M scientist—accidentally made an adhesive that was strong enough to hold paper, but was easily removable. No one found a use for the glue until Fry had the inspiration.

It took Fry four years to convince his superiors that his product innovation would be a commercial success. Another two years passed before Post-It Notes were introduced to the marketplace. 3M started with two sizes of Post-It Notes, 31/2" × 5" and 11/2" × 2". These two sizes were available only in yellow. Initially, Post-It Notes sold slowly. Fry believed sales were falling short of expectations because potential customers were not aware of the product's value. Based on this belief, Fry argued strongly that Post-It Notes should be given away in Boise, Idaho. Almost all recipients of the free products said that they would buy them if they were available in stores. This feedback renewed 3M's conviction that Fry's innovation would probably be commercially successful.

Recently, 3M was producing over 350 varieties of Post-It Notes in a range of colors and sizes. Many of the notes have cartoon characters or messages on them. Because the Post-It division is internal to 3M, the company does not release sales figures. Nonetheless, it is known that Post-It Notes are one of the top-selling office items in the United States, along with tape, copy paper, and file folders. They also sell in Japan, where the shape of the notes is long and narrow to accommodate the vertical writing of characters in the Japanese language. The product also sells well in Europe and most other developed countries.

Historically 3M has been known for its ability to foster internal innovation. The Post-It Notes product is one of the most famous outcomes from the firm's internal innovation processes. However, it took the company almost seven years to accept the idea and get it into production and marketing. Seven years appears to be a long time period for an innovative company such as 3M. If this is the case for a company known for its internal innovation abilities, what might it be like to foster innovation in companies that are not known for such an ability? In a general sense, the Post-It Notes example suggests that for a more complicated product, even more product championing or political forcing would be necessary to get a new product accepted, given the bureaucracy of large firms.

*Post-it Notes are an example of a successful product innovation developed in a large firm. Sold originally in a single color and in two sizes only, the product is now sold in a wide variety of colors and sizes, as shown in this picture. Large firms are challenged to promote an environment and culture that allow innovative products to be developed and championed.*

This example shows the difficulties of pursuing entrepreneurial activity and product championing in large firms. 3M, known for its internal innovativeness, found it difficult to produce and market the Post-It Note, an innovative product with great commercial potential. 3M is known for its entrepreneurial culture. Thus, it would be more difficult to produce a complex and innovative good or service in an organization where bureaucracy is rampant. Of course, successfully innovating and commercializing a new product idea outside large corporations is not an easy task, either. Putting together the funding, marketing plan, and production facilities, along with completing the regulatory paperwork, is no easy task for entrepreneurs seeking to start their own private company. Nonetheless, small new technology-based firms have fostered the growth of many industries, including semiconductors, CAD, and other software. Another industry benefiting from small firms is biotechnology. These examples illustrate the importance of entrepreneurs and small firms in the development of new products and the diffusion of innovation.

What can large firms do to act small and be innovative? First, many firms, through the types of restructuring described in Chapter 7, are organizing themselves into more manageable units.[64] Accompanying these restructurings, firms are reengineering to reduce organizational processes to the essential functions, share risks with partners, and listen more fully and effectively to customers. Second, large companies are trying to make themselves attractive places to work and are also seeking to bind employee interests to those of the company. This is accomplished through arrangements such as self-managed teams and customer-satisfaction bonuses. For example, Herbert Kelleher, CEO of Southwest Airlines, has sought to keep a small-firm culture by using traditional profit-sharing plans and a buddy system linking long-time and new employees. However, many large firms have handled decreasing competitiveness by laying off tens of thousands of employees on a worldwide basis. The downsizing approach has not realized the gains anticipated. Although head-count cuts happen fast and the stock market sometimes reacts favorably, research indicates that 75 percent of the firms end up worse after their downsizing.[65] Much to large firms' chagrin, massive layoffs can sometimes merely erode morale. Restructuring divestitures, and spin-offs such as those accomplished by Thermo Electron Corp., have produced much more favorable results.[66] In the long run, large firms must practice a delicate balancing act that allows autonomy at the lowest levels, while maintaining the advantages of size.

The advantages of size cannot be dismissed. At least some large enterprises possess significant amounts of capital. This capital can be used for investment purposes and/or to endure the negative effects encountered during prolonged recessionary periods. The advantages of scale also go beyond mass production. What firms can easily match the advertising capabilities and distribution networks of Coca-Cola, Anheuser-Busch, and Nike? Although EMI was the first firm to develop a scanner in the medical electronics field, creating worldwide demand for scanner technology, it did not have the distribution and sales network to compete with General Electric worldwide.

An increasing number of large and small firms are joining together.[67] While thinking small may be important for large firms, this may often be more easily stated as a goal than as an accomplished fact. Sometimes it may be easier to form a strategic alliance with a smaller firm than to try to become one. For instance, Eli Lilly & Co. needed a way to administer its heart blockage drugs after an angioplasty, a procedure used to open blocked arteries. A start-up firm, Zynaxis, Inc., had developed a drug-delivery device needed by Eli Lilly. However, Zynaxis lacked the funds required for clinical trials to test its product's effectiveness. Eli Lilly provided the funds, and both firms got what they needed. However, such cooperative enterprises need more than complementarities to succeed. Corporations need to develop a culture of cooperation and communication in order to succeed in such ventures.

## Summary

- Three basic strategic approaches are used to produce and manage innovation. The first approach is called internal corporate venturing. This approach emphasizes the development of autonomous strategic behavior wherein product champions pursue new product ideas and executives help them manage the political process to commercialize them within a larger firm. Induced strategic behavior is a top-down process wherein incremental product changes and adjustments are made to the original product. This is a process driven by the organization's current corporate strategy, structure, and reward and control systems.

- There are three stages in the innovation process. Invention is the act of creating and developing a new product idea. The next stage, innovation, is the process of commercializing products from invention. Ultimately, other firms in the industry imitate the new product and diffuse the innovation. Imitation results in product standardization and market acceptance.

- In the past, internal innovation was done serially. Now, more parallel innovation is done through cross-functional teams. Facilitated by cross-functional teams, interfunctional integration can reduce the time a firm needs to introduce innovative products into the marketplace, improve product quality, and ultimately help a firm create value for its targeted customer. When innovations decrease the time to market and create product quality and customer value, it is likely that a firm will be able to appropriate (or extract) value from the innovation process.

- Another approach to producing and managing innovation is to obtain innovation through contracting or strategic alliances. Because knowledge is exploding and is often located in specialized firms, the only way a firm may be able to take advantage of the knowledge necessary to create new products is through strategic alliances and/or joint ventures.

- There are two basic types of strategic alliances—product-link alliances and knowledge-link alliances. Product-link alliances may fill out a firm's product line to help it remain competitive on a global basis. However, product-link alliances may not allow a firm to create a sustainable competitive advantage.

Knowledge-link alliances have a higher probability of leading to a sustainable competitive advantage, especially when a firm can learn from its strategic alliance partners.

- A final approach for large firms to produce and manage innovation is to acquire innovation. Innovation can be acquired either through direct acquisition or through indirect investment. An example of indirect investment is the formation of a wholly owned venture capital division and/or the use of actions that result in the private placement of venture capital. Buying innovation, however, may be risky and detrimental to the internal innovation process a firm uses to create new products.

- An alternative approach is to pursue innovation by investing in new ventures through a venture capital division. Venture capital operations, however, should be managed as such and should only secondarily contribute to the firm's strategic benefit. Thus, the best way to succeed with a wholly owned venture capital operation is to consider the venture capital as an investment and only secondarily as a strategy to acquire innovation. Alternatively, a firm may seek to invest venture capital directly in small firms or to spin off firms into a network of affiliate companies.

- Small firms are particularly well suited for fostering innovation that does not require large amounts of capital like semiconductors and chemicals do. Small firms have therefore become a vibrant part of industrialized nations, accounting for more job creation than large firms over the last decade. Where there are low-cost ways to invent, for example, through mechanical inventions, small firms are likely to have a higher patent rate than large firms.

- Large firms are needed to foster innovation due to capital requirements. Small firms are often found to be better at creating specialty products and diffusing the innovation through spin-offs from large corporations. This was the case in semiconductors and computer-aided design software. Large firms are seeking ways to think and act smaller in order to become more entrepreneurial. Often, however, the best way for both small and large firms to solve technological problems is to form strategic alliances that benefit both partners.

## Review Questions

1. What are three strategic approaches firms can use to produce and manage innovation?
2. Define and describe the two processes that make up internal corporate venturing: autonomous strategic behavior and induced strategic behavior.
3. Name and describe the three stages of innovation.
4. Some believe that when managed successfully, cross-functional teams facilitate the implementation of internal corporate ventures and a firm's innovation efforts. Describe how cross-functional teams should be managed to achieve these desirable outcomes.

5. Some firms use strategic alliances to contract for innovation. Explain the actions taken to use strategic alliances for this purpose.
6. How can a firm create value when it acquires another company to gain access to its innovations and/or its ability to produce innovations?
7. How do large firms use venture capital to create innovations and to identify new product opportunities?
8. What are the differences in the resources and capabilities large and small firms have to produce and manage innovation?

## Application Discussion Questions

1. In the 1980s, there was an acceleration in the number of external acquisitions. There was also an acceleration in the number of dollars being spent as venture capital. Discuss whether or not you think there is a relationship between the wave of external acquisitions and the increase in venture capital funding.
2. In your opinion, is "corporate entrepreneurship" an oxymoron? In other words, is it a contradiction of terms? If so, why?
3. Discuss the current increased interest in horizontal organization relative to the increase in the use of cross-functional teams as an increasingly popular approach to new product design.
4. Given the constraints on ownership among U.S. firms, is it desirable and/or possible to create keiretsu-type networks (of either the horizontal or the vertical varieties)?
5. How would you suggest that developing countries with a tradition of centralized bureaucracy, such as Russia, begin to compete in a global economy that emphasizes product innovation? What should be emphasized in

these countries to make firms and their countries more competitive on a global basis? Should they encourage entrepreneurial firms (as is the case in Taiwan)? Should they encourage large firms (as is the case in South Korea)? Should both forms be emphasized? Be prepared to justify your views.
6. The restructuring movement (e.g., acquisitions, divestitures, and downsizing) of the 1980s and early 1990s has apparently made U.S. firms more *productive* (as measured by traditional output-per-employee ratios). But, in your opinion, are U.S. firms more innovative due to the restructuring and downsizing activity? Why or why not?
7. Are strategic alliances a way to increase existing technological capacity, or are strategic alliances used more by firms that are behind technologically and trying to catch up? In other words, are strategic alliances a tool of firms that have a technological advantage, or are they a tool of technologically disadvantaged companies?

## Ethics Questions

1. Is it ethical for a company to purchase another firm in order to gain ownership of its innovative products? Why or why not?
2. In this chapter, it is mentioned that entrepreneurs are sometimes more effective when they work against existing product standards. How do entrepreneurs know when their new products might harm consumers? Should organizations establish guidelines to assist entrepreneurs in terms of this issue? If so, what might some of those guidelines be?
3. Is using an internal venturing process to produce and manage innovation inherently more ethical than

obtaining innovations by acquiring another company? Why or why not?
4. When participating in a strategic alliance, partners may legitimately seek to gain knowledge from each other. At what point does it become unethical to gain still additional and competitively relevant knowledge from a strategic alliance partner? Is this point different when partnering with a domestic, rather than a foreign firm? If so, why? When is it
5. Small firms often have innovative products. When is it appropriate for a large firm to buy a small firm for its new products and new product ideas?

## Notes

1. C. A. Lengnick-Hall, 1992, Innovation and competitive advantage: What we know and what we need to learn, *Journal of Management* 18: 399–429.
2. C. Farrell, 1993, A wellspring of innovation: Factories have changed relentlessly from 18th century mills to today's worker-empowered auto plants, *Fortune* (Special Bonus Issue), 62.
3. J. P. Womack, D. T. Jones, and D. Roos, 1990, *The Machine That Changed the World* (New York: Rawson Associates), 14.
4. J. Schumpeter, 1934, *The Theory of Economic Development* (Cambridge: Harvard University Press).
5. B. Czarniawska-Joerges and R. Wolff, 1991, Leaders, managers, entrepreneurs on and off the organizational stage, *Organization Studies* 12: 529–546.
6. A. Taylor III, 1994, Iacocca's minivan, *Fortune,* May 30, 56–66.
7. B. M. Bass, 1984, Leadership: Good, better, best, *Organization Dynamics* 12: 26–40.
8. M. Magnet, 1994, The marvels of high margins, *Fortune,* May 2, 73–74.
9. J. P. Kotter, 1990, *A Force for Change* (New York: Free Press); H. Mintzberg, 1971, Mangerial work: Analysis from observation, *Management Science* 18, no. 2: 97–110.
10. Taylor, Iacocca's minivan.
11. J. Pinchot, 1985, *Intrapreneuring* (New York: Harper and Row).
12. R. A. Burgelman, 1983, A model of the interaction of strategic behavior, corporate context and the concept of strategy, *Academy of Management Review* 8: 61–70.
13. A. D. Chandler, 1962, *Strategy and Structure: Chapters in the History of Industrial Enterprise* (Cambridge: MIT Press), 233–236.
14. A. Deutschman, 1994, How H-P continues to grow and grow, *Fortune,* May 2, 90–100.
15. A. Farnham, 1994, America's most admired company, *Fortune,* February 7, 50–54.
16. Intel, 1994, *Value Line,* January 28, 1064.
17. D. Kirkpatrick, 1994, Intel goes for broke, *Fortune,* May 16, 62–68.
18. Intel, 1994.
19. Intel Corp., 1993, *Standard & Poor's,* December 10, 49H.
20. K. Bryor and E. M. Shays, 1993, Growing the business with intrapreneurs, *Business Quarterly,* (Spring): 40; R. M. Kanter, 1985, Supporting innovation and venture development in established companies, *Journal of Business Venturing* 1:47–60; D. F. Kuratko, K. V. Montagno, and J. S. Hornsby, 1990, Developing an intrapreneurial assessment instrument for an effective corporate entrepreneurial environment, *Strategic Management Journal,* 11(Special Issue): 49–58; R. S. Schuler, 1986, Fostering and facilitating entrepreneurship in organization: Implications for organization structure and human resource management practices, *Human Resource Management* 25: 607–629; W. Souder, 1981, Encouraging entrepreneurship in large corporations, *Research Management.* (May): 18–22; H. B. Sykes and Z. Block, 1989, Corporate venturing obstacles: Sources and solutions, *Journal of Business Venturing* 4: 159–167.
21. J. A. Byrne, 1993, The horizontal corporation: It's about managing across, not up and down, *Business Week,* December 20, 76–81.
22. J. E. Ettlie, 1988, *Taking Charge of Manufacturing* (San Francisco: Jossey-Bass).
23. P. R. Lawrence and J. W. Lorsch, 1969, *Organization and Environment* (Homewood, Ill.: Richard D. Irwin).
24. J. D. Orton and K. E. Weick, 1990, Loosely coupled systems: A reconsideration, *Academy of Management Review* 15: 203–23.
25. R. Henkoff, 1994, When to take on the giants, *Fortune,* May 30, 111.
26. K. M. Eisenhardt, 1989, Making fast strategic decisions in high-velocity environments, *Academy of Management Journal* 32: 543–576.
27. W. Q. Judge and A. Miller, 1991, Antecedents and outcomes of decision speed in different environmental contexts, *Academy of Management Journal* 34: 449–463.
28. M. B. Lieberman and D. B. Montgomery, 1988, First-mover advantages, *Strategic Management Journal 9* (Special Issue): 41–58.
29. W. Davidson, 1988, Technology, environments and organizational choice. Paper presented at the conference on Managing the High-Tech Firm. The Graduate School of Business, University of Colorado.
30. Judge and Miller, Antecedents and outcomes.
31. Deutschman, How H-P continues.
32. M. A. Hitt, R. E. Hoskisson, and R. D. Nixon, 1993, A mid-range theory of interfunctional integration, its antecedents and outcomes, *Journal of Engineering Technology Management* 10: 161–185.
33. B. Borys and D. B. Jemison, 1989, Hybrid arrangements as strategic alliances: Theoretical issues in organizational combinations, *Academy of Management Review* 14: 234–249; J. E. Forrest, 1992, Management aspects of strategic partnering, *Journal of General Management* 17, no. 4: 25–40.
34. J. L. Badaracco, Jr., 1991, *The Knowledge Link: How Firms Compete Through Strategic Alliances* (Boston: Harvard University School Press).

35. T. Steinert-Threlkeld, 1994, TI, Microsoft forming software tool alliance, *Dallas Morning News,* May 2, 1D.

36. Corning Inc., 1994, *Value Line,* January 28, 1004.

37. Ibid.

38. G. Hamel, 1991, Competition for competence and interpartner learning within international strategic alliances, *Strategic Management Journal* 12: 83–103.

39. J. B. Treece, 1991, Why GM and Daewoo wound up on the road to nowhere, *Business Week,* September 23, 55.

40. C. K. Prahalad and G. Hamel, 1990, The core competence of the corporation, *Harvard Business Review* 68, no. 3: 79–93.

41. D. Lei and J. W. Slocum, Jr., 1992, Global strategy, competence building and strategic alliances, *California Management Review* 35, no. 1: 81–97.

42. Hamel, Competition for competence.

43. D. C. Mowery and D. J. Teece, 1993, Japan's growing capabilities in industrial technology: Implications for U.S. managers and policy markers, *California Management Review* 35, no. 2: 9–34.

44. M. A. Hitt, R. E. Hoskisson, R. D. Ireland, and J. S. Harrison, 1991, Effects of acquisitions on R&D inputs and outputs, *Academy of Management Journal* 34: 693–706.

45. M. A. Hitt, R. E. Hoskisson, and R. D. Ireland, 1990, Mergers and acquisitions and managerial commitment to innovation in M-form firms, *Strategic Management Journal* 11 (Special Issue): 29–47.

46. T. E. Winters and D. L. Murfin, 1988, Venture capital investing for corporate development objectives, *Journal of Business Venturing* 3: 207–222.

47. G. F. Hardymon, M. J. DeNino, and M. S. Salter, 1983, When corporate venture capital doesn't work, *Harvard Business Review* 61, no. 3: 114–120.

48. U. Gupta, 1993, Venture capital investment soars, reversing four-year slide, *Wall Street Journal,* June 1, B2.

49. R. E. Hoskisson and M. A. Hitt, 1994, *Downscoping: Taming the Diversified Firm* (New York: Oxford University Press).

50. R. E. Hoskisson and R. A. Johnson, 1992, Corporate restructuring and strategic change: The effect on diversification strategy and R&D intensity, *Strategic Management Journal* 13: 625–634.

51. M. L. Geralch, 1992, *Alliance Capitalism: The Social Organization of Japanese Business* (Berkeley: University of California Press).

52. M. Aoki, 1990, Toward an economic model of the Japanese firm, *Journal of Economic Literature* 28: 1–27.

53. M. J. Roe, 1990, Political and legal restraints on ownership and control of public companies, *Journal of Financial Economics* 27: 7–41.

54. M. Maremeont, 1990, The first acid test of the drug megamergers, *Business Week,* February 19, 62–63.

55. The stateless corporation, 1990, *Business Week,* May 14, 52–60.

56. P. Patel and K. Pavitt, 1992, Large firms in the production of the world's technology: An important case of non-globalization. In O. Granstrand, L. Hakanson, and S. Sjolander (eds.), *Technology Management and International Business: Internationalization of R&D and Technology* (New York: John Wiley & Sons), 53–74.

57. B. O'Reilly, 1994, The new face of small business, *Fortune,* May 2, 82–88.

58. J. Johanson and J. E. Vahlne, 1977, The internationalization process of the firm—a model of knowledge development and increasing foreign market commitments, *Journal of International Business Studies* 8: 23–32.

59. R. Rothwell, 1984, The role of small firms in the emergence of new technologies, *International Journal of Management Science* 12, no. 1: 19–29.

60. J. A. Byrne, 1993, Enterprise: Introduction, *Business Week* (Special Bonus Issue), 12.

61. P. Coy, 1993, Start with some high-tech magic, *Business Week* (Special Bonus Issue), 24–28.

62. C. Burck, 1993, The real world of the entrepreneur, *Fortune,* April 5, 62–81.

63. J. Huey, 1993, Managing in the midst of chaos, *Fortune,* April 5, 38–48.

64. R. A. Melcher, 1993, How Goliaths can act like Davids, *Business Week* (Special Bonus Issue), 192–201.

65. Ibid., 193.

66. Hoskisson and Hitt, *Downscoping.*

67. K. Kelly, 1993, Turning rivals into teammates, *Business Week* (Special Bonus Issue), 222–224.

# Preparing an Effective Case Analysis

In most strategic management courses, cases are used extensively as a teaching tool. A key reason for this is that cases allow opportunities to identify and solve organizational problems through use of the strategic management process. Thus, through analyzing cases and presenting the results, students learn how to effectively use the tools, techniques, and concepts that combine to form the strategic management process.

The cases that follow involve actual companies. Presented within them are problems and situations that managers must analyze and resolve. As you will see, a strategic management case can focus on an entire industry, a single organization, or a business unit of a large, diversified firm. The strategic management issues facing not-for-profit organizations also can be examined through the case analysis method.

Basically, the case analysis method calls for a careful diagnosis of an organization's current conditions (internal and external) so that appropriate strategic actions can be recommended. Appropriate actions not only allow a firm to survive in the long run, but also describe how it can develop and use core competencies to create sustainable competitive advantages and earn superior profits. The case method has a rich heritage as a pedagogical approach to the study and understanding of managerial effectiveness.[1]

Critical to successful use of the case method is your *preparation*—that is, the preparation of the student or case analyst. Without careful study and analysis, you will lack the insights required to participate fully in the discussion of a firm's situation and the strategic actions that are appropriate.

Instructors adopt different approaches in their use of the case method. Some require their students to use a specific analytical procedure to examine an organization; others provide less structure, expecting students to learn by developing their own unique analytical method. Still other instructors believe that a moderately structured framework should be used to analyze a firm's situation and make appropriate recommendations. The specific approach you take will be determined by your professor. The approach we are presenting to you here is a moderately structured framework.

Discussion of the case method is divided into four sections. First, it is important for you to understand why cases are used and what skills you can expect to learn through successful use of the case method. Second, a process-oriented framework is provided that can help you analyze cases and effectively discuss the results of your work. Using this framework in a classroom setting yields valuable experiences that can, in turn, help you successfully complete assignments received from your employer. Third, we describe briefly what you can expect to occur during in-class discussions of cases. As this description shows, the relationship and interactions between instructors and students during case discussions are different than they are during lectures. Finally, a moderately structured framework is offered for effective completion of in-depth oral and written presentations. Written and oral communication skills also are attributes valued highly in many organizational settings; hence, their development today can serve you well in the future.

## Using the Case Method

The case method is based on a philosophy that combines knowledge acquisition with significant student involvement. In the words of Alfred North Whitehead, this philosophy "rejects the doctrine that students had first learned passively, and then, having learned should apply knowledge."[2] The case method, instead, is based on principles elaborated by John Dewey:

> Only by wrestling with the conditions of this problem at hand, seeking and finding his own way out, does [the student] think. . . . If he cannot devise his own solution (not, of course, in isolation, but in correspondence with the teacher and other pupils) and find his own way out he will not learn, not even if he can recite some correct answer with a hundred percent accuracy.[3]

The case method brings reality into the classroom. When developed and presented effectively, with rich and interesting detail, cases keep conceptual discussions grounded in reality. Experience shows that simple fictional accounts of situations and collections of actual organizational data and articles from public sources are not as effective for learning as are fully developed cases. A comprehensive case presents you with a partial clinical study of a real-life situation that faced practicing managers. A case presented in narrative form provides motivation for involvement with and analysis of a specific situation. By framing alternative strategic actions and by confronting the complexity and ambiguity of the practical world, case analysis provides extraordinary power for your involvement with a personal learning experience. Some of the potential consequences of using the case method are summarized in Table 1.

As Table 1 suggests, the case method can help you develop your analytical and judgment skills. Case analysis also helps you learn how to ask the right

## TABLE 1

### Consequences of Student Involvement with the Case Method

1. Case analysis requires students to practice important managerial skills—diagnosing, making decisions, observing, listening, and persuading—while preparing for a case discussion.
2. Cases require students to relate analysis and action, to develop realistic and concrete actions despite the complexity and partial knowledge characterizing the situation being studied.
3. Students must confront the *intractability of reality*—complete with absence of needed information, an imbalance between needs and available resources, and conflicts among competing objectives.
4. Students develop a general managerial point of view—where responsibility is sensitive to action in a diverse environmental context.

*Source:* C. C. Lundberg and C. Enz, 1993, A framework for student case preparation, *Case Research Journal* 13 (Summer): 134.

questions—that is, the questions that drive to the core of the strategic issues included within a case. Students aspiring to be managers can improve their ability to identify underlying problems, rather than focusing on superficial symptoms, through development of the skills required to ask probing, yet appropriate, questions.

The particular set of cases your instructor chooses to present to you and your classmates can expose you to a wide variety of organizations and managerial situations. This approach vicariously broadens your experience base and provides insights into many types of managerial situations, tasks, and responsibilities. Such indirect experience can help you make a more informed career decision about the industry and managerial situation you believe will prove to be challenging and satisfying. Finally, experience in analyzing cases definitely enhances your problem-solving skills.

Furthermore, when your instructor requires oral and written presentations, your communication skills will be honed through use of the case method. Of course, these added skills depend on your preparation as well as your instructor's facilitation of learning. However, the primary responsibility for learning is yours. The quality of case discussion is generally acknowledged to require, at a minimum, a thorough mastery of case facts and some independent analysis of them. The case method therefore first requires that you read and think carefully about each case. Additional comments about the preparation you should complete to successfully discuss a case appear in the next section.

## Student Preparation for Case Discussion

If you are inexperienced with the case method, you may need to alter your study habits. A lecture-oriented course may not require you to do intensive preparation for *each* class period. In such a course, you have the latitude to work through assigned readings and review lecture notes according to your own schedule. However, an assigned case requires significant and conscientious *preparation before class*. Without it, you will be unable to contribute meaningfully to in-class discussion. Therefore, careful reading and thinking about case facts, as well as reasoned analyses and the development of alternative solutions to case problems, are essential. Recommended alternatives should flow logically from core problems identified through study of the case. Table 2 shows a set of steps that can help you develop familiarity with a case, identify problems, and propose strategic actions that increase the probability that a firm will achieve strategic competitiveness and earn superior profits.

## Gaining Familiarity

The first step of an effective case analysis process calls for you to become familiar with the facts featured in the case and the focal firm's situation. Initially, you should become familiar with the focal firm's general situation (e.g., who, what, how, where, and when). Thorough familiarization demands appreciation of the nuances as well as the major issues in the case.

▼ **TABLE 2**

### An Effective Case Analysis Process

| | |
|---|---|
| *Step 1:*<br>*Gaining Familiarity* | a. In general—determine who, what, how, where, and when (the critical facts of the case).<br>b. In detail—identify the places, persons, activities, and contexts of the situation.<br>c. Recognize the degree of certainty/uncertainty of acquired information. |
| *Step 2:*<br>*Recognizing Symptoms* | a. List all indicators (including stated "problems") that something is not as expected or as desired.<br>b. Ensure that symptoms are not assumed to be the problem (symptoms should lead to identification of the problem). |
| *Step 3:*<br>*Identifying Goals* | a. Identify critical statements by major parties (e.g., people, groups, the work unit, etc.).<br>b. List all goals of the major parties that exist or can be reasonably inferred. |
| *Step 4:*<br>*Conducting the Analysis* | a. Decide which ideas, models, and theories seem useful.<br>b. Apply these conceptual tools to the situation.<br>c. As new information is revealed, cycle back to substeps a and b. |
| *Step 5:*<br>*Making the Diagnosis* | a. Identify predicaments (goal inconsistencies).<br>b. Identify problems (discrepancies between goals and performance).<br>c. Prioritize predicaments/problems regarding timing, importance, etc. |
| *Step 6:*<br>*Doing the Action Planning* | a. Specify and prioritize the criteria used to choose action alternatives.<br>b. Discover or invent feasible action alternatives.<br>c. Examine the probable consequences of action alternatives.<br>d. Select a course of action.<br>e. Design an implementation plan/schedule.<br>f. Create a plan for assessing the action to be implemented. |

*Source:* C. C. Lundberg and C. Enz, 1993, A framework for student case preparation, *Case Research Journal* 13 (Summer): 144.

Gaining familiarity with a situation requires you to study several situational levels, including interactions between and among individuals within groups, business units, the corporate office, the local community, and the society at large. Recognizing relationships within and among levels facilitates a more thorough understanding of the specific case situation.

It is also important that you evaluate information on a continuum of certainty. Information that is verifiable by several sources and judged along similar dimensions can be classified as a *fact*. Information representing someone's perceptual judgment of a particular situation is referred to as an *inference*. Information gleaned from a situation that is not verifiable is classified as *speculation*. Finally, information that is independent of verifiable sources and arises through individual or group discussion is an *assumption*. Obviously, case analysts and organizational decision makers prefer having access to facts over inferences, speculations, and assumptions.

Personal feelings, judgments, and opinions evolve when you are analyzing a case. It is important to be aware of your own feelings about the case and to evaluate the accuracy of perceived "facts" to ensure that the objectivity of your work is maximized.

## Recognizing Symptoms

Recognition of symptoms is the second step of an effective case analysis process. A **symptom** is an indication that something is not as you or someone else thinks it should be. You may be tempted to correct the symptoms instead of searching for true problems. **True problems** are the conditions or situations requiring solution before an organization's, unit's, or individual's performance can improve. Identifying and listing symptoms early in the case analysis process tends to reduce the temptation to label symptoms as problems. The focus of your analysis should be on the *actual causes* of a problem, rather than on its symptoms. It is important therefore to remember that symptoms are indicators of problems; subsequent work facilitates discovery of critical causes of problems that your case recommendations must address.

▲ A **symptom** is an indication that something is not as you or someone else thinks it should be.

▲ **True problems** are the conditions or situations requiring solution before an organization's, unit's, or individual's performance can improve.

## Identifying Goals

The third step of effective case analysis calls for you to identify the goals of the major organizations, units, and/or individuals in a case. As appropriate, you should also identify each firm's strategic intent and strategic mission. Typically, these direction-setting statements (goals, strategic intents, and strategic missions) are derived from comments of the central characters in the organization, business unit or, top management team described in the case and/or from public documents (e.g., an annual report).

Completing this step successfully sometimes can be difficult. Nonetheless, the outcomes you attain from this step are essential to an effective case analysis because identifying goals, intent, and mission helps you to clarify the major problems featured in a case and to evaluate alternative solutions to those problems. Direction-setting statements are not always stated publicly or prepared in written format. When this occurs, you must infer goals from other available factual data and information.

## Conducting the Analysis

The fourth step of effective case analysis is concerned with acquiring a systematic understanding of a situation. Occasionally cases are analyzed in a less-than-thorough manner. Such analyses may be a product of a busy schedule or the difficulty and complexity of the issues described in a particular case. Sometimes you will face pressures on your limited amounts of time and may believe that you can understand the situation described in a case without systematic *analysis* of all the facts. However, experience shows that familiarity with a case's facts is a necessary, but insufficient, step to the development of effective solutions—

solutions that can enhance a firm's strategic competitiveness. In fact, a less-than-thorough analysis typically results in an emphasis on symptoms, rather than problems and their causes. To analyze a case effectively, then, you should be skeptical of quick or easy approaches and answers.

A systematic analysis helps you understand a situation and to determine what can work and probably what will not work. Key linkages and underlying causal networks based on the history of the firm become apparent. In this way, you can separate causal networks from symptoms.

Also, because the quality of a case analysis depends on applying appropriate conceptual tools (such as those presented in this book), it is important that you consider which ideas, models, and theories seem to be useful for evaluating and solving individual and unique situations. As you consider facts and symptoms, a useful theory may become apparent. Of course, having familiarity with conceptual models may be important in the effective analysis of a situation. Successful students and successful organizational strategists add to their intellectual tool kits on a continual basis.

## Making the Diagnosis

▲ **Diagnosis** is the process of identifying and clarifying the roots of the problems by comparing goals to facts.

▲ **Predicaments** are situations in which goals do not fit with known facts.

The fifth step of effective case analysis—**diagnosis**—is the process of identifying and clarifying the roots of the problems by comparing goals to facts. In this step, it is useful to search for predicaments. **Predicaments** are situations in which goals do not fit with known facts. When you evaluate the actual performance of an organization, business unit, or individual, you may identify over- or under achievement (relative to established goals). Of course, single-problem situations are rare. Accordingly, you should recognize that the case situations you study probably will be complex in nature.

Effective diagnosis requires you to determine the problems affecting longer-term performance and those requiring immediate handling. Understanding these issues will aid your efforts to prioritize problems and predicaments, given available resources and existing constraints.

## Doing the Action Planning

▲ **Action planning** is the process of identifying appropriate alternative actions.

The final step of an effective case analysis process is called action planning. **Action planning** is the process of identifying appropriate alternative actions. Important in the action planning step is selection of the criteria you will use to evaluate the identified alternatives. You may derive these criteria from the analyses; typically, they are related to key strategic situations facing the focal organization. Furthermore, it is important that you prioritize these criteria to ensure a rational and effective evaluation of alternative courses of action.

Typically managers "satisfice" when selecting courses of actions; that is, they find *acceptable* courses of action that meet most of the chosen evaluation criteria. A rule of thumb that has proved valuable to strategic decision makers is to select an alternative that leaves other plausible alternatives available if the one selected fails.

Once you have selected the best alternative, you must specify an implementation plan. Developing an implementation plan serves as a reality check on the feasibility of your alternatives. Thus, it is important that you give thoughtful consideration to all issues associated with the implementation of the selected alternatives.

## What to Expect From In-Class Case Discussions

Classroom discussions of cases differ significantly from lectures. The case method calls for instructors to guide the discussion, encourage student participation, and solicit alternative views. When alternative views are not forthcoming, instructors typically adopt one view so students can be challenged to respond thoughtfully to it. Often students' work is evaluated in terms of both the quantity and the quality of their contributions to in-class case discussions. Students benefit by having their views judged against those of their peers and by responding to challenges by other class members and/or the instructor.

During case discussions, instructors listen, question, and probe to extend the analysis of case issues. In the course of these actions, peers or the instructor may challenge an individual's views and the validity of alternative perspectives that have been expressed. These challenges are offered in a constructive manner; their intent is to help students develop their analytical and communication skills. Commonly instructors encourage students to be innovative and original in the development and presentation of their ideas. Over the course of an individual discussion, students can develop a more complex view of the case, benefiting from the diverse inputs of their peers and instructor. Among other benefits, experience with multiple case discussions should help students increase their knowledge of the advantages and disadvantages of group decision-making processes.

Comments that contribute to the discussion are valued by student peers as well as the instructor. To offer *relevant* contributions, you are encouraged to use independent thought and, through discussions with your peers outside of class, to refine your thinking. We also encourage you to avoid using "I think," "I believe," and "I feel" to discuss your inputs to a case analysis process. Instead, consider using a less emotion laden phrase, such as "My analysis shows. . . ." This highlights the logical nature of the approach you have taken to complete the six steps of an effective case analysis process.

When preparing for an in-class case discussion, you should plan to use the case data to explain your assessment of the situation. Assume that the case facts are known to your peers and instructor. In addition, it is good practice to prepare notes before class discussions and use them as you explain your view. Effective notes signal to classmates and the instructor that you are prepared to engage in a thorough discussion of a case. Moreover, thorough notes eliminate the need for you to memorize the facts and figures needed to discuss a case successfully.

The case analysis process we described above can help you prepare effectively to discuss a case during class meetings. Adherence to this process results in consideration of the issues required to identify a focal firm's problems and to propose strategic actions through which the firm can increase the probability it will achieve strategic competitiveness.

In some instances, your instructor may ask you to prepare either an oral or a written analysis of a particular case. Typically such an assignment demands even more thorough study and analysis of the case contents. At your instructor's discretion, oral and written analyses may be completed by individuals or by groups of two or more people. The information and insights gained through completing the six steps shown in Table 2 often are of value in the development of an oral or a written analysis. However, when preparing an oral or written presentation, you must consider the overall framework in which your information and inputs will be presented. Such a framework is the focus of the next section.

## Preparing an Oral/Written Case Presentation

Experience shows that two types of thinking are necessary to develop an effective oral or written presentation (see Figure 1). The upper part of the model in Figure 1 outlines the *analysis* of case preparation.

In the analysis stage, you should first analyze the general external environmental issues affecting the firm. Next your environmental analysis should focus on the particular industry (or industries, in the case of a diversified company) in which a firm operates. Finally, you should examine the competitive environment of the focal firm. Through study of the three levels of the external environment, you will be able to identify a firm's opportunities and threats. Following the external environmental analysis is the analysis of the firm's internal environment. This analysis results in the identification of the firm's strengths and weaknesses.

As noted in Figure 1, you must then change the focus from analysis to *synthesis*. Specifically, you must *synthesize* information gained from your analysis of the firm's internal and external environments. Synthesizing information allows you to generate alternatives that can resolve the significant problems or challenges facing the focal firm. Once you identify a best alternative, from an evaluation based on predetermined criteria and goals, you must explore implementation actions.

Table 3 outlines the sections that should be included in either an oral or a written presentation: introduction (strategic profile and purpose), situation analysis,

**FIGURE 1**  **Types of Thinking in Case Preparation: Analysis and Synthesis**

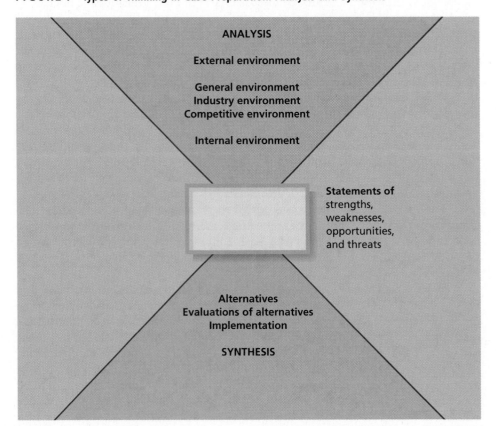

## TABLE 3

### General Outline for an Oral or a Written Presentation

I. Strategic Profile and Case Analysis Purpose
II. Situation Analysis
   A. General environmental analysis
   B. Industry analysis
   C. Competitive environmental analysis
   D. Internal analysis
III. Identification of Environmental Opportunities and Threats and
     Firm Strengths and Weaknesses (SWOT Analysis)
IV. Strategy Formulation
   A. Strategic alternatives
   B. Alternative evaluation
   C. Alternative choice
V. Strategic Alternative Implementation
   A. Action items
   B. Action plan

statements of strengths/weaknesses and opportunities/threats, strategy formulation, and implementation. These sections, which can be completed only through use of the two types of thinking featured in Figure 1, are described in the following discussion. Familiarity with the contents of your book's 12 chapters is helpful because the general outline for an oral or a written presentation shown in Table 3 is based on an understanding of the strategic management process detailed in those chapters.

## Strategic Profile and Case Analysis Purpose

The strategic profile should state briefly the critical facts from the case that have affected the historical strategic direction and performance of the focal firm. The case facts should not be restated in the profile; rather, these comments should show how the critical facts lead to a particular focus for your analysis. This primary focus should be emphasized in this section's conclusion. In addition, this section should state important assumptions about case facts on which the analyses may be based.

## Situation Analysis

As shown in Table 3, a general starting place for completing a situation analysis is the general environment.

**General Environmental Analysis** First, your analysis of the general environment should consider the *effects of globalization* on the focal firm and its industry. Following that evaluation, you should analyze general environmental trends. Table 4 lists a number of general environmental trends that, when studied, should yield valuable insights. Many of these issues are explained more fully in Chapter 2. These trends need to be evaluated for their impact on the focal firm's strategy and on the industry (or industries) in which it competes in the pursuit of strategic competitiveness.

▼ **TABLE 4**

### Sample General Environmental Categories

| | |
|---|---|
| *Technology* | • Information technology continues to become cheaper and have more practical applications.<br>• Database technology allows organization of complex data and distribution of information.<br>• Telecommunications technology and networks increasingly provide fast transmission of all sources of data, including voice, written communications, and video information.<br>• Computerized design and manufacturing technologies continue to facilitate quality and flexibility. |
| *Demographic Trends* | • Regional changes in population due to migration<br>• Changing ethnic composition of the population<br>• Aging of the population<br>• Aging of the "baby boom" generation |
| *Economic Trends* | • Interest rates<br>• Inflation rates<br>• Savings rates<br>• Trade deficits<br>• Budget deficits<br>• Exchange rates |
| *Political/Legal Environment* | • Anti-trust enforcement<br>• Tax policy changes<br>• Environmental protection laws<br>• Extent of regulation/deregulation<br>• Developing countries privatizing state monopolies<br>• State-owned industries |
| *Sociocultural Environment* | • Women in the work force<br>• Awareness of health and fitness issues<br>• Concern for the environment<br>• Concern for customers |

**Industry Analysis**   Once you analyze the general environmental trends, you should study their effect on the focal industry. Often the same environmental trend may have a significantly different impact on separate industries. Furthermore, the same trend may affect firms within the same industry differently. For instance, with deregulation of the airline industry, older, established airlines had a significant decrease in profitability, while many smaller airlines, with lower cost structures and greater flexibility, were able to aggressively enter new markets.

Porter's five force model is a useful tool for analyzing the specific industry (see Chapter 2). Careful study of how the five competitive forces (i.e., supplier power, buyer power, potential entrants, substitute products, and rivalry among competitors) affect firm strategy is important. These forces may create threats or opportunities relative to the specific business-level strategies (i.e., differentiation, low cost, focus) being implemented. Often a strategic group's analysis reveals how different environmental trends are affecting industry competitors. Strategic group analysis is useful for understanding the industry's competitive structure and the profit possibilities within those structures.

**Competitive Environmental Analysis**   Firms also need to analyze each of their primary competitors. This analysis should identify competitors' current strategies, strategic intent, strategic mission, capabilities, core competencies, and a competitive response profile. This information is useful to the focal firm in formulating an appropriate strategy and in predicting competitors' probable responses. Sources that can be used to gather information about an industry and companies with whom the focal firm competes are listed in Appendix I. Included in this list is a wide range of publications, such as periodicals, newspapers, bibliographies, directories of companies, industry ratios, forecasts, rankings/ratings, and other valuable statistics.

**Internal Analysis**   Assessing a firm's strengths and weaknesses through a value chain analysis facilitates moving from the external environment to the internal environment. Analysis of the primary and support activities of the value chain provides opportunities to understand how external environmental trends affect the specific activities of a firm. Such analysis helps highlight strengths and weaknesses (see Chapter 3 for an explanation of the value chain).

For purposes of preparing an oral or a written presentation, it is important to note that **strengths** are internal resources and capabilities that have the potential to be core competencies. **Weaknesses,** on the other hand, are internal resources and capabilities that have the potential to place a firm at a competitive disadvantage relative to its rivals. Thus, some of a firm's resources and capabilities are strengths; others are weaknesses.

When evaluating the internal characteristics of the firm, your analysis of the functional activities emphasized is critical. For instance, if the strategy of the firm is primarily technology driven, it is important to evaluate the firm's R&D activities. If the strategy is market driven, marketing functional activities are of paramount importance. If a firm has financial difficulties, critical financial ratios would require careful evaluation. In fact, because of the importance of financial health, most cases require financial analyses. Appendix II lists and operationally defines several common financial ratios. Included are tables describing profitability, liquidity, leverage, activity, and shareholders' return ratios. Other firm characteristics that should be examined to study the internal environment effectively include leadership, organizational culture, structure, and control systems.

▲ **Strengths** are internal resources and capabilities that have the potential to be core competencies.

▲ **Weaknesses** are internal resources and capabilities that have the potential to place a firm at a competitive disadvantage relative to its rivals.

## Identification of Environmental Opportunities and Threats and Firm Strengths and Weaknesses (SWOT Analysis)

The outcome of the situation analysis is the identification of a firm's strengths and weaknesses and its environmental threats and opportunities. The next step requires that you analyze the strengths and weaknesses and the opportunities and threats for configurations that benefit or do not benefit the firm in its efforts to achieve strategic competitiveness. Case analysts, and organizational strategists as well, seek to match a firm's strengths with its external environmental opportunities. In addition, strengths are chosen to prevent any serious environmental threat from impacting negatively on the firm's performance. The key objective of conducting a SWOT analysis is to determine how to position the firm so it can take advantage of opportunities, while simultaneously avoiding or minimizing environmental threats. Results from a SWOT analysis yield valuable insights into the selection of strategies a firm should implement to achieve strategic competitiveness.

The *analysis* of a case should not be overemphasized relative to the *synthesis* of results gained from your analytical efforts. There may be a temptation to spend most of your oral or written case analysis on results from the analysis. It is important, however, that you make an equal effort to develop and evaluate alternatives and to design implementation of the chosen strategy.

## Strategy Formulation—Strategic Alternatives, Alternative Evaluation, and Alternative Choice

Developing alternatives is often one of the most difficult steps in preparing an oral or a written presentation. Development of three to four alternative strategies is common (see Chapter 4 for business-level strategy alternatives and Chapter 6 for corporate-level strategy alternatives). Each alternative should be feasible (i.e., it should match the firm's strengths, capabilities, and especially core competencies), and feasibility should be demonstrated. In addition, you should show how each alternative takes advantage of the environmental opportunity or avoids/buffers against environmental threats. Developing carefully thought out alternatives requires synthesis of your analyses' results and creates greater credibility in oral and written case presentations.

Once you develop strong alternatives, you must evaluate the set to choose the best one. Your choice should be defensible and provide benefits over the other alternatives. Thus, it is important that both alternative development and evaluation of alternatives be thorough. The choice of the best alternative should be explained and defended.

## Strategic Alternative Implementation—Action Items and Action Plan

After selecting the most appropriate strategy (that is, the strategy with the highest probability of enhancing a firm's strategic competitiveness), you must consider effective implementation. Effective synthesis is important to ensure that you have considered and evaluated all critical implementation issues. Issues you might consider include the structural changes necessary to implement the new strategy. In addition, leadership changes and new controls or incentives may be necessary to implement strategic actions. The implementation actions you recommend should be explicit and thoroughly explained. Occasionally, careful evaluation of implementation actions may show the strategy to be less favorable than you thought originally. A strategy is only as good as the firm's ability to implement it effectively. Therefore, effort to determine effective implementation is important.

## Process Issues

You should make sure that your presentation (either oral or written) has logical consistency throughout. For example, if your presentation identifies one purpose, but your analysis focuses on issues that differ from the stated purpose, your logical inconsistency will be apparent. Likewise, your alternatives should flow from the configuration of strengths, weaknesses, opportunities, and threats you identified by the internal and external analyses.

Thoroughness and clarity also are critical to an effective presentation. Thoroughness is represented by the comprehensiveness of the analysis and alternative generation. Furthermore, clarity in the results of the analyses, selection of the best alternative strategy, and design of implementation actions are important. For example, your statement of the strengths and weaknesses should flow clearly and logically from the internal analyses presented.

Presentations (oral or written) that show logical consistency, thoroughness, and clarity of purpose, effective analyses, and feasible recommendations (strategy and implementation) are more effective and will receive more positive evaluations. Furthermore, developing the skills necessary to make such presentations will enhance your future job performance and career success.

## Appendix I

### Sources for Industry and Competitor Analyses

#### Abstracts and Indexes

| Periodicals | ABI/Inform |
|---|---|
| | Business Periodicals Index |
| | InfoTrac (CD-ROM computer multidiscipline index) |
| | Investext (CD-ROM) |
| | Predicasts F&S Index United States |
| | Predicasts Overview of Markets and Technology (PROMT) |
| | Predicasts R&S Index Europe |
| | Predicasts R&S Index International |
| | Public Affairs Information Service Bulletin (PAIS) |
| | Reader's Guide to Periodical Literature |
| Newspapers | NewsBank |
| | Business NewsBank |
| | New York Times Index |
| | Wall Street Journal Index |
| | Wall Street Journal/Barron's Index |
| | Washington Post Index |

#### Bibliographies

| | Encyclopedia of Business Information Sources |
|---|---|
| | Handbook of Business Information |

#### Directories

| Companies—General | America's Corporate Families and International Affiliates |
|---|---|
| | Hoover's Handbook of American Business |
| | Hoover's Handbook of World Business |
| | Million Dollar Directory |
| | Standard & Poor's Corporation Records |
| | Standard & Poor's Register of Corporations, Directors, and Executives |
| | Ward's Business Directory |
| Companies—International | America's Corporate Families and International Affiliates |
| | Business Asia |
| | Business China |
| | Business Eastern Europe |
| | Business Europe |
| | Business International |
| | Business International Money Report |
| | Business Latin America |
| | Directory of American Firms Operating in Foreign Countries |
| | Directory of Foreign Firms Operating in the United States |

*Hoover's Handbook of World Business*
*International Directory of Company Histories*
*Moody's Manuals, International* (2 volumes)
*Who Owns Whom*

Companies—Manufacturers
*Manufacturing USA: Industry Analyses, Statistics, and Leading Companies*
*Thomas Register of American Manufacturers*
U.S. Office of Management and Budget, Executive Office of the President, *Standar*
*d Industrial Classification Manual*
*U.S. Manufacturer's Directory*

Companies—Private
*Million Dollar Directory*
*Ward's Directory*

Companies—Public
Annual Reports and 10-K Reports
*Disclosure* (corporate reports)
*Q-File*
*Moody's Manuals:*
    *Moody's Bank and Finance Manual*
    *Moody's Industrial Manual*
    *Moody's International Manual*
    *Moody's Municipal and Government Manual*
    *Moody's OTC Industrial Manual*
    *Moody's OTC Unlisted Manual*
    *Moody's Public Utility Manual*
    *Moody's Transportation Manual*
Standard & Poor's Corporation, *Standard Corporation Descriptions:*
    *Standard & Poor's Handbook*
    *Standard & Poor's Industry Surveys*
    *Standard & Poor's Investment Advisory Service*
    *Standard & Poor's Outlook*
    *Standard & Poor's Statistical Service*

Companies—Subsidiaries and
Affiliates
*America's Corporate Families and International Affiliates*
*Ward's Directory*
*Who Owns Whom*
*Moody's Industry Review*
*Standard & Poor's Analyst's Handbook*
*Standard & Poor's Industry Report Service*
*Standard & Poor's Industry Surveys* (2 volumes)
U.S. Department of Commerce, *U.S. Industrial Outlook*

## Industry Ratios

Dun & Bradstreet, *Industry Norms and Key Business Ratios*
*Robert Morris Associates Annual Statement Studies*
*Troy Almanac of Business and Industrial Financial Ratios*

## Industry Forecasts

International Trade Administration, *U.S. Industrial Outlook Predicasts Forecasts*

## Rankings & Ratings

Annual Report on American Industry in *Forbes*
*Business Rankings and Salaries*
*Business One Irwin Business and Investment Almanac*
*Corporate and Industry Research Reports (CIRR)*
*Dun's Business Rankings*
*Moody's Industrial Review*
*Rating Guide to Franchises*
*Standard & Poor's Industry Report Service*
*Value Line Investment Survey*
*Ward's Business Directory*

*Statistics*

American Statistics Index (ASI) Bureau of the Census, U.S. Department of Commerce, *Economic Census Publications*

Bureau of the Census, U.S. Department of Commerce, *Statistical Abstract of the United States*

Bureau of Economic Analysis, U.S. Department of Commerce, *Survey of Current Business*

Internal Revenue Service, U.S. Treasury Department, *Statistics of Income: Corporation Income Tax Returns*

*Statistical Reference Index (SRI)*

## Appendix II

## Financial Analysis in Case Studies

### ▼ TABLE A–1

#### Profitability Ratios

| *Ratio* | *Formula* | *What it Shows* |
|---|---|---|
| 1. Return on total assets | $\dfrac{\text{Profits after taxes}}{\text{Total assets}}$ <br><br> or <br><br> $\dfrac{\text{Profits after taxes + interest}}{\text{Total assets}}$ | The net return on total investment of the firm <br><br> or <br><br> The return on both creditors' and shareholders' investments |
| 2. Return on stockholders' equity (or return on net worth) | $\dfrac{\text{Profits after taxes}}{\text{Total stockholders' equity}}$ | How profitably the company is utilizing shareholders' funds |
| 3. Return on common equity | $\dfrac{\text{Profit after taxes} - \text{preferred stock dividends}}{\text{Total stockholders' equity} - \text{par value of preferred stock}}$ | The net return to common stockholders |
| 4. Operating profit margin (or return on sales) | $\dfrac{\text{Profits before taxes and before interest}}{\text{Sales}}$ | The firm's profitability from regular operations |
| 5. Net profit margin (or net return on sales) | $\dfrac{\text{Profits after taxes}}{\text{Sales}}$ | The firm's net profit as a percentage of total sales |

### ▼ TABLE A–2

#### Liquidity Ratios

| *Ratio* | *Formula* | *What it Shows* |
|---|---|---|
| 1. Current ratio | $\dfrac{\text{Current assets}}{\text{Current liabilities}}$ | The firm's ability to meet its current financial liabilities |
| 2. Quick ratio (or acid-test ratio) | $\dfrac{\text{Current assets} - \text{inventory}}{\text{Current liabilities}}$ | The firm's ability to pay off short-term obligations without relying on sales of inventory |
| 3. Inventory to net working capital | $\dfrac{\text{Inventory}}{\text{Current assets} - \text{current liabilities}}$ | The extent to which the firm's working capital is tied up in inventory |

## TABLE A–3

### Leverage Ratios

| Ratio | Formula | What it Shows |
|---|---|---|
| 1. Debt-to-assets | $\dfrac{\text{Total debt}}{\text{Total assets}}$ | Total borrowed funds as a percentage of total assets |
| 2. Debt-to-equity | $\dfrac{\text{Total debt}}{\text{Total shareholders' equity}}$ | Borrowed funds versus the funds provided by shareholders |
| 3. Long-term debt-to-equity | $\dfrac{\text{Long-term debt}}{\text{Total shareholders' equity}}$ | Leverage used by the firm |
| 4. Times-interest-earned (or coverage ratio) | $\dfrac{\text{Profits before interest and taxes}}{\text{Total interest charges}}$ | The firm's ability to meet all interest payments |
| 5. Fixed charge coverage | $\dfrac{\text{Profits before taxes and interest} + \text{lease obligations}}{\text{Total interest charges} + \text{lease obligations}}$ | The firm's ability to meet all fixed-charge obligations including lease payments |

## TABLE A–4

### Activity Ratios

| Ratio | Formula | What it Shows |
|---|---|---|
| 1. Inventory turnover | $\dfrac{\text{Sales}}{\text{Inventory of finished goods}}$ | The effectiveness of the firm in employing inventory |
| 2. Fixed assets turnover | $\dfrac{\text{Sales}}{\text{Fixed assets}}$ | The effectiveness of the firm in utilizing plant and equipment |
| 3. Total assets turnover | $\dfrac{\text{Sales}}{\text{Total assets}}$ | The effectiveness of the firm in utilizing total assets |
| 4. Accounts receivable turnover | $\dfrac{\text{Annual credit sales}}{\text{Accounts receivable}}$ | How many times the total receivables has been collected during the accounting period |
| 5. Average collection period | $\dfrac{\text{Accounts receivable}}{\text{Average daily sales}}$ | The average length of time the firm waits to collect payments after sales |

## TABLE A–5

### Shareholders' Return Ratios

| Ratio | Formula | What it Shows |
|---|---|---|
| 1. Dividend yield on common stock | $\dfrac{\text{Annual dividends per share}}{\text{Current market price per share}}$ | A measure of return to common stockholders in the form of dividends. |
| 2. Price-earnings ratio | $\dfrac{\text{Current market price per share}}{\text{After-tax earnings per share}}$ | An indication of market perception of the firm, usually, the faster-growing or less risky firms tend to have higher PE ratios than the slower-growing or more risky firms. |
| 3. Dividend payout ratio | $\dfrac{\text{Annual dividends per share}}{\text{After-tax earnings per share}}$ | An indication of dividends paid out as a percentage of profits |
| 4. Cash flow per share | $\dfrac{\text{After-tax profits} + \text{depreciation}}{\text{Number of common shares outstanding}}$ | A measure of total cash per share available for use by the firm. |

## Notes

1. C. Christensen, 1989, *Teaching and the Case Method* (Boston: Harvard Business School Publishing Division); C. C. Lundberg, 1993, Introduction to the case method, in C. M. Vance (ed.), *Mastering Management Education* (Newbury Park, Calif.: Sage).

2. C. C. Lundberg and C. Enz, 1993, A framework for student case preparation, *Case Research Journal* 13 (Summer): 133.

3. J. Soltis, 1971, John Dewey, in L. E. Deighton (ed.), *Encyclopedia of Education* (New York: Macmillan and Free Press).

# Name Index

# Company Index

## PHOTO CREDITS

## TEXT CREDITS

*News.* **45** Brent Bowers, 1993, FDA regulatory tide swallows up McCurdy Fish Co., *Wall Street Journal,* May 18, B2, Reprinted by permission of *Wall Street Journal* © 1993 Dow Jones & Company, Inc. All Rights Reserved Worldwide. **66** Z. Moukheiber, 1993, Our competitive advantage, FORBES, April 12, 59–62. Reprinted by permission of FORBES Magazine © Forbes Inc., 1993. **68** Associated Press, 1993, 970 Woolworth Stores to close, *Dallas Morning News,* October 14, D1, D14. **76** A. Taylor 1993, Making up for lost time, FORTUNE, October 18, 78–80, © 1993 Time Inc., All rights reserved. **81** P. Sellers, 1993, Brands: It's Thrive or die, FORTUNE, August 23; 52–56, © 1993 Time Inc., All rights reserved. **90** J. Huey, 1993, How McKinsey does it, FORTUNE, November 1; 56–81, © 1993 Time Inc., All rights reserved. **100** A. E. Serwer, 1994, Business is bad? It's time to grow! FORTUNE, January 24, 88, © 1994 Time Inc. All rights reserved. **105** S. Caminiti, 1994, How to get focused again, FORTUNE, January 24, 85–86, © 1994 Time Inc. All rights reserved. **107** B. R. Schlender, 1993, The perils of losing focus, FORTUNE, May 17, 100, © 1993 Time Inc. All rights reserved. **117** A., Taylor III, 1992, Now hear this, Jack Welch! FORTUNE, April 6, 94–95, © 1992 Time Inc. All rights reserved. **120** R. S. Teitelbaum, 1993, Keeping promises, FORTUNE (Special Issue, Winter/Autumn), 32–34, © 1993 Time Inc. All rights reserved; T. Maxon, 1994, Southwest's '93 profits sky-high, *Dallas Morning News,* February 3, ID, 4D. **122** E. S. Browning, 1994, U.S. tire ventures travel rough road, *Wall Street Journal,* March 22, p A11. Reprinted by permission of *Wall Street Journal,* © 1994 Dow Jones & Company, Inc. All rights reserved worldwide. **130** R. L. Hudson, 1993, BT faces a line of potential international competitors: Rivals will produce major changes in British telecommunications services, *Wall Street Journal,* April 29, B4; J.J. Keller and M.L. Carnevale, 1993, MCI–BT tie is seen setting off a battle in communications. *Wall Street Journal,* June 3, A1, A6. Reprinted by permission of *Wall Street Journal,* © 1994 Dow Jones & Company, Inc. All rights reserved worldwide. **136** E. Lesly, 1993, A&W's summer plans: Hitting the warpath, *Business Week,* April 12, 53–54; W. Kimbrell, 1993, Niche hitters, *Beverage Industry,* February, 28–33; A&W: Here, there and everywhere, 1993, *Beverage World,* August, 10. **141** A. Fleming, 1993, Money machine, *Automotive News,* October 4, 36; E. Lapham, 1993, Chrysler hopes Neon will be the new Beetle, *Automotive News,* September 13, 1–2; A. Taylor III, 1994, Will success spoil Chrysler? FORTUNE, January 10, 88–91; D. Woodruff and K.L. Miller, 1993, Chrysler's Neon: Is this the small car Detroit couldn't build? *Business Week,* May 3, 116–126. **145** R. E. Hoskisson and M. A. Hitt, 1994, *Downscoping: How to Tame the Diversified Firm* (New York: Oxford University Press). **154** M.A. Hitt, B. B. Tyler, C. Hardee and D. Park, 1994, Understanding strategic intent in the global marketplace, *Academy of Management Executive,* in press; D. Darlin and J.B. White, 1992, Failed marriage: GM venture in Korea nears end, betraying firms' fond hopes, *Wall Street Journal,* January 16, A1, A12. **162** B. O'Brian, 1993, Tired of airline losses, AMR pushes its bid to diversify business, *Wall Street Journal.* February 18, 1A, 8A. Reprinted by permission of *Wall Street Journal,* © 1993 Dow Jones & Company, Inc. All rights reserved worldwide. **166** B. Pulley, 1991, Wrigley is thriving, despite the recession, in a resilient business, *Wall Street Journal,* May 29, 1A, 8A. Reprinted by permission of *Wall Street Journal,* © 1991 Dow Jones & Company, Inc. All rights reserved worldwide; *Value Line,* 1994, Edition 10 (February 18): 1494. **171** M. Siconofi, 1993, Merrill Lynch, pushing into many new lines, expands bank services, *Wall Street Journal,* July 7, A1, A14. Reprinted by permission of *Wall Street Journal,* © 1993 Dow Jones & Company, Inc. All rights reserved worldwide. **177** S. McMurray, 1993, U.K.'s Hanson to buy maker of Polyethylene, *Wall Street Journal,* July 1, A3. **187** U. Gupta, 1991, Sony adopts strategy to broaden ties with small firms. *Wall Street Journal,* February 28, 2B; Reprinted by permission of *Wall Street Journal,* © 1991 Dow Jones & Company, Inc. All rights reserved worldwide. *Value Line,* 1994, Edition 10 (February 18): 1562. **194** L. Landro, J. L. Roberts, and R. Smith, 1993, Time-Warner sees synergy in partnership, *Wall Street Journal,* May 18, B1, B7. Reprinted by permission of *Wall Street Journal,* © 1993 Dow Jones & Company, Inc. All rights reserved worldwide. M. Sikora, 1990, Deals and misdeals: A sampling of M&A hits and strikeouts in the 1980s, *Mergers and Acquisitions* (March-April): 100–103, Reprinted with permission of Mergers & Acquisitions, Philadelphia. **199** A. Choi, R. L. Hudson, and O. Suris, 1994, BMW to buy 80 percent control of Rover Cars, *Wall Street Journal,* February 1, A3, A6. Reprinted by permission of *Wall Street Journal,* © 1994 Dow Jones & Company, Inc. All rights reserved worldwide. **202** Adapted from W. C. Kester, 1991, *Japanese Takeovers: The Global Contest for Corporate Control* (Boston, MA: Harvard Business School Press), 118–127. **206** S. McMurray, 1993, ICI changes tack and splits itself into two businesses: Diversified company hopes spin off with speed its reaction to marketplace, *Wall Street Journal,* March 5, B4, Reprinted by permission of *Wall Street Journal,* © 1993 Dow Jones & Company, Inc. All rights reserved worldwide. **211** Adapted from M. Maremont, and P. Dwyer, 1992, How Gillette is honing its edge: CEO Zeien is busily expanding and launching new products, *Business Week,* September 28; 60–65; P. Sellers, 1993, Brands: It's thrive or die, FORTUNE, August 23, 52–56; M. M. Royce, 1994. Gillette, *Value Line,* January 14, 823. **214** J. Bussey, C. Chandler, and M. Williams, 1993. The other shoe: Japanese recession prompts corporations to take radical steps, *Wall Street Journal,* February 24, A1, A8; Japan's fallible firms (editorial), 1993, *Economists* February 27, 17; J. Templeman, G. E. Schares, J. Levine, and W. Glasgall, 1993, Germany fights back: There's a revolution under way. *Business Week,* May 31, 48–51. **226** J. Barnathan, P. Engardio, L. Curry, and D. Einhorn, 1993, China: The emerging economic powerhouse, *Business Week,* May 17, 55–68; R. Keatley, 1993, Sticks and carrots: As Washington tries to spur reform in China, business people often get caught in the middle, *Wall Street Journal* (Special Report on China), December 10, R8; J. Leung and C.S. Smith 1994, Some chinese factory bosses live it up, *Wall Street Journal,* March 15, A21. **232** M. Moffett, 1993, U.S. firms yell ole to future in Mexico, *Wall Street Journal,* March 8, B1, Reprinted by permission of *Wall Street Journal,* © 1993 Dow Jones & Company, Inc. All rights reserved worldwide. **236** D. F. Abell, 1993, *Managing with Strategies: Mastering the Present and Preempting the Future* (New York: Free Press), 210–214; C. A. Bartlett and S. Rangan, 1992, Komatsu Limited, in C. A. Bartlett and S. Ghoshal (eds.), *Transnational Management: Text, Cases and Readings in Cross-Border Management,* Homewood, Ill.: Irwin, 311–326. **240** R. A. Melcher, 1993, Ford of Europe: Slimmer but maybe not luckier, *Business Week,* January 18, 44–46; R. L. Simison and N. Templin, 1993, Ford is turning heads with $6 billion cost to design world car, *Wall Street Journal,* March 23, A1, A6. **248** J. B. Levine, 1993, The knives come out in Europe's software market, *Business Week,* February 8, 37–38; D. P. Hamilton, 1993, U.S. companies rush to fill Japanese software void, *Wall Street Journal,* May 7, B4; G. P. Zachary, 1994, Consolidation sweeps the software industry, *Wall Street Journal,* March 23, A1, A7. **260** J. B. Treece, 1992, The board revolt: Business as usual won't cut it anymore at a humbled GM, *Business Week,* April 20, 30–36; J. B. White, 1992, GM concludes sale of 55 million shares, raising funds for major restructuring, *Wall Street Journal,* May 20, C15; B. A. Stertz, and J. B. White, 1992, GM's top buyer shakes up motor city, *Wall Street Journal,* June 17, B1, B11. **269** B. Marshi, 1991, More small firms are employing outside directors, *Wall Street Journal,* June 11, B2. Reprinted by permission of *Wall Street Journal,* © 1991 Dow Jones & Company, Inc. All rights reserved worldwide. **271** J. A. Byrne, 1993, Executive pay: The party ain't over yet, *Business Week,* April 26, 56–64; J. Lublin, 1991, Are chief executives paid too much, *Wall Street Journal,* June 4, B1; A. Bennett, 1989, A great leap forward for executive pay: Stock options propelled by CEOs in '88, *Wall Street Journal,* April 24, B1. **277** J. Neff, 1993, What do Japanese CEOs really make? *Business Week,* April 26, 60–61; J. S. Lublin, 1991, Are chief executives paid too much? *Wall Street Journal,* June 4, B1; T. Mroczkowski and M. Hanaoka, 1993, Continuity and change in Japanese management, in S. Durlabhji and N. E. Marks (eds.), *Japanese Business* (Albany: State University of New York Press), 271–287. **284** G. A. Patterson and F. Schwadel, 1992, Sears suddenly undoes years of diversifying beyond retailing field, *Wall Street Journal,* September 30, A1, A6. Reprinted by permission of *Wall Street Journal,* © 1992 Dow Jones & Company, Inc. All rights reserved worldwide. **293** D. Milbank, 1991, Quaker State slips in market share battle, *Wall Street Journal,* February 13, A4. Reprinted by permission of *Wall Street Journal,* © 1991 Dow Jones & Company, Inc. All rights reserved worldwide. **298** T. A. Stewart, 1992, The search for the organization of tomorrow, FORTUNE, May 18, 92–98. © 1992 Times Inc. All rights reserved. **308** N. J. Perry, 1992, Bausch & Lomb: Trust the locals, win worldwide, FORTUNE, May 4, 76–77. © 1992 Time Inc. All rights reserved. **310** C. Rappoport, C., 1992, A tough Swede invades the U.S., FORTUNE, June 29, 76–79. © 1992 Time Inc. All rights reserved. **318** G. P. Zachary, 1993, After a fall from grace, Oracle gets back on its feet: Software maker undone by a culture of greed, rebuilds with new blood, *Wall Street Journal,* April 15, B4. Reprinted by permission of *Wall Street Journal,* © 1993 Dow Jones & Company, Inc. All rights reserved worldwide. **323** P. Burrows and S. A. Forest, 1993, Dell computer goes into the shop: It's assembling a new executive team and retooling its business, *Business Week,* July 12,138–140; M. Fitzgerald, 1993, Dell trying to get back on track. *Computerworld,* 27, 34:15; Dell's formula defies rules in competitive PC market. 1992, *Computerworld,* 27, 1:78; T. Steinert-Threlkeld. 1994, Dell to end sales through chains, *Dallas Morning News,* July 12, 1D and 7D. **327** R. Johnson, 1993, Tenneco hired a CEO from outside and he is refocusing the firm, *Wall Street Journal,* March 29, 1A, and 14A; J. Cole, 1993, New CEO at Hughes studied its managers, got them on his side, *Wall Street Journal,* March 23, 1A, 8A; 1994, *Value Line,* Tenneco, Inc., April 1, 466. **332** A. K. Naj, 1993, Shifting gears: Some manufacturers drop efforts to adopt Japanese techniques, *Wall Street Journal,* May 7, 1A, 12A. Reprinted by permission of *Wall Street Journal,* © 1993 Dow Jones & Company, Inc. All rights reserved worldwide. **346** B. R. Schlender, 1992, How Sony keeps the magic going, FORTUNE, February 24, 76–84. © 1992 Time Inc. All rights reserved. **351** R. A. Burgelman, 1991, Intraorganizational ecology of strategy making and organizational adaptation: Theory and field research, *Organization Science* 2: 239–262. **354** B. A. Stertz, 1992, Chrysler is making solid progress in spite of executive turmoil, *Wall Street Journal,* March 3, A1, A5. Reprinted by permission of *Wall Street Journal.* © 1992 Dow Jones & Company, Inc. All Rights Reserved Worldwide. **358** C. Mitchell, 1988, Partnerships are a way of life for Corning, *Wall Street Journal,* July 12, 6. Reprinted by permission of *Wall Street Journal,* © 1988 Dow Jones & Company, Inc. All rights reserved worldwide. **364** J. Reese, 1992, Thermo Electron: How to grow big by staying small, FORTUNE, December 28, 50–51. © 1992 Time Inc. All rights reserved.; Thermo Electron, 1994, *Value Line,* February 11, 1396. **368** E. Stych, 1990, Post-it notes turn 10 years old, *Houston Chronicle,* February 5, 4B. Reprinted by permission of Associated Press (AP), Copyright © 1990, AP.